To Eleanor:

I hope you enjoy
this book about Bethlehem's
rich historical legacy.

William Thomas
"Mentor chapter"

Best wishes

Peter R. Christoph

To Eleanor —
Appreciation for your
interest in Town history

Floyd Brewer
MAY 1, 1993

I hope you enjoy this
book, Eleanor, as much
as we enjoyed writing
it.

R. Hugh Hewitt

BETHLEHEM REVISITED
A Bicentennial Story 1793-1993

by the
BICENTENNIAL HISTORY COMMITTEE
Floyd I. Brewer, Senior Editor

Published Under the Auspices of the
Bethlehem Bicentennial Commission

February 1993

Copyright 1993 by the
Bicentennial Commission
Town of Bethlehem, New York

Library of Congress
Cataloging-in-Publication Data
92-085272

ISBN 0-9635402-0-3

Printed by
Lane Press of Albany, New York, Inc.

Manufactured in the United States
of America

Cover jacket: Nicoll-Sill home, ca. 1795. Original painting by Len F. Tantillo, noted area painter of historic homes and buildings.

Title page: Original sketch of Bethlehem welcome sign by Margaret G. Foster, founding member of the Bethelehem Art Association.

Introduction

Almost 8,500 years ago Indians arrived at the confluence of the Vloman Kill and Hudson River, an area that would later become part of the town of Bethlehem. Europeans began farming the land nearby as early as 1630. Chapter one is the story of an archaeological excavation that produced direct evidence of Indian cultures living on Bethlehem land over many centuries. Chapters two through four offer an overview of life here since 1630, and provide a sense of the interrelationships among several aspects of town history. Later chapters concentrate on specific subject areas that detail the rich history of our town.

The writers have had considerable freedom to present divergent interpretations of our history.

An interdisciplinary team of editors has worked long and hard to present a balanced and integrated story of life in Bethlehem over the ages by following a process of multiple reviews and extensive discussions with each author.

Every reasonable effort has been made to assure the accuracy of information presented in this volume. Still, one of our basic purposes is to encourage debate over unsettled questions. If you find errors in presentation or interpretation, please contact the Senior Editor. Where original documents or related evidence is submitted to support a different version of the facts, we pledge to publish corrections in *Bethlehem Diary*, the second book in the bicentennial series, scheduled for release in 1994.

Acknowledgements

In 1988, the Town of Bethlehem Bicentennial Commission authorized the formation of the Bicentennial History Committee to develop a comprehensive history of the town. Already serving informally for a couple of years, the writers and editors pictured in the appendix embarked on a team effort to produce this volume. Along the way considerable help was received from a number of people and organizations. Especially helpful were Allison P. Bennett, Dr. Kendall A. Birr, Gordon Conklin, Dr. Robert E. Funk, Dr. Charles T. Gehring, Helen E. Hobbie, Dr. Paul R. Huey, James C. Leyhane, M.D., Dr. Leslie G. Loomis, John H. McCashion, Kenneth J. Ringler, Jr., Dr. William A. Ritchie, Dr. David W. Steadman, Charlotte Wilcoxen, and the staff of the Bethlehem Public Library.

Significant help was received from dozens of citizens and town employees who granted interviews and supplied original documents. Extended help was given by Barbara A. Asprion, David B. Austin, Ruth Oliver Bickel, Richard D. Bollam, John E. Brent, Alice P. Boutelle, Lynn Corrigan, Thomas V. Corrigan, Martin J. Cross, Margaret G. Foster, Evelyn and Helen Frazier, John B. Geurtze, Susan Graves, J. Robert Hendrick, Scott A. Horton, Gloria M. Johnson, Judith E. Kehoe, Thomas A. Knight, Marion E. Koch, Philip Maher, Kathleen A. Newkirk, C. Terri Picazzi, Rodney W. Raynor, James Reagan, Sue Ann Ritchko, Gregg Sagendorph, Claudia K. St. John, Martha Dickinson Shattuck, Martha Slingerland, Len F. Tantillo, Pieter S. Van Derzee, and Richard S. Webster.

Obtaining the archaeological information used in chapter one and the family chapter was a labor of love for a dedicated group of individuals who have worked long and hard since 1981. An average of sixteen members of the Bethlehem Archaeology Group worked more than 10,000 hours each year, excavating, preserving, identifying, and interpreting thousands of objects recovered from six sites in Bethlehem. Members serving more than five years included Jean A. Adell, Floyd I. Brewer, Florence A. Christoph, Roy A. Dietert, James T. Engleman, Benjamin and Virginia French, Adrienne R. Gordon, Edward D. Homiller, Ann S. Jacobs, Jeanne M. Knouse, Bernard J. Lamica, Jean M. Lyon, Charles D. (Chuck) McKinney, Eleanor J. Norrix, Nanci E. Page, Eleanor E. Turner, Carol L. Wock, and Ralph B. Wood.

Finally, the editors are grateful for the financial support received from the General Electric Foundation through the efforts of James R. Conheady of the General Electric Plastics Division at Selkirk. Additional financial help over many years was received from the Bethlehem Town Board, members of the Bethlehem Archaeology Group, and dozens of individuals who contributed funds to defray the cost of this publication.

Contents

1 Buried Secrets

Ice Age hunters roamed this area about 11,000 years ago in search of edible wild plants, fish and game. The living environment was relatively harsh; the climate was cool and wet and a spruce woodland covered the landscape.

Excavations on the Goes farm in Cedar Hill uncovered evidence of Indian visits to Bethlehem as early as 6500 B.C. Conditions then were more moderate, much like today. From that period until the time of Henry Hudson's historic visit to present-day Albany, various cultures lived at the Goes farm site, leaving behind a record of their life and times.

The excavations were conducted over four summers by the Bethlehem Archaeology Group. Another four years were spent in the laboratory studying the evidence.

This is the story of that dig and what it revealed.

Bill Goes got off his tractor and wandered over to watch members of the Bethlehem Archaeology Group digging on the Nicoll-Sill estate, a few hundred feet north of the land he rented from landowner Pieter Van Derzee. He told them he had been picking up Indian stone tools over the last thirty years on a ridge about 700 feet south of the Nicoll-Sill home. The next day he showed them about 600 stone tools in his collection, ranging from inch-long projectile points to large, round, sandstone rocks with shallow indentations on each side. Called hammerstones, such rocks were used by Indians over many centuries in Bethlehem.

The collection was clearly significant. But could the group find enough evidence on the Goes farm, along with information from associated sites in the Northeast, to re-create Indian life in prehistoric Bethlehem? Further, there were serious doubts about their ability to handle the Nicoll-Sill site and a prehistoric site at the same time. Nevertheless, Bill Goes agreed to lend his collection for a few months so it could be studied carefully at the laboratory.

From a pragmatic point of view, senior author Floyd Brewer had been making it clear to all who asked that he was a retired graduate education professor with ten years of part-time experience working with professional archaeologists in this country and abroad. Given this limited background, would a prehistoric dig be too much of a challenge? It was the summer of 1983, a full ten years before the town's bicentennial. The lead time was there to complete the project, but could the necessary resources be organized to accomplish such ambitious goals?

William A. Ritchie, former State Archaeologist, identifying the Goes collection at the Bethlehem Archaeology Group laboratory in 1983.

Doubts continued until the Goes collection was shown to William A. Ritchie, former New York State Archaeologist, who lives in Delmar. "All of this? For heaven's sake, there must be a big site there. I have a notion that if Goes found all this stuff in that field, there could be some pits and subsurface accumulation."[1] He identified all of the stone tools and made it clear that we had a multicomponent site, which means many cultural groups lived there for several thousand years before the arrival of Europeans. This was exciting news. Permission to do some exploratory digging was requested and granted.

The results of test excavations in the summer of 1984 were disappointing. Volunteers recovered a few projectile points on the surface, and several pottery fragments of European manufacture. Still, it was a good time for organizing the research team. Volunteer Virginia French agreed to supervise the work and keep a detailed set of notes on each day of digging.

Serious Digging Begins

In late July 1985, after the corn had been harvested, the volunteer crew concentrated on a low-lying ridge, about 300 feet south of the Nicoll-Sill cemetery, where Goes had found most of the stone tools in his collection. Control was established over the site with a grid system of ten-foot squares marked by stakes in the ground. Progress was slow. Days of wilting sun went by with very few finds, but the crew understood that patience is a virtue in archaeology. They joked about a huge pile of manure Bill Goes stored below the ridge where they were digging. His plan was to spread it over the grid area after the digging season was done. New volunteers were occasionally asked to open a new square in the middle of the manure pile, only to be stopped the last minute when a supervisor got "wind" of the practical joke.

All excavated soil was sifted through metal screens, just in case artifacts were missed when the soil was removed. Now the crew was finding Indian projectile points by the dozens. The finds were frequently checked against a handy chart showing distinctive New York State projectile points.[2] The field notes are peppered with sentences such as "A perfect Lamoka point, a kaolin clay pipe stem fragment, and some Indian pottery shards were the most significant finds today."[3] Later, the laboratory's kaolin clay pipe specialist, Jim Engleman, dated the clay pipe fragment to the 1640s, the earliest years the land was used by European settlers.

The Goes Farm

On cool days the crew often sat in the middle of the corn field having lunch and contemplating the beauty of the setting. We were working on a low-lying glacial terrace overlooking a large flood-plain, near the point where the Vloman Kill flows into the Hudson River. For Indians dependent on foot and canoe travel, it was a perfect spot to spend the summers over the centuries.

Landowner Pieter Van Derzee, son of S. Vint Van Derzee, who descended from the legendary Storm van der Zee, lives on a wooded hill to the west. The farmer, William M. Goes, lives in a nine-teenth-century farmhouse a few hundred feet to the south. The plow zone is rich mostly because Bill fertilizes it with manure every fall. The corn he grows on the ridge is highly prized among his customers at farmers' markets in Bethlehem.

The crew found a layer of yellow sand at the bottom of the plow zone about twelve inches down, and the sand continued as far down as they excavated. A common question asked by visitors was, how do you know how far down to dig? Our usual answer—as far down as a sterile level where there are no more materials or features left by the Indians.

More and more Normanskill projectile points were recovered, confirming the presence of native groups living here during the River phase, a hunting-gathering culture of the mid-Hudson region radiocarbon-dated between 1900 and 1600 B.C. The crew was so captivated with these long, slen-

William Goes, farmer, showing a recent find to Pieter Van Derzee, landowner.

der points, often made of grayish green chert, that we had one specimen drawn by Delmar signmaker, James Ralson, on our laboratory road sign.

A Normanskill point from the Goes farm, one-third actual size.

Exciting Find

Occasionally, the field notes dealt with sensitive information. On August 10, 1985, Chuck McKinney unearthed some human bone frag-ments in his square. Over lunch the crew had a spirited discussion about the bones. Were they digging in an ancient cemetery? Did freezing and thawing expose these bones, or were the bones dragged to the surface by the tip of a plow?

Virginia French cataloguing prehistory artifacts in the B.A.G. laboratory.

Later Jan Vine uncovered a full skeleton, an event that caused a lot of excitement among the crew and concern that word of the find might get out. Worried that vandals might be attracted by the finds, we decided not to publicize these fascinating discoveries.

Trained in physical anthropology as well as archaeology, Dr. Ritchie said that Vine had found the bones of an Owasco Indian. Virginia French was careful to get all the details down: the skeleton faced east with the head pointed south, the knees were drawn up toward the chest, and there were no grave goods. However brief, it was a sample of mortuary customs around A.D. 1300. The crew measured and photographed the skeleton and left it in the ground. It was the first of nine skeletons they would encounter over the next two summers, all but one with exactly the same burial pattern.

In late August 1985, Ben French and John Gold reached the layer of yellow sand beneath the plow zone in their square, and began to shave off thin slices of soil with their trowels. Soon, bits of animal bone and streaks of charcoal appeared, followed by a circular pattern of small rocks.

Bone about four inches in length from the back of a sturgeon fish.

A typical Owasco Indian burial, ca. A.D. 1300.

Within minutes they exposed a large butterfly-shaped bone among the blackened rocks. Great care had to be exercised since the plate-like bone was thin and very fragile. Dr. Ritchie identified it as a bone from the back of a sturgeon. A triangular Levanna point appeared near the hearth after another hour of careful digging. We were beginning to document Owasco/Mahican life in the centuries on either side of A.D. 1500.

Although the group tried to keep a low profile to avoid interruptions, it was inevitable that visitors would find the dig site. Some were especially welcome. On August 31, Henry Meyer came with his daughter, Ruth Russell, who brought her collection of projectile points found on her father's farm. The points were photographed for later identification. Emerson Martin, another regular visitor, had collected Indian artifacts at the site for many years. He agreed to lend his collection to the group for study. The same arrangements were made with the Perry family of Albany. These collections considerably enhanced our knowledge of the many Indian cultures occupying the Goes farm over the centuries.

In the Beginning

As the 1986 digging season evolved, and hundreds of additional stone tools and Indian pottery fragments were recovered, the crew began to look at the broad picture of Indian life on the farm. We wondered what the land and the climate were like before the Indians arrived, and sought answers from geologist Robert Dineen at the New York State Museum.

We learned that about 20,000 years ago, most of New York State was covered by the Wisconsin glacier. Five thousand years later, the glacier had retreated, leaving a huge lake that occupied a large part of the Hudson Valley. It was later called Lake Albany. The lake began to drain about 13,000 years ago as the ice withdrew into present-day Canada. Later, park-tundra conditions covered the land—great open spaces and very few trees, followed by spruce and fir forests about 11,000 years ago. At this point the climate was cold and dry.

By mid-summer 1986, it was getting easier for the diggers to recognize distinctive point types as they emerged from the soil. Dozens of Lamoka points identified by Dr. Ritchie, made between 2500 and 1900 B.C., were recovered by several excavators. Were the people who made them

related to the well-known Lamoka culture described by Dr. Ritchie in his work on Lamoka Lake in the western part of New York? If so, why weren't we finding the beveled adz, a cutting tool used by the Lamoka people? This was a summer in which dozens of questions were raised about where the Indians living in Bethlehem came from and why they came here. Answers were few and far between.

Continue Digging or Close the Site?

In late August it was obvious that our evidence was incomplete in several time periods. There was just enough evidence to show that the land had been occupied during the centuries after 3500 through 1900 B.C., but not enough to make a strong case in print. Further, the evidence of life during the two milleniums after 600 B.C. was thin to non-existent. The crew began to debate the issue of whether or not another summer's digging would strengthen the record of prehistoric life in the bicentennial history. There was an urgent need to move the crew to an archaeological site near the First Reformed Church of Bethlehem in Selkirk, but several key people felt another summer of digging on the Goes farm could be productive.

The Owasco Mystery

Toward the end of the digging season in 1986, Ann Jacobs and John Kohl uncovered another skeleton. We groaned because nothing new was being learned about Owasco mortuary customs. Skeletons demand meticulous excavation and careful attention to measurement and photography, which adds up to a great deal of staff time.

Still, this one was different. The skeleton was stretched out, instead of lying flex-style with knees drawn up toward the chest, and the arms and hands appeared to be behind the back. Further, there was a reddish-brown stain in the middle of the skull. Inexplicably, some isolated bones of a child were found less than a foot east of the skeleton. Minds raced ahead with tantalizing questions. Was death caused by a blow on the head? Were the hands of this person tied behind the back? We looked for traces of a decayed leather thong, but found none.

The case was made for removing the skeleton to the laboratory for further study. It was later examined by Dr. Ritchie, Dr. John E. Manne, a Delmar dentist, and by Dr. Jeffrey D. Hubbard, a forensic pathologist. Dr. Hubbard took the mystery out of the find:

> He was male, about forty-five to fifty years old, and pretty healthy since the bones show no evidence of disease. His diet was tough and full of fiber. He was about five feet seven inches tall. There is no evidence of a violent death. The stain on the underside of the skull probably came from iron in the soil. The cause of death will have to be listed as undetermined. One thing about him is unusual: his right ulna (lower arm bone) is much larger than his left ulna.[4]

We were disappointed to discover that he was like all the others. Our mystery skeleton was dubbed the right-handed canoe-maker of his time, and returned to the exact spot of his burial to lie peacefully on his side where he had lain for more than 600 years.

The 1986 digging season ended in September with a number of unresolved questions and limited evidence about several cultural groups living on the farm. The debate about returning to the farm another summer or moving to the First Reformed Church of Bethlehem was still underway and it was obvious that we needed more outside advice.

Two Experts Get Together

The need to settle these unresolved questions about some of our recent finds prompted a call to Dr. Robert E. Funk, current New York State Archaeologist, to ask if he would join Dr. Ritchie and our prehistory team in a meeting at the laboratory. They agreed to come on November 20, 1986.

It was a crucial meeting for us. They identified more than a dozen types of Owasco/Mahican pottery, most of which dated between A.D. 1300 and 1400. They agreed that our fat, stubby Indian clay pipe fragments were the ring bowl type probably made during the Owasco/Mahican period. Further, they thought that two little-used strike-a-lights were probably manufactured in the Snook Kill phase shortly after 1500 B.C.

The two scientists were accustomed to discussing and debating one another's ideas. Dr. Ritchie summed up one long discussion: "My guess is that this spoolstone, ulu knife, and gouge go with this Vosburg point and they're about 2500 B.C."[5] It was a relief to discover where some of the general tools fit in and to get a clearer picture of Indian life during a period in which our evidence was very limited. A few minutes later, they were pondering over two curiously-shaped fist-sized stones and decided they were bannerstone preforms, meaning atlatl weights in process of manufacture. They were asked about an unusual group of small, human bones unearthed in late August, and Dr. Ritchie immediately recognized them as a good example of a baby bundle burial.

Earliest Evidence of Indian Life in Bethlehem

Dr. Funk talked at length about three odd-looking points he thought were bifurcates made around 6500 B.C. He was then shown a similar point made out of the same kind of flint. It required only a few minutes of thought for him to label it "a Kirk made around 6000 B.C."[6] This was exciting news for the laboratory staff. It was firm evidence of Indian visits to Bethlehem about 8,000 years ago.

Early Archaic projectile points comprising evidence of early Native American visits to Bethlehem, ca. 6500-6000 B.C.

The Final Season of Digging

During a tour of the laboratory, a sixth-grade pupil asked, "After removing all of your stakes from the previous year, and after the farmer planted and harvested his corn, how do you find where you dug before?"[7] Good question! It was an opportunity to explain that we rely on our transit, an instrument archaeologists use for setting up a grid from an easy-to-find fixed point. An iron stake driven into the ground below the plow zone marked our fixed point. Accuracy was especially important since we had excavated so many skeletons.

We returned to the Goes farm in 1987 determined to establish an entirely new grid, closer to the

The sifter team in action. Left to right: Ann Jacobs, James Engleman, Florence Christoph, Virginia French, and Bernard Lamica, who constructed the motorized soil sifter.

Nicoll-Sill cemetery, where flatter land might show some evidence of permanent Indian housing.

Lamica's Soil Sifter

Some way had to be found to move the soil quickly if we were to finish our digging by September 1987. Bernard Lamica, the laboratory's iron restoration specialist, heard this remark several times over the previous winter. In a burst of creative zeal, he purchased a motorized belt conveyor on Rogers Island near Fort Edward and converted it to a soil sifter. Some of us were a bit skeptical that it would work, but Barney and his two sons, Stephen and Kevin, brought it to the Goes farm on August 1.

A sifter team was quickly organized. Two people dug and filled pails with soil, two people carried the pails to the sifter and dumped the contents into the hopper and two people watched for artifacts as the soil sifted down through the screenbed. Only topsoil that had been disturbed by the plow was put through the machine. Two hours later it was clear that the team could sift four times more soil with the machine than it could by hand.

Encouraged by the successful test of the sifting machine, Floyd Brewer queried, "Why not go all the way and bring in a front-end loader to remove the topsoil in the new grid?"[8] Although we would not be able to recover artifacts in topsoil removed by the loader, it would help us check a wide area rather quickly for evidence of permanent Indian housing. Bill Goes approved the plan after assurances that the topsoil would be replaced. Martin Cross, the town's superintendent of highways, said he would provide the equipment and an operator.

As we waited for the heavy equipment, the soil sifting machine was operated day after day, and

Notched ulu knife, approximately four inches in length.

artifacts tumbled onto the screenbed in greatly increased numbers. Two more precious bifurcates were found, further evidence of an early hunting party around 6500 B.C.

On August 8, Chuck McKinney found a wide-bladed ulu, similar in shape to a modern butcher knife. It was the find of the week as we knew it was the kind of tool commonly used by the Vosburg people in the centuries after 3000 B.C. The knife was beautifully ground from slate, and notched along the top edge toward the point. The following Monday, an eared-notched point from the Vosburg period was found in the same square at the same level. In view of our limited evidence for this period, we hoped these finds were omens of good things to come.

A highway department equipment operator brought a front end loader to the farm on August 24, and removed the topsoil in the plow zone from a flat area a few dozen feet south of the Nicoll-Sill cemetery. We watched the process closely to be sure the blade didn't bite into the yellow sand below the plow zone. Edward Homiller immediately created a new grid on the flat land and, within minutes, members of the crew began to dig a representative pattern of squares across a very large area.

Significant Finds

On September 7, 1987, working slightly below the plow zone in the new grid, Martha Shattuck found five near-perfect Brewerton projectile points on the edge of a huge pile of flint chips she had unearthed gradually the week before. It was an important find and sufficient reason alone for this final season of digging. These points are especially meaningful to archaeologists who know the Vosburg culture. Martha had uncovered a Brewerton tool-making station, and we were now sure of a Vosburg presence in Bethlehem between 3000 and 2500 B.C.

Martha Shattuck uncovering a Brewerton tool-making station, ca. 3000 B.C. Looking on from left to right: Bernard Lamica, Virginia French, and Roy Dietert.

Florence Christoph recovering a polished celt (ax), ca. A.D. 1400.

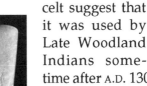

Celt find, approximately four inches in length.

Meanwhile, other diggers, working with trowels, reached the layer of yellow sand below the plow zone in their squares. Flo Christoph found a celt, an ax-like tool that tapered down to a sharp edge. Materials around the celt suggest that it was used by Late Woodland Indians sometime after A.D. 1300. It was the fourth one found, and further evidence of Owasco/Mahican woodworking activity.

15

Fragment of Chance Incised Native American pottery, ca. A.D. 1400, and particles of nepheline syenite used to temper the pottery.

Barney Lamica uncovered a strange-looking black mineral similar in appearance to a piece of hard coal. He applied a blowtorch to a sample and the material glowed, but produced no ash. He wondered if it could be the same material as the tiny black specks in the Indian pottery found on the farm. Lamica consulted a mineralogist who labeled the mineral nepheline syenite. We believe he correctly identified the tempering material used by Owasco/Mahican Indians in making their pottery between A.D. 1300 and 1450.

Later, Lamica recovered several large pieces of Owasco corded horizontal pottery, some of them heavily ornamented rim shards with everted lips. It was one more type of pottery to add to our list of about a dozen types found on the farm.

Over lunch, we talked about the nature and uses of Indian ceramic pots. Somewhat rounded on the bottom, the pots were nestled among the coals and supported by large rocks. Indians learned long ago that boiling acorns in water with wood ashes would destroy the bitter tannin taste. After they were boiled, the acorns were dried in the sun and pounded into meal or flour. Acorn meal was added to soups or made into a mush similar to the mush made today with corn meal. [9]

No Sign of Permanent Housing

There was general agreement that work on the Goes farm should end on September 28, 1987. For weeks we had searched in vain for telltale, circular, dark stains in the squares we excavated, which would indicate post holes for either a house or a protective palisade. Not a single post hole pattern was found after sampling 3,500 square feet of land. It is our belief that Indians on the Goes farm lived in small wigwams or open-faced shelters, primarily during the late spring, summer, and early fall seasons.

Roy Dietert, the group's cartographer, returned with us the following month to finalize all pertinent measurements for the site map. His plan was to tie both the Nicoll-Sill and Goes farm sites together in one master site map that could be used in all future publications and by future scientists. Methods improve over time and archaeologists in a later period may need such a map to dig undisturbed areas.

Filling in the Gaps

Two thousand prehistoric artifacts were recovered from the Goes farm by Bill Goes and the Bethlehem Archaeology Group. Six hundred remained to be identified and catalogued. Additionally, several significant features had been uncovered, which would help us tell the story of Indian life on the farm. The lab's prehistory team identified many of the artifacts but soon asked for more help from Bob Funk who returned to the laboratory in February 1988. He confirmed our identifications, added a few dozen of his own, and helped us examine the entire collection against a backdrop of current knowledge of New York State prehistory. His comments were helpful in determining which cultures lived on the farm over many centuries:

> The more productive the site is, the more frequently people came back over a long period of time. Your site starts about 6500 B.C., then there is a long hiatus we don't fully understand, then you have evidence of Vergennes from 3500 to 3000 B.C. and Vosburg from 3000 to 2500 B.C. The Otter Creek points are typical of Vergennes, the Brewerton points are typical of Vosburg in eastern New York.[10]

We knew that most of the names of local cultural groups came from sites where diagnostic point types were first found, but wondered if the groups that made them were linked together just as families today can be traced back for centuries. Dr. Funk continued:

> A succession of phases or cultures have been defined for the Hudson Valley, and we have type sites to define these phases. Your evidence shows Vergennes, Vosburg, Sylvan Lake, and River cultures in the late Archaic period, and Snook Kill, Orient, Middlesex, Fox Creek, and Owasco/

State Archaeologist Robert Funk examines recent Goes farm finds at the laboratory in 1988.

Mahican cultures in the Transitional and Woodland periods. The Vergennes may be ancestral for the groups that followed.[11]

The February meeting was helpful in filling in the gaps. Now the Bethlehem Indian story could be told at a meeting of the New York State Archaeological Association in April 1990. An earlier version of the chart on page 18 was presented at this meeting, and later refined in accordance with professional criticism received there.

The chart lists our evidence in summary form for the many Indian cultures that lived in Bethlehem from the earliest hunting parties to Mahican times when agricultural practices enriched their diets and fostered larger settlements.

Some stone tools, such as hammerstones, scrapers, knives, and choppers, were used by many

				Native American Cultures on the Goes Farm*	
Stage	**Tradition**	**Local Phase**	**Begin. Date**	**Type & Number Projectile Points Found**	**Other Artifacts Found**
LATE WOODLAND	Owasco	Mahican	AD 1000	Levanna 10	Amulet, Bone Awl, Sinew Stone, Clay Smoking Pipe, Clay Pot Fragments, Arrowshaft Rubber, White-tailed Deer & Sturgeon Bones, Polished Pendants & Celts
MIDDLE WOODLAND	Point Peninsula	Fox Creek	AD 400	Fox Creek 5 Greene 3	
EARLY WOODLAND	Adena	Middlesex	300 BC	Adena 9	Scrapers, Drills, Perforators
TRANSI-TIONAL			700 BC	Meadowood 4	
		Orient	1000 BC	Orient Fishtail 115	Oyster Shells, Netsinkers (used by many cultures)
	Susquehanna	Snook Kill	1500 BC	Susquehanna 19 Snook Kill 4 Genessee 18	Strike-a-lights, Bi-face Knives, Adz
ARCHAIC	Narrow Point	River	1900 BC	Normanskill 117	Mortar, Nutting Stone, Atlatl Weights (bannerstones), Pebble Hammerstones, Shallow-lipped Gouges, V-shaped Abrading Stones, Edge-grooved Anvil Stone, Spearpoint
		Sylvan Lake	2200 BC	Sylvan Side-Notched 1 Sylvan Stemmed 217 Bare Island 27 Wading River 8	
	Laurentian	Vosburg	3000 BC	Vosburg 3 Brewerton Eared-Notched 10 Brewerton Side-Notched 19	Gouge, Ulu Knives, Spoolstones, Cylindrical Pestles, Notched Maul
		Vergennes	3500 BC	Otter Creek 6	Fire-cracked Rocks
EARLY ARCHAIC			6000 BC	Kirk 1	End & Side Scrapers, Hammer-stones, Choppers, Blades
			6500 BC	Bifurcates 6	

*By Virginia L. French & Chuck McKinney, 1991. Adapted from Figure 27 in *Recent Contributions to Hudson Valley Prehistory* by Robert E. Funk, 1976.

Re-creation of the life of Ice Age people at West Athens site in Greene County about 10,500 years ago.

cultures over thousands of years. Similarly, white-tailed deer were hunted in Bethlehem from earliest times, yet deer bones are listed in the Late Woodland period simply because they were found only in Owasco/Mahican hearths on this site.

Further, Indian life in Bethlehem must be viewed against a backdrop of Indian cultures throughout the northeastern United States. Names designating broad traditions of Indian life such as Laurentian, Narrow Point, and Susquehanna on the left side of the chart illustrate where local groups fit into the broader picture.

Finally, little attention has been paid to languages spoken here in prehistoric times. When the Europeans arrived, Indians west of Amsterdam spoke the Iroquoian language and Indians in the greater Fort Orange (Albany) area spoke the Algonquian tongue. We can only assume these languages were spoken by their ancestors over many generations.

Earliest Visitors

Toward the end of the Ice Age in the Northeast, the land and climate became more hospitable for human life. Ice Age hunters were the first people to inhabit New York State about eleven thousand years ago, and roamed this area in search of edible wild plants, fish and game.

Evidence from a hilltop site in West Athens, Greene County, about thirty miles south of Bethlehem, shows these nomadic Indians quarried flint and manufactured stone tools there around 8500 B.C.

The climate grew warmer and more moist over the next three milleniums, as coniferous vegetation gradually gave way to mixed, deciduous forests. Our evidence suggests that the first visitors to Bethlehem were small hunting parties around 6500 B.C. These parties traveled for miles within a defined territory, and their stays here may have been of short duration. From other sites throughout the Northeast, we know they ate fish, small game, and the white-tailed deer, and supplemented their diet with nuts and berries. Bifurcate points were used to bring down game around the Goes farm and simple scrapers and choppers were used to prepare food.

Regular Spring and Summer Visits
after 3500 B.C.

The finding of only six Otter Creek projectile points on the Goes farm suggests that small numbers of Indians visited Bethlehem infrequently during the **Vergennes** period after **3500 B.C.** Fires were probably started by twirling a wooden bow drill. Food was cooked by dropping heated stones into bark containers. Evidence of this early form of cooking can be seen in the many fragments of fire-cracked rock found on the farm. The climate and terrain were very similar to those of today. These Indians hunted among mixed hardwoods and some conifers, particularly spruce, hemlock and pine. They fished along the lakes and streams.

Life may have been easier in the **Vosburg** period after **3000 B.C.** Ulu knives were sharp enough to cut meat and fish easily. One of the specimens found on the Goes farm is still very sharp after more than 4,500 years in the ground. The same can be said of Vosburg gouges, which were effective in all kinds of woodwork. From careful research elsewhere, we know that Indians in this period used stone axes to chop down large trees, from which they made their canoes. The center of the tree was removed by fire, and the remaining part of the core was hollowed out with gouges similar to those found on the farm.

Spoolstone, approximately two inches in length.

We are still hearing theories about the purpose of two intriguing spool-stones found on the Goes farm, a type found only in the Hudson Valley. No proof, just theories. The twenty-nine Brewerton projectile points in our collection associated with the Vosburg culture suggest larger numbers or more frequent visits than the preceding culture.

A pestle, approximately eight inches in length.

Most spectacular of all are the ten long, cylindrical pestles in the Goes collection that were probably made in the Vosburg phase, but also used by other groups to grind acorns into meal. To the lab crew, the pestles are both artistic and functional in the tradition of better things for better living.

During the **Sylvan Lake** phase after **2500 B.C.**, many of the projectile points found on the farm were both narrower and smaller, part of the Narrow Point tradition throughout the northeastern section of the United States. Points that were identified as Lamokas by Dr. Ritchie in 1983 are now known to have been made by the Sylvan Lake people in eastern New York. Evidence for this culture was uncovered by Dr. Funk and others in the mid-1960s at a rockshelter about thirteen miles southeast of Poughkeepsie. Other small, narrow points used by the Sylvan Lake people, called Bare Island and Wading River, were found on the Goes farm as well as in Poughkeepsie. From a lengthy list of stone tools found at the rockshelter,[12] it appears that hunting was the major activity, and faunal remains show that these people mainly hunted "white-tailed deer, raccoon, turkey, beaver and elk."[13]

Spear throwers with attached weights were used heavily by Laurentian, Sylvan Lake, and River Indians over many centuries. They attached a bannerstone to their spearthrower to add weight. The combination of spear and weighted spearthrower is called an atlatl. Our finds are bannerstone preforms, large stones made of garnetiferous gneiss, which would eventually be shaped to final form. Another few hours of work and they would have been reduced to nicely polished, reasonably slim stones, with a winged or crescent shape.

A prize spearpoint in the Goes collection crafted by a **River** culture Indian after **1900 B.C.** is a work of art as well as a deadly weapon. Made of greenish gray Normanskill flint, it is three-and-a-half inches long and an inch-and-a-quarter wide. It has a very sharp point and finely ground, slightly serrated edges. The person who turned out this spearpoint clearly took pride in his work. He would have used a pebble hammerstone and the percussion method to remove large flakes from a flint core, and probably a deer antler to break off increasingly smaller flakes. Since the spearpoint was done to perfection, the final stage would have involved pressure-flaking in which an antler tine was applied to one area at a time—twisting the wrist to chip off tiny additional flakes.

River Indians, ca. 1900 B.C., used atlatls to spear their quarries. Drawing by Margaret Foster.

Prize River culture spearpoint, ca. 1900 B.C.

Mystery Stone

One day, the experts may learn why the River people created shallow, conical pits in large, lap-sized stones sometimes called nutting stones. The nutting stone found on the Goes farm is similar to one found near Scotia[14] but neither site provides a clue as to their use.

A more obvious use can be described for the hollowed-out stone mortar found on the farm. Acorns were placed in the mortar for grinding into meal with a pebble hammerstone. Similarly, a clear purpose is known for the 117 Normanskill projectile points in the Goes collection. Sharp and presumably effective against humans or animals, these small, narrow points were deadly weapons when fastened to the end of spears.

Better Method of Starting Fires

For reasons not understood by archaeologists, the **Snook Kill** Indians living here after **1500 B.C.**

Stone mortar and pebble hammerstone believed to have been used for grinding seeds into meal during the River phase, ca. 1900 B.C.

turned to making heavy, wide-bladed projectile points, a radical departure from the Narrow Point tradition. We knew they were part of the Susquehanna tradition throughout the Northeast, but wondered how they were different from earlier cultures.

Named for a site on the Snook Kill in Saratoga County, the Snook Kill people used flint strike-a-lights and the percussion method to create a spark for their fires, a major improvement over the bow drill. The two strike-a-lights in the Goes collection have squarish bases similar to bases on the Snook Kill points in that collection. Although strike-a-lights were used in earlier centuries, the Snook Kill people may have been the first to use them in Bethlehem.

Strike-a-lights, two-thirds actual size, ca. 1400 B.C.

Earliest Indian Pottery

Better methods of cooking evolved in the **Orient** period after **1000 B.C.** As the chart on page 18 shows, the Orient people are known as a transitional group because of their use of soapstone and Vinette 1 pots, an early ceramic form. No soapstone pottery fragments were found on the farm, but a few Vinette 1 fragments in the collection attest to the earliest use of ceramic pots for cooking in Bethlehem.

On Long Island, the Orient people ate a lot of shellfish, and they may have done so here as well. The marine shells uncovered in the yellow sand below the plow zone on the farm are mostly "eastern oyster or crassostrea virginicus," according to the laboratory's shell specialist, Clark Galloway, and his consultant, Dr. Stephen Brown, a professor of biological sciences at the University at Albany.[15] The twelve netsinkers in the Goes collection are tangible evidence of fishing activity. One hundred fifteen Orient fishtail points found on the farm suggest frequent visits by the Orient people over a long period of time, and the likelihood of Orient burials on a hilltop near the Goes farm.

The Great Wasteland

Except for a few Adena, Meadowood, Greene, and Fox Creek projectile points, not a great deal is known about the 1,900 years in Bethlehem after **600 B.C.** The **Meadowood** people are worthy of mention because tantalizing bits of their innovative lifestyle are known from other sites: possible use of fish nets, bone and copper awls, stone gorgets, ornaments, and birdstones whose function is unknown.

The **Adena/Middlesex** people left nine of their sleek-looking points with a rounded base, a well-known style in Ohio, but less frequently found in the Northeast. Some scientists believe that a few of these people moved east and north from Ohio following a "political disruption of the Adena civilization, with the displacement of some of their more dissatisfied groups."[16]

The Rise of Agriculture

An important development among the **Owasco/Mahican** Indians living in Bethlehem after A.D. **1000** was their experimentation with growing corn, beans, and squash. When added to their usual diet of fish, animal meat, nuts, and other wild vegetable foods, such horticulture would have significantly improved their well-being and encouraged larger and more permanent settlements.

Better things for better living in Owasco-Mahican times, ca. A.D. 1300-1600. Sinewstone, left; arrowshaft smoother, top center; amulet, bottom center; and bone awl, right.

Ten triangular Levanna points found on the farm indicate that Owasco/Mahican Indians used the bow and arrow, a major advance in hunting weapons and an effective instrument of war. The single arrowshaft smoother in the Goes collection is tangible evidence of their use of arrows.

Owasco/Mahican women made clothing from animal skins by stretching strips of hides over a sinew stone, and sewing them together with bone awls similar to the tools pictured on page 23. One amulet or tiny pebble with a hole in the top was the only evidence found on the Goes farm of necklaces used by young girls or women in this period. We know that the men smoked, since a few fragments of their ring bowl, trumpet style pipes were recovered along with hundreds of Indian pottery fragments.

Pottery fragments showing female artistic ability in the Owasco/Mahican period.

Mahican Female Artisans *Par Excellence*

Perhaps the most significant evidence of Mahican female artistry in the Goes collection are the fragments of pottery styles, which include incised Chance, Deowongo, and Kingston ceramic pots, as well as Oak Hill Corded pots. All are elaborately decorated around the rim, with designs that some modern artists would envy, and all are significant improvements over the less well fired pottery styles in earlier centuries.

The pots were used by Algonquian-speaking people, part of a large cultural group ranging from southern Ontario down through eastern New York, and as far south as the Delaware Valley. The record suggests that they were often in conflict with Iroquoian-speaking Indians, and sometimes Mahican braves "captured women potters from their neighbors to the west."[17] This

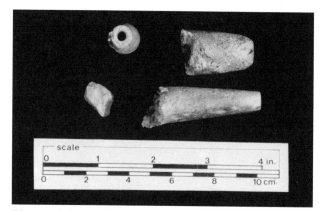

Ring bowl clay smoking pipes used by Mahicans, ca. A.D. 1400.

could explain why both Mahican and Iroquois pottery types were found on the Goes farm.

European Contacts With Mahicans

Although the Mahicans may have been driven out of the area after conflicts with the Iroquois in 1628, they were still negotiating the sale of land in Bethlehem as late as 1652, about 22 years after Brant Peelen, Bethlehem's first resident, began to farm the land on Westerlo Island. One such sale shows Aepje (pronounced Ap ya), chief of the Mahicans, and two men from his tribe confirming the sale of land to colony director Johan B. van Rensselaer, on September 12, 1652. Other Bethlehem citizens mentioned in the bill of sale are Aert Jacobs, who farmed the land immediately north of the Vloman Kill, and Cornelis van Voorhout, who had a farm in the area now called Glenmont.[18]

The bill of sale is typical of others negotiated during the seventeenth century: vague boundaries, and figures of small animals or birds to identify the Indians selling the land. In exchange for the land, the Indians received "a certain parcel of goods named separately," a record that could not be located. The usual items exchanged for land by the Dutch ranged from glass beads, iron tools, and woolen textiles to guns, liquor and ornamental trinkets. Europeans realized that trading guns and liquor with the Indians brought trouble but never discontinued the practice.

BILL OF SALE FOR LAND IN BETHLEHEM
Mid-Seventeenth Century

Appeared before us the subscribed witnesses in the presence of Aepje alias Skiwias, Chief of the Mahicans, Nosinaawe, owner and proprietor of a certain piece of land extending from the Molenkil (which is also included) southward to the first stream, south or past the house of Cornelis Cornelisz van Voorhout, and as far inland as is convenient without special limitation. Item Na'ckonan owner of the land at Bethlehem from the large stream there (which is included together with the falls and lands around it) northward to the mountain where Aert Jacobsz lives (including the aforesaid mountain); and from there northward to the flats that are being cultivated by the aforesaid Aert, together with the woods inland according to convenience as before; and we, the aforesaid owners of the respective parcels of land, acknowledge to have freely and voluntarily sold the same, as previously mentioned, to the honorable Mr. Johan Baptista van Rensselaer, director of the colony of Rensselaerswyck, for a certain parcel of goods named separately, which they acknowledge by the acceptance of this to have received to their complete satisfaction; therefore, the grantors eternally transport and convey the aforesaid lands to his honor the before mentioned director on behalf of his honor, the patroon, and co-directors of the aforesaid colony; and for this purpose the contents of this has been translated and proposed to the aforesaid owners in their language, whereupon they acknowledged that this was their exact meaning, and that they were in full agreement with the sale. In confirmation whereof we as witnesses and the grantors have affixed our signatures hereto. Done this 12th day of September Anno 1652 in the aforesaid colony.

The mark of Nosinaawe done with his own hands.

The mark of Na'ckonan done with his own hands.

The mark of Aepje as witness done with his own hands.

[Signed:] A: van Curler as witness
G: Swart

The common mark of Cornelis Cornelisz van Voorhout done with his own hands.

Thus approved and signed in my presence and cognizance, the secretary of the aforesaid colony. [Signed:] Antonius De Hooges Secretaris

[Endorsed:] Bill of sale of lands of Cornelis Cornelisz van Voorhout, and Aert Jacobsz 1652: 12 September.

Translation by Charles Gehring.

How the Mahicans Appeared to One European

No history of local Indian life in the Late Woodland period would be complete without mention of the observations of Adriaen van der Donck who wrote *A Description of the New Netherlands* in 1655.[19] His first-hand observations are often the best answers to difficult questions asked by members of groups touring the laboratory.

Van der Donck, the first legal officer for the colony of Rensselaerswyck, earned a doctor of laws degree from the respected University of Leyden in Holland. He was a young man in his twenties when he arrived here in August 1641.

When the temporary nature of housing on the Goes farm is described to groups touring the lab, the quick rejoinder is often, "Yes, but they had houses elsewhere in the area when Henry Hudson arrived in 1609."[20] Of course they did, as van der Donck confirms:

> When they build a house, they place long slender hickory saplings in the ground, having the bark stripped off, in a straight line of two rows, as far asunder as they intend the breadth of the house to be (usually no more than twenty feet) and as far as it is intended the length shall be.

> The sapling poles are then bent over towards each other in the form of an arch, and secured together, having the appearance of a garden arbour. The sapling poles are then crossed with split poles in the form of lathing, which are well-fastened to the upright work. The lathings are the heaviest near the ground.

> For covering they use the bark of ash, chestnut, and other trees, which they peel off in pieces of about six feet long, and as broad as they can. They have one door in the center of the house and an opening in the crown of the roof to let out the smoke.[21]

And the subject of ancient burials often comes up in group discussions at the lab, both within the staff and during group sessions with students or adults visiting the lab. People wonder why the Owasco Indians interred on the Goes farm were buried flex-style, with knees drawn up toward the chest. Van der Donck offers a clue:

> Whenever an Indian departs this life, all the residents of the place assemble at the funeral. Whenever a soul has departed, the nearest relatives extend the limbs and close the eyes of the dead; and after the body has been watched and wept over several days and nights, they bring it to the grave, wherein they do not lay it down, but place it in a sitting posture upon a stone or block of wood.[22]

His description suggests that relatives simply placed the body in a flex or sitting position, just before it was buried on its side in a shallow grave. Admittedly, this is a shortened version of the ceremony that may not tell the whole story.

Although it is not possible to tell the entire story of mid-seventeenth century Indian life here, the inquisitive reader who takes the time to locate van der Donck's book will find that he covers a wide range of Indian subjects. Almost all of our visitors to the lab know about the Mahican diet of corn, beans, squash, animal meat, and fish, but they are curious about how the food was prepared by Indians. Van der Donck explains as well as titillates with stories about roasting beaver and serving fatty raccoon meat to special guests.

Probably not all of van der Donck's observations are accurate, since he wrote his famous book after returning to Holland. Still, he offers much food for thought, a solid basis for final impressions of the Indians after the arrival of Europeans.

In the Final Analysis

The preceding story of a dig and its aftermath emphasizes Indian life in Bethlehem between 6500 B.C. and A.D. 1655. The evidence is far from complete and it is hoped that future digs will fill in the gaps, particularly during the 1,900 years after 600 B.C.

Although the Mohawks claimed sovereignty over Hudson Valley tribes after 1628, and the Mahicans lost most of their riverfront property, Algonquian-speaking Mahicans continued to live independently in this area well into the last quarter of the seventeenth century and beyond. Some moved to the Schaghticoke settlement established by Governor Edmund Andros on the Hoosic River north of Albany in 1678, making it necessary for them to abide by New York laws.[23]

Life under English rule was not without its problems. A smallpox epidemic killed hundreds throughout the valley in 1679. Dozens of Mahicans fought on the side of England in its war with France in 1689. Many returned from Canada in 1690 with still more smallpox. By 1691, more than half of all the valley Indians had died or left their homes.[24]

By 1700, almost 100,000 Europeans had settled in the Hudson Valley and fewer than 3,000 Indians remained. A paltry few hundred Indians were living in the greater Albany area at this time. The few remaining Indians resisted selling their lands and avoided any involvement in white man's wars. Their numbers grew smaller with each passing year and by 1800, Mahicans in Bethlehem were few and far between.[25]

Roughly 40,000 Indians remain in the entire state of New York today, and some thirty-five percent of the total live on reservations. Gone are the ancient bark longhouses and domed thatched houses. In their place stand frame houses, mobile homes, and apartment houses. Today's Native Americans live, work, and play like their neighbors.[26]

2 Colonial Beginnings

Henry Hudson's Expedition

Henry Hudson.

The Dutch East India Company in 1609 sent out the ship *de Halve Maen* (the Half Moon), with Henry Hudson as master, to search for a northeast passage to the Orient. Failing in that, Hudson then took his ship across the Atlantic, sailed along the North American coast, and finally decided to explore the river that now bears his name. He anchored on the evening of September 19, a little north of the present city of Albany, some 150 miles upstream at latitude 42° 40'.[1] The next day, the mate went ashore (the log does not indicate on which side of the river) and was a guest at the house of "a Governour of the Countrey."[2] Hudson remained at anchor there for six days, allowed some of the local Indians on board, and traded beads, knives, and hatchets for furs. Hudson and the mate plied a few chiefs with "so much Wine and Aqua vitae, that they were all Merrie.... In the end one of them was drunke ... and that was strange to them; for they could not tell how to take it." Later the mate took a boat upstream, reported back that the river became too shallow for further progress, and on September 23 *de Halve Maen* swung about to begin the journey back to Europe.[3]

Replica of *de Halve Maen* (the Half Moon), built in Albany in 1990.

Although Hudson's expedition in search of a passage to the Orient was a disappointment to his employers, they and others saw in his reports some possibilities for profit in what would be

The Hudson River, 1827. Crayon drawing by Charlotte Bonaparte.

called New Netherland. Several independent trading expeditions were outfitted over the next four years, and then in 1614 a group of traders formed the New Netherland Company, which was granted a four-year monopoly.[4]

Trading Posts

In 1614 Hendrick Christiansen van Cleef of the New Netherland Company erected a fort (actually a redoubt) on Westerlo Island in the Hudson River, just east of the mouth of the Normanskill. He named it Fort Nassau, after the Dutch royal family, and served as its first commander. This first structure to be erected by Europeans within the future bounds of Bethlehem was surrounded by a moat eighteen feet wide, mounted with two cannon and eleven smaller guns, and garrisoned with ten or twelve men.[5]

A spring flood in 1617 destroyed the fort, but New Netherland Company traders established a new post at (probably meaning against, not on top of) the heights of the mainland, overlooking the mouth of the Normanskill.[6] This site was abandoned after the company's trading license expired a year later.

Fort Orange and the First Settlers

West India Company House, Amsterdam.

A new company, called the West India Company, was formed in 1621. It was chartered by the Dutch government to wage war on the nation's enemies, take prizes of enemy shipping, and govern all Dutch colonies facing the Atlantic in Africa and the Americas, including New Netherland. In 1624 the West India Company erected Fort Orange on the west shore of the Hudson River just north of Westerlo Island. Eighteen families, mostly Walloons, were settled there that year to raise food for the fort's traders

Mauritz, Prince of Orange, for whom Fort Orange was named.

West India Company cannon from Fort Orange, later in possession of Rensselaerswyck.

and soldiers. However, in 1626 the fort commander, Daniel van Kriekenbeeck, at the request of the local Mahicans joined a war party against the neighboring Mohawks. This was contrary to orders not to meddle in native affairs, but the Mahicans were offering as an enticement a gift of land adjacent to the fort and the Dutch soldiers probably foresaw little risk in the venture. They walked into an ambush—Kriekenbeeck and three of his men were killed. Three others escaped, one of them wounded in the back by an arrow while swimming to safety. The colony's director-general, Pieter Minuit, resettled the farm families on Manhattan Island for their own safety, leaving only sixteen soldiers and traders at the fort.[7]

The Founding of Rensselaerswyck

The war between the Mohawks and Mahicans ended in the spring of 1628 when the Mahicans were overwhelmingly defeated and forced to abandon the area. Thus, in the autumn of that year, there were no Indians residing within several miles of Fort Orange, nor for that matter any Europeans living outside the walls of the fort.[8]

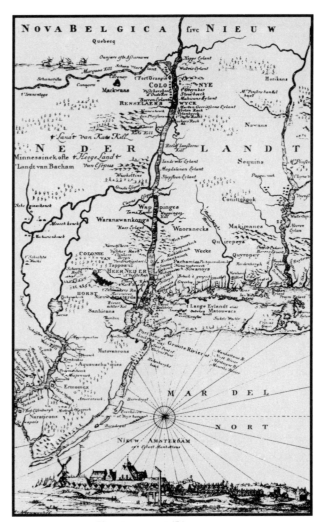

New Netherland. Visscher map, 1656.

Settlement throughout New Netherland progressed slowly. Therefore, the West India Company directors in 1629 decided to stimulate immigration by permitting private colonies to be formed within New Netherland. Any principal stockholder of the company willing to buy a tract of land from the Indians and able to settle fifty people there, aged fifteen or above, within four years would receive land title and various privileges, as well as the personal title of *patroon*. The land meant potential wealth, the title prestige; neither was an insignificant consideration to untitled merchants in a title-conscious age.[9]

Amsterdam in the eighteenth century. Engraving by T. Jefferys.

Three applicants informed the West India Company on January 13, 1629, that they were sending agents to America to seek out likely sites for colonies. Only one of these three potential patroons would succeed—the director of the company's Amsterdam chamber, Kiliaen van Rensselaer. The two agents, Gilles Houset, sailor, and Jacob Jansen, cooper, arrived in New Netherland to find the relocated Mahicans willing to sell the area around Fort Orange. Van Rensselaer registered his intentions of founding a colony on November 19, and was granted the title, "Patroon of Rensselaerswyck."[10]

By January 16, 1630, the patroon had engaged Wolfert Gerritsen to be supervisor and Rutger Hendricksen and Brant Peelen as farmers. They

would become the first settlers within the eventual Bethlehem town boundaries. These men,

"Wigwam in the Forest." Engraving by J. Cousen after a painting by W. H. Bartlett, 1840. Archaeological evidence (see Chapter 1) suggests that Indians in Bethlehem used temporary housing.

A River Indian. Engraving by I. Faber, 1710.

together with another farmer, their families, and five laborers, left Holland March 21 on the ship *de Eendracht*. They arrived at New Amsterdam May 24, and with luck may have reached Fort Orange a few days later. Instructions from the patroon to Bastiaen Jansen Krol, the company's business agent at the fort, requested that he purchase land in the neighborhood from whatever Indians had claim to it. The actual purchase, however, was made by van Rensselaer's agent Gillis Houset, much to the surprise of company officials and the chagrin of Krol, who had been reporting that the Indians refused to sell. Houset, it seems, had sailed upriver and on July 27 "came to the place where Jan Jansse Meyns camped with men to cut timber for the ship." To that place "there came also by accident" five owners of land which Houset proposed to buy and they agreed to sell.[11]

On August 13 the five Mahicans[12] appeared in New Amsterdam to declare to Director-General Minuit and the Council that they were satisfied with the terms of the sale and had been paid. The sale included land on both the east and west banks of the river, that on the west including one parcel extending from Petanock[13] north to Negagonse. Petanock is today the Normanskill; within a few years of the sale there was some uncertainty as to the location of Negagonse.[14]

On April 18, 1631, several Mahicans agreed to sell another parcel called Sanckhagag, extending from a little above Barren Island north to Shad Island, and two days' walk inland.[15] According to a map received by the patroon from Pieter Minuit, there were included about 200 morgens (400 acres) of cleared land, some seeded by the Indians. This gave van Rensselaer, according to his reckoning, all the land on the west shore and two days'

The Hudson River, about 1630. Places named (from left to right) are: Barren Island, Three Clovers, Smacks (Shad) Island, Castle (Westerlo) Island, and Fort Orange.

journey inland from Barren Island (below Coeymans Creek) to Peebles Island (by the mouth of the Mohawk River). This presents some problems, since van Rensselaer did not indicate how and when he acquired the land between Shad Island and the Normanskill, nor are there any deeds from that time for the area.[16]

Following an inventory in 1651 of Rensselaerswyck's holdings, there seems to have been some concern that the colony's deeds of 1630 and 1631 were deficient. This could explain why two of the colony's directors, Jan Baptist van Rensselaer in 1652 and Jeremias van Rensselaer in 1661, made additional purchases from the Mahicans of land between the Normanskill and the Vloman Kill.[17]

Westerlo Island: the First Settlement

Two farms were erected during that first summer in 1630, one on the east shore on the site of present-day Rensselaer; the other, named Rensselaersburgh, was on Westerlo Island, just off the west shore of the Hudson and for the most part south of the Normanskill. Twelve morgens (about twenty-four acres) were seeded with wheat and four with rye by the fall of 1631. By 1632 the farmers were planting wheat, rye, oats, green and gray peas, and barley. Livestock included horses, cattle, sheep, hogs, chickens, and pigeons.[18]

The patroon described the Rensselaersburgh farm as "provided with a convenient dwelling, the sides and gable built up with brick," and the farm provided with two hay barracks, a barn, a sheepcote, and other necessities. A brick house with several outbuildings is not the primitive farm in the wilderness we usually picture, but Rensselaerswyck was a well-financed operation. Van Rensselaer since 1620 had been supporting the establishment of farms in the Netherlands on land being reclaimed from the sea; he understood farming, was organized, and was prepared for long term investment.[19]

The initial farm on Westerlo Island was established on the western half of the island. Van Rensselaer anticipated from the beginning that the island would have more than one farm, and in 1632 he sent detailed instructions to Rutger Hendricksen to designate workers and livestock for a second farm and to have a house erected. The name of the farm was to be Welysburgh, for the patroon's wife, Anna van Wely. "Brant Peelen from [Nykerck] shall be farmer, who shall have half of the said island for his use." This farm on the southern and eastern half of the island was occupied on January 1, 1634, by Peelen, who had previously assisted Rutger Hendricksen in developing the Rensselaersburgh farm.[20]

Bethlehem's First Resident

Brant Peelen may be considered the first permanent resident within the eventual bounds of Bethlehem. The original employees' contracts with the patroon expired in 1634 and only Peelen renewed his, thereafter managing both of the Westerlo Island farms. He was born about 1589 in the village of Nykerck, also the home town of

Kiliaen van Rensselaer, who undoubtedly either knew Peelen or had had good reports of him. The early reports of his work in Rensselaerswyck were also favorable, and in 1632 the patroon directed that Peelen be appointed a *schepen* (alderman), although it does not appear likely that a governing council ever actually functioned at this early date. He was also appointed *voorlezer* (layreader), there being no clergyman in Rensselaerswyck until 1642, and van Rensselaer sent him a Bible and a book of homilies to be read on Sundays and before council meetings.[21]

Little is known of Brant Peelen's personal life, but it can be presumed that his wife, Lubbertje Wouters, and their children Lysbeth, Geert, and Gerritje accompanied him to New Netherland in 1630. Lysbeth and Gerritje are listed as passengers from Holland to America on the ship *den Waterhondt* in 1640, but this was most certainly a second trip, rather than an indication of a ten-year family separation.[22]

In the spring of 1634, van Rensselaer sent over Jacob Albertsen Planck as *schout* (court officer) for the colony and in his contract included instructions to settle "in the middle of the east side of Castle now West Island [modern Westerlo Island], on the river side, [and] cause a suitable dwelling to be erected." This would put a third house on the island, and in that same year van Rensselaer wrote to his nephew, New Netherland Director-General Wouter van Twiller, "There must be not two only but three farms on West Island, each of which would have more than forty morgens of land. They must draw their hay from

"Hofstede Renselaar," the van Rensselaer farmstead in Nijkerk.

another island."[23] He noted that Rensselaer (the family farm in Nykerck),

> has not even 20 morgens of cultivated farm land, at least not much more; and what a fine farm that is.... There could easily be six farms on the island. This must come gradually as more cattle and people come.... I will send people enough hereafter if only I have cattle.[24]

And this was the problem, not a shortage of people. Few cattle survived the ocean voyage to America, so that new herds were developed chiefly through the slow process of natural increase, or purchased from older, more established colonies.

Relations between Brant Peelen and van Rensselaer became rather chilly after 1638, due in part to van Rensselaer's being eight years in arrears in settling Peelen's accounts.[25] However, the amount due to Peelen was small in comparison to his income from the sale of wheat to the West India Company in America and furs in the Netherlands. Comfortable in his situation, Brant Peelen remained on Westerlo Island the rest of his life. Peelen married twice: his second wife was Marritje Pieters, a widow whom he married in July 1643. He died before May 1, 1644.[26]

The explorer David Pietersen de Vries visited Rensselaerswyck in 1640 and described a common problem for those living in the lowlands:

> The 30th of April while I lay here at Fort Orange, there came such a flood upon the island on which Brand Pijlen [Brant Peelen] dwelt (my host for the time being) that we had to abandon the island, and to use boats in going to the house, for the water stood about four feet deep on the island, whereas the latter lies seven or eight feet above ordinary water. This high water lasted three days before we could use the houses again. The water came into the fort. We had to resort to the woods, where we set up tents and kept great fires going.[27]

The *schout*, Jacob Planck, probably settled on Westerlo Island as instructed. However, he remained in the colony only until 1638. Presumably Brant Peelen thereafter kept up all three farms on the island.

As for government for the colony, from Planck's departure until 1641, Rensselaerswyck was supervised by a commission of three officials: Cornelis Teunissen van Slyck as the patroon's representative, Pieter Cornelissen van Munnickendam as receiver of tithes and supercargo, and eighteen-year-old Arent van Curler (his mother was the patroon's cousin) as *commis* (business agent), secretary, and bookkeeper.[28]

Adriaen van der Donck was engaged by the patroon in 1641 as *schout* and was sent over with instructions to settle on Westerlo Island. After his arrival, he remarked that there was room for only two farms there, and moved to Schuyler Flats.[29] Van Rensselaer did not see how a *schout* could operate effectively from the "extreme upper end" of the colony, and forced van der Donck to move back to Westerlo Island. Early in 1642 the *schout* was farming at the south end of the island "near brandt peelen." By June he had moved away again, leasing his farm to Peelen for 200 guilders a year. Peelen intended to settle some sort of in-law there, perhaps Goosen Gerritsen van Schaick, husband of Peelen's daughter Geertie. However, van Rensselaer again had his way, this time for good—van der Donck was back on the island soon thereafter and remained on the farm until January 1646.[30]

Brant Peelen praised the island's rich alluvial soil to the Reverend Johannes Megapolensis in 1642 or 1643, telling him "that he had raised fine wheat on one and the same piece of land eleven years successively without ever breaking it up or letting it lie fallow."[31] Spring floods, such as the one in

1640 mentioned by David Pietersen de Vries, brought fresh soil to the island. Adriaen van der Donck affirmed Megapolensis's report in his own account of the colony: "I owned land adjoining the land referred to, and have seen the eleventh crop, which was tolerably good."[32] On the other hand, floods could sometimes ruin a farm. The farm of Jan Helmsen at Bethlehem was one of several along the river that were spoiled by knee-deep deposits of sand during the winter of 1668.[33]

The First Sawmillers

In 1631 and 1632 van Rensselaer sent more people. In 1631 two sawmillers named Laurens Laurensen from Copenhagen, Denmark, and Barent Thonisen from Hellesund, Norway, signed a contract with him to settle either on the Normanskill or on the east side of the river on a creek "where there is a good waterfall." The next year the patroon sent over "all kinds of ironwork and the like for the erection of a saw and grist mill, tobacco planting and farming purposes." The millers seem to have settled on the east side where a gristmill was erected,[34] but someone in the colony, perhaps the millers themselves, advised van Rensselaer against putting the sawmill there. The two Scandinavians may have later erected the sawmill on the Normanskill "where there is much timber," van Rensselaer writing in June 1634 to Johannes de Laet that "the mill [creek] on the west side at the end of Castle [Westerlo] Island, where the first sawmill was erected, I have named Godyns kil." Yet a month later, he was telling a committee of the West India Company that he had sent equip-

ment for the saw and gristmills, "whereof is still in existence the gristmill," which sounds as if the sawmill no longer existed. Perhaps the millers built the sawmill but never operated it, since they were not listed in the colony's pay records after 1633.[35]

Albert Bratt, Norwegian Settler

In 1636 two more prospective sawmillers signed a contract[36] with van Rensselaer for seven years' service: Pieter Cornelissen from Munnickendam, aged forty-three, millwright, and Albert Andriessen Bratt[37] from Frederikstad, Norway, aged twenty-nine, tobacco planter. Pieter Cornelissen would spend a decade in Rensselaerswyck; Albert Bratt's career would span forty-nine years, nearly a third of the entire colonial period.[38]

Bratt was a Norwegian, but that was not unusual in New Netherland, where there eventually were hundreds of Scandinavians. He grew up in Frederikstad, the principal sawmilling city of Norway, then went to the Netherlands where there were no forests, working for a while as a sailor in the merchant marine.[39] Sometime after 1632 he took up tobacco farming, which was what he was doing when he and Pieter Cornelissen signed the contract.

They arrived at Fort Orange on April 7, 1637, the Tuesday before Easter, about three o'clock in the morning according to the ship's log. An earlier entry in the log for November 2, 1636, noted that, "This day a child was born on the ship, and

"Ships in a Tempestuous Sea." Engraving by Schelte Adams Bolswert, after a painting by Andries van Eertvelt.

named and baptized in England stoerm," the third of the Bratts' eight children; "the mother is annetie baernts." In later life the son would call himself Storm van der Zee, "Storm from the Sea."

The fort where the settlers disembarked consisted of a few small buildings within a rather unsturdy palisade. Among the personnel stationed there were West India Company officials, soldiers, laborers, and slaves; regular visitors included free traders, smugglers, and Indians. Outside the fort was Rensselaerswyck, which for the most part was still wilderness, the total working personnel consisting of one official, three farm managers, six common laborers, and a wheelwright, together with some families. To this total the ship suddenly added twenty-seven men, five housewives, and a half-dozen children.

The sawmill on the creek known variously as Petanock, Secktanock, Tawasentha, and Godyn's

Kil was put in working order. According to the contract, Bratt was to help Pieter Cornelissen with the sawmill and also to operate the tobacco farm. Before the end of the first summer, however, the partners had a fight and Bratt left the sawmill. The patroon wrote to Pieter Cornelissen, "I hear that he is a strange character and it is therefore no wonder that he could not get along with you."

Bratt's Tobacco Farm

For the next several years, Albert Bratt concentrated on the tobacco farm, having the help of his brother, Arent, and five employees. He also dabbled in the illegal fur trade.

The 1638 tobacco crop was bad, and van Rensselaer wrote of the next year's crop, "The tobacco was so poor and thin of leaf that it could not stand being

"Albert Bratt's Tobacco Farm." Painting by Jean Eaton.

rolled." The 1640 crop was of a good grade but Bratt had overpriced it and van Rensselaer had trouble selling it.

The fur trade was opened to private citizens in 1639 and thereafter became a mainstay of Bratt's income. In 1643 Bratt was convicted of smuggling, in response to which "he abused the lord patroon and the whole council, so that he was condemned to pay a heavy fine," which he refused to pay, and the court had to deduct the fine from his tobacco credits.

In addition to the tobacco plantation and smuggling, he was involved at various times with sawing, fishing, cattle, real estate, and apple orchards, often with several simultaneously. Van Rensselaer had noted in 1632 that the Normanskill "has quantities of fish, principally bullheads and lampreys, and nearby is much beautiful, arable meadow land." In 1682 Bratt's orchards on the Normanskill were subleased to Teunis Cornelissen Slingerland for 150 *schepels* a year, which, if they represented the usual tenth, meant that the orchards were producing 1500 *schepels* (about 1100 bushels). The degree of freedom that Bratt and the other Rensselaerswyck tenants enjoyed enabled them to pursue secondary careers which were often as lucrative as their lease-holdings. Bratt was not lacking in ambition, and the diversification was necessary to guarantee an income from season to season and year to year.

Bratt's Mills

In 1646 Albert and his brother Arent left the tobacco farm, Arent becoming a cattle and grain farmer elsewhere in Renselaerswyck while Albert succeeded his former partner Pieter Cornelissen as manager of two sawmills on Godyn's Kil (now the Normanskill). Albert had picked a lucky time to go into the lumber business—during at least part of this period he was selling 6,000 board feet a day. Spring floods in 1646 and 1647 washed away all but three of the houses at Fort Orange; in the next five years some one hundred houses were built in and around the fort. By 1651 the colony had some ten mills in operation, providing not only building supplies for local consumption, but a major commodity for export to other colonies along the eastern seaboard.

An inventory of Rensselaerswyck in 1651 stated that Bratt's two mills were driven by a powerful

Normanskill Falls. Engraving.

New Amsterdam, about 1660.

Mohawks for 120 guilders worth of furs.

In addition to his business career, Albert Bratt was an active lay leader in the Lutheran Church. This was a patently il-

Beaver. Engraving by William Daniell, 1807. Fortunes were made by trading in beaver pelts.

legal activity under the charter to the West India Company, which established the Dutch Reformed Church as the only church, and in 1656 Bratt, as elder, was fined for organizing a public service. After the 1664 English conquest of New Netherland, the Lutheran Church was officially tolerated. Bratt continued as elder until at least 1680.

In 1672 he retired from work, turning over control of his mill to his eldest son, Barent, who in 1682 released it to his own sons, Anthony and Dirck. By then the mill creek was usually referred to as the *Normans Kil* (Norwegian's Creek, in Dutch) which, of course, is what it is still called today.

Albert Bratt died in 1686 at the age of seventy-nine, having outlived his younger brother, three of his eight adult children, and two of his three wives (he was separated from the third). Van Rensselaer said he was cruel to his family, neighbors complained that he trespassed on their property, burned their fences, fought with them, and threw a knife at one, and yet he was a respected businessman and an elected church leader at a time when that required some courage. Some people do not fit into easy categories.

waterfall and that the operation was worth a thousand guilders rent a year, but that he was being charged only 250. Eight years later, Jan Baptist van Rensselaer noted, "He ought to give more than 250 guilders for the mills and the land, although he always complains, but that is an old habit of his." Not that it really mattered greatly what the annual rent was, because Bratt only paid it ten times in twenty-six years.

Business Diversification

As his operations expanded, Bratt bought an office and warehouse on Manhattan Island for storing imported trade goods, and furs and lumber for export. Profits in the fur trade were astounding, with a markup for most materials of two thousand percent. For instance, a musket that cost six guilders on delivery could be traded to the

A New Family on Westerlo Island

Less than a month before Kiliaen van Rensselaer's death in October 1643, Cornelis Segers van Voorhout, aged forty-four, sailed for America with his wife, Brechie Jacobs, forty-five, and six children, aged eight to twenty-two. The ship reached New Amsterdam the following March, and within the month Cornelis had occupied the farm of the recently deceased Brant Peelen. By 1646 neighbor Adriaen van der Donck had left Rensselaerswyck, and Cornelis agreed to take over his farm as well for the three years remaining on the lease.[40]

The temper of Cornelis Segers is evident in frequent court records. In October 1648 he was obliged to retract some derogatory comments about magistrate Andries de Vos made in a tavern, as well as remarks he had made in August that Jan Barentsen Poest was a rascal, thief, and the greatest liar in the colony. Court records of the next summer show him in a fight provoked by his former employee, Jacob Aryaensen the wheelwright. In August 1649 Cornelis was accused by the *schout* with suddenly and without provocation striking Gysbert Adriaensen in the face with a glass, cutting a deep gash and severing some arteries.[41]

In a long-running dispute over his accounts with Rensselaerswyck's director, Brant van Slichtenhorst, Cornelis was charged with refusing to allow his farm to be appraised, and in August 1649 was ordered to obey his contract. Cornelis and his son-in-law, Jacob Jansen Schermerhoorn, were charged in January 1650 with having assaulted Director van Slichtenhorst, but the case never came to trial. However, since Cornelis's contract had expired, Westerlo Island was offered for lease to anyone interested. The next lessee was Gysbert Cornelissen from Weesp, but since he was another of Cornelis Segers's sons-in-law, Segers continued in fact as farmer of Westerlo Island, Gysbert apparently signing the contract so that the equally and notoriously stubborn Segers and van Slichtenhorst could avoid having to agree with each other.[42]

The inventory taken of Rensselaerswyck in 1651 recorded that Cornelis was indeed in possession of "a good farm on Castle [Westerlo] Island" comprised of seventy morgens, some of the land recently cleared, with thirteen horses and twenty-two cattle, for all of which he was supposed to pay 1,210 guilders annually.[43] This farm was by far the most valuable in the colony, the next best being assessed at 810 guilders.

It was therefore no insignificant matter for Rensselaerswyck that Cornelis year in and year out neglected to pay his rent. The director was understandably tired of waiting for the grain that was due as payment on the lease when he armed himself with a court order, and on March 30, 1652, went to Westerlo Island to obtain at least partial payment. Cornelis refused to release the grain and had previously nailed the door to the loft shut. The court ordered him to transfer 150 *schepels* within four days to the loft of Gysbert Cornelis, where it should remain until the case could be settled. Finally on September 29, by which time

Slichtenhorst had been succeeded as director by Jan Baptist van Rensselaer, Cornelis signed a new lease for Westerlo Island, agreeing to pay 3,000 guilders in partial satisfaction of the old account. He continued to work the farm until 1659 when his son Seger married, and Cornelis turned over the lease to him.[44] Cornelis last appears in the records on January 2, 1677, and Maria van Rensselaer in a letter of November 1683 mentioned that he was deceased.[45]

Hot-Headed Offspring

The van Voorhout sons had tempers to match their father's. Cornelis Cornelissen was something of a tavern brawler, charged with fighting in 1649 and 1650 with Jan van Bremen, Thomas Chambers, and Jan Labatie, and drawing a knife on Christoffel Davids.[46] Another son, Claes Cornelissen, was in Hendrick Jochimsen's inn on August 31, 1658, when he began a heated argument with Daniel Nonvou, a soldier. A fight ensued with the two combatants wrestling each other to the floor several times. Nonvou drew his rapier and tried to stab Claes, but bystander Jan Eeraerts took the sword from him. Claes tried again to punch Nonvou, who drew a knife and stabbed Claes in the breast, killing him.[47]

On June 23, 1662, Claes's brother Seger became involved in a tavern dispute with Andries Herpertsen Constapel, a former ship's gunner (*konstabel*). Seger struck Constapel in the head with a pool cue, severely injuring him. Then, according to a witness, Andries stabbed Seger "in

his left side, below the short ribs. After having stabbed him, Andries dealt him five blows on the head, so that they claim his skull is cracked." The next day at Seger's bedside they forgave each other, and that night at the age of thirty-three Seger died, leaving a wife but no children. His parents, brothers, and brother-in-law signed an agreement also forgiving Andries but requiring that "in order to prevent further mischief" he make every effort to avoid Seger's relatives. Constapel himself died before October 12, but whether or not as a result of the fight is not known.[48]

Such tumultous behavior was not a peculiarity of life on the colonial frontier. Records throughout Europe reveal a general turbulence. The seventeenth century was a violent age.

Marten Gerritsen on Westerlo Island

Seger Cornelissen's widow, Jannetie van Vechten, married Marten Gerritsen van Bergen[49] sometime prior to August 4, 1664. Marten, formerly a servant of Rensselaerswyck director Jeremias van Rensselaer,[50] took over the lease of Seger's farm and renewed it several times thereafter. A flood in April 1666 swept away the house, barn, and hayricks, all the cattle and horses perishing except one mare. By November 1667 Marten had replaced the house with a new brick one valued at 1,000 guilders, and by 1668 Jeremias van Rensselaer could say, "The island, occupied by Maerte Gerretsen, is again in full posture." After the flood, Marten had moved to the other house on the island and apparently remained there, since in 1683 his father-in-law, Teunis Dircksen van Vechten, was living in the house Marten had built.[51]

By this time the early history of European settlement on the island had long been forgotten. Jasper Danckaerts, who visited Albany in 1680, recorded a local legend in his journal:

> In the afternoon, we took a walk to an island upon the end of which there is a fort built, they say by the Spaniards. That a fort has been there is evident enough from the earth thrown up, but it is not to be supposed that the Spaniards came so far inland to build forts, when there are no monuments of them to be seen down on the sea coasts.... This spot is a short hour's distance below Albany.[52]

The fort, of course, had been built on Westerlo Island by Dutch traders in 1614.

Gerritsen's long occupation of the island resulted in its often being called Marten Gerritsen's Island, as in Albany's city charter in 1686. Jeremias van Rensselaer in 1671 called Gerritsen "our best farmer" at a time when he was threatening to leave if he could not get better terms than van Rensselaer was offering. Incidentally, van Rensselaer noted, "The land produces so many weeds that it is unbelievable."[53]

After the death of Jeremias, the Holland branch of the van Rensselaer family and the business partners of the first patroon sought to sell off the colony, either as a unit or piecemeal, in order to settle the family estate. Jeremias's widow Maria opposed every effort of that sort, and was eventually able to buy out the partners and relatives and take absolute control of the colony as her children's inheritance. Before that, though, there were lean years, and one or another of the van Rensselaers did occasionally manage to sell a farm or two.

Marten Gerritsen tried to buy his island but was turned down by Richard van Rensselaer, who wrote Maria, "That being sold, we should have lost the best part." Richard would say, as late as 1684, "We have no intention of selling," but on January 12, 1688, he did sell the island to Samuel and Jochim Staats for 10,500 guilders. Maria expressed her "great displeasure" with the transaction "to which I cannot consent at all, and which I cannot deliver either," but Marten Gerritsen by 1690 had been dispossessed and had moved to a farm just to the south on the nearby mainland.[54]

Settlers along the Shoreline

Not all the heirs of Cornelis Segers had remained on Westerlo Island. Two deeds of 1652 and 1661 mention his son Cornelis ("Young Kees") Cornelissen[55] as living just north of a creek between the Normanskill and Vloman Kill.[56]

Young Kees first leased his farm in 1650. Jeremias van Rensselaer wrote in 1659 that "the gray mare, which was leased to young Kees, was this spring drowned in the river, close to the shore, as she was going to the river to drink." Van Rensselaer was not reimbursed for the horse, "for the farmer is as poor as a rat and I can not get a single schepel of grain from him," and in fact had to give Cornelissen a rebate in 1661 after his grain field was flooded.[57]

In 1668 Cornelis took over some old debts of Jan Labatie, perhaps a tradeoff for a house Labatie had built on the farm, but then left shortly thereafter. He was succeeded by Pieter Winne, about whom van Rensselaer wrote, "Whether the latter will succeed better than he [Cornelis], I can not yet tell, but, please God, I hope so, for Kees made nothing at all." To van Rensselaer's surprise, Winne was able to thatch the barn, repair the house, and build a barn and hay rick in less than two years. Van Rensselaer contributed a barrel of beer at the barn raising.[58]

Winne had problems with his neighbors. He sued Teunis Slingerland in 1670 for failure to fence the land between their fields, and in 1676 brought suit against Albert Bratt for burning down his fence and for planting on Pieter's land.[59]

After Winne left the farm in 1679, Maria van Rensselaer wrote that the house needed repair, and a year later that a new one should be built. Maria next rented the farm to Juriaen Teunissen, who after a year turned over the lease to Jan Caspersen Halenbeck. A court record in 1682 reports that Albert Bratt "has committed trespass against Jan Casperse by drawing and throwing a knife, pulling up the corn in his field and tearing down his fences, and [magistrate Marten Gerritse] presumes that the matter deserves the attention of the court." It was the sort of thing Bratt's neighbors could expect but one more nuisance on top of floods and unfenced fields and worn-out soil.[60]

Halenbeck renewed the lease in 1683 for three to six years. However, Maria wrote to her brother Stephanus van Cortlandt that year, "The land is not good," and since she was in no financial position to put costly improvements into a mediocre farm, sold it outright to Myndert Harmensen van den Bogaert.[61]

Teunis Slingerland Settles near Albert Bratt

Located on the Normanskill somewhere near Pieter Winne's farm on the river shore and also adjoining Albert Bratt's farmland, was the farm of Teunis Cornelissen Slingerland. He first appears in the colonial records in 1654, applying for a building lot in Beverwyck.[62] This may have been about the time he married Engeltie, daughter of Albert Bratt, and he had probably been in the colony a little while before that.

He was often called a "trader at Beverwyck," and references to him at the fur trade are frequent. Like many of the smaller traders who were at a disadvantage competing with the wealthiest merchants, he occasionally transgressed. He was one of a half-dozen men said to be in the woods to trade illegally in June 1659; among the others were his wife's brother Storm van der Zee and her sister's husband Roeloff Swartwout.[63]

By 1676 Slingerland owned two buildings in Albany—a trading office or warehouse on (or against) the hill, and a residence on the plain south and west of the fort. He had an office on Manhattan Island next door to his father-in-law's office and in fact it had been a gift from Bratt. He also had land on the Normanskill, probably the farm bordering the creek behind Westerlo Island mentioned in Pieter Winne's suit. In 1677 the Albany court ordered him not to cut off the path across his land on the "Noorman's kil" and in 1680 denied him permission to tear down his dilapidated house in Albany, which he wanted to move "near the land of the old Noorman." Obviously his farm was adjacent to Bratt's, and, in fact, in 1682 he took over management of Bratt's apple orchard.[64]

In about 1682 Engeltie died, and on April 9, 1683, Slingerland married Geertje Fonda, widow of Jan Bicker. In 1685 he received a deed from the Mohawks to land on Onesquethau Creek (Voorheesville area), part of which he gave to his sons Arent and Albert in 1687, and another portion to his eldest son Cornelis in 1701.[65]

Settlers at Cedar Hill

Kiliaen van Rensselaer in 1641 anticipated sending "20 persons who will establish 3 farms in bylers dal ... between beeren [Barren] Island and smackx [Shad] Island." By sailing time the number had dropped to head farmer Cornelis Hendricksen van Nes, master carpenter, and Andries de Vos and their families.[66]

They arrived in Rensselaerswyck late in the summer of 1641. The farm that Cornelis van Nes started—today known as the Nicoll-Sill property—may have been located on land already planted by the Mahicans and ready to use, since van Nes was charged rent for a working farm beginning in 1642.[67]

An account in the Rensselaerswyck court minutes of a family misadventure helps to locate the farm.

> Quiryn Cornelisen declares that in the fore part of the year 1643, as the wedding guests were going over the ice to the wedding of the daughters of van Es, a mare of the said Cryn [Quiryn] and a stallion of van der Donck were drowned near the swarte, or paerde hoeck [Black, or Horse Point].[68]

Since the destination of the party was the minister's house and chapel on the east side of the river, their starting point had to be at or below Parda Hook, and therefore near the Vloman Kill. The brides were probably Gerritie van Nes who married Quiryn's brother Roelof Cornelissen, and her sister Grietie who married Pieter Claessen Wyckoff.

Andries de Vos, a farmer and carpenter, immigrated with the van Nes family and undoubtedly lived with them for a few years while developing

The Wyckoff House. Flatlands (now part of Brooklyn). Occupied by Pieter Claessen Wyckoff from 1652 to 1694, after leaving Bethlehem. Now a historic site.

an adjoining farm north of the creek, together with a sawmill. In 1648, by which time de Vos had been appointed a member of the Rensselaerswyck Council, there was a falling out between the van Nes and de Vos families, and Van Nes's wife "greatly slandered" de Vos.[69]

There was also great animosity between van Nes and Director van Slichtenhorst, van Nes accusing the director of cheating his son-in-law Pieter Claessen, and Pieter calling van Slichtenhorst a liar and no Christian. Van Nes was cited in court on October 29, 1648, "for having out of spite threshed out a quantity of oat straw, which in the winter is the best fodder, and thrown the straw on the manure pile."[70]

Origin of the Name Bethlehem

It would appear that Andries de Vos built the first mill on the Vloman Kill. A court ruling of January 21, 1649,[71] states that "Andries de Vos is to pay the patroon's dues on his mill at Bethlehem [to] the sum of *f*62:10—[i.e., sixty-two guilders and ten *stuivers*] a year," but there is no indication of how many years' rent was due. Since, however, this is the earliest use in the records of the name *Bethlehem*, the entry is worth further consideration.

The first patroon had divided Rensselaerswyck into districts, calling the area south of Fort Orange—roughly the town of Bethlehem as it would be formed in 1793—Byler's dal (the name did not survive him) in honor of his first wife, Hellegond van Byler. The general assumption has been that not long after the patroon's death, someone renamed Byler's dal as Bethlehem. But the term Bethlehem in the seventeenth century was limited to a much smaller area,[72] comprising only the two farms adjacent to what was then called *Bethlehem's Kil*[73] (the present Vloman Kill), together with the offshore islands. In terms of today's topography, allowing for changes in the shoreline caused by landfill and dredging of the river channel, the area would include Bear Island, Parda Hook, the Putney property, Henry Hudson Park, the sewage treatment plant, the Nicoll-Sill property, the cemetery lot, and Schermerhorn Island.

After Andries de Vos, the next farmer north of the Vloman Kill was Aert Jacobsen. It is in connection with him that the name *Bethlehem* occurs for the second time in the records:

> Gerrit van Wencom declares that a certain Mahican, whom he [found] at [Aer]t Jacobsen's, at Bethlehem, on Wednesday, the 8th of December 1649,

[said Indian] being quite drunk with anise water, assaulted and fell upon him in cold blood and almost strangled him, in such a way that his head was extremely swollen, but that he was accidently released by another Indian.[74]

This was the fourth assault on the deputy *schout* that year, but perhaps the greater annoyance to van Wencom was Aert Jacobsen's refusal to sell him liquor on credit, which is why he had gone there in the first place. In that same month Jacobsen's wife defied an order to turn over one of Rensselaerswyck's heifers to Jan Reyers. A second order, which included a penalty of "three guilders for each day's delay after sight hereof," seems to have ended the squabble.[75]

In 1677 the mill was leased to Pieter Winne, often called *de Vlamingh* (the Fleming) since he came from Ghent in Flanders, and the stream eventually became the Vloman Kill (variously spelled). Although Winne's lease began in 1677, he does not seem to have left his farm on the Normanskill until November 1679. In 1681 he took on as a full partner the earlier sublessor Hendrick Martensen Beeckman.[76]

Island Farms at Original Bethlehem

Other early farms within the original Bethlehem were on offshore islands. The present Schermerhorn Island, extending from the Vloman Kill to Shad Island, was leased to Ryck Rutgers in 1648

for six years. Ryck transferred the lease to Jan Reyersen van Houten on March 17, 1650, and it is probably only coincidence that two weeks earlier Kit Davids had hit Ryck in the head with a post. The fight seems to have been part of a general melee: on the same court day, Davids was charged with beating his servant black and blue and hitting Jan van Bremen in the head with a tankard, while Jacob Flodder was charged with using a tankard on the head of Poulus the Noorman.[77]

Jan Reyersen leased Schermerhorn Island until 1663. He and his wife then moved to Claverack where they and another family were killed by two Onondaga Indians, sometime prior to July 1665, during a war principally between Mahicans and Mohawks.

Early Activities at Original Bethlehem

During a 1660 uprising of Esopus Indians, Jeremias van Rensselaer wrote to his brother Jan Baptist, "I gave everybody some [powder] according to his needs and ordered them to keep a good watch, as at Bethlehem and in the Grene Bos [Greenbush, now the city of Rensselaer], where I formed a corporal's guard to keep watch these days."[78] The colony's account books on October 30, 1662, credit Eldert Gerbertsen with building a blockhouse at Bethlehem.[79] This was apparently not maintained; in 1689 when an invasion from Canada was expected, the inhabitants of Bethlehem were ordered to build themselves a fort "for their oune security to retreat unto."[80] There is also reference to a tavern at Bethlehem, although this would probably have been just the front room of someone's house, as was the custom. We noted earlier Aert Jacobsen's tavern, and Marten Cornelisssen in 1660 mentioned having a conversation with Harmen Harmensen Gansevoort in a Bethlehem tavern. Although there were no schools, churches, or other public buildings here (or anywhere else beyond Albany), both the tavern and the blockhouse suggest a sizeable community at Bethlehem in some proximity to these gathering points.

We conclude that the name Bethlehem was originally applied only to the community of farms that bordered on the confluence of the Vloman Kill and the Hudson, the mills on the creek, and the nearby islands—Bear, Shad and Scher-merhorn. It is somewhat amusing that many residents of the Delmar area at the far edge of town are unaware that Cedar Hill and Selkirk are "part of Bethlehem."

New Netherland Becomes New York

Charles II, King of England, 1649-85.

In the seventeenth century, trade wars were literally that: wars fought for control of trade. Principal combatants were England, France, the Netherlands, and Spain. In 1664, King Charles II of England decided that too much of the North American trade was going to the Netherlands.

James, Duke of York, proprietor of New York, 1664-88.

His solution of the problem was to give New Netherland to his brother James, the Duke of York. That summer James sent over three warships to settle the matter. They arrived off New York harbor in late August, and on the thirtieth Colonel Richard Nicolls demanded the surrender of the Dutch government. Neither the fort nor the town of New Amsterdam was capable of mounting an adequate defense. On the eighth of September, Director-General Petrus Stuyvesant ratified the terms of capitulation, and New Netherland became an English colony to be called New York. Fort Orange surrendered on September 20, and the neighboring village of Beverwyck was renamed Albany.

Petrus Stuyvesant, director-general of New York, 1664-88.

The appropriate status for the privately-owned colony of Rensselaerswyck was a subject of negotiation for the next two decades, especially since the patroon's heirs were claiming that the entire city of Albany had been illegally seized by Stuyvesant and by rights belonged to them. The English acknowledged that although they were right, they should not expect to have the colony's second largest community as private property. In 1685 a compromise was reached, whereby Rensselaerswyck was given the status of an English manor, with its own representative in the colony's General Assembly, in return for recognizing the independence of Albany, and surrendering a mile-wide strip of land running northwest from the city to the northern boundary of the manor. Still within Rensselaerswyck Manor lay the territory of the future town of Bethlehem.

3 Life in an English Colony

In the little more than a half century between Henry Hudson's exploring and the arrival of the English, the lands of Bethlehem had been purchased from their Native American owners and European settlement and development had begun. Farms and mills lined the river shore as well as the principal creeks for some distance back.

Following the English conquest of the Dutch in 1664, the people of the colony of New York suffered great economic, political, and emotional turmoil for a quarter-century. Trade with the Netherlands was reduced to insignificance and colonial Dutch merchants at first lacked the contacts for entering London markets. The colonist who did not speak English lacked the ability to secure a political office. Residents of Albany, Kingston, and New York had to provide room and board in their homes for English soldiers.

A Dutch military and naval force captured the colony in 1673, to the joy of Dutch colonists and disconcerting English settlers, then surrendered it a year later under terms of a peace treaty between England and the Netherlands. For some in the colony it was a terrible turn of events.

While these changes had great effect on the residents of the merchant towns, the impact was less upon the rural population of Bethlehem, although the price and availability of such important items as steel farming equipment were affected by trade and war. The markets for Bethlehem's wheat and lumber also depended upon the outside world. But farmers were used to making do with what they had, and so the community survived.

The number of farms in Bethlehem and their relative sizes increased throughout the remainder of the colonial period, despite Indian wars that occasionally spilled over into Bethlehem. Four intercolonial wars between 1689 and 1763 did not reach Bethlehem's borders, though their economic and political effects were felt. Bethlehem's sons marched off to fight in these wars. They fought again after 1776 when the opponent was Great Britain herself.

After the Revolutionary War came the birth of the Town of Bethlehem, established by State law. The world thereafter continued to see wars and economic crises, yet in Bethlehem change came more slowly. The population grew; small businesses began to gather around the several crossroads.

Rapid, suburban growth finally came toward the middle of the twentieth century. For a while, local government continued to be a part-time occupation, administered after stores and business offices had closed for the day. But an era was passing, and a new one beginning.

Background

The Glorious Revolution came to England in 1688. King James lost his throne to his son-in-law and daughter, William of Orange and Mary. The change of rule led to chaos and anarchy in New York, for William and Mary forgot to send new commissions for New York

King James II of England.

officials, leaving the colony without a government. Jacob Leisler, the ranking New York City

Pieter Schuyler, first mayor of Albany.

militia officer, finally took control of Manhattan and attempted to bring the whole colony together under his rule. In Albany County, former sheriff Richard Pretty and Joachim Staats were among his supporters. Distrustful Albany officials, including mayor Pieter Schuyler and city clerk Robert Livingston, resisted until French troops and Canadian Indians massacred the settlement at Schenectady, forcing Albany to accept military protection from Leisler.

His methods of governing were sometimes high-handed—he jailed opponents without trial, among them Nicolaes Bayard, member of the government council and nephew of former Dutch governor Petrus Stuyvesant, and attorney general William Nicolls, son of provincial secretary Matthias Nicolls. When regular government was reestablished, Leisler was prosecuted by William Nicolls for treason and put to death. The animosity between Leislerians and Anti-Leislerians lasted for decades.

Leaseholds

After the tumults of the preceding decade, the eighteenth century opened with life in

The Van Rensselaer manor house in Albany, built about 1666, where rents were paid.

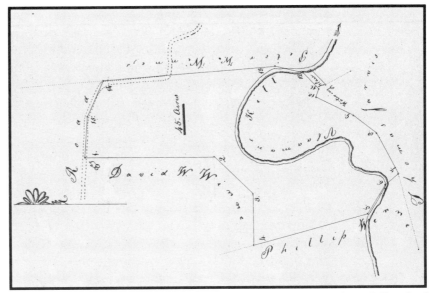

Peter W. Winne of David W. Winne

Beginning at a point in the Road leading from Benoyd. Winne to the Bethlehem Church, South twenty five degrees and forty five minutes West eighty four links from d. Hickory tree standing on the north side of said road, and runs thence —

1. .. South .. ... 15 . 84 To d. Marked Hickory .. .. hill
2. .. S 43 . 00 W .. 6 . 32 To d. Mark. Hicory Sapling near top of the
3. .. S 09 . 10 W .. 6 . 03 To d. Stake set 23 links West of Apple tree
4. .. S 14 . 30 E .. 14 . 20 d. stake near the Vlamans Kill
5. .. S 57 . 00 E .. 4 . 00 Along the North Bank of the Kill
6. .. S 42 . 00 E .. 2 . 10 To d. Stake set in Thomas Jarvis line
   .. 41 link west of d. Chesnut Oak Sapling
   Stand, on d. Ridge or Boog[d]land then
   along Thomas Jarvis line
7. .. N 61 . 00 E .. 5 . 45 To two hard maples
8. .. N 36 . 00 E .. 3 . 52 four links West of d. Blazed Chesnut Sapling
9. .. N 25 . 00 E .. 4 . 90 Stake 5 links N W of d. Large White pine
10. .. S 71 . 00 E .. 1 . 00
11. .. N 45 . 00 E .. 2 . 60 Stake on the West Bank of the Vlamans Kill
    N 5 E 1 . 00 from d. Beach tree Marked W W.
    = 1709
12. .. N 12 . 00 E .. 3 . 45 To the East side of the Vlamans Kill
    N 31 E 2 . 15 from d. White pine Sapling then
13. .. N 4 . 00 W .. 25 . 25 [...]
    at 14.90 to the Bend of the Road
    To d. Stake Bottom in the fence
    in the Original line
14. .. N 64 . 45 W .. 40 . 62 in the Road
15. .. N 06 . 45 W .. 4 . 00 To the place of Beginning
    Containing 45 Acres of Land

Surveyed the 28th Day
of June 1832. —

By Ab. Roskrance

Survey in 1832 of the Peter W. Winne farm, near the First Reformed Church of Bethlehem (Selkirk).

Rensselaerswyck calm and the state of the Manor generally improving. The fourth patroon (and the third named Kiliaen van Rensselaer) had made a decision which was to change the direction of the manor's fortunes from a sixty-year history of unbroken deficits into a profitable enterprise. Short-term leases in the manor had never proved particularly attractive, and so van Rensselaer began offering his tenants lifetime leases.[1] This was much like a quit rent, and entitled the lessee to bequeath his farm to his children, or divide it up and sell parts as he saw fit. There were only a few conditions that separated a manor lease from a freeholding. The tenant owed the manor lord annually two fat fowl (four for a large farm), a bushel of wheat per five acres of tilled fields, and a day's labor on public works projects, such as clearing land for a new farm or cleaning a clogged stream. Transfer in title required payment to the manor lord of only one quarter of the value of the property; thus, one could purchase a farm worth forty pounds for only ten pounds. This had political implications since, under English law, voting was the privilege of persons either owning, or holding a lifetime lease to, forty pounds worth of property. Tenancy in the manor therefore entitled persons to vote, many of whom would otherwise have been denied the privilege. In fact Rensselaerswyck was entitled to its own elected representative in the colonial assembly.[2]

Rensselaerswyck's farms averaged about 153 acres, and were better planned than those on other manors. Although maps of the manor show a crazy quilt of irregularly shaped farms of no apparent pattern, each was drawn so that it would include cropland, meadow, woodlot, and water. Established farms came with buildings and animals, with the leaseholder receiving a share of the animal increase. A new farm was not charged any fee for the first few years while it was under development. Van Rensselaer Manor offered the most generous leasehold terms anywhere in the Hudson Valley, which, together with the right to vote, led to a steady growth in the number of its farms for the next one and a half centuries.[3]

Prior to the inauguration of the lifetime leasehold system in about 1688, there were seventeen farms. Within the next twenty-five years that number had grown to eighty-two, perhaps a quarter of them in the Bethlehem area. The number of farms increased over the next forty years under successive patroons[4] until in 1752 there were 345 taxable persons in the manor.

Population

The population of seventeenth-century Rensselaerswyck, including Bethlehem, had been a mixture of nationalities (like that of the rest of New Netherland, and Holland itself for that matter), for the Netherlands received political, economic, and religious refugees from across Europe. In addition to the native Dutch, Flemish, and Frisians of the Netherlands, the most common national types to be found among Rensselaerswyck's "Dutch" population were Scandinavians and Germans, French and Walloons, British (English, Scots, Welsh) and Irish, with a scattering of people from more distant countries. The English takeover in 1664 led to a sharp reduction in immigration from continental Europe for the rest of the seventeenth century, except for French Huguenots. These religious refugees, together with retired British soldiers, made up most of the new settlers in the later part of the century. In addition to the Europeans, there were African slaves on the larger farms and Mahican Indians living in their own communities (if not in Bethlehem then at least close by—they are mentioned in 1690 at Catskill and Barren Island, and in 1744 in a village on Lower Schodack Island[5]).

The eighteenth century in New York was marked by immigration of free settlers and some transported prisoners from Great Britain and Ireland, black slaves from Africa and the Caribbean, and Germans. Immigration from western Germany, principally the Rhineland Palatinate, was perhaps greater than from Great Britain herself.

Palatine communities developed in Rensselaerswyck in the western part of Guilderland and in Center Brunswick, and there were individuals scattered across the future area of Bethlehem.

In unsettled times the nearness of the frontier, with its dangers, could depress settlement. Dr. Alexander Hamilton, sailing up the Hudson in 1744 at the outbreak of King George's War, put ashore near Van Wie's Point (often called at that time Dominie's Hook or Rock, for which Hamilton seems to offer some explanation, identifying it as "Prec Stone, or Preaching Stone, from its resemblance to a pulpit"). He "found the poor people there in great terror of the Indians," although Jeremiah van Rensselaer could boast "that he has a great number of tenants upon his manor, and ... could muster 600 men fit to bear arms."[6]

Growth was also retarded during the youth of the third Stephen van Rensselaer (1764-1839), when the manor was operated by his mother and other guardians. They were more interested in quick profits than in steady growth and long term investment, and stopped granting lifetime leases. Even so, by the middle of the Revolutionary War there were about a thousand farms in Rensselaerswyck.

While leaseholds were ideal for people who could not afford to buy a farm, they were also attractive to well-to-do Albany merchants who enjoyed having a large garden near the city for their household needs. One such was leased to Captain Cortlandt Schuyler in 1768, on the south side of the Normanskill. It was described as abutting on the creek, the river, the flat "where Ryck Mackielor lived" (perhaps Ryck Michaelsen), and the houselot and lowlands held by heirs of Albert and Arent Slingerland between the creek and the foot of the hill called Kittenbergh. (One of the more fanciful derivations for the name is provided in a local legend, which has Captain Kidd burying treasure there.) Schuyler's lease also included an island in the river called Jonge Jans Plaat (Young Jan's Shoal).[7]

Country Living

Swedish naturalist Peter Kalm, travelling to Albany in 1749 by ship, provides a description of the scenery just south of the city:

> The country on both sides of the river was low and covered with woods, only here and there were a few little scattered settlements. On the banks of the river were wet meadows, covered with sword grass (Carex), and they formed several little islands.... The land on both sides of the river was chiefly low, and more carefully cultivated as we came nearer to Albany. Here we could see everywhere ... [hay barracks][8] with movable roofs.... As to the houses which we saw, some were of wood, others of stone.[9]

Kalm wrote a great deal about the houses of the area. Construction began with putting up the

House on Beaver Street in Albany, built in 1679.

one could almost drive through them with a horse and sleigh." Brick ovens for baking were placed on a hill apart from the house.[10]

Dr. Hamilton also wrote about the interiors of Dutch homes he had seen, presumably all belonging to residents of the better classes:

> The Dutch here keep their houses very neat and clean, both without and within. Their chamber floors are generally laid with rough plank, which in time, by constant rubbing and scrubbing, becomes as smooth as if it had been planed. Their chambers and rooms are large and handsome [Warren Johnson thought Albany "worse than Edinburgh in Scotland for little Houses"[11]].... They affect pictures much, particularly scripture history, with which they adorn their rooms. They set out their cabinets and buffets much with china. Their kitchens are likewise very clean, and there they hang earthen or delft plates and dishes all round the walls, in manner of pictures, having a hole drilled thro' the edge of the plate or dish, and a loop of ribbon put into it to hang it by; but notwithstanding all this nicety and cleanliness in their houses they are in their persons slovenly and dirty. [An old New England saying was that the Dutch kept their houses cleaner than their bodies, and their bodies cleaner

framework upon which the rafters and roofs rested, and then the framework was filled in with unfired bricks. The inner side was brushed over with lime and whitewashed, and the outside generally covered with clapboards so that the unfired brick might not be damaged by weather. The roof was either of boards or shingles of white pine. "It is claimed that such a roof will last forty years." There were several rooms, nearly always a cellar with masonry walls the length of the house, and an attic reached by a ladder or staircase within the house, where miscellaneous household goods were stored. The fireplace for about six feet or more from the ground consisted of nothing more than the brick wall of the house. In country houses it was possible to sit on three sides of the fire, but in Albany the fireplaces were closed off by ends fronted with Dutch tiles, "with a white background and blue figures." Stoves for heating were unknown and "chimneys are so wide that

House on the corner of Steuben and Chapel streets in Albany.

than their souls.] They live here very frugally and plain, for the chief merit among them seems to be riches, which they spare no pains or trouble to acquire, but are a civil and hospitable people in their way, but at best rustic and unpolished.... They live in their houses in Albany as if it were in prisons, all their doors and windows being perpetually shut.[12]

After his arrival in Albany, Peter Kalm visited Westerlo Island, which he reported was planted chiefly with grain and potatoes. The leaseholder also sublet lots "to the inhabitants of Albany for kitchen gardens." Although the island was treeless, Kalm noted wild plum trees along the main-

land shore, and grapevines. "The grapes are eaten after the frost has touched them, for they are too sour before. They are not much used in any other way." Elsewhere he saw walnut, chestnut, butternut, and mulberry trees. He also noted that ginseng for medicine could be found in the woods. Touring about the countryside, he remarked chiefly on the farms but also noted the many sawmills. At night he was fascinated to find that "fireflies are seen in abundance."

Dr. Hamilton also visited Westerlo Island, and in fact stayed there as guest of the owner, the Reverend John Miln, former rector of the Anglican church at Albany. Hamilton noted the "fine grass of different sorts, and very good crops of wheat and pease, of which they bring up great quantities here for the use of the ships."[13] He called the trip from there to Albany "a pleasant walk of two miles from the island."[14]

Health Care

The practice of medicine in colonial America was not up to the highest European standards. Persons with a doctorate in medicine were rare in Europe and rather more so in America. The primary healer for most people was the oldest woman of the family. When her skills proved inadequate, the sufferer went to a chirurgeon ("barber-surgeon"), whose training was through an apprenticeship program that provided practical experience, but not university training.[15]

Dr. Hamilton, whose observations on Albany County life in 1744 appear frequently in this chapter, was a chirurgeon trained in Scotland. His general assessment of the local residents was that "they are a healthy, long-lived people, [but] they are subject to rotten teeth and scorbutic [afflicted with scurvy] gums."[16]

Hamilton stayed on Westerlo Island[17] and walked daily into the city, where he met several of his fellow practitioners. His opinion of their skills was not high.

> After dinner Mr. Shaekesburrough, surgeon to the fort, came in, who by his conversation seemed to have as little of the quack in him as any half-hewn doctor ever I had met with. The doctors in Albany are mostly Dutch, all empirics [persons with practical experience], having no knowledge or learning but what they have acquired by bare experience. They study chiefly the virtues of herbs, and the woods there furnish their shops with all the pharmacy they use. A great many of them take the care of a family for the value of a Dutch dollar a year, which makes the practice of physick a mean thing, and unworthy of the application of a gentleman. The doctors here are all barbers.

On another day, Hamilton wrote of visiting Dr. Rosaboom, "a man of considerable practice in administering physick and shaving." His only reference work was a German book on medicinal plants.[18]

Bethlehem in 1767

Bethlehem at the two-thirds mark in the century was heavily agricultural, with a few sawmills, gristmills, and fulling-mills on the principal creeks and an occasional blacksmith, wheelwright, storekeeper, dockowner, or other tradesman or merchant necessary to the farming communities. Population records for 1767 in the area south of the city of Albany show that the vast majority of residents were descendants of early settlers who had emigrated between 1630 and 1675. The number of new names in the area is surprisingly low, considering the numbers of laborers, sutlers, and other camp followers who came from Great Britain and New England to the area during the last two wars against French Canada, when Albany was the major supply base for the British army. Many of those newcomers may have settled in the city itself, although a colony of Scots was developing at New Scotland, then still called Onesquethau, together with a few Yankees. A century after the English conquest, the primary language of Bethlehem was probably still Dutch.

A list of taxpayers in the Bethlehem area in 1767[19] shows some 318 names, 200 of which date from the Dutch period. Of the rest, forty appear to be British, thirty-nine German, eighteen French Huguenot, and twenty-one uncertain, given the vagaries of spelling. (Family names, of course, do not tell the whole story— there were many families where the father was English but the mother Dutch). Similar results can be obtained from lists of leaseholders and militia men. The newcomers tended to be absorbed into existing society rather than to form ethnic communities. Written instruments of the time show that many of the older French and English families could write Dutch, and most children in the Albany area were taught both English and Dutch,[20] although English was probably lacking in the education of those from the more remote regions.

The Reformed Church at the corner of State Street and Broadway in Albany, about 1805.

Religion in Bethlehem

Conservative in language, Bethlehem was also religiously conservative, most residents holding on to Reformed traditions. Peter Kalm in 1749 found it curious that at meals, "The host himself generally says grace aloud," a custom he apparently had not encountered among either Anglicans or Swedish Lutherans. He also wrote,

> The inhabitants of Albany and its environs are almost all Dutchmen. They speak Dutch, have Dutch preachers, and the divine service is performed in that language. Their manners are likewise quite Dutch; their dress is however like that of the English.

Dr. Hamilton was not impressed by the local spiritual community. "As to religion they have little of it among them, and of enthusiasm not a

grain." However, he did not investigate the subject particularly thoroughly, since he wrote at the same time, "The bulk of them, if anything, are of the Lutheran Church." Perhaps in his mind, the continental varieties of Protestantism were all more or less the same. There actually were Dutch Lutherans back along the Normanskill (known, therefore, as the Normanskill people), mostly on the Guilderland side of the line. They were oriented toward Albany where they had a church, but hardly the majority church of the city. The Dutch in that congregation were soon outnumbered by Palatine Germans—at almost the same time that the Reformed Church was changing from Dutch to English services, the Lutherans were changing from Dutch to German.

Such Anglicans as there may have been in Bethlehem would also have had to go into town for church. Dr. Hamilton wrote of one July Sunday, "We went to the English Church, where was

The English Church (St. Peters) on State Street in Albany in 1714. The English fort is in the background.

the meanest congregation ever I beheld, there being not above fifteen or twenty in church besides the soldiers of the fort, who sat in a gallery."

Later in the century there were Presbyterians in New Scotland. A congregation was organized in Albany in 1763, to which residents of New Scotland undoubtedly belonged until after the Revolutionary War, when they formed a separate congregation.

Rensselaer Nicoll

Government of Albany County was run by descendants of Dutch settlers, with Englishmen allowed to participate if they were of a proper sort, and had Dutch wives. A good example of the power structure can be found in the Albany County militia rolls for 1767. They show that 85 percent of the officers had Dutch surnames, but only 3 percent of the enlisted men, the other 97 percent of whom were German, Irish, Scots, and Yankee.[21]

Among the county's militia officers was Bethlehem resident Rensselaer Nicoll. (His forebears spelled the name as Nicolls, his son as Nicoll; his own signature ends with an indecipherable flourish.) His father was William Nicolls, speaker of the colonial general assembly, former attorney general, and (as noted before) special prosecutor appointed to try Jacob Leisler. Renssaelaer's grandfather Matthias Nicolls served the colony in a variety of offices, including provincial secretary over a period of sixteen years, and judge for five more. Rensselaer Nicoll's other grandfather was Jeremias van Rensselaer, third director of Rensselaerswyck and son of the first patroon.

When Anna van Rensselaer Nicolls died in about 1715, her youngest son Rensselaer (baptized Killian van Rensselaer Nicolls) was sent from the family estate at Islip, Long Island, to live at the Watervliet manor house of his mother's brother, the fourth patroon, after whom he had been named. When Uncle Kiliaen died four years later, the boy was taken in at Schuyler Flats by his "Aunt Schuyler"—Maria, wife of former Albany mayor Pieter Schuyler and sister of Anna Nicolls. The patroon in his will left to Rensselaer Nicoll the 1300 acres of farms and sawmill of what had historically been known as Bethlehem. The will[22] grants:

All that farm at Bethlehem now in possession of William van Allen, with the island called Nieffes Island,[23] beginning at the south side of Bethlehem Creek and extending to the bounds of Barent Peterse Coeymans, and backwards into the woods from Hudsons River one English mile, and the farm on the north side of Bethlehem Creek, ten or twelve acres, as in fence, where the house and barn of Coysome[24] lately stood, with the right of keeping a sawmill on the south side of the creek, where a sawmill now stands.

However, a letter (unfortunately known only in a nineteenth-century copy) from William Nicolls to his late wife's brother Hendrick van Rensselaer states:

I was not a little surprised at what you mentioned of Brother [Kiliaen van] Rensselaers' will relating to those lands [Bethlehem]. You know, brother, that your sister had them of you in exchange for Craaloo [across the river], and that I have been possessed and seized of them in her right as her Inheritance for upwards of twenty years before her death.[25]

This document, if authentic, would place the original Bethlehem in the hands of William and Anna Nicolls at about the time of the final settlement of the first patroon's estate in 1695.

When William Nicolls died in 1723, Rensselaer was in his late teens or early twenties. On the one side he was from a prominent colonial English family. His father was the aforementioned prosecutor of Jacob Leisler, and later speaker of the general assembly. His grandfather, Matthias Nicolls, held major posts in the New York colonial government for a quarter of a century. Rensselaer's brothers and nephews served in the colonial general assembly, and his nephew William was one of the founders of Kings College, now Columbia University. Rensselaer was also Dutch, the grandson of Jeremias van Rensselaer, and thus related to the van Cortlandts, Livingstons, Schuylers, and other manor lords and landed gentry of the Hudson Valley.

In 1730 he married Elisabeth Salisbury of Catskill, whose background was similar to his own. Her grandfather, Captain Sylvester Salisbury, had been commandant at Fort Albany and close friend and comrade in arms (in the 1664 invasion force) of Matthias Nicolls. He had been one of the few popular English officers in Albany, undoubtedly helped by having a Dutch wife. Elisabeth's other grandfather had been the Reformed minister at Kingston; his widow later married Thomas Chambers, lord of the Ulster County manor of Fox Hall. Elisabeth, despite the English name of Salisbury, was three-quarters Dutch—just the wife for a man to have in Albany County.

Rensselaer and Elisabeth Nicoll lived in Bethlehem House, which was built about the time of their marriage in 1730,[26] or perhaps a few years later, on the estate later known as Cedar Hill. The house, much expanded over the years, is still standing.

Rensselaer's life, like that of his kinsmen, was comfortable but not leisurely. He was involved with the management of his estate, part of which he leased to tenant farmers, part he farmed himself through the use of a large staff of slaves. He was also a lawyer, like his father and grandfather before him, and perhaps he had already begun to read law with his father before moving to Albany County. In 1736 he was appointed assistant justice of the Albany County Court of Common Pleas, the beginning of a long judicial career, which suggests that he may have been closer in temperament to his grandfather, a government administrator and court justice, than to his flamboyant father, a trial attorney and leader of the popularly-elected assembly. Rensselaer Nicoll served on the county bench over a forty-year period in the courts of common pleas, general sessions, and oyer and terminer (a criminal court), and with the local sessions of the colonial supreme court.

In court he was English, but among his neighbors he was Dutch. In 1733 Rensselaer joined the Albany County militia as a lieutenant, and was later promoted to captain. That he became an officer strongly suggests that he was an accepted member of the local Dutch gentry. It is worth noting that although Rensselaer seems to have been raised in Trinity Episcopal Church in New York, he and Elisabeth in Albany normally attended the Dutch Reformed Church. Undoubtedly the language of the household was Dutch— a letter to Rensselaer from his father-in-law Francis Salisbury on family matters (including congratulations on the birth of a daughter) is in Dutch.[27]

Transportation

Settlement below Albany at the beginning of the eighteenth century was still limited to the Hudson shoreline and along the principal creeks—the Normanskill, Vloman Kill, and Onesquethau or Coeymans Creek. As the century progressed and population increased, a number of roads appeared. These were dirt roads; not even Albany's streets were completely paved. Warren Johnson, who did not like the Dutch at all, suggested that the people of Albany were so miserly that they did not pave their roads for fear the paving stones

State and North Pearl streets in Albany, looking well-paved in the early nineteenth century. From a painting by Milbert.

would wear out the iron wheels on their wagons.[28] But Peter Kalm, in Albany twelve years earlier, reported that, in fact, many of the streets were paved.[29] Both agreed the streets were very dirty.

The principal roads connected one community with another, as needed. A highway from Albany to New York did not appear in the colony until late in the 1700s, extending up the east shore to Greenbush (now Rensselaer), where the trip concluded by ferry to Albany. The west side of the river, with steeper hills in many places and fewer communities overall, had segments of road from one place to another, but nothing that extended the full length of the river. For residents of Bethlehem, the principal means of long distance travel was still by sail—faster and cheaper than any alternative. Mid-century traveller Peter Kalm wrote:

> The boats are quite large, and have a good cabin, in which the passengers can be very commodiously lodged.... They bring from Albany boards or planks, and all sorts of timber, flour, peas, and furs, which they get from the Indians, or which are smuggled from the French.[30]

Farming

The colony of New York was famous in the seventeenth century as the leading producer of quality wheat and flour, and the government strove to preserve that reputation with strict regulations and quality control of all exports. During the Revolutionary War, it was New York wheat that fed the Continental Army. Peter Kalm in 1749 wrote, "Wheat is sown in the neighborhood of Albany to great advantage." Rye and barley were grown in lesser quantities and "they do not sow more oats than are necessary for their horses."[31] Hemp and flax were likewise grown only for home consumption. Kalm also noted that "the people are forced to keep their cattle in stables from the middle of November till March or April, and must find them hay during that time,"[32] which would indicate that hay was purchased from a grain dealer rather than grown on each farm.

The traditional image of the self-sufficient farm, growing a little bit of everything, is not an accurate picture of most farms in this area. From the beginning, people were interested in raising cash crops. Particularly after the outlying areas were shut out of the fur trade, most farmers' efforts were put into what made the most money. An important factor in the development of Bethlehem as an agricultural area was the act of the colonial government in 1686 to grant Albany a monopoly in the fur trade. This shut out non-residents of the city, and forced them to focus their attention on other sources of income. By the end of the seventeenth century, Bethlehem was concentrating on the exporting of grain and lumber. Dr. Hamilton wrote, "The country about is very productive of hay and good grain, the woods not much cleared."[33] Winne's dock near Van Wies Point

West view of the General Market of the city of Albany in the summer of 1819.

became a focal point of trade. Albany, once a place to take one's furs, became for Bethlehem a place to buy supplies or go to church. There were several cash crops. "The Dutch and Germans who live hereabouts sow peas in great abundance; they grow very well, and are annually carried to New York in great quantities," according to Peter Kalm. They also sold locally: "There are two marketplaces in town, to which the country people come twice a week."[34] He also noted that, "They sow corn in great abundance.... Potatoes are planted by almost everyone."[35] By the end of the century Bethlehem would be noted for its butter.[36]

There were other cash crops as well. "Each farm has a large orchard. They have some apples here which are very large, and very palatable; they are sent to New York and other places as a rarity. People make excellent cider in the autumn in the country round Albany." However, pear and peach trees "do not succeed here."[37]

The housewife had a kitchen garden and an herb and spice garden, to produce variety and some flavoring for the family meals. Hogs provided meat—they required little effort to raise—and a cow or two would keep the family in milk and cheese. The traditional meals of the time were not highly nutritious, and as Peter Kalm wrote of the Dutch in and around Albany, "Their food and its preparation is very different from that of the English."

Food and Drink

Breakfast consisted of bread and butter with slices of dried beef or grated cheese, or buttered bread toasted over the coals, or a bowl of bread and milk. The principal drink was tea, introduced into the area in the first quarter of the eighteenth century. It was commonly drunk without milk, and "they never put sugar into the cup, but take a small bit of it into their mouths while they drink."[38]

Dinner at midday was bread, "to which they add sugar on special occasions," and either buttermilk or fresh milk, often served with boiled or roasted meat and always a large salad flavored with much vinegar and little or no oil. They sometimes boiled buttermilk into a thin porridge "that tastes very sour but not disagreeable in hot weather." In the afternoon, about three o'clock, tea was served again. Supper consisted generally of a cornmeal porridge called *sappaan*[39], or bread and butter, or a bowl of milk with small pieces of bread in it. Even Warren Johnson, who had very little good to say about the Dutch at Albany, admitted they made bread "good and white."[40] Sometimes they had chocolate, and occasionally grated cheese. The usual drinks were weak beer and plain water.[41]

Other foods that Kalm mentioned were coleslaw (from the Dutch, meaning cabbage salad), watermelon, and, in particular, pumpkins. Pumpkins were cut in pieces, buttered and roasted before the fire, or boiled in water and eaten with meat. At Albany, the Dutch made a kind of porridge out of them with fresh milk, or made a thick pancake of mashed pumpkin and cornmeal which was either boiled or fried. They also used pumpkin for pudding and pie. Kalm noted that "the Indians do not raise as many pumpkins as they do squashes."[42]

Brandy was cheap in the Dutch period, rum in the English, and the consuming of these beverages or beer took the place of the modern coffee break. Many workmen were in a state where their work was unreliable before noon, and by midafternoon any work at all was impossible. However, it is interesting that Peter Kalm wrote that the Dutch "are not so given to drink as the English, and the punch bowl does not make a daily round in their households."[43] An implausible tale comes from Warren Johnson, apparently not something he actually witnessed. "A Gent. at Albany drank 27 Bowls of Punch one Night."[44]

The English introduced a variety of drinks into the colony for the evening tavern entertainment; the Dutch had some of their own. In cold weather, rum and brandy were flavored with spices and beer and heated with a hot poker—two such spiced hot drinks, flannel and kill devil, were popular among all nationalities. The sophisticated Englishman would vary his evening's imbibing with lemonade and other fruit flavorings, all with a potent base.

Local Customs

Visitors to the area always seemed intrigued with the local customs. Among the observations of Peter Kalm were these:

> In many houses in the town they had partitioned off the part of the room where the beds stood by placing large doors before them like cupboards, and thus completely concealing the beds from view. [This was typically Dutch.][45]

"The women ... rise early, go to sleep very late, and are almost superstitiously clean in regard to the floor, which is frequently scoured [with sand] several times in the week," although elsewhere he noted, "Saturday was the day especially set aside for scrubbing the floors."[46]

"Inside the homes the women are neatly but not lavishly dressed." [This contrasts sharply with the earlier statement of Dr. Hamilton, that the Dutch were "slovenly and dirty."] "Some of the inhabitants wear their own hair very short, without a bag or queue, because these are looked upon as the characteristics of Frenchmen." Elsewhere he also reported, "When the men go out of doors they frequently have only a white cap under the hat and no wig."[47]

Dr. Alexander Hamilton noted, "I went thro' the farce of kissing most of the women, a manner of salutation which is expected from strangers com-ing there.... This might almost pass for a penance, for the generality of the women here, both old and young, are remarkably ugly."[48]

Warren Johnson, in America to visit his brother, Sir William, wrote in January 1761 of the Dutch around Fort Johnson (presumably not so different from the Dutch of Bethlehem), that when they stop by one's house, they start right in to "Smoke in Ones Parlour," and though not asked to sit down, "always seat themselves without bidding. Their Children at Seven years Old, Smoak, & their Parents think it a great Qualification."[49] We should note that one is generally bewildered, rather than enlightened, by the mixture of gossip, exaggeration, and invective in Johnson's diary, but we must presume that he witnessed at least one seven-year old puffing away in his parents' presence. Peter Kalm remarked about old women gathered about the fireplace smoking, and even young wives in their twenties with pipes in their mouths.[50]

Weather

Contemporary reports on the climate are contradictory. According to Peter Kalm, "There is hardly a month in summer during which a frost does not occur."[51] Geologic evidence suggests that conditions were not that extreme, and Dr. Hamilton wrote that "the mornings and evenings all summer long [are] cool and pleasant, but often, about noon and for three hours after, the sun is very hot."[52] Beginning in October it was customary for women, even servants and little girls, when seated to put warming pans filled with live coals into a sort of small stool under their skirts. During the winter,

> The ice on the Hudson is commonly three or four feet thick. On the third of April some of the inhabitants crossed the river with six pairs of horses. Great pieces of ice come down about that time, which sometimes carry with them the houses that stand close to the shore.

This last was, of course, based upon the testimony of others since Hamilton himself was in Albany only in the summer. The same might be said of his tale, "Their winter here is excessive cold, so as to freeze their cattle stiff in one night in the stables."[53]

Eighteenth-Century Politics

The people of Bethlehem, and the residents of Rensselaerswyck generally, were comfortable with the local manor government with its strongly Dutch flavor, with the Reformed religion as practiced in the area (although there was a colony-wide dispute as to whether authority should rest in America or in Amsterdam), and with the economic division of Albany for the merchants and the manor for the farmers. As in the rest of Rensselaerswyck, local sentiment was probably generally anti-New York City and anti-Boston (or any other place that could be a mercantile competitor for Albany), as well as against colonial

government and almost anything else English. While New Englanders and foreigners invariably ran down the backward-looking, conservative Dutch of Albany and the Hudson Valley generally, the Dutch continued to be well-satisfied with themselves and disinclined to change things. Though they sided with the Yankees and Virginians finally in the Revolution, that had more to do with the English trade laws raising the cost of imports than any particular desire to associate with Yankees and such.

The reputation of the Dutch of the upper valley in the eighteenth century as being stubborn and insular is certainly due to the particular circumstances in which they found themselves. They resented that the government at New York had eliminated Dutch law, language, and customs from the courts, from government, and from official documents. The government also controlled the city of New York and did all it could to enrich its friends and comrades there, which increased the resentment of the upstate area. It is a resentment which is understandable, and it is very old, and, while it no longer has to do with being Dutch or English, it is still with us. Anyway, the defense for the upstate area was to resist, to be Dutch with a vengeance. The only language heard on the streets of Albany or out in country farmhouses was Dutch, even though the people were perfectly capable of understanding and speaking English. Peter Kalm noted, "In their homes and between themselves they always speak Dutch, so that rarely is an English word heard. Nearly all the books found in the homes are Dutch and it is seldom that an English book is seen." Kalm also wrote that the people were "permeated with a hatred toward the English whom they ridicule and slander at every opportunity."[54]

With the pressure to cooperate with other colonies against the English Parliament, which began with the trade acts of 1763, Albany learned English, or finally admitted to outsiders that it understood the language. Even the Reformed Church, and churches are the most conservative of institutions, adopted English as the liturgical language in 1770. Some of the rural churches seem to have continued to use Dutch up to 1800 or a little after.

As the Revolution approached, the leading forces in Bethlehem were represented by residents at opposite ends of the town—Francis Nicoll at Cedar Hill and, at the north end of town, Philip van Rensselaer at Cherry Hill and his nearest neighbor, Philip Schuyler.[55] They were part of the old guard of Albany; Nicoll and van Rensselaer were cousins of each other and of their wives (their own and each other's) so that they were connected by blood and marriage to almost everybody of importance in the Hudson Valley, including Schuyler. In an age when station in life counted for something, their opinions were considered respectfully by all the inhabitants of the town, probably more so than those of the underaged patroon to whom they owed fealty.[56]

Francis Nicoll

Francis Nicoll was born in 1737, the son of Judge Rensselaer Nicoll. Francis served briefly as a lieutenant in the Albany County militia at the end of the French and Indian War. Six days after his regiment was called up, he married his second cousin, Margaret van Rensselaer; in time they would have three children, two boys who died young, and a girl, Elisabeth.

With the close of the French and Indian War in 1763, the British government had an enormous debt to settle. Since the war had been fought to protect the American colonies, it seemed reasonable to Parliament that the colonies should foot the bill. A series of revenue laws, including the stamp act and the tea act, hit the colonial merchants particularly hard and resistance sprang up immediately. Throughout the colonies, while young men of the working class rioted, young gentlemen from fine families formed clandestine associations such as the Albany County Committee of Correspondence. It is a significant coincidence that in Albany County, and in many other communities as well, these angry young gentlemen also comprised the bulk of the junior officer corps of the militia. Among them was Francis Nicoll, tied by blood and marriage to the Albany merchant community.

As the critical year of 1775 opened, Rensselaerswyck's delegates to the Albany Committee of Correspondence included Francis Nicoll and his wife's uncle, Kiliaen van Rensselaer. Nicoll was elected to the Provincial Congress that met in New York City and promoted to lieutenant colonel of militia. In November 1775 he was in New York where the burning subject under debate was support for Boston, whose harbor was under British naval blockade, an act of retaliation for the Boston Tea Party. Although the colonies were still professing loyalty to England, a Continental Army under the command of George Washington was trying to lift the blockade. That winter, Henry Knox wrestled Fort Ticonderoga's cannon over to Boston, forcing the British to retreat. Meanwhile, Francis Nicoll was progressing up the Hudson with a boatload of New York City's cannon, and although he was blocked by ice for a time at Poughkeepsie, he eventually reached Albany.

By June of 1776, Nicoll was a full colonel in the militia, but there being no immediate prospects of fighting in Albany County, he was appointed by the Committee of Correspondence to sound out local sentiment on the idea of setting up a new form of government. Two weeks later that government became a reality with the Declaration of Independence.

In October 1776 Colonel Nicoll applied to the Committee of Correspondence for wagons to move the regimental baggage. The militia was getting ready for war. The opportunity to act came in the following year. The British marched out of Canada in a pincers movement to cut off the Continental Army's vital supply center at Albany. The force moving east along the Mohawk was stopped at Oriskany; the other, coming south from Lake Champlain, was defeated at Saratoga. Saved from invasion, Albany in the autumn of 1777 concentrated its attention again on supplying provisions to the Continental Army. The war moved on to other theaters and there was little for the Albany County militia to do. In June 1778 Francis Nicoll resigned his commission to devote his time to the family estate at Cedar Hill. Family tradition, unusually unreliable in this family, has his father dying in 1776 by drowning on his property (presumably in the Vloman Kill). A reference to him toward the end of the war makes the date of his death, if not the manner, suspect.[57] Nonetheless, he would be getting on in years in 1778 and in need of his son's assistance in running a large plantation.

Robert Sanders, father-in-law of Philip Van Rensselaer, in the 1750s.

At the other end of town, Philip van Rensselaer (born 1747), destined to be the first supervisor of the Town of Bethlehem, was from the East Manor branch of the family, moving to Cherry Hill about the time of his marriage to Maria Sanders in 1768.[58] He was a merchant, perhaps taking over the business of his father-in-law Robert Sanders, dealing in imported goods as well as shipping produce to New York City from his thousand-acre farm. During the Revolutionary War he served under his cousin, General Philip Schuyler, as quartermaster for the New York State region, and after the war served as Albany city alderman and county justice of the peace. As he grew in wealth (and in family—there were 12 children), he had a home built to reflect his station in life, the present Cherry Hill Mansion, erected in 1786. He was elected supervisor of Bethlehem in 1794, and died in 1798.[59]

of Albany's representatives at New York's Provincial Convention, and delegate to the Second Continental Congress. During the war he served in the Congress and as Major General and commander of the Northern Department of the Continental Army. Removed from command for supposed incompetence in abandoning the indefensible Fort Ticonderoga, Schuyler demanded a court martial at which he was vindicated in 1778. He left the Continental Congress in 1780 for the New York State Senate.

Philip Schuyler.

Although not remembered as having played an active part in the formation of the town, no doubt due to pressing national concerns, Philip John Schuyler, cousin and neighbor of Philip van Rensselaer, deserves to be mentioned. Certainly Schuyler was the most widely known resident at the town's beginning. In the colonial period he had served as an officer in the French and Indian War, then almost continuously in the New York General Assembly from 1768 until the Assembly was dissolved in 1775. Before the year was out he had served as one

First meeting of Washington and Hamilton.

One of his important contributions to the war effort was his service in the Continental Congress, where he was a strong supporter of his friend and confidant, General George Washington. Adding to the close alliance of the two men was Schuyler's son-in-law, Alexander Hamilton, who served on Washington's headquarters staff. The end of the war and the victorious beginning of the United States was due in no small part to the contribution of Philip Schuyler.

4 Bethlehem in the New Nation

A great desire of colonial Americans, and an immediate goal of the revolutionary generation, was to create local governments responsive to the will and needs of the people. During the country's early period of independence, New York was a leader in opposing strong, centralized government.

In Albany County, then the largest county in New York, some people lived more than 100 miles from the county seat. To bring government closer to the people, all or parts of eight new counties were created from Albany County between 1772 and 1809.

Within the county, subdivisions were created, beginning as districts in 1772. One of them was called Rensselaerwyck (without the possessive 's'), which was now both a manor and a district. This district was deemed unwieldy by the revolutionary state government in 1779, and was di-

The signing of the U. S. Constitution: Alexander Hamilton seated at far right.

vided into two districts separated by the Hudson River. The two parts were given the burdensome names of the West District of the Manor of Rensselaerwyck and the East District of the Manor of Rensselaerwyck, but were called by manor officials (and probably everyone else) the West and East Manors. In 1788, even as the state's proponents of home rule were disputing with advocates of nationalism over whether to ratify the proposed Constitution of the United States, all of the county districts within the state were reorganized as towns. The West Manor became the Town of Watervliet (the East Manor retained the name Rensselaerwyck and in 1791 became part of Rensselaer County). Five towns would be formed from Watervliet between 1790 and 1809.

North Pearl Street, Albany, about 1815. From a drawing by James Eights.

The Formation of Town Government

Bethlehem was formed from Watervliet March 12, 1793, some 163 years after the arrival of the first settlers. Originally bounding the town were Albany and Watervliet to the north, Rensselaerville to the west, Coeymans to the south, and the Rensselaer County line in the middle of the river to the east. New towns were formed from old ones between 1795 and 1822 so that Berne, Guilderland, Westerlo, and Knox replaced Rensselaerville and Watervliet on our western and northern borders. New Scotland was formed from Bethlehem April 25, 1832, replacing Berne, Knox, and Westerlo as our western neighbor. The borders have since remained stable, except that portions of northern Bethlehem have been ceded to the City of Albany from time to time.

Within these changing borders there was a changing population. Following the peace treaty ending the Revolutionary War, American citizens began moving about, seeking better opportunity. James Selkirk, a Scotsman who had settled in the Argyle or Galway area of Saratoga County before the war, leased a Bethlehem farm that included the present hamlet of Selkirk.[1] Many sixth-or-seventh-generation New Englanders, whose once-large farms had been divided into ever smaller units as the family grew, moved into Bethlehem.

A year after the creation of the town of Bethlehem, local citizens met to form a government. Philip Van Rensselaer, one of the town's most prominent residents, was chosen supervisor. His death only four years later, and the frequent absences and lack of involvement of Philip Schuyler, who was involved in state and national politics, left the way open for non-patrician citizens to take control of local government.

Schuyler certainly was Bethlehem's most famous resident. His organizational and political skills had been integral to the success of the struggle for independence. Then in the closing years of the American Revolution, he left the Continental Congress for a seat in the New York State Senate, where he served until 1797, with only one brief interruption (1789-1791) when he served in the United States Senate. He returned to the U.S. Senate in 1797, but resigned the next year to become a federal judge. In addition to his senatorial and judicial service, Schuyler concurrently held several state offices, among them Commissioner of Indian Affairs, Surveyor General, and Regent of the University.[2]

While Schuyler's attention was often concentrated on national and state affairs, he must have been aware of the interest in erecting the town of Bethlehem. In fact one would presume he was the member to introduce the bill in the State Senate. However, nothing has been found among his papers to identify his role in the town's establishment.

A Rural Town

At its formation Bethlehem was very much an agricultural town. A gazetteer of 1797 describes it as "Bethlehem, a town in Albany co., New York,

West view of the general market of the city of Albany in the summer of 1819.

grape, and the large tough fox grape." He was informed that on some of the islands there were grape species unknown in other parts of the United States. While he was picking grapes, his companions caught "a mess of fish," which he defined elsewhere as "a dishful of yellow perch."[6]

very fruitful in pastures, and has large quantities of excellent butter."[3] Howell and Tenney's county history, published nearly a century later, mentions Bethlehem's "fertile alluvial flats on the Hudson," and in the town generally, "The soil, under good tillage, produces a great variety of fruits, vegetables, and other farm and garden products for the Albany market."[4] Jacob S. Markle in the same volume notes that "the islands and alluvial lands are largely planted with potatoes and cabbages. Fruit culture is connected with general farming, and certain portions of every farm are planted with apple, plum, pear, cherry, and peach trees." He further notes that berries, garden vegetables, and dairy products were finding a ready market in Albany. Several farmers were experimenting with specialized breeds of cattle.[5]

Untilled areas were like the garden of Eden. An English traveller, John Maude, found sour cherries on an island called Overberg (high hill) Island, a little north of Cedar Hill. On a smaller island closer to Cedar Hill, he found good timber and two varieties of grapes, "the small black frost

Stephen Van Rensselaer. Engraving by A. B. Durand after a painting by A. Dickinson

Under Stephen van Rensselaer (the eighth patroon[7] and the third named Stephen), farms in Rensselaerswyck Manor grew in number until, at his death in 1839, there were over 3,000. These manor farms were quite popular until the 1840s, when vastly changed circumstances led to taxpayer revolts in a few of the towns in the hills, where people on the newest and poorest farms were having trouble scratching a bare existence out of the soil, and even minimal rents were a burden. The ensuing Antirent War did not affect Bethlehem and other older areas near the river where the land was fertile and the farms well-developed. Although it is difficult to look at this period objectively through the obscuring haze of the anti-renters' propaganda and the interpretations of twentieth-century Marxist historians, the fact remains that most of the farms were started and leases granted, not in some mythical feudal period, but after the American Revolution when people were free to travel and live anywhere in the country. Most of the post-Revolution leases went to New Englanders who

Van Rensselaer Manor House, north of Albany, in the time of Stephen Van Rensselaer. Drawn by Eugene Sintzenich.

saw Rensselaerswyck (also known as Van Rensselaer Manor) as affording a better opportunity than they had had at home.

Van Rensselaer Manor House. Painting.

Finally in 1846 a new state constitution was adopted that put an end to most of the manors of the Hudson Valley, except Van Rensselaer Manor, whose leases were still constitutional and could have continued forever. In truth, the Van Rensselaers saw the handwriting on the wall and decided it was time to get out of the land business and go into something else. They sold out for the most part to Walter Church, the real estate investor, who, in turn, sold most of the farms to the tenants then occupying them. While most were sold between the 1850s and 1880s, some were not sold and their occupants contin-

ued to lease. Some persons were still paying rent in the 1930s and perhaps some even after that.

Changes in Population

Even though English became the language of ordinary commerce, Dutch was used in the conversation of many rural families well into the nineteenth century. For many the last item to survive (the meaning of the words often forgotten) was the old nursery rhyme "Trippe troppe troontjes," which was handed down among many families throughout the region.

Although English became the language of home and trade in nineteenth-century Bethlehem, the town continued to receive and absorb immigrants from a multitude of nations. In the early years of the century the numbers of foreign-born residents were low—twenty-three aliens in 1820, fifty-seven in 1830. A dramatic increase came at midcentury following the Revolution of 1848 in Germany and the potato famine in Ireland, when the arrival of 1,000 Germans and 300 Irish almost entirely accounted for a population increase of seventy-three percent. However, almost every nationality in Europe was represented to some degree in the population.

African-American families, freed from slavery in the period from 1799 to 1827 under the state's program of emancipation, were among the town's older families.[8] Census figures show the results of gradual emancipation. In 1800, the year after the beginning of freedom for all newborn children, the black population included thirteen free and 254 enslaved persons. Ten years later there were 109 free and 137 slaves, and in 1820 for the first time more free black persons than slaves: seventy-three to fifty-five. In 1830 all 167 black persons were free and ten years later, following the creation of the town of New Scotland, Bethlehem still had 161 blacks (as compared to 2,877 whites).

With universal emancipation completed by 1827, rural black neighborhoods developed in time. A community with roots reaching back into at least the 1830s survives in the area east and south of Beckers Corners, although it is now a bedroom community rather than a farming hamlet.

The size of the population was rather large in the early years of the country's history—in 1810 it was three times larger than that of the entire state of Arkansas, and only a few hundred persons less than that of Michigan. A steady population growth rate was fairly balanced by periodic reductions in the town's boundaries. From 1810 to 1830 the town population grew from 4,430 to 6,082. Spafford's *Gazetteer* in 1825 shows the town's population as 5,114. That number included 943 farmers, ninety-seven mechanics (manual workers), and only four traders. The population declined by half when New Scotland[9] was taken off in 1832, so that in 1840 the population remaining in Bethlehem was 3,238. French's *Gazetteer* in 1860 shows Bethlehem with a population of 2,646 males and 2,505 females, comprising 981 families living in 795 dwellings. There were 476 freeholders.

Much of the town had not yet been developed—of the more than three hundred thousand acres of land in town, only 26,800 were improved farmland and 6,600 unimproved. Of the nine towns in the county at that time, Bethlehem had more landowners, more families, more children, more dwellings, more males and females, and a greater value of real estate than any except the huge town of Watervliet. The value of personal property was less than that of Coeymans. Bethlehem was fifth of nine towns in number of improved acres and seventh for unimproved acreage. All in all it was a middling town in terms of improved acreage but high in number of people, value of land and personal property, and in the raising of swine, grain, and potatoes. It was low in producing cloth, cheese, oxen, calves, sheep, and apples, somewhere in the middle in horses, cows, and butter.

By 1870 the population had risen to 6,950. Another ceding of territory—Cherry Hill (formerly a mile outside of Albany[10]) and Groesbeckville to Albany in 1870—reduced the population in half again, leaving the town with a population in 1875 of 3,746. It has increased steadily ever since. Even though the town population from 1800 to 1930 increased from 3,000 to but 7,000, by 1990 it was 27,000.

Growth of Roads and Hamlets

In the colonial period the settlement pattern had followed the shoreline and the creeks. A network of roads developed in town in the nineteenth-

View of the Hudson Highlands. Engraving by H. Adlard from a drawing by W. H. Bartlett, 1839.

The first steam railroad passenger train in America, the Mohawk & Hudson Rail Road Company, which ran between Albany and Schenectady.

century, both organized turnpikes and informal beaten paths between farms. This freed settlement somewhat from the restriction of following major waterways. Crossroads became the meet-

The Clermont. Contemporary engraving.

ing places of people, post offices appeared there, and general stores and other businesses, until we had the various "corners" of the town—Beckers Corners, Babcock Corners, Mallorys Corners, and so on.

Many of the roads were built and maintained by the residents themselves. Well into the nineteenth century, road repair was the duty of residents along the road, under the supervision of the town's road commissioners, rather than the town sup-

porting a professional staff of highway personnel.

The nineteenth century was Bethlehem's great toll road period. Numerous turnpike companies were formed between 1804 and 1854, connecting Bethlehem with Albany, Catskill, Schoharie, and other neighboring towns and nearby counties, as well as more distant points such as Delaware County. There were at least six railroad companies that owned or leased roads in Bethlehem, operations of the various companies beginning between 1851 and 1883. Numerous steamboats docked at Cedar Hill, which was known at one

Albany & Susquehanna Rail Road Company. Lithograph by Harry E. Pease.

time as Steamboat Landing. Stagecoaches ran daily through Bethlehem Center to New Scotland, New Salem, Berne, Clarksville, Westerlo, and Rensselaerville.

The road records of the town show that thirty-one roads were laid out or extended during Bethlehem's first ten years, 120 either created or extended in the forty years prior to the separation of New Scotland in 1832, and another eighty additions of various sorts over the next half century. The 1866 Beers map of Bethlehem shows that a number of hamlets had developed— Slingerland's Corners (originally Normanskill, now Slingerlands), Groesbeckville, Kenwood (Lower Hollow), Upper Hollow (Normansville), Adamsville (also called Adams Station, now Delmar), Bethlehem Centre (earlier Babcock's Corners and Wemple), Cedar Hill (Steamboat Landing), South Bethlehem (Janes Corners), Beckers Corners, and Callanans Corners. Communities that the mapmaker missed included Selkirk and Van Wies.

A number of settlements developed such requirements of civilized life as a church, a school, a physician's office. By 1886 the largest community in town was Adams Station (Delmar) with 360 residents, several shops, a cigar factory, and, of course, the Adams Hotel. Nearby Slingerlands had 230 people, a print shop and cigar factory, and a hotel. Other communities with at least a hundred residents included Bethlehem Center, South Bethlehem (which had a barber shop and O.S. Jolley's band of twelve musicians), and the two mill towns on the Normanskill—Kenwood

The horse-drawn Albany railway: cars at the corner of Clinton Avenue and Ten Broeck Street.

and Normansville. Kenwood was also known for Cherry Hill, where the Van Rensselaers lived, and for Mount Hope, site of the Academy of the Sacred Heart and the Prentice estate. It was important enough to be connected to Albany by a horsecar line.

Country Estates

An Englishman, I. Finch, visiting Albany in 1824 wrote of a local site that a friend insisted he see. "The rapids of Norman Kill are worthy a visit. A small river dashes over ledges of rock, and the stream is confined by precipitous banks covered with forest trees."[11] A writer in 1825 reminisced of trips from Albany to Kenwood in an earlier time. "The ride to this spot [Rensselaer's Mills], and to the hospitable mansion of the late venerable Col. Francis Nichols, on the Bethlehem Flats, used to be one of the pleasantest in the vicinity of Albany."[12]

The Nicoll-Sill House. Painting by L. F. Tantillo, 1992.

Whitehall. From a sampler made by Hester Gansevoort Ten Eyck in 1810.

Attractive scenery and a quiet countryside attracted the harried city dweller. A number of prominent Albany residents began to make their homes in Bethlehem, beginning with Albany Mayor (1838-1841) Jared L. Rathbone, who purchased Rensselaer's Mills on the Normanskill (at the time two and a half miles from Albany[13]) and named the site Kenwood after a spot in Scotland. Others selected similar locations just outside the city in that area or at scenic points along the river.

Several notable homes were built as a result, scattered among older but equally grand residences. Some buildings that drew the attention of writers, such as local historian Jacob Markle and gazetteer writer Horatio Gates Spafford, included the Nicoll-Sill house on the Vloman Kill, the homes of Peter van Wie and S. Baumes, Cherry Hill Mansion (at that time still in Bethlehem), Mount

Hope (then the property of Ezra P. Prentice), the elegant Abbey Hotel, and Whitehall Mansion near the Delaware turnpike road (now Delaware Avenue). This last was originally built by General John Bradstreet in the 1760s. It had served as a Loyalist hideout during the Revolution, before being acquired by Bradstreet's namesake, John Bradstreet Schuyler, son of Philip. Schuyler sold it in 1789 to Leonard Gansevoort, an important local figure in the Revolution and the brother of General Peter Gansevoort. Later, Leonard Gansevoort served in several state offices and as an Albany County judge. He greatly expanded Whitehall Mansion to truly impressive proportions, with a frontage of 110 feet and depth of seventy feet.[14]

One house that barely survived was Schuyler Mansion. After Philip's Schuyler's death in 1804, his family moved away and his mansion was sold

Schuyler Mansion. Photograph.

Merino Sheep. Painting by R. Vandusen. The worth of these creatures was recited by prominent Americans from Sir William Johnson to Robert Fulton.

at auction. In 1824, when it was owned by Albany furrier John Bryan, one writer described the house as "now a grey venerable ruin, though occupied and in repair."[15] From 1846 to 1854 it was the home of Ezekiel McIntosh, and then of his widow until her marriage in 1858 to former president Millard Fillmore. From 1886 to 1914 it was St. Vincent's Home for Orphans. It was purchased by the state of New York in 1912, and in 1914 was opened to the public as a state historic site. Meanwhile, Philip Van Rensselaer's Cherry Hill Mansion remained in family hands until 1961 when it was sold to a private corporation and opened as a historic site. Both houses are now within the Albany city limits.

Farming in Bethlehem

Most residents of the town continued to be farmers, not suburbanites commuting to Albany from country mansions. State census records from 1835 to 1875 show that Bethlehem's principal export crops were corn, rye, potatoes, and apples for human consumption, and oats for New York City's horses. Sheep were an important cash product until the closing of the local fulling mill, around 1850. Home production of cloth was an important source of income until just before the Civil War. There were almost as many cattle and hogs as people, the cattle providing salable dairy products, the hogs raised for home consumption.

It was not an industrial town. The 1855 census lists five coach and wagon factories, three sawmills, two gristmills, a plaster mill, a blacksmith

The New York Agricultural Fair at Albany, 1850. Lithograph by R. H. Pease.

shop, a tannery, and a broom factory, which altogether employed a mere forty-seven persons.

Many of the leading lights in town were those persons who were the most progressive in farming. Ambrose Wiltsie, Jr., (born 1828) increased the profits of the family farm he had inherited by specializing in the production of cider and vinegar. He supplemented his income by working as a surveyor, a skill in much demand in the nineteenth century as Van Rensselaer Manor was broken up and sold off.[16] Jurian Winne, one of the four organizers of the Albany County Agricultural Society and vice president of the State Agricultural Association, raised prize-winning Leicester sheep and was a published authority on winter feed.[17]

The 1875 census shows that most of the trades practiced in the town were related to agriculture. Residents of Bethlehem included milk peddlers, pork packers, tanners, butchers, and an apple pruner. Other individuals were involved in moving the produce to market—teamsters, hay freighters, railroad employees, and boatmen. Supporting the transportation were the wagon makers, wheelwrights, blacksmiths, and harness makers. There were significant numbers of domestic and other servants. Carpenters and masons provided services useful to the entire community, as did small numbers of such necessary tradesmen and professionals as shoemakers and dressmakers, tavern keepers and hotel keepers, a grocer, doctors and a lawyer, teachers and ministers, surveyors, a civil engineer, and two gate keepers for the toll road. Two persons were involved in cigar manufacturing in Slingerlands.

Manufacturing

Milling was one of the most ancient of the town's industries. Rensselaer's mills, once the property of Philip van Rensselaer, were described in 1825 as

> consist[ing] of a very excellent grain mill, saw mill, plaister[!] mill, a carding and clothier's works, and a snuff mill. They are on a good stream, near the city, and of great use to the inhabitants, mills in this quarter being rather scarce.[18]

Obviously the situation had changed greatly from the 1650s when Rensselaerswyck had ten sawmills. Trees were fast disappearing so that sawmills were closing rapidly, and wire was replacing wooden-rail and stone fences. However, the town did have some industry beyond the usual sorts found anywhere. Westerlo Island, where Bethlehem's earliest settlers had planted their first crops, by the 1880s had two iron works—the Corning Iron Company, founded in 1870, which became in 1873 the Jagger Iron Company, and the Albany City Iron Company, founded in 1878—with docks, railroad tracks, and other evidence of the industrial age. The other islands by then were being used largely for the storage of ice, with housing for 275 thousand tons.

Another manufacturing firm of note was J.C. Huyck and Co. at Kenwood. This firm, which later moved to Rensselaer, is best remembered for wool felts, produced for papermakers, and for wool blankets.

There were firms that excavated molding sand for foundries, and for stove and hollow ware manufacturers. A Mr. Clow is said to have begun the first company in the area. The soil in Selkirk was good for this purpose, and the pitted landscape shows the results of the innumerable wagonloads carted away. A few quarries provided stone for railroad bridges and other building purposes. Callanan's was, and still is, the best known.

Communications

Communications media developed in the nineteenth century and opened the town further to the rest of the country. The American Telegraph Co. was operating by 1855. The Hudson River Telephone Company began operations in 1883, and by 1886 had communication from Albany to the Abbey Hotel, Cedar Hill, Hurstville, Slingerlands, Delmar, and Bethlehem Center.

Religious Practice

As the population in the early federal period grew to the point that people could begin to contemplate the formation of a town, so they also considered establishing local church congregations.

Between 1770 and 1870 a number of Christian congregations developed—Reformed, Presbyterian, and Methodist. Persons of other denominations and faiths had to be content with visits from circuit riders, or attend services outside of town.

That the first church would be anything but the Dutch Reformed Church was not even a question. The First Reformed Protestant Dutch Church of Bethlehem and Jericho (now the First Reformed Church of Bethlehem) applied on December 28, 1791, for incorporation under the state's religious corporation laws. The treasurer's records of contributions for building materials and books begin in October 1792. A delegate was sent to the General Synod for the first time in June 1794, and finally in December 1795, the elders, deacons, and other members transferred their letters from their former congregations, and purchased from Stephen van Rensselaer land at Jericho (not the present hamlet of that name but what is now called Selkirk). Regular services began in January 1797, conducted by supply ministers until the arrival of the Reverend Christian Bork in March 1798 as minister to the congregations at Bethlehem and Schodack (Rensselaer County). Prior to this, most town residents had attended services in Albany or Schenectady.

Several other Reformed congregations were formed at about the same time, including Jerusalem (Feura Bush) and New Salem, both then in the town of Bethlehem, and Heldeberg in Guilderland. Records of the churches show a slow increase of names not Dutch, until Scotch, English, and German names had become fairly common. Both black and white people participated in the sacramental life of the congregations from the beginning. At the Bethlehem church, both Dutch and English services were held each Sunday until 1811, when the frequency of Dutch services was reduced, a first step toward their inevitable elimination.

By the 1880s there were churches of several denominations—three Reformed, three Methodist (and a chapel), one Presbyterian, and a Baptist chapel. Following the First Reformed Church organized in 1793, a Reformed church was built at Adamsville (Delmar) in 1841, originally as a chapel sponsored by the Union Reformed Church at Unionville (in the town of New Scotland). In 1827 the separatist True Reformed Church established a congregation in Bethlehem, which in 1854 built a church near Bethlehem Center. The First Presbyterian Church of Bethlehem was organized in 1835 and was situated one and a half miles west of Hurstville. The first Methodist church in town was the Methodist Episcopal Church, originally located a short distance east of Beckers Corners, formed in 1823. This church was taken down in 1845 and the timber used for a church at Janes Corners (South Bethlehem) and dedicated in 1846 as the First Methodist Episcopal Church of Bethlehem. The Methodist Episcopal Church at Adams Station was organized about 1830 and a building erected about 1833. A division of this congregation in 1871 resulted in the formation of the Methodist Episcopal Church at Slingerlands. A free chapel was erected by Methodists in 1877 at Cedar Hill. A Baptist mission chapel at Kenwood was built in 1866 by William Sawyer and conveyed to the Baptist Missionary Association.

Education

At the beginning of the new nation, quality education was not equally available to all. A river traveller in 1800 wrote, "On the W. shore I noticed Colonel Nicol's house, where we landed the accomplished tutor of his children on my voyage up."[19] Not everyone could afford a tutor. Education in the town developed in the nineteenth century with the formation of local school districts and efforts by the state and county to enforce standards. The public school system, established by law in New York State in 1851, decreed that every child thereafter not only had the opportunity but in fact was required to have an education, which did much to raise New York to its long preeminence among the states in all fields of endeavor. That this law permitted a variety of schools—public, private, and parochial—has allowed and encouraged a variety in education, and perhaps recognized the variety in people that has been New York's hallmark from the beginning. Thus we find by 1886 the Bethlehem countryside dotted with one- and two-room school houses, and a Catholic institution on Mount Hope in Kenwood, the Academy of the Sacred Heart, which was the only secondary school in town. Unlike some neighboring towns, Bethlehem had no public high schools in this time period. Besides

Albany High School, non-Catholic pupils pursued further education at the Albany Academy for boys, the Academy for girls, St. Agnes, the Episcopal school for girls, or similar institutions farther afield.

The rural towns of the county were divided into three districts, with Bethlehem falling within the First District. Between 1856 and 1886 the school commissioners of the district included four from Cedar Hill, three from Coeymans, and one each from Bethlehem Center, Albany, Callanan's Corners, and New Salem. In 1860, some 1,806 children were being taught in fifteen school districts. In 1883 there were fourteen school districts with fourteen schoolhouses, twenty teachers, and 769 pupils.

Wars

Although no wars were fought upon Bethlehem's territory, she sent her sons off to fight in numerous battles elsewhere. The 1840 census shows four men in Bethlehem receiving pensions for Revolutionary War service. Their names and ages were Conrad Goss, ninety, Jacob Laraway, eighty-two, Joshua Bailey, seventy-six, and Minardt P. Vandenburg, eighty-three. Residing in New Scotland, which had separated only

Solomon Van Rensselaer, as a young officer. Engraving by H. B. Hall & Sons.

Solomon Van Rensselaer, in his later years. Engraving by H.B. Hall & Sons.

eight years earlier from Bethlehem, were three veterans of that war and one widow receiving a pension—John Ramsay, eighty-one, Garret J. Sager, eighty-seven, Christopher Winne, eighty, and Rachel Van Hosen, eighty. In the War of 1812 Major General Solomon van Rensselaer was the highest ranking officer among Bethlehem's residents, and exceedingly popular among his men, if one can judge by the number who named sons after him. He had earlier (1797) fought against the Indians in the Battle of Fallen Timbers under General "Mad Anthony" Wayne, and formed a lifetime friendship with fellow officer William Henry Harrison. In the War of 1812 he captured and briefly held Queenstown Heights in Ontario, Canada, and was for many years a major general in the state militia.

The war with the greatest effect upon any town in the nineteenth century was the Civil War. The subject is well covered in our military history chapter by William Howard, who discusses all of Bethlehem's military history. One effect of all the wars was to take young men out of their familiar surroundings and expose them to life's varieties and the world's opportunities.

Politics

It is said that until 1987, only Republicans had been elected to office in the town since the founding of that party. However, Jurian Winne is remembered as having been active in the shortlived Greenback Party, not only as one of the founding members but as the party's unsuccessful candidate for State Treasurer in 1879.[20] Town historian Joseph Allgaier, in his chapter on town government, further dismantles this old-wives' tale of Republican monopoly. However, it is certainly

Encampment of New York troops in the Civil War, Camp Butterfield, Virginia.

true that in living memory this uninterrupted success held true until 1987. But not, however, the oft-repeated statement by Albany journalists that the town has had only Republicans since its founding—fifty-seven years before the establishment of the Republican Party. No doubt there was fervent political activity in the years prior to 1854, but to what purpose or of what political orientation is often unknown.

A leader in early Bethlehem town politics, as he had been in the Revolutionary War period, was Francis Nicoll of Cedar Hill. His son-in-law, Richard Sill, who had read law in the office of Aaron Burr, served in the State Assembly from 1789 until his untimely death on June 4, 1790. Nicoll then served two terms in the Assembly, a term in the State Senate, and another in the Assembly.

After the death of Francis Nicoll in 1817, the influence of the Nicoll-Sill family waned rapidly. A grandson with poor financial judgement brought the family into difficulties, and before the end of the century the property had been sold off in pieces. Part of the property did remain in the family; Cornelius Baker married Caroline Lasher, a relative of the Nicoll family, and purchased the 450-acre main farm, which he called Grand View. In addition to farming, Baker had a considerable income from shipping lumber and other products to New York.

The leading role of the Van Rensselaer family of Cherry Hill also declined as the town developed. When Elizabeth Van Rensselaer married her cousin Solomon Van Rensselaer, her father Philip gave the couple as a wedding present Mount Hope, the southern part of the Cherry Hill property. After Philip's death, Solomon acquired also Cherry Hill. However, as a professional soldier, and later Congressman, Solomon was seldom home (although in his later years he served as Albany postmaster). His son Rensselaer Van Rensselaer engaged in politics and commerce in Latin America, then became so involved in Canada's unsuccessful war of independence in 1838 that he was found in violation of

Rensselaer Van Rensselaer. Engraving by H. B. Hall & Sons.

American neutrality laws and imprisoned. Catherine Bonney, Solomon's daughter, and her husband Samuel spent most of their lives in the Orient as missionaries (their correspondence includes letters from King Monkut II of Siam, made famous by the book *Anna and the King of Siam* and the musical *The King and I*). Henceforth politics in Bethlehem was democratic rather than patrician. With the old patrician families generally involved with the world beyond Bethlehem's borders, town politics was democratic, and local.

One presumes that in the national formative period 1783-1800, local contests had a Federalist versus Anti-Federalist orientation. By 1793, when Bethlehem was formed, President Washington had abandoned his earlier stance above party interests and was cooperating strongly with

Alexander Hamilton.

Alexander Hamilton's Federalists, one of the reasons for Thomas Jefferson's leaving the cabinet (we should not forget that Hamilton's father-in-law, Philip Schuyler, and Washington were good friends who corresponded several times a month). Closer to home, the popular governor George Clinton, although also publicly taking a stance above politics, in fact was considered by everyone to be Anti-Federalist. The family ties of such men as Francis Nicoll and Philip van Rensselaer would have been to the patrician element of Philip Schuyler and his famous son-in-law Hamilton. The solidarity of that faction ended with the deaths of Hamilton in 1803 and Schuyler in 1804.

George Clinton. Engraving by Buttre.

By the state census of 1796, 388 of Bethlehem's inhabitants were electors.[21] In comparing this to total population figures, we have to remember that numerous groups in society, in particular women and slaves, were not permitted to vote.

In the early nineteenth century, the Federalist party collapsed and left the field to Jefferson's "Republicans," eventually renamed Democrats (at first intended as an insult, implying supporters of mob rule). Election campaigns for some time thereafter were intramural affairs, rather than party opposition, but soon enough Free-Soilers, Anti-Masons, Know-Nothings, Whigs, Abolitionists, and Temperance groups all fielded, or lent support to, candidates. Again, the strength of these or other more local organizations has not been traced. Local Anti-Renters—their heyday was from 1839 to 1846—would eventually join with western Free-Soilers, abolitionists, and Whigs to form the Republican party, although what elements went into Bethlehem's local organization at first is open to speculation.[22]

Following the sale of much of the Van Rensselaer lands in the 1860s, local issues for Bethlehem in the latter part of the nineteenth century must have been largely those of a settled and mature agricultural region. Low tariffs on imported goods would have been welcome, but since the principal markets for local farmers were in Albany and New York, export taxes were of no concern. Immigration did not threaten farmers' livelihoods so the ethnic disturbances of the cities would not have spread to Bethlehem. The town could hardly have escaped the religious prejudices of the day, but no evidence of virulent expression has reached us.

Medicine

For a rural town, Bethlehem had a significant number of physicians. There were seven practicing in the mid-1880s, located in Adams Station, Slingerlands, South Bethlehem, and Callanans

Corners. Eighteen others had served the town earlier in the century.[23] Dr. Babcock, a native of Bethlehem Center (originally Babcocks Corners), practiced at Beckers Corners and is perhaps the best known. His medicinal cabinet is on display at the Town of Bethlehem Historical Association museum in Cedar Hill.

Societies

In an age when meetings of social and business organizations were avidly attended, Bethlehem had its share. There was an insurance association and a society to protect against horse thieves, in both of which organizations town supervisor Albertus W. Becker (in private life a farmer) was active. Other groups included the Grange at Beckers Corners, the Good Templars, the Odd Fellows, and the Masons at Babcocks Corners. The Sons of Temperance met from 1868 to 1871, at first at Adamsville and later in Slingerlands; perhaps their early dissolution indicates a lack of solid support for their cause. There were also several cemetery associations, some of which still exist; a list can be found in the Appendix.

Caverns

In the nineteenth century, natural curiosities were a favorite area of investigation, whether mental or physical. One writer pokes fun at the sport of cave exploring, or spelunking.

In the limestone of this Town, there have been discovered some extensive Caverns, one of which has been explored for a quarter of a mile in length, and the other about 40 rods. The principal one is at Bogardus's, or Mrs. Ludlow's 12 miles SW. from Albany, where people, fond of such excursions, may go a great distance underground, and see a long, dark, crooked, dirty, great hole, where the water once ran, perhaps see some toads, and bats, spiders, and so forth, get comfortably tired, dirty enough, and make a good escape in getting out of it. I have explored some of those wonderful Caverns, and, excepting now and then a stalactite, have found nothing worth the trouble. A gentleman tells me he can perfectly recollect seeing a smart stream issue from one of these Caves, some years since, and well remembers the time, though not the year, when it ceased to flow out of it, having probably found some other passage, underground.[24]

Spelunkers still enjoy exploring these caves, some of which are in what is now the town of New Scotland. In 1990 a flash flood trapped five explorers in a cave for several hours. Twice in the spring of 1992, spelunkers needed rescuing by the Clarksville Rescue Squad.

Concluding Thoughts

As Bethlehem neared the twentieth century, it remained very much what it had always been—a peaceful town, not in the sense of bucolic, but one without class strife, and not suffering invasion by either foreign or native forces. While the national and state populations had doubled several times over, Bethlehem held steady, although slowly eroded by the expanding city to the north.

In 1900 the name of the person behind the store counter was the same as the name over the door. Such businesses remain, but they are proportionately fewer. The train and the automobile have ushered in an age when more and more people live here but work someplace else. Bethlehem becomes more obviously an integral part of the region, one of many towns that are interconnnected and interdependent. Yet it continues to maintain a character of its own.

5 Business and Industry

Profit from a business enterprise and resultant power and fortune were the motivations for settlement by the Dutch in the region of New York, unlike religious convictions, which attracted Pilgrims from England to nearby New England.[1] Financial gain would compensate for the hardships of a long sea voyage and day-to-day living under primitive conditions. We can imagine the expectations of Dutch businessmen, who made the journey to the new world, and their visions of wealth from the trading of furs with Indians of the area. Trading was initially undertaken from Fort Nassau, constructed in 1614 by Hendrick Christiansen van Cleef of the New Netherland Company, on Westerlo Island at the mouth of the Normanskill. It became the starting point for the evolution of agricultural, industrial, and residential growth that exists today.

In 1630, Kiliaen van Rensselaer, Patroon of Rensselaerswyck, engaged Wolfert Gerritsen as supervisor and Rutger Hendricksen and Brant Peelen as farmers. They would become the first settlers within the eventual boundaries of the town.

Settlement and Business Growth

During the seventeenth century, settlement progressed slowly in the area that was to become Bethlehem. It was most notable along the Hudson River and the Normanskill because of the practical advantages during that period of living near a source of water. By the year 1700, up to forty families had settled in the area. A map of 1767 identifies a total of 127 households.[2] These settlements were primarily agricultural and most early farmers were interested in raising cash crops. For example, wheat was a popular and valuable commodity for a long time.

Besides raising agricultural products, the enterprises that developed during the seventeenth and early eighteenth centuries to satisfy the needs of the community were sawmills, gristmills, wheelwright shops, and smithies. Early records also disclose inns and taverns as popular establishments.

The Early Years

Common early businesses were shops connected with a hamlet or a farm dwelling, providing services to family and neighbors. There was also the investment business, as a gristmill or sawmill, operating under an agreement with the owner. Early owners of a business operated in much the same manner as today, engaging in legal contracts, like leasing work privileges, in return for a profit share. One such owner was Eldert Gerbertsen Cruyff, who owned at least one sawmill in Bethlehem on the banks of the Vloman Kill and land in the area of Catskill.

Cruyff shows up frequently in the Dutch court records of the county of Albany.[3] He seems to have been a very quarrelsome man, given to abuse and defamation, going to the court both as plaintiff and defendant. In 1657, he was prosecuted for defaming Vredrick Kleyn's wife and the following year for calling Jochim Kettlehuyn a thief. Representing Mr. Cruyff as his attorney, although he was not trained in law, was his stepson, Albert Janse Ryckman. Acting as a lawyer and having power of attorney was not unusual in early days.

Money problems surfaced in 1671 when Eldert Gerbertsen Cruyff acknowledged debt to Jan Heyndricsen Bruyns and Hans Heindricksen, pledging his sawmill as collateral. He entered into contracts with people to run his sawmill in 1671, 1672, and 1673. Eldert went back to Holland in 1672, leaving his stepson to manage financial

affairs. Accounts were finally settled, including the sale of his sawmill in Bethlehem, after Cruyff died in 1675.[4]

The Period of Revolution

As the 1700s progressed and events leading up to the Revolutionary period unfolded, the town of Bethlehem felt the forces which affected life in the city of Albany. The farmers of Bethlehem were major agricultural producers in the area and they seized opportunities to feed the expanding military population in and around the city. This was not a normal circumstance but arose from the French and Indian wars. Military forces numbered 15,000 men in 1758, almost four times Albany's population.[5] Wheat was a major cash crop for the farmer. The Continental Army, in the Revolution, survived on New York wheat. Because wheat was used in producing flour, the gristmill operator also had a great advantage and opportunity to profit. Undoubtedly, local Bethlehem sawmill operators and smithies also participated in an economic upturn to satisfy the needs of so large a contingent of soldiers.

Although the forces of the Revolution surrounded the area that was to become Bethlehem, there was little impact on settlement in the community after the war. Soldiers, who were predominantly German, Irish, Scotch, and Yankee, were given land in undeveloped areas or settled within the city of Albany. Settlement in the town of Bethlehem and establishment of stores, shops, and other forms of

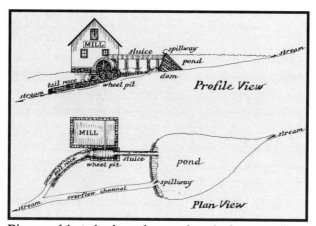

Diagram of the technology of an overshot wheel system mill.

business linked to people and households, varied little until about 1850 when the Federal census recorded a population of 4,102.

The Nineteenth Century

The great influx of immigrants from Europe to the United States after 1850, seeking relief from famine and oppression, had an impact on the town. About 1,000 Germans and 300 Irish settled in Bethlehem during the next two decades, a seventy percent increase in population.[6] Most involved themselves in agriculture, which remained the dominant industry in Bethlehem. A century would pass before another radical increase in population took place, because of the desire of people to live in a more placid, semi-rural environment rather than within the city.

The last half of the nineteenth century saw the start of the industrial revolution in the United States, symbolized by foundry and iron-works smokestacks, huge textile mills, and powerful steam engines. Factories, which were located on the major waterways, the Hudson and Mohawk Rivers, became a source of employment for immigrants in the communities to the north of Albany—Cohoes, Waterford, and Mechanicville.

Bethlehem, however, did not participate in the development of large-scale manufacturing facilities but remained an agricultural community during this time of industrial growth. The Corning Iron Company was formed in 1870 (renamed in 1873 Jagger Iron Company in recognition of its president, Ira Jagger) and began to produce iron in 1871 on Westerlo (formerly Castle) Island.[7] In 1878, two blast furnaces were erected on the north

Late nineteenth century mills on the Wynant's Kill in Troy. Such industrialization did not take place on the Normanskill.

end of the island and the Albany City Iron Works began production. Other than these two enterprises on Westerlo Island, which was at that time within the borders of the town, Bethlehem did not participate in the prevailing image of growing industry in the area surrounding Albany.

A Native Product

In a notable way, Bethlehem was important to industrial revolution industries. To manufacture cast metal products such as coal-burning stoves, moulding sand, a type of sand that retains its shape when compressed, was required. Bethlehem land contained such sand and the mining of moulding sand became a major industry in the town. One 1897 historical publication indicated 500,000 tons were shipped to Albany for distribution throughout the country.[8]

Two firms that mined the sand in the town were the Whitehead Brothers Company and the New York Sand and Facing Company. They purchased or leased land for mining or entered into other agreements with property owners. The first such recorded transaction in the town was in 1884. A contract was initiated by Whitehead Brothers to mine four and one-half acres of the Bailey Farm in Selkirk, adjacent to the tracks of the New York West Shore Railroad. The first recorded agreement for mining sand by New York Sand and Facing was in 1905. However, a map of about 1880 shows the company with a location in Glenmont, next to the West Shore Railroad. A

short distance east and south on the river were sand docks.[9] Both companies were active until about 1920, when the demand for moulding sand dropped off.

Farms throughout the town furnished the sand, from Selkirk to South Bethlehem to Slingerlands. The process of mining was to remove topsoil until the sand was reached, which would be from ten inches to two feet in depth. After the sand was removed, the topsoil would be restored. Typical prices paid to the property owners during the early 1900s were $200 to $300 an acre mined. Andrew Koonz of Selkirk, whose family sold sand from its farm to Whitehead Brothers, recalls that a siding to accommodate six freight cars was located near his present home on Beaver Dam Road.

Some requirement for moulding sand persisted; for example, sand was necessary for producing accurate and detailed castings of brass and iron. As late as 1946, the Selkirk Moulding Sand Company was incorporated by Selkirk residents, Michael J. Miller and his son, to mine and market the product. Michael J. Jr., commonly known as Joe, recalls shipping sand to Canada, Pennsylvania, the midwest, and other locations where small foundries existed. By 1960, the business was no longer profitable due to the small demand for the sand. A primary reason for the decline was the widespread use of molded plastic rather than cast metal products.

Into the Twentieth Century

The assessment rolls for 1917 provide a picture of the business development at the time within the town. A total of 157 farms and thirty-two business establishments was identified. Businesses included ten stores, three hotels, five shops, and six mill sites. The ratio of farms to businesses started to change during the 1920s when Bethlehem emerged as a suburban community. Today, assessment rolls suggest a different composition of the community. One hundred parcels of farm and agricultural products land and 250 commercial parcels are on the rolls. The dominant assessment unit is the residential category with about 8,600 parcels.

Several conditions influenced business development in Bethlehem. Included were natural resources, perception of the town as a favorable location for business establishments, the growth of

various industries, and an increase in the population of the town, which fostered the need for people to have convenient access to goods and services.

The River

The Hudson River is the major natural resource that influenced business development. It carried all the early settlers to the town and was the only avenue for trade until the advent of the land transportation industry. As commercial vessels and pleasure boats travelled the river, Bethlehem shared the fruits of economic investment by providing labor to the shipping industry and various

Hudson River Day Line steamboats, like the luxurious *New York*, travelling between New York City and Albany, would pass numerous docks such as the Winne dock and the Van Wie dock.

forms of service. Two prominent examples of such service are the dock at Van Wies Point and the Winne dock at Cedar Hill.

The docks became regular stops for steamers such as the *City of Hudson* and barges like the *Harvest Queen* and *Empress* travelling between Albany and points south. Many types of merchandise were either delivered or picked up. Agricultural products, ice, and lumber were popular exports. For example, oats were transported to New York City to feed horses. Furniture, hardware products, and coal were imported. At the Winne dock, a general store became a profitable business along with coal bins and storage facilities for grain and hay. Business at the docks was brisk during the late 1800s through the 1920s.[10] During later years, residents along the river commuted to Albany by boat. The Winne store may be considered the first convenience market in the town. Its stock was extensive. In addition to goods and produce, a variety of other products needed on farms and in households were sold. Marie Weidemann, a long-time resident of Cedar Hill, former teacher and an active member of the Bethlehem Historical Association, remembers buying kerosene and coal at the Winne store in the early 1920s.

In 1835, the Hudson River Steamboat Company leased the Van Wie dock for use as its Albany terminal. It was a thriving commercial enterprise.

The river continued to provide a livelihood for the people of Bethlehem during the winter months, even though travel ceased because of freezing temperatures. At the beginning of the twentieth century, before home refrigeration became commonplace, a large ice industry existed. It is said to have had an accidental start in 1828 when a sloop, loaded with cakes of ice from an early break-up of the river, sold its cargo in New York City for $300.[11]

Icehouses were a familiar sight alongside the river. Two examples are the Cedar Hill Ice Company, which was locally owned, and the Knickerbocker Ice Company, which was owned by New York City interests. The Normanskill also was dammed to produce ice. The Pappalau icehouse was located at Normansville and the Kelly icehouse at Kenwood. Henry Meyer, a local resident for more than ninety years, recalls ice harvesting at the turn of the century. Horses and manual labor were the main source of power. Ponds were constructed adjacent to the river to form smooth ice. The ice was cut into uniform blocks and stacked between layers of hay in the icehouse. Export of the ice on steamship freighters to the homes, restaurants, and hotels of New York City continued throughout the summer.[12]

Display of ice harvesting implements in Bethlehem Historical Museum.

Although much ice was exported, local ice merchants also supplied the needs of the town. In 1917, two icehouses were located in Bethlehem, one owned by A.C. Rowe and the other by G.G. Wilfert.[13] The industry began to decline during the 1920s because refrigerators became a common appliance in the home, but many local residents recall deliveries of ice well into the 1940s. Robert Westervelt was listed as an ice dealer in the Tri-Village Area Directory as late as 1949.

Beckers Corners Hotel in 1921. Today, calling it a "bed and breakfast" accommodation might be more appropriate.

Land Transportation

Almost three centuries would pass before significant transportation of commercial products and groups of people would take place over land routes within the town of Bethlehem. The dominant avenue for travel in the early centuries was the Hudson River. Over land, paths developed from Indian trails. They were eventually widened to accommodate horse-drawn vehicles. For the most travelled routes, turnpike companies were formed to construct and maintain a road, financed through tolls collected from users of the road. Maintenance of most dirt roads in the town, however, was the obligation of individual property owners who were assessed days of labor for the purpose. This method of maintenance lasted until the late 1800s. Results were poor. During winter, snow would make roads impassable. Periods of rain during the rest of the year turned earth to mud and made most of the paths unusable or difficult to traverse during these times.

Travel was very tedious. Any trip of consequence would require overnight stays. In the nineteenth century, inns were common and most often associated with an individual residence. Early records of meeting places in the town from 1794 through 1819 identify the inns of Henry Burhans, James Wands, William Burhans, George Houck, Peter Barrager, John Rosenkrans, and William Wayne.[14] In later records, reference to hotels as meeting places is prominent.[15] These hotels were located at Normansville (Smith's), Slingerlands (Home Lawn), Glenmont (Abbey), Delmar (Van Cott's), Cedar Hill, and Bethlehem Center. Also mentioned were the hotels of William Munsing, A.C. Woods, Crippen Fowler, Henry Paar, William Selkirk, and Daniel Waters.

The Road and Turnpike Business

At the beginning of the nineteenth century, the legislature of the state introduced laws to provide for the construction of major highways or turnpikes. The laws established corporate bodies, defined methods of raising capital and revenues, and provided for other administrative matters. The corporation was empowered to acquire land needed for the road. Owners were given cash settlements and the legislation outlined procedures to resolve disputes. The Albany and Schenectady Turnpike Company was the first venture, incorporated by law on April 1, 1797.[16] During the next half century, similar corporations were established throughout the state.

On April 9, 1804, the Albany and Bethlehem Turnpike Company was incorporated by act of the State Legislature for construction of the first turnpike in the town. It was to run from the Albany city line on the Bethlehem road, renamed South Pearl Street in 1870,[17]

The Kenwood tollgate.

> to the Norman's-kill bridge, including the same, thence running westerly on the Bethlehem road to the house of Joshua Babcock, junior, then from the Norman's-kill bridge, southerly, to a small bridge south of James Van Rensselaer's, including the same.[18]

The distance was about five miles and the road had one tollgate at Kenwood.[19] The act also contained specifications for the turnpike that were standard for the period:

> The said president, directors and company shall cause a road to be opened and kept open, four rods [sixty-six feet] wide, and which shall be thirty feet between the ditches on each side thereof, twenty-eight feet whereof shall be faced with broken stone, or gravel well compacted together...and sufficiently level to form a good road for sleighs, and where other roads shall intersect said turnpike road, shall be so formed as that

carriages may conveniently go on and off said turnpike road.[20]

The Bethlehem Turnpike passed by Mount Hope, a favorite visiting place for Albanians during summer days, the Abbey Hotel, and the newly constructed brick house of the Haswell family. The Abbey in Glenmont is believed to have been built by one of the Van Rensselaers in the early 1700s.[21] It was razed in 1961. Over the years, it served as an overnight stop for travelers on horseback along the turnpike or travelling by steamboat on the river. In later years it became a favorite spot for clambakes, picnics, and other gatherings.

The Haswell house served as a tavern and resting place for stagecoach travelers.[22] Additional income was derived through use of the house and surrounding fields for military training during the War of 1812, the Mexican War, and the Civil War.

On March 2, 1805, an act passed by the New York State Legislature incorporated the Albany and Delaware Turnpike Company.[23] The route of this turnpike was to be through the hamlet of Adamsville, the towns of Rensselaerville, Bristol, and Blenheim, thence to the Susquehanna River near Brink's Mills in the town of Otego. Construction specifications called for a stone roadbed. The turnpike, which started in the city of Albany, was renamed Delaware Avenue on July 1, 1870.[24]

Improving Road Surfaces

During the mid-1800s, a method of improving dirt roads became popular and several business ventures were formed. The improvement involved the laying of wood planks over a dirt roadbed, thereby providing a firm and relatively smooth surface. These were known as plank roads. On May 7, 1847, the New York State Legislature passed an act providing for the incorporation of companies to construct plank roads and turnpike roads.[25] This legislation facilitated the development of roads throughout the state. It outlined the conditions of incorporation and authorized the company to buy land for road construction and to collect tolls. Provision was made for the settlement of any disputes that might arise from land acquisitions. Also, specifications were stated for plank roads and turnpikes. Both were required to be at least four rods wide (sixty-six feet). The plank roads were to be:

> made of timber, plank, or other hard material, so that the same shall form a hard and even surface, and be so constructed to permit carriages and other vehicles conveniently and easily to pass each other.[26]

Plank roads functioned mainly as branch lines off the major turnpikes of the day and were usually less than ten miles in length. The first company to be formed in Bethlehem under the provisions of the 1847 act was The South Bethlehem Plank Road Company, which was incorporated in July 1851.

The road it constructed linked Babcocks Corners (Bethlehem Center) with South Bethlehem. Investors in Albany and Bethlehem subscribed to the 240 shares (at fifty dollars per share) authorized by the company. Philip Kimmey, near the end of the line and a resident in the town of Coeymans, was the largest stockholder with twenty-four shares.[27]

Other plank roads constructed were the Albany and Clarksville plank road (Feura Bush Road) and the Albany-Rensselaerville plank road through Slingerlands (New Scotland Road). Life span for the wood was about five years, when rotting and decay started. Maintenance proved to be unfeasible and uneconomical. Engineers of the day realized that stone and gravel provided the more permanent road bed and the days of the plank road ended about 1860. Later, asphalt and concrete were used to provide a smooth surface.

Eventually, all turnpike and plank road companies ceased operating A legislative act passed on April 18, 1938, provided for the disbandment of private road companies. The act stated:

> Whenever any turnpike corporation shall become dissolved, or the road discontinued, its road shall become a public highway and be subject to all the legal provisions regulating highways.[28]

Today, the town maintains about 150 miles of road and the county and state about sixty-five miles within the boundaries of Bethlehem.[29]

The Railroad Era

The railroad came to Bethlehem when a section of the Albany & Susquehanna Railroad opened in 1863 through Adamsville and Slingerlands on the way to New Scotland and, ultimately, in 1869, to Binghamton. The fare in July 1864 was twenty cents for the ride from Albany to Adamsville and twenty-five cents to Slingerlands.[30] The railroad offered the advantage of a scheduled trip to and from Albany, establishing the pattern for a future Bethlehem commuter town. An 1869 timetable shows a 9:00 A.M. arrival in Albany for passengers boarding in Slingerlands at 8:37 and in Adamsville

The Delmar station.

100

Albany (D. & H.) ...	Ravena ....N	0 ALBANY...................
Kenwood Jct.........	So. Bethlehem ....D	MADISON AVENUE..........
Glenmont...........	Feura Bush..................N	5 ELSMERE....................
Wemple............	New Scotland ....D	6 DELMAR....................
Selkirk............	Voorheesville..... ....N	8 SLINGERLANDS.............
Selkirk Jct..........		9 FONT GROVE................
		11 VOORHEESVILLE.............
WEST SHORE R. R.	DELAWARE & HUDSON R. R.	WEST SHORE R. R.
TO WEEHAWKEN	TO BINGHAMTON	TO UTICA
1947	1909	1908

Early timetable listings of stations in Bethlehem.

at 8:42. The 5:30 P.M train out of Albany would arrive in Adamsville at 5:50 and in Slingerlands at 5:55. A century later, the same trip by modern bus takes about eight minutes longer. For example, the 1991 Capital District Transportation Authority schedule shows a departure of 5:00 P.M. from the old D&H building, now SUNY Plaza, in downtown Albany, with arrival at the Four Corners in Delmar at 5:27 and at Grove Street in Slingerlands (which is near the old Slingerlands railroad station) at 5:33.

The Delaware and Hudson Canal Company, which acquired the Albany and Susquehanna in 1866 and other railroads in northern New York, established an office in Albany. A principal executive employed in the Albany office was Charles Darius Hammond, who moved to Slingerlands and lived in a house near the railroad station. He was held in high esteem in Albany and Bethlehem. The only son of an itinerant Methodist preacher,

he was active in the Slingerlands Methodist Episcopal Church, becoming a trustee in 1877, superintendent of the Sunday school in 1882, and president of the Board of Trustees in 1899.[31]

Fate dealt Mr. Hammond a unique place in history when President McKinley was shot in Buffalo, New York, on September 5, 1901. Five days later, Vice President Teddy Roosevelt, believing the president was recovering, made way to the Adirondacks, finally camping at Lake Colden. Unfortunately, President McKinley took a turn for the worse, and in anticipation of his death, D&H corporate officials were contacted by the government to provide standby transportation for the vice president. Mr. Hammond took personal charge of a special train which sped to the North Creek station of the old Adirondack Railway. On the night of September 13, 1901, at the North Creek station, he handed Roosevelt the telegram which informed the vice president that

The Slingerlands station.

Hungerford bus in 1918.

President McKinley had died. The ninety-eight mile return to Albany was made without delay.[32]

Expanding Public Transportation

As the system of roads within the town grew and the automobile for transportation became more popular, starting about 1915, a business to transport people became a practicable venture. In 1918, Frank Hungerford, who lived at 505 Kenwood Avenue in Delmar, purchased a Denby bus. It had wooden spoke wheels and solid rubber tires. This vehicle was the start of the Tri-Village Bus Service by the enterprising former farm boy from Selkirk.[33]

Service was provided between Albany, Elsmere, Delmar, and Slingerlands. Bus fare at the time was five cents. By the 1920s, the service had a fleet of up to fourteen buses providing transportation throughout the year. Hungerford's base of operations was a garage located at 500 Kenwood Avenue. In 1934, Frank Hungerford sold the business to the United Traction Company, forerunner of the current Capital District Transportation Authority.

Aviation in Bethlehem

The aviation industry in Bethlehem has not been commercially significant, but the town has an historical place in the development and promotion of aviation. In 1910, Glenn Hammond Curtiss, an aviation pioneer from Hammondsport, New York, took off from Westerlo Island and completed a flight to New York City. The purpose of his mission was to pick up a $10,000 prize offered by the *New York World* newspaper for the first aviator to complete such a flight. The offer was made in connection with the Hudson-Fulton Celebration of 1909. No claim

Historical marker located by the administration building of the Albany Port Authority.

of success was made during 1909 and the offer was extended for another year.

Newspaper reports of the day provided extensive and competitive coverage of the event.[34] As an example, the *New York Times*, not to be outdone by the *New York World*, which initiated the challenge, chartered a train from the New York Central to follow the Curtiss aircraft down the Hudson, filing daily news reports along the way. The airfield of departure was identified as Albany. However, the land used as the departure airfield, occupied by a tenant farmer, was actually in the town of Bethlehem. At this location, just south of the present-day office building of the Port Authority of Albany, the dirt area used for takeoffs and landings became

1910 flight to New York City from Westerlo Island. Painting by Linda Jordan Bunzey.

known as the Albany Airport and the first municipally owned and operated commercial airport in the country. This status came in 1915 when the city purchased 131 acres of land on Westerlo Island, including the airport site.[35] It was not until 1926, after establishment of the Albany Port District, that the land serving as the Albany airport was annexed to the city of Albany.[36]

World War II stimulated public interest in flying. Improvements in aircraft reliability and practicality changed the image of aviation from a daredevil adventure to an exciting and promising means of transportation for the average citizen. Aircraft for civilian use were manufactured and sold to former military pilots and other individuals who had the desire to fly. In 1946, laws were enacted which required that authorization be obtained from the appropriate local governmental jurisdiction before a privately owned airport could be established.[37]

In 1942, William Van Valkenburg, an avid pilot who had started flying in 1929, purchased property in Selkirk to construct a commercial airport facility. His wife, Marie, still lives at their home on Jericho Road, adjacent to the airport. She recalls her husband's efforts to construct the airport runway with an old backhoe, the building of a basic hangar, and establishment of a snack bar, which subsequently burned. Mr. Van Valkenburg requested permission of the town to operate the airport. The town board authorized the airport location during its meeting on July 1, 1946. The

South Albany Airport, as it was named, attracted people interested in flying to fulfill dreams and to satisfy transportation needs. One such person who quickly established a bond of friendship with the Van Valkenburg family was Santo (Sam) Italiano of Albany. He was the airport flight instructor, charter pilot, and general helper. South Albany Airport was sold to Mr. Italiano in 1959 and he ran the operation as a labor of love until September 20, 1971, when he died as a result of a tragic automobile accident that occurred shortly after he had left the airport for his home. His wife, Dorothy, maintained ownership until a group of sixteen local enthusiasts purchased the airport in 1978 as the South Albany Airport Corporation.

Shelly Edmondson's airport as shown on a 1947 U. S. Geological Survey map.

Near Selkirk at Pictuay Road, on land now occupied by the Wickes Lumber Company, an auxiliary airfield existed at the site of a home owned by Shelly Edmondson, who also operated the Ravena Airport. He established the field in the early 1940s, using it for private purposes and for flying lessons.

During 1947, two additional commercial venture airports started within the town. Ralph Mosher leased land on the Garry McBride farm off New Scotland Road and established a turf strip for aircraft takeoffs and landings. He named it the Tri-Village Airport.

Authority for operation of the Tri-Village Airport was granted by the town of New Scotland on May 2, 1947. Mr. Mosher did not realize that part of the airport was situated within the town of Bethlehem. In September 1947, the town board of Bethlehem approved a request by Dominic J. Chiore and Santo Italiano, both of Albany, to operate an airport for commercial purposes on the Sutter-Gettel farm, located off Blessing Road. It was later purchased by Walter Bonneau. This field, named Normanside Airport, was two miles from the Tri-Village Airport and Mr. Mosher objected to the authorization to operate Normanside, citing safety concerns and requirements of New York State laws relative to spacing between airports. A controversy resulted which was ultimately resolved through involvement of the Civil Aeronautics Authority and the New York State Department of Commerce.[38]

Normanside airport.

The status of Normanside Airport was finally decided during the town board meeting of February 3, 1954, when a request for renewal of the permit authorizing operation of Normanside was denied, and all operations were to cease as of March 17, 1954.

Ralph Mosher purchased the McBride farm in 1954. He died in September 1984 at the age of seventy-four because of a motorcycle accident. His widow sold the airport property shortly thereafter. Mr. Mosher's accumulation of aircraft, parts, and supplies was sold on a warm November day in 1984, during an auction that attracted the area aviation community.[39]

Utilities To Serve the Public

The establishment of New Scotland in 1832 and annexation by Albany of a large portion of the Kenwood area in 1870 defined the present land area of Bethlehem, except for some minor subsequent alterations. For the next fifty years, until 1920, the population of the town remained stable and averaged 4,200. The decade of the roaring twenties saw a dramatic increase of sixty percent in town residents. Subsequent decades also reflected continued substantial growth—thirty-seven percent from 1930 to 1940, thirty-three percent to 1950, forty-five percent to 1960, twenty-four percent to 1970. By 1980, town population totalled 24,296. In 1990, the census total was 27,552, a thirteen percent increase during the decade of the 1980s.

The business of providing basic utilities such as water, electric power, communication service, and treatment of waste to support and encourage the increase in population was a factor in the growth of the town. In early stages of development, some utilities, such as water and sewers, started within the town and expanded. In other cases, such as telephone and electric power, service was extended into the town.

Water

A water supply, other than from individual wells, was designed and built in 1902 by William Henry Slingerland, a civil engineer and surveyor in the town of Bethlehem, when he organized the Suburban Water Company. The water, from a spring in the Helderbergs known as the Helderberg Cold Springs, flowed by gravity to the Martin Spring Farm at New Salem, where it was then pumped to a reservoir constructed above New Scotland. From there, the water again flowed by gravity to Slingerlands. The system expanded and by 1918 gravity mains served New Salem, New Scotland, Font Grove, Slingerlands, Delmar, and Elsmere.[40] These lines, however, proved to be inadequate to

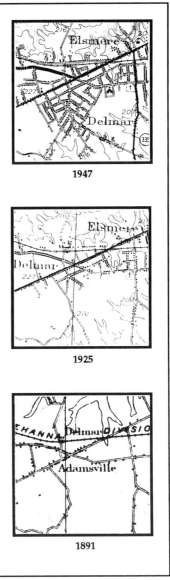

1947

1925

1891

Growth in the Delmar-Elsmere area as shown on U. S. Geological Survey maps.

service the growing number of households which requested access to the water line.

In 1927, Water District #1, Town of Bethlehem, was formed and the Suburban Water Company was purchased from the Slingerland estate. During succeeding years, lines were replaced and extended to serve the expanding population. By 1940, the district served about 5,000 people. In 1956, construction started on the Vly Creek Reservoir, the current water supply for the town. During the 1960s, a significant number of extensions were added. They included the area around Houcks Corners and Feura Bush Road, Colonial Acres, Selkirk, Cedar Hill, Corning Hill, and New Scotland Road. A major addition to the water plant, completed in 1971, increased capacity to a flow of almost five million gallons per day. By 1990, the water district served close to 24,000 people.

Waste Water Treatment

Population growth also dictated the establishment of waste water treatment facilities to replace individual septic tank systems. In 1927, the first sewer district, Delmar-Elsmere, started. It served an area of about 1.25 square miles, containing a population of around 3,000 people. In 1951, the district expanded to include the Fernbank Avenue area. By 1965, 630 miles of sewer lines were in place, serving almost 12,000 people, about fifty-six percent of the town population. In 1969, extension number eight to the Delmar-Elsmere

Sewer District was proposed, and approved by the residents of the town. It was a major addition providing service to expanding residential areas, essentially coinciding with water extensions, to serve roughly ninety percent of the town population.

Telephones

Telephone service was started in Albany in 1878 by the American District Telegraph Company. By 1883, the Hudson River Telephone Company, which became part of New York Telephone in 1910, was the provider of service in Albany.[41] As the twentieth century began, the public demand for telephones grew at an unprecedented rate. Lines extended from the Hudson River Telephone Company office in Albany to serve customers in Bethlehem. Primary routes were extensions from South Pearl Street to Kenwood and beyond, and from Delaware Avenue through Normansville.

The South Bethlehem Telephone Company, incorporated in 1904, was the only company formed and located within the town to provide telephone service. The Clarksville Telephone Company, which was located in the town of New Scotland, had one subscriber in Bethlehem, Doctor Hiram Becker of Slingerlands. With the acquisition of the South Bethlehem Telephone Company in 1923, New York Telephone became the sole franchised provider of telephone service. At present, switching centers exist in South Bethlehem and in Delmar. These modern centers replaced earlier manual

The Delmar telephone office constructed in 1927.

cord switchboards that required operators to answer a subscriber request and establish a connection with another party through inserting plugs into the jack associated with the subscriber. Marjorie A. Terrell, a retired telephone company employee and town resident since 1924, recalls being hired in 1925 as an operator. The telephone office was located in the dining room of a house near the corner of Kenwood Avenue and Adams Street. At the time, four board positions were in place. These grew to eight, reflecting the growth of the community and the increasing demand by residents for telephone service. In 1927, a new telephone office building was constructed on Adams Place near Kenwood Avenue to house electromechanical switching equipment, replacing the local operator. On June 24, 1928, the new dial switching system became operational.[42]

Electric Power

Thomas Edison's invention of the incandescent lamp in 1879 stimulated the need to furnish electric power to the general population. Prior to that time, illuminating gas was the major source of lighting. In the late 1800s, many companies existed in the area to provide gas and electric power. In Albany, alone, there were the Albany Gas Light Company, Peoples Gas Light Company of City of Albany, Peoples Gas Company of Albany, Albany Electric Illuminating Company, and Edison Light and Power Company of Albany.[43] Other companies existed in Troy, Cohoes, Rensselaer, Kinderhook, and Hudson. These companies, and more than 500 others throughout the state, consolidated in 1950 as the Niagara Mohawk Power Corporation, the franchised provider of electric power in Bethlehem.[44] Service to the town was furnished through extensions of lines from generating facilities located outside of Bethlehem. These lines were separate from telephone lines and it was not unusual to see a pole line on each side of a road. Later, agreements developed so telephone and electric companies could use the same pole.

In 1952, Niagara Mohawk constructed a steam generating plant on River Road in Glenmont to serve Capital District area needs for electric power. This facility was the first large-scale industrial site established within the town after World War II. The plant has a prominent brick building 162 feet in height from which four stacks, each standing 175 feet above the roof, reach to the sky. Each of

The Niagara Mohawk station in Glenmont.

An Early Major Industrial Enterprise

The geography of Bethlehem is suitable for agricultural pursuits but it also has rock formations adaptable for the processing of good stone. It was a valuable commodity in early days and remains so today. Stone, in various sizes, provided the basic product for one of the town's earliest and largest manufacturing enterprises that still exists— Callanan Industries, Inc.

Peter Callanan engaged in the business of raising and selling hay during 1880 at Callanans Corners in South Bethlehem. However, he saw greater economic opportunities in the growing land transportation industry. A ready market existed

A remembrance of the founder of the Callanan Road Improvement Company. Located in the South Bethlehem United Methodist Church.

the stacks serves one of four identical 100,000 kilowatt generating units that produce enough power to serve a population of nearly 500,000 people. Originally constructed to burn coal as its primary fuel, increasing environmental constraints prompted conversion of the plant by 1970 to burn fuel oil to generate the steam required for the turbine generators. In 1981, the capability to burn natural gas was added in order to maintain cost efficient operation. Oil cost had risen from $1.67 per barrel in 1970 to $32 per barrel in 1980. Today, the fuel source can be switched on short notice between oil and gas for maximum cost efficiency.[45]

for broken stone and gravel needed for construction of the West Shore Railroad line along the Hudson River. In 1883, he succeeded in convincing a local physician, Dr. J.R. Davidson, an 1869 graduate of Albany Medical College, and two businessmen, store owner Philip Scharbauer and icehouse owner John Newton Briggs, to enter into partnership and establish a quarry.

In 1895, Callanan Road Improvement Company was incorporated and received its first state contract, for a road leading out of Northern Boulevard in

Camp at South Bethlehem for transient immigrant laborers.

Albany. One year later, in 1896, Callanan died of a heart attack. His wife, Hannah Whitbeck Callanan, assumed leadership of the young company.

Operations during the early years required heavy labor. Workers using steel points and sledgehammers would drill blasting holes to fragment the rock. Stone crushing in the mill would follow. As many as 150 transient laborers were employed for this task. During such operations, on May 12, 1909, an explosion occurred which took the lives of twenty-nine men including Charles and John Hoyt Callanan, two of the six children of Peter and Hannah.[46]

In 1967, Penn Dixie Company purchased the Callanan firm. Today, it is owned by an international conglomerate, CRH, a major manufacturer and supplier of a wide range of materials for the construction industries in the United States, Britain, The Netherlands, Spain, and Ireland. The corporation is headquartered in Ireland.[47] Tradition of family involvement in the Callanan company continues, with John Callanan as a project manager.

An Industry Develops In the Town

As families established their households in town, starting in the 1920s, residential building offered increasing business opportunities. Minimal requirements existed regarding the type and location of structures being built. Essentially, an owner of a piece of property could build what he wanted and where he wanted it on the property he owned, guided by common sense and agreements made with the seller of the property. Virtually all building of houses was done on an individual basis with an owner contracting with a builder, or an architect, for a particular structure. It was not uncommon for an individual property owner to undertake the task himself, securing help from family members or independent craftsmen. An effective zoning law was not passed until December 15, 1944. One stipulation was the requirement to apply for a building permit. These applications document the growth in residential units and reveal the emergence of neighborhoods within the suburban areas of Delmar, Elsmere, and Glenmont.

During the decades of the 1950s and 1960s, individual home construction emerged as a growing industry in the town. Some examples of residential neighborhoods developed during that era

are: Kenaware—bounded by Kenaware, Kenwood, Cherry, and Delaware Avenues; Kenholm—bounded by Kenwood Avenue, Elsmere Avenue, and the Delmar By-Pass; Birchwood Acres—bounded by Mosher, Murray, and Elm Avenues; and Colonial Acres in Glenmont. Town streets, many of which are now familiar, were also created—for example, Brockley Drive, Brookview, Dumbarton Drive, Devon Road, Huron Road, Marlboro Road, Mosher Road, Tierney Drive, and Wellington Road. After the early 1960s, multi-residential units satisfied a demand for maintenance-free housing. Apartment units developed, such as Village Drive, Elsmere Arms, Bethlehem Terrace, and Kensington Court (which was subsequently converted to condominium ownership). The town house—attached individually-owned homes—also came to town. Owners of town houses usually belong to a community association that provides some exterior maintenance in accordance with deed requirements. Woodgate in the Kenaware area and Chadwick Square in nearby Glenmont are examples of town house communities.

Single home construction continued and new streets emerged —Jefferson Road, Journey Lane, Huntersfield Road, Hancock Drive, Fairlawn Drive, and others. These areas resulted from the enterprise of several local residents who engaged in the business of building homes. Included are Fred and Bill Weber, who started development of Birchwood Acres; Henry Klersey, the Hamagrael area; Bob Wiggand, development in Glenmont; Kent Jenkins, developer of Dowerskill; Bill Swift, the Quail Hollow project; and Dick Daniels, Normansgate in Elsmere. Based on history, continued development is forecast as the areas of population in the town expand.

Population Growth and Business Opportunities

The opening of retail stores and the establishment of service-oriented businesses grew as population in the town increased. This commercial development was most pronounced in the hamlet of Delmar, previously Adamsville. Rapid growth started after the end of World War II and continued throughout succeeding decades. The focal point of this activity was the intersection of Delaware and Kenwood Avenues, which became known as the Four Corners. Within a few hundred feet of this intersection, a business community formed starting in the late nineteenth century. The beginning was very modest. In a 1930 interview, Charles Allen of 509 Kenwood Avenue in Delmar recalled the area of Delaware Turnpike and Kenwood Avenue as it looked about 1870. "There was one store in Delmar. Albert Rosencrans was storekeeper. At Paddock Block was a blacksmith shop and wheelright shop owned by Lawrence Van Schaick."[48]

Over the succeeding years of the twentieth century, various structures at the four corners housed a post office, hotel, bank, hardware store, grocery store, tavern, drug store, automobile showroom, gasoline station, and other small shops. Alice Porter, who came to Delmar in September 1926 and lived in the first house to be built on Furman Place, recorded her remembrances of the period between 1926 and 1974.[49]

> The 'Four Corners' had a beautiful large home, owned by the Blanchard family, situated where stores were later built .... Spreading elm trees graced the corner where a service station now stands.

Winter scene at the Four Corners, about 1920.

She recalled former businesses such as Lang's Department Store, Schnurr and Wood (feed store), Waltermire's Pharmacy, and the Three Elms tavern. Of the 1920s she wrote:

> Delmar transportation to Albany was mostly by train. When the six o'clock evening train arrived, one would have thought that a factory had been let out. Long lines of commuters stretched from the little D&H railroad station on Adams Street to Kenwood Avenue where each walked in a different direction on his merry way home.

Vincent (Jim) Spinosa, a long-time local meat market proprietor (Van Allen Farms store in Glenmont), went to Delmar at the age of fifteen during 1931, working in the Delmar Meat Market owned by Nick Ippolito. The market was located on Delaware Avenue by Paddock Place. Mr. Spinosa recalls the food stores around the Four Corners—Schaeffer's, Barcelow's, A&P, Karpel's, and Empire Market.[50]

Expanding Elsmere and Delmar

In 1928, a new viaduct was built over the Normanskill replacing the steep grades and winding road through Normansville. The viaduct improved travel between Albany and the town. An Albany newspaper hailed it as a great improvement over one of the most heavily travelled routes to and from Albany.[51] As travel became less time consuming and inconvenient, more opportunities arose for customers to shop in Albany, Elsmere, or Delmar. Local businessmen of the time recognized the potential impact on business in the town and a group of fifteen met on April 15, 1930, in the office of Howard P. Paddock, a real estate broker and active community leader, to discuss establishment of a chamber of commerce.[52] The group, called the Delmar-Elsmere Community Organization, advertised in the *Albany County Post* (a newspaper published in Delmar) a general meeting of residents for May 14, 1930. The meeting was cancelled without explanation, and years would pass before an effective chamber of commerce organization was ultimately formed.

The Four Corners in 1957.

The traditional idea of downtown (i.e., center of town) stores was also changing with the development of shopping centers, offering customers ease of parking and limited walking to a variety of shops and services. In the early 1950s, the impact of this change became evident in Delmar with the building of Delaware Shopping Plaza in Elsmere. At the time, a loosely knit group of individual businessmen, primarily operating in the area of the Four Corners, formed an organization called the Bethlehem Business Men's Association. The initial intent, according to Alan Hilchie, hardware store owner and one of the early organizers of the association, was to enhance the area of the Four Corners and provide a pleasant shopping opportunity for customers as a means to stimulate business and maintain the loyalty of customers. One primary motivation for the cooperative

effort was recognition that the newly developed Delaware Shopping Plaza would mean a significant increase in competition and would tend to lure customers away from the Four Corners.

The group, under the leadership of such individuals as Charles Oliver, William Schoonmaker, and Raymond Brownell, recognized and stimulated a broader goal of business development within the town. Consequently, the Bethlehem Chamber of Commerce was formed in 1954. The organization incorporated on October 14, 1957. Among its stated purposes was "to foster good feeling, comity, trade and commerce in and for the Town of Bethlehem and vicinity." There were roughly 100 members in 1957. During the early years of the Chamber, attention focused on beautification projects such as the planting of dogwoods, providing flower boxes on the sidewalks of town, and decorating the streets for Christmas. The Chamber experienced steady growth and undertook more ambitious projects as the years went by. In 1962, a separate corporation formed under the umbrella of the Chamber called The Bethlehem Chamber of Commerce, Opportunities For Growth. The major purpose was to advertise the advantages of establishing an industrial enterprise in the town of Bethlehem. Identification of building sites took place and brochures were developed for mailing to prospects, inviting consideration of the town for business purposes. The organization assisted in attracting business interests to establish commercial facilities within the town.

Today, the Chamber of Commerce operates with a full-time professional staff and continues to promote the business interests of the town. The Chamber has a membership roster of about 300, which includes a large number of business interests that view Bethlehem as a market area but are located elsewhere. One example of such a service-oriented business is Tebbutt Funeral Home, which started in 1850 in Albany and opened a branch home in Delmar in 1949. The establishment of a location in the town was indicative of changing attitudes toward funerals. In former years, an individual's home was the focal point for birth and death. In the latter case, the mortician was summoned. In today's world, the funeral home is generally used for last respects.

Representative Old Businesses

Some businesses moved to Delmar for a permanent home. An example is Price Greenleaf store and nursery. This business was started by William Thorburn in 1831 as the Albany Seed Store.[53] In 1875, the name of Price was associated with the store as Price and Knickerbocker. In succeeding years, the names were Price and Reed, George H. Price, and Price Greenleaf. For the last fifty years, the business has been in the Plummer family. Edmond Plummer moved from Connecticut to Delmar in 1936, as related by his wife, Edith. They rented a home on Booth Road, which they purchased in 1940 from the estate of Andrew A. Booth. After working as an employee of Price's, Plummer purchased the business and in 1958 opened greenhouses at Elsmere Avenue, on the north side of the present Delmar By-Pass. The greenhouses at this site are still used to grow the nursery stock sold at the store. Originally, it was planned to relocate the store from Albany to the site on Elsmere Avenue. The plan changed, however, and in 1961 the present store was constructed on Booth Road. The old Plummer house was razed in 1963. At the time, Booth Road was still an unpaved street. David Plummer, with his sons Dean and James, manages the enterprise today.

The family owned and operated business has been common in Bethlehem. However, relatively few continue to be actively managed by a member of the original family after two or three generations. The oldest continuously run family business that started in Bethlehem and still exists may be Lehmann's Garage in Selkirk. The great-grandfather of Bert Lehman, the current proprietor, operated the original portion of the garage as a blacksmith shop, starting in 1913. Why the garage name contains an extra letter is unexplained. As the automobile replaced the horse, so the work of smithing gave way to automotive mechanics.

Being precise about when a business started is often very difficult. In the past, as today, it was common for an individual to start a business or career from a residence location before establishing a business location. LeGallez Electric Company was such an early business, started by Clayton LeGallez, working out of his home in Delmar. His daughter, Lois Bub, displays in her home the first job proposal recorded by Clayton LeGallez, dated December 11, 1914, to install wiring in a house owned by Mr. Frazer. The total charge was one hundred twenty-four dollars. Work was completed the following month and a final bill was prepared on January 31, 1915. After LeGallez died, his wife, Wilda, ran the business for twenty years until William Bub, Lois's husband, took over in 1972. Today, their son, Steven Bub, a third generation family member, runs the business.

Bennett's plumbing business in Delmar is another example of the family-run enterprise that has survived three generations. Daniel Bennett, the oldest of five children of Frank Bennett, started working in the trade out of the family farmhouse, which still stands at 578 Delaware Avenue in Delmar. He started an account book in 1913, listing various jobs done. His first entry for a plumbing job was September 6, 1915, when he worked on a pump for O.S. Haswell, charging eight dollars and seventy-five cents. Operation of the business passed to his daughter, Evelyn, and son-in-law, Gilbert Drake, then to their son, Thomas. Their present business location at 341 Delaware Avenue was established in 1915.

During the early years of Daniel Bennett's plumbing business, his brother, William, better known as Bill, worked with him. They dissolved their business relationship about 1930 and Bill worked as a plumber in Selkirk. In 1934, he formed a plumbing supply company called the Save Supply Corporation with Earl Vadney and Harold Williams, Sr., who had been working for Bill Bennett. In 1936, the name was changed to the current Security Supply Corporation. The company has developed into a large and successful plumbing and heating supplies concern. From its main office in Selkirk, third generation Keith Bennett, grandson of Bill and vice president of the firm, oversees operations in eight branch locations in northern New York and North Adams, Massachusetts. Harold Williams, Jr., is president of the firm and his son, Kenneth, is a branch manager. Other second and third generation family members involved with the company are Kenneth Mortenson, Sr., son-in-law of Harold Williams, Sr., his son, Kenneth, Jr., and son-in-law Patrick Reed.

A Large Slingerlands Business

One example of a large business that was developed within the town by a local resident, but has not survived, is the printing company started by Cornelius H. Slingerland. After a two-year apprenticeship with an Albany printer, Slingerland started his own business in 1879 at the age of nineteen, on family property at the intersection of the Albany, Rensselaerville, and Schoharie Plank Road (New Scotland Road) and the railroad tracks in Slingerlands. He advertised a specialty in railroad and express printing, and also dealt in paper, envelopes, and twine. Timetables and

C. H. Slingerland's printing plant.

various business forms were his main products, along with items such as posters and election forms. In 1910, construction was started on a major addition to the printing plant. One year prior to the death of Cornelius H. Slingerland in 1916, the company was incorporated as Slingerland Printing Company. Ownership was transferred to his daughter, Mary Andrews, who held a fifty percent ownership interest, her husband, Dr. Clarence E. Mullen, with forty-nine percent interest, and Andrew C. Couse, general manager of the plant, with one percent interest. Dr. Mullen's daughter, Betsey Andrews Tolman, still lives in the family home on Mullens Road, across the railroad tracks and opposite the former site of the plant. She recalls that the plant was an active location in earlier days, employing over 100 people.

In 1935, as recalled by Mrs. Tolman, stock ownership of the plant was sold to the Burland Printing Company. Although a sign was painted on the building naming it Burland Printing Company, the corporate business name of Slingerland Printing Company remained until the company was dissolved in 1940. That same year, the plant was sold to the newly formed Bethlehem Printing Company. The president and twenty-five percent owner of the new company was John O'Hagan, who had been working as a printer in the plant. The end of the facility as a printing establishment came in 1946, when the building was converted to apartment units.

The Emergence of Large Business Interests

As the twentieth century progressed, the typical business in the town was much as it was in past years, small in scope and family owned and operated. The rural character of the town, however, was declining as farming became less attractive as a career path toward financial security. Availability of large tracts of land close to the city of Albany became an attraction for companies wishing to expand or build new plants.

A Major Railroad Facility

Location was a major consideration when the New York Central decided to build a large freight classification yard near Selkirk. The yard, in conjunction with a new railroad bridge across the Hudson from Selkirk to Castleton, eliminated two problems that caused serious bottlenecks in handling freight traffic going to the west from Albany through the West Albany Yards. First, trains needed to go up a steep grade to West Albany, requiring pusher locomotives. Second, the railroad bridge across the Hudson at Albany, which handled traffic from New York City and Boston, was a drawbridge that would be closed to traffic for up to eight hours a day during the season of river navigation.

Andrew Koonz, a Selkirk resident, recalls working on the railroad yards when construction was started in 1922. He worked alongside his father, Abram. The Walsh Construction Company of

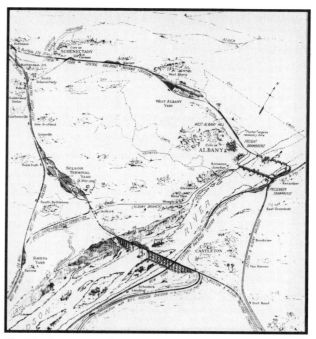

The "Castleton Cut-Off" project.

Davenport, Iowa, was awarded the contract and hundreds of men were employed. Koonz estimates eighty percent of the men came from the Capital District. Houses, dormitories, and dining halls were constructed for the work force, including a two-story YMCA with approximately 100 sleeping rooms. A large number of mules were imported to haul the dump wagons used in the grading process, which required that huge amounts of soil be relocated in order to establish level grades for the train tracks. Mr. Koonz recalls that four mules were used for each wagon. Heavy-duty earth-moving trucks were not available in those days. Two large roundhouses were constructed; each could accommodate approximately thirty engines. It was a time when steam was a major source of power. Much water was needed to generate the steam and a six-inch line was built to the Hudson River. Water was pumped from the river to the rail yard into five storage tanks with a total capacity of 1,650,000 gallons.

The project, which was named The Castleton Cut-Off, cost $25,000,000, a significant sum in 1922. The yard became operational in November 1924, when the Castleton bridge was opened to rail traffic.

In 1968, the New York Central and the Pennsylvania Railroad merged to become Penn Central. The new company invested $29 million to upgrade and build, at Selkirk, the most technologically advanced facility in the country for rail car classification and maintenance. It was named the Alfred E. Perlman Yard, in honor of the president of New York Central for fourteen years and the first president of the merged Penn Central Railroad.[54]

An Industrial Area Grows

The 1960s and 1970s were particularly active times for attracting large business interests to the town. Local government fostered a positive environment for commercial growth, and the business community, primarily through the Chamber of Commerce and its member firms, extolled the virtues of doing business in Bethlehem.

The General Electric plastics plant in Selkirk in 1986.

One of the first and largest of the companies to take advantage of this environment was the General Electric Company. Corporate commitment to the expanding field of plastics resulted in a decision to build a plant for the production of thermoplastic resins, the raw material used in the manufacture of plastic products. The site selected for the plant was an area of 500 acres in Selkirk, including the Becker farm and homestead occupied by three generations of Beckers. Farming on the land had stopped in 1962. Reasons for the selection included land area, access to rail transportation via a spur from the Selkirk rail yards, and community acceptance encouraged by local

117

politicians. At the twentieth anniversary celebration of the plant, the General Electric Chief Executive Officer, Jack Welch, paid tribute to the town for the positive influence which attracted the company to Selkirk.[55]   Mr. Welch, a Delmar resident at the time construction of the plant started, was appointed General Manager of the facility in 1965 after successfully spearheading efforts within General Electric to develop practical production processes for the new resins. Initially, about twenty people from operations in Pittsfield, Massachusetts, came to Selkirk to establish the plant. This group, later known as the Selkirk Pioneers, worked with Welch to develop what is humorously referred to as "the plant that Jack built." William (known as Billy) Mack, a member of the group that came to Selkirk in 1965, was assigned responsibility to open the Finishing Plant, the process which converts the resin to pellets. He recalls the busy but fulfilling days culminating in start-up of operations in December 1966. Notable was a team spirit of accomplishment and resolution of day-to-day problems through involvement of employees, regardless of job status.

The company had a concern for the environment and interest in being a good neighbor in the town. One expression of that concern was to save the Becker homestead from demolition and to integrate the structure into the building space used for research and development. It stands today as a unique landmark on the site, along with the Becker family burial plot, which is also maintained. Through the General Electric Foundation, the company has extended monetary grants within the community. Some examples are the purchase of a senior citizen van for the town, contribution to the Tri-Village Little League, and support for the Audubon Wildlife Cooperative Sanctuary. Growth of the plastics plant has continued. From 1965 through 1989, the town issued 115 building permits. Acquisition of an additional 200 acres of land has brought the total site up to 700 acres. There are almost 700 employees at the plant.

In 1973, Owens Corning Fiberglass Company purchased parcels of land that totaled over 250 acres, located across the road from the General Electric site. The company's purpose was to build a fiberglass-insulation manufacturing facility to serve the northeast market area. Reasons for selection of the site included availability of low-cost electric power and a good water supply,  factors important in the production process for fiberglass-insulation material. Construction of the plant was delayed due to local community opposition and a depressed building industry, resulting in a lessening of demand for insulation products. When construction started, the company maintained a sensitivity to the concerns of its neighbors and kept them aware of progress through direct mail and newspaper announcements.[56] Production started in June 1976. Two years later, a second insulation machine went into production. The plant currently employs about 450 people and fosters involvement in community activities such as Junior Achievement and Little League. As a remembrance of former days, a granite block smokehouse still stands on the property. It houses the athletic equipment used by employees on the nearby ball field. The graveyard of Baltus Crewell and his wife, Eva, is in a wooded area north of the plant. He farmed the land in the early part of the nineteenth century.

Shortly after Owens Corning began production, AIRCO Industrial Gases, located near the General Electric plant, started operation in April 1977. AIRCO's major products are nitrogen and oxygen which it distributes throughout the northeast. The plant employs about fifty-five people and is owned by an international concern, the BOC Group, with corporate headquarters in London, England.

Business and the Future

For 300 years after the first settlers arrived in Bethlehem, the primary business interest was agriculture, using the natural resource of land. Sawmills and gristmills were constructed along the Normanskill and Vloman Kill, taking advantage of the abundant water power. The owner of a mill was able to provide for his needs and also create a business opportunity by selling services or products to others in the community. The mills were most often associated with family names such as the Gansevoort sawmill, Van Zandt's

mill, the mills of Conrad LaGrange, Albert Vanderzee's gristmill, Adam Spawn's sawmill, and Harder's Mill. The association of a family name with a business enterprise was customary in early years. Surnames were associated with inns, hotels, taverns, grocery stores, docks, icehouses, barber shops, hardware stores, blacksmith shops, garages, and other forms of owner-operated businesses. John Soop's Grocery Store, Winne Dock, George Best Ice House, Pappalau's Ice House, Folsing's blacksmith shop, Ginder's store, and Adams Hotel are examples.

Today, more often than not, a franchise business name or a unique, functionally descriptive name is used to identify a small business or a segment of a large business concern. A review of the more than 300 business establishments associated with the Bethlehem Chamber of Commerce indicates that only forty percent bear the name of the owner, or former owner.

Most small businesses have a limited life span for a number of reasons. For example, as forest areas decreased, so did the number of sawmills; when refrigeration became common, icehouses declined; as farms stopped growing grain, the mills closed. Children of an owner-operated business usually were expected to work in the enterprise and ultimately operate the business. This expectation was not always realized and consequently, few businesses operated under three or more generations of ownership.

A satisfactory financial return was another fact dictating the life span of a business. Competition for the consumer dollar increased during the past half century. The automobile and telephone were particularly instrumental in broadening the market area of potential customers. These factors, which influenced the longevity of a business during the past three centuries in the town, will continue in the future.

Bethlehem, as a suburban community, is inexorably linked to the Capital Region. It has available land, access to transportation, and desirable residential environments. As larger business interests seek a presence within the region and existing regional businesses expand their facilities, location in Bethlehem is an attractive option.

6 Houses of Faith

From the early 1600s, Europeans brought their religious traditions and practices with them when they crossed the Atlantic to settle in the New World. The official, established church in Virginia in the early seventeenth century was the Church of England, and later, in the first half of the eighteenth century, it became the official church in Maryland, South and North Carolina, Georgia, and, as some church historians believe, in southern counties of New York.[1] In the colonies of Massachusetts, Connecticut, and New Hampshire, English Puritans, mainly Congregationalists, were dominant. And in Rensselaerswyck, the West India Company established the Dutch Reformed Church as the official religion. In 1664, with the English conquest, the Lutheran church was tolerated.

> During its first twenty years in Albany, the Dutch Reformed church had no organized competition. The Dutch West India Company had become more tolerant of other faiths during the 1640s in an effort to encourage settlement, and this change increased the religious diversity of New Amsterdam and the lower Hudson Valley. In Albany, however, the city's remote location, its predominantly Dutch population and the intolerance of local Dutch leaders prevented the establishment of a second church until the late 1660s, when a small group of mainly Dutch Lutherans began to hold regular meetings.[2]

One hundred fifty years before any religious congregation was organized in what was to become Bethlehem, settlement was taking place along the Hudson River south of Albany, on offshore islands, and at the falls and along the banks of the Normanskill, Vloman Kill, and Onesquethaw Creek. Since there were neither organized congregations nor services, nor even a minister, in Rensselaerswyck until 1642, the early settlers most probably worshipped in their own homes. However, Patroon Kiliaen van Rensselaer was concerned for the religious welfare of his colonists, and Brant Peelen was appointed "to take charge of the Sunday services, reading and explaining one of the texts from the Bible...."[3] In 1632, van Rensselaer instructed the Rensselaerswyck sheriff that the inhabitants of the colony

> shall not neglect to invoke the name of the Lord, and every Sunday and on the usual holidays they shall come together to read aloud some chapters from the Holy Scriptures, for which purpose a Bible is herewith sent to them....[4]

Although settlement began here in the second decade of the seventeenth century, no religious congregations were organized until the second half of the eighteenth. Because of the proximity of these early settlers to Albany, they probably attended church in the city or met in the homes of others with similar religious beliefs. But when settlers moved southward and westward, travel to Albany was a hardship, particularly when dirt roads were muddy or covered with ice and snow. So, in the latter part of the eighteenth century, religious congregations developed near the present-day hamlets of Selkirk, New Salem, Unionville, Feura Bush, and Onesquethaw. When the size of the congregation made it feasible, a church building was constructed.

As the population of Bethlehem increased, so did the number and diversity of religious organizations. Over the years, some churches have ceased to exist because changes in population affected memberships. In several instances, churches for various reasons divided. In other instances, churches of entirely new denominations developed in the town, particularly in the first half of the twentieth century. Today, Bethlehem has representatives of three great religious denominations—Protestant, Catholic, and Jewish.

The Beginnings

The first settlers resided near the city [of Albany],
and thither they wended their way for instructions and
social communion in sacred things.[5]

When the Town of Bethlehem was formed in 1793 it contained four congregations, the First Dutch Reformed Church of Bethlehem, the Protestant Dutch Reformed Church of New Salem, the New Scotland Presbyterian Church, and the Jerusalem Reformed Church.

When discussing the churches of Bethlehem, it is necessary to include churches which today are in New Scotland, since that town was part of Bethlehem until April 25, 1832. Because of this, Presbyterian and Reformed churches in the hamlets of New Salem, New Scotland, Clarksville, Unionville, and Onesquethaw, dating from the eighteenth and early nineteenth centuries, are mentioned in this chapter.

A pattern emerges as we survey the development of most of our town's religious organizations. First, an itinerant or circuit minister, sometimes a missionary, visited the groups of his denomination. Because there were no church buildings, services were held out-of-doors, in the house of one of the members, or in some other available location—an abandoned blacksmith shop in one instance, a hotel's summer kitchen in another. Later, after the number of members increased, it was financially possible for groups to construct their own churches. As we shall see, this pattern continued even into the second half of the twentieth century.

Rev. H.S. Van Woert, pastor of the First Reformed Church of Bethlehem in the early twentieth century, has left us a description of a pre-Sunday service scene in, probably, the 1820s:

There might be seen on a Sabbath day, approaching the meeting-house from every direction, worshipers sitting in double chairs in thimble-skein, linch-pin, wooden-box wagons drawn by horses or oxen. Many of both sexes came on horseback; and some also might be seen coming with shoes and stockings in hand, which they put on before entering the church.[6]

Although this scene took place some forty years after the first congregation was formed, it was no doubt representative of Sunday mornings in Bethlehem from the 1780s until the early decades of the twentieth century when automobile travel became commonplace.

The First Reformed Church of Bethlehem.

The Reformed Dutch Church In Bethlehem

The First Reformed Church of Bethlehem
Route 9W and Clapper Road, Selkirk
The Reverend Allan Janssen, Pastor

The early history of the First Reformed Church of Bethlehem is given in Peter Christoph's chapter, "Bethlehem in the New Nation."[7]

On December 28, 1791, "The Declaration of Incorporation" of the Reformed Protestant Dutch Church at Bethlehem and Jericho, as the church was named then, was signed by the following elders and deacons: Barent I. Staats, Johannis Burhans, Benjamin Post, Francis Nicoll, Peter D. Winne, and Wouter Becker. Thirty-one years later,

the name of the church was changed to the Reformed Dutch Church of Bethlehem. Since 1912, it has been known as the First Reformed Church of Bethlehem.

In 1795, Stephen van Rensselaer, the eighth patroon, gave the church society 105.84 acres of land, formerly known as the Parsonage Farm, later known as the Church Farm, and now as the Van Rensselaer Forest and Wildlife Preserve. On this land is the site of the first parsonage (1800 to 1946). This preserve stretches along Route 9W from the church and parsonage north to Elmwood Cemetery (1861).

Sixty-eight years later, on March 9, 1890, during the pastorate of Rev. Lawrence Dykstra, the church building burned to the ground. But at a meeting held the next day, church members decided to rebuild at once. Work began in April, the cornerstone was laid in May, and the church was finished and dedicated on November 20. The Methodist Episcopal Church of South Bethlehem offered use of the church on Sunday afternoons or evenings until the new church was erected, and during the summer months the congregation worshipped in the Grange Hall at Beckers Corners.

On December 8, 1947, the Bethlehem Church Reforestation Commission was established. The original committee, appointed by Rev. Theodore W. Luidens, consisted of Andrew Koonz, Sr., chairman, and members Richard Thayer and Clifford Lasher. The sign was made by Peter Van Kempen and the cutting and erecting of posts done by James Wiedemann. The preserve was originally planted with 45,500 trees (red, white, and Scotch pine, Norway and white spruce, Douglas fir and European larch) and shrubs for wildlife food and shelter.

Reformed Churches In New Scotland

Four Reformed churches were formed in the western part of Bethlehem before New Scotland was erected as a town: the churches in New Salem, Unionville, and Onesquethaw, and the Jerusalem Church.

The New Salem Reformed Church, whose pastor is Rev. David Cooper, dates from about 1783.

Again, as in the case of the First Reformed Church, early records are scarce or nonexistent. But people of the Dutch Reformed faith met for worship in Salem, as New Salem was earlier called, as early as 1783, and the first church building of record was erected there about 1813. The present building dates from 1893.[8]

The Jerusalem Church was organized in 1791. It was probably built of stone and located on present-day Waldenmaier Road, between Delaware Turnpike and Feura Bush Road. Its pastor was Rev. Harmanus Van Huysen who also preached in churches in New Salem and Guilderland. When he retired in 1825, the Old Jerusalem Church apparently ceased to exist. When the building was razed, Peter Bradt, a church member, transferred the door to his own house on Delaware Turnpike, known as Smoke House Farm, and now owned by Ronald J. and Judy Von Ronne. Those members of the congregation living north of the Old Jerusalem Church, with some members of the New Salem church, erected a building on Delaware Turnpike and named it Union Church. Those living south of the Old Jerusalem Church

Door from Old Jerusalem Church.

Jerusalem Church, Feura Bush.

also pastor of the New Salem Reformed Church. He was followed by Rev. Simon V.E. Westfall. Over the years, there have been many devout pastors ministering to the spiritual needs of the parish-oners. The original windows of the church were of clear glass, upper and lower sashes containing twelve panes each. They were replaced in 1911 with large panes of milk glass in each sash. In 1925, in time for the

Stained glass window, Unionville Reformed Church.

church's one hundredth anniversary, the present windows were installed. The accompanying photograph shows one of these stained glass windows.[10] The present pastor of the Unionville Reformed Church is Rev. Thomas Kendall.

In 1841, the pastor and congregation decided that a branch should be opened in Adamsville (now Delmar). There were two reasons for this move. The Unionville church

built their new building in Feura Bush and named it Jerusalem Church. Both new churches date from 1825.[9]

The hamlet which grew up near Union Church became known as Unionville. The first pastor of the church was Rev. Ira C. Boice, who was

> was serving a large rural area including Adamsville.... Often the long distances of travel along the Delaware Turnpike and other dirt roads became difficult due to the mud following heavy spring rains or the deep snows and cold of

winter, thus keeping some families from attending church regularly. Also a Methodist Church had been started in Adamsville and some found it more convenient to attend this church than travel the long distance to the church located in what is now Unionville.[11]

The Onesquethaw Reformed Church started as a Presbyterian church when, in December 1824, six men and eight women left the Presbyterian church at New Scotland and organized the Onesquethaw Presbyterian Church. In the following year a church building was erected on land which Cornelius A. Slingerland (1775-1845) and his wife Anny Earls (1779-1835) deeded to the church.[12] However, in 1838 the congregation's ties with the Presbyterian faith were dissolved, apparently because there were "too few people of the Scottish Presbyterian persuasion in the vicinity...."[13] It then successfully petitioned to be a congregation of the Reformed Protestant Dutch Church.

The Onesquethaw Reformed Church is located on Route 301 at Groesbeck Road between Meads Corners and Tarrytown.[14] The pastor is Rev. Boyd Holdring.

Onesquethaw Reformed Church.

When the church was constructed, stone was being cut in the neighborhood for use in the building of the Erie Canal locks and aqueducts. "Barent Spose was the stone mason who constructed the [church] building, by tradition using stones that were rejected as too small for use on the canal."[15]

True Reformed Dutch Church of Bethlehem
Feura Bush Road, Bethlehem Center

In 1822, because of differences in doctrine and practice, several congregations seceded from the Reformed Dutch Church and organized as the True Reformed Dutch Church. In Bethlehem, a society of the organization was formed about 1827. The first and only pastor was Henry Bellinger (d. 1877), who served for fifty years.

The church building, constructed about 1854, was located on Feura Bush Road near the Niagara Mohawk power station. The first officers of the society were Peter Kimmey, Storm Vanderzee, and David Kimmey. After the congregation was disbanded about 1919, the building stood idle for many years and was dismantled in 1949.[16]

Delmar Reformed Church and parsonage. From a 19th century post card.

Delmar Reformed Church
386 Delaware Avenue, Delmar
The Reverend Dr. Robert A. Hess, Pastor

The Adamsville branch of Union Church, logically known as East Church, was built on land donated by Nathaniel Adams across the Delaware Turnpike from his hotel, the Adams House. It was completed in 1842, and during the following six years, Pastor Westfall served both it and the church in Unionville. Because of increased duties he had to give up the church in New Salem. He resigned his position as pastor of the church in New Salem when he became pastor of the church in Adamsville He resigned his pastorates in Adamsville and Unionville in 1847 to become a missionary to the Indians in Illinois, whereupon members of the congregation of the Adamsville branch successfully petitioned to become an independent church. The division was made in 1848 and the new church was incorporated as the Second Reformed Dutch Church of Bethlehem. Since 1927, it has been known as the Delmar Reformed Church.

Over the years, additions and renovations have occurred. In 1851, the first parsonage was constructed next to the church. It was torn down in 1935 and the present parsonage was built on the same site. The church building has been enlarged several times. The entire building was raised on its foundation in 1927 so that a new basement could be excavated, thus providing additional space for various activities. The sanctuary has been enlarged by the addition of the chancel, the balcony rebuilt, and a wing constructed to the west which provided space for church school classrooms and offices.

Glenmont Community Church
(Reformed Church in America)
1 Chapel Lane, Glenmont
The Reverend Lynn T. Joosten, Pastor

The predecessor of the Glenmont Community Church (Reformed) was the Glenmont Chapel Association, organized on November 11, 1956. The Extension Committee of the Reformed Church in America chose Glenmont as a desirable place for a church. A door-to-door canvass in the area was made and about fifty people expressed an interest in becoming members. The Reverend Theodore W. Luidens of the First Reformed Church of Bethlehem played an important part in the establishment of the church.

The cornerstone, built on land donated by two Glenmont residents, was laid on Sunday, May 18, 1958. On this Sunday, the Reverend Harvey W. Noordsy was installed as the first minister. The first worship service in the new church was held on May 25, 1958. The first deacons were W.H.

Waldbillig, Robert Wiggand, W.M. Mueller, and Willis Smith. The architect was Gilbert Van Auken, assisted by Kenneth Mallary.

At present, a new entrance is being constructed. It will contain space for pre- and post-worship service gatherings, additional classrooms, and an elevator to provide accessibility to the church for people with physical disabilities.

An active outreach program is carried on by the minister and members of the church, in keeping with the original goal of the Glenmont Chapel Association, to "extend the cause of Jesus Christ in the Glenmont Parish."[17] In addition, in association with First Reformed Church of Bethlehem, United Methodist Church in South Bethlehem, and Lord of Life Lutheran Church, Glenmont Community Church (Reformed) is a member of the Focus Church Group, which sponsors a food pantry for the needy in Glenmont, Selkirk, and South Bethlehem.

The Presbyterian Persuasion

The Presbyterian Church in New Scotland is generally considered to date back to 1776. At that time, a Presbyterian missionary preached out-of-doors under two massive oak trees near the present town hall. But it was not until 1787 that the Presbytery of Suffolk, Long Island, organized a mission church in New Scotland. From then until 1795, when the church installed its first pastor, the Albany Presbytery supplied itinerant clergymen who ministered to the spiritual needs of the people. This was two years after Bethlehem was formed and thirty-seven years before New Scotland became a town.

It is presumed that members of the Presbyterian faith met for worship in the houses of other like-minded people until, as records indicate, the first building for church services was erected in 1791. In 1793, Stephen van Rensselaer, the eighth patroon, gave the trustees 156 acres which were to contain a house for the minister and a half-acre burying ground.[18] In 1849, "due to the initiative, persistence, vision and consecration of Mr. Blodgett"(the sixth minister), the first building was torn down, and a new one built and dedicated.[19] Since then, the building's size was increased in 1868 and an educational annex added in 1957.

In 1824, six men and eight women left this church and organized the Onesquethaw Presbyterian Church, between Meads Corners and Tarrytown. In 1838, this church's relationship with the Presbytery was dissolved and the church was "organized according to the constitution of the Reformed Protestant Dutch Church...."[20] This congregation is discussed above in the section on the Reformed Dutch Church in Bethlehem.

Over the years, the New Scotland Presbyterian Church has had thirty-three ministers and three church buildings. The present minister, Gregory John Pike, commenced his pastorate in 1977.

First Presbyterian Church of Bethlehem
Krumkill Road, North Bethlehem

The next Presbyterian church in chronological order of founding was the First Presbyterian Church of Bethlehem on Krumkill Road in North Bethlehem. It was organized in 1835. Two men were responsible for its organization, Rev. John H. Campbell and Rev. William P. Davis. According to a late nineteenth-century county history,

> It [the congregation] consisted of fifty-three members. The first pastor was Rev. Wm. P. Davis, who was ordained and installed December 1, 1835. The first house of worship was erected the same year at a cost of $1,800. It was enlarged and refitted in 1869 at a cost of $4,000. It will now seat 300. Connected with it is a commodious parsonage, and the society is prosperous. The church is located about one and a half miles west of Hurstville. ... The pastor reports fifty families, ninety communicants, ninety-five Sabbath-school scholars and teachers.[21]

After the building was abandoned by the Presbyterians, it housed other religious groups. At present the Unity of Faith Christian Fellowship holds services in the building.

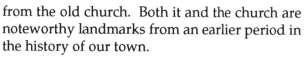

The former parsonage of the Presbyterian Church is located across Krumkill Road from the old church. Both it and the church are noteworthy landmarks from an earlier period in the history of our town.

The former parsonage.

Delmar Presbyterian Church
585 Delaware Avenue, Delmar
The Reverend Larry A. Deyss, Pastor

To serve the people with energy, intelligence, imagination and love. (The Presbyterian Charge)

The Delmar Presbyterian Church began in 1955 as a mission church of the Albany Presbytery. In 1956, the church body was formally organized with seventy-six charter members. Since its founding, it "has been committed to reaching out in service to the Bethlehem community, to the Capital District, and through mission opportunities, to those in need across the nation and around the world, in the name of Jesus Christ and for the glory of God."[22]

From 1956 until 1961, when the present sanctuary was completed, the congregation met at the Masonic Temple on Kenwood Avenue in Delmar. During that time the block at the northwest corner of Delaware and Cherry avenues was bought with gifts from all of the churches in the Albany Presbytery.

It was decided at one of the earliest meetings of the congregation that the two Great Commandments of Jesus would be spoken during each Sunday worship service.

This tradition is maintained. The commandments as spoken are:

Jesus said: You shall love the Lord your God with all your heart, with all your soul, with all your mind and with all your strength. This is the first and great commandment, and the second is like it: You shall love your neighbor as yourself.

Mission has been a keystone in the development of the Delmar Presbyterian Church. It was decided around 1956 that at least ten percent of the church budget would be dedicated to mission. Great emphasis, too, is placed on the mission of Christian education in the church. Growth in the Christian faith is encouraged through educational programs for all people of the church and the community.

In the thirty-seven years since it was founded, the Delmar Presbyterian Church has had two dedicated pastors. The first, Rev. George H. Phelps, served for twenty-three years. During his pastorate, the church was organized, the land for the new building was cleared, and the sanctuary was built. A second wing was constructed in 1968 and major renovations were made in 1979. He retired on Easter Sunday in 1980. The current pastor, Larry A. Deyss, began his ministry here in 1981.

During recent years, the church has invited the wider community to share in studies on national and international issues, such as aging and the Middle East. The church has also hosted ecumenical services, including Ash Wednesday, Good Friday evening, and prayer services for peace. Outreach services to the community include the senior citizens' Tuesday lunches, the "School's Out" child care center, and summer camping for children with special needs.[23]

The Growth Of Methodism

Tradition has it that the first Methodist church south of Albany and west of the Hudson was the Old Stone Church (1791-1792) near Coeymans. It was built for the Methodist congregation formed in 1788 in the Coeymans Patent by Rev. John Crawford and was located about three miles south of South Bethlehem. Although this was not in Bethlehem, town residents attended services there.

In 1823, members who lived north of the Old Stone Church erected a building for their use a short distance east of Beckers Corners on present Route 396. It was dedicated on November 20, 1823.

South Bethlehem United Methodist Church
Willowbrook Avenue, South Bethlehem
The Reverend Richard Reynolds, Pastor

In 1845, the Methodist church near Beckers Corners was taken down and some of its materials used in the construction of a new church building in South Bethlehem. This move may have been caused by a shift in population or because of the larger First Reformed Church of Bethlehem which

131

was nearby.[24] At that time, South Bethlehem was known as Janes Corners and the church was located on Church Street, now Willowbrook Avenue. It was dedicated in February 1846.

Over the years, many improvements have been made to the building through the financial assistance of such church groups as Willing Workers, Epworth League, and the Sunday school. It is because of their efforts and those of other church members that the building has the annex adjacent to the sanctuary, the front entrance and belfry, choir loft, stained-glass memorial windows, kitchen, and the Callanan-Scharbauer Memorial Auditorium given in honor of the two families who contributed in large part to the undertaking. This addition at the rear of the church building contains a stage, an auditorium which doubles as a dining room, kitchen facilities, and other rooms which may be used for Sunday school classes or meetings.[25]

Methodists In Delmar And Slingerlands

In 1830, a group of nine Methodists formed a fellowship in Adamsville (Delmar). Within three years, fifty people had become Methodists. The congregation was named the Second Methodist Episcopal Church in the Town of Bethlehem. Since early church records do not list a resident minister for the Adamsville church, it is assumed that the people were ministered to by itinerant preachers until 1852, when Rev. Manly Witherill became the first pastor of record.

In 1834, a piece of land was acquired by the fellowship on the north side of Kenwood Avenue, and a small church building was erected there. In 1852-1853, this building became a parsonage and a new and larger church was erected to the east, approximately at 415 Kenwood Avenue.[26]

Until 1871, Methodists in Slingerlands attended the Adamsville church. The congregation then divided into two groups, one wishing to keep the Adamsville building and the other, the majority, wanting to tear it down and erect a new one in Slingerlands.

Many of the details of what occurred within the congregation at that time are lost, but we do know that the building in Adamsville was indeed torn down. It was recorded in the Board of Trustees minutes for October 3, 1871: "Resolved that we take the old church down and begin tomorrow morning."[27] For about two years, the Adamsville Methodists had no church building. The Slingerlands church was built in 1871 and the Adamsville church was rebuilt in 1873.

Community United Methodist Church
1499 New Scotland Road, Slingerlands
The Reverend Jeffrey A. Matthews, Pastor

The Slingerlands Community United Methodist Church building and the land on which it was built were given to the Board of Trustees by Albert I. Slingerland and dedicated on Sunday, December 14, 1871. Mr. Slingerland probably had much to do with its planning and construction, as he did with many dwellings in the hamlet of Slingerlands, including the Methodist parsonage. From an early trustees' record book we learn that on February 24, 1872, it was "resolved that Albert I. Slingerland be authorised to use the stone, timber, and lumber of the old church [in Adamsville] in building a house for a parsonage."[28] Then the record shows that on April 14, 1873, "Mr A I Slingerland offered the new brick house and lot for a parsonage for one thousand and seven hundred dollars ($1700)...."[29]

The tower bell, cast at the famous Meneely Bell Foundry in West Troy, New York, in 1877, was presented to the church in that year by the Ladies Aid Society. In 1899, the pressed tin ceiling in the sanctuary was installed—an interesting and unusual relic. Electric lights supplanted a gas lighting system in 1910, and the present chandeliers were installed in the early 1940s, given to the church by Charles Sanders of Slingerlands in memory of his parents. Among the many memorials in the sanctuary are the stained-glass windows (1920-1929), the Wallace Cross on the altar (1945), the Birchenough Sunburst Cross above it (1983), and the hand-hewn Conklin Lenten cross (1985). The chimes and carillon (1987), which provide the community with the sound of bells and hymn tunes at noon and six o'clock in the evening, were given by Arthur Ahr in memory of his wife, Frances. In 1960, the

Community United Methodist Church, Slingerlands. Rendition by Frank Sheridan of Delmar.

educational wing, which was planned and designed by architect, church member, and artist Charles A. Schade, was consecrated.[30]

The Slingerlands Community United Methodist Church is, as are other Tri-Village churches, actively involved in services to the community. These include providing a meeting place for Alcoholics Anonymous, aerobics classes, a weekday nursery school, and the women's choral group, Friendship Singers. It also supports local and foreign mission programs.

First United Methodist Church
428 Kenwood Avenue, Delmar
The Reverend Dr. Donna Meinhard, Pastor

The House of Worship for All People.
(Church designation suggested by
Rev. Leon M. Adkins, Sr., in 1929.)

Within two years of the 1871 division referred to above, the Adamsville congregation had sufficient funds to purchase from Nathaniel Adams the land now occupied by the church. The amount paid was $500. In December 1873, the new church building was completed and dedicated. By 1907, the building and facilities were insufficient for the growing membership of the church and Sunday school. The building was raised on its foundation, providing space in the basement for Sunday school rooms, and the sanctuary was enlarged. The church building has been altered and enlarged several times since then. The educational wing was designed by Charles A. Schade, architect. In 1980, the nearly century-old section of the sanctuary was reconstructed following plans by the architectural firm of Schade and Wizenaar.

First United Methodist Church, Delmar. From a 19th century post card.

The sanctuary was enlarged, new walls installed, and the stained glass windows restored. As reported in *The Spotlight* in 1980, Rev. P.P. Harrower, who supervised the building of the 1873 sanctuary, might feel at home in the renovated structure and the pastor, Rev. Leon M. Adkins, said that the renovation "will complete our building, we believe, for the next 100 years."[31]

From a small religious organization in the early 1920s, the First United Methodist Church in Delmar, through inspired pastoral and lay leadership, has become one of the largest Methodist churches in the Troy Conference.[32] The following words occur near the end of the 1913 history of the church, as applicable today as then: "Thus the House of our God becomes a place more fit for His worship, a temple for His gracious indwelling."

Convent of the Sacred Heart.

The Catholic Presence In Bethlehem

**The Convent of the Sacred Heart
and Kenwood Academy**
799 South Pearl Street, Albany

In 1858, the Catholic Diocese purchased fifty-two acres of the Joel Rathbone estate at Kenwood, south of Albany near the mouth of the Normanskill. The grounds, "laid out in gardens and terraces, orchards and groves," would serve as the home of the convent and the girls' Academy of the Sacred Heart.[33] The cost was $45,000 and the purchase was effected through the efforts of the Very Reverend J.J. Conroy and John Tracey.[34] The Rathbone mansion, built in 1841, was included in the purchase.

The Academy of the Sacred Heart moved into the mansion in September 1859. During the next five years, enrollment in the school increased and the number of nuns helping with the school increased as well. By 1866, it was apparent that a larger establishment was needed, and in March of that year, excavations for an addition began. By 1867, part of the main section was ready for occupancy, the cornerstone of the chapel was laid, and the Rathbone mansion was demolished.

Materials from the old house helped to build the new novitiate wing, the West Wing, as the children named it. Rafters from the former Albany State House were used in the erection of the Chapel. The hardwood floors of the old mansion were made into the beautiful parquets which are still to be seen in the Reverend Mother's parlor and in what was known in early days as the Bishop's parlor.[35]

The chapel, completed in 1869 and consecrated on December 13, 1871, has been the spiritual center of Kenwood's life for almost a century and a quarter. It has been the scene of the daily celebration of mass, baptisms, first communions, ordinations, and ceremonies of the Novitiate and of Final Profession. In short, the chapel at Kenwood has had a long history of prayer and dedication.[36]

The Church of Saint Thomas the Apostle
35 Adams Place, Delmar
The Reverend James D. Daley, Pastor

The parish of Saint Thomas was formed in July 1907 with the Reverend Thomas F. Phibbs, a native of Troy, as the first pastor. Since there was no church building at that time, mass was celebrated in parishioners' houses throughout the three hamlets. Even before the advent of Father Phibbs, Catholic families worshipped in various locations. Mrs. Maurie Gleason Flanigan, former Slingerlands postmistress, remembers hearing about a visiting priest's coming from Albany to celebrate mass before 1907. The services had been held in the summer kitchen at the rear of the house at 1465 New Scotland Road in Slingerlands. This building, formerly a hotel for workers on the Delaware & Hudson Railroad, was later bought by Mrs. Flanigan's father and served as the Gleason, and then Flanigan, family home for seventy-one years.

The membership grew slowly. In 1910, two important events occurred. First, the church was

The former Church of Saint Thomas the Apostle.

incorporated on April 10, and second, the property on the southeast corner of Borthwick and Kenwood Avenues in Delmar was purchased in July and became the first church building of the parish.

Father Phibbs was pastor until 1922. He was followed by Rev. William C. Heffern (1922-1947), during whose pastorate the second building was completed. It was located on Delaware Avenue where the parking lot of the present church building is situated. The next pastor was Rev. Daniel H. Markham (1947-1955), who laid plans for a large building program, but whose greatest work was in things spiritual.[37] During the pastorate of Monsignor Raymond Rooney (1955-1968), Saint Thomas School was completed in January 1957, a new rectory was occupied in October 1958, and the present church building was begun in July 1961 and dedicated on September 16, 1962. The clergy and parishioners reverently believe that "'If God build not the house, they labor in vain who build it'. With prayerful confidence we say that God has here built Himself a home. May it serve to glorify His name to generations yet to come."[38] Monsignor Rooney was followed by Monsignor Matthew Brennan (1968-1970). The present pastor of Saint Thomas is Father James Daley, who came to the parish in 1970.

Saint Michael's Chapel
Route 9W and Beacon Road, Glenmont
Bishop J. Vida Elmer, Pastor

Saint Michael's Chapel was established in 1975 at the request of a group of traditional Catholics. They were unable to accept what they considered to be the un-Catholic innovations resulting from the Second Vatican Council during the years 1962-1965. The pastor, Father Elmer, was born in Hungary, but came to the United States in 1957 after the Soviet army defeated the Hungarian freedom fighters.

At first, a house on Route 9W between the present rectory and the road served as a rectory, and church services and masses were held in temporary quarters in motels in Albany. The house on the corner of Route 9W and Beacon Road was purchased and remodeled to become the chapel. Then, a new rectory was constructed behind the former rectory, which was torn down, and the present rectory was completed and opened for use in 1990.

Since the founding of the chapel, Father Elmer has been serving his congregation the True Mass and Sacraments in the old way. The church has approximately one hundred twenty members who come for worship from Pittsfield, Amsterdam, and Glens Falls, as well as Albany. Father Elmer adheres to the public celebration of the traditional Latin (Tridentine) Mass and ministers to the needs of "the remnant faithful, alienated from their parishes by the changes following II Vatican Council."[39]

The Episcopalian Denomination

Saint Stephen's Episcopal Church
Corner Elsmere Avenue and Poplar Drive, Delmar
The Reverend Darius Mojallali, Rector

Eighty-five years ago, a small group of men imbued with the Episcopal spirit met in Elsmere. It was their hope to establish an Episcopal Church congregation in the Elsmere-Delmar area. They acquired land on Elsmere Avenue near the Delaware & Hudson railroad station, but until it was financially possible to build a church, they worshipped in a former blacksmith shop. During the twelve years that the group worshipped there, lay readers and priests from the Cathedral of All Saints in Albany conducted the religious and sacramental services. Until about 1922, the congregation was known as Saint Stephen's Mission. Dr. Roelif H. Brooks, rector of Saint Paul's Church in Albany and priest-in-charge of the mission, was responsible for the mission's becoming a full parish of the diocese.

Within two years, the $10,000 necessary for the construction of the church building had been raised and on All Saints Day in 1925, the cornerstone of the original church was laid. This was at the corner of Elsmere Avenue and Poplar Drive, the present location of the church. Several priests-in-charge held services in St. Stephen's Church during the 1920s and 1930s, until finally, in 1938, the Reverend John J. Paulsen became the first rector.

Following World War II, the area southwest of Albany began to grow and the character of Elsmere and Delmar changed from that of a semi-rural community to a suburb on the outskirts of Albany.[40] With this growth came an increase in the membership of the church. By the late 1940s it was necessary to increase the size of the building and in 1952, land adjoining the church property was purchased. As the result of a successful fund drive, money became available for a new sanctuary. The present church and parish building were dedicated in 1957.

Saint Stephen's Episcopal Church, ca. 1950.

In the sanctuary behind the altar is a stained glass window in the shape of the cross. It was given in memory of William A. Glenn, one of the founders of the parish and a senior warden from 1909 to 1954. "The central figure of the window is The Lamb who, through the power of The Holy Ghost, overcomes the pain of the cross and brings salvation to all men."[41]

Over the entrance to the sanctuary are ceramic figures of the major missionary saints of the Episcopal Church. The central figure is that of St. Stephen with the

Missionary saints of the Episcopal Church.

stones with which he was killed. His hand is raised in blessing. At the left are Saints Simon and Jude, Andrew, Thomas, and James. To the right are Saints Paul, Peter, and the Four Evangelists, Matthew, Mark, Luke, and John. They are interpreted as representing Humanity, Royalty, Sacrifice, and Divinity, the principle themes of the four gospels.

Lutheran Growth In Bethlehem

Bethlehem Lutheran Church
85 Elm Avenue, Delmar
The Reverend Warren Winterhoff, Pastor

A Friendly Church in a Growing Community
Sharing the Good News of Jesus Christ

The forerunner of the Bethlehem Lutheran Church was the Delmar Lutheran Mission. It was formed in 1933 under the direction of St. Paul's and St. Matthew's Mission Society of Albany. Presumably because of insufficient numbers of Lutherans, the mission was disbanded after a few years. However, by 1953 the population had increased sufficiently to encourage the Reverend Lawrence Heuchert to reopen missionary services in Elsmere, Delmar, and Slingerlands. Two years later, in April 1955, the Community Lutheran Church congregation was formed and seven acres of land at the corner of Murray and Elm avenues were purchased on which to build a church. The congregation's first worship service was held on May 29, 1955, in the former Delmar Public Library at 90 Adams Place. Eighty-five people attended the service.

Construction of the church building began in March 1956 and on April 8 the cornerstone was laid. In October, the name of the congregation was changed to Bethlehem Lutheran Church. The building was dedicated on November 11, 1956. The first elected officers of the congregation were president, Earl Pinney; vice president, Frank Markus, Sr.; secretary, Carl Rappe; treasurer, Otto Rauch; financial secretary, James Michaels; and elder, Alton Marshall. Because of the growth of the congregation, a larger building was erected in 1970. The co-chairmen of the building committee were James Michaels and Rudy Gehr; the congregational president was John Gold. By 1989, it was decided to construct a large addition to the church

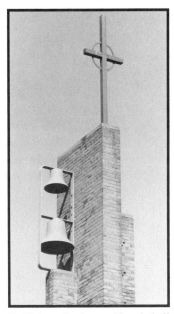

Bethlehem Lutheran Church bell tower.

building to accommodate the growing congregation and to facilitate the expansion of the church's outreach to the community. The building committee co-chairmen were Jerry Jonas and Michael Mineau. The dedication took place on September 23, 1990.

An active outreach to youth is a major focus of the church. The senior high and middle school youth groups meet regularly for programs centered on discussions of Christian issues affecting daily living and for service projects and "fun" outings. General church activities include visitation to shut-ins, monthly birthday parties at The Good Samaritan Home in Elsmere, social ministry outreach to the needy, and congregational fellowship programs.

The Bethlehem Lutheran Church has had four pastors during its thirty-eight-year history— Lawrence Heuchert (1953-1958), Harold W. Scheibert (1959-1965), Paul H. Gassman (1965-1976), and Warren Winterhoff (1977-present).

A plaque on the bell tower on the church grounds states that

> THE CARILLON
> IS DEDICATED TO
> THE GLORY OF GOD
> AND
> **PAUL C. MICHAELS**
> BELOVED SON OF
> JAMES AND MARION MICHAELS
> OCTOBER 1963

Agonizing Decision

In 1976 and 1977, the members of the Bethlehem Lutheran Church agonized over a matter of conscience. A schism occurred in the Missouri Synod, to which the church belonged, relating to matters of doctrinal theology, specifically, the ordination of women and the interpretation of scripture. This schism "confronted them with a deeply personal choice: remain with the established synod or affiliate with the newly formed East Coast Synod of the AELC [Association of Evangelical Lutheran Churches]."[42] On Palm Sunday about one-third of the congregation left the Bethlehem Lutheran Church, affiliated with the AELC, and established Faith Evangelical Lutheran Church.

Faith Evangelical Lutheran Church
1 Chapel Lane, Glenmont

The first pastor of Faith Evangelical Lutheran Church was Rev. Richard Gall. He was followed by Rev. John S. Macholz, who remained with the congregation for ten years.

The congregation met first in the community room of the Delmar Key Bank and then in the Masonic Temple in Delmar. In 1980, services were moved to the Glenmont Community Church. In the mid-1980s, the congregation was able to purchase about three and one-half acres of land on Route 9W for the site of the future church building. The members hoped to start a ministry in the southern part of Bethlehem. However, Faith Lutheran disbanded in November 1990, and in December about two-thirds of the membership transferred their affiliation to the Lutheran Church of the Holy Spirit on Hurlbut Street in Albany.

Lord of Life Lutheran Church

Bethlehem Grange Hall 137
Beckers Corners
The Reverend Wayne D. Moritz, Pastor
Future church site on Route 9W (opposite Jericho
Drive-In Theater)

In the meantime, the dream of having a ministry in the Glenmont, Selkirk, and South Bethlehem area continued to be viable. In October 1990, the Albany South Ministry, now known as the Lord of Life Lutheran Church, was created. This religious organization is the joint venture of the Evangelical Lutheran Church in America, the Upstate New York Synod, and the Lutheran Church of the Holy Spirit in Albany. With Rev. Wayne D. Moritz as its pastor-developer, its goal is to develop a new church in the Route 9W area serving the towns of Bethlehem and Coeymans. During the past several years, Pastor Wayne, as he is called by church members, has gone from door to door, ringing over 1,000 doorbells and inviting people to join the Lord of Life Lutheran Church.

The organization meets in the Grange Hall on Route 396 in Beckers Corners for regular Sunday morning services. The church has occasional outdoor worship services at its Route 9W building site.

Other Area Churches

Mount Moriah Assembly of God Church

Route 9W, Bethlehem Center
The Reverend Stephen Giles, Pastor

The Alcove Full Gospel Church, forerunner of the Mount Moriah Assembly of God Church, started in Alcove, New York, in 1943. Rev. Giles became pastor in 1981. Because of a growing feeling that the church should move to a more populated area, and because the congregation had outgrown the Alcove building, land was purchased on the east side of Route 9W north of Bethlehem Center and construction began on a 22,000-square-foot church building. At present (1992), construction has been stopped because of financial and legal problems. "The congregation is using other sites for its services and it says it cannot afford to go ahead with any more work until its financial situation is straightened out."[43] The congregation is currently meeting in the Howard Johnson motel on Route 9W near Thruway Exit 23. The church-related Mount Moriah Christian Academy meets in three homes in the area.

Members of the Assemblies of God believe that God's purpose concerning man finds fulfillment in a priority reason-for-being: to be an agency of God for evangelizing the world, to be a corporate body in which man may worship God, and to be a channel of God's purpose to build a body of saints being perfected in the image of His Son.

Baptist Mission Chapel
Kenwood

A Baptist chapel was built in the hamlet of Kenwood in 1866 by William "Poppy" Sawyer of Albany. He was devoutly religious, very wealthy, and eccentric. "He loved to build churches. Hope Baptist Church, a Baptist chapel on Madison Avenue, and a chapel at Kenwood were among his benefactions. He is also remembered as the principal founder of Memorial Hospital."[44] The chapel was conveyed by him to the Baptist Missionary Association as an absolutely free gift, to be used forever for worship and Sunday school purposes.[45] However, it was destroyed by fire in the 1890s and not rebuilt. It was rumored that the fire was started by "several rowdies from the saloon" nearby.[46]

Cedar Hill Free Chapel

A nondenominational chapel was erected in 1877 near Cedar Hill on the farm of Stephen Baumes. The Good Templars, mentioned by Floyd Brewer in his chapter on organizations, met in this building during the 1880s.[47]

Normansville Community Church
10 Rockefeller Road, Delmar
Edwin A. Tompkins, Treasurer

The Normansville Community Church was built in 1889 and incorporated on September 6 of that year. Its original name was Normansville Free Chapel. The first trustees were Mrs. Charles Phelps Stevens, Mrs. Horace Allen Lightbody, Mrs. George S. Leith, Mrs. Hester J. Rockefeller, and Mrs. Henry Onderdonk.

Around 1920, the Albany Bible School became the sponsor of the chapel and conducted regular Sunday school services. Blanche Long was the teacher. At a meeting in 1921, the following trustees were elected: Mrs. Horace Allen Lightbody, Miss Mary A. Rogers, and Mrs. William Scrafford. Mr. Leon F. Wardell became the first salaried pastor of the chapel in October 1953; he was also chairman of the board of trustees.

The Normansville Community Church has always been a nondenominational church. There is now no permanent minister. Edwin Tompkins, treasurer of the church, and his wife Charmaine, are extremely interested in the history and preservation not only of the church but of the hamlet of Normansville. He is president of the Normansville Neighborhood Association. Mrs. Tompkins recalls that, as late as twenty-five years ago, baptisms took place in the Normanskill.

The church is presently undergoing a major restoration and renovation program, consisting of exterior and interior painting, installation of new flooring in the sanctuary, and a general sprucing up, including raising the church on a restored foundation. As much as possible of the original clapboard siding has been preserved. The original bell hangs in the tower and is rung Sunday mornings before the Sunday school classes and

Normansville Community Church.

Purposes of the church are to teach parishioners about Jesus Christ, His reason for coming, and to give His salvation message.[48]

First Church of Christ, Scientist
555 Delaware Avenue, Delmar

On April 12, 1879, a small group of people in Boston who called themselves Christian Scientists met and voted "To organize a church designed to commemorate the word and works of our Master [Christ Jesus], which should reinstate primitive Christianity and its lost element of healing."[49]

The discoverer of Christian Science and the founder of the church was Mary Baker Eddy (1821-1910). Her beliefs are communicated through the textbook she wrote, *Science and Health with Key to the Scriptures* (1875). The well-known *Christian Science Monitor*, a daily international newspaper, and other Christian Science publications are available for purchase or perusal in the Christian Science Reading Room, located at 397 Kenwood Avenue near the Four Corners. Many of us are familiar with MonitoRadio, produced in Boston and carried on more than 200 public radio stations around the United States, including our own FM radio station, WMHT.

church services. The circular window over the entrance door used to contain a stained glass window which was illuminated at night. An oil painting by Eleanore Kirchner, *Sunday Morning in Normansville*, hangs in the sanctuary. Current membership is twenty-five adults and twenty children in the Sunday school.

A group of Christian Scientists began meeting in members' homes in Delmar in September 1955 in order to make Christian Science services available to local residents. There were sixteen charter

members in the society. As membership increased, the Masonic Temple on Kenwood Avenue was rented for both Sunday morning services and mid-week testimony meetings; a Sunday school was begun at the same time. On June 22, 1959, ground was broken for a church building on Delaware Avenue and the new edifice was dedicated in December 1963. Four years later, a Sunday school addition was necessary.

Bethlehem Community Church
201 Elm Avenue, Delmar
The Reverend Miles A. Hall III, Pastor

The Bethlehem Community Church was founded in 1966 by a group of town residents who wished to have an interdenominational church responsive to the spiritual needs of members of the community. Beginning in September 1966, Sunday morning services were held in the former Delmar Public Library and evening services in the basement of a member's home. However, within a year the size of the congregation had increased to such an extent that it had outgrown the library and had begun holding services in the community room of National Commercial Bank, now Key Bank, in Delmar. Soon after the formation of the congregation, Arthur Gay became the first pastor. By November 1967, the group had purchased property and begun construction of the church building. The church building, containing a fellowship hall, offices, and classrooms, was completed in June 1968. Soon, however, the size of the congregation grew, necessitating an addition to the original building. Miles A. Hall III has been pastor since the summer of 1987.

The constitution of the Bethlehem Community Church states:

> The purpose of this church shall be to glorify God by presenting the Gospel of Jesus Christ with the guidance of the Holy Spirit and presenting the Holy Scriptures as the divine revelation of God's word, will, and authority, for the spiritual growth and unity of all who believe.

Fundamental beliefs of members of the church are: The Bible was given by divine inspiration and is the word of God. As a body of God's believing children, the faith of the membership is based on the revelation of God's holy will found in the Scriptures. The Scriptures are the sole authority in all matters of faith and doctrine. Members desire to grow in grace and in knowledge of the Lord Jesus Christ, to the end that they may glorify God and be used as witnesses to His saving grace.

In each July since 1966, the church has been offering opportunities for personal growth and development by presenting enjoyable and instructive courses through Bethlehem Christian Workshop for the young people of the community. Two hundred eighty children participated in the 1992 workshop.

The church offers a nursery school program for three- and four-year-old children, men's and women's Bible study groups, a youth group, and meetings of the Christian 12-Step Program for recovery from compulsive abusive behavior. Throughout the year, opportunities are presented to learn about a variety of topics, such as home schooling, the occult, abortion alternatives, and child abuse.[50]

Emmanuel Christian Church
31 Retreat House Road, Glenmont
The Reverend Stephen P. Lalor, Pastor

> And all that believed were together,
> and had all things common....
> (Acts 2:44)

In 1972, three Catholic charismatic prayer groups in Albany combined for weekly Sunday evening prayer meetings. From the members' fellowship and deliberations came the establishment of Emmanuel Community, incorporated May 2, 1974. At the same time, the former Jesuit retreat center on Retreat House Road in Glenmont was purchased.

During the past fifteen years, the group has withdrawn from the Catholic church, become nondenominational, joined with an evangelical Protestant fellowship, and become associated with Resurrection Churches and Ministries. Stephen P. Lalor became the first full-time pastor in 1986. In 1988, the name became Emmanuel Christian Church. Three years later, the church moved to the Hilton Music Building in Albany for Sunday services. Emmanuel Center on Retreat House Road, a ministry outreach of Emmanuel Christian Church, continues to serve "as an oasis where God's people can come to be refreshed, restored, and sent out to serve God with renewed vigor."[51]

The aim of the church is to help people mature as Christians so that every aspect of their daily lives will reflect the life of Christ. Furthermore, the church attempts to help as many as possible to mature to the point where they, in turn, can teach and train others in the Christian life. The motto of the church is: Mobilizing people to fulfill the purposes of God in this generation.

Emmanuel Center, Retreat House Road, Glenmont.

Solid Rock Family Outreach Center
1 Kenwood Avenue, Glenmont
The Reverend Justin T. Metcalf, Pastor

Solid Rock Family Outreach Center.

The nondenominational Solid Rock Church started in Rensselaer some thirty-five years ago. The Reverend S.R. Hanby was pastor. He was succeeded by Rev. Gerald Metcalf, whose son, Justin, is the present pastor. The church building, on the corner of Kenwood Avenue and the Delmar By-Pass, across the street from Magee Little League Field, was built in 1975.

The church has about 125 members. There are Sunday worship services for adults and children, Sunday school for families, evening bible study Wednesdays. Some biblical precepts which are features of the worship service are:

Clapping of Hands
O clap your hands, all ye people; shout unto God with the voice of triumph. (Psalm 47:1)

Lifting of Hands
Lift up your hands in the sanctuary, and bless the Lord. (Psalm 134:2)

Speaking with Tongues, Interpretation of Tongues
The manifestation of the Spirit is given to every man to profit withal. ... To another ... divers kinds of tongues; to another the interpretation of tongues.... (I Corinthians 12:7, 10)

Prophesy
He that prophesieth speaketh unto men to edification, and exhortation, and comfort. (I Corinthians 14:3)

Jehovah's Witnesses
Selkirk Congregation
Kingdom Hall
Elm Avenue, Selkirk

In Pennsylvania in the early 1870s, Charles Taze Russell (1852-1916) and some friends began to make a thorough, nondenominational study of the Bible with regard to Christ's return. They also began to seek Bible Truth on many other basic teachings. This was the beginning of the modern-day activities of Jehovah's Witnesses.[52]

Jehovah's Witnesses constitute a society of ministers. They meet three times a week, usually in the Kingdom Hall which they built on Elm Avenue in 1972. In the meetings, they study and discuss Bible teachings and prophecy, aspects of Christian living, how to gather material on Bible subjects and to teach it effectively, and how to present the good news from house to house.[53] The congregation, consisting of some 100 members, is currently constructing a larger Kingdom Hall. This is at the corner of Elm Avenue and Feura Bush Road.

Delmar Chabad Center
109 Elsmere Avenue, Delmar
Rabbi Nachman and Clara Simon

The Delmar Chabad Center, founded in 1987, is a branch of an international Hassidic Jewish outreach organization. The purpose of this center of traditional Judiaism is to provide programs, classes, and seminars for Jews regardless of their backgrounds or denominational affiliations. Programs designed to fulfill varying needs of the Jewish community are offered, such as classes in Hebrew and Yiddish, philosophy, and Kabbalah-Jewish mysticism. The Friday evening service is at sunset and the Saturday service is followed by Kiddush. The center also sponsors a Tiny Tot Program on Sunday, a nursery camp in the summer, and the television program, "The Jewish View," on Channel 32.

Then and Now

Looking back over the past two centuries, we see that religion has been important in the lives of our predecessors. Even before the formation of our town, Kiliaen van Rensselaer, the first patroon of Rensselaerswyck, made arrangements in 1632 for Sunday religious services in the colony. Among his instructions for the inhabitants was the following: "Every Sunday and on the usual holidays they shall come together to read aloud some chapters from the Holy Scriptures, for which purpose a Bible is herewith sent to them...."[54] The first ordained minister in Rensselaerswyck was Domine Johannes Megapolensis (1642). The earliest services of the Dutch church, "and until the English takeover, the only church permitted by law," were probably on the east side of the Hudson. The meeting-house was later moved to a remodeled warehouse (1647) near today's Church Street and Madison Avenue in Albany.[55] Probably the earliest settlers in our area attended services either in the houses of like believers or in the church in Albany. This was in the years preceding the construction of churches. In the eighteenth century, congregations were often ministered to by mission pastors and circuit ministers. Eventually, congregations were able to support their own pastors or, in some instances, pastors were shared by two or three groups of the same denomination. Today, we have more than twenty churches in our town.

Throughout our history, we have enjoyed a high degree of religious tolerance, not only from our various governments but from our neighbors whose religious beliefs are different from ours.

> With the formation of new state governments following the Declaration of Independence, separation of church and state came about more or less as a matter of course where establishment [of official or state churches] had been more a matter of theory than of fact.[56]

It was Thomas Jefferson who proposed an Ordinance of Religious Freedom in 1785 in Virginia (it was adopted almost verbatim by the House of Burgesses). He "ranked his authorship of this act with the drafting of the Declaration of Independence and the founding of the University of Virginia as his most significant accomplishments."[57]   This ordinance served as the model for the first Amendment of the Constitution of the United States: "the Statute declared that no man could be compelled to attend or support any church nor suffer any discrimination because of his religious beliefs."[58]

Thus, the religious beliefs of the earliest settlers of this region were the elements that gave them the strength, courage, and determination to establish this town. Fortunately, these elements continue to endure and have become significant factors in the life or our town today.

7 Community Organizations

Community organizations have filled a variety of needs and enriched the lives of Bethlehem citizens since the town was established. Although few original records exist of early organizations, it is possible to reconstruct group activity through an examination of life in the larger community. The record of community organization activity in this century is voluminous, especially during the last fifty years, and a concerted effort has been made to describe the origins and purposes of these groups and to list the people who started them.

A handy chart is included in the appendix[1] to provide readers with a quick reference to all organizations for which records are available. That many groups have survived for decades is adequate evidence they were needed. They have contributed extensively to the gradual development of a dynamic community, and the many opportunities for group involvement is one of the major reasons newcomers cite for moving to Bethlehem.

Early Social Life

The record suggests that the earliest Bethlehem families, such as the Bratts, Peelens, Cruyffs, and Flodders, participated in occasional baptisms, marriages, and funerals. Most of these gatherings were occasions for social participation—events not to be missed. Food and drink were the dominant features. It was common for men to set aside a barrel of brandy toward their own funerals, a practice that probably occurred at the funeral of Jeremias van Rensselaer in 1675:

> The church rented a pall (covering for the coffin) to the family of the deceased. No one attended without an invitation. The women, who never accompanied the body to the cemetery, stayed in the home of the deceased, drinking spiced wine and eating little cakes. When the men returned they found a table laid with a sumptuous amount of food and drink. Pipes and tobacco were set out, and eating, drinking and smoking often continued far into the evening. As a result of much drinking, fights often broke out at funerals and sometimes the law had to intervene.[2]

Seventeenth-century residents played a variety of games which we know about primarily because they were prohibited on Sundays. Early Bethlehem families, sometimes with their Beverwyck friends, played card and ball games, cricket or ninepins, and tennis. They raced boats in the summers and skated in the winters as well as raced sleighs on the ice.[3]

Mutual support given by groups of neighbors has been crucial for Bethlehem citizens from the earliest days. Logging bees and barnraisings were occasions for helping a neighbor and socializing with others. The women cooked for the crowd of helpers, and served a heavy meal that was sometimes topped off with Dutch *oliekoeken,* a small, dough-like round cake filled with a mixture of chopped apples, raisins, milk, eggs, shortening, and nutmeg fried in hot lard.[4]

During the Revolutionary War years, special groups were formed outside the court system to exert control over citizens believed to be disloyal. On May 17, 1777, the Albany Committee of Safety, a group sanctioned by the court, considered the cases of Bethlehem citizens John Van Aelen (Alen) and Henry Ten Eyck, along with James Dole, Peter Sharp, John Roff, William Hogan, Peter Yates, Gysbert Merseles, and Richard Cartwright, who were labelled:

> Persons whose characters are suspicious and who by their influence in this County are suposed dangerous to this state And it is resolved that in order to give said Persons an Opportunity to wipe away such an Aspersion that they be tendered the Oath of Allegiance and that Time be Given them till Morrow afternoon at 5 O'clock.[5]

All of the persons appeared except Dole, Merseles, and Roff, and it is assumed they signed the oath of allegiance although there is no mention of action taken by the defendants in the record.

Farseeing groups of citizens in the fledgling nation often noticed problems developing and campaigned for solutions. One such group placed a notice in the *Albany Journal* on March 2. 1789, expressing the hope that citizens would soon see a law

> To put a stop to the numerous race of Quacks and Pretenders who are daily committing murder and entailing uncurable difeates under the sanction of Doctors, a character they assume at pleasure, without having the least pretensions thereto. A law is now in force in New Jersey and Massachusetts which establishes prices to regulate all their charges, and prevents persons from entering the practice of physican or surgery unless he has studied a certain number of years...goes through a regular examination and is approved.[6]

Early Bethlehem residents could join a group to increase their social skills. One purveyor of social skills advertised the opening of a new dancing school in which James Robardet pledged to

> give 36 lessons, three a week, during a new Quarter beginning on March 13, 1788. The price: two Guineas. Each Scholar will pay One Dollar for the Music and a PUBLIC BALL will be given every fortnight.[7]

Groups and Human Needs

Groups of early residents formed churches and schools to pass along knowledge, values, and social standards to the citizens, especially to the younger generations.

A mix of human needs is met in the organizations described hereafter, but in one form or another, they reflect citizen needs for social participation, mutual support, social control, education, economic gain, and spiritual values.

In later years, the same needs are in evidence, but modern residents use different words to describe how groups fill their needs. A few excerpts from their own words tell the story well:

> The community has gained from a better-informed and vibrant citizenry; this is a great community to live in, and I want to give something back. The artists give each other wonderful support, and I've made friends with stimulating and talented people. The need to preserve our historical and natural resources, our open spaces and rural quality ... is a very challenging endeavor which should be of vital concern to all responsible residents. It is an exciting and fascinating exploration of how people relate to one another and to their institutions and develop a more

caring community. The group has helped me become and remain an informed advocate for my children.[8]

Some of these highly personal reasons for involvement in various Bethlehem groups show that there are probably 101 purely individual reasons for joining groups in our town. More reasons for group involvement can be seen in the following descriptions of Bethlehem community organizations.

Charter Members: Bethlehem Masonic Lodge 1096. 1948 Photo. **Front Row** (left to right): Ernest Shufelt, William Vogel, Charles Sanford, Ray Hicks, Ellsworth Cramer, Charles Spore, Daniel Bennett, George Meyer, Frank Patterson, and J. Walter Hotaling. **Second Row:** Stuart Van Derzee, Walter J. Hotaling, Alvah Mallory, James Coates, Alton C. Rowe, Jr., Floyd Lounsbury, Floyd Hiller, Carl Cronk, Chester Anthony, and W. Jack Weaver. **Third Row:** Howe K. Cassavant, Stanley Crocker, George C. Porter, John A. Cromie, Frank Gates, Arthur Main, Harry Waltermire, Albert D. Potter, Sr., and Alton C. Rowe, Sr.

Early Organizations

Joshua Babcock appears in many town records for everything from road construction to taking in stray animals, but his participation in founding the **Bethlehem Masonic Lodge** in 1820 earned him a special place in local history. It is one of the earliest examples of citizens joining a well-established society. We do not know when the first Bethlehem lodge disbanded; however, the Masons reappeared in 1928 with the formation of Bethlehem Masonic Lodge 1096.

Mason's Past Master's Jewel.

In recent years under the leadership of Alan C. Lewis, Lodge 1096 has engaged in a variety of service projects including support of the Bethlehem Tomboys softball team and the Masonic Nursing Home in Utica. The Lodge's companion organization, the **Order of the Eastern Star**, takes considerable initiative in helping the Masons achieve their goals through card parties, bake sales, and dinners. Former officer and long-term member Flossie Smith gives credit to Installing Grand Officer Irwin Conroe for the shortest dinner speech on record. He said, "I'm glad to be here. Now let's eat."[9]

Almost all Masonic and Eastern Star meetings and programs are held in the historic Masonic Hall at 421 Kenwood Avenue in Delmar, where an early district school was built in 1852. It was replaced by Delmar Elementary School in 1908 and purchased by the Masons for $8,000 in 1929.

Organizing for the Hereafter

The formation of groups to provide a basic service is sometimes stimulated by new laws. The Rural Cemetery Association Act of 1847 encouraged the formation of local cemetery associations and laid down requirements for their operation. Prior to 1847, most citizens were buried in family or church cemeteries or in a regional burial ground such as the Albany Rural Cemetery.

One of the earliest churches to take advantage of the new law was the First Reformed Church of Bethlehem at Selkirk where Robert Selkirk, Peter Niver, and Daniel P. Winne were named to a committee to establish a cemetery in 1860. They were joined by Dr. John Babcock, Lewis Myers,

Scenic Bethlehem Cemetery. 1992 Photo.

and Zachariah Riker in forming the **Elmwood Cemetery Association of Bethlehem**, an association independent of the church that would be obligated to sell a lot to anyone desiring to purchase space.

Burial customs changed over the years and many cemeteries were developed with park-like landscaping. Founded in 1865, the **Bethlehem Cemetery Association** is a good example of this trend. Town supervisor George C. Adams was the cemetery's first superintendent. In recent years, Gilbert O. Drake, treasurer, and John Pangburn, superintendent, have continued a long tradition of discreet service to bereaved families and further development of the cemetery's scenic beauty.

Organizing Against Lawlessness

Stray animals have been a problem in Bethlehem since the beginning of town government and they often caused problems among neighbors. A record of the earliest transgressions was made in the *Book of Strays*,[10] which listed names of citizens on whose property animals strayed between 1794 and 1823 as well as cattle marks for some of the owners of cattle on the loose. Lost or stolen animals were still a big problem in 1875, when recently retired town supervisor Albertus W. Becker teamed up with former town clerk William Kimmey to found the **Bethlehem Conscript Society**. The name sounds as if they drafted the members but, in fact, they chased after horses and wagons stolen from the members.

Twentieth-Century Groups

Automobiles, newspapers, and radio encouraged local ties to the larger community in the early part of this century. Constitutions and by-laws of national organizations brought considerable influence to bear on the conduct of many local group meetings and on the behavior of group members. Groups such as the Boy Scouts of America, Masons, and Bethlehem Lions are typical of a substantial number of local organizations that receive direction from state and national offices. The Delmar Progress Club, Selkirk Fire Company, and the Bethlehem Tennis Association are examples of purely local organizations.[11]

Delmar Progress Club

Founded in 1901 by Elva Hinman Dyer, with eleven members and Carolyn Rouse as its president, the **Delmar Progress Club** aims to "promote an intelligent interest in literature, art, science, philanthropy and the vital questions of the day,"[12] and spends a lot of time dreaming up ways to improve the quality of life in Bethlehem. From spearheading the building of a new schoolhouse in 1904, publishing a Delmar directory in 1913, and establishing Bethlehem's first free library in 1913, the club has moved on to an expanded vision of service to society with CARE packages for Korea in the 1950s and volunteer work at the Veterans Administration Hospital in recent years.

Delmar Progress Club past presidents. **Front Row** (left to right): Mrs. Richard W. (Vivian) Bennett, Mrs. V.A. (Catherine) Van Volkenburgh, Mrs. Robert (Sybil) Selkirk, and Mrs. Neal C. (Midge) Baldwin. **Second Row:** Mrs. G. Earl (Margaret) Hay, Mrs. Kenneth S. (Joy) Ford, Mrs. William P. (May) Blackmore, Mrs. Clifton C. (Vivian) Thorne, and Mrs. Harry K. (Eunice) Spindler.

The Progress Club has had top-flight leadership over its long history and earned a reputation in which membership personifies dignity, gracious living, intellectual stimulation, and community service. It is one of the busiest groups in town with a variety of program sub-divisions offering members considerable choice in pursuing their own interests within a range of helpful projects.

In the Name of Service

A number of additional groups in Bethlehem have service goals. Especially noteworthy are the **Bethlehem Lions Club** (1955) programs to help the hearing and visually impaired. Known as "Knights of the Blind against darkness,"[13] Lions Club members help underwrite dog guides, eye banks, and glaucoma and vision tests. Their

Lions Lighting the Community, ca. 1979. **Left to Right:** John Thompson, Maynard "Red" Goyer, and Richard Clark.

local program for the deaf started in 1975 with the installation of a teletypewriter at the State Police Headquarters in Albany. The Bethlehem Lions Club motto, "We Serve," is an umbrella for a wide range of other services to the community, including support for establishing a senior citizens program a few years ago and the popular Bethlehem police bike rodeo today.

In a similar vein, the **Delmar Rotary Club** (1957) supports a number of helpful Bethlehem projects such as the Delmar Job Corps Support Project, Bethlehem Police Canine Program, Bethlehem Ambulance Program, the Rotary Essay Contest at the Middle School, and the Community Bethlehem movement started by town

THE DELMAR MEN'S ORCHESTRA
PRESENTS
"Sounds of Music"
WITH A COMMUNITY CHORUS
AT BETHLEHEM CENTRAL SENIOR HIGH SCHOOL
SPONSORED BY
KIWANIS, LIONS and ROTARY CLUBS
8:30 P.M.
FRIDAY, APRIL 13, 1962   N° 301
Admission $1.00

supervisor Kenneth Ringler. Through Community Bethlehem, the club has increased the number of trees it has planted over the years to beautify selected locations in town. Its unique membership plan (one person from each business and profession) assures wide representation from all parts of the community.

The amount of help given by service groups to a wide range of individuals and organizations is a source of inspiration to citizens in general, as well as to the members of such groups. **Kiwanis Club** members have served Bethlehem for more than fifty years. The group's first president in 1940 was Dr. S. Benjamin Meyers, and his son, Benjamin L. Meyers, served as president in the club's fiftieth year in 1990. Under the motto, "We Build," Kiwanis clubs everywhere promote good citizenship, effective law enforcement and the work of public service agencies. The club is especially known for its sponsorship of the Key Club at Bethlehem Central High School and for its role in establishing the Tri-Village Little League in 1954.

Fraternally Yours

Known for its fellowship and occupancy of former Governor Martin Glynn's historic summer home in Cedar Hill since 1962, Bethlehem's chapter of the **Benevolent and Protective Order of Elks**

2233 has preserved a slice of the town's colorful history as well. Often called the BPOE, the local group makes its headquarters available to other groups and serves delicious food in pleasant surroundings. Bethlehem Elks support Selkirk Troop 81, Boy Scouts of America, disabled veterans, and a range of educational and charitable programs from drug awareness to cerebral palsy.

Architect Marcus T. Reynolds designed the home in 1907, although it was not completed and occupied by the Governor until 1910. In 1926, the home was sold to Daniel Prior, a well-known criminal lawyer and Albany judge, who defended the notorious Jack "Legs" Diamond in the 1920s. While out on bail, Diamond allegedly was a house guest of Prior at the Cedar Hill home. Since 1961, the **Elks Ladies Auxiliary** has concerned itself with supporting Elks goals, programs, and building upkeep. Their annual country store flea market was widely attended for many years and the members have been especially faithful in their volunteer work at the Veterans Administration Hospital.

Politics

The normal image of politics in the early years of this century is of smoke-filled rooms and a group of men hammering out solutions to town government problems. In Bethlehem, however, women organized first and involved themselves heavily in the political process. Political activist Ruth M. Miner working with

Bethlehem Republican Club officers in 1992. Left to Right: David Austin, treasurer; Paul Wagner, vice president; Robert Oliver, president; Bernard Kaplowitz, director; and Brian Murphy, secretary.

Nettie Glenn, wife of attorney William Glenn, formed the **Bethlehem Women's Republican Club** in 1926. The group evolved into an organization with 2,000 members—advocating women's rights, encouraging women to enter politics, and recruiting members for the party.

Over the years, the club supported a variety of projects ranging from giving employment assistance to women and organizing marches for Republican campaigns to providing a sundial for the town park near the railroad overpass on Delaware Avenue. In January 1992, the Women's Republican Club merged with the Bethlehem Men's Republican Club under the title **Bethlehem Republican Club.**

The record suggests that the **Bethlehem Men's Republican Club** was organized in 1961 by Charles Redmond and Arthur McCormick in response to criticism leveled in 1960 by Republican William Schoonmaker, among others, who organized the Lincoln Club and mounted a full slate of candidates in the 1962 primary. This story is told in more depth in the government chapter.

Some thirty years later, the Bethlehem Republican Club now includes both men and women and pushes an aggressive agenda of grass roots participation in the ongoing affairs of the party. Togetherness and frequent communication on the issues of the day are often a by-product of regular social events such as a "World Series Party" at the Normanside Country Club and a "Steak Roast" at an area park, typical events held in 1990-1991.

Documenting the Past

Bethlehem's Tawasentha Chapter, **Daughters of the American Revolution,** has been documenting our history since 1907, a remarkable record of longevity and usefulness. The group takes its name from Tawasentha, a word Longfellow used in his introduction to the poem, *Song of Hiawatha,* to describe the creek known as the Normanskill.

The group has always worked toward patriotic, historical, and educational objectives. It supports national DAR schools for underprivileged children and annually gives "Good Citizen" awards and a $500 scholarship to a local high school senior interested in pursuing historical studies. Additionally, scholarships are awarded to local students to study special interest subjects in a summer enrichment program.

Further, the Tawasentha Chapter donates money and supplies to the Veterans Administration Hospital in Albany, distributes citizenship manuals to new United States citizens, and offers assistance to Native Americans in need. The group maintains an extensive file of genealogical papers and has donated many historical books and related materials to the Bethlehem Public Library.

One highlight of the 1992 program was the construction of a viewing platform and rededication of a bronze plaque, to commemorate pioneer geologists of the Helderberg region in Thacher Park. This was one of four plaques installed by the chapter in Albany County in 1933 to commemorate historical sites.[14]

The second oldest historical organization in Bethlehem traces its origin to Mrs. Norma June's concern about what would happen to the historic Cedar Hill School (1859) after it closed in 1960. Town historian Ruth Dickinson and her assistant, Allison Bennett, shared her concern. Together, they framed a resolu-

Jean Lyon, left, and Mary Elizabeth Van Oostenbrugge.

tion for adoption by the town board that made the Cedar Hill School "available for the use of residents of the town and others for the keeping and display of historical data and other items of historical interest."[15]

The **Town of Bethlehem Historical Association** was chartered by the New York State Board of Regents and incorporated as a tax-free educational organization in 1965. Since then, thousands of elementary school children and hundreds of history-minded adults have been exposed to the town's rich history. Through the efforts of long-term members such as Jean Lyon, Mary Elizabeth Van Oostenbrugge, James Weidemann, Marie Weideman, and many group officers over the years, the Cedar Hill School was transformed into a first-rate museum that now harbors thousands of objects from Bethlehem's past.

Ralph B. Wood, first president of the Bethlehem Archaeology Group.

Next to appear on the scene was the **Bethlehem Archaeology Group**, a small research organization established to collect data for this volume and two additional books to be published soon after the bicentennial year. The group is an outgrowth of a continuing education class in archaeology taught by the author of this chapter in 1981. The group's work has been funded by the town, the members, and the General Electric Foundation. Its laboratory was initially housed in the old Adams Hotel at the Four Corners in Delmar, but after the town sold this building in 1983, the laboratory was moved to the former Waldenmaier meat processing plant on Route 32, site of the town's waste disposal recycling center.

Retired engineer Ralph B. Wood served as the group's first president, as well as its supervisor in the organization of its permanent laboratory. He negotiated the group's charter as a tax-free educational organization under the New York State Board of Regents in 1986. James T. Engleman, vice president and laboratory supervisor for many years, has continued the good work begun by Ralph Wood. An average of sixteen regular members have worked over 10,000 volunteer hours every year since 1982, excavating, identifying,

and interpreting thousands of objects from local historic sites. Results of the group's research have been presented at statewide meetings in recent years and have been published in several professional journals.

The Golden Years

When senior citizens talk about their lives in Bethlehem, they complain about the cost of living, but often say it is worth it because there are so many things for older citizens to do and there are good support services available through town hall. Further, many acknowledge the rich variety of restaurants, shopping, and entertainment values open to them in the greater Albany area after a mere ten or fifteen minute drive.

Bethlehem Senior Citizens was organized by the Lions Club and the Bethlehem Central School District in 1955. The group developed further under its own leadership after 1958, incorporated in 1966, and blossomed under a co-sponsorship arrangement with the Parks and Recreation department after 1974. Bethlehem Senior Citizens has enjoyed a much expanded program since the group's move to town hall in 1980, where it has a close working relationship with Karen Pellettier, director of senior citizen services, and Joyce Becker, program coordinator. A related group called **Sunshine Seniors** has provided opportunities for education and socialization for older citizens living in the southern section of Bethlehem.

Past presidents of Second Milers. Front Row (left to right): Frederick Knapp, William Reuter, John Longley, George Chesbro, Vincent Hummell, and Harold Hastings. Second Row: Donald Stevens, Howard Gmelch, Jack Pellettier, Alan Hoffman, Neil Smith, John Klim, Wayne Fry, and Carlton Gordon.

One of the most appreciated services is the transportation program. Fifty-five volunteer drivers currently use bus, van, and sedan to transport needy senior citizens to and from doctors' offices, hospitals, grocery stores, and many more places.

One notable program is the Senior Lunch Bunch at the Delmar Presbyterian Church, where citizens over eighty years of age meet once a week to share common interests and delicious lunches provided by Bethlehem churches. It is typical of the nice things available to members of the Bethlehem Senior Citizens organization and one more in a long list of reasons why numerous citizens stay here long after retirement.

Another organization serving senior citizens, **The Second Milers,** was begun at the First United Methodist Church in 1964. It is a men's organiza-

tion interested in fellowship and in keeping up with the issues of the day. Long-term member Colonel Howard Gmelch remembers the time "when the men prepared their own simple lunch for about thirty-five cents from food supplied by the church. Now a Methodist Church staff member prepares a meal that costs each man an average of three dollars."[16] Gmelch enjoys mixing with many men "of varying religious faiths who are highly respected in our community, who enjoy hearing the latest in fields such as travel, science, health, and public affairs."[17]

A large group of seniors attends meetings of the **American Association of Retired Persons** through the local chapter organized in 1973—one more example of a national group expanding into Bethlehem. Over the last fifteen years, the group's newsletter, *The Bethlehem Star*, has been a medium for communicating to the membership dozens of stories about recent actions by government and industry which affect the welfare of older citizens. Under their motto, "to serve, not to be served,"[18] the members of AARP Chapter 1598 sponsor a 55 Alive defensive driving course, programs for seniors about combating crime in their own neighborhoods, and a tax advisory service that is widely appreciated in Bethlehem.

Perhaps the most important role of the AARP is its support of legislation affecting older citizens and its lobbying campaign for the laws it deems absolutely necessary. Former town supervisor and current vice president of the local chapter, J. Robert Hendrick, is well aware of senior citizen needs in Bethlehem. He joined the group to help out on the legislative front, as well as to enjoy the fellowship of other retirees. To him, "Influencing change at the state and national levels is both challenging and important for senior citizens everywhere."[19]

Alcohol and Drugs

A never-ending problem for Bethlehem citizens from the earliest days has been the control of addictive substances. Strict penalties were imposed for selling alcohol in the seventeenth century. Government officials struggled with the problem all through the eighteenth century and private groups joined the fray in the nineteenth century. The first substance abuse organization in Bethlehem for which records are available was called the **Star of Bethlehem 305**, Sons of Temperance. Organized in Adamsville in 1868, the group moved to Slingerlands soon after and disbanded in 1871. Undaunted, temperance advocates tried again, this time through a group called the **Light of Bethlehem,** which met at the Baumes Chapel in Cedar Hill for a number of years before fading into oblivion. This group was affiliated with national organizations known as the Good Templars and the Women's Christian Temperance Union.

In recent years, several exotic drugs have been added to the addiction repertory, and people who abuse drugs and alcohol are helped to overcome their problems by highly-trained specialists. A special effort is made to educate young people and the community through organizations known as the **Bethlehem Networks Project** and **Bethlehem Opportunities Unlimited**.

Holly Billings, the first president of Opportunities Unlimited, has been in the forefront of this new approach to overcoming substance abuse. She finds it "exciting to see how a sense of community can be nurtured, and fascinating to observe how people relate to one another and to their institutions."[20] In a note to the editor, she writes that "such relationships can be fostered and preserved. A fine sense of community is a sense of caring—for others, for ourselves, for a place. Working toward a more caring community is part of providing alternatives for teens."[21]

Environmental Concerns

Strong concern about the environment in which we live is a relatively recent phenomenon although similar needs were addressed by local officials in earlier years with words such as preservation and conservation. The first major environmental protection program in Bethlehem was, and still is, the **Five Rivers Environmental Education Center**, created after passage of the 1972 Environmental Quality Bond Act by the New York State Legislature. The area now occupied by the center was covered by extensive orchards a century ago and was turned into an experimental game farm in 1933. Some 400 Civilian Conservation Corps workers created a pond, built dams, and put up two buildings on the property in the mid-1930s.

A group known as **Five Rivers Limited** was organized in 1972 to support the center's work. In past president Robert S. Alexander's words, "Five Rivers Limited is a group of dedicated citizens working quietly behind the scenes to provide an important community and regional service which could not exist without their support."[22] The success of this group's work can be seen in visitor attendance figures—some 6,000 school children now receive structured lessons annually and an additional 10,000 visit the center with their teachers. Further, another 10,000 family members are attracted to the center each year following advertisements in the local media.

One more option open to lovers of wildlife and outdoor activity is the 138-acre sanctuary on Rarick Road, near South Bethlehem. Founded by Robert and Leona Train Rienow in 1940, **Hollyhock Hollow Sanctuary** is a paradise for lovers of birds and other wildlife. The sanctuary is open to the public, free of charge. It was deeded to the Audubon Society of New York State in 1989 and the society's headquarters are located on the grounds. The sanctuary is administered and protected in its natural state. Hiking is permitted during daylight hours, although pets are not allowed. The Audubon Society of New York State also administers the New York Loon Conservation Program and the Cooperative Sanctuary Program for golf courses, municipalities, schools, and individuals.

A more activist role in protecting the environment is open to members of **Bethlehem Citizens for Responsible Planning** which had its origin with a group of eight concerned citizens meeting in the home of John Smolinski of Delmar in February 1987. Word of the new organization spread and within two years membership grew to 250. From the beginning, the group's purpose was to serve as an advocate of effective and consistent planning in the town of Bethlehem. In recent years, the group exerted its influence through a petition with 1,500 signatures to have the town hire a professional planner and update the master plan for Bethlehem. Both objectives were realized. Members of the group are now working closely with the newly formed Land Use Management Advisory Committee on a variety of ongoing problems with the goal of rendering Bethlehem a more desirable place to live and work.

Organized in 1965 with help from the Bethlehem Chamber of Commerce and with a highly specific goal, the **Bethlehem Garden Club** now fills forty-nine flower boxes in Bethlehem every spring and fall, creating a splash of color near businesses and public buildings in the main shopping areas. Further, the club awards an annual scholarship to a Bethlehem Central High School graduate who plans to continue in natural science, forestry or agriculture. Funding for both the boxes and the scholarship is derived from an annual plant sale in May and contributions from merchants where the boxes are located.

Delmar Concert Orchestra, ca. 1935.

For the Love of Music

Bethlehem residents have taken advantage of musical events in large numbers on many occasions, particularly in the twentieth century. The best evidence of interest in music by local citizens is the Albany Symphony mailing list of season ticket subscribers; well over half are listed as living in Bethlehem. But the homegrown variety of music is widely appreciated as the record for this century clearly shows.

The **Delmar Concert Orchestra** and the **Delmar Choral Society** worked together to bring semi-classical music to the people of Bethlehem in the 1930s. Like so many other good things in the community, these groups were first sponsored by the Progress Club, which spurred community interest with a major organizational meeting at the Delmar Reformed Church in mid-March 1929. Professor Lucius S. Ades, known for his successful conducting of other choruses, attended the meeting along with the personnel of seven subcommittees and a number of Bethlehem residents

who wanted to play or sing. Professor Ades may have conducted the first few performances but, before long, other talented conductors took their turns.

Donald S. Dewire directed the orchestra and his wife, Ethel, served as accompanist for the Choral Society when *The Mikado* was presented in 1931. It was an immense success and was attended by a record number of Bethlehem residents. On February 17, 1939, Frederick W. Kerner directed the two groups in a gala performance of *H.M.S. Pinafore*, a memorable program that is still remembered by old-timers today.

Now in his eighties, George Alfred Lansing has fond memories of playing a Stradivarius violin on loan from the Smithsonian Institute. Claude White's love of the trombone was so dominant in his life that he organized a dance band in addition to playing in the concert orchestra. A picture of the concert orchestra taken in 1935 shows eight women and twenty-one men in elegant formal dress performing on the stage of the present Middle School.

By 1940, when the **Delmar Men's Orchestra** was organized, the coeducational aspect of orchestral music in Bethlehem seems to have gone by the wayside as seven men got together to play at the First United Methodist Church in Delmar. The men's orchestra was gradually expanded into a non-denominational group as more and more men wanted to play. The group gained national fame through a two-page picture in *Life* magazine in 1955 showing forty-eight men in rehearsal. The caption, "Amateurs All,"[23] was an apt description of the farmers, doctors, lawyers, businessmen, and clerks who gathered regularly under the baton of Rolland Truitt, music supervisor of the Bethlehem school system.

Ralph Mead remembers the early days of the orchestra: "It was pure enjoyment for the members who liked to play light classics, waltzes, and show tunes."[24] The legendary Charles Lacy enjoyed his membership in the orchestra so much that he continued playing violin in the orchestra well beyond ninety years of age.

As women joined the group in the 1960s, the name was changed to **Delmar Community Orchestra**. Robert McGowan, a music teacher in the Albany school system, became conductor in 1974, and continued in this role until his death in 1990. His assistant, Millie Stahl, picked up the baton, finished the season, and remained on as the orchestra's conductor, determined to continue the group's mandate of "promoting an art form for the pleasure and entertainment of its members and audiences."[25] The group now gives six or seven concerts a year in churches, nursing homes, and local clubs. Concerts became especially enjoyable for audiences when sing-a-long numbers were introduced as a regular feature in programs.

Young people in Bethlehem got involved in a special kind of music after the **Village Volunteers Fife and Drum Corps** was formed in 1956. This group was originally sponsored by the Delmar Fire Company and was then known as the Village Fire Fifers. From its first public appearance in 1957 at the Albany Tulip Festival, the corps has gone on to record an album, *Music of American Liberty*, and to win numerous medals throughout the United States and Canada. The corps' annual program in the Bethlehem Public Library's summer series always draws a large audience.

William F. Bub, music master, his wife, Lois, and their five children kept the organization going over most of the early years. Their son, William C., liked the experience so much that he is still with the corps. They were aided by Mrs. Beninati, business manager, her husband, Carl, and their three children. Mrs. Beninati was instrumental in arranging many trips and competitions, the best route to keeping the group at a peak performance level.

A highlight in the group's history took place in September 1976, when the Corps hosted a muster of fourteen fife and drum corps from other states in a gala parade and performance on Bethlehem Central High School's athletic fields. News reports of the event label it as "one of the most spectacular and epochal weekends in Bethlehem's history."[26]

Young peoples' interest in good music got another boost when the **Bethlehem Music Association** was formed in 1975 to provide music enrichment opportunities not normally available in the schools for students. Mrs. Bailey Bloom, the first president, and Kathleen Kaplowitz, vice president, worked closely with Samuel S. Bozzella,

Village Volunteers Fife and Drum Corps, Memorial Day parade, 1992.

music department supervisor, to come up with interesting and helpful programs that first year. The organization has waxed and waned according to the number of parents with children in school who are seriously interested in music, but it has been on the upswing in recent years. Kathleen Bragle was a strong influence in the 1980s when the annual June Pops Concert at the Middle School was the featured event.

Thespians at Heart

Eighteenth- and nineteenth-century church plays gave way to Progress Club plays, performances by the Fellowcraft Club in the Bethlehem Masonic Lodge, the Slingerlands Community Players, and

the Village Stage in this century. So many groups in Bethlehem began with a modest idea, but success bred continuation and expansion.

Such was the case with the **Slingerlands Community Players,** which evolved from a successful performance of *The Male Animal* at the Slingerlands Community Methodist Church in 1952. Vera and Morris Schaeffer organized the play. Before long, eighteen friends and neighbors were staging other plays at the Middle School and Bethlehem Central High School.

Over the years, hundreds of talented people helped with the plays, which were attended by thousands of Bethlehem residents. Four of the most talented Slingerlands Players—Zaida Johnson,

Joanne Kimmey, Betty Taylor, and Ruth Wilber—formed a professional group known as the Quarto Playhouse and traveled throughout the Northeast presenting short plays to women's groups and college audiences. After almost twenty years, the older players gradually drifted away and productions became too costly. A great idea faded into oblivion.

But good quality drama wouldn't die. An elaborate pageant was staged in 1976 to celebrate the nation's bicentennial.[27]

Slinglerlands Quarto Players. Left to Right: Zaida Johnson, Joanne Kimmey, Betty Taylor, and Ruth Wilber.

Mrs. George (Ruth) Bickel was general chairman of the celebration and Richard Feldman coordinated the writing. Groups such as the Hamagrael Players and the Middle School Players portrayed different times in Bethlehem's history. Mrs. Dominick (Patricia) DeCecco was program chairman of the event and has been a key figure in many Bethlehem dramatic events since 1976. One of her greatest successes was the variety show she wrote, organized, and directed for the Bethlehem Central School District's fiftieth anniversary in 1984.

Basking in the glow of audience reaction to the school district variety show at a cast party following the event, the key players agreed they wanted to stay together and do more plays in Bethlehem. Although extremely busy as a wife, mother, and full-time speech pathologist for the South Colonie School District, Pat DeCecco needed very little encouragement to keep the cast together for her favorite pastime.

Attorney William Schoonmaker suggested the name, **The Village Stage**, and the group was

Patricia DeCecco and Lars Allanson of the Village Stage.

tice over many years of helping the needy with knitted items and of helping the Red Cross in several wars with rolling and packaging bandages.

The women worked on fashionable items for themselves such as hug-me-tight sweaters in the 1920s and knitted dresses in the 1930s. It was a time when knitting was thought to be "a cure for nervousness, agoraphobia, rheumatism, insomnia, smoking, mental strain, and guilt. Further, from time to time women were warned to stay out of men's affairs and tend to their knitting."[29]

born. Tom Watthews, a biology teacher at Bethlehem Central High School for over thirty years, played Hucklebee (the boy's father) in the group's first performance of *The Fantastiks* in 1985. My wife, Coleen, and I have enjoyed many performances by The Village Stage from *Ballroom* and *Little Mary Sunshine* in the early years to *Pajama Game* and *The Bells Are Ringing* in 1989-1990. And all of these good things are just a three-minute ride from our home!

The modern counterpart of the Sewing Society is the **Embroiderers' Guild of America** which was formed in 1967. Although this is the capital district chapter of the national organization, all of the group's meetings are held at the First United Methodist Church on Kenwood Avenue. Great skill is needed to carry out some of the projects sponsored by this group, and there is considerable emphasis on educating the members to do the fine work needed. One of their recent projects involved threading gold fiber material into twenty-six drapes for the Executive Chamber in the Capitol building.

In Pursuit of Crafts and Hobbies

Most people have long since forgotten the **Delmar Sewing Society** but the record is there. A 1960 story in the *Altamont Enterprise* asserted that "the society has an interesting history. In 1902 six women met once a week for lunch and afterwards would do their personal sewing during the afternoon."[28] The minutes confirm the group's prac-

Mrs. Thomas Sanvige saw an urgent need to maintain the highest ideals of home life and to share a growing knowledge of homemaking at its best, a purpose she attributed to Dr. Ruby Green Smith and a philosophy on which she founded the Glenmont Home Bureau in 1945. Groups with such a fundamental purpose last for years. Fifty-five strong in 1990 and now called **The Glenmont Homemakers**, the group has sponsored workshops on subjects from nutrition to furniture repair. A safe driving theme was integrated into the Homemakers programs in the 1970s.

Clubs have a habit of springing up around things people like to do, as was the case with a group at Saint Stephen's Church in 1957. Father Charles Kaulfuss was aware that some of the church members shared his interest in photography. He invited them to meet in the church parlor. The early members of the group soon drafted a constitution and the **Delmar Camera Club** came into being. Past president Florence Becker joined the group during its second meeting and has been a top scorer in many of the club's competitions in both black-and-white prints and color slides. Alice Porter, long-known for her work in photography

Prize-winning photo of abandoned Wemple Road home by Florence Becker.

around Bethlehem, joined at the same time and went on to win several awards in national competitions for pictures submitted through the *Times Union* newspaper.

Today, the club holds memberships in the Photographic Society of America and the Hudson-Mohawk Council of Camera Clubs, which offer outlets for their best work. Prizes are awarded regularly in black-and-white prints, color prints, and color slides. Florence Becker summed up the reason for her involvement in the club. "A musician needs his or her music played, a writer needs to be published, a photographer's work should be shown. Public display encourages further production, an exchange of ideas, and the will to do more."[30]

Another group enjoyed by dozens of Bethlehem residents was established by Charlotte Reinhardt, whose lifelong love of quilting caused her to organize **QUILT** in 1977. Years ago, a member of the group thought this should mean **Quilters United in Learning Together**, and the idea stuck. Beautiful quilts abound everywhere, tangible reminders of historic events and group activity. Some of Mrs. Reinhardt's former students are presently working on a bicentennial quilt designed by Barbara Boynton.

Quilts are often major community projects, as was the quilt done for the Bethlehem Public Library's seventy-fifth anniversary in 1988. Lorre Smith of the library staff organized the project using Charlotte Reinhardt's design. Joyce Strand, a quilting enthusiast as well as president of the library's board, was heavily involved. Many adult quilters in the community submitted designs for the squares, and Ann Jacobs won the coveted center spot with her design depicting the library's logo. Art departments in the schools were active in working on parts of the quilt, and winning designs by a selected number of children were incorporated in the plan. The final quilt, done in shades of orange and black, was indeed a community project of the first order.

In the Spirit of Competition

Few records remain, but papers in Alice Boutelle's possession mention the **Echoes Baseball Team** of Slingerlands, a group that played the game with strenuous intensity between 1890 and 1895. Equipment was scarce and the players were without gloves. The catcher didn't wear shin guards or a chest protector and masks were few and far between. In those days a foul ball was not called a strike. Old-timers say the baseball field in the 1890s was on New Scotland Road, near the site of the old Slingerland Printing Company, the present Zautner apartment building.

An early twentieth-century team called the **Village Wonders** earned the title through diligent practice and a competitive schedule. The team's pitcher, Ira Pier, reminisced with Allison Bennett in an April 1970 interview. They played "on Kenwood Avenue where Union Avenue now intersects.... spectators had to find their own seats—no grandstands in those days!"[31]

Young people got their chance to play ball with the formation of **Tri-Village Little League** in 1954. With help from the Delmar Kiwanis and the Bethlehem Shrine Club, and with the driving force of Arthur Fleahman, president of the

Tri-Village Little League hitter, Jill Kaplowitz.

new organization, the group soon purchased land for a playing field from Harold J. McGee. Located on Kenwood Avenue where it intersects the Route 32 By-Pass, the land cost $2,000. The first four Little League teams were sponsored by Crannell Lumber, Carroll's Pharmacy, Main Brothers, and Studler Sales.

Adrian "Ade" Arnold, Tri-Village Little League coach: 1954-1988.

Long-term coach Ade Arnold rarely missed a practice. Further, he kept a detailed scrapbook of the league's activities which is full of great sports stories. One page tells the story of Joey Marotta, son of Colonel James V. and Clara Marotta of Paxwood Road, Delmar, who hit five home runs in five consecutive times at bat at the Little League National Playoffs in 1960. Another explains how Jill Kaplowitz broke the gender barrier by insisting on playing with the "majors" in 1978-1979. She ended the 1978 season with a decent .333 batting average, then zoomed to a .563 average by the end of the 1979 season. [32]

Boys who want more body contact in sports can try out for **Pop Warner Football,** a group organized about 1963. Early records appear to be lost. However, former players such as Charles W. Reeves, Edwin D. Reed, and Robert F. Verstandig

are full of stories about their experiences. Football competitions were built around age and weight groupings of boys between nine and fourteen years of age.

Another kind of ballplaying grew in popularity in the last third of the current century following the organization of the **Bethlehem Tomboys** and the group's opening game on July 5, 1972. Coach Irving VanWoert, Jr., had enrolled his team in the Miss Softball America organization under their initial name, the Tri-Village Tomboys. An enthusiastic audience of 300 heard speeches that first day about the national playoffs to be held near

Bethlehem Tomboys: 1972. Front Row (left to right): Meg Johnson, Shelly Richter, Kris Congemi, Heather Leslie, Ann Campbell, Mary Moriarity, Karen Welch, and Rhonda Rush. **Second Row:** Irving Van Woert, coach; Dave Richter, assistant coach; Donna DeBiase, Kelly Ann Keller, Sue Ciccio, Sue McGarrahan, Debby Valentine, Amy Collen, Judy Ciccio, manager; Joe Keller, sponsor, and Carol Owens (missing).

Disneyland in California. Months of hard work, backed by elated audiences, carried the Tomboys to victory over three capital district teams in 1972 and to third place in the national competition in Anaheim, California.

As both medical adviser and coach, Dr. VanWoert worried about cranial damage from speeding balls, and worked to obtain a helmet rule in the early years of competition. Further, VanWoert and manager Susan Singer deftly handled criticism from conservative members of the public who objected to labeling girls Tomboys. The term was stoutly defended by mothers of the Tomboys, one of whom signed her letter, "mother of two sexy Tomboys."[33]

Another sport with wide appeal for young people in Bethlehem is soccer—a fact realized by Connie and George Tilroe who did something about it in 1978. They coached a team of boys, eleven and twelve years of age, that year and arranged a few games with teams in nearby towns. The Capital District Youth Soccer League was formed, followed soon after by an affiliate group called the **Bethlehem Soccer Club**. The growth of this group is nothing short of phenomenal—increasing from fourteen in 1979 to 350 in 1984 and 1,500 in 1990.

Now more than 100 parents help the coaches and as many as eighty teams (with over 900 young people) participate in an "Off the Wall" tournament every year. Off the Wall means a tournament inside Bethlehem Central High School gyms in which local teams struggle against sharp teams from places as far away as Lynn, Massachusetts, and Manchester, Vermont. More important than numbers are the innumerable opportunities for young athletes to learn the art of team play, a skill that is likely to stay with them for life.

Lest we think that sports are primarily for children, attention should be called to the presence of the **Bethlehem Tennis Association**, which grew out of tennis clinics conducted by Donald Camp in 1966. He now has an honorary life membership and has been in the association for twenty-four years. Maynard Parsons organized the association and persuaded his wife, Adele, to play the game.

In her eighties, Adele is still enjoying tennis. She slams the ball with gusto and refuses to give in to those minor aches and pains that come with advancing age. She recently enrolled in a teaching clinic at the Southwood Indoor Tennis and Golf facility where Linda Burtis, the teaching pro, regards her as "the star of some of

Adele Parsons.

my clinics and a player with a lot of spunk."[34]

Adults enjoy running with Doris Davis who organized the **Delmar Sunday Morning Running Group** in 1981. Now some twenty members pad around well-worn trails in different parts of Bethlehem—mostly for pleasure, sometimes to prepare for races. The members gather at 8:30 A.M. every Sunday morning at Stewart's Ice Cream store in Delmar and run various routes ranging from five to fifteen miles.

Head, Hands, Heart, and Health
—the 4-H Creed

Records at the Cornell Cooperative Extension of Albany County in Voorheesville suggest that The Delmar Stitch and Chatter Girls (1946) were the first to organize in Bethlehem, although earlier 4-H groups probably existed here since the national movement originated in 1914. A spate of groups followed, including the Selkirk Jolly Workers (1948), Elm Avenue Elves (1954), Delmar Zip and Whip (1955), Selkirk Jolly Homemakers (1956), and the Selkirk Harvesters (1957). Additionally, groups called the Happy Stitch and Cook Family (1960) and Little Lassies (1963) enriched dozens of young girls over a period of several years. Other groups were organized in Bethlehem after 1963, but most were short-term in nature.

More important than records is the vital contribution made by these groups to the development of young people (mostly girls) in such important areas as self-confidence, public speaking, home-making skills, community service, and good citizenship, all accomplished under the 4-H motto "To Make the Best Better." Carol Northrup, author of the farm chapter in this volume, and her friend, Joan Prusik, have keen memories of the helpful programs planned for the Elm Avenue Elves by Joan's mother, Helen Prusik, between 1954 and 1964. Jean Olson has similar memories of programs planned for the Jolly Homemakers by her mother, Helen Olson, between 1957 and 1971. The above groups reflect a broadening of the 4-H organization in the 1960s to include more groups in urban and suburban areas. By 1970, about twenty-five percent of the members lived in urban areas.

Scout's Honor

The oldest Boy Scout group in Bethlehem is probably **Troop 16, w**hich is believed to have been organized in 1912 at the Methodist Church in Delmar.[35] This may be one of the earliest groups in the United States, since the movement was incorporated in this country in 1910 and chartered by the United States Congress in 1916. The photograph on page 172, taken in 1916, shows scoutmaster Charles Stine with twenty-four scouts flanked by two flags. Two of the scouts, Harold and Raymond Geurtze, went on to found businesses that are well known to hundreds of Bethlehem residents.

Boy Scouts of America Delmar Troop 16, ca. 1916. First Row (left to right): Clayton Rosboro, Reynold Becker, Wesley Vrooman, and Kenneth Hunt. **Second Row:** Ernest Smith, Dave Kirk, Walter Kunz, Charles Stine, scoutmaster; Adrian Johnson, Harold Geurtze, and Lloyd VanCott. **Third Row:** Fred Baxter, Ray Kirk, John Carpenter, and Edward Garry. **Fourth Row:** Chester Smith, George Yager, Paul VanNess, Ernest Hunt, Wyman Osterhout, Raymond Geurtze, Harris Becker, Harold Stine, and Burnside Wynkoop.

Another early group with similar goals was the **Boys Brigade**, formed in 1917 at the First Reformed Church of Bethlehem in Selkirk by the Reverend H. S. Van Woert. Within two years the group had reorganized under the leadership of the Reverend Charles G. Mallory as **Troop 1, Selkirk**, Boy Scouts of America, meeting at the church. In the early years, all Boy Scout troops in this area were under the administration of the Fort Orange Council in Albany. Several older citizens believe that troops were organized in Elsmere and Slingerlands at about the same time, but no record can be found of their existence.

Kenneth Van Allen, now eighty-five years old, was a member of Selkirk Troop 1. He remembers with pleasure looking forward to Friday evenings with scoutmaster James Killough. It was the highlight of the week for the dozen or so boys in Troop 1, since there was very little organized activity for young people in Bethlehem at that time.

Records for a later **Selkirk Troop 81** are lost, but notes in Allison Bennett's files show that it began around 1934 with Elmer Bleezarde as scoutmaster. The group met at the Selkirk School. Further, a strong Cub Scout pack was organized at Selkirk and South Bethlehem in the 1950s with Clair S. Snyder as cubmaster.

Troop 1 was formed in Elsmere under Kenneth Swallow's leadership in 1919. This troop disbanded soon after it was organized, but another group formed under the same designation in 1920, changing its name to **Elsmere Troop 58** in 1926. Still going strong after decades of existence, Troop 58 has exposed hundreds of Elsmere boys to an array of outdoor experiences and healthy life values unequaled in most other organizations. The group is sponsored by American Legion Post 1040.

By 1930 another group had formed at the Methodist Episcopal Church in Delmar, an early name for the present First United Methodist Church on Kenwood Avenue. **Delmar Troop 75** was formed that year under the watchful eye of pastor Leon

Delmar Troop 75 Eagle Scout project. Surface search in 1987 for evidence of seventeenth-century sawmill near mouth of the Normanskill. **Front Row** (left to right): Billy Proper, Floyd Brewer, Bethlehem Archaeology Group field director; Ryan McKinney, prospective Eagle Scout; John Keck, Jon Schroeder, and Mike Bonneau. **Second Row** (left to right): Matt Begg, Steven Downs, scoutmaster; Scott Watkins, Mike Yovine, and Steven Dorsey.

Adkins. This is one of very few troops in the Capital Region to remain with its original sponsor and in its original location since the troop's beginning. Troop 75 has grown to more than sixty members in recent years, partly because of the popular Winter Sports Mart, held at Bethlehem Central High School, where people throughout the Capital Region can buy second-hand winter sports and scouting equipment every year. Profits from the Sports Mart have fueled trips and an energetic program of local activities for the members. Eagle awards were granted to thirty-six Boy Scouts in Troop 75 between 1933 and 1989.

Delmar Troop 71 was organized in 1974 when it became clear that a number of boys in Bethlehem wanted a scouting experience but couldn't get into existing groups because of overcrowding. Assistant scoutmaster Ralph T. LaBarge became involved because of his own experience in scouting in Connecticut in the 1940s. He was one of five boys in his troop to contract polio. He remembers praying a lot with his parents and of feeling immensely relieved to learn that doctors labeled his case "a weakness rather than the full paralysis."[36] He made up his mind then and there to give something back to scouting when he was old enough to accept a leadership role in the movement. That opportunity came in 1974 when his own boys were ready for scouting. He served as scoutmaster Roger Dandeneau's assistant for a few years and took over the troop when Dandeneau withdrew. The troop is sponsored by the Church of Saint Thomas the Apostle and its leaders have recommended ten Eagle Scout awards since the group was organized. All were granted.

Character Building at its Best

Not to be outdone by the boys, **Delmar Girl Scout Troop 1** was organized in 1917 with a view toward helping young girls with matters of character, conduct, patriotism, and service to others.

There were three patrols in the early 1920s led by Jane MacConnel, Dorothy Best, and Helen Karpel. Early Girl Scouts could work toward a cook merit

Girl Scouts of America, Delmar Troop 1, ca. 1917.

through the Girl Scout movement. Her membership card shown below indicates that the Delmar Troop was administered from a headquarters in Albany in those days. Now, top level direction comes from the Hudson Valley Girl Scout Council located in Delmar.

Alice Porter Boutelle, Girl Scout leader in 1939.

badge. Several girls working toward this badge in these early patrols cooked an entire banquet. The girls passed their tests and did so well that "a box supper was given in their honor."[37] Later, the Scouts made up a Christmas basket for a poor family at the City Mission in Albany. Delmar's Marcelle M. Olsen had heard stories about these early groups and was helpful in filling in the details because of her forty-five-year association and many leadership roles with Girl Scouts in this area.

Alice Porter Boutelle recalls serving as a patrol leader in **Delmar Troop 33** in the early 1930s. She had risen to the rank of lieutenant by 1939 when 30,000 Girl Scouts of America converged on the World's Fair in New York City for a major procession and pageant stressing world-wide peace

Fond memories abound of **Troop 48** formed by Mrs. Ira (Jessie) Winne around 1934. Former troop member Allison Bennett remembers regular meetings at the Selkirk School and camping at Burden Lake where twelve to fourteen girls enjoyed outdoor activities.

Few records have been kept of other Girl Scout troops in Bethlehem, but some stories have survived. Margy Jo Lilly Borofsky, the Hamagrael School secretary, remembers starting in a Brownie troop around 1956, a group that was upgraded to **Troop 321** by her mother, Peg Lilly, in 1958. Evelyn Bennett Drake was assistant leader of Troop 321. The 1960s found Joy Ford, assisted by Dorothy Starkweather, working with **Glenmont Girl Scout Troop 315**, although no records have been located for this group.

First officers, American Legion Post 1040 in 1931. 1953 photo. Front Row (left to right): George Fowler, Jon Carpenter, installing officer; Winthrop P. Robinson, and Otto D. deHeus. Second Row: George Lauer, Harry Keelan, Edwin Piper, Alfred Brown, and Earl McGuirk.

and an outpost of the State Police here in the 1950s, to mention a few of the Legion's many projects. One of the Legion's exciting youth projects in the early years was the Sons of the American Legion Band, a group of twenty-six musicians that added color to many of the Legion's parades. Additionally, the group sponsors Boy Scout Troop 58 based in Elsmere.

American Legion Post 1040's first home, the former Elsmere School, was moved to a site on Herber Avenue in 1931. Spiraling membership and the desire for more modern facilities encouraged the members to build the present Legion Hall on Herber Avenue in 1970 when the old school building was demolished. This attractive, spacious building is used by 700 members today. A **Ladies**

Veterans Groups: United in War and Peace

The military chapter in this volume describes **American Legion Post 1040**, but more should be said about the post's dynamic role in the development of the community. From its beginning under Winthrop P. Robinson's leadership in 1930, American Legion Post 1040 has supported constructive change in Bethlehem. A scrapbook compiled by William Campbell carries stories about the Legion's role in stimulating community interest in vital matters ranging from zoning and new sidewalks in the 1930s to establishing a community skating rink behind Legion Hall in the 1940s

First American Legion Post 1040 home.

Auxiliary has actively supported the work of Post 1040 from the earliest months of its existence when president Winifred R. Butler banged the opening gavel in 1931.

Another opportunity for friendships with men and women of like interests can be found at the **Veterans of Foreign Wars, Bethlehem Memorial Post 3185**. James Austin, the first commander, handled 101 organizational details when the group got underway in 1946, and Hazel Martin, first president of the **Ladies Auxiliary** worked hard to get their group firmly established the following year. They have a cozy headquarters on Delaware Avenue near the Four Corners. The Ladies Auxiliary supports the group's objectives, runs an annual children's Christmas party for about 100 children, and supplies volunteers for the Veterans Administration Hospital in Albany.

In the Spirit of Business

Although the subject of business in Bethlehem is covered nicely in the Business and Industry chapter, a little more should be said about the primary business organizations. The **Delmar Business Men's Association** was organized in 1949 with Arthur Starman as its first president. The officers wanted to foster good feeling, comity, trade, and commerce in the Tri-Village area. The association is regarded as the forerunner of organized business cooperation in Bethlehem and a clear sign of the intent of several local businesses to become more customer-centered in their work.

The following year Evelyn Sanvidge urged that women in business organize as the **Bethlehem Business Women's Club**. Soon, twenty-five women accepted her call and, by 1951, the group had joined the New York State Federation of Business and Professional Women's Clubs, then part of an international organization working to promote qualified women to higher level jobs in their fields. Dorothy Brown said, "We broke away from the national organization in the middle 1960s, when we wanted to do more locally and send less of our money out of the area." [38]

Organized in 1954, the **Chamber of Commerce** is covered fully in Chapter Five. It is noteworthy that Bethlehem businesses have supported hundreds of worthy projects and groups, especially athletic, dramatic, and musical events over the town's entire existence. This vital help has continued through good times and bad times. One merely has to look through a few dozen program booklets for entertainment and athletic events scheduled in Bethlehem in the twentieth century to appreciate the consistency and significance of business support of local group activities.

Mixing Fun, Friends, and Skill Development

When the **Normanside Country Club** comes up in conversations, many people think of the word fun. There they meet friends, enjoy a relaxing meal, swim, or improve their golf game. No doubt attorney William A. Glenn had all of these things in mind when he proposed the establish-

Normanside Country Club in 1992.

ment of the club in 1926. Several key members of the community approved his ideas at a meeting at the Elsmere School in 1927, and the group purchased three farms along Salisbury Road soon thereafter. A prominent golf architect was engaged and the first nine holes were completed in 1928. By 1930, a nine-hole addition was opened for play.

Today, golf is still king at the club but formal committees plan many events every year, including the president's ball, men's guest day, a semi-formal dinner dance, and a traditional New Year's Eve party. A major fire in 1960 destroyed many of the club's records. A new clubhouse was built and some 275 members now enjoy its many conveniences before and after their golf games. It is a home away from home and a way of life for many citizens who consider membership in the club a priority in their lives.

Another group with a clubhouse and related sports facilities is the **Bethlehem Sportsman's Club**. The club has 200 acres atop the Helderberg Escarpment—a paradise for the outdoorsman with a hillside of red pines, a small stream winding along a valley floor, and a view of the distant Catskills and nearby Helderbergs.

The Bethlehem Sportsman's Club was established in 1946 with Harold Ochner as its first president. From the beginning the leaders and officers have stressed their educational programs. Safe gun handling is a special emphasis. Long-term member John E. Manne, a Delmar dentist, has been taking his family to the club's popular facility on Dunbar Hollow Road in Clarksville for many years. He likes the fun a family can have at club dinners and at the well-known pancake breakfast, but, most of all, he is proud of the educational programs they sponsor—the hunter training program, the hunting-fishing trips, and the New York State Conservation camps to which they send two young people every year.

Civil War History: A Never-Ending Interest

Mention the Civil War to any member of the **Capital District Civil War Roundtable** and one is riveted to the spot where the conversation began for at least a half hour. Maybe more! The group has met at the Bethlehem Public Library since its beginning in 1984 under its first president, Michael Aikey.

Part of a national network, the local group has a reputation among similar groups in the United States for outstanding programs. In 1989, the Capital District group joined with leaders at West Point in sponsoring a program that featured leading academic Civil War specialists from different universities throughout the country. The group's annual banquets with top-flight speakers are so popular among its 125 members that two a year are likely to be scheduled beginning in 1993.

Under John Hennessey's leadership, the Capital District group prepared a booklet listing Civil War preservation causes. It was distributed widely and is utilized by Roundtable organizations throughout the county. Additionally, William Howard, author of the military chapter in this volume, and Michael Aikey have written a number of articles and books on the Civil War.

The Best Bargain in Bethlehem

This facetious sub-title aptly characterizes how many citizens feel about the **Tri-Village Directory Association's** popular publication, which was started by Mrs. Alton (Caroline) Rowe, Sr., and the First Methodist Episcopal Church (now the First United Methodist Church) in 1930. Publication costs are recovered from donations of five to ten dollars given by many residents when they receive their copy from one of more than 400 community workers who help with the project.

The directory was initially printed by the Slingerland Printing Company, and the first issue of 1,000 copies cost $625. The issue carried sixty-eight advertisements. At that time, the people were more interested in "the names of all residents of the hamlets of Delmar, Slingerlands and Elsmere, together with their occupation, home address and business affiliation, and other names in the family,"[39] an early pledge that has been kept in all of the editions thus far. Now the advertiser's index and classified buyers guide in the yellow pages at the back of the book are being used heavily by hundreds of residents. It is a quick way of finding out who sells what or offers the service one needs.

Some people call the directory "The Snoop Book," not in a pejorative sense but in testimony to the book's helpfulness. One can look up who lives at a particular address in the green pages at the back of the book or, if the name is known, it is easily found in bold type in the main section. It helps newcomers get to know entire families who have befriended them, and there is a widely used list of phone numbers in the yellow pages at the front of the book, a quick way to locate government, school, and church officials, along with professional people and the heads of community organizations.

Some of the profits still go into Methodist Church accounts, and in recent years the association has voted substantial donations to worthy community groups. Bethlehem Opportunities

Unlimited, Senior Projects, and the Bethlehem Community Festival Fund all received $750 during the current year. Whatever the cost in volunteer time and expense, this is one publication that most users feel is well worth the effort!

Last But Definitely Not Least

When a fire company is mentioned in Bethlehem, the chances are the conversation will turn to stories of appreciation and pride. It doesn't matter whether the conversation occurs in Selkirk, Slingerlands, North Bethlehem, or other hamlets. People often say, "I always give." By that they mean a contribution during the fire companies' annual donation fund drives. Almost everyone wants and appreciates competent lifesaving and property protection.

Fire fighting in Bethlehem was mostly neighbors helping neighbors until 1911 when the **Delmar Fire Company Chemical No. 1** was formed with Alton C. Rowe as captain. Floyd Irons organized the first Rescue Squad in 1939 and Peter Applebee donated an ambulance in 1960. Now called the **Delmar Fire Department**, this group of hardy volunteers is on call day and night, in good weather and bad. Rigorous training has reduced the number of serious injuries to a bare minimum but the risk is always there.

Former chief Henry Kleinke, a fifty-three-year veteran with the department, remembers the spectacular fire at the Three Elms restaurant in 1948.

The popular Delmar hangout at 359 Delaware Avenue was gutted by flames, which had burned through the roof by the time firemen arrived. Damage was estimated at more than $10,000, a kingly

Award in 1989 to Dorothy and Henry Kleinke for fifty years of service to the Delmar Fire Department.

sum in those days. Henry's wife, Dorothy, worked with the Ladies Auxiliary for the department during the same years. In 1989, they were awarded the beautiful sculpture shown here, commemorating fifty years of service to the Delmar Fire Department.

The second oldest company in Bethlehem (1922), the **Elsmere Fire Company A**, was whipped into shape by the legendary chief, Peter N.A. Klein, who served as a lieutenant and captain before being named chief in 1933. A 1952 news article in a scrapbook compiled by former chief Kenneth E. McNary, a sixty-two-year veteran with the department, tells the story of the Elsmere Company's "first fire engine, a 1917 Model T Ford purchased second hand, equipped with two chemical tanks, a ladder, hose and lanterns."[40] Called "Old Dinky" today, this early fire engine is still in working order and can be seen by citizens who take the time to visit the fire station on Poplar Drive.

The present Elsmere fire station was built in 1929, nicely planned and still very useful. Two additions have been made to the original building

Fred Webster comparing 1917 "Old Dinky" to the Elsmere Fire Department's new snorkel truck in 1972. **Left to Right:** Wayne Johnson, Carl VanHoesen, Paul Kleinke, Jerry Smith (in snorkel truck), and Fred Webster.

Chief J. Robert Hendrick witnessed another disastrous loss at the Normanside Country Club in 1960. Toward the end of his tenure in 1968, prevention-minded Elsmere residents voted sufficient money to purchase a new fire truck with a snorkel and platform at the end that extended eighty-five feet into the sky. A major fire at the Agway fertilizer plant in Albany in 1970, to which several outside companies were called, provided the first opportunity to use the new equipment, and it helped to keep the fire from reaching tanks containing thousands of gallons of fuel oil. Despite

over the past sixty-two years. The calls coming in to the station are always unexpected and the risks to individual firemen cannot be accurately predicted. In a spectacular blaze at the United One Hour Cleaners and Shirt Launderers plant at 156 Delaware Avenue in Elsmere around 7:45 A.M. on May 8, 1960, three firemen were overcome by smoke at the scene. The building was a total loss.

this, acting chief Frederick C. Webster said the building was heavily damaged.

T. Bronk Van Derzee, chairman of the Board of Fire Commissioners of **Selkirk Fire District No. 1,** called a meeting of residents of the hamlet on July 3, 1928, "for the purpose of organizing a volunteer fire company."[41] Assistant chief Walter

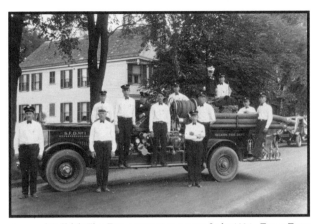

A proud Selkirk Fire Department at a parade in 1931. **Front Row** (standing on pavement, left to right): William M. Bennett, J. Bronk Van Derzee, chief; and George Young. **Second Row** (on truck): William Pausley, C. J. Woerhmann, Jr., A. J. Lehmann, Rubin White, Allen Winnie, C. J. Woerhmann, Donald Hansen, Charles Hansen, William Newberry, and Peter Hoffman.

Miller and fifty-eight others in the group made it clear that they were ready to fight fires, and all were directed "to familiarize themselves with the apparatus and pump according to a set of rules worked out earlier."[42] Although the minutes start with this meeting, a small group of dedicated people had been working for two years to obtain funding, develop a charter, and explain the plan to the public. W.L.L. Peltz was one of these dedicated supporters, a strong benefactor of Selkirk Fire Company No. 1 who provided money for equipment and for social events for the firemen and their families at his Hudson River home in Selkirk.

With strong leadership from Sanford Vint Van Derzee, the **Selkirk Fire Department** expanded to include Company No. 2 in Glenmont in 1952 and Company No. 3 in South Bethlehem in 1956, all under one Board of Fire Commissioners. Sometimes fire companies become involved in a huge fire as was the case with the LaCasa restaurant fire on Thatcher Street in Selkirk in 1979. Selkirk Company No. 1 could do little to stem the flames. Strong winds caused a reverse air current to reach the broiler, and co-owners Edward and Bernard Mocker said the loss was well above $225,000. It was a favorite meeting place for a number of community groups and a popular restaurant for hundreds of Bethlehem residents. Big fires are often in Bethlehem's end of the Port of Albany, where Selkirk firemen have sometimes spent days bringing a single fire under control.

On October 12, 1928, the **Slingerlands Fire Department** held its first meeting under the leadership of chief George Fowler. In the early months of the department's existence, the siren was sounded at 7:30 P.M. on meeting nights. A Sanford fire truck was purchased in 1929. Then, as now, fire protection was especially appreciated by the residents. The department's minutes for May 11, 1931, say that "a box of cigars was received from Father Charles [Kaulfuss] for help with the Banfil farm fire."[43] A new firehall was built in 1933 at a cost of $10,000.

The Slingerlands Fire Department was the first to install radio equipment in 1956, under the leadership of chief George Martin. "It was not only a first in Bethlehem but the first in Albany County."[44] No easy task to staff, the base radio station required the assistance of eighteen part-time operators that first year. The old Slingerlands railroad station Firehouse No.1 outlived its usefulness by 1964 and a new firehouse on New Scotland Road was completed in 1966. Today a second pumper station is located on New Scotland Road in the Karlsfeld section, now part of Albany but still operated by the Slingerlands Fire Department.

Last to organize was the **North Bethlehem Fire Department,** a movement spearheaded by chief Stephen B. Fliegel in 1948. Houses were going up in the hamlet by the dozens and protection was badly needed. A second-hand 1923 Brockway fire truck was purchased from Altamont for $450. This was just the beginning of a long struggle to acquire money for a firehouse and better equipment during a nine-year period before the department's incorporation into the town of Bethlehem on a contract basis. The firehouse was built in 1952 "with $500 in the bank and a lot of nerve."[45] From the beginning, the firehall has been a meeting place for dozens of community groups, an unusual community-centered philosophy for a fire company in any town.

Today, the North Bethlehem Fire Department is on much firmer ground with a contract with the town and a new Central States pumper purchased at a cost of $180,000. Further, there is a new pumper station serving North Bethlehem on Russell Road.

Ladies Auxiliaries

Firemen often acknowledge the crucial support provided by members of the ladies auxiliaries in all of the companies. They answer the telephones at the stations, help with fundraising, prepare publicity releases, handle correspondence, serve coffee at fires, and sponsor social events including holiday parties for children, to mention just a few of the 101 ways they help bring effective fire protection and community involvement to all of the hamlets throughout Bethlehem.

Rescue Services

From a single ambulance donated to the **Delmar Fire Department** in 1960, rescue services in Bethlehem have expanded to include several kinds of emergency service. The **Delmar Rescue Squad** offers Tri-Village residents advanced life support and paramedic assistance with the aid of two fully-equipped ambulances. The **Slingerlands Fire Department** goes anywhere in town where heavy rescue equipment is needed. "Jaws of life" equipment is used at major accidents. **Bethlehem Volunteer Ambulance** service has operated out of several different stations over the past forty years and is currently planning a permanent building on Route 9W near Selkirk. North Bethlehem offers its

Selkirk Fire Company No. 1 Emergency. Ray Keim on the hose with an unidentified assistant.

residents ambulance service under the hamlet's contract with the Western Turnpike Ambulance Service.

Dedicated volunteers have dealt with all types of emergencies over the years, from the tragedy of death and dying to the wonder of childbirth. A recent letter to the editor of *The Spotlight* is typical of the feelings of dozens of residents who benefit from emergency service every year:

> I cannot give enough thanks for my family to Bethlehem Police Officers Paul Roberts, Louis Corsi and Timothy Beebe, plus the crew of the Bethlehem Volunteer Ambulance, for their assistance in my wife's recent illness. With their help, an impossible situation became positive. They understand all the reasons for my gratitude.[46]

Following a request from the **Volunteer Fire Officers Association** in the town of Bethlehem, an Emergency Medical Services Task Force was formed in 1990 by supervisor Kenneth Ringler. The group will deal with a variety of problems facing the rescue services in a modern age. Volunteers are becoming less and less available at a time when the volume of calls in Bethlehem has exceeded 1,700 per year. Consideration is being given to using a mix of paid and volunteer personnel.

Growth and Nature of Fire Departments

Space limitations make it impossible to list the many firemen who have served their hamlets over the years since the **Delmar Fire Company** was established in 1911. The equipment now in use throughout Bethlehem would have a value well into the millions of dollars compared to the paltry sums expended as each company began. In terms of equipment, fire protection is big business today. The public is fortunate indeed that the service is still handled by volunteers.

Fire fighting is, in part, a family affair. A number of fathers, sons, and grandsons have been active in fighting fires in almost every hamlet. For most, the love affair with fighting fires probably began with dad taking his son to the station for an imaginary ride in a shiny red truck. Such was the case with Richard Webster who has been with the **Elsmere Fire Company** for eighteen years and is now serving as chief. His dad, Frederick C. Webster, a former chief of the company, has been a member for thirty-two years. Similarly, chief Charles A. Wickham, Jr., has served **Selkirk Fire Company No. 1** for fifteen years. His dad was a former chief of Company No. 1 and a long-term member until his death in 1989. His grandfather, Arthur Wickham, was a former chief of the Coeymans Hollow Fire Department. Charles Wickham's brother, Craig, liked firefighting with Selkirk Company No. 1 so much that he became a professional fireman with the City of Albany Fire Department.

The spirit of adventure, friendships with people of like interests, a desire to learn something new, and the wish to be really helpful to others in the community are still the main reasons young men stay with the departments today, but there is change afoot. Many younger wives are working, and a great many of the younger men have more responsibility at home. They have less time for socializing at the firehouse. Government regulations now require many hours of safety instruction and OSHA rules require more documentation when fires occur.

Owners of large businesses and industrial plants have a special reason to value the work of these dedicated volunteers. When a fire is too big for one volunteer company, companies from other parts of town and/or outside of town come to help. Cooperation among fire companies can spell the difference between light and heavy losses.

Some Final Thoughts

Looking back over the mass of data on community organizations assembled for this chapter, one is struck by the enduring quality of a large number of Bethlehem groups, especially during the present century. Many were founded by forceful leaders who left a legacy of group structure to fill varying needs, to resolve problems, and to enhance the cultural life of a dynamic, growing community.

A careful perusal of "Bethlehem Community Organizations in Brief"[47] in the appendix shows that most groups started with a good idea and grew in size and effectiveness over many years. There were Boy and Girl Scouts early in this century. We still have them. The need for an activist Progress Club is as great today as it was when the group was formed in 1901. There was a Bethlehem Conscript Society in 1875 to help government resolve its problems in the early years, and we have groups such as Bethlehem Citizens for Responsible Planning today. In short, citizens will find ways of addressing their problems and needs through organizations in every age.

But signs of change abound. Volunteerism is under assault as more women accept paid employment. Men have to do more around the house and have less time for organizational work. Many church groups are falling by the wayside as fewer parishioners are available to keep them going. Membership in some social and service groups is down, raising the specter of a higher rate of dissolution of such groups over the coming decade.

Still, as current supervisor, Kenneth Ringler, Jr., points out:

> A true spirit of volunteerism exists in our town and rarely is someone called upon who does not respond. We have many individuals who work quietly and effectively without being recognized for what they do.[48]

This book was turned out by volunteers. **Community Bethlehem** is one of the most recent organizations to demonstrate that where there is a will there is a way. And **Tri-Village Welcome Wagon** has exuded the very spirit of community for almost forty years, an impressive record of community service. Further, large numbers lend a hand when they believe in the cause. We fully expect that such causes will be around in 2093 and organizations will be there to do something about them.

Bethlehem report

SUMMER 1992 • Volume 18, No. 1

From the Supervisor's Desk

"Poor government comes around when good citizens sit on their hands instead of standing on their feet."

-- Robert Baker

This certainly is not a problem in Bethlehem, and as I sit back and think about the difficult problems confronting us, it is nice to reflect and realize what a wonderful community this is. The basis of this good community is the willingness of our residents to "stand on their feet" and assist government in any way to make our town a better place to live.

A true spirit of volunteerism exists in our town and rarely is someone called upon who does not respond. We have many individuals who work quietly and effectively without being recognized for what they do. The services and activities provided our Senior Citizens could not be accomplished without the many hours donated by volunteers to the community. A tally taken indicated that these services would cost close to $150,000 per year, if we had to pay for them.

On May 16, we celebrate **Community Bethlehem!** . . . a day in which volunteerism is once again in the forefront. The Bicentennial Commission, Reserve Police Force, EMS Task Force, Fire Departments, Ambulance Squads, Solid Waste Task Force, Bethlehem Opportunities Unlimited, Little League Pop Warner, Soccer, and Scouts are all examples, as the list goes on and on, of how residents give back to our town.

In this brief space, I wish to say thank you to all of you who are so willing to give.

Ken Ringler
Kenneth J. Ringler, Jr.
Supervisor

COMMUNITY BETHLEHEM!

Join your friends and neighbors at **Community Bethlehem!** on Saturday, May 16. This third annual celebration is a townwide series of events that encourage special spring cleanup projects for both neighborhood and public areas, a forum for environmentally related town issues, and an afternoon family outing featuring food and festivities.

This event was introduced in 1990 by Town Supervisor Kenneth J. Ringler, Jr. to encourage community spirit and pride in Bethlehem and to bring into focus a partnership of business, government, and residents. Each year, dozens of clean-up and improvement projects have been undertaken by a variety of groups in our town. Some are new projects, and a few have become repeat favorites.

The volunteer committee is chaired this year by Delmar resident, Mark Stuart. Coordinating involvement throughout the town of Bethlehem are: Lynn Corrigan, afternoon event coordinator; Cyndi Reilly for Scout troops; Carolyn Kaufman for volunteer fire companies; Holly Billings for school organizations and youth groups; Marty Cornelius for businesses; the Senior Services Office for senior citizens; Dave Austin, Town Hall liaison; Phil Mahar, treasurer; Karen Singerle, data coordinator, and Lorraine Smith, promotion coordinator.

The committee is organizing projects suggested by residents by assigning organizations offering their labor with the materials, talents, or financial resources donated by local businesses.

If you, your family, your office, your club, a group of your friends, or your neighborhood would like to volunteer a morning toward a spring assignment, or if you would like to suggest a project for Saturday, May 16, please call one of the following area coordinators:

North Bethlehem	Joseph Arnold	489-5762
Slingerlands	Pat Brewer	439-6365
Delmar/Elsmere	Cyndi Reilly	439-3481
Glenmont	Diane Smith	439-0512
Selkirk	Faith Fuller	767-2986
South Bethlehem	Joan Jurevis	767-2368

Afternoon festivities begin at 11:30 a.m. at the Slingerlands Volunteer Fire Company Park on New Scotland Avenue in Slingerlands. The afternoon includes music, entertainment by local groups, food and table displays by community organizations.

The afternoon events are open to the public and parking is available on site.

Community Bethlehem! is a special day set aside to celebrate and enhance our community. Join us!

Example of volunteerism *par excellence*, 1992.

8 Changing Families

Fellow Citizens: You have taken an oath of allegiance to a great ideal, to a great body of principles, to a great hope of the human race. And while you bring all countries with you, you come with a purpose of leaving all other countries behind you—bringing what is best of their spirit, but not looking over your shoulders and seeking to perpetuate what you intended to leave behind in them.

Woodrow Wilson, 1915.[1]

President Wilson could just as well have been talking to arrivals almost three centuries earlier, a mix of families and cultures who brought the best customs and values their countries had to offer and blended them with others in the rough and tumble of the New World. Although that "great body of principles" had yet to be firmed up, there was certainly a pioneering spirit among the early immigrant families and an almost inevitable need to compromise and adapt to the lifestyles of others.

Although the Dutch culture was dominant in our early history, there was a healthy linguistic and ethnic mix in the early immigrant group. For example, Albert Bratt, a Norwegian, married Annatie Barents, a German, before moving to this country in 1637. Here they worked and socialized with Dutch neighbors and other residents from a variety of European countries. The influence of these early immigrant families has persisted from the mid-seventeenth century to modern times. One merely has to look in a phone book to be reminded that life is an inexorable process of marriage that links family to family and century to century.

One such marriage united William Nicoll and Anna van Rensselaer whose son, Rensselaer, born in 1706, married Elizabeth Salisbury and constructed a beautiful home at the confluence of the Vloman Kill and Hudson River in Bethlehem. Built around 1735, Rensselaer and Elizabeth's home stands today as a monument to the lives of a privileged few in Bethlehem's early history. Other marriages require a discussion of well-known family stories in our history including the Babcocks, Kimmeys, Slingerlands, Van Derzees, and Van Allens, to mention just a few.

Bratt and Van Derzee Families Then and Now

Albert and Annatie Bratt, mentioned frequently in chapter two, deserve more space in order to describe their family life more fully and to trace the development of their descendants to modern times. Peter Christoph speculates that the home in which Albert and his family lived would have been an improvement over the primitive mill house they stayed in following their arrival on

April 7, 1637. The house they moved into on March 25, 1638, was located on the south side of the Normanskill near its entry into the Hudson River:

> The chimney would be stone instead of wood, and the main room would have an attractive birch floor. Wainscoting decorated the lower half of the walls, and there would be a real cupboard. Eventually, the fireplace would be bordered with decorative Dutch tiles. And Albert and Annatie would have a real bed, with a curtain for privacy. A brother, Arent, and other workers slept on the floor with the older children while Storm, now eighteen months old, had a shelf above the heads of his parents. However, the comfort that Albert and Annatie enjoyed was a relative thing, for in the short bed of that day they had to sleep in a semi-sitting position with a bolster and pillows supporting their backs. Such a position was thought to be good for their health.[2]

The move into their new house took place about six weeks prior to the couple's sixth wedding anniversary, and they may have reminisced about their beginnings as a family. Albert married Annatie Barents in the Dutch Reformed Church at Amsterdam, Holland, on Easter Sunday, April 11, 1632. Their daughter, Eva, was baptized early in 1633 in the Lutheran Church in Amsterdam as was their son, Barent, who was baptized in 1634. Albert is listed as a sailor in his marriage record, but became interested in planting tobacco prior to his arrival in the New World. His contract called for him to help build a sawmill and then experiment with a crop of tobacco.

Rowdy Family

Records suggest that it was a rowdy family, a pattern firmly established by Albert. A son, Andries, born after the couple's arrival in the New World, was charged with fighting in 1666 and fined thirty guilders.

In 1670, Andries and a partner were charged with giving lodging to three Indians with packs of beaver pelts. He said the Indians had only two or three beaver pelts, and were put up in a small house in the backyard. The court thought that was a flimsy story and fined Andries and his partner. Andries owned some farm land and a sawmill on the Normanskill and indulged in some fur trading on the side.[4]

The eldest son, Barent, married Susanna Meyer in 1654. She didn't get along with her brother-in-law, Storm, and twice took him to court for beating her. Storm was fined six guilders for calling her a whore. In another legal action in 1670, Susanna asked the court to order Storm, a tavern operator, not to give her husband either liquor or credit. The court warned him not to let Barent have any more credit under penalty of losing his money.[5]

In 1680, Susanna complained to the court about her husband's godless life of drinking, clinking, beating, and throwing. The court charged him with bad conduct and ordered him to conduct himself better and to live with his family in peace. He promised to behave and the record suggests that he did. Like others in the family, he operated a sawmill, farmed, and traded in furs. He paid off many of his debts with lumber.[6]

Perhaps the most colorful of the Bratt children was Storm, whose tavern was the center of many incidents in the last half of the seventeenth century. One court case underlines the intricate currency problems of the early colonists:

> Storm Bratt sued Roeloff Janse in 1675 for f136:19:8 in seawan, and brother Dirck, for twenty beaver pelts plus f6:4 in seawan for a total of f406:4, the beaver pelt being counted as f20 seawan. In the latter case, Dirck said he never refused to pay in seawan, and that he never promised to pay in beaver pelts, but if Storm would swear that he promised to pay in beaver pelts then he would pay in pelts, and Storm so swore.[7]

Storm Bratt was born on a ship during a harrowing storm on November 2, 1636, as the family traveled to the New World. By 1662, he was signing his name as Storm van der Zee (from the sea) in keeping with the Dutch custom of identifying oneself by place of origin, a clear case for the origin of the Vanderzee family name in Bethlehem's history.

Storm's tavern became a major center of community life. Although there is no record of his marriage, it is believed that he married in 1665, since his daughter, Anna, was born in 1666.[8] After his first wife's death, Storm married Hilletie Lansing who bore him three sons. Hilletie and Storm filed a joint will on February 2, 1679, prompted by his illness. The will directed that the children be taught reading, writing, and an honorable handicraft. He died sometime before May 6, 1679. His wish that his children be taught an honorable handicraft was fulfilled in part, for a contract has survived that apprenticed Gerrit to a tailor.[9] With four children, Hilletie could not afford the luxury of a long period of mourning. Within a few months she married William Ketelhuyn, who took over the management of Storm's tavern.[10]

The Bratts apparently were intrigued by the name Storm. Even the branch of the family that retained the original surname used the name frequently. On April 15, 1797, Bratts listed as working under overseer Wormer included "Storm Bratt, Storm D. Bratt, David Bratt, and Gerrett Bratt."[11] The name was often written as it sounded to the recorder. Some Bratts preferred to spell the name Bradt.

Albert and Annatie Bratt's daughter, Engeltie, married Teunis Slingerland, who created a family dynasty that would become a key element in Bethlehem's growth in the nineteenth century.

No record of the wedding survives, although the evidence points to a union of the two families around 1654. Teunis was apparently a family favorite, since he is shown in the record as having served as a business associate of his father-in-law, Albert Bratt, and as guardian of Albert's daughter Eva's children. The record also suggests that Teunis was a loyal helper when others in the family were in trouble. In contrast to the brawling Bratts, and in an age of hard-drinking tavern crowds, Teunis was a family man who stayed out of court and out of the limelight.[12]

The Slingerland Story

It was Teunis Slingerland who bailed Engeltie's younger brother, Dirck, out of jail after one of his more outrageous pranks. And during an epidemic in 1677 when Engeltie's sister, Gisseltie, and her husband, Hendrick Willemsen, were mortally ill, it was Teunis and Engeltie who cared for them. Hendrick's will was drawn when he was sick in bed at Teunis Slingerland's house.[13]

A 1663 incident shows that family support worked both ways. Teunis suffered a cash flow problem when he was unable to pay for a boatload of trade goods from Holland on which he owed 103 beaver pelts. With 103 beaver pelts, one could buy 103 muskets, or hire eleven common laborers for a year. Therefore, it was a transaction he badly wanted to finalize.[14] Teunis sold his wife's one-eighth interest in the Bratts' Manhattan house for forty beaver pelts. He paid off the remaining sixty-three pelts of his debt in wooden planks, valued at twenty planks to the pelt, 1,260 planks in all. His father-in-law's sawmill was the likely source of the planks.[15]

The above story underscores the advantages of close family relationships in Bethlehem's earliest period. It is the story of a compassionate family, a model for future generations. Family role models may have meant a great deal to descendant John I. Slingerland, since his exemplary record of service and leadership established a high standard for later Bethlehem residents to follow.

John I. Slingerland

No citizen is more deserving of praise for his impact on Bethlehem's progress in the nineteenth century than John I. Slingerland (1804-1861), son of John Albert and Leah Britt Slingerland, and grandson of fifth generation American Albert Slingerland. Much has been written about John I. Slingerland's advocacy of tenant rights, his work on early versions of the Homestead Act, and his role as one of the founders

John I. Slingerland.

of the Republican Party, an outcome of his membership in the Congress after 1848. Several of his eloquent speeches in the House of Representatives contain passionate statements against slavery, "that direful curse of human bondage that must be kept within constitutional limits."[16] His father is the first person listed in the town's record of the manumission of slaves: "John Slingerland, being the proprietor of a negro woman slave—which said slave had a child—born the tenth day of September 1799, being a boy named Jhack."[17] All newborn children of slaves were automatically freed under New York State law beginning in July 1799.

Less attention has been paid to John I. Slingerland's family life. He was married first in 1823 to Elizabeth Vanderzee, daughter of Harman Vanderzee and Axie Slingerland, and second, in 1835 to Sally Hall, daughter of Robert Hall and Sarah van Schaack. One of the most revealing records of John I. Slingerland's family life can be found in an account book he kept during the 1850s. Some entries show both a generous and controlling nature. In 1853 he listed many payments of cash to his wife Sally, but grew tired of her extravagances by February 1854 and penned the following item:

> Salley agrees to take one Dollar a week from the first day of March 1854 'till the first day of March 1855, and is to have no more than one Dollars per week, not another ct. signed: S. Slingerland and J. I. Slingerland.[18]

This confrontation may have been precipitated by an incident recorded in the same book in February 1854 when Slingerland wrote "cash to Sally she got it when A. Slingerland paid me in five dollar gold pieces—$25."[19] Sally may have demanded all of the gold.

However when tempers cool, hard feelings between husband and wife often fade as they probably did in this instance. Payments to Sally during the ensuing months far exceeded one dollar a week. In later entries the payments reflect an affluent woman's needs in the mid-nineteenth century:

> 1854—cash to Salley for dress, 3.25; shues, 2.50; new hat, 5.00. Cash to Dutch peddler Sally drove him away he would not go. 1856—cash to Sallay to get hat repaired, 2.75; to trim hat, 2.50; to trim her head for Pease's weding, 2.50.[20]

Evidence of Slingerland's innate leaning toward doing the human thing is sprinkled throughout the account book. As Jack, the family's black servant, grew older, he became a trusted friend and supervisor of the children when the parents were away. It was a bond of friendship and service that would last through several generations of the John Albert and John I. Slingerland families. The record suggests both personal support and a tenant/farmer relationship with Jack in July 1854:

Cash to Jack for 8 bush of rie, 35.00; load of hay, 10.00; cash to Jack for new coat and his cap. 8.50; for mendin his boots, 1.00; for himself to get close [clothes], 4.00; to go to minstrals, 1.00.[21]

Slingerland was generous with the church as well as with family members and servants. The account book lists many payments to the Delmar Reformed Church in the mid-1850s, including his share of Reverend John Lansing's salary, repairs to the church, donations to other churches, and payments to his employees so they could keep up their pledges to their own churches.

Locally, the account book reveals an honest man respected for his leadership and for opening his purse to worthy causes. Nationally, the record suggests a preoccupation with the common man, the rights of tenants, the key role of farmers, and the right of all people to be free.

John I. Slingerland died at the family home at 1575 New Scotland Road where he spent much of his life, a few hundred feet from the Albany and Susquehanna Railroad line he worked so hard to secure for Bethlehem. Owned and occupied by George and Kathleen Bragle in recent years, the exterior of the house is little-changed from Mr. Slingerland's days there.

William Henry Slingerland

William Henry Slingerland, 1906.

It is important to mention William Slingerland (1820-1910), younger brother of John I., because of his stature as a surveyor, his successful effort to obtain a post office for Normanskill (renamed Slingerlands through his intervention in 1870), and his pioneering contribution to Bethlehem when he organized the Suburban Water Company in 1901, a service that would last nearly a century. He won high praise for his work on federal and state projects, which may have helped him in gaining election to the New York State Assembly in the 1880s. He was responsible for the removal of the beautiful but unsafe stone ceiling in the assembly chamber, and for the installation of the present wooden ceiling.

William Henry married first, in 1842, Elizabeth Wayne, daughter of George Wayne and Elizabeth Coughtry, who bore him six children. His second marriage in 1868 was to Maria J. Whitbeck, daughter of Andrew Whitbeck and Charlotte A. Bronck.

Beautiful Slingerland Home and the Family Vault

William Henry's 1837 Greek revival home at 1620 New Scotland Road was the center of family activities for much of his life, and continues today as one of Bethlehem's finest examples of this style of architecture. He moved to a more palatial residence in the 1500 block of New Scotland Road late in life, close to the post office and railroad in which the family had a vested interest. The house no longer exists, but the family vault is located on land nearby.

The burial vault was the site of the Bethlehem Archaeology Group's first excavation in 1981, where research to support authentic restoration was the primary goal. Pieces of a long-lost marble marker were recovered from the soil in front of the vault. When reassembled, it read:

> THE FAMILY VAULT OF
> JOHN I. AND WM. HENRY SLINGERLAND
> ERECTED IN A.D. 1852.[22]

William Henry Slingerland died in 1910. He rests in a sarcophagus on the floor of the vault. The marble marker of a second sarcophagus was broken and carried off by vandals in the 1940s, but a careful search of the records revealed its occupant as John H. Slingerland, who died in 1914. He was the son of William Henry Slingerland.

Rensselaer and Elizabeth Nicoll

Rensselaer Nicoll and his wife Elizabeth Salisbury, mentioned above, are shown on the 1767 Bleeker map on page 317 (Chapter 11), along with several dozen other early Bethlehem families. Nicoll was a judge. His grandfather Mathias Nicoll was both a chief judge and a major official in the colonial government, and his father, William Nicoll, was attorney-general and speaker of the assembly.

Kiliaen van Rensselaer Nicoll (ca. 1706-1776), son of William Nicoll and Anna van Rensselaer, married Elizabeth Salisbury, daughter of Francis Salisbury and Maria van Gaasbeck of Catskill, around 1730. He inherited a farm at the confluence of the Vloman Kill and Hudson River in Cedar Hill, land that was first farmed by Cornelis van Nes in the 1640s. It is possible that Rensselaer dropped the 's' from the end of his family name, although his only surviving signatures leave this matter in doubt. In any event, the land he inherited is part of the property to which the name Bethlehem was first applied, and the home he and Elizabeth built on the property around 1735 is called Bethlehem House.

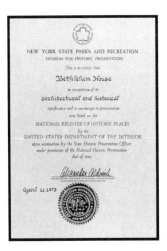

Nicoll-Sill Home in Cedar Hill, 1991 photo.

Historic Bethlehem House

The recently restored Bethlehem mansion is a spacious twenty-four room Dutch-style home with cut stone foundation walls. The exterior walls are of load-bearing brick laid up in Dutch cross bond. The original section and 1795 addition feature a gambrel roof.[23] The house was restored recently under the supervision of the late town historian, Thomas E. Mulligan, and his son, Paul, the present occupant.

The Sill Connection

Elizabeth and Rensselaer Nicoll, builders of Bethlehem House, had four children including Francis (1737-1817), who married Margaret Van Rensselaer in 1762. Colonel Francis Nicoll took over the house when his mother died in 1790.

Margaret and Francis Nicoll's daughter Elizabeth married Major Richard Sill at the house in 1785. Their oldest son, William Nicoll Sill (1786-1844), lived much of his early life with his grandparents, Francis and Margaret Nicoll, and inherited the house when Francis died in 1817. Thereafter, Sill families occupied Bethlehem House until it was sold by Lydia Sill in 1875.

Exciting Archaeological Finds

Excavations conducted on the estate from 1982 through 1986 produced thousands of artifacts and an excellent picture of the life-styles of the many families who lived in the house between 1735 and 1960. Only the highlights are presented here.

Elizabeth Salisbury Nicoll (1712-1790) may have owned some beautiful underglaze-decorated

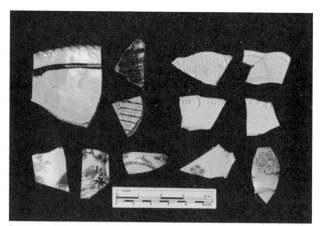

Representative sample of probable ceramic choices of Elizabeth Salisbury Nicoll, ca. 1712-1790.

Chinese porcelain prior to her marriage in the early 1730s, and the record suggests that she bought a wide variety of high quality English pottery during the years she lived in the building. Fine quality English saltglazed stoneware gave way to English creamware for everyday service, and attractive but fragile English delftware may have been used as serving plates and bowls. The accompanying photograph shows all of these types of pottery, as well as pie-edged slipware and thick, strong redware, which were probably used in the kitchen.

A careful analysis of about 13,000 pottery fragments recovered from the property in the 1980s shows that a large percentage of the dishes used by many families over the building's 250-year existence were manufactured in England. Since these were affluent families, the findings suggest that owning pottery imported from England was probably a mark of status, a validation of one's success in life.

Leisurely Living

Although this was a successful farm that involved a great deal of hard work, especially by servants, the archaeological record shows that the residents enjoyed a number of recreational activities such as hunting with muskets in the early years, and high powered rifles in this century. Further, recovery of several clay and stone marbles suggests that the residents played Chinese checkers around the turn of the nineteenth century. Bone

dominoes, found on the estate and dating to the 1830s, recall the timeless nature of some games which have delighted generation after generation.

A common activity, at least for the men during the first two centuries of the existence of Bethlehem House, was smoking long, white, clay pipes. Twenty-five hundred stem and

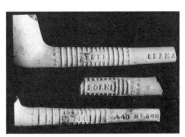
Nineteenth-century smoking pipes.

bowl fragments were found around the estate, indicating that this was a major leisure time activity. Men living in the house in the nineteenth century smoked a highly ornamental pipe made by the German pipe maker, Peter Dorni. Only one nearly complete pipe was found, which could mean that pipe smokers in the early years smoked a bowl of tobacco, broke off the tip, and then put the pipe away for another smoke, at which time the process was repeated.

Children used to write on slate in the eighteenth century, however the "chalk" used in the early years was like the type shown in the accompanying

School at home in the 1740s.

photograph. It was recovered from the north lawn of the estate, along with a piece of slate marked with the initials "FN" (Francis Nicoll?). The pottery with it dated to the 1740s, about the time of his childhood.

Daily Living Around the House

The soil around Bethlehem House yielded evidence of sumptuous living—fragments of wine glasses and bottles, quality buttons, beads, works of mantlepiece clocks, and thousands of bottle fragments which tell stories about the products used by the families down through the centuries. Some of the bottle fragments indicate usage of alcohol-laced patent medicines, a nineteenth-century phenomenon that lasted until the passage of the Food and Drug Act in 1907.[24]

One such medicine was sold by Dr. J. Hostetter, whose advertisements for his stomach bitters suggested that one should take one wine-glassful three times a day. His product was touted as a swift and certain cure for dyspepsia, liver com-

Strong medicine about 1860.

plaint, and every species of indigestion—an unfailing remedy for intermittent fever, ague, and all kinds of flux, colies, and choleric maladies.[25] Swift is the key word in the advertisement. Hostetter's product, enjoyed by someone in Bethlehem House, was forty-seven percent alcohol or ninety-four proof. It was so potent that the government bought it by the carload as an aid to Union soldiers in facing up to the enemy during the Civil War.

Excavators noticed fragments of three dark, olive-green wine or spirits bottles under the trunk of a huge sycamore tree, when it was removed from the south lawn of the estate in the mid-1980s. Legend holds that the tree was planted by Colonel Francis Nicoll and his wife, Margaret Van Rensselaer, in the 1790s. All of the bottles were free blown and were probably manufactured in Europe. The three wine bottles suggested a party to some of the excavators and one said, "How about a toast to Elizabeth Nicoll, daughter of Francis and Margaret, who married Major Richard Sill in the house in 1785?"[26]

The suggestion brought shouts of affirmation, but the group learned later that a descendant of Elizabeth and Richard Sill found an undertaker's bill for Rensselaer Nicoll's funeral in the garret of the old house and two items attracted attention—a charge for five gallons of rum and five gallons of gin.[27] This would support the concept of funerals as festive occasions in eighteenth-century Bethlehem, although there is no way of learning whether the above wine bottles are related to the marriage, the funeral, or to regular dining in the mansion. One thing is sure—such wine or spirits would have been served by black servants in the Nicoll home.

Of Slaves and Servants

Caesar: Nicoll-Sill family servant, 1737-1852.

Occasional references in the record to black families living in Bethlehem House suggest that they were treated as servants rather than slaves. However, the word slaves was used on December 19, 1800, when Francis Nicoll asked town clerk Jacob Ten Eyck to record the birth of two black children:

Being a proprietor of two Negro wimen Slaves which Said Slaves head each a Child Born the one was born on the Eighteenth Day of March & being a male Name Ceasar the Other a female Born on the third day of May 1800 Named Diaune[28]

Whether or not the male named "Ceasar" mentioned above was related to the senior servant with the same first name who had been with the family since 1737 is open to question, but such a relationship is logical. In any event, a 1799 New York State law required Francis Nicoll to register the births and to free the children when they could care for themselves. Colonel Nicoll is shown in later pages of the same record freeing "Dian" and several additional slave children in 1814. All slaves in New York were emancipated by 1827. There is no need to repeat the story of the well-known Caesar (1737-1852), who served the Nicoll and Sill families through three generations, since it was nicely told in one of Allison Bennett's books,[29] but it is important to show the relationship between these early Caesars and modern-day black families in Bethlehem.

Ruth Geddies Blackmore: Story of a Black Family

Ruth and Charles Blackmore live on Route 396 in Selkirk, very near her family's ancestral home at the point where Beaver Dam Road intersects Route 396. Ruth's mother, Ida VanDeusen, and grandmother, Grace Knott VanDeusen, trace their family back to Caesar Augustus VanDeusen who married Ann Marie Scofield in 1860. His parents and grandparents served early Bethlehem families during the turbulent transition from slavery to servants between 1799 and 1827. Caesar and Ann VanDeusen passed away in 1929 and are buried in Graceland Cemetery on Delaware Avenue in Albany, which was formerly part of the town of Bethlehem.

Ruth Blackmore in recent years.

tional Harvester Company clerk, Charles likes sports and many outdoor activities. Ruth shares his interest in sports, having served as secretary for the Capital Area Golfers Club for a number of years. In many ways, Ruth and Charles have answered a query posed by Ralph Ellison in 1964:

> Can a people live and develop over three hundred years by simply reacting? Are American Negroes simply the creation of white men, or have they at least helped to create themselves out of what they found around them.[30]

Clearly, Ruth and Charles Blackmore have created their own stable family and maintain close ties to their children who live in places as close as Watervliet and Athol, Massachusetts, and as far away as Denver and Houston.

Local Families in a Free America

After the American Revolution and as the full meaning of a free America developed in the minds of local families around 1800, it was time for taking stock. By now, most area citizens who did

Ruth and Charles Blackmore, ca. 1950.

Ruth Geddies was born in 1931, attended the one-room elementary school just off Route 396, and graduated from the old high school in Ravena in 1949. She worked at Jacobsen's Shirt Factory for a year before her marriage to Charles J. Blackmore in 1950. They had five children between 1952 and 1958 and found time to pursue their favorite hobbies as well. Ruth loves jazz and has a large record and tape collection. A retired Interna-

First Reformed Church of Bethlehem at Selkirk farmhouse and barns, 1800-1946. Sketch by Margaret Foster.

Probable key to front door of the First Reformed Church of Bethlehem at Selkirk, ca. 1825.

vials suggest visits by the doctor, and long, white clay pipe fragments show that pipe smoking was practiced in the shadow of the church. A key believed to fit a lock on a door to the original church building was found near the back steps, mute testimony to the need for security in the late 1700s.

After 1821, the property was leased to farmers. Margaret and Marcus Lasher paid $125 per year for the use of the farm. In 1836, the rent was $225, a fee that would remain constant during their last five years on the farm. Elizabeth and John Leedings took over the farm in 1841 and stayed until 1855. They were followed by Margaret and Jurian Leedings, who remained from 1856 to 1880. Thereafter, a number of families rented the property for short periods, except for Anna and Spencer Gallup who ran the farm between 1910 and 1925, and Dorothy and Henry Golden who were there between 1936 and 1946, the year the farmhouse burned to the ground.

Quality of Life on the Church Farm

They lived surprisingly well, judging from the possessions they left behind. During excavations conducted by the Bethlehem Archaeology Group between 1986 and 1989, it was learned that several

not want to live under the new government had gone to Canada. Jacob Ten Eyck had replaced Philip Van Rensselaer as town supervisor following Van Rensselaer's death in 1798. His task was to search for solutions to Bethlehem's three main problems: roads, bridges, and predatory wolves.

It was a time when farms covered most of the town, a subject amply documented in the chapter on farms in this volume. It may be useful to show how several average families lived on the farm of the First Reformed Church of Bethlehem where light farming was practiced and the man of the house was often the sexton of the church. Here, living was easy, at least in comparison to the larger farms where there was pressure to raise large crops for sale.

The church farmhouse was used by several ministers and their families for twenty years after it was built in 1800, and the objects they left behind reflected their status in life. High quality hand-decorated pearlware adorned the table, medicine

of the early families owned attractive English whiteware transfer-printed with pastoral and historic scenes and probably reserved for company. A silver baby-spoon inscribed with the initials "JL" and probably owned by John or Jurian Leedings was found near the house, along with good quality scissors, straight-edged razors, and a number of metal objects used with horse harnesses.

 A little-worn Bank of Montreal halfpenny dated 1842 was found near the front doorstep. The find raised a spirited discussion among the excavators who questioned whether or not Margaret and Jurian Leedings actually traveled to Montreal. It was a time when plank roads were in vogue and railroad travel was but a gleam in the eyes of the big financiers. Most of us doubted that such a trip took place.

An archaeologist's dream—artifacts dating to about 1860 found by Ann Jacobs.

There was no such thing as recycling waste around the middle of the nineteenth century. Instead, the residents dug a hole and buried their waste near the house as the accompanying photograph amply demonstrates. This scene from about 1860 shows that one of the families used a cross-cut saw to cut up their fireplace wood, stoneware crocks to store their food, hair dye to maintain a youthful appearance, medicine to cure their ills, transfer-printed whiteware to impress their guests, and spirits to liven up the party. The nature of nineteenth-century life is more clearly revealed when the contents of dozens of similar trash pits are excavated and interpreted as a whole.

Hair dye came in small bottles. The families living on the church farm used brands manufactured by J.H. Thompson and Bachelors prior to 1850 and Blasies and Hills after 1850. In the same vein, they liked linaments manufactured by Hunts and Birdsalls and ink bottled by Dovells and Staffords, all commonly used products throughout the nineteenth century. Additionally, stoneware bottle fragments found on the farm show that the families living after 1875 indulged in the

Nineteenth-century hair dye bottles. First Reformed Church of Bethlehem Farm.

well-known mineral water "cure," which was so popular in the last quarter of the century and well into this century.

A pit along the front of the farmhouse yielded a small, thin, medicine vial dating to the 1860s. It was a time when Dr. John Babcock refilled such vials during home visits from large bottles in his carriage.

Medicine vial about 1866.

Bottles were scarce and Dr. Babcock was happy to refill a container owned by the patient and/or take unneeded vials back to his office at Beckers Corners. We will take an imaginary tour with Dr. Babcock in 1866, and look in on several families encountered on his rounds.

John Babcock, M.D., ca. 1866.

A Tour With the Doctor in 1866

Following his visit with Margaret and Jurian Leedings at the church farm, during which he might have refilled their medicine vials, Dr. Babcock traveled south on the present Route 144 to the farm of Caroline and Cornelius Baker. Caroline Lasher Baker was being fitted for a new dress:

> Her beige suit was trimmed with gray and white plaid and consisted of a skirt, overskirt, round waist, and mantle. The skirt was being cut from taffeta silk, and measured forty-two inches and a half in the front, forty-five inches and a half in the back and two yards and an eighth around the bottom. It was trimmed with a plain beige pleating three inches deep.[31]

The doctor joked with Caroline about her modest beginning as the daughter of Margaret and Marcus Lasher on the church farm, and went directly to her husband's bedroom. It was nothing serious.

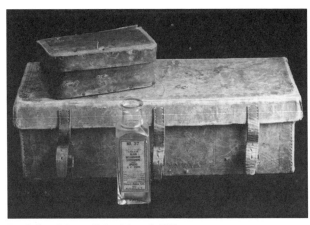

Dr. Babcock's medicine kit and pillbox.

Cornelius Baker had a mild ague, or fever, and needed mostly rest from his busy work schedule. Baker was a successful businessman who owned many acres on both sides of the road near the Coeymans/Bethlehem town line, land that had been in the family since 1791.

After a bite of lunch back at his Beckers Corners home, Dr. Babcock set out for two visits at Vanderzee homes along the main road in South Bethlehem. He stopped at the Baumes Chapel in Cedar Hill on the way because Mr. Baumes wanted to talk about means of dealing with the problem of alcoholism in the community. Then, as now, it was a difficult social problem and organizations such as Sons of Temperance were having little success in saving souls. The two men talked about the inadequacy of their training for dealing

with such social problems. Dr. Babcock graduated from the Vermont Academy of Medicine in the early 1840s. Most American medical schools in the mid-nineteenth century had "extremely low standards. They usually required the completion of two school years of nine months each, plus a term of service with a medical practitioner."[32] By the early 1860s, he was routinely granted a license to practice medicine upon payment of ten dollars a year to the Internal Revenue Department. Still, these credentials were of little help when he was faced with an alcoholic in his office.

It was like visiting family during his stops at Vanderzee homes, since Babcock married Hester Vanderzee around 1842 and was well acquainted with all of her relatives. The Vanderzee name is spelled differently by various members of the family, but this spelling was common in 1866. It was a family that would persist over the centuries down through Bronk and John Van Derzee, who lived in Selkirk during the early decades of this century, and Henry C. and Henry M. Van Derzee, who lived in South Bethlehem around the same time. Many trace their lineage back to Storm Van der Zee through John and Elizabeth Vanderzee. Some specialized in the law, such as Newton B. Van Derzee, Sr., and others in investment work such as S. Vint Van Derzee and his son, Pieter, who is currently vice president of Kidder, Peabody and Company, an affiliate of the General Electric Company.

Dr. Babcock's license, 1864.

A messenger on horseback caught up with Dr. Babcock as he left the H.M. Vanderzee home and urged him to ride up to John Wiltsie's old home just a little to the north. Old John died before the Civil War and his son, John Ambrose, was running the farm at age twenty. John Ambrose still had heavy problems with skin blemishes. Little was known about the cause of such rashes at the time. The doctor suspected a disease of unknown origin but could only prescribe an ointment and regular washing with Pear's Soap.

On his way back to the office at Beckers Corners, Dr. Babcock crossed the Hudson-Saratoga railroad tracks deep in thought. Railroad travel might help him eventually but, for now, it was no substitute for a good horse and carriage. He thought about a patient, Barent Staats Winne, Sr., he would see that afternoon. Although he was mainly concerned with healing people, not their family histories, it was common knowledge that his well-known patient was a descendant of Pieter Winne, the original Winne who arrived here in 1652. Barent, Sr., was a descendant of Pieter and son of Daniel Winne. Daniel built a stone house near the Winne dock on the Hudson River a little north of present-day Henry Hudson Park

Winne Dock and Barge Business

Barent Staats Winne, Sr., tore down the old stone homestead and built a stately house on the same site in 1857 with profits from his successful barge business at the Winne dock. His son, Barent Winne, Jr., married Lena Gallup Van Derzee in 1910 and continued the business until his death in

AUCTION

CARL G. BRUST   -   AUCTIONEER

WILL SELL AT PUBLIC AUCTION TO SETTLE THE ESTATE OF THE LATE LENA WINNE, AT THE PROPERTY LOCATED 7 MILES SOUTH OF ALBANY — OFF OF ROUTE No. 144, ON

Winne Road, Cedar Hill

SATUR., NOV. 18

AT 10 O'CLOCK, SHARP, THE FOLLOWING PROPERTY:

COMPLETE CONTENTS OF HOME
ANTIQUES
AND
HOUSEHOLD GOODS

(Weber) square body grand piano	Gold mirrors (various sizes)	Porch furniture, 3 Radios
Victorian cameo back settee	Gold frames, Brass bed	Candlesticks, Foot-stools
Victorian lady's rocker and man's rocker	American and Oriental rugs	Card tables, Many old books
4 Straight Victorian chairs	Marble-top hall tree	2 Antique dolls with china
Large sofa, Large baby cradle	O. G. mirrors, Vases	heads, Chafing dish
3 Combination book case and	Drop-leaf mahogany table	2 Electrolux vacuum cleaners
desk, Large wooden bowl	Tilt-top table	Rrfrigerator, Electric stove
7 Pieces marble-top furniture:	Sewing stands with 2 drawers	Kitchen table and chairs
Stands, dressers, commodes	Child's high chair	Ironing boards, Toaster
Victor record player with horn	China, Silverware, Glassware	Kitchen cabinet, Card tables
Several pine blanket chests	Cut and pressed glass, Dishes	Kitchen utensils
Wash bowl and pitcher sets	Several clocks, Sheets	Speed Queen washer
2 Spinning wheels	Blankets, Quilts, Linens	Folding chairs, Stepladders
Oil paintings, Jugs and crocks	3 Bedroom sets, complete	2 Electric heaters, Jardinieres
Many pictures and frames	Dining room set	Straight ladders, Scales, Crocks
	2 Sewing machines, Flatirons	Wheelbarrow, Small tools
	2 Wicker chairs, Bear rug	Lawn mowers, Etc., etc.

1955 CHRYSLER SEDAN (WINDSOR — Full power, two new snow tires, 27,000 miles, excellent condition.

REFRESHMENTS   SERVED
TERMS   CASH

No Property Removed Until Settled For   Sale Positive — Rain or Shine.

By Order of THE EXECUTOR

CARL G. BRUST, AUCTIONEER --- 31 GARDNER TERRACE, DELMAR. PHONE HE 9-4697.

an automobile accident in February 1932. He handled the company during a period of declining river traffic when the barge-freight business faced increasing competition from the railroads.

When the contents of the Winne home were sold at auction after Lena Winne's death in the early 1960s, the items reflected a transition from the nineteenth to the twentieth century, as well as a life-style of privilege and the end of an era for this industrious family in Bethlehem's history. The house is occupied today by Freeman and Sherry Putney.

Richard Kimmey, ca. 1866.

Another patient of Dr. Babcock was Richard Kimmey, who talked business as well as his health with the doctor, because both men were directors of the Bethlehem Mutual Insurance Association. Sooner or later, the talk turned to Richard's problems as the first president of the Association. Now called Bethlehem-New Scotland Mutual Insurance Company, this venerable institution is still serving citizens in our area. Dr.

Babcock had been treating many members of the Kimmey family since the 1840s. In the early years, they were concentrated around Philip Kimmey's beautiful home at Kimmeys Corners in South Bethlehem.

Family Health Problems

Most citizens had various ailments in 1866. Some were afflicted with such problems as ague (fever), jaundice, consumption (tuberculosis), and dropsy, now called edema in which the legs swell due to heart or kidney failure. Indeed, galloping consumption, or aggressive tuberculosis, had sent a good many Bethlehem residents to the cemetery before Dr. Babcock could do much to help them.

However, some Kimmeys lived on, married, had children, and their children had more children in this century. The late Warren Kimmey of Slingerlands traced his family lineage back to the earliest Kimmeys through his father, Clarence Peter (1880-1945) and grandfather Peter D. (1819-1898), who is believed to have been one of Dr. Babcock's patients. Warren Kimmey married Joanne Glenn, daughter of John Glenn and granddaughter of William A. and Nettie Glenn, who made their home at 248 Delaware Avenue in Elsmere. It was a union of two well-known families in Bethlehem's history.

Judge William Alexander Glenn: former Bethlehem town attorney, and first president of the Normanside Country Club.

Nettie Vanderzee Glenn: cofounder of the Bethlehem Women's Republican Club.

Home of William A. and Nettie Vanderzee Glenn in Elsmere. Built by John Vanderzee, ca. 1905.

Facing up to the Modern World

Early in the twentieth century, life in Bethlehem was decidedly on the upswing. Sarsparilla was the beverage of choice for those who didn't want the hard stuff, main street shopping was in vogue, homemakers cleaned with Fels Naphtha, experimental automobiles excited the well-to-do, a potato peeler was the latest gadget in the home, electric irons took some of the drudgery out of pressing clothes, and the box camera enabled amateurs to capture all of this on film.

Dr. John Babcock passed away in 1879, but by then a new group of better-trained medical practitioners was visiting families all over town. They rode in attractive horse-drawn surreys with comfortable, padded seats and front wheels much smaller than the rear wheels. The family doctor could purchase such a surrey for seventy to ninety dollars from a Sears Roebuck catalogue as late as 1898. A more modest phaeton, seating two people, could be purchased for about forty dollars.

Popular physician Edward J. Bedell took over many of Dr. Babcock's patients after 1878, culminating in a name-recognition advantage that enabled

Ca. 1885.

him to run for the position of town supervisor in 1899. He won hands down with 619 votes to Charles Coonley's 406 votes. He served as the grand old man of the local Republican party and as a consultant to those in power well into this century, through his office at his son Joseph's home on Borthwick Avenue in Delmar.

Cedar Hill home built by John Taylor Cooper, ca. 1836.

James B. Lyon's "summer home" in Cedar Hill, ca. 1915. Note Cooper's 1836 home, right side of picture.

Dr. Bedell continued to see some of his elderly friends in his twilight years, including James B. Lyon of Cedar Hill, who founded a printing business in 1876 and built a large plant on Beaver Street at Market Square in Albany. Lyon sold the business in 1916. It became part of the Williams Printing Company in 1923. The Lyons were typical of several well-to-do families with business interests in Albany and homes in Bethlehem along the Hudson River. In 1890, Lyon purchased the former John Taylor Cooper home in Cedar Hill and moved the family here permanently after his retirement in 1916. The accompanying photograph shows the original Cooper home and the palatial

John Taylor Cooper, ca. 1866.

mansion it became under Lyon's guiding hand. An empire builder in everything he did, Lyon's life-style matched his boundless ambition.

Together, James and his wife, Anita Thompson Lyon, entertained business associates and government leaders in their Cedar Hill home with quiet parties in gracious surroundings. Evidence of such entertaining was still visible in 1986 behind the outbuildings on the property. The Bethlehem Archaeology Group recovered dozens of early twentieth-century dish fragments and bottles from the estate between 1985 and 1988, along with several hundred

James B. Lyon, 1906.

Entertainment at the James B. Lyon Home, ca. 1920.

record of this remarkable family is maintained by the senior Lyon's granddaughter, Mary Elizabeth Lyon Van Oostenbrugge, who lives on part of the estate today.

The New Generation

Daniel C. Case, M.D., 1906.

As we continue to look at life in Bethlehem through the eyes of physicians, the record shows that several doctors were helping early twentieth-century families. Dr. J. R. Davidson's practice was largely in South Bethlehem, Dr. D.C. Case worked from his Slingerlands home, and Dr. J. B. Washburn had an office in Delmar. All of these dedicated professionals were paid seventy-five dollars a year from the town coffers for their service to the poor, while Dr. Bedell's more experienced service was worth $100.[34] Dr. Hallenbeck of Delmar also served the poor during some of the early years of this century.

objects which await analysis in the laboratory. Judging from the number of containers recovered, various brands of imported spirits were enjoyed by Lyon guests who stayed for delicious steak meals graced with Maggi sauce. Mr. Lyon also entertained at a rustic bungalow on the Hudson River from where he took as many as two dozen friends at a time on boat rides in his steam-powered launch.

Anthony Catalano, a chauffeur on the estate after 1922, said the senior Mr. Lyon "owned a 1914 Pierce Arrow Coach"[33] and the artifacts confirm a gradual transition from the horse and buggy phase of our history to extensive use of the automobile after 1910. James B. Lyon, Jr., managed the estate and Lyon business interests after his father's death in 1929. The house burned in 1964, but a detailed

By 1916, young Thomas Holmes, a recent medical school graduate, was well into a career of service to Bethlehem residents from his Kenwood Avenue residence. People came from all over the

207

area to see Dr. Holmes. Although home visits were less frequent, he started up his car two or three times a day and traveled over dusty roads to all corners of Bethlehem before and after his service in World War I, a story told in the military chapter in this volume. When the heavy snows arrived, he drained the fluids and put his car up on blocks of wood in the garage and reverted to the tried-and-true horse and sleigh.

1912 Buick Phaeton, ca. 1914. Front seat: William A. Glenn (hand on wheel) and John M. Vanderzee (holding Elizabeth Eleanor Glenn). **Rear seat (left to right):** Hannah Conger, Catherine M. Vanderzee, and Nettie V. Glenn (holding Catherine M. Glenn).

Dr. Holmes liked to talk cars and did so occasionally with William A. Glenn, attorney for the town and a strong Republican ally. Glenn was proud of a 1912 Buick Phaeton he owned in earlier years that was powered by a thirty-eight horsepower four cylinder engine. It featured carbide tank headlights, all leather seats, and a roof that could be folded back in nice weather. Glenn often took the whole family for a ride in the countryside in the Buick. He traded it for a new Buick touring car in 1916, but the new car didn't have the pep the old car had. It was designed to go a little faster than older cars, although most drivers were honoring the signs limiting automobile speed approved by town board in 1909. In that year, residents of Delmar asked members of town board to

take some action to stop the furious driving through town. Town attorney Glenn read the law on speeding autos and Town Board directed that signs be erected requiring drivers to slow down to one mile in four minutes (15 MPH) and one mile in fifteen minutes (4 MPH) on the bridges.[35]

Dr. Holmes's associate at his 455 Kenwood Avenue office in 1942 was Dr. Robert L. MacDowell, who carried on a general practice here after Dr. Holmes retired. Dr. MacDowell's son, Richard, epitomizes the new generation through his current practice as a surgeon at the Albany Medical Center.

Toward the end of his career, Dr. Holmes consulted frequently with Dr. Harold R. Browne when both served different generations of the same families, among them Frank Boutelle, the stationmaster in Slingerlands, and his son, Edward Boutelle, who later moved to Delmar. Browne's office was in his home, which was next to Edward and Marietta Boutelle's home at 413 Kenwood Avenue in Delmar. It was a cozy, neighborly relationship in which patients learned that they could reach him in an emergency by calling the Boutelle number when Dr. Browne was making his rounds.

Bethlehem on the Map

Edward Boutelle was a talented draftsman whose hand lettering could not be distinguished from mechanical lettering. He took an International Correspondence course in the early 1920s and was certified as a professional engineer and surveyor when such certification was begun by New York State in 1923. His son, Lindsay, joined the firm in 1949, following his graduation from Duke University's School of Engineering. Records in the company's files show considerable

involvement of the Boutelle company in many building projects and developments since 1925. Father and son provided property-line surveys, site plans, and utility designs for dozens of Bethlehem projects, ranging from Mayfair Estates and the Kenholm Subdivision in the early years to the Town Squire Shopping Center in Glenmont and the Delaware Plaza in later years.

Changing Fashions, Foods and Gadgets

Doctors Bedell, Case, Holmes, and Browne not only watched the parade of change in this century, they were part of it. Dr. Bedell's stories were colored with references to clothing worn around

The well-dressed Bethlehem man in 1908.

Charles and Emma Frazier with daughter, Helen, 1905.

the turn of the twentieth century. His relationship to the firm of Bedell-Corscadden and Youngs at Maiden Lane and James Street in Albany is unclear, but the firm was well-known as the place for well-dressed Bethlehem men to go for advice and fine clothes.

The Albany company carried a line of clothing manufactured by Hackett, Carhart and Company of New York City, which had a reputation for setting standards of dress in the early decades of this century. The company issued an illustrated booklet with advice on what to wear and when to wear it. Men could discover when to wear their brown derby versus their silk "topper," and what jewelry to wear at major events. Women in less affluent Bethlehem families got similar advice when they shopped at B. Lodge and Company at 109 North Pearl Street in Albany. This was a favorite stop because the store carried clothing for all members of the family, as well as a selected line of home necessities.

Dr. Case tried to avoid making house calls on Saturday evenings but sometimes duty called and he often ran into well-dressed families going out for dinner or special events. They were sometimes dressed like Charles and Emma Frazier, shown with their daughter Helen in the accompanying photograph taken in 1905. The Fraziers lived at 30 Maple Avenue in Slingerlands. Dresses were often long and ornate. Men wore bowler hats, and the faces of little girls were sometimes surrounded with a flaring lace-like bonnet that made them look like the dolls with which they played.

Around the turn of the century Emma Frazier made pie crusts from scratch, but her daughters watched this basic household practice change to making crusts from a mix in the 1930s to buying the whole pie in a store in the 1960s. Similarly, food was sweetened with honey by Emma Frazier, and her daughters saw this practice change to sugar in the 1930s, saccharin in the 1960s and aspartame today. Of course, sugar and honey are still used. Homemade cookies were a big treat in Emma Frazier's time, whereas her daughters enjoyed ice cream more frequently in the 1930s, various junk foods in the 1960s, and a wide range of fast foods and frozen delectables in the 1980s.[36] Although heavily committed to railroad travel because of his long years of work for the Delaware and Hudson Railroad Company, Charles Frazier succumbed to the lure of automobile travel when he purchased a used Buick in 1921. Now the family could enjoy a wider range of entertainment without having to wait for the next train. They drove to Albany for Charlie Chaplin movies, to visit relatives with whom they occasionally stayed for two or three days, and to places of business in Delmar and Albany. In later years, Bethlehem residents could purchase a four-door sedan in the 1930s, a station wagon in the 1960s, and a mini-van in the 1980s.

The evolution of clothing styles from one century to the next can be seen in a photograph showing Mrs. John S. Van Allen in a long, billowing black dress, her daughter Elizabeth in clothing more typical of the first decade in this century, and Marjorie, daughter of Elizabeth and Emmett A.

Elizabeth Van Allen Terrell, standing, her mother, Mrs. John S. Van Allen, and her daughter, Marjorie Terrell.

Terrell, with a loose, high-necked white dress, a common style worn by young girls around 1912.

Marjorie Terrell lived through the flapper period in the 1920s, knitted, bag-like dresses in the 1940s and 1950s, and wide swings in dress lengths well above and well below the knees in recent years. Mention changes in this century in Bethlehem and Marjorie has been there. She worked hard on the Van Allen farm during her teen years and moved on to a job with the telephone company in 1925. She changed from using an iron heated on the stove to an electric iron when it came along, but developed a healthy skepticism about all the new gadgets that have supposedly made life easier for families. Marjorie absolutely refuses to buy the microwave oven so popular with young families today. "Don't need it," she says. "The stove cooks perfectly well."[37]

Modern Families With Roots in the Community

The few families presented thus far were selected mainly to illustrate change over Bethlehem's long life as a growing, dynamic community. It is not possible to include very many of the dozens of worthy families who have helped to make Bethlehem one of the most desirable places to live throughout the greater Albany area. Still, it may be useful to browse through some early twentieth-century telephone directories and present some facts about a few families chosen at random, simply because they remind the writer of events in this century.

Early Telephone Directories

The 1908 Hudson River Telephone Company directory lists an E. A. Niver in Selkirk. He was related to D. M. Niver, author of a history of Bethlehem in 1887, whose stories about slaves and their masters in early Bethlehem are fascinating, but unfortunately undocumented. He mentioned the Houghtalings as early Bethlehem residents, a fact backed up by no less than 105 listings under the name in *People of Bethlehem*, published by the Town of Bethlehem Historical Association in 1982.[38] The spelling of this name has been shortened over the years and the directory shows Reverend B. J. Hotaling living in Selkirk along with Charles R. Hotaling. John Hotaling is listed under South Bethlehem in the same directory. Hotalings in Bethlehem have built houses, taught school, run businesses, operated farms, and generally contributed to most phases of life here.

The 1908 directory also lists Spencer Gallup living in South Bethlehem. He is probably the same Spencer Gallup who married Anna Becker and rented the First Reformed Church of Bethlehem farm between 1910 and 1925. Spencer was paid $150 a year to serve as sexton of the church in 1910. Archaeological research in the barn area shows considerable building activity during Gallup's tenure. A new machine toolshed was built, an equipment storage building was renovated, and extensive repairs were made. Further, Dr. James E. Gallup and B. H. Gallup are listed in a later directory as living on Kenwood Avenue. All of these Gallups are probably related and can very likely be traced to either Elias M. or Isaac Gallup, early members of this family who are buried in the Elmwood Cemetery on Route 9W in Selkirk.[39]

The same directory shows William A. Glenn living at 248 Delaware Avenue in Elsmere. He was the town's attorney over many decades. His wife, Nettie Van Derzee Glenn, worked closely with Ruth Miner in founding the Bethlehem Women's Republican Club and was well-known for her delightful parties at the Normanside Country Club, which her husband helped found in 1927.

Further, the directory lists William H. S. Miner, admired by some for his sharp business deals as a Slingerlands milk dealer. Much of his business was done on the telephone. The New York Telephone directory in 1917 indicates that a call to Ballston Spa was twenty-five cents and to Glens Falls forty cents. His daughter, Ruth, mentioned above, became an attorney who served the town, county, and state in a variety of responsible positions. She was in much demand as a speaker at local and Albany area events, a bright, energetic woman who blazed a trail in the world of work for other women to follow.

The 1917 directory also shows Alton C. Rowe, a charter member and first captain of the Delmar Fire Department, a charter member of Bethlehem Masonic Lodge 1096, and town supervisor between 1924 and 1931. His wife, Caroline, started the Tri-Village Directory in 1930. Telephone numbers in 1917 represented the best technology of the day. When others wanted to talk to the Rowes they asked the operator to ring 131-M.

Finally, it would be remiss of me not to mention the listing of Frederick Goldring's Greenhouse in the 1908 and 1917 directories. This recalls for many older residents the beautiful flowers and plants he sold at his Slingerlands home. "As a young man, Goldring worked at Kew Gardens just outside of London, one of the great botanical gardens in the world."[40] "They lived on Font Grove Road, then a rural oasis among the milieu of suburbia,"[41] in a large home of French design. "Joyce Goldring, a tall, spare woman whose agility belies her years, and whose warmth and humor is so reminiscent of your favorite aunt of past years, tends to the lawn and keeps the house in immaculate order."[42]

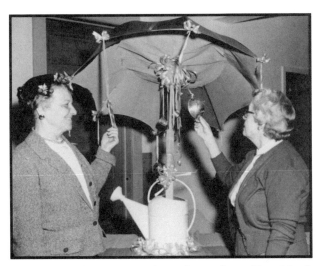

Ruth Miner (left), attorney and popular speaker, with unidentified hostess.

Family Directory of Delmar—1913

The first page of the 1913 *Family Directory of Delmar*, issued by the Progress Club, shows Nathaniel Adams, his wife, and three children living on Kenwood Avenue. It is assumed that this is Nathaniel, Jr., son of Nathaniel, Sr., who bought land in 1835 near the Four Corners and built a hotel there. The original records describing the land transfer of the hotel property are owned by William Howard of Delmar, author of the military chapter in this book. They show the transition from payments to the patroon, to ownership of the land by Dexter Brown, and the sale of the land to Nathaniel Adams, Sr., on February 13, 1835. Nathaniel Adams, Sr., and George C. Adams, town supervisor from 1867 to 1870, left an indelible impression in Bethlehem's history, a record rarely matched by other families. Many residents remember Earl C. Adams, who owned Adams Hardware at 380 Delaware Avenue near the Four Corners. The family is listed in the 1917 New York Telephone directory. Earl and Irma Adams were living at 17 1/2 Adams Place in 1930, a convenient location to get to their hardware store in a hurry when a valued customer had a special problem on a weekend. Earl Adams's son,

Details of the Adams land purchase at Four Corners from Dexter Brown in 1835.

Earl C. Adams hardware store at the Four Corners in Delmar, ca. 1929.

Robert, ran the store in recent years. His former store is now the Village Furniture Company.

Mrs. Catherine E. Bennett is listed in the *Family Directory* as living on Delaware Avenue with Frank Bennett, author of the Bennett family history, and Daniel A. Bennett, originator of the plumbing business so well-known among Bethlehem homeowners. Others shown at the same address are Emily M., William M., H. Alton and Walter Bennett. Additionally, Mary E. Bennett is listed as living on Kenwood Avenue. William M. and William D. Bennett are familiar names among area residents because of their affiliation with the Security Supply Corporation in Selkirk. Finally, Allison Chesebro Bennett, wife of William D., has a large following throughout the greater Albany area for her books on local history. If he were alive today, the original Daniel Bennett (1777-1813), who came by sailboat to Albany and tramped westward through heavily wooded, sparsely settled country looking for work, would be amazed to see the family's progress over the last two centuries.

The *Family Directory* also lists the Henry Geurtze family living on Hudson Avenue, which included his wife, sons Harold H., Raymond J., Henry K. [Kenneth], Paul, and daughter Pearl. Later records show that Harold married Ruth Rose, moved to Woodbridge Road, Elsmere, in 1926, and founded the contracting business familiar to so many Bethlehem residents today. Henry passed away in 1961 and his son, Harold Geurtze, Jr., has continued the business.

In the 1940s, many Bethlehem families sent their children to college, financed, in part, by the GI Education Bill introduced after the close of World War II. John B. Geurtze, son of Harold, completed a program in poultry husbandry at Cornell University toward the end of the decade. His chicken barbecues for numerous Bethlehem social events are an institution in themselves. Harold, Jr., enrolled in a civil engineering program at the Clarkson Institute of Technology.

Boutelle Directory of *Property Owners at Delmar and Elsmere*

Edward W. Boutelle completed a map of part of Bethlehem in 1930, and published a directory of *Property Owners at Delmar and Elsmere*[43] to go with the map. In addition to many of the families mentioned above, the Boutelle directory lists David R. Main, popular constable and later the first chief of police, whose story is told in the government chapter. Main married Ella A. Mynders on August 15, 1893. He was prone to discuss his antique clock hobby with anyone who entered his home.

Wedding invitation of David Main.

The Boutelle Directory shows John and Florence Glenn living at 37 Herrick Avenue. John is remembered for his tireless and effective service on Bethlehem's Board of Education between 1942 and 1959. The Hamagrael School and Bethlehem Central High School buildings were built during his tenure. John Glenn once journeyed to Oxford, Ohio, where the famous author of *McGuffey Readers*, William Holmes McGuffey, formerly taught at Miami University. Glenn brought back a supply of *McGuffey Readers* for the Hamagrael School, and this led to naming the street that passes by the school McGuffey Lane. The son of William A. and Nettie Glenn, John is typical of many citizens in Bethlehem who have held high level leadership positions in the greater Albany area in this century. He served as chairman of the Salvation Army's Advisory Board, a position also held by his daughter, Joanne Glenn Kimmey, in recent years. He was a lawyer and employed in his father's law firm.

The same directory shows the growth in property owned by Alton and Caroline Rowe, mentioned earlier in these pages. The former town supervisor and his wife are listed as owners of twenty-two parcels of property on five different streets in Delmar, but mostly along Roweland Avenue. Other families owning many parcels of property in Delmar or Elsmere in 1930 were Edward and Sara Bedell, Theodore and Jennie Burhans, George and Madge Casey, Julius and Clementine Fox, John and Anna Herber, and George and Belle Paddock.

It was a time when the big building boom had yet to come. Many additional parcels of land were tied up in the George Adams estate and the Elsmere Development Corporation. Howard and Frances Paddock were living at 400 Delaware Avenue in 1930, the base for Howard's beginning as Bethlehem's real estate entrepreneur par excellence. His deals over the next few decades would accelerate the pace of development and change the face of Bethlehem in dramatic fashion.

The Changing Family

Looking back over everything I have learned about Bethlehem families during the twenty-six years Coleen and I have lived here, I am struck by the explosive growth in numbers in selected time periods and by the shoulder-to-the-wheel behavior of so many families at crucial times in our history. When roads were needed in the beginning, men of all ages pitched in to get the job done and women were with them every step of the way. Farm families, in which everyone worked hard, created outstanding crops and a reputation for quality agricultural products unmatched by other communities in the greater Albany area.

Over the centuries, as more and more families were attracted to Bethlehem's rural landscape, and in later years, as the railroad delivered hundreds of visitors and commuters to our doorsteps, thousands of men and women thought of Bethlehem as the best place to live while pursuing their jobs in Albany. Buses and automobiles accentuated this trend, and today numerous families are struggling to control the factors unleashed by their presence in such large numbers, destined to reach 30,000 within a few years.

Despite all of these trends and problems, average family members living here in recent years like their life in Bethlehem. Many have tried moving elsewhere for short periods, but moved back because they liked the life-style here better. The reasons are individual, but collectively they add up to one undeniable fact—after a period of adjustment to everything new, most families enjoy living in Bethlehem.

PROMINENT PEOPLE IN LOCAL HISTORY. Upper left: Rhogenia Adams, ca. 1835. **Lower left:** Nathaniel Adams, Sr. (1802-1892), ca. 1835. **Above:** Clarence A. Blanchard, Sr. and his wife Grace Adams Blanchard at home, 403 Delaware Avenue, ca. 1935.

⑨ From Oxen to Diesel

Farming in the town of Bethlehem began in the early 1600s. It was the mainstay of colonial life and would continue to have a vital role in Bethlehem's development.

As the farm population grew, so did its agricultural concerns and problems. As non-farm communities became more prevalent, their increasing demands influenced farm production and prices. In addition, government initiated and developed farm policies, laws, and regulations. It therefore became evident to the farmers that they needed agricultural guidance and representation in government. Consequently, agencies such as the New York State Agricultural Society and the New York State Farm Bureau Federation (now New York Farm Bureau) and organizations such as the Grange were founded to promote agriculture and represent farmers' interests in local and state governments. Several Bethlehem farmers held offices in these associations and many farmers supported them through memberships.

Local farmers participated in state and county fairs. These events played a vital role in the promotion of agriculture and related products. Dealers exhibited farm equipment and new machinery. Farmers entered fine livestock and garden specimens that were evaluated by judges, with prize money awarded to top winners. Fairs also provided the opportunity for farmers to exchange views on farming techniques and theories.

Agriculture has had and continues to have a vital role in our lives. Daniel Webster, once United States Secretary of State, said, "When tillage begins...other arts follow. The farmers are the founders of civilization."[1]

Over the years, farmers have faced monumental challenges, but through their dedicated efforts they have produced a bounty of farm products, livestock, and livestock feed for local and world markets.

This chapter focuses on several local farmers but is dedicated to the hundreds of farmers who have tilled Bethlehem's soil.

A Region to be Developed—Dutch Farmers Arrive

Kiliaen van Rensselaer was among the few men in the early 1600s who were willing to start colonies in New Netherland. Acting on van Rensselaer's instructions, an agent was to purchase flat and arable land, islands, and inland to include forests and mountains.[2] The selected region provided areas for farms both large and small to be established in the Colony of Rensselaerswyck, which would be under the jurisdiction of Patroon van Rensselaer.

On March 21, 1630, forty-year old Brandt Peelen left Holland. He accompanied patroon-appointed supervisor Wolfert Gerritsen, thirty-two-year old Rutger Hendricksen, and five laborers on the ship *de Eendracht*, bound for the colony of Rensselaerswyck in New Netherland[3]—a new world filled with opportunities and many uncertainties. After an arduous two-month voyage, they arrived at New Amsterdam and settled near Fort Orange. It was not long before two farms were established. To the east of the river was a farm called Laetsburg, and located on Castle (Westerlo) Island was the farm Rensselaersburg.[4] This area is located on the Hudson River at the present-day Port of Albany. The distant scenic Berkshire Mountains are to the east and the picturesque Heldebergs are to the west of the area.

Since life was concentrated on or near waterways, the Hudson River provided a convenient highway to the outside world for trade and travel. The river and local creeks furnished the early settlers with an unlimited supply of fish. In addition, the region provided a suitable environment for a variety of wild game and berries to supplement the settlers' diet.

Agricultural opportunities abounded for those who recognized and understood the value of good soil and possessed the determination to work the land to its potential. Much work was in store for these pioneer farmers who chose to make their home on Bethlehem's soil. Taming a hostile wilderness, enduring severe winters, living under unpredictable conditions, and farming with crude equipment (by modern standards) are circumstances many people of today would relate to with difficulty. However, early farmers persevered and built a future for themselves and their families.

Agriculture—Vital To a Successful Colony

Even though the Rensselaerswyck colony was a business venture, van Rensselaer seemed to be concerned with the well-being of his colonists and realized how vital agriculture would be to his colony. In correspondence dated 1632, he stated:

> Now at first we must have a little patience and necessarily spend money to obtain possession. After the first harvest, which is at hand, I hope that our people will no longer have lack of wheat, milk, butter or cheese; they can catch plenty of fish with little trouble and in the course of time they will also have plenty of meat as they have already oxen in the field, of which they can slaughter one at killing time. I intend now by this ship to send six or eight more heifer calves. If we had cattle we should have money and if we had horses we should have wheat. I take good care to avail myself of all opportunities to acquire cattle, which makes many jealous of me, but they have to stand it, as every one is free to do what is best for himself.[5]

Farm implements and wagons were available in the colony. Additionally, the livestock included horses, cows, sheep, and hogs. In some instances, any increase in livestock was divided between the farmer and patroon. Then if the patroon so desired, he could sell them or establish new farms with his portion.

Rensselaersburg was established with a house, barn, two hay barracks, a sheepcote, and a variety of farm equipment. It was farmed by Rutger Hendricksen and Brandt Peelen. The amount of grain harvested on their farm was twelve morgens (about twenty-four acres) of winter wheat and four (approximately eight acres) of winter rye. It was anticipated that eight to ten morgens of summer seed would be planted. The following year, the amount of land plowed was eight morgens (perhaps this was designated for the summer seed). By 1633, the livestock on Rensselaersburg was to include six horses, five head of cattle, six hogs, and sixteen sheep. The grains grown had amounted to fourteen morgens of winter wheat and two morgens of rye, and four morgens were devoted to oats, peas, and other crops. As additional farms were established, Peelen would later work Welysburg, another farm located on the island.[6]

Van Rensselaer understood the importance of livestock and perhaps realized the difficulties encountered with preparing the land to make it suitable for farming in his colony. He stated:

> ...our principal profit will come from the cattle, for which there is plenty of fine pasture and hay for nothing but the labor...the clearing of the land proceeds with slowness but a certainty of which I have no doubt at all if the Lord preserves us from surprisals.[7]

Essential crops for farmers, grains were used as payment for rent and sold in New Netherland. "No better farmers ever came to America than the Dutch. They were industrious and above all knew how to till the soil to make it produce."[8] Working assiduously, their grain fields were planted by mid-May and harvested by mid-August. The common grains grown were wheat, barley, oats, buckwheat, canary seed, and flax. Their gardens eventually included beans, corn, peas, potatoes, turnips, and other crops.[9]

Van Rensselaer enriched the existing farms and established new ones in Rensselaerswyck by supplying additional farm animals, tools, and equipment. His leasing terms for farms attracted additional farmers. Since farm animals were considered property, the leases also dealt with livestock increases and how they were to be divided. Records were kept on agricultural activity in Rensselaerswyck including the number of livestock, the animals' gender, how many were born, and how many died. Records were also kept on the type and amount of each grain grown and harvested in the colony.

Van Rensselaer seemed to have wanted his colony to be self-sufficient. He contracted with people to build houses, barns, sawmills, and gristmills. In addition, he specified in some contracts that these persons were to be available for hire to do other types of work whether it be felling trees for logs, carpentry, or farm labor. Farmers were encouraged to furnish each other with various tools and other essentials critical to colonial farm life and to keep written records as to what was received and/or given out.[10] These were some of the significant factors that structured the successful Rensselaerswyck.

What Became of these Earliest Pioneers?

During the period from 1634 to 1638, five farm hands, Hendrick Carstensen, Thomas Jansen, Jacob Pietersen, Gijsbert Adriaensen, and Claes Gerritsen, served under Peelen's guidance. These farm workers eventually relocated elsewhere. The two men who sailed from Holland and started with Peelen were Wolfert Gerritsen and Rutger Hendricksen. Gerritsen was released from duty at Rensselaerswyck in 1632, and Hendricksen left the colony in 1634. Brandt Peelen helped develop the land on Westerlo Island into productive farms. Although he contracted for four years as a farmer, he stayed and faithfully farmed the land on Westerlo Island until his death sometime before May 1, 1644. The Welysburg farm then went to Cornelis Segersen van Voorhout.[11]

Devoted Tillers of the Soil

Interestingly enough, even in the beginning, leases and contracts had significant roles in the lives of farmers and their patroon. Since farms were rented from the patroon, payment was usually a predetermined percentage of grain or whatever provisions were stipulated in the farmer's contract.

Farmers Pieter Claesen (Niclaesen), Albert Andriesen (Bratt), Aert Jacobsen, Pieter Winne (Winnen), and Jan Labatje were among those who leased land or farms and thus helped build Bethlehem's agricultural foundation. The following brief history of each farmer and his farm was obtained from the *Van Rensselaer Bowier Manuscripts*:

- Records indicate Pieter Claesen (Niclaesen) occupied a Bethlehem farm for one year and left the colony by June 5, 1649.[12]

- In 1637, Albert Andriesen (called Bratt after 1670) joined Rensselaerswyck. He was a tobacco planter and helped construct a mill in the colony. In May 1652, he rented property and two mills on the Normanskill.[13]

- Aert Jacobsen leased a farm. In 1651, there were six horses and eight cattle (three mares, three stallions, three cows, three heifers, and two bull calves) on his farm. Sometime before February 1654, a fire destroyed the house, barn, and barracks. The settlement for damages amounted to

300 guilders of wheat at ten guilders a mudde (3.056 bushels) for which he was responsible to pay in two installments. After farming for six years in Bethlehem, he moved to Greenbush and farmed there for twelve years.[14]

• Pieter Winne occupied a farm from 1652 to 1655. In April 1655, he leased it with permission from Rensselaerswyck's director, Mr. Johan Baptista van Rensselaer, to Eldert Gerbertsen Cruyf for 275 guilders a year in addition to the tithes. Wheat and oats, at ten and four guilders a mudde respectively, would be used as payment. The buildings were valued at 2,400 guilders. The lease stated the number of livestock that came with the farm as three full grown mares, one yearling mare, one stallion, one gelding, four cows, and one yearling bull. Any increase in livestock would be divided. If the young mare should die, the lease indicated a way Cruyf could make good for the loss of the animal. Cruyf operated the farm until May 1, 1658. In addition, he leased a sawmill and two horses that were used at the mill for a two-year period.[15]

• From 1654 to 1661, Jan Labatje leased a farm from Johan Baptista van Rensselaer for 300 guilders a year, payable in wheat and oats. The farm, previously rented by Jan Barentsen Wemp, included a house, barn, and three barracks which were valued at 1,760 guilders. Labatje was responsible for the general maintenance of the buildings.[16] Provisions in his lease specified that the livestock (mares, stallions, a filly, three cows, and a heifer) that came with the farm were considered property of the farm. The livestock were not to leave the colony without approval from van Rensselaer or the person in charge. Labatje's lease dealt with increases of farm animals and how the increases were to be divided.[17]

Indians Influenced Farming Practices

In spite of occasional conflicts with the Indians, the colonial farmers were influenced by the natives' farming methods. According to author Lymann Carrier, "crops and their method of culture developed by the Indians have been appropriated by the white man and have proved of untold value to humanity."[18]

Most farmers, Indian or colonist, realized that fertile soil was important. Since land at the time was plentiful, the Indians practiced field rotation rather than crop rotation. Referred to as "resting the land," it proved to be a valuable method of restoring fertility to the soil.[19]

Carrier also mentioned the crops, techniques, and practices shared by the American Indians with colonial farmers. They included the following:

• Indians had successfully grown corn, kidney beans, lima beans, varieties of squashes, and pumpkins.

• Hill planting was adopted by many farmers. Small hills were formed by mounds of soil spaced two and one half feet apart with five to six grains of maize (Indian corn) planted in each. This method continues to be recommended not only for corn but for melons, squash, and cucumbers.

• A beneficial practice was "clean cultivation." Indians hand-cultivated the soil around the planted seeds. This process discouraged weed growth and encouraged crop growth. The Indians kept the soil loose and free of weeds on and around the hills.

• Underground pits were used by the Indians to store certain foods during the unproductive months. A hole was dug in the ground and then lined with mats. A covered basket filled with foodstuff was inserted, another mat was placed on top, then all was covered with soil.

• To preserve certain foods, the Indians used drying or smoking methods. Corncribs were popular as they allowed the corn to air dry. The process could be hastened by building a small fire underneath the corncrib and regulating the heat. This method prevented weevils from destroying stored grains.

• The Indians made cornmeal, a coarse flour, by grinding dried corn. Cornmeal was used to make breads with variations that were considerably tastier when wild nuts or in-season wild fruits like strawberries, huckleberries, or raspberries were added to the batter.[20]

Farming—A Family Affair

The children tended to the lighter chores. They helped feed the animals, cleaned stalls, and placed clean straw down on the stall floors as bedding for the animals. Children fetched water and gathered wood for the fire. They collected the eggs from the henhouse, picked fruits and vegetables, and were of help during planting and harvesting times.

The farm wife grew accustomed to long days and hard work. She cared for her family's vegetable garden, gathered eggs, herbs, and berries, and preserved vegetables and meat. She also cared for her children and modest home, made clothes for herself and her family, and helped her husband whenever an extra hand was needed in the barn or fields.

Serving hearty meals could have presented an occasional culinary challenge for the cook. In an open-hearth fireplace, wild game or roasts were cooked on a spit and stews and soups were simmered in large, heavy, iron kettles and pots.[21] Corn, wheat, and rye breads were made by placing the bread dough into an iron kettle with a tight fitting lid, then covering it with hot embers and baking until done.[22] "A common dish was *erwten* [peas] or pea soup [*erwtensoep*] served most often with *olykoeks*, a roll that has been likened to doughnuts or bagels, and pumpkin bread, made from the vegetable the Indians showed them [the Dutch housewives] how to use."[23] In a kitchen furnished with basic utensils, the farmer's wife made butter, cheese, breads and cakes, toast, and waffles served with cinnamon and sugar. In some homes, when tea was served, an unusual item and practice was the "bite and stir" sugar box. The container was divided into two sections. One was filled with regular sugar for stirring into tea and the other contained sugar cubes that were nibbled with tea.[24] The kitchen also served as a focal point in family life where meals were eaten and shared chores such as candlemaking and sewing took place.[25]

Occasionally, clothing would be purchased for special occasions. The woman's cloth dress had mid-length sleeves and a full skirt gathered at the waist, overlaying several petticoats. Her dress was accented with a white shawl. She usually wore a cap and an apron. "The farmer wore a coat-shirt of cotton or wool called a *hemdrok*, over it a larger cloth *paltrok* for warmth, a steeple hat, and wooden shoes for work-days and leather shoes for Sundays."[26]

The kitchen was also a place to entertain an occasional visitor or two. A fire in the fireplace provided light, heat, and enhanced the delicate fragrances of dried herbs and spices and provided an atmosphere to warm the hearts of those who entered the kitchen. Even in the twentieth century, the kitchen continued to be a focal point. Most of the interviews for this chapter, the conversations that followed, and reminiscing of times-gone-by took place in the warm, friendly atmosphere of the kitchen.

Establishing a Farm Was Hard Work and Took Time

Agriculture continued to play a vital role in the lives of colonists. "In spite of wasteful methods and poor tools, the colonial farmer was as prosperous as any farmer of the day, anywhere in the world."[27] "Hardships, privation and self-denial were the first fruits of their venture; the harvest was in the future to be reaped by their descendants and those who followed after."[28] They were the pioneers of agriculture and helped to establish a foundation upon which later generations built.

Hand-tools—Vital to Pioneer Farmers

Farmers used basic tools to clear land and work the soil. Essential to their work were axes, spades, shovels, hoes, and rakes. The mattock, a simple tool similar to a pick axe on one end with a flat blade on the other (or possibly on both ends), was especially useful for loosening soil and for cutting roots from the ground. Hay knives and scythes were used to clear thick foliage and cut hay crops and clover, which were left to dry and then harvested as winter feed for the livestock. The sith and mathook were used to harvest grains.[29] The sith had a small handle attached to a short, straight section with a long curved blade on the end. The mathook, however, had a much longer and straighter handle with a tapered hand grip area. On the opposite end of the handle was a short, narrow hook. The farmer held the sith in one hand, and with a sweeping motion cut the collected grain held upright in the mathook that was held in the other hand. With a sweeping motion in the opposite direction, he then tossed the cut, bundled grain off the mathook to the side creating rows. These bundles of grain were collected, placed on horse-drawn wagons, and transported to the barn. The bundled grain was then placed on the floor where it was flailed, a process of threshing (beating) the grain by hand to remove the seeds of grain from the straw. The grain could then be ground into flour, used to make livestock feed, or sold. The straw was used for bedding livestock and for stuffing mattresses for beds. Other grain harvesting hand-tools introduced much later were the reaping hook and cradle scythe. The reaping hook (similar to sickle) was used to cut the grain. The cradle scythe had a long handle with two hand grips attached. On the other end was a curved blade situated just under several wooden "fingers." The farmer would swing the hand implement into the standing grain, thus cutting and cradling it, then on the back swing, dump the loosely bundled grain in rows for easier handling.

Cradle scythe, used for harvesting grain.

Clearing the Land

Manual labor was used to clear additional farmland. Men worked diligently using axes to fell trees, a quicker method than girdling. (Girdling was done by stripping a section of bark from around the tree thus stopping the flow of sap and killing the tree.)[30] Several long days could pass before the task of clearing the land would be completed. "A skilled woodsman, it is estimated, could clear an acre [approximately 208 feet by 208 feet] in seven to ten days. The average pioneer could hardly hope to clear and sow ten acres the first year even if he did little else."[31] Some of the logs were hewn into boards and used to construct dwellings for colonists and shelters for the animals.

Preparing the Soil

Preparing the soil for cultivation was another arduous task. Plowing required a workhorse or an ox to be harnessed to a one-blade wooden plow, a simple but valuable implement. Gradually, the plow was improved by making the section in front of the wooden moldboard of bar-iron. It was called a hog plow, and it penetrated the soil easier than its predecessor.[32] However, no matter how skilled the farmer was, it must have been challenging to maneuver the animal and plow over the ground. If the soil required further manipulation, hoeing or harrowing broke the clumps into a finer consistency, making it suitable for planting.

If the weather were cooperative, there would be enough rain to moisten the earth so the seeds would germinate. With God's will and the farmer's devoted care, the fields of grains and other crops flourished into a bounty for harvest.

A Need to Improve

Farming progressed slowly in spite of successful crops. The farm implements and tools, methods of fertilization and cultivation, crops, seeds, and grasses needed improvement. There was an increasing awareness that better overall farming techniques were necessary. Therefore, the 1700s were geared to developing mechanical implements and improving crops, grasses for hay, and farming techniques.

The first agricultural machine considered modern was the seed drill developed by Jethro Tull in 1701.[33] This mechanical implement enabled the farmer to seed fields efficiently and reduce manual labor. Manufacturers also continued to modify the plow. Even though the cast-iron plow was patented in 1785 in England, it was not until around 1797 that it would be used in some American fields.[34] These implements made a significant impact in the farm communities.

Colonial farmers continued to learn more about replacing soil nutrients, the importance of crop rotation, and fertilization with manure or by other methods. After the farmer cleared some land, he burned the brush or smaller tree branches and applied the ashes to the soil. Phosphates could be restored to the soil by applying compost made from waste material and ground bones.[35]

Another concern for farmers was soil erosion, particularly for those farms located near and around hills or gullies. Remedial and preventive methods needed to be studied and applied. Although knowledge was gained in both these areas, they would continue to be among the concerns faced by farmers.

During this era, clover and various hay crops were introduced which improved the quality of livestock hay for winter feeding. Timothy was sprouting in the fields around 1746, red clover was grown by 1749.[36] These hay crops, in addition to ryegrass, orchard grass, alfalfa, and other varieties of hay, became popular with area farmers.

Wheat continued to be an important crop. During the winter months, most local farmers transported their grain to Albany, a central marketplace. There it was sold to flour and feed merchants or exported. February 8, 1794, was recognized as a record day on which 25,000 to 30,000 bushels of wheat were handled.[37]

Advancements Are Made

Many changes were made in the 1800s. The Dutch continued to improve their farming skills and increase their crops and herds. In addition to fields planted with a variety of grains, Dutch farmers planted "orchards of apple, pear, cherry and peach trees and had introduced the best foundation stock of horses and cattle to be found in any of the American colonies at the time."[38] Other nationalities, particularly Irish, German, and English, immigrated and established farms.

Agencies Founded For Farmers

As farming became a viable economic industry, the importance of proper representation in local, state, and federal governments became evident to the farmers. Local farmers were among the founders, officers, and members of such agencies and organizations. These agencies and organizations also set standards, promoted better farming methods and breeding practices that improved herds, and provided information that had a profound effect on the industry.

Scientific farming received a boost during the 1800s. The "experiments of gentlemen farmers, the exhibits at county fairs, and the spread of information in the press helped to popularize the principles of sound husbandry."[39]

A Board of Agriculture was formed by the New York State Legislature in 1819. The Board published an annual report and, until 1825, provided financial support to county societies by allocating $10,000 a year in prize monies.[40]

The New York State Agricultural Society was reorganized in 1841 with Bethlehem's Joel B. Nott as president.[41] Its members held annual fairs and published books crammed with detailed information and statistics relevant to farmers. The Society's annual cattle show and fair were held at Auburn, New York, in September 1846. Prize money recipients were Mr. Corning (Albany) and Mr. Sotham (Jefferson County[42]) for their joint cattle entries: a young bull named "Waxie" and two three-year old cows, "Matilda" and "Anna," for which ten dollars, fifteen dollars, and ten dollars were awarded respectively. The Herefords (beef cattle) exhibited were first class.[43]

In January 1847, the annual meeting was held in Albany. Nott was corresponding secretary when James Callanan of New Scotland submitted his farm management report.[44]

On February 15, 1855, two Bethlehem farmers were rewarded for their entries. Jacob Wally received "Third Place" and was awarded two dollars in prize money for his grain and seed entry. Henry Schoonmaker received "Best" and two volumes of the *Transcriptions of the New York State Agricultural Society, 1854,* for his entry of five bushels of buckwheat.[45] In spite of a severe drought in the summer of 1854, the agricultural and horticultural entries showed "strong evidence of superior culture." The next fair was again held in September at Albany's Washington Parade Ground.[46]

L.G. Ten Eyck and Richard Kimmey, two Bethlehem farmers, held offices in the New York State Agricultural Society in 1855. During the same year, Erastus Corning and Erastus Corning, Jr., were listed as life members.[47]

Agricultural societies, private organizations, and public agencies had a significant impact from the beginning. They inspired area farmers and were successful in convincing them to use improved farming techniques, including fertilization, and seeds, and to plant fallow crops.[48]

Farm implements, machinery, and tools were steadily modernized. Consequently, farmers became more productive and efficient than their forefathers. The improved plow, disk, steel harrow, and cultivator allowed the farmer to prepare his fields for planting much faster, and harvest grains more efficiently with reapers and threshing machines. Later, combines were invented. This machine would cut grain and separate the kernels from the straw in one process. Horse-drawn hay mowers and rakes helped the farmer harvest hay crops faster. Plowing contests were held showing spectators "the superiority of the cast-iron plow over the inefficient wooden plow."[49] In "1850 a horse-powered mowing machine had started to replace the scythe, a reaping machine was cutting grain, a threshing machine was replacing the flail. By 1870, steam was doing some of the plowing, [and] more of the threshing."[50]

Farm machines and implement manufacturers such as Emerson and Company, J.I. Case Co., The Standard, International Harvester, and John Deere became farmhouse names. Ford, Massey Ferguson, McCormick-Deering and other manufacturers would be added to the list in the early 1900s. These manufacturers would have their names on such items as hay, grain, and corn machines, plows, harrows, drills, seeders, culti-packers, planters, cultivators, threshers, tractors, engines, cream separators, feed grinders, corn shellers, farm wagons, and manure spreaders.

Pennsylvania 4, corn sheller. Machine was designed to remove dried corn kernels from the cob. One ear at a time was put in the opening on top, a crank on the other side was turned, and the cob was pushed out the side as the kernels fell out the bottom into a bushel basket.

Local Farmers—Bethlehem Farms Are Productive

Cornelius Vroman Baker and his wife, Caroline Lasher, owned and operated the "Grand View Farm" in 1846. The mid-1800 homestead consisted of 450 acres, 120 of which originally were part of the Sill farm. This farm contained riverfront property with rich alluvial bottom lands. Baker, a gentleman farmer, did much to promote agriculture. His farm was recognized in 1872 as the largest productive farm in the county.[51]

As cities grew, the public's demand for dairy products and farm produce increased. Therefore, to satisfy those demands, dairy farms became more prevalent. In addition, farmers planted a variety of crops and continued their pursuit of improved farming practices. In 1864, Bethlehem farmers produced:

> 210 bushels of grain
> 14,217.5 tons of hay
> 97,902 bushels of potatoes
> 34,061 bushels of apples
> 106,135 pounds of butter
> 296,013 pounds of pork[52]

Bethlehem's improved and unimproved lands totaled 32,673.75 acres in 1865 and the farmers' livestock consisted of:

> 1,213 horses and colts
> 1,382 cows
> 2,986 sheep and lambs
> 638 other animals

The sheep produced 6,946.5 pounds of wool that year.[53]

The record book of Robert Frazier, an Adamsville (Delmar) farmer, showed he grew gardens of squashes and potatoes, fields of timothy, clover, barley, rye, oats, and corn, and orchards of apple and peach trees. Entries in his detailed ledger included the type and amount of goods and seeds purchased as well as the products sold from his farm. The amount of butter made and sold indicated he probably had several head of dairy cattle on his farm. Milking was done by hand, a tedious and tiring job since cows are milked twice a day.

Excerpts from three pages of his record book showed prices and their fluctuation in the late 1800s.

Barley, Rye, Oats, Hay, & Straw Sold in 1867				
Jan. 15	about 90 bushels of Barley	@ $1.10	$94.00
Mar.	12 " " Oats	@ 0.52	6.24
Mar. 20	12 " " "	@ 0.53	6.36
Nov. 2	4 loads of Rye Straw		49.50
Dec. 11	14 bushels of Rye	@ 1.70	23.80

The data also revealed fluctuating prices for eggs and butter. Between the months of March and December 1866, the low price per dozen was twenty-four cents with thirty-six cents as the high. Butter prices during the period of February to December 1867 ranged from a low of twenty-five cents to a high of forty-four cents per pound. The ledger entries suggested that keeping farm hands for any length of time must have been a problem as well, because the lists of names changed frequently.[54]

Jurian Winne, another prominent local farmer, raised sheep and cattle on his 200-year old family farm located on Jericho Road in the vicinity of today's Selkirk railroad yards.[55] The following is quoted from a brief profile of Jurian Winne in the *History of the County of Albany:*

> Mr. Winne has taken an active interest in everything pertaining to the advancement of agriculture. He was one of the four organizers of the Albany County Agricultural Society, and was for two years vice-president of the State Agricultural Association. Sheep-raising and winter-feeding is the specialty in which he excels. Among his Leicester sheep he exhibited one that weighed 290 pounds at eighteen months old. Another had wool twenty-four inches long at two and a half years. His address on winter-feeding before the Agricultural Society of the State of New York attracted the most favorable attention, and 5,000 copies were printed and distributed throughout the State.[56]

Winne was the first Master of the local Bethlehem Grange 137 that was formed by George Sprague in 1874,[57] one year after the New York State Grange was established. This organization, founded for the benefit of farmers and in the interest of agriculture, encouraged farmers to be open-minded and willing to learn. As a result of members' efforts, the New York State Grange helped establish experiment stations, agricultural colleges, farm bureaus, and extension services. It formed co-ops, insurance companies, promoted dairy products and interests, and represented farmers in government through its executive and legislative committees.[58] The newly formed Bethlehem Grange consisted of thirty charter members and provided local farmers with a place for meetings, social events, and discussions of agricultural matters. At one time, there was a well-stocked store established on the premises providing groceries, provisions, and animal feed for the convenience of its members. Some of the members who operated the store were: Henry Meyer, Harry Creble, Howard Lasher, Sr., Bert Blodgett, and Walter Miller.

The members at first met in Albany, then moved to a hotel located at Beckers Corners. Property was purchased from Albertus Becker on Route 396 in 1880. A two-story Grange Hall was built that had a spacious dining room and store on the first floor. Some of the history of the Bethlehem Grange follows:

- To accommodate the increased membership, additional property was purchased from Adam Winnie in 1900 and the existing building was enlarged. A kitchen and store room were included in the expansion.

- Another piece of land was bought in 1905 from L.A. Winnie where additional sheds were constructed. In 1920, the Grange Hall was destroyed by fire. Another building was constructed on the original foundation with the assistance of members headed by the building committee: Harris Creble, Ellsworth Cass, and LaGrange Adam Winnie.

• A Juvenile Grange 115 was organized in 1926 attracting fourteen youths as charter members. Elsie Hallenbeck was leader and its first master was David Mead.

• As the organization prospered and membership increased, two additions were built onto the hall, one in 1935 and another in 1949. Central heating was installed in 1948.

• The Grange incorporated in 1941, when William Comstock filed the necessary papers.

• In 1949, the Grange's diamond jubilee anniversary was celebrated. Recognized with fifty years of membership in the local organization were: Mr. and Mrs. Harris Creble, Mr. and Mrs.

Howard M. Lasher, Edgar Osterhout, Elmer Osterhout, and Burton Blodgett.[59]

To improve marketing conditions in the Capital District, it was through the efforts of many granges and their members that the Albany Market Gardeners Association was organized in 1917. Approximately 700 farmers from Albany County and nearby counties were shareholders in The Capitol District Cooperative, Inc. The twenty-five acre Menands Market opened in 1934, providing space for 300 farmers to display and sell their produce, along with 100 buyer stalls. In the summer of 1937 during a twelve-week period, the successful cooperative market handled 7,427 loads of locally-grown produce and approximately 1,500,000 containers of fruits and vegetables. Mr. L. Huested Myers, 1959 cooperative secretary, was past master of Bethlehem Grange 137 (1944-45, 1949-50, and 1952-54). He stated in 1959, "15,301 loads of produce [were] sold on the farmers' section of the market. About 3,500 car loads

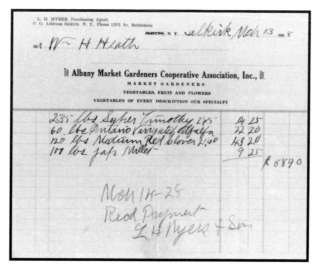

1928 receipt.

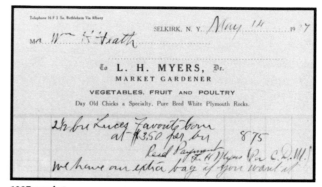

1927 receipt.

were sold on the wholesale section..." and numerous truck loads.[60]

The Cooperative Grange-League-Federation-Exchange, Inc. (G.L.F.) was formed in the early 1900s.[61] The G.L.F. farm store was located on Route 32 in Albany.

As society changed over the years, the Bethlehem Grange has placed more emphasis on community services. The Grange continues to serve Bethlehem and surrounding areas at its location on Route 396.

Farmers contended with the typical problems associated with farming but, as Robert Frazier's ledger disclosed, fluctuating market prices for farm products were an issue that would continue to concern farmers.

The problem of marketing dairy products led to the formation of several organizations on local and state levels. The formation of county farm bureaus in the decade after 1910 was rapid. In 1917, representatives of these bureaus formed the New York State Association of County Farm Bureau Associations, which later shortened its name to New York State Farm Bureau Federation.[62]

The Albany County Farm Bureau continues to represent farmers in government and provides information and services to area farmers. John Mead, a long-time Bethlehem resident and farmer, is currently vice president of the Albany County Farm Bureau. The Mead farm, established in 1791, is located on Meads Lane between Routes 32 and 443 (Delaware Avenue). James Frueh recently became a county board member in this organization. His farm is located in Glenmont. Both men engage in general farming in addition to raising beef cattle.[63]

Another agency that deals with agriculture is the New York State Department of Agriculture and Markets. This regulatory agency was established in 1926 and controls "such matters as plant and animal diseases, insect pests, the grading of fruit, feeds, fertilizers, seeds, weights and measures."[64]

As the public's demand for milk and dairy products increased, dairying progressed in Bethlehem. Farmers valued and improved their herds. Some farmers specialized in a particular breed: Erastus Corning raised Herefords (beef cattle) and Jerseys and was succeeded by his son in the business; John S. Perry's cattle were Guernseys; C.L.G. Blessing had a herd of Friesland (Dutch cattle). Other local successful cattlemen included C.C. La Grange, Abraham Fitch, and George Treadwell.[65]

Some area farm families developed retail and/or commercial enterprises. Heath's Shady Lawn Dairy and 3 Farms Dairy were among the local farm businesses that served Bethlehem's residents and surrounding communities with fine quality products for many years and contributed to the town's economic structure and growth.

Dairy Farming in Bethlehem

Heath's Dairy
An Interview with Richard and Margaret Heath Thayer

William H. and Elvira Heath chose the Glenmont area as a place to make their home and raise their four children, Aileen, Jerold A., Margaret, and William L. At first they rented a market farm on Weisheit Road. Then, in 1920, they purchased sixty-seven acres on Route 9W and Wemple Road from the Marcus Lasher family and established Heath's Dairy with nineteen cows. With additional land purchases, the farm eventually expanded to 450 acres consisting of six small farms and 225 registered "Shalawn" Holsteins. Their average milking herd consisted of 110 cows. The three youngest children assisted their father in the dairy operation.

In 1922, William H. started a daily home-delivery service with fifty quarts of milk left as free samples to prospective customers. The milk, sold in glass bottles, was delivered to customers by horse and wagon. Later, the horse and wagon were replaced with a Dodge panel truck. As time went on, five milk routes were established to serve the increase in customers. The Heaths continually updated their machinery, equipment, and service. The milk route was enlarged in 1936, when William H. purchased the Lansing Vroman milk route. This expansion provided service to residents in the Selkirk/Cedar Hill area. In 1937, Richard Thayer (son-in-law) delivered an average of twenty-eight cases of pasteurized and raw

Aerial view of Heath's Dairy, Route 9W around 1975. The two dark, round circles are watering receptacles for cattle.

milk on his daily milk route. Milk sold for seven cents a pint and fourteen cents a quart.

Jerold and William L. Heath became active managers of the family operation in 1940. The business was successful enough to warrant construction of a larger barn and investment in modern equipment. The Heaths opened a store and sold fresh dairy products from the dairy's location on Route 9W in Glenmont. The daily delivery service continued but, in 1943, it was temporarily affected by World War II and the deliveries were made every other day. As time went on, the business prospered. On January 1, 1951, William H. formed a family partnership with Jerold, William L., and Margaret and Richard J. Thayer.

The use of glass bottles remained a tradition with the dairy. Cardboard or plastic containers were definitely more economical than glass bottles, but the bottles were reusable, the milk stored and tasted better, and the glass containers allowed the customer to view the contents. These became collector items, particularly the smaller ones. Consequently, a forty-cent deposit was imposed on the bottles to encourage their return.

Gradually as business increased, as many as two thousand quarts of milk were processed and bottled daily. The fresh, rich cream was put into pint and half-pint bottles. During the earlier years, the bottles were washed by hand, scrubbed by a brush machine, rinsed, and sterilized. The milk was dumped into an ice cooled vat. The

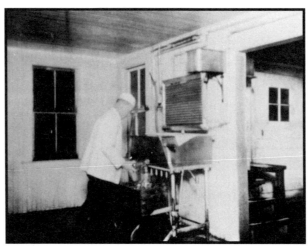

Bottling and capping process, late 1920s. Martin Lehfelt, from Germany, worked at Heath's dairy for a few years, then left to study and become a Lutheran minister.

An unidentified worker attends modernized bottling and capping system.

clean, empty bottles were placed in wooden cases and filled by pulling a lever that actuated filling valves. Eventually, this process was upgraded to a semi-automated process. An operator watched the conveyor-belt system as it transported the washed and sterilized bottles to a machine that filled and capped them automatically. The operator removed the bottles of milk and placed them in wooden cases that went into a cooler for the next day's deliveries. This was a process effective enough to be handled by one man, but generally two men worked the operation.

Even though Heath's Dairy was licensed to deliver milk only in Albany County, this restriction did not prevent satisfied customers from driving as much as twenty miles to the store for their purchases. One such customer was the Roraback Garden Market, a business located in Chatham. A buyer for Roraback's Garden Market drove to Heath's Dairy store, made purchases, and returned to the Chatham area, thus providing customers with the popular Heath's dairy products. The Heaths expanded their family operation when they purchased a pig farm located on Clapper Road from George J. and Florence E. Diederich in September 1950. The Heaths converted the buildings to accommodate chickens. In 1951, with the purchase of 22,000 hens, William L. Heath became manager of the poultry farm. Fresh eggs were available both in the store and through the home-delivery service. Six thousand hens were purchased four times a year creating a rotation cycle so Heath's Dairy could offer small, medium, large, and extra large eggs to its customers. The eggs, gathered three times a day, were cleaned, candled, cooled, and boxed for delivery the next day.

Those who desired to till the soil and reap the reward of their efforts had an opportunity to rent a garden plot (2,000 square feet) from the Heaths for a nominal charge for the growing season. In the spring, the land was plowed, disked, harrowed, fertilized, and staked out in pre-measured plots. Since manure from the dairy had been applied, the organic concept of farming appealed to many customers. For some, it was a family venture. The Heaths provided a parking area and water was available at the dairy for those who wished to do additional watering. The garden program started in 1973, and attracted fourteen participants. By 1980, that number had increased to 260 participating gardeners.

As on most farms, work began early. On a large commercial farm or a small family farm the work was basically the same—only more of it. Milking began at 5:00 a.m. and again late in the afternoon. The use of milking machines saved many hands and a tremendous amount of effort. In 1955, a milking parlor was conveniently located adjacent to the store so children and adults unfamiliar with the milking process could view it from behind a glass window. Children on school field-trips experienced the joy of touching a calf and learning about the cows and farm life.

Heath's Dairy provided many area residents with quality dairy products and home delivery service with a little extra hometown friendliness for many years. As with many of the local farms, an era has ended and the operation ceased. The farm was sold in 1985.[66]

3 Farms Dairy—The Newell Farm
An Interview with Thomas Newell

Minor Newell and his wife Mabel Winans sold the Newell homestead in Durham, New York, and purchased a farm in Coxsackie. In 1938, the couple and their son, Ernest, relocated and made their new home on the 165-acre "Sandy Creek Farm" on Wemple Road in Glenmont. The current barn, located opposite the house, was built by George Diederich from Coxsackie. Mr. Newell and his family did general farming and dairying. The small herd of Holstein cattle provided milk for their use and the remainder was sold to

Normanskill Dairy. In addition, the Newell family raised corn, wheat, oats, rye, and hay crops.

In the early 1950s, Minor's son, Ernest A., a 1930 graduate of Cobleskill Agricultural College, took over the operation. He and his wife, Florence Somerville, continued the tradition of general farming and dairying. Ernest logged during the winter months and took the logs to the Beinkafner Saw/Cider Mill on Feura Bush Road for processing. He used the lumber to construct two houses on Wemple Road near Beacon Road. For a while, he also was employed at the Port of Albany.

In 1954, a partnership was formed to establish 3 Farms Dairy on Route 144. Ernest Newell merged his "Sandy Creek Farm" with Bernard and Edward Mocker's farm located on Route 144 and Neil Goes's farm on the banks of the Hudson River in Cedar Hill (part of the Newton VanderZee estate). Beginning with approximately 215 head of dairy cattle, 3 Farms Dairy would serve the public for many years with fine dairy products. These products were processed and sold in the store located on the premises. The store was stocked with delicious homemade ice cream, cottage cheese, buttermilk, cream, sour cream, milk, and churned butter. For many years, folks enjoyed fine dairy products through the convenience of 3 Farms Dairy's home delivery service.

During the next several years many changes occurred in the business. Ernest Newell retired from the partnership in 1969 and his cows were sold. In 1971, Ernest died and his son, Thomas, who earned a bachelor's degree in agricultural economics from Cornell University, returned to the farm (he currently manages 3 Farms Dairy). The dairy, a retail and wholesale business, began a gradual phasing-out process in the early 1970s. In 1973, Neil Goes's cows were purchased, and a new barn and milking parlor, to accommodate approximately 200 cows, were built on the Mocker farm located behind the dairy store. By 1975 the home-delivery service was discontinued, but the wholesale business continued. In 1982, 3 Farms Dairy sold the raw milk to Fairdale Farm of Bennington, Vermont, which is now owned by Garelick, a Massachusetts dairy. In 1981, Edward Mocker died and Bernard Mocker continued farming.

When the dairy was established, there were ten producer/dealers in New York State. That number steadily declined. In the late 1970s, the three producer/dealers remaining in Albany County were 3 Farms Dairy, Heath's Dairy, and Van

Bernard Mocker and Thomas Newell at work on the Koch farm. Harvest will be stored in the bunker silo on the Mocker farm and later fed to livestock.

Wie's Dairy (Meadowbrook Farm), located in Clarksville.

The acreage farmed by 3 Farms Dairy, including rented property, is about 600 acres. Currently, Thomas Newell's "Sandy Creek Farm" houses some young stock and the milking cattle are at Mr. Mocker's farm, where an average of 175 cows are milked twice daily. Mr. Newell and Mr. Mocker continue to raise hay, corn, oats, and wheat. Most hay is processed in round, 2,000-pound bales rather than square bales, and all forage is stored in a bunker silo. The 4,000-ton capacity concrete bunker is horizontal and measures 60 feet wide, 145 feet long, by 10 feet high. The corn or hay-crop silage is dumped into the bunker and a four-wheel drive tractor is used to level and pack the feed. Front-end loaders are used to remove silage that is to be fed to cattle.

Hay bales 1990s style. The popular rolled bales have, to a large extent, replaced square bales.

Bernard Mocker, on field maintenance.

John Deere, and International machinery are used on the farms. Even with modern equipment, diesel tractors, a self-propelled combine (used for harvesting the grains), a self-propelled chopper (used for corn and grass silage), tractor-trailers ("eighteen wheelers"), and feeder wagons, the days are long and demanding.

With the high cost of equipment and machinery, one must take care of it not only because repairs are costly, but because it could take several days to repair or receive an ordered replacement part. The age of the equipment plays a vital role as well. With crops ready for harvest, a prolonged breakdown could have a devastating effect on the farmers. To keep costs to a minimum, most repairs are done by the few employees. Even with modern technologies, and equipment today's farmers face challenges.

The acreage of the Newell's "Sandy Creek Farm" has decreased gradually. Chadwick Square, Windham Hill, and Somerset Woods occupy farm land once owned by the Newell family.[67]

The Mocker Farm
An Interview with Bernard Mocker

Bernard and Edward's parents, Bernard and Mary Cross Mocker, did not farm. They lived in Albany and Mr. Mocker worked for General Electric in Schenectady. Therefore, the history of the Mocker Farm begins in 1889 when Bernard and Edward's maternal grandparents, Joseph and Margaret Cross, settled in Bethlehem from Poland. Mr. Cross worked on Charlie Baker's farm located in Cedar Hill. Melons, tomatoes, strawberries, and orchards of fruit including apples were grown on the farm.

In 1911, Joseph and Margaret Cross established a farm of approximately ninety-two acres on Route 144 (the location of the 3 Farms Dairy). The dairy herd on the Cross Farm included Holsteins and Guernseys. They also engaged in general farming and raised a variety of garden crops and had

Farmers Market 1990s style in St. Thomas's Church parking lot, Delmar.

a small orchard containing various fruit trees. Some of the produce was transported by horse and wagon and sold at the Albany Farmers Market located on State Street. Horses were "parked" head to head creating several rows for customers to stroll down and select fresh farm produce. Later, the marketplace was moved to Grant and Beaver Streets, in the vicinity of the present-day Albany Knickerbocker Arena.

During the 1930s, the number of dairy businesses in the county increased. After their grandfather's death in 1943, Bernard and his brother, Edward, carried on the farming tradition. The Mockers did

3 Farms Dairy on Route 144.

some gardening, but concentrated their efforts on dairying and increasing the dairy herd. During the 1950s, they joined the 3 Farms Dairy's partnership. The Mocker brothers purchased adjacent property of approximately 108 acres which enlarged the range of their homestead. For many years, Bernard's wife, Phyllis Goes, ran the dairy store located on the premises. The 3 Farms Dairy store and Mocker farm are still operating.[68]

Family Farms

Farmers and their families work many long and hard hours together, sharing workloads both within and outside the house, barn, and various farm buildings. They often possess a natural love for the land and have an appreciation for all life associated with it. They work until tasks are completed. It is a way of life that is affected around the clock every day throughout the year. The cows are milked morning and night, stalls are cleaned, and animals are fed. Some animals require special attention. Farmers care for sick animals and assist a difficult birthing—even during the night. Celebrations including holiday festivals are worked in during the chores, plantings, harvestings, and other types of farm work. Vacations are few.

In addition to farming, some farmers and family members join organizations or pursue further education while others balance careers or full/part-time jobs. Earlier farmers, at times, depended on their "egg money" to supplement their income.

As children developed lives of their own, some carried on the farming tradition, some did not. There are many outside influences that farmers must consider, e.g., weather, laws and regulations, market demands, fluctuating farm prices and costs of seeds, fertilizers, machinery and repairs, and many other concerns that have significant impacts on their livelihood.

Multigeneration Family Farmers and Related Stories

The Koch Farm
An Interview with Marian Koch (daughter)

Konrad Koch, a graduate of Hohenheim (Germany's oldest agricultural college), emigrated from the Black Forest, Germany, in 1926 and settled in Rensselaer County. There, he worked for several years on his uncle's farm and saved his earnings. In 1930, when his fiancée, Anna Laidig, arrived from Germany, they married. With his savings they purchased livestock and farm equipment and rented a farm in Rensselaer County for two years. In 1932, they moved to Glenmont and for two years rented a farm on Wemple Road. When the farm was sold, they moved to South Bethlehem and rented Callanan's farm. In 1938, they purchased a beautiful 100-acre farm that is situated upon a hill overlooking Route 396 in South Bethlehem. From the backyard, one can view the acres of flatland that were once part of Rensselaerswyck. Looking east, beyond the view of the towering Blue Circle cement plant's smoke-

Thomas Newell (on left) and Bernard Mocker in front of their farm equipment and trucks on the Koch farm.

stack near Ravena, the Berkshire Mountains are visible; looking to the west from the front lawn, the Heldeberg Mountains can be seen.

Konrad, Anna, and their two daughters, Evelyn and Marian, engaged in dairying and general farming, growing hay, corn, and oats for their livestock feed and a variety of garden vegetables for the family's use. The dairy herd, including young stock, consisted of seventy-five Holsteins. Corn silage was stored in three wooden, upright silos. Later, a concrete silo was constructed to replace the wooden silos. To accommodate the livestock within the huge, beautiful barn, a large section of one of the haylofts was removed, transforming the lower section into calf pens and an area to house other young stock. The wood from the wooden silos was used to construct a ceiling/floor above this area and, therefore, made the hayloft above still usable. An addition to the barn enlarged the milking facilities. In this area, fourteen stanchions were installed which increased the number of stanchions to a total of fifty. In 1953, to store the herd's milk production and conform to new regulations at the time, a bulk tank was installed in the milk house. The milk was sold to Normanskill Dairy. During this time, while helping with the farm, the two daughters continued their education. Evelyn graduated from Cobleskill Agricultural College and returned to work on the family farm until her marriage in 1960. Marian earned a bachelor of arts degree from the New York State College for Teachers (SUNY at Albany) and a master of arts from the College of Saint Rose. She then taught elementary school in the Ravena-Coeymans-Selkirk School District. After Mr. Koch died in 1965, the cows, machinery, and farm equipment were sold. Marian retired after thirty-one years of teaching. The Kochs rent the farmland to the owners of 3 Farms Dairy.

Most of the original buildings have been removed; only the barn, concrete silo, and farmhouse remain. The spacious barn and house, with a beautiful wrap-around porch, can be seen from Route 396. The well kept grounds and manicured shrubbery and lawns accentuate the beauty of the buildings.

The following list shows the transfers of the Koch farm property over the years:

> 167.2 acres from Stephen Van Rensselaer to Derrick Soop

Koch farmhouse on Route 396.

Abraham and Marie Soop March 20, 1824, to John Niver

Jacob Soop to John Niver November 18, 1828

John Niver from June 30, 1834 to April 21, 1861

Peter Niver from March 24, 1832 to January 12, 1904

Charles D. Niver from October 18, 1903 to December 4, 1931

Mary Ida K. Niver from July 21, 1931 to March 18, 1937

Jean V. Kirtland (Charles D. Niver's niece) from January 15, 1937 to October 17, 1938 and sold the property to Konrad and Anna Koch.

Small property sales/exchanges took place between 1824 and 1938 which will account for the 67.2 acres.[69]

The Waldenmaier Farm
An Interview with Charles Waldenmaier and his son, Charles, Jr.

George Waldenmaier, Sr., emigrated from Germany in 1898 to Albany County and later married Amelia B. Strohmaier. They established a homestead in 1908, operated a hotel on Route 32, and later established a meat packing business with sons George, Michael, and Charles. George Waldenmaier and Sons served the area for many years.

Parker Corning, a Congressman in 1922 and uncle of Albany's later Mayor Corning, owned a farm on Route 32 near the Waldenmaier homestead. From 1927 to 1943, "Sunnybrook Farm" was predominantly a holding farm for cattle on their way to the Corning Farm on Retreat House Road in Albany. Trefoil [birdsfoot trefoil, *lotus corniculatus vulgaris*, is a legume][70], a new hay crop, was later grown in the fields.

In 1943, Charles Waldenmaier and his wife, Virginia Elmendorf, bought approximately 225 acres from Parker Corning and established their home on Route 32. Like most area farms, general farming was practiced. Hay, oats, and wheat were some of the crops grown. Loose hay was purchased in Durham, New York, and trucked in to feed the cattle that were housed on the premises. Charles continued to operate the farm under the "Sunnybrook Farm" name, selling an assortment of apples from its 500-tree orchard. A few Alexander, Wolf River, Greening, and Delicious apple trees were in the orchard. Cortland apples were sold to Freihofers Bakery in Albany; MacIntosh were purchased by Aiello, a wholesaler, and Bradley (a jobber), who sold to different produce companies and businesses. These tasty varieties of apples were prepared, served, and no doubt enjoyed by many passengers in the dining cars of the Delaware & Hudson and New York Central Railroads. The immaculate grounds and manicured lawns complement the beautiful old buildings, including a very large barn, that remain on the property. Some bricks used to construct the house came from ships where they were used as ballast. After the bricks were removed, grains were loaded and the ship embarked to England. Buried on the Waldenmaier property are Revolutionary War veteran Frederick Britt and his wife, Helena Burhans.[71]

Typical wooden barrel for storage/transport of produce.

The Strohmaier Farm
An Interview with Charles Waldenmaier

In 1912, Charles Waldenmaier's uncle, Christian Strohmaier, purchased property located on the corner of Elsmere Avenue and Feura Bush Road from the Haswell family, and established his farm where he gardened and raised pigs. On this property, once owned by Strohmaier, corn has been planted and harvested for several years by another farmer. On occasion, especially in the fall, several deer can often be seen grazing on the corn crop.[72]

The Zdgiebloski Farm
My Family's Farm

In 1926, my grandparents, Henry and Helen Zdgiebloski, purchased a farm on Elm Avenue that was at one time owned by William and Rosa Pomykai. Henry, Helen, and their sons established general farming that, for a while, included truck farming. The fruit and produce, especially tomatoes, potatoes, cabbage, and strawberries were taken to the Albany Farmers Market for sale. Gradually, a variety of crops and fruit trees were introduced that eventually included a very large Concord grape arbor. The orchard included Bartlett pears, peaches, plums, cherry, a Seckle pear tree, and several varieties of apples. In time, the truck farming aspect was phased out and my parents, Peter and Dorothy Sitterly Zdgiebloski, established dairying in the 1940s which continued until the early 1960s. My brother, Pete, and I helped the family with the daily chores and all work associated with farming. By this time, most of the milking was done by machines with only a few cows that required hand-milking. The bulk of raw milk was sold to a dairy. Periodically, a portion of the family's supply of milk was set aside for my grandmother so she could make "pot" cheese (similar to today's farmer's cheese) and hand-churned butter, a time consuming process, but well worth the effort. When the butter

was removed, the remaining liquid was buttermilk, a palate pleaser by itself or as an ingredient in recipes such as buttermilk biscuits and pancakes.

Like most local farms, in addition to the cattle, there were many other farm animals including a dog trained to herd cattle. For several years wheat, rye, sorghum, and corn were grown and harvested. The corn was produced for silage and was stored in an upright concrete silo adjacent to the barn. The hay raised in the fields included alfalfa, clover, timothy, and trefoil.

The fruit trees and Concord grape arbor planted years earlier still bore fruit that was enjoyed by family members year round. When in season, the fresh fruit was used in recipes, canned, or to make preserves.

In the fall, the "drop" apples were gathered and taken to Charlie Beinkafner's Saw/Cider Mill located on Feura Bush Road opposite McCombe Drive. The apples were dumped into a bin; a large press squeezed the apples and extracted the delicious juice from them leaving only thick pulp and a sweet aromatic fragrance that lingered long enough to stimulate the taste buds. Several large wooden-staved barrels were filled with the cider and transported home along with the pulp. The pulp provided a treat for some of the livestock, thus completing the cycle.

In earlier years, horse-drawn implements were used to cultivate the soil, harvest grains and hay, and transport those products from the fields to

Horse-drawn plow manufactured by Oliver and used on the Zdgiebloski farm in the early 1900s.

This Dutch barn's exterior measurements are approximately 45 feet in width by 71 feet in length by 34 feet in height.

the barn and sheds located in the vicinity of the farmhouse. As years passed and equipment improved, the team of horses and appropriate machinery were replaced with several modern gas-engine tractors, power-driven machinery, and modern implements and wagons.

Most of the original buildings on the property have survived the elements of time with the aid of the family. Among these buildings is a Dutch barn. The barn is well constructed with several large hand-hewn vertical beams and six horizontal beams each measuring roughly nine inches thick by nineteen inches

Bought in the late 1930s, this grain machine was used on the Zdgiebloski farm. Markings on the machine read: N°. 6 BRYAN GRANT, Grain...Made for Gilbert H. Ackerman.

wide and approximately twenty-six feet in length. These support a center hayloft twelve feet above the main floor in the front of the barn. The large, heavy double doors (on both ends of the barn) slide on roller tracks. Located on both sides of the front portion of the barn are livestock facilities. On the right, there are two large pens (one with an access door to the front of the barn). On the left, there are stanchions that were used when milking the cows and an access door to the north barnyard. The nearby harness room was converted into a grain and feed storage area. Located above the livestock facilities are smaller lofts (on both sides) just under the front center hayloft. In the back of the barn are two huge hay bays with another center hayloft between them. Two smaller doors, also on tracks, are conveniently located on each side of the barn. The downstairs section has two large rooms. The one on the south side of the barn was used years ago to house chickens. During the dairying years, the room on the north side

Scotch Highland cattle, like this one, graze with Holstein cattle in the pastures on the Zdgiebloski farm.

contained two rows of stanchions. These have since been removed to provide adequate open space for the livestock currently raised on the farm. The Holsteins and Scotch Highlands are content to wander from pasture to pasture grazing peaceably. Hay and corn are still grown and harvested on the property.

There are only a few Dutch barns remaining in Bethlehem. They are located on the properties of Harrison Malary on Jericho Road, Selkirk, Jay Harold Jakovic (farm previously owned by his grandfather, Harold J. Magee) on Feura Bush Road, Glenmont, Hallenbeck's barn on the corner of Route 53 and Elm Avenue, and Frances Ott's barn off Route 9W.[73]

Harry and Ruth Eyers purchased a farm from Arthur Dubuque (previously Deckers). This farm borders the Zdgiebloski farm to the north. The

adjacent farm land to the east, located on Elm Avenue East, belonged to the Kimmey family. During most of the 1950s, the Martin family farmed some of the land, raising grain, corn, or hay. Next to the Kimmey's farm, near the Dowerskill, was the McCullough farm. William and Eleanor Van Derpool's 140 acre farm was across from them on the south side of Elm Avenue East.

Neighbors John H. and Myrtle Radley owned a fifty-five acre farm located on both sides of Elm Avenue near the intersection of Elm Avenue and Elm Avenue East. They engaged in general farming with apples as their chief product. I visited the older couple on many occasions during my childhood. I entered their home through the attached woodshed. While approaching the kitchen, the pleasant fragrances of different chopped woods blended with aromas of cooking that came from the kitchen, which was where the elderly couple and I visited. A woodstove was used to cook the meals and provide heat. A basket of fresh, brown chicken eggs sat next to the sink for cleaning. Mr. Radley would visit with us, but disappeared occasionally to complete his chores and tend to his only cow and horse. Age was slowly creeping up on them but I admired their spirit and energy.

In the summer, Mr. Radley would hand-cut the hay crop with a large scythe and let it dry in the hot sun. He used a pitchfork to pile the dry hay into small stacks, stab the stack dead-center, lift the whole thing, and place it on his horse-drawn wagon. Mr. Radley used voice commands to control his horse. The horse obediently pulled the wagon ahead to the next stack and stopped. This continued until the haying was done.

The farmhouse and a small barn remain at the original site. The other buildings have deteriorated until they collapsed or were taken down. The farm property has been parceled off and sold since my childhood visits. Some of the land that was once painstakenly attended to is now overgrown with trees and underbrush. On the farm property, previously owned by the Radleys, there are several individual homes, and the Jehovah's Witness Kingdom Hall on Wildwood Lane. The remainder of the farm property is planned for development.

A Hundred or More Years in Farming

The Haswells: A Family Tradition Ends
An Interview with Samuel Van Buren Haswell's Grandson, Richard Hale

John Haswell, his wife, and ten children arrived in Albany in November 1774, from England. The Haswell family rented 300 acres of farmland that stretched from present-day Elsmere Avenue to Elm Avenue, on both sides of Feura Bush Road and Murray Avenue, from Patroon Van Rensselaer. They established a homestead that would remain in the family for six generations. As each son married, a portion of the rented farmland was given to him. William Haswell, the youngest, chose the site across from Murray Avenue on Feura Bush Road to build his home.

A 1877 map shows the forty-three acres north of Feura Bush Road and east of Murray Avenue (including the five acres containing various farm buildings) and seventy-two acres south of Feura Bush Road were owned by Samuel J. Haswell, grandfather of Samuel Van Buren Haswell. After Samuel J. died in 1874, Samuel J.'s son, Oscar (Richard Hale's great-grandfather) and Samuel V.B. Haswell (Richard's grandfather) operated the farm to the middle 1900s. Oscar died in 1925. Joseph and William Haswell, brothers of Samuel J., owned some of the adjoining property and sold some land prior to 1960, thus leaving the above described acreage as the Haswell property.

In 1930, the Haswells built a roadside stand where they sold a variety of homegrown vegetables and fruits (pears, plums, peaches, and apples—their largest crop) and other specialties that included delicious homemade preserves, relishes, pickles, fresh brown eggs, and ready-to-cook chickens. These products were also delivered to customers in Albany and Bethlehem. Later, to accommodate the business, a larger stand was constructed at the same location. No longer in operation, these two roadside stands still exist along Feura Bush Road across from Murray Avenue.

Farming at the Haswell homestead reached its peak during the 1940s and 1950s. In addition to general farming and the roadstand business, the owner and his family engaged in dairying. Twenty Guernsey cows were milked twice a day and the milk was sold to a dairy affiliated with the Dairymen's League (now Dairylea), a dairymen's organization in which Samuel and Emily Haswell were members. The Haswells had grown and harvested their own livestock feed which consisted of wheat, oats, field corn, and hay (mostly alfalfa, trefoil, and timothy).

Samuel Van Buren Haswell operated the farm from the early to mid-1900s with the help of family members. Later, the family discontinued dairying and in 1966, the cows were sold. After Samuel died in 1971, the family continued the phasing out process and sold the chickens. A few years earlier, a sharpening service was established by Samuel's son-in-law, Richard F. Hale, and the business prospered. In 1973, Mr. Hale's son, Richard, joined the business. With few family members to operate the roadside stand, a decision was made to end this service. By 1980, farming ceased, thus ending a family tradition of six Haswell generations. Most of the acreage has been sold and many private homes are situated on property once belonging to the Haswell's multigeneration farm. However, Richard Haswell Hale (seventh generation) resides and operates his sharpening service at the original homestead site.[74]

An aerial view of the Mead farm on Creble Road taken sometime in the 1940s. Small dots are chickens wandering near their coop.

The Mead Farm
An Interview with Warren "Pete" and Marie Mead

This farm is located in a small valley close to the Vloman Kill south of Delmar on Creble Road. This property was once part of Peter D. and Ann Marie Winne's farm. Zebulon Lee purchased the property from the Winnes on April 1, 1842, and farmed there for several years. On April 2, 1856, Lee's widow, Nancy, their son and his wife, Stephen F. and Juliette Lee, sold seventy-two acres to David N. Mead and his wife, Elizabeth

George E. Mead, Warren's grandfather, hard at work haying in the 1920s.

were used for haying. Pitchforks were used to handle the loose hay.

While living at the homestead, George E. and Elizabeth Mead celebrated their fiftieth wedding anniversary. George died October 14, 1933, and Elizabeth continued farming with her family until her death in 1943. Her son, Warren J., and his wife, Alma Gallup, continued the operation and concentrated more extensively on dairying. Warren raised a mixed herd of about thirty Holstein and Jersey cows. Milk was sold to the Second Avenue Dairy, the Glendale Dairy, and to Clarence Crocker, a local farmer. To keep the milk as fresh as possible, a dairy truck would come to the farm every day and pick up the cans of milk produced the previous day. The cans of milk were stored and kept cold in the ice house located near the barn until they were picked up. Ice was harvested in the winter months from the nearby creek.

Warren owned a hay press. When the haying season was over, in late fall Mr. Mead would travel to neighbors with the press and process their hay into bales. Loose hay was packed into a large upright press. Using horse power, pulleys and cables, the hay was pressed into large, heavy bales weighing up to 200 pounds. Horses helped maneuver the bales onto skids for transport to

Onderdonk. David farmed it for many years with his family. On May 28, 1901, the ownership was transferred to David and Elizabeth's son, George E. Mead. George and his wife, Elizabeth Hotaling, continued the farming tradition for many years with the assistance of their children, Warren, Allen, Grace, and George E., Jr. The family grew a variety of garden vegetables and fruit along with oats, wheat, and hay. They did dairying and raised chickens. The milk, butter, cheese, and eggs were delivered to many Bethlehem families.

The soil on the hills and flatlands was worked by the farmer and a guided team of workhorses harnessed to farm machinery. Horse-powered implements were used for plowing, harrowing, and cultivating, and for harvesting the crops. Horse-drawn hay mowers, rakes, and wagons

storage. Gradually the machinery was updated and the horses were replaced with a Fordson tractor which later was traded in on a Farmalls-F12 with cog wheels.

In 1957, Warren S. "Pete" Mead and wife, Marie Braman, took over the family farming tradition. Dairying continued for many years with the milk sold to the Second Avenue Dairy, and to Dairymen's League (Dairylea).

In July 1966, Pete held a farm auction and sold the cows and some equipment and machinery. He continued farming on a part-time basis while working for a trucking company. During the late 1970s to the early 1980s, he raised a small herd of about eighteen Brahman beef cattle. Today the land remains productive and is worked by a local farmer.

The ice house remains as well as a barn (not the original barn, but the third one which was built around 1976). The location is an attractive setting for a farmhouse with the various farm buildings so near to the creek. In the 1950s, the creek occasionally flooded up to their home during heavy rainstorms and Jericho Road was closed to traffic until the waters receded.

The creek was also a source of entertainment, a welcomed break after working so hard in the hot fields or barn. Children enjoyed the rope swing over the old swimming hole in the summer. In the winter, the creek was excellent for ice skating.

The creek also provided a challenge for many local fishermen, old and young alike. There was an abundant supply of bullheads, suckers, eels, and sunfish to satisfy both the novice and experienced angler. The surrounding slopes provided an area for children's hiking trips and picnics during the warmer months, and for sleigh-riding, skiing, and tobogganing in the winter.[75]

A History of Diversification

In spite of the dairy trend, many Bethlehem farmers continued to grow a wide variety of farm produce. From small farms consisting of only two acres to larger farms of 600 acres, they existed harmoniously producing various vegetables, root crops, fruits, orchards of various fruit trees, grains, corn, and hay crops. Farmers raised various breeds of horses, beef cattle, dairy cattle, pigs, goats, sheep, chickens, ducks, geese, and other livestock. These were the general farmers in Bethlehem who, along with the local dairies and large farm businesses, contributed significantly to the local economy. This is supported by the data contained in the following charts prepared by M.C. Bond for an Albany County Farm Report in 1953. The detailed report revealed that in 1949 Bethlehem's farmers produced the following:

Number of Farms Reporting	Total Acres and Crops
61	811.0 acres of corn
39	314.0 acres of corn for grain
33	499.0 acres of winter wheat, the largest amount grown in Albany County
49	16.0 acres, 1,507 bushels of potatoes
3	0.5 acres of lettuce
9	12.5 acres of snap beans
16	42.0 acres of cabbage
11	53.5 acres of sweet corn
15	28.5 acres of tomatoes
17	43.4 acres of cantaloupes & muskmelons
7	11.6 acres of cauliflower
10	9.6 acres of sweet peppers

According to the above figures, the combined crop acreage of Bethlehem farms participating in the 1949 survey was 1,841.6. Of this, 1,125 acres were devoted to corn for grain; 499 acres to wheat; 43.4 acres to melons; and 174.2 acres to vegetables including sweet corn.[76]

With regard to fruit grown in Bethlehem, the report revealed data that compared the number of apple and pear trees grown in 1939 and 1949 on local farms and the total bushels grown of both fruits. These figures are represented in the table at the bottom of the page.[77]

Farms Decline—Auction Sales Held

Farming began to decline, especially in the mid-1900s. A common practice was to hold a public auction to sell the farm contents. Some auctions also included the contents of the farmhouse and personal belongings. The farm auction would be advertised in local newspapers, usually the *Altamont Enterprise,* and by word-of-mouth, but more often it would be advertised by displaying very large informative posters throughout the town and surrounding communities. I attended many such auctions during the 1950s and a few in the early 1960s.

On a research visit to the local Bethlehem Historical Association on Route 144, I came across a farm auction poster, rather tattered and torn but readable. This particular auction took place in 1920, but the format was typical. A facsimile of that poster is shown on the next page.

Number of Farms Reporting/Total Acres Devoted to Fruit						
1939			**1949**			
81 farms/268 acres			43 farms/172 acres			
	Farms Reporting Trees of Bearing Age 1949	Trees of Bearing Age 1939	1949	Trees of Non-bearing Age 1939	1949	Total Bushels 1949
Apples	29	5,131	4,182	1,284	940	5,977
Pears	14	1,229	112	349	6	35

AUCTION SALE
FARM STOCK and IMPLEMENTS
Wesley Simmons, Auctioneer, will sell on
TUESDAY, NOV. 9, 1920 11 o'clock sharp, for the subscriber,

One mile North of Selkirk and one Mile West of Cedar Hill, on the farm known as

"THE ASA BAILEY FARM"

THE FOLLOWING PROPERTY:

Pair Gray Horses, wt. 2550 lbs.	Light 2-seated Wagon, Surrey,	Wagon Box, Dump Box
Sorrel Mare, wt. 1300 lbs., 7 yrs old	Buggy, New Top Wagon,	2 1-horse Cultivators,
Holstein Cow,	2-seated Sleigh, pole & shafts,	Marking Plow, Scotch Harrow
Brood Sow, 12 Shoats,	Cutter, Heavy Bob sleighs,	Spring-tooth cultivator,
2 Lumber Wagons, 12-bbl. Truck	Pressed Hay Rigging,	7 Pitchforks, 4 Barley Forks,

Adriance Mower, Adriance Rake, New Oliver Sulkey Plow, Syracuse Plow

2 Iron Scoops, Manure Fork,	2 Jack screws, Grain box	3 Potato hooks, 4 Corn knives,
Heavy Team Harness, Breeching,	4 Corn planters, New corn sheller,	Wire stretcher, 2 Hot-bed sash,
Light double and single Harness,	Horse clippers, Potash kettle,	Emery wheel, Grind stone,
Heavy single Harness, New Fly Nets,	3 Scythes and snaths, 4 Log chains,	2 Gravity Separators,
Heavy and Light Blankets,	2 Swivel clevises, 3 Crowbars,	Davis swing churn, 3 hay hooks,
4 sets Whiffletrees, 4 Neckyokes,	Lot of rung chains, 2 cross-cut saws	Hog hook, Hog box, 2 Hog scrapers,
2 sets little Neckyokes, new,	2 wooden vises, hand saws,	Lot of lumber, 2 pair hedge trimmers,
Double & triple Block and Fall, with rope	Lot of carpenter tools, staple puller,	Wagon umbrella, 18 & 20-ft. ladders,
Set double blocks, with rope,	1 long handle, 5 good iron shovels,	Lot of corn stalks, oats, sacks,
Set extra heavy blocks, with rope,	Spade, Bog hoe, Post auger and maul,	Wrenches, hammers, etc.,
2 single blocks, 4 binding ropes,	3 Sledges, Steel sledge,	30 Cotton bags.

TERMS OF SALE:

All sums of $20 and under, Cash; over $20 a Credit of 12 months will be given, without interest, if paid when due, if not paid when due with interest from date. Good approved endorsed notes will be required, and no property is to be removed until these terms of sale are complied with.

By order of J. B. BAUMES.

ENTERPRISE PRINT, ALTAMONT

Auction sale poster.

The Rural Character of Bethlehem Changes

The decline in the number of farms reporting was reflected in the Bond Report data regarding chickens and milk cows. In 1935, 308 Bethlehem farms reported a total of 46,394 chickens. In 1940, 150 of the reporting farms showed the number of chickens as 36,579. In 1950, there was a decrease in reporting farms to 119 but an increase in chickens to 38,626. Data extracted from the same report revealed that in 1940, 148 farms reported a total of 1,450 milk cows. In 1950, the numbers declined to 91 farms reporting with a total of 924 milk cows.[78]

In the 1950s, there was a farm auction at Stanley Van Allen's farm at which a set of snack plates was purchased for me. The farmhouse and barn, once part of the farm, can be seen from Elm Avenue. The nearby Elm Estates is situated on former farmlands owned by the Alfred Williams family located on Elm Avenue, and G. Schwartz, located on Wildwood Lane. These farms, like so many other area farms, have been sold to residential and/or commercial developers.

The dairy farms of Howard Becker and S. Cady Schoonover were located on Long Lane where the General Electric Plastics plant is situated. The Owens-Corning plant is constructed on the dairy farm property once owned by the Dabravalskas family.

According to John Scharff, his grandparents, William and Ann Clare Glasser, farmed land where the Niagara Mohawk Steam Plant is now located on Route 144. They engaged in general farming during the period from about 1901 to the 1930s. John's great uncle, William Scharff, worked on the George and Mary Dettinger Schmitt farm located in Cedar Hill, and rented a parcel of land from them for his own use. The land now houses the Samaritan Shelters.[79]

A Questionable Future For Farms

Radical changes in the agricultural industry have taken place since the first seeds were planted in Bethlehem's soil on Westerlo Island. The farm industry has progressed. From the hand tools and implements used in Peelen's days to the modern diesel and self-propelled machinery, the farmers have served the town of Bethlehem and surrounding communities well. During the twentieth century, farming suffered a dramatic decline. Statistics from the Bond Report[80] supports the statement with the following:

Number of Reporting Farms	Total Acreage	Year
358	31,549 acres	1875
259		1930
214	17,506 acres	1940
163	14,070 acres	1950

There are seventy-six farms remaining in Bethlehem.[81] With each beautiful sunrise over the Berkshires and each spectacular sunset behind the Heldebergs, the world changes. Therefore, the fate of these farms and the resulting impact on the community and future generations in the Town of Bethlehem remains to be seen. The following is a quotation from *Memoirs of the Board of Agriculture of the State of New York*, published in 1821.

> THIS earth, as we all know, is a round and firm globe, carrying upon its surface men and beasts. These, however, would soon perish, and the earth become void of inhabitants, if the means of preservation were not abundantly and conveniently provided for them. By a beautiful providential arrangement of our Creator, the earth is endowed with a capacity to produce vegetable matter, fitted to sustain and preserve the beings which inhabit it.[82]

Man is not separate from earth, but rather greatly depends on it and all its valuable resources for survival. This chapter is dedicated to a multitude of hardworking farmers and their families both past and present, and to the descendants of past farmers who are still residing in Bethlehem, some living on or farming the land of their ancestors. Many area streets and crossroads bear the names of past families: Creble Road, Blessing Road, Meads Lane, Niver Avenue, Waldenmaier Road, Callanans Corners, Becker Corners, and Mallorys Corners, to mention a few.

The following information obtained from the *American Agriculturist Farm Directory and Reference Book of 1916*, allows the reader to envision earlier Bethlehem farms and the wide variety of products grown around the 1920s.[83] The accompanying map allows one to conduct a farm tour of Bethlehem. Although homes, industrial and commercial buildings, and other modern features have replaced most of the once open and fertile farmlands, it is important to remember that agriculture was a major industry in the town that made significant contributions to Bethlehem's history.[84]

Hwy No.	Name	Main Crop	Owned/ Rented Acreage	Location & Farm Name
61	Hugh & Susan Alexander		Owned 13	
20	Jacob & Rita Arnold	hay	Owned 33	Elsmere
61	William & Nellie Atchinson	hay/vegetables	Owned 60	Glenmont
54	Anna Babcock	corn	Owned 34	Glenmont
7	Samuel & Emma Ball	hay	Owned 48	Slingerlands
99	Charles M. & Marion Baker	fruit	Owned 400	Selkirk, "Grand View Farm"
4	Almond & Bina Barber	hay	Owned 54	Slingerlands, "Lilly Field"
79	Joseph S. & Ida Baumes	melons	Owned 50	Selkirk
78	Jacob B. & Emma Baumes	apples	Owned 85	Selkirk
33	William & Minnie Barkuff		Rented 116	Delmar, "Pine View"
62	Howard & Joanna Becker	hay	Owned 172	Selkirk
44	Mathew & Josephine Becker	wheat	Owned 67	Glenmont, "Oakwood"
39	Madison & Mary Becker	rye	Owned 86	Delmar
39	John H. & Ellen Becker	hay	Owned 96	Delmar
40	John C. & Mary Becker	hay	Owned 6	Delmar
39	Charles & Ella Becker	hay	Rented 130	Delmar
51	Henry G. & Libbie Beckman		Owned 68	Selkirk
43	William N. Bender	hay	Owned 35	Delmar
20	Justin E. & Jessie Bender	fruit	Owned 18	Delmar
39	Charles & Elizabeth Bender	melons	Owned 200	Slingerlands,"Bender Melon Farm"
57	George & Frances Bernkafner	hay	Owned 130	Selkirk
30	Frank Bennett	apples	Owned 57	Delmar, "Evergreen"
80	George & Ursula N. Best	hay	Owned 55	Selkirk
55	Anna L. Binck	hay	Owned 90	Selkirk
87	George & Elizabeth Blankenhorn	rye	Owned 156	Selkirk
101	Willard J. & Ada Blessing	hay/grain	Owned 105	Albany, "Cohassett"
44	William Blodgett		Owned 50	Glenmont, "Elmdale"
65	Chirstopher & Catherine Bombeck	hay	Rented 123	Glenmont
7	Peter J. & Barbara Brown	onions	Owned 32	Slingerlands
21	Theodore E. & Jennie Burhans	hay	Owned 43	Elsmere
61	Fred & May Burnell	rye	Rented 150	Glenmont
99	Mrs. Jennie K. Bull	hay	Owned 170	Selkirk, "The Pines"
57	Elmer E. & Loretta Carkner	hay	Rented 96	Selkirk
85	Elsworth & Elizabeth Cass	rye	Owned 182	So. Bethlehem, "Brookside"
43	John J. & Grace Casey	corn	Owned 85	Delmar
35	George & Eliza Chamberlain	milk	Owned 20	Glenmont
21	George U. Clark	tomatoes	Owned 5	Delmar
16	A.L. & May Clark		Owned 20	Albany
64	John P. & Catherine Collins	hay	Owned 84	Selkirk
29	Barent W. & Carrie Coonley	hay	Owned 145	Delmar
10	Frank & Mary Couse	rye/hay	Owned 110	Slingerlands
46	Rudolph C. & Anna Craft		Owned 32	Glenmont, "Pines"
82	Garrett B. Crebel	hay/grain		Selkirk, "Ashmore Park"
71	Harris R. & Catherine Creble	hay	Owned 108	Selkirk
60	Herbert M. & Margaret Creble		Rented 110	Glenmont
60	Winslow M. & Anne Crocker	milk	Owned 100	Glenmont
78	Joseph & Maggie Cross	cucumbers	Rented 40	Selkirk
79	William W. & Lizzie Crum		Rented 45	Selkirk
52	Alonzo E. & Jennie De Freest	potatoes	Owned 180	Glenmont
61	Alexander A. & Elizabeth DeLong	hay/corn	Owned 7	Glenmont
30	George E. & Nettie Dickson	rye	Rented 53	Delmar
16	Jacob & Caroline Dolch	hay	Owned 104	Albany
54	Miss Emma Dow	strawberries	Owned 14	Glenmont
n.a.	G.H. & Alice Earle	berries	Owned 1	Delmar
42	John H. & Elizabeth Epsey	potatoes	Owned 15	Delmar
16	John & Henrietta Etling		Owned 35	Albany, "Pine Ridge"
64	Matthew J. & Bertha Felter	hay	Owned 86	Selkirk, "Clover Knoll Farm"
12	David D. & Myra Fisher	rye/poultry	Owned 85	Slingerlands
21	Mrs. Sarah A. Fix	hay	Owned 83	Delmar
19	Leonard & Myrtle Frazier	rye	Owned 62	Delmar
101	Andrew T. & Clara Frichs	hay	Rented 63	Albany, "Valley View Farm"
23	John & Mary Fryer	rye	Rented 140	Slingerlands
78	Ellery & Mary Furman	hay	Owned 100	Selkirk
44	James T. & Mary Gardner		Rented 85	Delmar
16	George H. & Charlotte Gill, Jr.	potatoes	Owned 114	Albany
79	William J. & Anna Gimlick	hay	Rented 212	Selkirk
54	Peter & Anna Gise	rye	Owned 84	Glenmont "Elms"
61	William H. & Anna Glasser	hay/tomatoes	Rented 150	Glenmont
4	John & Caroline Goedtel	hay	Owned 106	Slingerlands
53	John U. & Eliza Graulich	strawberries	Owned 56	Glenmont
61	Albert Hakes	melons	Owned 30	Glenmont
67	Charles & Anna Hallenbeck	fruit/vegetables	Owned 8	So. Bethlehem
64	Walter & Elsie Hallenbeck	hay	Owned 125	Selkirk
97	Garrison & Cerenia Hallenbeck	hay	Owned 100	So. Bethlehem
74	Nicholas & Mary Halsdorf	tomatoes	Owned 12	Selkirk
35	Edward & Sarah Hannay		Owned 100	Kenwood Station
54	Oscar S. & Anna Haswell	hay	Owned 116	Delmar, "Homestead Farm"
22	Harmon & Minnie Hazelton	rye	Owned 120 Rented 20	Delmar
35	Theodore L. & Charlotte Heller	milk	Rented 165	Kenwood
73	David & Mary Henzler	rye	Owned 100	Selkirk
55	Christopher J. & Sophia Herber	hay	Owned 50	Feura Bush
75	Joseph M. & Mary Herbert	hay	Rented 108	Glenmont
88	Adam Hoffman	fruit	Owned 14	Selkirk
33	Susan E. Hogancamp	berries	Owned 6	Elsmere
63	Gottliet & Mary Hoight	hay	Owned 10	Selkirk
46	John S. & Viola Hotaling	hay	Owned 76	Glenmont, "Hilcrest"
10	John & Fannie Hotaling	rye/fruit	Owned 54	So. Bethlehem, "Willow Brook"
22	Albert H. & Jennie Hotaling	hay	Owned 100	Delmar, "West View"
64	Frank F. & Veronikah Hungerford	hay	Owned 186	Glenmont

Hwy No.	Name	Main Crop	Owned/Rented Acreage	Location & Farm Name
96	Wylie & Minnie Hunter	rye	Owned 10	So. Bethlehem
10	Peter D. Johnson	hay	Owned 117	Slingerlands
19	William Kilmer	rye	Owned 81	Delmar
78	Elvin M. & Ella Kinney	melons	Owned 80	Selkirk
16	M. & Anna Klapp		Owned 124	Albany
16	Nicholas & Barbara Klapp		Owned 38	Albany
34	William H. & Helena Kleinke	hay	Owned 60	Glenmont, "Pine Grove"
52	Charles & Etta Kline	hay	Owned 12	Delmar
44	August & Elizabeth Knapp	corn	Rented 45	Glenmont
54	John & Mary Knauf	corn	Rented 60	Glenmont
67	Milton F. & Augusta Knowles	hay	Rented 94	Feura Bush, "Shady Grove"
62	Charles W. & Florence Kunz	rye	Rented 100	Selkirk
61	John Laden		Owned 500	Glenmont
80	William D. & Isabel Laing		Rented 2	Selkirk
29	Jacob C. & Mary Lang	hay	Owned 146	Delmar, "Sunnyside"
83	Mans S. Lamoreaux	hay	Owned 8	So. Bethlehem
34	Julius & Anna Langush	hay	Owned 52	Glenmont
60	Marcus & Ida Lasher	hay	Owned 67	Glenmont
77	Howard M. & Eva Lasher	hay	Owned 125	Selkirk
79	Asa B. & Clara Lasher	melons	Owned 18	Selkirk
10	Christian C. & Mary LaGrange	hay	Owned 265	Slingerlands
33	James & Margaret Lavery	vegetables	Owned 18	Delmar
64	Arthur & Anna Lawton	hay	Rented 130	Glenmont
4	J. T. & Annie Lawton		Owned 8	Slingerlands
66	John J. Leedings	hay	Owned 100	Glenmont, "Evergreen Farm"
57	Edward & Ella Leonard	strawberries	Owned 11	Selkirk
29	Jacob Long	hay	Owned 80	Delmar, "Willowview"
30	Hugh & Ida Lyons	vegetables	Owned 40	Delmar
30	John & Jane Lyons	potatoes	Owned 94	Delmar, "Centre View"
76	Stephen O. & Lena Lyons	rye	Owned 72	So. Bethlehem
35	John H. & Mary Magee	hay	Owned 128	Glenmont, "Shady Crest"
8	James H. & Nellie Maher	hay	Owned 94	Slingerlands, "Maple Farm"
22	David R. & Ella Main	cabbage	Owned 10.5	Delmar
64	Ira & Hannah Malary	hay	Owned 88	Selkirk
63	Henry Mallory	hay	Owned 125	Selkirk
70	John & Anna Mallory	oats	Owned 98	Selkirk
10	Joel F. & Nettie Martin	hay	Owned 80	Slingerlands
62	Alton C. & Elizabeth Masher	apples	Owned 82	Feura Bush, "Willow Brook"
67	Henry & Elizabeth Mathias	apples	Owned 113	Feura Bush
17	Garrie B. & Carrie McCormick	hay/grain	Owned 105	Delmar, "Mt. Healthy"
69	William & Grace McCulloch	hay	Owned 72	So. Bethlehem
14	Walter McMillan	hay	Rented 156	Slingerlands, "Tower Stock Farm"
33	Seward J. & Augusta McMillen		Owned 40	Delmar
49	Baltice Mead	hay	Owned 310	Delmar, "Volomanskill"
49	Edwin B. & Ida Mead	hay	Owned 150	Delmar, "Ulaumans Kill"
70	George E. & Lizzie Mead	hay	Owned 72	Selkirk
60	Stephen D. & Mary Mead	hay	Owned 113	Glenmont, "Evergreen Farm"
7	Andrew L. & Lillian Miller	hay	Owned 117	Slingerlands
7	Charles V. & Sarah Miller	hay	Owned 68	Slingerlands, "Witchall Farm"
43	Frank & Martha Mizener	rye	Rented 116	Glenmont
15	Archibald T. & Lavina Moat	hay	Owned 61	Slingerlands, "Tawesentha"
96	Charles B. & Gertrude Mosher	hay	Owned 10	So. Bethlehem
93	Henry L. & Anna Mosher	rye	Owned 350	So. Bethlehem
85	John B. & Mary Mosher	hay	Owned 10	So. Bethlehem
46	George I. & Ella Mosher	milk	Rented 20	Glenmont
53	Martin & Anna Murray	potatoes	Owned 30	Glenmont
62	Lambert & Mary Nasner	hay/grain	Owned 100	Selkirk
67	Alvin & Ella Neahr	rye	Rented 80	So. Bethlehem
70	Eugene & Castella Niver	hay/oats/potatoes/corn	Owned 8	Selkirk
96	Veeder & Hester Niver	hay	Owned 115	So. Bethlehem, "Breezy Hill"
29	Eugene & Bertha Norehouse	hay	Owned 100	Delmar
93	Harvey J. & Viola Northrup	hay	Rented 150	So. Bethlehem
28	Andrew V. Oliver	hay	Owned 133	Delmar, "Fairview Farm"
22	John & Sadie Oliver	hay	Owned 90	Delmar
77	Elias N. & Melissa Osterhout	hay	Owned 98	Selkirk
53	Elmer & Lucy Osterhout		Owned 27	Glenmont, "Ferndale"
28	Anthony & Frances Pangbum	hay/milk	Owned 101	Delmar
40	Frank M. & Susan Patterson	hay/milk	Rented 72	Delmar, "Spring Farm"
34	Lewis & Cordellia Petrie	hay	Owned 15	Glenmont
43	James B. & Maria Platt		Owned 12	Delmar, "Three Pines"
57	William W. & Rosa Pomykai	hay	Owned 55	Selkirk
60	Henry L. & Caroline Price		Owned 25	Glenmont
73	Herbert W. & Sarah Pyle	potatoes	Owned 4	Selkirk
57	John H. & Myrtle Radley	apples	Owned 55	Selkirk
52	Charles A. & Ellen Reitz	rye	Owned 195	Glenmont, "Maple Grove"
51	Jacob M. Relyea	hay	Owned 90	Selkirk, "Elm Shade"
56	Richard & Abigail Reynolds	rye	Owned 120	Selkirk, "Snyder Hill"

Hwy No.	Name	Main Crop	Owned/Rented Acreage	Location & Farm Name
38	Fred Y. & Julia Rider	tomatoes	Rented 90	Glenmont
67	John H. & Anna Robertson	berries	Owned 44	Feura Bush
83	Oscar Rupert	apples/rye	Owned 188	So. Bethlehem
19	Edward & Margaret Ryan	rye	Owned 150	Delmar
18	William & Emma Saulsbury	hay/grain	Owned 121	Elsmere, "Cloverdale"
78	Mrs. Anna B. Saunders		Owned 68	Selkirk
21	William & Grace Schafford	hay	Rented 108	Delmar
71	Leonard & Anna Schaap	rye	Owned 53	Selkirk
71	Joseph & Margaret Schapp	cucumbers	Owned 93	Selkirk
61	William Scharff	melons/chickens	Rented 15	Glenmont
61	George & Mary Schmitt	hay	Owned 110	Glenmont
61	Augustus & Minnie Schmitt	tomatoes	Owned 64	Glenmont, "River View"
73	Adelia J. Schoonmaker	rye	Owned 185	Selkirk
60	Harry H. & Anna Schoonmaker	hay	Rented 30	Glenmont
2	Frederick & Elizabeth Schwarts	rye/potatoes	Owned 105	Albany
16	Mathew & Mary Schwinn		Owned 33	Albany
18	Charles & Elizabeth Secor	hay	Owned 83	Delmar
61	James H. & Mary Selkirk	pears	Owned 50	Glenmont, "Four Pines"
56	Sarah Shanks	hay	Owned 81	Selkirk
60	William & Caroline Shaver		Owned 7	Glenmont
100	Alfred & Minerva Smith	hay	Owned 196	Selkirk
93	Bernard C. & Alinda Smith	rye	Owned 145	So. Bethlehem
55	Milo & Jennie Smith	hay	Owned 69	Selkirk
61	August & Wilhemine Smultz	tomatoes		Glenmont, "Riverview"
83	Wesley W. & Isabella Snyder	apples	Owned 45	So. Bethlehem
55	Frederick & Hannah Spore	hay	Owned 74	Selkirk
53	Frederick & Anna Stattler		Owned 11	Glenmont
53	Valentine & Anna Stang	dairy/hay	Owned 150	Glenmont, "Spring Valley"
61	Harvey H. & Nora Steenburgh	apples	Rented 22	Glenmont, "Appledale"
61	Edward E. & Anna Stephens	potatoes	Owned 52	Glenmont
61	John E. & Grace Stephens	tomatoes	Owned 61	Glenmont
60	George F. & Josephine Stoffels	dairy/milk	Owned 3	Glenmont
42	Christian & Gertrude Strohmier		Owned 96	Delmar
16	Charles F. & Helen M. Swarts	hay	Owned 80	Albany
60	Christopher Traeger	hay	Owned 93	Glenmont, "Millbanks"
51	Harvey G. & Martha Taylor	hay	Owned 247	Selkirk, "Winding Brook"
65	Theodore C. & Carrie Trenchard	hay	Owned 117	Feura Bush
39	Charles G. & Henrietta Tierney	hay	Owned 112	Delmar
67	Jay & Elizabeth Tryon	fruit	Owned 90	Feura Bush
55	Charles & Mary Tryon	hay	Owned 73	Delmar
65	Aaron & Laura Tygert	melons	Owned 32	Glenmont
62	Edward A. & Maria Van Allen	hay/grain	Owned 110	Selkirk
57	James H. C. & Dora Van Allen	hay	Owned 72	Selkirk
62	John S. & Albertina Van Allen	hay	Owned 100	Selkirk
57	James Stanley & Susan Van Allen	hay	Owned 44	Selkirk
65	Mary E. Van Allen	hay	Owned 100	Glenmont
97	Mamie B. Van Allen	hay	Owned 44	Selkirk
69	Ezra & Sarah Van Alstyne	hay	Rented 136	So. Bethlehem
76	Peter L. & Harriet Van Alstyne	hay	Rented 114	So. Bethlehem, "Willow Brook"
57	Winnie Van Atten	hay	Owned 80	Selkirk
82	Newton B. & Anna Van Derzee	apples	Owned 136	Selkirk, "Apple Orchards"
76	Henry & Hattie Van Derzee	rye	Owned 226	So. Bethlehem
70	Albert & Carrie Van Derzee	hay	Owned 72	Selkirk
98	Abram & Emily Vanderbilt	berries	Owned 4	So. Bethlehem
89	Martin Vanderpool	melons	Owned 70	Selkirk
89	William W. & Anna Vanderpool	hay	Owned 112	Selkirk
57	William & Eleanor Van Derpool	hay	Owned 140	Selkirk
44	William J. Van Wie	milk	Owned 77	Glenmont
87	Leonard & Mabel Vincent	melons	Owned 46	Selkirk
66	Cornelius & Catlena Wagner	melons	Owned 93	Glenmont
97	Sidney & Cornelia Wagoner	hay	Owned 100	So. Bethlehem
68	Andrew & Helena Waldron	hay	Owned 156	So. Bethlehem
56	George and Emma Waldenmaier		Owned 3	Selkirk, "Snyder Hill"
7	Walter G. & Sarah Warren	milk	Owned 10	Slingerlands, "Far View"
93	Harry G. & Louise Weaver	poultry		South Bethlehem
74	William E. & Elizabeth Weisheit	strawberries	Owned 80	Glenmont, "The Pines"
52	Rudolph Westfall	hay	Owned 111	Delmar
65	Charles & Hannah Whitbeck	fruit	Owned 3	Glenmont
73	James & Mary Whitterick	hay	Owned 140	Selkirk
53	Jacob J. & Gertrude Wieland	corn	Owned 71	Glenmont
78	William & Anna Wilkie	pears	Owned 12	Selkirk
93	Franklin A. & Harriet Wiltsie	rye	Owned 200	So. Bethlehem, "Homestead"
97	John & Jane Wiltsie	hay	Owned 135	So. Bethlehem, "Pictaway Farm"
68	John & Minnie Wiltsie	rye	Owned 120	So. Bethlehem
80	Barret & Lena Winne	alfalfa	Owned 20	Selkirk
30	Esley Winne		Owned 8	Delmar
30	Francis A. & Flossie Winne	corn	Rented 106	Delmar, "Crystal Brook"
34	Harry H. & May Winne		Owned 60	Glenmont
62	Herbert H. & Eva Winne	rye	Owned 110	Selkirk
75	Ira & Luella Winne	rye	Owned 65	Selkirk
70	Garrett & Helen Winne	hay	Owned 30	Selkirk
85	Maynard & Jennie Winne	hay	Owned 250	Selkirk
17	Francis F. & Elizabeth Wright	hay	Owned 100	Delmar
83	George & Eunice Wright	dairy	Owned 100	So. Bethlehem
79	Michael & Agnes Zakens	melons	Owned 50	Selkirk

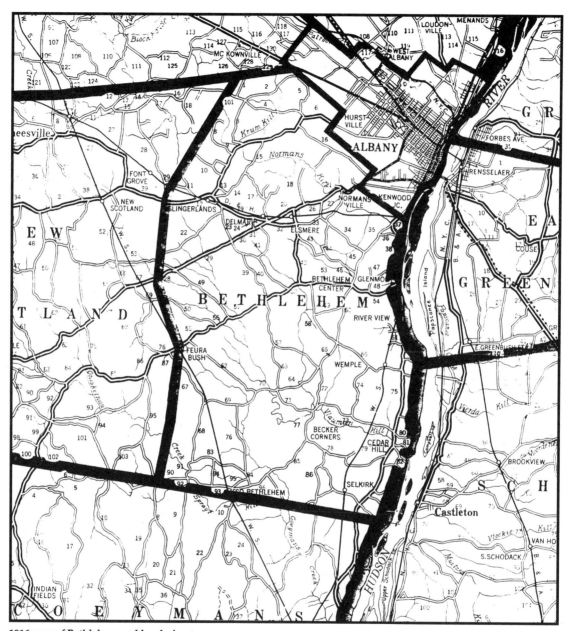

1916 map of Bethlehem and bordering towns.

10　Will of the People

In June 1640, colonists from the town of Lynn in Massachusetts Bay emigrated to Long Island and founded Southampton, the first English settlement in New York.[1] During subsequent years, more settlers moved from Massachusetts and Connecticut, establishing additional communities on the island and forming local governments like the townships they had left. The township form of government was prevalent in New England, starting with the *Mayflower* settlers.[2] Because of unknown dangers in a new land, New Englanders settled in areas large enough to produce food and small enough to be adequately defended from hostile Indians. Calling these communities towns appears to trace back to early Germanic tribes, who organized settlements in a similar manner. It is interesting that the word "town" is related to the Teutonic word *tun* (enclosure).[3]

The Dutch settled the land north of New Amsterdam and both east and west of the Hudson River. Many became leaseholders in privately owned patroonships such as Rensselaerswyck, which belonged to Kiliaen van Rensselaer. Rensselaerswyck encompassed about 850,000 acres around Fort Orange, the center of population in the area during the 1630s. The Patroon leased farmland to settlers, in lots generally sized between fifty and 100 acres.[4] In other cases, such as Schenectady, settlers purchased land directly from the Indians and established communities.

When the Dutch surrendered to the English in 1664, and New Netherland became an English colony called New York, Dutch authority, with its views of government, was replaced by the ruling monarchy in England. Rensselaerswyck was accorded the status of an English manor and was represented in the colony's general assembly, established to legislate affairs in the colony. The English bias to organizing all of New York State in towns or townships received impetus during the meeting of the general assembly held in Albany on August 22, 1754. The assembly presented an address to Lieutenant Governor James DeLancey, stating, "The other Colonies make themselves strong and defensible by settling in Townships, or some other close Order, while our frontier Lands are granted away in Patents, almost without bounds or number, regardless of Settlements, or the Public Welfare." DeLancey agreed "that settling in Townships, tends to make a County strong and defensible." [5]

The American Revolution was underway in 1777 when representatives from the fourteen counties of the State of New York met in convention in Kingston. One outcome was the ratification of the Constitution of the State of New York on April 20. The distinction of signing the document into law was conferred on a twenty-five-year-old Albany lawyer and political activist, Leonard Gansevoort, who was president pro tem on the day the constitution was ratified.[6] In later years, he gave up his political activities to carry on the family mercantile tradition in order to restore the family fortune.[7]

The constitution provided the framework and ideals under which the State would function. One fundamental principle was that governing officials at the state and local level would be elected to office by the people, thereby assuring the will of the people would prevail.

The state legislative body was established with an assembly consisting of at least seventy county representatives, and a senate of twenty-four representatives, apportioned by districts. Executive power was vested in a governor. Provision was also made for local governments, defined in the constitution as towns.

Bethlehem Formed

In succeeding years, as population increased, local governmental entities were established as towns, and representation within state government was broadened. During the eleventh session of the New York State Legislature held at Poughkeepsie, the town of Watervliet was defined and established on March 7, 1788.[8] Five years later, on March 12, 1793, during the sixteenth session of the legislature, the town of Bethlehem was formed from Watervliet. The effective date of the new town was to be the first Monday in April 1794.[9] The Act forming the town of Bethlehem also provided that no further towns be erected or divided without an application to the legislature by the inhabitants of the town or towns involved. Evidently, application was made to divide Bethlehem, and on April 25, 1832, the town of New Scotland was established. The separation, splitting the town about in half, resulted in the present-day land area of Bethlehem (afer annexation by Albany of some northern sections of the town).

Town Government

The legislation enacted in 1788 creating the town of Watervliet, along with others throughout the state, also provided for elections. Town meetings were required to be held on the first Tuesday in April in every year. The law stated that towns were:

then and there to elect and choose one supervisor, one town-clerk, not less than three nor more than seven assessors, one or more collectors ... two overseers of the poor, and three commissioners of highways ... and so many constables, overseers of the highways, fence-viewers and pound masters ... as necessary and convenient.[10]

The functions associated with official positions in town government provide some insight into the day-to-day problems faced by early residents. Overseers of the highways were responsible for the maintenance of roads in their respective districts. This was accomplished by requiring those living along a road to repair it. Fence-viewers inspected new fences and settled disputes arising from trespass by livestock that escaped enclosure. They also resolved disputes between adjacent land owners over who was responsible for making and maintaining a fence. Social needs were satisfied at the local level. Two overseers of the poor were elected, as required by law, in the first Bethlehem town meeting. For support of the poor, 100 pounds was to be raised. During the nineteenth century, additional town positions were established that faded away by the turn of the century. They included excise commissioner, inspector of weights and measures, inspector of cattle and slaughtering, health officer.

The Town Supervisor

Under English rule, the "Duke's Laws" provided for the laying out of the province of New York in towns and counties.[11] This followed the example set in New England by English settlers. However, the concept of "selectmen" to administer the affairs of a township was not adopted. Instead, the office of supervisor emerged. The earliest reference to the office and the functions to be performed was in 1702, in connection with an act passed for destroying wolves within the counties of Suffolk, Queens, and Kings. It stated, "The Supervisors ... shall be appointed and Authorized to Supervise, Audit or allow of the Accot's [accounts] and payments of the respective Treasurer."[12]

In the following year, the colonial assembly passed an act to increase the effectiveness of local government. The act provided for the annual election of supervisors, assessors, and collectors in every town. The supervisors within a county, responsible for the fiscal status of their towns, were required to meet annually to determine taxes to be levied in support of the county.[13]

After the states won independence from the English, the New York State Legislature granted similar powers to the supervisor.[14] The fiscal responsibilities of the supervisor to audit bills and make appropriate payments are, to this day, unchanged.[15] As the years progressed and the town grew, additional functions were added, requiring increased energy and time for the administration of town affairs and development of specialized departments.

It was on April 10, 1794, at the house of Henry Burhans, an innholder, that the first meeting of the town of Bethlehem took place. Philip Van Rensselaer was chosen as supervisor and John Van Derheyden as town clerk.

Philip Van Rensselaer.

Philip Van Rensselaer, who was both a merchant and farmer, served as supervisor until his death in 1798. He resided in the mansion he built in 1786 on his farm, called Cherry Hill, just south of the city of Albany. The area, at the time, was within the town of Bethlehem. Van Rensselaer was active in public service and during the Revolution served under his cousin, General Philip Schuyler, as a colonel and quartermaster of the Army of the Northern Region (New York), responsible for supplying the army with provisions.[16]

Very little is known about Philip Van Rensselaer during the period from 1794 to 1798, when he served as supervisor of Bethlehem. Although he was a prominent individual, few, if any, personal documents from this period have surfaced. More than 500 people were invited to attend his funeral, which was held at Cherry Hill on March 7, 1798.[17] An interesting fact, which can lead to some speculation, is that only one name on the invitation list, John Van Allen, coincides with the name of any of more than 150 town officials (two-thirds of whom were involved with highway matters) who served in various capacities during the 1794 to 1798 period. A John Van Allen served in 1797 as an overseer of highways for the town.

John M. Oliver.

Through 1992, a total of forty-three supervisors have served the town. The office holder with the longest period of service was John M. Oliver, who served from 1942 to 1959. He was born in Slingerlands in 1887. A graduate of Slingerlands Public School, his several careers included operating a dairy business, playing semi-professional baseball, serving as a combat soldier in the Argonne Forest of France, and selling automobiles. John Oliver's political career started in 1927 when he was elected town assessor. A significant addition to the tax roles occurred in 1931, during his tenure as an assessor, when the city of Albany purchased 256 acres of land for a park and golf course. The Albany Municipal Golf Course opened in 1933 and was a

Bethlehem taxpayer until 1967, when residents of the Karlsfeld section of the town voted in favor of annexation by the city of Albany.[18]

During Oliver's term of office, the town almost doubled its population, from a census count of 9,782 in 1940 to 18,936 in 1960. Within the period, World War II and the Korean War took place. In 1942, town government was involved in civil defense, blackout practices, rationing, and registration of draft-age youth. An aircraft observation post was organized to spot enemy aircraft.[19] During the early 1950s, the Korean War revived citizen concerns over the possibility of enemy attack. The rise of Communist aggression and the realities of an emerging nuclear age heightened tensions. In Bethlehem, as in other locations in the state and country, civil defense procedures were established, an aircraft observation post reactivated, basement bomb shelters constructed, and school children drilled in what to do if nuclear attack was imminent.

The face of Bethlehem changed during the 1940s and 1950s, as farms and woods gave way to residential and business growth. Local government was also on the rise. In 1941, Bethlehem became eligible under state law for classification as a "First Class Town" and a budget system was adopted. In 1947, officers and employees of the town were included in the New York State Retirement System.[20] More space for added functions and employees was needed. After the election in 1940, town board meetings were held in the office of the town clerk, Robert F. Westervelt, at 388

Kenwood Avenue (at present, Ehrlich's Auto Parts Store). The monthly rent of thirty-five dollars was authorized by the board to be paid by the town. A proposition to the voters to purchase the building was rejected in 1947. Instead, the old Adams Hotel at 393 Delaware Avenue was purchased in

Supervisor Thomas V. Corrigan (1978-1984) and future supervisor, J. Robert Hendrick (1985-1989), in May 1980 when the public was invited to visit the new Town Hall.

Aircraft observation post—at Cedar Hill. Former carriage house on the George Best estate, currently owned and occupied by Mr. and Mrs. Vincent Giordano.

1950 and renovated. The first town board meeting in the new Town Hall was held on December 30, 1950.[21] Thirty years later, in 1980, the former Delmar School building at 445 Delaware Avenue was renovated to accommodate town operations and became the present Town Hall.

Oliver was a devoted Republican and dedicated to his role as supervisor. His daughter, Mrs. Ruth Bickel, confirms the story, which many citizens recall, about his habit of going out with the snowplows in the dead of the night, but said "he did that to check on a driver who accepted drinks from grateful citizens and, on occasion, ran the plow into the ditch."

When John Oliver died in November 1959, shortly after being elected for another two-year term, the Bethlehem Town Board appointed Bertram E. Kohinke as supervisor. He had been serving at the time as sewer commissioner. Mr. Kohinke retained the post until 1974, thereby establishing his tenure of fifteen years in office as the second longest in the history of the town, matching the administration of David Delong who served from 1804 to 1818. Long-term tenures as supervisor were unusual. With the exception of David Delong, terms of office prior to the year 1900 were six years or less, averaging two and one-half years. Since 1900, the average term has been ten years in length.

A notable achievement of Bertram Kohinke's administration was the solicitation and courting of large business interests to establish facilities within the town. General Electric Plastics (1965) and Owens-Corning Fiberglas (1973) are two prominent examples. Both are located near the Selkirk rail distribution yards of Conrail, in an area zoned for industrial development.

Bertram E. Kohinke.

Politics and Government

Politics and the wide variety of definitions and emotions generated by the term are inseparable from government. From colonial times to the present, in our nation, state, county, and town, political factions have competed for control of the governmental process. During the history of the town, factions included Whigs, Tories, Federalists, Anti-Federalists, Know-Nothings, Republicans, and Democrats. There was, undoubtedly, public representation in Bethlehem of all these factions and, in all likelihood, of other splinter groups that formed during the past 200 years.

For the last 100 years, supervisors and other elected town officials have been associated with the Republican party. This dominance of a political party did not exist during the first century of our town government. Many of the political parties previously mentioned were represented in town government. Election results for supervisor, reported by the press in Albany, usually gave a party affiliation. For example, the last Democrat elected as supervisor was W. Chauncey Hotaling (1881-1882 and also 1877).[22] Jeremiah Mead (1848-1850) was associated with the Loco-Foco party.[23] Leonard G. Ten Eyck (1831-1832 and 1855-1858) was identified as a Know-Nothing party member.[24]

Although the Republican party has succeeded in maintaining its representation in the town for a long period of time, internal dissension and development of political factions within the party have occurred in Bethlehem. A prominent example is the emergence of the Lincoln party in 1961.

A group of Republicans organized the Lincoln group because they believed the Republican party in town was being dominated by a few individuals, referred to as the "Old Guard," and becoming a political machine of the undesirable type, not responsive to problems of the town. The Lincoln party headquarters was, interestingly, at 388 Kenwood Avenue in Delmar, which had served for ten years as the meeting place of the town board. Two major issues precipitated formation of the party: first, an attempt by the party in

power to influence election of candidates to the Board of Education of the Bethlehem Central School District, an intrusion considered highly inappropriate; second, an investigative report of tax delinquencies, mostly in the city of Albany, which led to Bethlehem, along with other towns in the county, being forced to pay additional taxes to offset the loss.[25] An election campaign was launched in 1961, and a third party slate of candidates was chosen to run for supervisor (against the incumbent Republican, Bertram Kohinke), two town council seats, and the town clerk. Other campaign issues raised by the Lincolns included the caucus system to endorse party candidates, lack of a police chief, and less than full-time availability of the supervisor.

The Lincoln group received substantial support. Mr. Kohinke won with 5,231 votes; the Lincoln candidate, Arthur P. Fisher, received 3,140 votes; and the Democratic candidate, John Clyne, received 1,155 votes.[26] Although the Lincoln party had a short life and did not participate in further elections, issues that existed and were introduced during the 1961 election received attention during subsequent years in both the town and the county.

At the county level, the traditional involvement of the town supervisor as a member of the Albany County Board of Supervisors came to an end in 1967, when the county charter was revised. On January 1, 1968, the first meeting of the Albany County Legislature was held, and Bethlehem, defined as the thirty-sixth legislative district, was represented by Edward H. Sargent, Jr. The invocation at this first meeting of the legislature was given by Monsignor Rooney, pastor of Saint Thomas Roman Catholic Church in Delmar.[27]

The police force was strengthened in late 1961 with the appointment of Peter Fish as police chief. At the time, the eighteen-man force was under the direction of the supervisor. The Lincoln group had voiced objection to this arrangement.

Another issue raised during the Lincoln party campaign in 1961 focused on the supervisor as a part-time official. The Lincoln candidate pledged to work full-time at Town Hall. Prior to the 1961 election, Mr. Kohinke announced retirement from his managerial responsibilities with an Albany tire company and pledged daily availability at Town Hall starting at 8:00 A.M.

During the fall of 1961, a group of Republicans led by Charles Redmond, a member of the planning board, and Arthur McCormick, the town attorney, organized and incorporated a club for men, separate from the Bethlehem Republican Organization, which was perceived to be politically controlled by a few individuals. The goals of the club were to give Republicans of the town an opportunity to participate in party affairs and to inform residents of the aims and achievements of town government. The first organizational meeting of the club was held during February 1962, and Mr. Redmond was elected president. Since that time, the Bethlehem Men's Republican Club exerted a strong influence in local affairs and was a focal point for Republican party activities in Bethlehem.

The advantages of an organized political group were recognized by the women of Bethlehem many years prior to the formation of the Bethlehem Men's Republican Club. On July 1, 1926, fifteen ladies met at the home of Mrs. William Glenn and organized the Women's Republican Club of Bethlehem. Miss Ruth Miner of Slingerlands, who initiated the organization, was elected president and Mrs. Glenn, vice president. Over the years, the group has been active in local politics through sponsoring various events and speaking out on the issues that were of concern to voters in the town.[28] In 1992, both clubs dropped the gender designation and merged as the Bethlehem Republican Club.

For some time, the local Democratic organization has been unable to muster the votes necessary to place its candidates in town government positions, with one exception, a Democratic councilman elected in 1987. But they have succeeded in maintaining the integrity of the election process through fielding a slate of candidates and providing the opportunity for residents of the town to express diverse views.

The Continuum of Town Government

As time went on, issues that concerned the residents and involved town government were those that had an impact on their daily lives. The government was structured in response to the needs of the day. It remains so today, although the scope of activity increased as the town grew, and adjustments were required to keep pace with the times.

Highways

Early road records of the town indicate a high degree of attention to the laying out of roads through land of property owners and the assignment of citizens to provide the labor for their maintenance. One evidence of that attention is the number of officials in Bethlehem assigned to highway concerns. In 1794, during the first town meeting, three commissioners of highways and nineteen overseers were appointed. Keeping roads passable during various weather conditions was a continuing effort of both the citizen and the overseer responsible for making sure the work was done. This method lasted well into the late 1800s, but it was, at best, a marginal way to maintain roads. In 1871, a total of fifty-five overseers were appointed. The system was unwieldy and change was required. Town meeting minutes do not record the action taken, but, since 1857, only one commissioner of highways has been in office at any one time, rather than the usual three that existed in prior years. No commissioner was named during the years 1872 through 1874. It was in 1909 when the name of commissioner was replaced by superintendent. The title of superintendent of highways has persisted to this day. Garrett Winnie was the first, followed in 1916 by Edgar Scrafford, who served for six years. From 1922 until his death in 1953, Allen D. Mead was the superintendent of highways. David Mead, son of Allen, followed and was elected to the office in 1954, serving until his death in 1966, when Martin J. Cross was appointed to the vacancy. Mr. Cross retired in 1991 after thirty-six years of service to the town.

The Highway Department garage on Elm Avenue Extension.

Martin (Marty) Cross, during his tenure of twenty-five years as superintendent, contributed much to the development of the town, in addition to the primary task of maintaining roads. For example, until more recent times, development of new residential streets was undertaken by the town. Streets in Kenaware, Kenholm, Birchwood Acres, Colonial Acres, Glenmont, Schuyler Meadows, Hamagrael, and North Bethlehem were constructed by the highway department. In addition, the pavilions at the town park on Elm Street and at the park by the Hudson River were completed by the department. When asked about the most memorable event during his term as superintendent, Marty Cross recalls "the biggest catastrophe and the biggest job that I handled while I was a highway superintendent ... was the October 4, [1987] storm." On that date, heavy snow fell and caused tree limbs, still containing leaves, to crack under the strain. He tells of calling together all highway department personnel and directing,

"Everyone is going to work eleven hours a day ... six days a week." Mr. Cross takes pride in the positive response of his work force to the emergency, the fact that only about $7,000 was spent for equipment rentals, and that the salary budget for the department was managed to include all overtime costs related to the storm. Neighboring communities did not fare as well.[29]

Perhaps the most contentious issue involving highways occurred in 1964, and left in its wake an oddity in the town, namely two modern state highways that end "nowhere." Known as the Slingerlands By-Pass project, the idea was to form a "loop" around the Tri-Village area by connecting Route 85 (the Albany By-Pass) to Route 32 (the Delmar By-Pass). The problem arose when the state highway department contended the only feasible manner of accomplishing the objective was to construct the road through the hamlet of Slingerlands. Citizens of the Slingerlands area and other individuals organized and forced abandonment of the project.[30]

Keeping the Peace

In 1675, magistrates were directed by the court of Albany, Rensselaerswyck, and Schenectady to choose constables annually, their duties "the same as constables in New York and other English places."[31] Some of their more common duties included carrying out such directives of the court as collecting fines, taking inventory of the estate of a deceased person, and making sure the stock-

118 Adams Street in Delmar. Location of Police Department and Town Court from 1968 to 1979.

ade or city gates were in good repair. As a badge of office and authority, it was directed that "Every Constable shall have a Staff of about six foot long, with the Kings armes on it as a badge of his Office which Staff shall be provided at the charge of the Town." [32]

The New York State Legislature, in establishing town governments, directed towns to elect as many constables as deemed necessary. Bethlehem apparently saw the need for at least four to five constables from 1794 through the early 1900s. One of the last constables in town, and the forerunner of our present police department, was David R. Main, who was appointed in October 1924 to fill a vacancy. Many older residents remember Constable Main, and humorously recall that he could not drive a car. He patrolled the town on foot with his pet white bulldog. In 1941, Main was appointed chief of police. At the time, C. Arthur Blodgett and John A. Hotaling were also serving as constables, a term since replaced by police. Chief Main died in 1949. Arthur Blodgett was appointed chief of police and John Hotaling was night chief, although many years would pass before police were actually assigned to twenty-four hour coverage. The first police car was purchased in 1951.[33] Over the next forty years, continuing expansion and improvement took place in police operations. In 1990, the town police force was accredited under the New York State Law Enforcement Accreditation Program. Bethlehem was one of the first towns in the state to receive the accreditation.

Controlling Animals

Animal control, a function under the police department today, has a long history in the town. In early days, the control of stray animals was a matter of concern and an important elected official was the pound master. His main duty was no different from that of the animal control officer of today, namely, to impound a stray animal and notify the owner. From 1794 until the late 1800s, pound masters were elected during town meetings and their names recorded in the minutes of the meetings. Thereafter, town minutes do not contain the names of pound masters. Presumably, they were no longer considered necessary. In more modern times, the chief problem with animals concerned dogs that were running loose, and dog wardens were appointed. One of the early control efforts was a quarantine on dogs running at large between the hours of sunset and one hour after sunrise. The Town Board passed the quarantine resolution on November 12, 1930, and published and posted the regulations. It appeared to be premature. Shortly thereafter, the Albany County Board of Supervisors issued a quarantine on dogs running at night for all towns in the county. On December 6, 1930, at a special meeting of the board, the town resolution was revoked based on county notification of its quarantine law, and the town dog warden, Frank Miller, was directed to cease operations.[34]

The issue of dog control has received recent attention in town history. In 1967, an ordinance was passed that prohibited dogs running loose, excessive barking, and other forms of nuisance. At a public hearing of the proposed ordinance in February 1967, an overflow crowd turned out at Town Hall to voice approval or opposition.[35] The ordinance proved to be unworkable and could not be enforced. In 1977, the ordinance was rescinded and a new resolution was adopted with the same intent, namely, to restrain the unrestricted running of dogs in the town. The resolution provided for penalties and fines for violations. Later, in 1991, another ordinance affecting dog owners was passed—the "pooper scooper" law. It led to sales of disposal devices and encouraged the owners of the more than 2,000 dogs licensed in the town to think of unique and creative ways to comply with the law.

Justice for All

From earliest colonial days, a system of courts existed to settle claims of violence or economic injury. Courts evolved at the state and county level. At the local or town level, fence-viewers were the elected officials responsible for assuring that property lines were honored and to resolve any disputes arising from claims of infringement. Justices of the peace were also appointed at the local level to hear disputes and mediate other legal matters.

In 1827, the legislature passed a law that provided for the election of justices of the peace.[36] Town Law, consolidated in 1890, directed that four justices were to be elected for a term of four years, one each year. At the time, and for many years thereafter, the four justices, with the supervisor, town clerk, and assessor, comprised the town board. Today, the town board consists of the supervisor and four elected council members. The transition to this composition of the board started in 1942 after William B. Phipps was elected the first councilman in the town. Ten years would elapse before the election of 1951 resulted in the present town council of four members.[37] There are now two justices of the peace who adjudicate the law of the town but are not directly involved in governing.

The Assessor and Collector

There is a familiar saying about the inevitability of death and taxes. Our forefathers in government made sure that taxes were satisfied by providing the office of assessor and the associated office of collector, the modern title for which is receiver of taxes. Taxation through assessment was among the early items of business addressed during the first session of the New York State Legislature. The law passed on March 12, 1778, provided for discharge of existing assessors and election of a greater number of assessors. The required oath called for the elected jobholder to "honestly and impartially assess the several persons and estates within the [place name]."[38] The system of local property taxation has existed for two centuries. It has been supplemented over the years in various creative ways at the county, state, and federal levels by taxing earnings and purchases in addition to property.

During the last fifty years, as residential construction increased along with inflation of the dollar, disparities arose between the property assessment of the older resident and the new homeowner in town. In 1991, the town contracted for a review of all property in order to arrive at full valuation assessment, as required by state law. In theory, total tax revenue would remain unchanged but would be more equitably borne by the citizen based on his, or her, property value. The reassessment of property was completed in May 1992, resulting in a record number of almost 1,700 grievances registered.

Evolving Government to Satisfy Needs

The needs of the time, during and after colonial days, determined when and in what way the structure of local government would change. As population increased, direct citizen involvement in handling the affairs of the town became more difficult and impractical. What evolved is a complex system of elected officials and town employees, whom the people of the town empower to meet the needs of the community. This structure of government is a relatively recent development, as seen from the following reports on some of the administrative departments in the town.

Planning for Growth

How land was being used became an item of importance in the community as more residents and businesses came to the town. In response to increasing concern over growth, the town board, in 1944, established a planning board to "preserve the attractiveness of our town."[39] Howard P. Paddock, a prominent Delmar real estate broker and developer, was appointed chairman, a post he held until his death in 1969. The initial thrust of the group was to develop a zoning ordinance and zoning map. The planning board, supported by zoning requirements, thereby became the forum for discussion and resolution of most issues related to land use within the town. In 1959, the planning board was authorized by the town board to review and approve or disapprove proposals for subdivision developments. Most of the current residential areas of the town were required to participate in this process.

In 1965, after two years of study by a planning consultant hired by the town, a comprehensive master plan was produced. Cost of the study was supported by federal and state grants. The master plan addressed the various characteristics of the town, including economics, population, land use, transportation, housing, community facilities, and schools. It developed plans for business districts, industrial areas, parks, and residential areas. The data presented were comprehensive and provided a base for consideration of future proposals.[40]

The planning board continues to be the overseer of development and change in the town. More recent considerations included the development of multiple-dwelling units and senior-citizen housing.

Public Works

Perhaps the new resident of our town, or the children of existing residents, will not relate to a private well for water and a septic tank to handle waste. Only during the last thirty years has the majority of the residents of Bethlehem been able to turn on a water faucet to receive safe water and utilize an indoor bathroom that directs waste to a treatment facility. The development and growth of water and sewer facilities is outlined in the chapter on business and industry. The demand for these conveniences—and most would argue they are necessities—evolved as the town grew in population. On June 10, 1981, the town board voted to make a major change in the administration of town public utilities and adopted a local law to establish the Department of Public Works. Included were functions associated with water, sewers, and engineering. Bruce Secor was appointed as the first head of the department.

Disputes within the town about water and sewer facilities are rare, but in 1957 and 1958 a water issue arose that dominated public attention. Purity and safety of a water supply have always been conditions not open to compromise by the residents of Bethlehem. Advancing technology, however, often provides opportunities to enhance a good thing, or cause concern. Such was the case in 1957 when a group of residents, known as the Bethlehem Community Association, proposed that controlled concentrations of flouride be added to the water from the new Vly Creek reservoir, as a means to curb tooth decay. Their proposal was based on the contention that:

> Fluoridation is endorsed by the American Medical Association, the American Dental Association, the American Public Health Association, the American Academy of Pediatrics, the U.S. Public Health Service, the New York State Department of Health, the New York State Dental Association, and by many other medical and dental groups.[41]

The proposal produced much controversy in the town. A public hearing was held and a vote taken on March 22, 1958, of the citizens of Water District No. 1. The proposal was defeated by a vote of 1,571 against and 915 for.

Parks and Recreation

On a national scale, the establishment of Yellowstone National Park in 1872 may be considered the start of governmental involvement in providing and maintaining facilities for recreational purposes. During the twentieth century, the provision of such public resources increased steadily at all levels of government.

In Bethlehem, recreational activities supported by public tax revenues were initiated in the schools. As new school buildings were erected, the integration of athletics and physical fitness programs into the school curriculum led to the construction of gymnasiums, swimming pools, tennis courts, and playing fields for various sports. The facilities were also used by the citizens of the town when not required for school needs and a cooperative arrangement between the town and the school districts developed. As an example, a nine-hole golf course was developed in 1937 on the grounds of the current Bethlehem middle school. It was really intended for practice and was a boon to novice golfers. There were no greens fees and the course was open to the public during daylight hours, except 1:00 to 5:00 P.M. on weekdays.[42]

In 1945, a law was enacted creating a state youth commission to encourage the development of recreational programs for children, defined by the state as persons under the age of twenty-one. Citing the existing war, the fact that heads of families were serving in the armed forces, and that mothers were filling the places of those men in industry, the legislature pronounced, "It therefore becomes necessary for government to supplement and aid in coordinating the care and guidance furnished to young people by the family and by existing religious and social institutions."[43] Projects sponsored by local government were eligible for matching funds up to $1,000 per annum in a municipality of less than 4,000 children.

Through the efforts of parent-teacher groups, the Bethlehem Recreation Committee was started. It developed plans for summer recreational and playground activities and solicited support from sixty-seven organizations throughout the town. In March 1946, committee representatives John McColl and Roy Curtis, who were associated with Central School District No. 6, asked the town board for sponsorship and suggested the appointment of a three-person commission to administer the program. With an estimated 1,000 children in the town, the plan was to raise $1,000 through volunteer contributions and apply to the state for matching funds, resulting in a working budget of $2,000. In May 1946, the board approved sponsorship of the program and appointed a recreation commission consisting of Clinton Hartzell of Slingerlands as chairman, John Clyne of Elsmere, and Mrs. Keith Callanan of South

Bethlehem. By the time the resolution was adopted, the Bethlehem Recreation Committee had raised more than $1,200 in contributions and expanded the effort to include the Selkirk and South Bethlehem parent-teacher organizations.[44]

The recreational and playground programs that existed were funded under school budgets. In 1947, the town board was requested to appropriate $1,000 to aid in financing the Youth Recreation Program. The fund was to be used for a three-week craft and music program at the Elsmere Grade School and the Delmar Grade School. The board approved the appropriation, transferring the amount from a contingency fund. Additionally, the board approved a resolution to establish a recreation project, intending to apply to the state for matching funds. By 1950, additional town funding for recreation was incorporated within the budget and $1,000 was added, supplementing the $200 allocated since 1948 for patriotic observances.[45]

A joint arrangement of school, town, and state funding continued as summer programs and other activities increased to satisfy recreational needs. During 1954, the school district opened a youth canteen at the high school (now the middle school), where Hamilton H. Bookhout was the supervising principal. The canteen was an offspring of a Youth Center Advisory Council of local citizens. The center, intended as an outlet for wholesome social contact among students, grew and expanded operations into evenings, weekends, and summer periods. It became known to the youth of the town as "The Pit" due to its location in the basement of the school. Despite the disparaging, or perhaps affectionate, name, it was the center of youthful activities for many years. The operation was not without peripheral problems, such as alcohol consumption on nearby grounds. About 1970, support and interest in the center waned, resulting in a gradual decline in participation during the early 1970s.[46] During that same time frame, a membership corporation called Bethlehem Coffee House, Inc., was started to operate a youth center at 125 Adams Street (currently, offices of *The Spotlight*).[47] Operating with parents, who volunteered their time, it failed to generate a substantial clientele and was phased out in the mid-1970s. In 1990, middle school students, teachers, and parents collaborated to reopen "The Pit." During the season of 1991-1992 the facility was open one evening per month after school hours until 4:00 P.M. With support of volunteers and the students of the middle school, "The Pit" continues to provide an opportunity for wholesome social activity.

During the early 1970s, with the opening of two parks, the town made substantial commitments to recreational programs for its citizens. The park on Elm Avenue became

operational in 1973 with a summer program. Currently, a wide array of summer and winter activities is offered for children and adults. In 1975, the Henry

Hudson Park at Cedar Hill, by the Hudson River, was dedicated. Family picnicking is a favorite pastime in this park.

Town Historian

In April 1919, the education law of the state was amended with a bill known as the "Historian's Law." The law provided for the designation of a local historian for each city, town, and village in the state. The historian was to gather and store material relating to the history of the political subdivision to which he, or she, was appointed and to cooperate with public officials in preserving historically valuable public records. New York was the first state in the country to direct the establishment of such a network of historians. Although the law was vigorously encouraged by the State Historian, Dr. James Sullivan, little interest was initially shown. By the end of 1920, only fifty percent of the 1,550 community jurisdictions in the state had appointed an historian.[48]

In 1921, Bethlehem appointed its first town historian, Harriet C. D. Wiltsie, of South Bethlehem.

She was succeeded in 1926 by Mrs. Lucius H. Washburn. Their efforts in promoting and preserving local history have, apparently, been lost to time since no documentation of their activities is evident in town records. Ruth F. Dickinson was appointed to the office in 1945, initiating an era of increased emphasis on the history of the town.

Ruth Dickinson, prior to her designation as town historian, was appointed to the town's War Council in 1940 when the country was on the verge of entering World War II. She compiled a record of all Bethlehem residents who served in the armed forces during the war. Ten years later, during her tenure as town historian, the Korean War arose and she was asked by Supervisor Oliver to set up a civil defense office. As chairman of administration of Bethlehem's Office of Civil Defense, she coordinated the recruitment of volunteers and oversaw other activities.

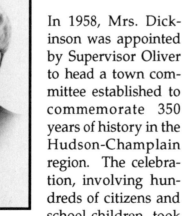

Ruth F. Dickinson.

In 1958, Mrs. Dickinson was appointed by Supervisor Oliver to head a town committee established to commemorate 350 years of history in the Hudson-Champlain region. The celebration, involving hundreds of citizens and school children, took place in 1959, designated by the state as a "Year of History." Additionally, she served as a catalyst in developing the Bethlehem Historical Association and the museum at Cedar Hill. In April 1965, she proposed to the town board a resolution to make available the Cedar Hill school for keeping and displaying historical artifacts. Ruth Dickinson, who devoted countless hours and unbounded energy to the job, ended her term as historian in December 1965.[49] She graciously agreed to serve as assistant historian to her successor, Allison Bennett.

Mrs. Bennett, a prolific historical researcher and writer, wrote a number of articles for publication in the local newspaper, *The Spotlight*. Many of these articles were later published in two books, *Times Remembered* and *More Times Remembered*. Allison Bennett also published in 1968 a popular booklet about the history of the town. She resigned as town historian after nine years but has remained active in historical matters through continued research, writing, and involvement with the Bethlehem Historical Association.

Subsequent historians were Thomas E. Mulligan (1974-1983, during which period the nation and the town celebrated the country's bicentennial in 1976), James E. Morgan (1983-1987), Valerie J.

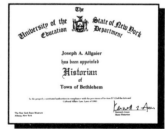

Thompson (1988-1990) and Joseph A. Allgaier (1991-to date).[50]

Senior Services

During the latter half of the twentieth century a social trend emerged affecting a significant portion of the population. For various reasons, such as health care, increased standards of living, social security income, and various forms of pension benefits, the older citizen of today lives longer and is more active than the older member of society of yesteryear. "Senior citizen" is the phrase most often used to describe an older resident. As reported in the 1990 census, Bethlehem has 5,200 citizens aged sixty and over.

Senior citizens formed a mutual interest group in 1955 with the help of the Lions Club and the Bethlehem Central School District. More information about this organization will be found in the community organizations chapter of this book. Town government became directly involved with the needs and concerns of the senior citizens when their group sponsorship and modest funding were transferred from the school district to the Parks and Recreation Department in 1974. In 1979, a volunteer position as coordinator became an hourly-paid job. By 1989, a separate Senior Services Department was created, headed by Karen Pellettier, and continues to serve the needs of the older members of the community through the efforts of more than 340 volunteers involved in more than thirty-five programs.[51] One of their more visible programs is the senior van service, offering transportation at no cost to seniors for medical visits, shopping, and other purposes.

1985 mini-van contributed by **General Electric Foundation.** From left to right: Norrine Cooke, Joyce Becker (Senior Services Coordinator), Thomas Corrigan, Charles Gunner, George Hernandez, and Warren Boutelle.

Town Government Administration

The Town of Bethlehem has fourteen departments with 180 employees to administer a budget that exceeds sixteen million dollars. Some departments result from the need to handle town functions efficiently—for example, the office of Comptroller, the Data Processing department, the Building Inspector, and the Board of Appeals to rule on proposed variances to town regulations.

Remaining town administrative units relate more directly to citizen and community concerns and tend to reflect issues of the day.

Some are temporary, as the Bicentennial Commission, established to celebrate the two-hundreth anniversary of the founding of the town. Other functional units are the Solid Waste Task Force to address options for disposal of waste, Recycling Coordinator to deal with stimulation of material recycling, the Youth Employment Service to coordinate needs and availability of teenagers for temporary jobs, Community Relations to foster and maintain communications between town government and the citizens of the town, Land Use Management Advisory Committee to reflect the attitudes and opinions of the residents of the town regarding development and environmental concerns.

Government and the Future

The pragmatic role of government is to provide for the safety and welfare of its citizens. Laws of the state, county, and town define the rules under which local government is to act. The administration of those rules through elected officials is a matter of local citizen concern. Politics is inherent in the system and the election process.

The will of the people is the ultimate determinate factor in governmental matters. Continuing involvement and participation of Bethlehem residents in the local government process and exercise of the voting privilege will assure succeeding generations a community life equal to, if not better than, that which we inherited from our forefathers.

11 Hamlets: A Bicentennial Tour

Several drives into the country south of Albany are recommended in nineteenth- and early twentieth-century guide books to the city and county. For example, the most frequented drive outside the city, according to *The Albany Hand-Book for 1881*, was on the "New Scotland turnpike, or the Hurstville road, as it is commonly called," a drive of "inexhaustable extent and variety."[1] Suggestions in the *Albany Guide Book*, published in 1917, include three drives in Bethlehem: along New Scotland Avenue to Hurst's roadhouse; on country roads to Slingerlands; and down along the Hudson River to the Abbey Hotel and Cedar Hill. It was also noted that people "of means and leisure" could travel around the suburbs and into the country for "$1.50 per hour for a carriage holding four persons and having a speed rate of about four miles per hour."[2]

This year, as we celebrate the two-hundredth birthday of Bethlehem, we, too, can go for drives around our town. By means of the bicentennial tours in this chapter, we can travel the length and breadth of Bethlehem, look at the hamlets as they are today, and, through such sources of information about our past as county histories, interviews, scrapbooks, and newspaper articles, learn about the history of the hamlets of Bethlehem.

A Drive Down the Hudson Shore
(From Albany to Cedar Hill)

We will start at Historic Cherry Hill, located on South Pearl Street between First and McCarty avenues in the southeastern corner of Albany. Then, the drive south on Route 144 (River Road) to the southern border of Bethlehem will include the hamlets of Kenwood, Glenmont, Van Wies Point, and Cedar Hill.

Historic Cherry Hill

It may seem strange that Cherry Hill, located in Albany, should be included in this tour of Bethlehem. When the house was built, in 1786-1787, it was in open country and surrounded by 900 acres of farmland. Bethlehem was formed in 1793, six years after the house was built, and from then until 1870, the house was in Bethlehem. Since 1870, when Albany annexed the land between the Normanskill and the city limits, Cherry Hill has been within the city of Albany.

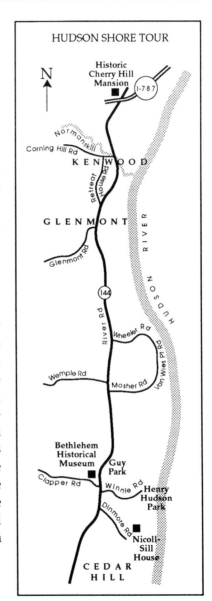

HUDSON SHORE TOUR

Cherry Hill was the country residence of Philip van Rensselaer, his wife Maria Sanders, and their twelve children. Roderick Blackburn has written:

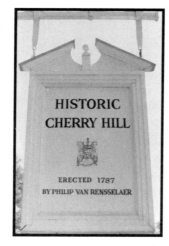

HISTORIC
CHERRY HILL

ERECTED 1787
BY PHILIP VAN RENSSELAER

> Cherry Hill is a significant landmark in American cultural history. It is one of the relatively few eighteenth century houses which have survived to the present day in the same family with a large portion of the possessions intact. Following nearly two centuries of continual family residence, Cherry Hill became a museum in 1963, established as a memorial to the Van Rensselaer family by the last owner.[3]

Philip van Rensselaer was a merchant-farmer with business interests and, in addition to Cherry Hill, a town house in Albany. He was a wealthy merchant, a politician (alderman in 1786), and one of the first trustees of the Albany Water Works, which was incorporated in 1801. During the Revolutionary War he was paymaster of the Army of the Northern Region (New York) and Deputy Commissary General.[4] In addition, he was Bethlehem's first supervisor.

Over the years, as Albany developed and expanded, and as ownership of the estate changed, Cherry Hill became encircled by the city and the extent of the estate was reduced to just a few acres. Now, the view east from Cherry Hill is of South Pearl Street, Route 787, and the Port of Albany, instead of a vista of lawns sloping down to the river.

Cherry Hill was only one of many mansions built along the Hudson River south of Albany in the eighteenth, nineteenth, and twentieth centuries. Immediately south of Albany, the country homes of the Prentices, Rathbones, and Townsends were situated between the Albany city limits and the Normanskill. The Corning estates were just south of the creek.

The Ezra P. Prentice estate was named Mount Hope. The property came into Mr. Prentice's possession in 1834, and, as reported later, he improved it

> to such an extent that it has for some years been a point of attraction for citizens, particularly women and children seeking a stroll out of the dense city in search of fresh air and pleasant scenes. ... The horse rail road cars, which have now superseded the omnibuses, pass Mount Hope every half-hour, on their route to Kenwood mills.[5]

The estate of 127 acres consisted of flower and vegetable gardens and orchards, in addition to herds of cattle, South Down and Cotswold sheep, swine, and horses. The feed for all the stock was grown on the farm. At one time, there was a "fine elliptical sheet of water, 150 feet long by 100 wide, bordered by trees ... in the center of which a perpetual fountain, in the form of a fine delicate silver jet," shot some fifteen feet into the air.[6]

Today, this part of Bethlehem looks very different from the way it looked in the first three decades of the seventeenth century when Dutch traders, trappers, and later, farmers, millers, and sawyers were becoming established in the new land. Gorham A. Worth has left us a word picture of the Hudson shore near Albany as it appeared nearly 200 years ago, which may help us to visualize the bucolic character of early Bethlehem:

> The margin of the river ... was over-hung with willows, and shaded by the wide spreading elm. The little islands below the town [of Albany] were feathered with foliage, down to the very water's edge, and bordered with stately trees, whose forms were mirrored in the stream below. As far as the eye could extend, up and down the river, all remained comparatively wild and beautiful....[7]

This could well be a description of the banks of the Normanskill today near its mouth at the intersection of Route 32 (Corning Hill Road) and Route 144 (River Road) in the area known as Kenwood.

Kenwood

A pretty suburb [of Albany] at the terminus
of the South Pearl street car line....[8]

Kenwood is much more a state of mind today than a political entity. In the late eighteenth and nineteenth centuries, it was an important settlement.[9] Although the place-name still appears on maps of Albany County and of Bethlehem, the hamlet itself disappeared about one hundred years ago. For our purposes, the borders of the area known as Kenwood are First Avenue in Albany on the north, the Hudson River on the east, Route 9W on the west, and Route 32 (Corning Hill Road) on the south.

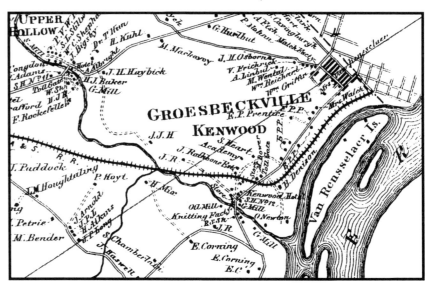

Detail of 1866 map of Bethlehem by S. N. and D. G. Beers; note hamlet of Kenwood near mouth of Normanskill.

One day not long ago, I set out to try to find some relic of the old hamlet. On South Pearl Street, just south of the entrance to the Doane Stuart School, is a street without a sign. A mailman told me it was South Pearl Street Extension. Actually, this street follows the original route of the old Albany and Bethlehem Turnpike, which was chartered on April 9, 1804, and was a continuation of South Pearl Street.[10] Later, as we shall see, the path of the turnpike was changed. The Albany street railway (1864), consisting of horse cars, ran on South Pearl Street as far as Kenwood.

The hamlet of Kenwood was located on both banks of the Normanskill below the hill on which the Convent of the Sacred Heart, Doane Stuart School, and Kenwood Day Care Center are situated. Kenwood is described in a New York State gazetteer of 1860 as being a village near the mouth of the Normanskill, containing an extensive mill and a factory for woolen and cotton knit goods.[11] Twenty-six years later, it was described as containing sixteen dwellings, thirty-six families, one hundred fifty inhabitants, a Baptist chapel, schoolhouse, store, and blacksmith shop.[12] By 1890, it also contained a saloon, several more stores and blacksmith shops, the administrative buildings for the mills, and tenement houses for the mill workers.[13] Over the years, the mills and factories were abandoned or burned, the turnpike was rerouted, and the settlement was abandoned.

The name Kenwood was given the settlement by the Rathbones, who had a mansion on the hill where the Convent of the Sacred Heart is now located. The Rathbones owned woolen mills on the Normanskill below the hill. It is said that while on a trip to Scotland,

> Mr. and Mrs. Rathbone had found a delightful mill village called Kenwood ... and hoped to build its duplicate here adjoining their estate. The plans fell through after a few [brick row houses] were built. Today a part of the Rathbone estate is the Sacred Heart Convent.[14]

Even now, when we hear the name, Kenwood, many of us think of the wool plaid Kenwood blankets which were manufactured in the mill on the banks of the creek. Kenwood was earlier called Lower Hollow, a name which referred to the gorge or ravine of the Normanskill at the lower falls near the mouth of the creek. The name differentiated this hamlet from another further up the Normanskill called Upper Hollow (present-day Normansville) at the upper falls.

I met George Albert in the vicinity of old Kenwood. In addition to being president of the Irwin Elevator Company on Second Avenue in Albany, George is an amateur geologist. On this day, he was out prospecting for mineral deposits.[15] Although George now lives in Altamont, he grew up on Fourth Avenue and his family lived there for several generations. Here in this part of what is still known as Kenwood, George used to hunt rabbits and fish for trout in the Normanskill when he was young, and here, too, his father used to spear eels and silver suckers. A short walk along the creek brings one to an island, some rapids, the falls where mills were located until the end of the nineteenth century, and the remains of a dam across the creek. This was the site of the hamlet of Kenwood, where the main street, the turnpike, crossed the creek via an iron bridge.

George remembers playing in an abandoned icehouse on the Normanskill near the present site of Glenmont Leasing, Inc., of New York, between the creek and Binghampton Street. In the latter part of the nineteenth century, this cleared and gravelled area was flooded in the winter and blocks of ice were cut and stored in the icehouses. Concerning the ice business in the Kenwood area, Thomas Davidson has written:

> The land between the town of Kenwood and the river was used for the creation of a giant artificial pond, which was flooded from the dam built across the Normanskill just above the town [of Kenwood]. An iron pipeline carried the water onto the flat in the early winter, and blocks of ice were cut out when this later became frozen. ... Icehouses, however, succumbed to the march of progress, being replaced in a short number of years by ice plants.[16]

Wilbur's icehouse was located here in Kenwood, and the ice was sold chiefly to restaurants in Albany, although some was sold to people living in the city.[17]

Just beyond the bridge over the Normanskill is the intersection with Corning Hill Road. It was here, between Route 9W (the old South Bethlehem Plank Road) at the top of the hill and Route 144 (the Albany and Bethlehem Turnpike Road along the river) that Erastus Corning, the great-grandfather of the late mayor of Albany, had his farm. He bought land in October 1833 along present-day Retreat House Road (former Albany and Bethlehem Turnpike) from Angelica van Rensselaer of Bethlehem, and more land in 1846 from Philip S. van Rensselaer. Erastus Corning raised Hereford and Jersey cattle here, and in the 1930s, Parker Corning, his grandson and a former Congressman, raised thoroughbred horses on the farm. After Parker Corning's death in 1933, the farm was divided and sold. The former Corning house on Retreat House Road has since been a Jesuit Retreat House, then in the 1960s it was the Center for Humanistic Education (the University at Albany), and finally the Emmanuel Community Center, an ecumenical Christian organization.

Retreat House Road follows the original route of the Albany and Bethlehem Turnpike Road. When the turnpike was improved in the 1930s, it was rerouted to where Route 144 is today. This, as Davidson writes, sealed the fate of the decaying hamlet of Kenwood—the land was purchased by the Cornings and others, and the buildings on the south side of the Normanskill were torn down.[18] The land between Retreat House Road and Route 144, which used to be pasture for cows and horses, is now partially used for light industry. Mrs. Elizabeth Corning, Mayor Corning's widow, continues to live on their estate at the top of the hill near Route 9W.

Glenmont and the Old Abbey Hotel

Glenmont is located at the intersection of Glenmont Road and Route 144. The place-name Frazertown is given on the 1851 Sidney-Arrott map, perhaps because of the J. Frazier family who, in the mid-nineteenth century, lived near this intersection. An 1897 Albany County history notes:

> Glenmont is a station and post-office on the West Shore Railroad about a mile below Albany. Considerable moulding sand is shipped from here. There are no stores or other business interests in the place.[19]

The Abbey Hotel was a former landmark along Route 144 in Glenmont. It was built about 1710 by, it is said, a van Rensselaer. During its 250-year history, it had many owners, two of whom were Hugh Jolley and Henry Parr. Hugh Jolley, who was born in Galway, Scotland, in 1721 and came to America in 1772, owned the hotel during the Revolutionary War.[20] Henry Parr, who was born in Germany in 1848, came to the United States in 1867, and managed the National Hotel in Albany before taking over the Abbey Hotel in 1881. The *Albany Guide Book* noted that the Abbey was, "A favorite old roadhouse at Glenmont, about a mile below

Kenwood. ... The ride there is attractive and the property has a fine frontage on the river."[21] The hotel was razed in 1961.

The road forked at Glenmont, just past the Abbey. The road to the right, known today as Glenmont Road, led up the hill and connected at Babcocks Corners (present-day Bethlehem Center) with the road which in 1851 became the South Bethlehem Plank Road. A late nineteenth-century county history noted that this was a pleasant and picturesque drive out of the city.[22] The old plank road through Bethlehem Center is now known as Route 9W.

Continuing on Route 144, our drive along the river takes us over the tracks of the West Shore Railroad and past the Niagara Mohawk Steam Power Station on the left and the entrance to radio station WQBK on the right. Our next side trip will be to Van Wies Point on the Hudson.

Van Wies Point

When we turn left on Wheeler Road, we start on a two-mile-long loop which takes us, via Van Wies Point Road and Mosher Road, back to Route 144. This is a winding and narrow road, and it is easy to miss several historic sites along the way. Wheeler Road is named for the Wheeler family which owned property in this area at one time. The large, square, white clapboard Wheeler house is on the left, set back in the field.

At the end of Wheeler Road, just at the turn onto Van Wies Point Road, one may get a glimpse of the Four Mile Light in the river. This lighthouse was tended for fifty-two years by William Welch who lived nearby. At his death in 1910 at the age of ninety-three, he was the oldest lighthouse keeper in the United States. He polished the big two-foot brass lantern, cleaned the glass, trimmed the wick, and filled the lantern with kerosene. In all the years that he tended the lighthouse, he did not miss a single day. For this he received a salary of $180 a year.[23]

Historic site marker on Van Wies Point Road.

Here, the road curves to the right and we drive south with the river on our left. There are two markers on the Van Wies Point Road section of this side trip. The first is at the site of the dock once owned by Peter G. and Henry Van Wie, and the second at Van Wies Point. From the dock, local hay, other farm produce, and ice were shipped to New York. In 1835 it was leased to the Hudson Steamboat Company and served as the Albany terminal for passengers going to and from Albany. This location for a passenger terminal was necessary because of navigational hazards nearer Albany.[24] In the nineteenth century, passengers used stagecoaches for the journey between the dock and Albany. It was not until the 1920s that the Hudson was dredged to its present depth to provide a deep-water channel to Albany.

Second historic site marker on Van Wies Point Road.

Van Wies Point is the site of the house which Hendrick Gerritse van Wie built in 1679 on land he leased from the van Rensselaers. Van Wie used this place for shipping farm produce to New York City. The road winds up and down hill and finally, one and a half miles from our turn off Route 144, we reach the highest point on the road. We are now on Mosher Road with a half mile of road straight ahead until we reach Route 144 again.

From Van Wies Point south, there used to be several huge ice houses. In the winter, ice was harvested from the river and from ice ponds located on the flatlands along the shore of the river. The ice was cut and stored in the barns. Most of the ice was shipped to New York. Harvesting ice was a welcome source of supplemental income during the winter months for the farmers in the area. Several of the old houses at Van Wies Point and Cedar Hill were built by men who made fortunes in the ice business.

It is probably difficult for many today to realize what life was like before the advent of electrical refrigeration. When I was a child and living in Elmira, New York, our ice-box was located in an unheated room off the kitchen. A pipe ran from the bottom of the ice-box through a hole in the floor for the runoff from the melting ice inside. The iceman delivered chunks of ice from a horse-drawn wagon. In retrospect, the slivers of ice he gave me and my friends in the summer were better than ice cream cones.

Historic Cedar Hill

Guarding the Lyon Estate.

As we drive on down Route 144, another well-known landmark on the left attracts our attention—two concrete lions on pedestals which mark the former entrance to the Guy Park estate of James B. Lyon. This was one of many nineteenth- and early twentieth-century estates along the shore of the Hudson. The lions signify the name, Lyon, and the name Guy Park is from the home of Guy Johnson, Sir William Johnson's son-in-law (and nephew). At the intersection with Clapper Road, the Cedar Hill School is on the right and the Elks building is on the left and up on a rise. The next road on the left is Barrent Winne Road, commonly called Winne Road, which winds through the woods to the river and Henry Hudson Park.

The red brick Cedar Hill School, designed by Walter Hunter Van Guysling and built in 1859, was originally a one-room schoolhouse facing Route

Cedar Hill School (1859). Home of the Town of Bethlehem Historical Association Museum. Route 144 (River Road) and Clapper Road.

144. Eventually, it was necessary to enlarge the building, and it was redesigned in 1907 by noted Albany architect Marcus T. Reynolds (1869-1937).[25] A second room, a new entrance vestibule on the Clapper Road side, and a noteworthy cupola were added. This building was used as a school until 1959

when it was closed by the Ravena-Coeymans-Selkirk Central School District. The "little red schoolhouse," as it is known locally, has been occupied by the Bethlehem Historical Association since 1965, the year in which the New York State Board of Regents chartered the association.

Here, historic items and information concerning the town's past are gathered and preserved by the Association. Exhibits in the museum located in the building feature the Home, the Farm, the River, Ice Harvesting, and the School.

Ruth Mendel has written of this area as it was at about the beginning of the twentieth century, "when three gracious summer homes held dominion over some 200 plus acres of land overlooking the still sparkling Hudson."[26] The houses referred to were the summer homes of J.B. Lyon, Dr. Willis G. MacDonald, and New York State Governor Martin H. Glynn. All of these houses were built on land which Mr. Lyon had bought from John Taylor Cooper (1798-1878), who was an Albany lawyer and a nephew of James Fenimore Cooper. James B. Lyon owned the Lyon Block building in Albany and had a lucrative printing business.

Dr. MacDonald studied in Switzerland and when he built his house on the Hudson in 1905, the architect Marcus T. Reynolds designed it to resemble a Swiss chalet.[27] This is now the home of Mary Elizabeth Lyon Van Oostenbrugge, grandaughter of J.B. Lyon. Mr. Lyon also built a one-room bungalow with a wraparound screened porch on the river in 1907. This is now the home of Mr. and Mrs. Thomas Evans. Mrs. Evans (née Lisa Lyon) is the great-grandaughter of J.B. Lyon.

The large white stucco-covered building with red Spanish tile roofs on the hill above the corner of Route 144 and Winne Road was the former summer house of Governor Glynn. It was built on land given to him by Mr. Lyon and designed in 1907 by Marcus T. Reynolds. At one time, it was the residence of Judge Daniel Prior, a famous criminal lawyer in Albany, his wife, and their eight children. Jack "Legs" Diamond, who was defended by Judge Prior in the 1920s, was a guest here when he was out of jail on bail. In 1962, the deteriorating building was sold to the Bethlehem Chapter of the Benovelent and Protective Order of Elks 2233 (BPOE), and since then it has had a new lease on life. The house on the right at the entrance to Winne Road was once the gate house of the Governor Glynn estate.

If we turn left here and follow the winding road toward the Hudson, we reach Henry Hudson Park. On the way, we pass two more Guy Park lions guarding another entrance to the former Lyon estate. Henry Hudson Park is on the shore of the Hudson and has a pavilion, ball field, cooking facilities, tables and benches

To Bethlehem's Henry Hudson Park.

among the trees, rest rooms, space for walking and running, and a stunning view of the river. A large granite boulder with a bronze plaque near the fence which separates the park from the river commemorates Hudson's visit.

James Weidemann and ice saw.

From the early decades of the nineteenth century until the advent of refrigerators and the production of artificial ice in the early years of the twentieth century, the ice harvesting industry flourished along the shores of the Hudson River here at Cedar Hill. In 1870, George Best, a lumberman, and his friend, a Mr. English, formed the Cedar Hill Ice Company. In 1908, Henry Myers of Cedar Hill, when only a boy, "led horse" as he expressed it, in those years before the advent of mechanized ice-harvesting equipment. At first, he

explained, large blocks of ice were cut from the river, but as the years passed, the quality of the river ice declined. By 1900, ponds with five-to-six-foot-high embankments were constructed along the shore. They were filled with water brought from the Vloman Kill through a flume. In the summer, the dry pond beds were sometimes used for growing corn and at least one of them contained a baseball field. The men who worked in the ice harvesting industry were, for the most part, local farmers and hired men. In the pre-gasoline engine years, they used their farm horses to pull the equipment needed for clearing snow from the ice and for making the marks to guide the men who wielded the ice saws. The icehouses have all disappeared—some burned, one was damaged by a hurricane in 1931, and others were torn down.[28]

Beyond Winne Road, on Route 144, we cross the Vloman Kill which was named for Pieter de Vlamingh (or Peter the Fleming) who settled on the bank of the stream in 1677 and built a mill at the falls. On the left, at Dinmore Road, is a sign for the Bethlehem Water Pollution Control Plant. Here, we turn left in order to visit the Nicoll-Sill House and the family cemetery.

The Nicoll-Sill House

The Nicoll-Sill House, also known as Bethlehem House, was built ca. 1735 and enlarged in the 1790s and in the nineteenth century. The house remained in the Nicoll and Sill families until 1875. Since then, there have been several owners. The historic house is now owned by prominent Scotia attorney Paul K. Mulligan, son of former Bethlehem town historian Thomas E. Mulligan.

The house, with its brick walls, twenty-four rooms, and gambrel roof, was built by Rensselaer Nicoll (1706-1776), a nephew of Kiliaen van Rensselaer, the fourth patroon of Rensselaerswyck. Rensselaer Nicoll's parents were Anna van Rensselaer, widow of Kiliaen van Rensselaer, third patroon, and her second husband, William Nicoll, of English birth and a lawyer and politician. Rensselaer Nicoll brought his bride, Elizabeth Salisbury, here when the house was completed. Her father was Francis Salisbury, whose father was Sylvester Salisbury, the English commander of the fort at Albany. Among the wedding presents were several slaves from the bride's father. According to family folklore, a baby named Caesar was born to two of the slaves a year later. Caesar remained in the family all of his life. It is alleged that he died in 1852 at the age of 115.[29]

Floyd Brewer and members of the Bethlehem Archaeology Group conducted a dig here at Bethlehem House in the mid-1980s and made a detailed record of the different occupants during its long history. In the field south of the house and adjoining cemetery, they discovered a cache of native American artifacts dating to 6500 B.C. (see first chapter, Buried Secrets).

Among the eight Revolutionary War soldiers buried in the cemetery across the road from the south lawn of the Nicoll-Sill House are Col. Francis Nicoll, 3rd Regiment, Albany County Militia, Maj.

Richard Sill, Continental Army, Lt. Arie Van Wie, 3rd Regiment, Albany County Militia, and James Selkirk of the 2nd Regiment. In James Selkirk, the immigrant, we have the beginning of the Selkirk name in Bethlehem and the family for whom the hamlet was named. A bronze plaque, affixed to a granite boulder and placed here by the Tawasentha Chapter of the DAR in 1977, lists the names of the eight soldiers.

James Selkirk (1756-1820) was born in Scotland, came to New York City at the age of seventeen, went first to Galway (between Saratoga Springs and Amsterdam), and then came to Bethlehem. He served for seven years during the Revolutionary War, some if not all of that time as a sergeant. After the war, he married Elizabeth Henry of this area. In 1788, at the time of the baptism of the first of their ten children, James, Jr., his occupation was listed in church records as a "Taylor" in Bethlehem.[30] At least three of the children are buried in the cemetery just south of the Nicoll-Sill House; others are buried in Cedar Hill Cemetery, Elmwood Cemetery, and Albany Rural Cemetery.

Because of industrialized areas south of Cedar Hill, Exit 22 of the Thruway, and increased population, there is a great deal of traffic on Route 144. The older houses in the area are located between the road and the river. To the west of the road, across the township to its western boundary, there are still farms. Even though the area is split by the Thruway, Route 9W, and the Selkirk railroad yards, several roads including Clapper Road, Beaver Dam Road, and South Albany

Road, take us through countryside which has maintained a pastoral quality. Jean Lyon, a Cedar Hill resident of long standing, has said, "On a misty morning you can still stand by the river and almost see Henry sailing up on that strange little ship."[31]

Along the Old Plank Road
(From Albany to New Scotland)

The drives in and about Albany are numerous and picturesque. ... The most frequented is the New Scotland turnpike, or the Hurstville road, as it is commonly called, which ... leads to a drive of inexhaustable extent and variety.
(*The Albany Hand-Book for 1881*[32])

The compiler of *The Albany Hand-Book for 1881* whets the reader's appetite with mention of sights along New Scotland Avenue (in Albany) and New Scotland Road (in Bethlehem), known then as the Albany, Rensselaerville, and Schoharie Plank Road. First, there is the "famous Log Tavern, the glory of which has somewhat faded under modern management." Several miles further west is "the pretty village of Slingerlands." From there, he writes, the plank road "takes us to the top of the mountain, from which the view is almost as sublime as is that from the hotel verandah [of the Catskill Mountain House] on the Catskills."[33]

Today, 112 years later, the reader may well wonder about the Log Tavern. The Log Tavern, kept by a first settler probably named either Derrick or William Hagadorn, was located on the northwest

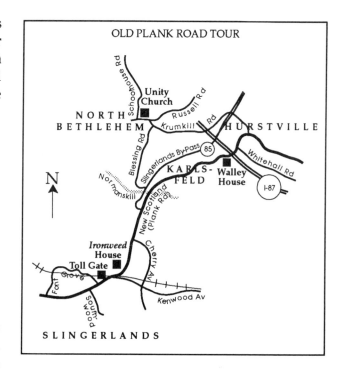

corner of Krumkill Road and New Scotland Avenue. The small settlement which developed there, and included the area at the intersection of New Scotland Avenue and Whitehall Road, was known as Hurstville. The hamlet was named for William Hurst who settled there in 1861 and built what became known as Hurst's Hotel on the site of the Log Tavern. However, it continued to be known as the Log Tavern for some time. Seven years later, in an entry in his daily journal for 1867, John Slingerland of Normanskill (present-day Slingerlands) wrote, "Paid Tax at Hursts Log Tavern...."[34] In addition to the hotel, William

Hurst operated a race track, known as the Pleasure Trotting Park for horses, on the east side of New Scotland Avenue between present-day Hurst Avenue and Whitehall Road. Hurst Avenue near New Scotland Avenue and Krumkill Road perpetuates the name of William Hurst. During prohibition days, the hotel was known as The Love Nest, and the proprietor was one "Pop" Johnson. It was a popular place in the Roaring '20s, with dance bands, floor shows, and the accompanying excitement and sense of adventure that some of us still associate with the out-of-town roadhouses of those times. It is easy to picture couples in roadsters with rumble seats, raccoon coats and flappers' short skirts, the Charleston and Black Bottom. Sadly for some, the building was destroyed by fire on election night in 1929.

The "New Scotland turnpike, or the Hurstville road," as the author of the 1881 hand-book referred to the plank road, was opened for traffic as a toll road in 1859. It ran from Lydius Street (present Madison Avenue in Albany) through Slingerlands, New Scotland, and New Salem, up on the Helderbergs, through Berne and Gallupville, and on to Schoharie. Although much of this road was originally covered with planks, the authors of a county history published in 1897 stated that "The use of plank on a large part of this road was abandoned some years ago."[35]

The Hurstville post office was first located in Hurst's Hotel but later transferred to the toll house, which was situated opposite O'Neil Road and the entrance to the present-day Albany Municipal Golf Course where the Walley farm was located. It was abolished in 1902 when rural free delivery came into existence. The plank road tollgate in the nineteenth century was located between the schoolhouse and the Walley farm, near Paddock Road. Many long-term residents remember Walley's Farm, where vegetables were grown and sold along with annuals and perennials. It was only a few short years ago that several rows of rhubarb grew just to the right of the white painted brick Walley house (1841), which still stands even though the farm has disappeared. Although Hurstville no longer exists, the name appears on maps published as late as 1989.[36]

The curious traveller driving west from Albany to Slingerlands may wonder about the sign announcing "KARLSFELD" across New Scotland Avenue from the Training Academy of the New York State Department of Correctional Facilities (the former Mater Christi Seminary, opened in September 1954). Karlsfeld is German for Charles's Field and was the name in the 1920s for the athletic field where the Training Academy is now located. It was set up by Rev. William R. Charles when he was pastor of St. Vincent de Paul's Church in Albany. Mrs. Mildred Flagler, who has lived in Karlsfeld since 1942, tells us that the people there petitioned Mayor

Corning in 1967 to annex the area so they could have water, sewerage, and electricity. They also received the Mayor's promise that their taxes would not be increased for five years, and, as Mrs. Flagler reported, he kept that promise. Karlsfeld today looks much as it did when Mrs. Flagler and her husband moved from Albany. It contains more houses than fifty years ago. Then, too, there was a small neighborhood store in the house next door to the firehouse on New Scotland Avenue. The store was run by Woodruff and Agatha Sorrell. Both of the Flagler sons are volunteers in the Slingerlands Fire Department, and while I was talking with Mrs. Flagler, the police-fire monitor near the front door went off several times. They have to go to the firehouse in Slingerlands, at least two and a half miles west on New Scotland Road, when there is an alarm. And now, since Karlsfeld is within the city limits of Albany, fire fighting equipment

Slingerlands firehouse. New Scotland Avenue, Albany side of the Normanskill.

must come from the firehouse on New Scotland Avenue near St. Theresa of Avila Church and School 19 in the city. The firehouse is a relic of the days when Karlsfeld was in Bethlehem township. It contains a fire engine, which is used for fighting fires in Slingerlands.

The plank road formerly crossed the Normanskill on a covered bridge, and the road to North Bethlehem (Blessing Road) went to the right just before the bridge. Another drive recommended by the complier of *The Albany Hand-Book for 1881* was

> on the New Scotland road ... to the covered bridge, three miles from Albany, and then turning to the right make the circuit, coming out at McKownsville, on the Western avenue road, and then to the city [of Albany]. This is a drive of about seven miles, and is simply exquisite, the view from Sunset hill, the road through the dense pine woods, and the little church in the forest, being the most attractive features. [37]

This section of road between New Scotland Avenue and Blessing Road no longer exists. To reach North Bethlehem, we must cross the Normanskill and turn right at the traffic light at the top of the hill where the Blue Cross-Blue Shield building is located, take the Slingerlands By-Pass to the next traffic light, just over the Normanskill, and turn left onto Blessing Road.

North Bethlehem

A 1977 newspaper article referred to North Bethlehem as "the forgotten corner of Bethlehem."[38] Those who drive through the hamlet between Albany's Western Avenue to the Slinger-lands By-Pass or on Russell and Krumkill Roads, as well as the people who live there, are, I am sure, well aware that the area is not forgotten. When I drove between Slingerlands and Western Avenue some twenty-six years ago, between home and work, Blessing, Krumkill, and Schoolhouse roads led through, for the most part, a slow-paced and rural landscape. In 1976, when we had a wedding in the family, wildflowers for bouquets at the reception were gathered in the fields along Blessing Road where the Meadowbrook Apartments, Bethlehem Terrace, and Eastmount Townhouses are now located.

In 1989, a newspaper article contained a list of eight major building projects in North Bethlehem and noted that the Albany County Engineer, Paul Cooney, had proposed two studies, one to analyze traffic problems and the other to evaluate the impact of development and roadway construction in the area.[39] This "forgotten corner" has indeed been found. Among the projects are two on Blessing Road and three on Krumkill Road, in addition to the large building housing the Albany County Association for Retarded Citizens on the southeast corner of Blessing and Krumkill roads (erected 1987-1989). Brookehill Village on Blessing Road is being built by John Quadrini Enterprises, Inc. Dutchbrook, Indian Hills, with streets named for Indian tribes, and Beverwyck, a retirement development, are located on Krumkill Road. Krumkill Road eventually meets New Scotland Avenue in Albany. It was in this general area that the former hamlet of Hurstville was located. Both Hurstville and Karlsfeld on the road to Slingerlands were annexed to Albany in July 1967. Also on Krumkill Road, between Russell Road and Schoolhouse Road, are two noteworthy landmarks which are discussed in the chapter on Bethlehem religious institutions, the Unity of Faith church, built by Presbyterians in 1833 and since then housing several different religious denominations, and across the street, the former parsonage, built in 1838.

Slingerlands

hoed potatoes ground Scyths shelld some corn[40]

When John Slingerland (ca. 1827-1882), son of the well-known John I. Slingerland and Elizabeth Van Derzee, wrote the above entry in his daily journal for 1867, he was forty years old. He and his wife, Betsey Andrews, and their two children, Cora E. and Cornelius H.V., lived on their farm across the plank road from present-day Southwood Drive in Slingerlands. Their first-born had, in the words of the family genealogists, "died young."[41]

Various houses and buildings in Slingerlands were built by members of the Slingerland family, including the Methodist church and parsonage

House built by William H. Slingerland, 1584 New Scotland Road; now owned by Robert H. and Elizabeth Deily.

(1871 and 1873), six houses in a row along Kenwood Avenue between Union Avenue and New Scotland Road (ca. 1870), and several houses on New Scotland Road. The houses on Kenwood Avenue had identical floor plans and exterior architecture, but over the years, the one on the Union Avenue corner burned and some have been modified. The most recent change has been to the house purchased by architect Andrew Prescott and his wife Kathy in 1979 and renovated in 1980 and 1989. The house directly across New Scotland Road from Bridge Street is owned by Garett Dillenback. It is sometimes called "The Ironweed House," since it was featured in the motion picture of that name. It was built by Albert I. Slingerland in 1876 for Charles D. Hammond, superintendent of the Delaware and Hudson Railroad.

Slingerland family members were still building houses in the hamlet in the early years of the twentieth century. My house at 1592 New Scotland Road was built by Harold Bullock Slingerland (1898-1985), known as "Sling." He was a graduate of Groton and the Harvard Law School, attended Cambridge University in England, and studied the cuneiform writings of the ancient Hittites, Babylonians, Assyrians, and Persians. In addition, he was an artist, painted the murals on the walls of my dining room, and, among other honors, won a Prix de Rome.[42] He was a lawyer by vocation. His cousin, Grace Slingerland (1874-1946), daughter of George Wayne Slingerland, designed and lived in the brick house just west of mine, now owned by John and Barbara Sommer. Miss Slingerland was an 1899 graduate of the Cornell University School of Architecture. All in all, it is little wonder that the settlement has been known as Slingerland's Corners, Slingerland's Station, and finally Slingerlands.

Its earliest known name was Normanskill, officially bestowed upon the settlement in 1852, the year the post office was established by William H. Slingerland (1820-1910). He was the first postmaster and served in that capacity for over twenty years. In addition, he was a civil engineer and town surveyor, one of the men who helped select the site of the Watervliet Arsenal (1890), surveyed the land for the railroad, and organized the Suburban Water Co. in Slingerlands (incorporated in 1901). In the parlance of today, he was that company's chief executive officer. The water flowed by gravity to Slingerlands from two springs, one in the Helderbergs above New Salem and the other in New Salem. Within a few years, the system was expanded to the main streets of Delmar and Elsmere. The management of the company passed to his son, George, and then to George's daughter, Grace. Finally, in 1927, the company was sold to the Town of Bethlehem (Water District No. 1).

It is interesting that on the front flyleaf of his daily journal for 1868, John Slingerland gave Normanskill as his place of residence, two years after a map was published which labeled the intersection of the roads from Albany and Adamsville (Delmar) as Slingerland's Corners. Old habits persist, as we have seen in the case of Hurstville and Karlsfeld. Two years later, in 1870, the name of the hamlet was officially Slingerlands. However, several peach-colored pasteboard tickets in the archives of the Slingerlands Community United Methodist Church use the place-name, Slingerland's Station. The tickets were for the Peach Festival of the Methodist Episcopal Church (the predecessor of the present church congregation), held on August 30, 1871.[43] This place-name, of course, came from the presence of the railroad station which was only a few hundred feet away from the church, where the firehouse is today. The old freight station is still standing between Kenwood Avenue and the

Pasteboard ticket for church Peach Festival (1871).

railroad tracks. The station, large and durably built, was closed in 1933. The building was then modified to serve as a firehouse. The present firehouse was designed by architect and artist, Charles A. Schade, who has lived in Albany and Slingerlands all of his life.

John Slingerland also referred to the settlement as "red Hook."[44] A newspaper article, written by Mrs. Arthetta Reed Blessing, wife of Frederick Slingerland Blessing, and probably dating from the first decade of this century, states:

> Tradition says the old store with its sheds, which stood where Mr. C.D. Hammond's [Garett Dillenback's] and Mr. W.F. Winship's residences are now located, and the old blacksmith shop directly opposite, the property of the late Henry Ostrander, were painted red. The village at that time consisted of store, blacksmith shop, and five or six houses, so it can readily be seen how the color of the buildings of the chief enterprise might have been responsible for a part of the name, and the sharp curve in the road at this point the part, the Hook.[45]

This location today is the curve in New Scotland Road at the Bridge Street intersection.

For a reason unknown at this time, many citizens of Slingerlands around 1890 petitioned to have the hamlet's name changed to Ruxton, after a village of that name in England. The name was changed on November 1, 1891, but members of the Slingerland family

> appealed to the Holland Society of New York which brought its influence to bear on President Olyphant of the Delaware and Hudson Canal Company [owner of the railroad] and the Dutch name of Slingerlands was restored on November 12th of the same year.[46]

In 1886, the hamlet of Slingerlands contained

> 44 dwellings, 50 families, 230 inhabitants; a commodious brick schoolhouse and M.E. church, printing establishment, hotel, marble and monumental works, store, 2 blacksmith shops, wheelwright and paint shop, shoe shop, cigar manufactory, R.R. station, several fine residences, [and] the buildings of the village.[47]

In the second half of the nineteenth century, downtown Slingerlands was on the Albany side of the railroad tracks. The Home Lawn Hotel (ca. 1800), post office, blacksmith shops, store, railroad station, brick schoolhouse, wheelwright and paint shop, and Methodist Episcopal Church (1871) were all located there. Only the printing company (1879) of Cornelius Slingerland, the sawmill, and the cider mill were on the south side of the tracks.

Today, the center of downtown Slingerlands seems to be at the intersection of New Scotland Road and Kenwood Avenue. The landmark Toll Gate Restaurant, famous since 1949 for such treats as peanut butter and jelly ice cream, the Double Sizzle, and The Bucket, was started by Arthur and Robert Zautner and is now run by Bob's sons. Their

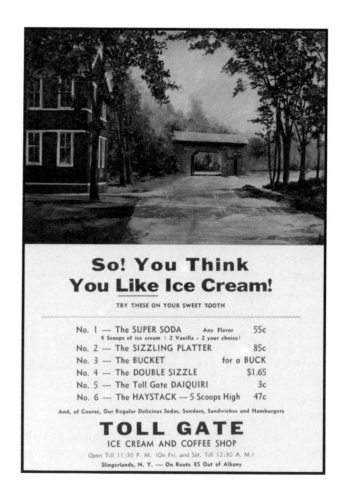

So! You Think You Like Ice Cream!

TRY THESE ON YOUR SWEET TOOTH

No. 1 — The SUPER SODA	Any Flavor	55c
4 Scoops of ice cream (2 Vanilla - 2 your choice)		
No. 2 — The SIZZLING PLATTER		85c
No. 3 — The BUCKET		for a BUCK
No. 4 — The DOUBLE SIZZLE		$1.65
No. 5 — The Toll Gate DAIQUIRI		3c
No. 6 — The HAYSTACK — 5 Scoops High		47c

And, of Course, Our Regular Delicious Sodas, Sundaes, Sandwiches and Hamburgers

TOLL GATE

ICE CREAM AND COFFEE SHOP

Open Till 11:30 P. M. (On Fri. and Sat. Till 12:30 A. M.)

Slingerlands, N. Y. — On Route 85 Out of Albany

aim, as stated on an early menu, was "to make an ice cream as good as Mom made forty years ago in the old hand-turned ice and salt freezer." The restaurant is a few dozen feet from where the tollgate on the old plank road stood from 1859 until about 1908. Inside the restaurant over the entrance door is a painting of the old tollgate by Charles Mullen. The Slingerlands post office was located in the right-hand section of the Toll Gate building until it was moved to its present location on the northwestern corner of New Scotland and LeGrange roads in July 1992.

In the days of turnpikes and tollgates, tolls were collected from those who passed through the tollgates, not those who by-passed, or shunned, them. There was no doubt a shunpike near practically every tollgate. And to be sure, there was a shunpike in Slingerlands—it was Bridge Street, which ran between New Scotland Road and Kenwood Avenue.

Across the street from the Toll Gate restaurant is Mangia (1991), a restaurant serving pizza and pasta. It is located where Charles Sanders's gas station and later his restaurant stood from the 1940s. Many people remember the large white-painted clapboard Victorian house which used to be behind Mangia. Originally the house of William H. Slingerland and later of Charlie Sanders, it was demolished in 1982. In the woods beyond the

Toll Gate Restaurant and former Post Office; watercolor by Charles A. Schade; collection Slingerlands Post Office.

Slingerlands Post Office (1992).

Charlie's (ca. 1940). Watercolor by Charles A. Schade; author's collection.

Slingerland's oldest store.

about the Jake Vagele horseshoe shop which was located near the present cul-de-sac on Bridge Street. Portions of the mills' foundations are still visible behind the two split-level houses between Adriance Lane and Cherry Avenue.

On a pleasant day in October 1991, while Ray, his wife Martha, and I were enjoying satisfying slices of a newly-baked cake and mugs of coffee on their glassed-in back porch, Ray pointed to a woodpile in his back yard and said that in his dad's day, that had been the location of home plate for the Village Wonders, Slingerlands's famous ball team. Other playing fields were at the corner of Kenwood and Union avenues and the corner of Southwood and New Scotland Road.

The large building between the railroad track and the Toll Gate Restaurant is now an apartment building. It was formerly the printing establishment of Cornelius Slingerland. Note the word "LITHOGRAPHER," barely visible under the roof line of the eastern wing of the building. Two doors west of the Toll Gate Restaurant is John I. Slingerland's former house, now owned by George and Kathleen Bragle. The part facing New Scotland Road was built in 1842, but the section at the rear, built ca. 1790, is the oldest structure in the hamlet.

parking lot is the Slingerland burial vault, visible from New Scotland Road when the leaves are off the trees and bushes. To the east, on the other side of the railroad underpass at 1526 New Scotland Road, is a painted brick building with a deli in the front part and in the rear a space which over the years has been the Slingerlands post office, a liquor store, a Baptist church, a pet store, and a baseball-card shop. This is the oldest commercial building in Slingerlands. Next to this building is the Slingerlands firehouse, and east of it the Slingerlands park with an old milestone near the sidewalk.

My friend Raymon Pastori has lived all his life on Lower Font Grove Road in Slingerlands. He usually has some nugget of interest about "old Slingerlands" for me when we see each other. Not long ago, he told me about the old Coonley saw-mill and cider mill across Kenwood Avenue from the former intersection with Bridge Street, and

Along the Old Delaware Turnpike
(Delaware Avenue, Route 443)

The Delaware Turnpike, as some people still refer to Delaware Avenue, started in Albany at the corner of

Lydius Street (present-day Madison Avenue) and Lark Street. It passed through Normansville and Adamsville (present-day Delmar) on the way to Unionville and Clarksville, which were then in Bethlehem. It continued through Rensselaerville and out of the county. The turnpike existed for almost seventy years, until it was abandoned in 1879 and its upkeep taken over by the town and state.

Normansville

Normansville, according to a nineteenth-century county history, was

> situated on both sides of the Normanskill, and through the water power supplied by that stream, considerable manufacturing came into existence in early years, some of which survived to later times. The Normanskill at this point has cut a deep ravine through the soil and down to the rock, over which it flows with a gradual descent.[48]

Before the present high bridge at Normansville was built in 1928, Delaware Avenue crossed the stream via Old Delaware Avenue, known affectionately as the Yellow Brick Road. One of the earliest bridges there was of wood, built by the turnpike company. It was carried away in 1868 by a spring

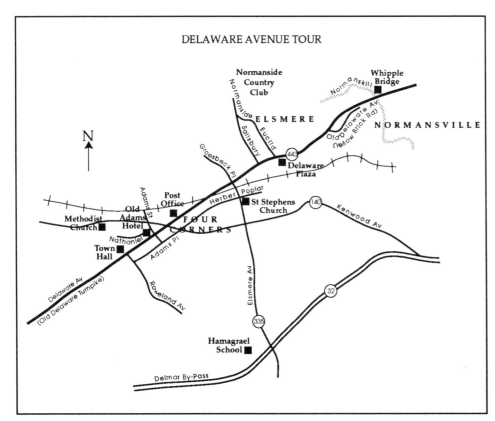

DELAWARE AVENUE TOUR

"YELLOW BRICK ROAD"

THESE ARE ORIGINAL BRICKS FROM ONE OF THE FIRST

"PAVED" ROADS PASSING THROUGH BETHLEHEM

CONSTRUCTED BY THE ALBANY AND DELAWARE TURNPIKE

COMPANY (CHARTERED 1805)

NORMANSVILLE · TOWN OF BETHLEHEM

freshet. The next year, it was replaced by an iron bridge with two spans which was built by the town of Bethlehem because the turnpike company had by then abandoned the road. Later, the iron bridge was replaced by the present concrete bridge. A few years ago, this bridge was declared unsafe for use and is now closed. Thus, Normansville is divided in two, by both the Normanskill and the closed bridge. The Yellow Brick Road on the south side of the creek (Old Delaware Avenue) has, for the most part, been blacktopped, but the roadbed of the bridge retains the paving bricks as does the continuation of the road (Normanskill Drive), which winds up around the hill and ends at Delaware Avenue on the Albany side of the creek. At the Four Corners in Delmar, on the traffic island at the intersection of Delaware and Kenwood avenues, is a walk paved with bricks salvaged from this road.

Another bridge is located in the hollow. One hundred thirteen feet long, this bridge spans the ravine between the Mark W. Stevens Farm and the brick road on the Albany side of the Normanskill. It is one of only two known surviving Whipple bowstring truss bridges and was accepted for the National Registry of Historic Places in 1971. It was invented and patented in 1841 by Squire Whipple (1804-1888), a graduate of Union College and an eminent civil engineer. In the mid-nineteenth century, hundreds of these bridges, which utilized a bolted and pinned form of construction, were installed over the Erie Canal across New York State. Later, when the canal was enlarged, many of the bridges were sold and set up elsewhere. This bridge was fabricated in 1867 for a site near Syracuse by Simon DeGraff whose factory was in that city. Around 1900, it was moved here from someplace in Schoharie County and re-erected over the ravine.[49]

Normansville has also been known as Upper Hollow and there are rapids and falls in the creek which have provided power for various industries. Over the years, on both sides of the stream, there have been sawmills, grist mills, mills for carding wool and for making wrapping paper, and Pappalau's icehouse, which burned in the 1930s. There have also been a hotel, dance hall, and bathing beach.

Today, Normansville is a quiet little residential settlement on the banks of the Normanskill. Houses line Mill Road and Rockefeller Road on the Bethlehem side of the stream. The Normansville Free Chapel, with its lancet arched door and windows and open belfry on the roof, stands as a sentry at the intersection of the roads.

Elsmere

The next hamlet on Delaware Avenue is Elsmere. The authors of *The Tale of Three Centuries* suggest that Elsmere may have been named for the hero of Mrs. Humphry Ward's *Robert Elsmere* (1888), an extremely popular novel in its day.[50] Robert E.S. Adams (1917-1992), former owner of the Adams Hardware, Inc., in Delmar, told the author he had heard that the name of Elsmere came from the following incident: Many years ago, when the land south of the Normanskill, near present-day Delaware Plaza, was undeveloped and swampy, an Englishman who crossed it on horseback on his way to Delmar referred to it as

"Hell's Mire." It is also noted in *The Tale of Three Centuries* that Elsmere has been known in the past as Groesbecks Corners; it may well have been so referred to because of the J. Groesbeck family living near the present intersection of Delaware and Elsmere Avenues and Groesbeck Place.[51]

It was not until after the turn of the century that Elsmere began to develop into a residential area. Before that, there were farms, a few houses, and the station built by the Albany and Susquehanna Railroad, which opened in 1863. The station was located on the corner of Elsmere Avenue and Poplar Drive, across the street from St. Stephen's Church. Note the Delaware Turnpike, Elsmere Avenue (formerly Cemetery Road), the Albany and Susquehanna Railroad (later the Delaware and Hudson), and the location of the railroad station in the accompanying plat included in the "Abstract of The Title of Part of the Groesbeck farm at Elsmere, Albany County, N.Y." Wide concrete steps on the southern side of the underpass still lead from Elsmere Avenue up to the former site of the station.

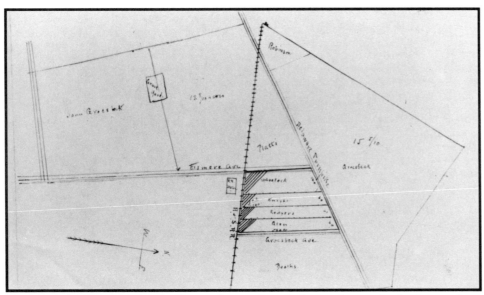

Plat (ca. 1903) of Delaware Avenue-Elsmere Avenue-Groesbeck Place intersection in Elsmere, from "Abstract of The Title of Part of the Groesbeck farm at Elsmere, Albany County, N.Y."

One of the men who was important in the development of Elsmere in the early part of the twentieth century was William A. Glenn, a long-time town attorney. He was in large part responsible for Elsmere's becoming an important suburb of Albany. Under his energetic and enthusiastic boosterism, "Houses began to spring up in all parts of the village and soon Elsmere was considered one of the prettiest little places of its kind in Albany county."[52] Both St. Stephen's Church and Normanside Country Club owe much to William Glenn's organizing abilities.

Elsmere was equipped with electric lights in the early decades of this century. Soon after, water mains were installed and a sewage system was put into operation.

Delaware Plaza, which was originally developed by Murray-Simon in the early 1960s, has been owned by Norris MacFarland and Senator Howard Nolan since 1974.

Delmar, the Four Corners Hamlet

In 1886, as a county history tells us, Adams Station (present-day Delmar) on the old Delaware turnpike contained a post office (established in 1840), a railroad station, and

> 85 dwellings, 90 families, 360 inhabitants, a Reformed church, M.E. church, school-house, 2 stores, tin shop, wheelwright and blacksmith

shop, cigar manufactory, tavern. One physician and lawyer reside here.[53]

Nathaniel Adams came to this crossroads in 1836 and built a hotel in 1838 which was long known as the Adams House. In 1840, he opened a post office in the hotel and became the first postmaster. It was probably at about this time that the earliest known name, Adamsville, began to be applied to the four corners. With the construction of the Albany and Susquehanna Railroad through the hamlet in 1863 and the building of the depot, at least the stop at the station became known as Adams Station. The station was situated on Adams Street at approximately the location of the empty lot or driveway between the railroad tracks and the cement block building housing the businesses of Delmar Auto Radiator and Havil's Auto Body. Across Adams Street, between the railroad tracks and the G.R. (George Rubinchuck) Auto Repair Shop, Inc., was the freight depot. In various records, among them the minutes of meetings of the trustees of the Second Methodist Episcopal Church of Bethlehem, the name Adamsville continued to be used for many years.[54]

In 1950, the old brick Adams Hotel was purchased by the town and became the Town Hall. (Since 1980, the Town Hall has been located in the former Delmar Elementary School building at 445

Delaware Avenue.) The Delmar Fire Department, formed in 1911, continues to be housed in the rear portion of the building, on the corner of Adams Street and Nathaniel Boulevard. After the town offices moved, the Bethlehem Archaeology Group, the Bethlehem Chamber of Commerce, the Bethlehem Art Association, and the Daughters of the American Revolution occupied space in the building. But in 1982, the Town Board decided to sell the old building because of high operating and maintenance costs and because it was felt that the rent would not cover costs.[55] The building was purchased in 1983 by the New York State Association for Retarded Children, Inc. After extensive and tasteful renovation, the historic landmark became the association's headquarters. It is now known as The Joseph T. Weingold Building.

Adams House (late nineteenth-century postcard).

Alice Porter, who was a long-time resident of Delmar, has written that during the Washington Sesquicentennial year of 1932,

> It was decided ... to plant a George Washington Memorial Tree on each school lawn, which included Glenmont and Houcks Corners. Few people know that the evergreen tree at the left of the entrance to the Delmar Grade School [present Town Hall] is a Memorial Tree.

> I was asked to put on the first shovel of dirt when it was planted.[56]

And speaking of schools, have you ever wondered where the name of Hamagrael School came from? In the Bethlehem Public Library files is a letter from Barbara Somers, who used to live in Delmar. According to Mrs. Somers, the name comes from the beginnings of four names: Ha from Harry, Ma from Marian, Gra from Grace, and El from Eleanor. These were the names of Mr. and Mrs. Goddard and their two daughters, who were related to Mrs. Somers's mother. Mrs. Somers's parents bought a 104-acre farm which they named Hamagrael, in the area where the school is located.[57] While this is not the only explanation of the name's derivation, it is perhaps the most logical.

Early Delmar post office.

street even had three names. Poplar Avenue ended at Elsmere Avenue, from there it was called Herber Avenue, and at Oakwood Place it became Adams Place. The Civic Betterment Committee petitioned the Town Board for mail delivery, but was told that first the houses had to be numbered and every street in Bethlehem named. The erection of road and street signs was authorized by the Town Board in June 1932. The author of the paper continues:

> Incidentally, the street with the three names still remains. The Civic Betterment Committee wanted it all called Helderberg Avenue as Adams Street and Adams Place seemed too confusing. It was discovered that these two streets were named after two different Adams families and a change was met with resistance. Also, Miss Wands, who lived on Adams Place and sold rock garden plants, opposed the issue. She had new stationary with the address of Adams Place. So much opposition was made that the committee had to go along with all three names.[59]

Since Nathaniel Adams opened the first post office in his hotel, mail has been processed in several different locations in the hamlet. The present post office building was opened on February 11, 1940. Noteworthy features in the lobby are the terrazzo floor, the marble wainscoting, and on the end wall, the mural of the Indian Ladder in the Helderbergs. It was painted by a Works Progress Administration artist named Sol Wilson from New York City. Although the exact date of the painting of the mural is not known, it was probably done just before the United States entered World War II.[58]

Street Signs in Delmar

There is an interesting footnote to history in Alice Porter's unpublished paper, "Delmar Then and Now 1926-1974." It seems that in the early 1930s, some streets had names, some did not, and in any event, there were no signs at street corners. One

Over the years, there have been many attempts to discover the source of the name, Delmar. Charlotte Wilcoxen writes:

> The naming of Delmar is something of a local mystery. It is not recorded what the earliest name of the Four Corners that are now a landmark was, though they must have had some local

designation in the 18th Century. ... A cryptic notation found in the files of the Bethlehem Public Library declares that the village was named for a suburb of St. Louis, Mo. This seems improbable—one reason being that place names in the United States usually traveled west, not east—yet it is possible and should be mentioned.[60]

Another idea is that the name is an "absurd misappropriation of [a] well-known town name on [the] border of Delaware and Maryland."[61] It could well be from Spanish *del mar*, of the sea. It has been pointed out, however, that the name "rarely has anything to do with the sea, and it appears to have become popular merely for its euphony and perhaps for a vaguely attractive suggestion."[62] Whatever its source, Delmar is the third known name for the hamlet.

Along Delaware Avenue
(From the Normanskill to the Four Corners)

It is quite clear, as we drive along Delaware Avenue from the bridge over the Normanskill to the Four Corners, that Elsmere and Delmar are two major commercial areas. Here one finds an extraordinary number of stores and shops, professional offices, banks, pharmacies, barber shops and beauty parlors, liquor stores, service and gas stations, and places to eat. This is by no means a comprehensive list of the goods and services available in that almost two-mile distance.

The Southern Hamlets
(Along Route 396)

Route 396 traverses the southern portion of Bethlehem westward from Route 144, south of Cedar Hill and the Selkirk entrance to the New York State Thruway (opened October 1954), through the hamlets of Selkirk, Beckers Corners on Route 9W, and South Bethlehem, to the extreme southwestern corner of the town at Callanans Corners, which is on the border between Coeymans and Bethlehem.

Selkirk

When reading nineteenth-century county and town histories, one finds that they usually include mention of the hamlets' post offices, dates when

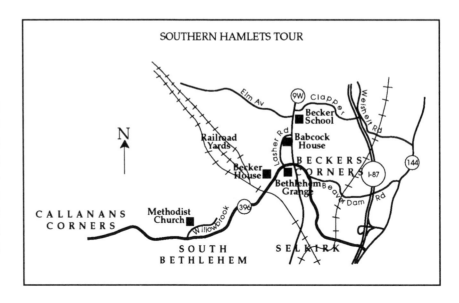

postal service was started, and the names of post-masters. One history, published in 1886, states:

> *Selkirk* is a post-office established in 1883; Jacob J. Soop, postmaster. This post-office is located at the station of the same name, on the N.Y. & W.S. Railroad, in the southeastern part of the town, upon lands belonging to the Selkirks. The Selkirks are of Scotch origin, and include two families whose buildings represent the commence-ment of the future village.[63]

Until the 1880s, what is now the hamlet of Selkirk was part of the farmsteads of such well-known Bethlehem families as the Vroomans, Selkirks, Van Derzees, and Ten Eycks. Parts of this south-eastern section of Bethlehem still retain rural char-acteristics of an earlier time: planted and fallow fields, farmhouses, barns and outbuildings, wood lots, herds of dairy cows and beef cattle, and winding roads such as Beaver Dam Road and further north, Clapper and Wemple roads. But after the coming of the railroad in 1883, houses began to be constructed at the end of the present hamlet near the Thruway bridge on Maple Av-enue. These were large houses, many built as summer residences for people from Albany, some for local farmers who planned to retire there. During the late nineteenth and early twen-tieth centuries, the hamlet contained a post office, general store, and the present Lehmann's Garage (which began as a blacksmith shop).

With the development of the Selkirk railroad yards in the 1920s, the settlement blossomed as homes were built by railroad men. The Hackett Gardens section of three streets near Security Supply Corpo-ration was a sub-division at that time. In addition, the West Shore line running through town meant that Selkirk would become a bedroom community for office workers who could commute to their jobs in Albany. Commuting between Selkirk and Al-bany was further facilitated by the regular schedule on Route 144 of the Mountain View Bus Line. In those years before widespread automobile owner-ship, many Selkirk people who were railroad work-ers had passes and were thus able to commute to Albany for work or shopping.[64]

The Selkirk Post Office

Although the post office at Cedar Hill was estab-lished in 1833, it was discontinued in 1901 and joined with that of Selkirk. The Beckers Corners post office, established in 1873, was also merged with that of Selkirk in 1899.

Seventeen years and three postmasters later, John J. Vrooman, who was then postmaster, received authorization to establish Rural Free Delivery in the southern part of the township. Edward K. Selkirk was appointed carrier and his father, Wil-liam Selkirk, was substitute carrier, the letter from the First Assistant Postmaster General stating, "one carrier, at a salary of $400 per annum, in-cluding horse hire."[65] A short excerpt from this letter gives us a hint of the sort of route followed:

Starting from the Post Office in the said town of Selkirk, and going East on Selkirk Road to River Road, 1/2 mile, thence North on River Road to Cedar Hill Bridge, 2 miles, thence East 1/4 of a mile thence North 1/4 of a mile to road leading to Cedar Hill landing....

The length of the route was twenty-four miles, the area covered twenty square miles, and the population served was 925 persons. Iron collection boxes were placed at Cedar Hill, Bethlehem Church, Bethlehem Center, and Beckers Corners. Further, the Selkirk postmaster was told that

> It is particularly desired by the Department that the boxes put up by the patrons of the delivery shall be of such a character as to be secure, not only from the weather, but from mischievous or malicious depredation. The U.S. mail should not be deposited in any but an appropriate receptacle, properly labeled and protected.

When Edward K. Selkirk retired thirty years later, in 1930, the Postmaster General of the United States wrote:

> I congratulate you on the loyal and efficient service which you have given and which must afford you abundant satisfaction. In your future years I hope that happiness, contentment and well-being may attend you.[66]

From Selkirk, we follow Route 9W north for a couple of miles to the hamlet of Beckers Corners.

Beckers Corners

The Beckers Corners road sign comes into view slowly as the driver approaches the intersection. The popular Bonfare store is on the right. At the Hess gasoline station across the road, the timid sounds of automobiles compete with the roaring sounds of heavy trucks approaching the Corners on 396 from the south. Such trucks have been carting crushed stone from the Callanan Quarry in South Bethlehem to all points north, south, east, and west for decades. Old-timer Frank Gifford remembers watching the trucks in the 1930s and 1940s when their drivers drove straight ahead on Beaver Dam Road toward the Schiffendecker Dock, which was on the Hudson River where the Henry Hudson Park now stands. There the crushed stone was unloaded onto barges with destinations to the south. Sitting there at the light, you notice Don Millious's Excavating and Blacktopping business beyond Hess on the right, followed by Country Carriage Auto Sales, and suddenly become aware that a few houses are sprinkled among all of the businesses. You wonder how the homeowners co-exist with all the noise and confusion from the traffic at the Corners. On this bright sunny day in 1991, I drove north beyond the light a few thousand feet to the intersection of Lasher Road and Route 9W where the state police barracks is located. A smiling state policeman said they had been in that location since 1966.

You think, there must be more to Beckers Corners than this and I drove back toward the Corners, passing Dan's Moving & Trucking Company, Inc., and Andy's Deli before turning right on Route 396.

This is more like it! A heavy truck passes now and then, but a pleasant scene unfolds as one drives southwest for a block or so. A short jog to the right on Lasher Road takes one past the old home of the legendary Bethlehem doctor John Babcock. It is now occupied by Helen Crowel, step-daughter of the doctor's grandson, John Babcock. It is a peaceful road with lots of trees and a large set of farm buildings at the end where Lasher Road intersects with 9W. There, G. Clifford Lasher, aged eighty-four, greeted me at the door and quickly introduced me to his sister, Mildred Irene Lasher, 86. They are the modern representatives of a family that has lived on this property for about 130 years.

Back on 396, and a short distance south on the right, a marker in front of an old brick house proclaims "Becker Homestead at Becker's Corners settled by Albertus Becker who married Helen Van Derzee." There is no one home on this day, but a quick glance at Howell and Tenney's *History of Albany County* shows that Albertus W. Becker built the home in 1800. He was the grandson of Albertus

Albertus W. Becker homestead (1800). Route 396 between Beckers Corners and South Bethlehem.

Becker, listed on the 1767 Bleeker map of Rensselaerswyck, which includes present-day Bethlehem (see p. 317). And it was Albertus W.'s grandson, Albertus Becker II, who was elected supervisor of Bethlehem in 1862 and again in 1871-1874. Now it is crystal clear where the name Beckers Corners comes from. The name appears in J.H. French's *Gazetteer of the State of New York*, published in 1860. It is quite possible that the name was used informally well before that year. It is easy to tarry in the driveway of the old Becker home. An artist painting the house would surely capture the beautiful, rolling farmlands in the valley below the house to the north.

A few hundred feet south on 396, a sign "Conrest" on the right raises a question. What is it? The sight of men in blue overalls talking in small groups as they look down the valley to the north from a bluff overlooking the Selkirk Yards provides a clue. Conrest must mean a restaurant for railroad men. A visit with

Doris Kelly, manager, revealed that Conrest is both a restaurant and a place for railroad men to stay overnight.[67] She said an average of "forty-five men have their meals and stay here every night." The old "Y" which stood just beyond the present building was torn down some years ago. The line of trees which led up to the entrance of the large hotel-like building is still visible.

Feeling much better about the human side of Beckers Corners, I turned the car around and drove back toward the intersection of routes 9W and 396, and passed in front of the large rectangular building of the Bethlehem Grange on the right. On this day, cars in the parking lot suggested some kind of activity and a visit confirmed this. The aroma of food cooking greeted me as I walked through the front door and there was a friendly welcome from several people who were busy in

the kitchen. Neita Raynor said they were preparing a spaghetti supper that would be served to the members beginning at 2:30 P.M. Frank Gifford brought out a large historical record book created by Helen Raynor for the Grange's one hundredth anniversary in 1964. Jurian Winne is listed as the first master of the Grange in 1874 and the highlights of Grange activity were spelled out in later pages. These are covered in the farm and Community Organizations chapters in this book. Jurian Winne owned a farm in Jericho in the early years. His home was destroyed in 1924 when the Selkirk Yards were built by the New York Central Railroad. Over the years, the Grange has served a wide range of farm folks from all over the town and some come from surrounding towns today. The stop at the Grange was truly a warm, friendly experience. There is a lot more to Beckers Corners than businesses and noisy trucks.

Leaving the Grange and heading east toward the intersection of 9W and 396, the name W.J. Riegel & Sons appears on a sign. The company is in the railroad construction and maintenance business—a handy location considering the huge amount of railroad activity just a few miles away. W. Jerry Riegel, Jr., said the firm started in Selkirk in 1968 and moved to this location near the Corners in 1975.

Deep in thought, I turned north on 9W and after about a quarter of a mile noticed the A.W. Becker Elementary School. It is an attractive brick building set back away from the road. One of the teachers said the school was built in 1962-1963 for kindergarten through fourth grade. There are 425 pupils enrolled today. All of this leaves me with the feeling that no part of Bethlehem should be dismissed by merely passing through on a heavily travelled highway. There are interesting people and unquestionably rich history everywhere along the tour.[68]

South Bethlehem

The hamlet of South Bethlehem is located in the southwestern part of the town on Route 396. In 1886, according to an Albany county history,

> The village has 30 dwellings, 33 families, 135 inhabitants, M.E. church, school-house, 2 stores [kept by E.C. Palmer and Peter Ginder], shoe shop, harness, blacksmith and wheelwright shop, barber's room and saloon. It has a band of 12 musicians, with O.S. Jolley as leader.[69]

At various times, South Bethlehem also contained a small hotel, a post-office, the plants of Henry Callanan, the farm of John Mosher, grist and sawmills, and a tannery for making leather which was built about 1825 and burned in 1883.

The South Bethlehem United Methodist Church on Willowbrook Avenue was built in 1845. The congregation, however, had been organized in 1823 and housed in a building located near Beckers Corners. Thus, as Allison Bennett writes, it is

South Bethlehem United Methodist Church (ca. 1848). Painting by Rita Buttiker.

"the oldest Methodist Episcopal Church group in the Town of Bethlehem."[70] This church is further discussed in the chapter on religious organizations.

Mount Pleasant Cemetery (1864) is located just west of South Bethlehem on Route 396, on nine acres which were a gift from John Callanan. In 1975, the Tawasentha Chapter of the DAR placed a plaque on the right brick post at the entrance to commemorate the burial here of Patrick Callanan. He was a soldier in the 3rd Regiment of the Albany County Militia during the Revolutionary War.

The hamlet of South Bethlehem has had two earlier names. One was Janes (or Jaynes) Corners, named in honor of the Janes family: William Janes was an early settler and Elishama Janes a tavern

Bridge Street, South Bethlehem (late nineteenth-century postcard).

South Albany

The hamlet of South Albany, on County Route 53 north of South Bethlehem and west of the Selkirk Yards, came into being with the arrival of the railroad in the 1920s. Land in this sparsely settled farming section was bought up by Charles P. Brate, owner of an Albany printing firm and a land developer and wealthy investor. The hamlet was developed for families coming into the area to work on the railroad or in related services. Some 350 homesites were laid out in South Albany with streets and a water supply system. Twenty-one dwellings were built and then the Great Depression put an end to Mr. Brate's plans. Currey Avenue in South Albany is named for Francis Currey, a World War II hero and holder of the Congressional Medal of Honor.

keeper. The other name was Kimmeys Corners (1856), for Philip Kimmey who settled here about 1825.

Any description of South Bethlehem must contain mention of the Callanan Road Improvement Company, which was founded in 1883 by Peter Callanan. The Business and Industry chapter in this book contains material on this most important company.

North to Feura Bush Road

Feura Bush Road may be reached by driving north on Route 53 and continuing on to Elm Avenue.

Houcks Corners and Eastward to Route 9W

Houcks Corners is located east of the Elm Avenue Park (opened 1973) in the area of the intersection of Elm Avenue and Feura Bush Road (Route 32).

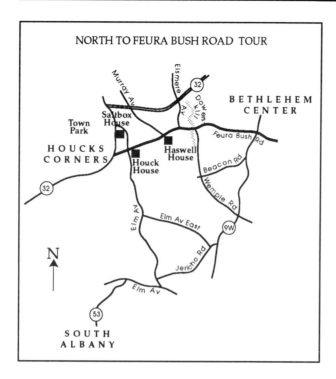

NORTH TO FEURA BUSH ROAD TOUR

front and three small windows above them. This was an early tavern, built in the mid-1800s by W. Haswell, and occupied by the Houck family when this crossroads was first called Houcks Corners. The building now contains apartments.

There are two more important houses on the right as we continue east on Feura Bush Road. Traveling toward Bethlehem Center, the fifth building on the right at 808 Feura Bush Road is the white painted brick house (1797), built by a Haswell on land leased from Patroon Stephen van Rensselaer. The original house had seven rooms and cooking cranes in the kitchen. It is now owned by Harold and Pamela Williams. The second is the Haswell homestead (1820) at 708 Feura Bush Road, which was built by William Haswell, youngest son of the original settler. Seven generations of the Haswell family have lived here, including present owner Howard Bennett Haswell and his nephew, Richard Haswell Hale. The present house, located across Feura Bush Road from Murray Avenue, has developed from the original three-room saltbox. There are still a couple of fruit and vegetable stands in front of the house along the road. At present, Richard Hale's Bethlehem Grinding Service is located in one of the outbuildings behind the house.

The original settler here, John Haswell, Sr., came from England in 1774 with his wife and ten children and rented over 300 acres from the patroon. They lived in a cabin near the Dowerskill, the creek which flows south, east of Murray Avenue. There are about eighty acres of the farm left today,

Elm Avenue bears right directly opposite the entrance to the main town park, and immediately on the right is a house worthy of notice. The saltbox portion of the old Becker homestead was built ca. 1770 and wings were added in the 1860s and 1900. This was the thirteen-room farmhouse of the farm on which the present park is situated. This historic house is owned by Steven and Roberta Sandler.

Diagonally across the intersection of Elm Avenue and Feura Bush Road is another noteworthy nineteenth-century building. It is a large, square, frame house with four square columns across the

Haswell homestead (1820), Feura Bush Road (opposite Murray Avenue).

and all commercial farming has been discontinued. On the farm is the Haswell family cemetery in which some of the original Haswells were buried.[71]

Now, as we continue along Feura Bush Road, we pass on the left the intersection with Elsmere Avenue, and further on the right, Wemple Road. Colonial Acres on the left dates from the early 1960s, and Adams Woods from 1991. Before we reach the Route 9W intersection, we pass the Niagara Mohawk Electric Service area and Holy Spirit Lutheran Cemetery. At the intersection are two shopping centers, both dating from about 1990, Glenmont Plaza on the southwestern corner (1990) and Glenmont Centre Square on the northwestern corner (1989-1990). On the northeastern corner is the Town Squire Shopping Center.

Bethlehem Center

One may with some justification wonder what happened to the hamlet here, which was known as Babcocks Corners in the mid-nineteenth century and after that as Bethlehem Center. The Garden Shoppe, Colonial Acres, and housing developments on Wemple Road use Glenmont in their addresses, as does the Capital Cities Imported Cars salesroom and service garage on Route 9W, not far from Wemple Road.

Bethlehem Center, known as Babcocks Corners in the mid-nineteenth century, is located at the interesection of Route 9W and Feura Bush Road (whereas Glenmont is located further east and near the Hudson, at the intersection of Route 144 and Glenmont Road). In an 1886 Albany County history, Bethlehem Center is described as follows:

> There are 40 dwellings, 45 families, 190 inhabitants, 2 blacksmiths, 2 wheelwright shops, school-house, church and hotel. Widow Van Buren, postmistress, and post-office kept at the toll-gate house. Four cemeteries are located here.[72]

Today, Bethlehem Center contains residential streets, several cemeteries, two schools, gas stations, three shopping centers, and on Route 9W some fine old houses, areas of light industry, and houses and lots for sale.

313

Mid-Twentieth-Century Developments

A 1989 map of the Town of Bethlehem notes many residential sections in and near the hamlets of Slingerlands, Delmar, and Bethlehem Center.[73] Brookehill Village, Dutchbrook, Indian Hills, and the apartments and townhouses on Blessing Road near the Slingerlands By-Pass have already been mentioned. Slingerlands has several areas of relatively new houses—Surrey Mall, Deerfield, and the sections north and south of New Scotland Road from Southwood Drive and Mayfair to Carstead Drive and Caldwell Boulevard. A drive along Cherry Avenue, crossing Delaware Avenue and continuing south on Elm Avenue, takes us past Woodgate, Kenaware, and Westchester Woods, which date from the late 1950s. Two developments off Elm Avenue, Park Edge and Adams Station, date from the late 1980s and early 1990s. Along the roads in Adams Station are signs for Derzee Court, The Commons, and Astor Court, each containing the representation of an old-time train engine, which calls to mind the railroad trains passing through the earlier Adams Station (which became Delmar). Wemple Road, south of Feura Bush Road, has its share of recent settlements, too—Chadwick Square, Windham Hill, Somerset, and The Crossroads. Not long ago, I drove along Beacon Road one Saturday morning from Wemple Road to Route 9W, a short ride through a delightful residential area. I noticed some large houses, an in-ground pool, raised-ranches, a gazebo in a back yard, few trees but many shrubs; people along the side of the road—a couple striding purposefully with arms swinging, a girl and her

dog, a boy waiting to cross the road. This scene could be duplicated in any of the locations in and near our hamlets.

As I drove along Beacon Road here at The Crossroads, along the winding roads in North Bethlehem's Indian Fields, and through Dowerskill Village near Myers Corners, I felt that these and the other developments in North Bethlehem and in and around Slingerlands, Delmar, and Elsmere, made a fitting conclusion to our bicentenial tour of Bethlehem. We commenced with the oldest, along the Hudson and its tributaries, and are ending with the newest.

IN RETROSPECT

The editor of a late nineteenth-century history of Albany County wrote that most of the hamlets in Bethlehem "have gathered about the post-office, or an early mill, or a store and a few shops."[74] He could have added that hamlets have also developed about a railroad station or at a crossroads. He continues: "So thickly placed throughout the town are these numerous hamlets that their description substantially constitutes the modern history of the locality."

The "Map of the Manor Renselaerwick," surveyed by John R. Bleeker in 1767, identifies the families living in the Bethlehem area some twenty-five years before our township was formed.[75] The portion of the map comprising present-day Bethlehem is delineated in the detail included here. At the bottom is the Hudson River with its many islands. At the extreme left is "Beren Ile," the present Barren Island just south of Coeymans. Three streams flow west from the "Hellebergh" hills to the Hudson: Onesquethaw Creek; the Vloman Kill with the house of Renselaer Nicolls, Esq., on its south bank (No. 4 on the map, the Nicoll-Sill, or Bethlehem, House); and the Normanskill. There were seventeenth-century mills on the Vloman Kill and Normanskill, where Cedar Hill, Normansville, and Kenwood developed.

Bleeker's map also indicates that in the eighteenth century, most houses were situated along the Hudson and the three streams mentioned above. Others were located beside the tracks or dirt roads which had developed from Indian trails and from paths which led from one farm to another. Except for mills on the main streams, Bethlehem was a farming community.

Other hamlets such as Slingerlands Corners (which became Slingerlands), Beckers Corners, and Houcks Corners, developed at a crossroads. And some hamlets evolved at the site of a railroad station—former names of Glenmont and Delmar, for example, were Glenmont Station and Adams Station. Other hamlets, such as Kenwood and Hurstville, waxed in the nineteenth century and waned in the twentieth, but they live on in people's memories.

In the nineteenth century, and to some extent into the first decades of the twentieth, each hamlet in the township had its own elementary school, grocery and dry goods stores, and post office. Many had a church, perhaps a physician's office, grist and sawmills, and blacksmith and wheelwright shops. Today's equivalents of dry goods or department stores are shopping centers and malls. The blacksmith and wheelwright shops of yesteryear are gas stations and garages today. The small-town hotel with its dining room featuring family-style dinners at noon is a thing of the past, too, and now we have the fast-food chain cafeterias and restaurants.

This brings us to the end of our bicentennial tour of Bethlehem's hamlets, which we visited as they were two hundred years ago and as they are today. Along the way we visited the eighteenth-century gristmill near the mouth of the

Normanskill, the precursor of Kenwood, and the many residential settlements and commerical centers which make up the present-day community. Bon voyage as you set out on your own tours of our hamlets.

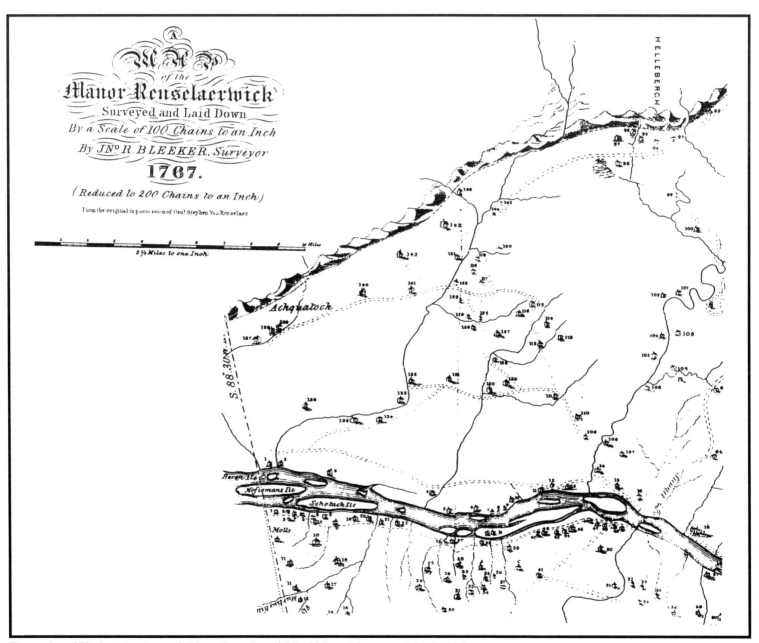

The portion of Bleeker's 1767 map of "Manor Renselaerwick" which contains present-day Bethlehem.

PROMINENT SCENES AND BUILDINGS IN LOCAL HISTORY. Top: First Delmar Fire Department pumper and crew, ca. 1917. **Bottom:** Essex House on Feura Bush Road, ca. 1830.

12 Schools and Library

Educational historians usually begin the story of public education in the United States with the enactment of the Massachusetts School Law of 1642, which stated that every town in the colony was required to provide instruction in reading to all the children in its jurisdiction. This initial step was built upon five years later by the famous "Olde Deluder Satan" law, whose purpose was to fight the Devil's attempts to " keepe men from the knowledge of ye scriptures." Further, the law's purpose was that "learning might not be buried in the graves of our fathers in Church and Commonwealth." The law specified that a town of fifty or more families was to support a teacher, over one hundred families, a school.[1]

Similar patterns were evolving in New Netherland, including Rensselaerswyck, the patroonship that later would become Albany, Bethlehem, and rural areas beyond these political boundaries. Both the English and Dutch colonies had been settled principally by Puritans and Dutch Reformed church members. John Fiske, the eminent American historian, reminds us that Calvinism required some form of universal and compulsory education, making it possible for the individual to read freely in the Scriptures without clerical assistance. Fiske points out that the state archives of Holland, Zeeland, and Friesland reveal that in the sixteenth century in the Netherlands free schools existed, supported by public taxation. We are told that even the peasants could read and write in the local idiom.[2] There is no reason to doubt that this early form of public schooling carried over to the Dutch colony in the New World, including Rensselaerswyck, in the early 1600s. Kiliaen van Rensselaer, the first patroon, appointed one Johannes Megapolensis to form a church in 1642. One writer suggests that the minister (or domine) may have been the first teacher in this area. If so, a church-school connection would have been made. It was further proposed that the comforters of the sick (laymen of the Dutch church) administer the schools.[3] Nevertheless, instruction was open to all in the colony and cannot be construed as narrowly sectarian.

Religious or not, early schoolmasters sometimes exhibited less than exemplary behavior. In April 1648, Evert Noldingh, a tailor by trade, was granted permission to support himself by teaching in the patroonship. In 1651, he was in court for seriously wounding a citizen in a fight. Other schoolmasters included Ludovic Cobus, Adrian Jansen van Ilpendam (who was forced to sue the citizens for back pay), and Adam Roelantsen. We are told that the latter had frequent quarrels with his neighbors. Later in life, after his schoolmaster days, he was found guilty of adultery and publicly flogged. Schoolmasters were burdened with a multiplicity of duties not associated with instruction. They were expected to help the domine by consoling the sick and performing sexton duties. While the church and school lines were tangential, we should expect that the schoolmaster's social role was not confined to his school duties.

When the English took over New Netherland, they found the principle of community-based schools, albeit religiously oriented, already firmly established. Jonathan Tenney tells us that "the crowning glory of New England, giving its sons everywhere prosperity, influence and power, came from its free school."[4] The colonial Dutch schools could make the same claim. Perhaps they were even more liberal. One authority states that English tourists in the Hudson Valley found that girls as well as boys attended the schools, learning reading, writing, and ciphering.[5] Nevertheless, Michael Kammen reminds us that schools were neither free nor obligatory in the modern sense, and did not educate very many people for very long periods of time. Consequently, they were less important than newspapers, artisans, lawyers, printers, and book-sellers as sources of education.[6] Kammen estimates that in "1770 only about three-sixteenths of the white children younger than sixteen were in school in any given year."[7] Bethlehem probably reflected the same general picture.

Such data might easily be misinterpreted. Schools do reflect social needs. We should remember that the town of Bethlehem in 1770 was an overwhelmingly agricultural society, whose rural landscape was broken by scattered hamlets. Girls and boys were needed to perform all the household and farm chores. They began at an early age and continued into adulthood. In the eighteenth century, schooling was indeed a privilege of the more fortunate.

Legacy of the Revolutionary War

The American Revolution represents a watershed in both our political and educational history. Social forces were at work. Democratic impulses were in the air. The spirit of social equality lent itself to initiating steps for a true system of public education. In Albany County the early nineteenth century would usher in the breakup of the manorial lands. Freehold farms began to dot the landscape. Rural towns and villages attracted a growing class of mechanics. The nascent industrialism and availability of land had attracted energetic and enterprising newcomers to the area—French, Germans, Welsh, Scots, and Irish. This new social mix gave enormous impetus to a new way of thinking in education.

The Jeffersonian ideas that swept through the colonies, soon to become states, were another moving force in educational reforms. In 1789, Virginia enacted a "Statute of Religious Liberty." This law, in effect, disestablished the Anglican Church as the official state religion and prohibited its maintenance by public taxation. By this act of the separation of church and state, public education was taken from the church and placed under the jurisdiction of the state. In a philosophical sense, and Thomas Jefferson was a classical scholar, the new republic's health and safety were felt to rest upon an enlightened and politically active citizenry. Thus was established the principle that has lasted to this day, namely, that political democracy and public education go hand-in-hand. The schools' overarching purpose was to prepare young Americans for citizenship.

District 3 School in South Bethlehem, early 1900s.

Cedar Hill School, early 1900s.

New York State began to respond. In opening the legislative session in 1795, Governor George Clinton said:

> While it is evident that the general establishment and liberal endowment of academies are highly to be commended... yet it cannot be denied that they are principally confined to the children of the opulent. The establishment of common schools throughout the state is happily calculated to remedy this inconvenience, and will therefore engage your early and decided consideration. [8]

The legislature acted. In perhaps the first instance of state aid to local school districts, the state legislature appropriated the annual sum of $50,000 for a period of five years. Albany County was to receive $3,975 of this amount. A firm precedent was set. With this general historical setting in mind, let us trace the evolution of public school education in the town of Bethlehem.

The Era of the One-Room Schoolhouse

In line with the quickening of democracy, the Albany area began to push ahead in the advancement of public schooling. According to Preston's Statistical Report, data compiled by a schoolmaster from Westerlo, Albany County, in 1820 had 155 common schools in addition to its private academies. An early step toward teacher professionalism was the opening of the state's first normal school in Albany in December 1844, with twenty-nine prospective teachers. At about the same time, provision was made for the establishment of countywide teacher institutes, from which

All in the family: Cedar Hill School graduates. From a photograph taken in 1959, the last year the school was open. **Left to Right:** Martin J. Cross, Sr., Martin J. Cross, Jr. (former Bethlehem superintendent of highways), and Martin J. Cross III.

practicing schoolmasters might gain new ideas in education. Additionally, certain academies were permitted to establish teaching departments, from which future schoolmasters might come.

Within Albany County, each town was empowered to establish school districts. The term "district" is really a euphemism for a one-room schoolhouse. For example, there were fifteen schoolhouses scattered throughout the town of Bethlehem, one in each of the districts. One of these districts was located in Hurstville, then a part of the town of Bethlehem, and referred to as the Hurstville School. Allison Bennett tells us that the first of these districts was the Cedar Hill School, built of log construction at the beginning of the nineteenth century. She reports that:

When the Clermont steamed up the Hudson River, the scholars were allowed to go to the river bank and watch the boat's passage.[9]

The locally famous Little Red Schoolhouse in Cedar Hill was constructed in 1859, in District No. 1. W.H. Van Guysling was its architect. In 1907, a second room was added and the building redesigned under the direction of Marcus Reynolds, architect. A. Miller was the first schoolmaster, hired in 1860. The original roster of twenty-four pupils still exists. To judge from its names, the Dutch heritage in Bethlehem was still strong.

In District No. 8 the freeholders got together to erect a new building, which opened in 1829. The cost was $107.50. Miss McHarg was employed as the first teacher, at an annual salary of $70.00. The yearly cost of maintenance was just $15.00. But by

Eighth grade, Selkirk School. Ca. 1916.

Slingerlands School, Mr. Adams, principal. Ca. 1913.

1883, things were beginning to look up. Jacob S. Markle tells us that the combined districts in Bethlehem then had twenty teachers educating some 769 pupils. This would result in a class load of thirty-eight pupils per teacher, with ages varying from six to thirteen. For this demanding and exhaustive work, teachers' salaries ranged from $290.00 to $520.00 per year. [10]

Let us try to reconstruct a one-room schoolhouse curriculum that would meet the needs of nineteenth-century rural children. Of course, the starting point would be the basic skills of readin'-writin'-'rithmetic. Yet American nationalism must be served. History centered on the great patriotic heroes, with plenty of attention to the national holidays, particularly the Fourth of July. Civic instruction was important, involving citizenship responsibilities and studying the American Constitution and the maintenance of its freedoms. Geography was of prime importance, we are told by Meredith Clapper and Marie Weidemann,

themselves former pupils at Cedar Hill.[11]. It was essentially place geography, locating states and memorizing their capitals. It took a later revolution in geographical education before schools began to probe the idea of geography as a cultural adaptation to the physical environment. Miss Weidemann tells us that poetry portrayed the seasons and there were outdoor field trips for nature study.

Physical conditions were primitive enough to require the students to bring drinking water acquired from neighbors. There were two outhouses, "his" and "hers." Wet shoes and socks, while drying out, provided a less-than-aromatic odor to the atmosphere. And we can't forget the ubiquitous *McGuffey Reader*, chockfull of historical anecdotes and functional moralities. This almost universally used teaching-learning tool was perfectly suited to the educational climate of a one-room schoolhouse, offering a splendid opportunity for self-instruction without too much teacher direction.

Delmar Public School, early 1900s.

School District No. 6, June 1909. Van Wies Point.

different from the Americanization process that permitted foreign newcomers to become assimilated into mainstream American life.

Important as these curriculum dimensions were, we are more impressed with what educators refer to as the "affective domain." There has been a revision in modern educational thinking about the values inherent in one-room multi-age education. The teacher was literally forced to depend upon the older children to teach the younger. The learning environment required a large degree of pupil interaction and sharing. If education involves pupil participation in the learning process, and it surely does, then one-room schoolhouses in the nineteenth century provided an exceptional opportunity for that to take place.

Bethlehem reflected the same practices. And its graduates, many of whom still reside in the town,

Science instruction, essentially nature study, was not ignored. And there was time for some group singing. Moral education was deemed to be important. This involved the kind of ethics found in *Poor Richard's Almanac*, and the qualities of hard work, thrift, punctuality, and striving for success were to serve well the capitalist socio-economic structure. Without being quite aware of it, the rural schools of Bethlehem, and the nation's for that matter, socialized young Americans into a kind of American creed, not at all

Bethlehem Center School, 1930s.

demonstrate that individual responsibility and social activism are the schools' end-products.

In the demographic sense, the one-room schoolhouse well served the needs of rural Bethlehem. Fifteen district schools were located in the scattered population centers. Those included Cedar Hill, Slingerlands, Bethlehem Church, Van Wies Point, Delmar, Elsmere, Bethlehem Center, North Bethlehem, and South Bethlehem. This kind of decentralized structure permitted an intimate relationship between school and community, very much akin to the neighborhood school concept.

We should not forget that the broad range of learning materials found in today's schools was largely missing in the rural one-room schoolhouse. Rough-hewn country kids were pretty unruly at times. Although education law permitted it and the popular image of spare the rod, spoil the child prevailed, Eric Sloane, eminent chronicler of American folkways, is persuaded that physical discipline was confined to a simple rap on the palm with a straight-edged ruler.[12] As is true today, classroom discipline meant rules, order, instruction, education, and knowledge.[13]

In an economy that did not require a sophisticated level of skills, the motivation for learning could be, at times, weak indeed. Nevertheless, the one-room schoolhouse worked. It represented a solid stepping stone in the evolution of Bethlehem's public school system.

In leaving this era in our educational history, let us pay tribute to those heroic figures who taught and guided Bethlehem's youngsters in their quest for intellectual and social maturity. We mention A. Miller, Cedar Hill's first schoolmaster,

Hamagrael School.

lum secondary schools were using to prepare their students. To construct the laboratories and equipment needed for these changes would require a substantial investment. With buses available to replace the horse and buggy, one feasible solution was to build a centrally located school and transport the students. In Bethlehem, as it turned out, this action would take place in two steps.

followed by such teachers as M. Van Vechten, Georgeanna Hungerford, Miss Udell, Etta Hotaling, Miss Dugan, Susie M. Glasser, Margaret Keyser, Mettie E. Sexton, Miss Ferguson, Miss Gilboy, Mrs. Stanton, Mr. Stott, Elsie C. Mead, and others whose identities have unfortunately been lost in the mists of history. Their ideas continue to live in the minds of their protégés.

The Centralization of Bethlehem Schools

As vital as the one-room schoolhouse had been, historical forces in the early part of the twentieth century dictated a move toward consolidation and centralization. The advent of the automobile, the telephone, electricity, motion pictures, and the typewriter had revolutionized both society and the world of work. Science and technology had a major impact on the content of the curricu-

On April 25, 1930, seven of the original fifteen one-room districts joined in the formation of Bethlehem Central School District No. 6, with an enrollment of 866 students. Included were Delmar, Slingerlands, Elsmere, Houcks Corners, Bethlehem Center, Glenmont-Normansville, and Van Wies Point. The key

Sign on Hamagrael lawn.

Olin Bouck, 1929.

figures in the transition process were W. Jack Weaver and Olin Bouck. Weaver, as board president, first proposed the centralization plan. A committee, consisting of Walter Tiedeman, James Coates, Harold Worden, T.E. Burhouse, H.L. Marvin, and Weaver drew up the plan. Olin Bouck was asked to administer the new arrangement.

Bouck had started as a teacher in 1925 in the Delmar School, then housed in the Masonic Temple on Kenwood Avenue. In the following year, he was appointed principal of the Delmar School on Delaware Avenue at a starting salary of $1,000. In 1931, Bouck became district superintendent with jurisdiction over four districts: Bethlehem Central, Guilderland Central, and two districts in Colonie. Bouck served some forty-five years as a public school educator.

The First High School

A particularly exciting episode in our school history was the formation of Bethlehem's first central high school building, the present Middle School, built at a cost of $317,000 in 1932. Heath Coons was appointed the supervising principal of fifteen teachers. He was to remain for eight years. Although by present-day standards the

Bethlehem Central Middle School.

curriculum was limited, its range was sufficiently broad to justify the centralization move. In addition to the standard history-civics, English, science, and mathematics courses, instruction was offered in Latin, French, art, music, and physical education. Later in the 1930s, agriculture and commercial subjects found their way into the program.

Another outstanding educator was Hamilton Bookhout, who succeeded Heath Coons as supervising principal in 1938. A graduate of Hamilton College, Bookhout began his teaching career in Baldwin on Long Island. He retired in 1964 from the Bethlehem system. In that interval it can be truly said that the Bethlehem Central

Hamilton H. Bookhout, 1950.

Slingerlands School, 1992.

School District came of age. Its reputation as one of the state's outstanding school districts was unchallenged. From a rather intimate and rural past, the schools had now become a thoroughly professional operation. It is to Bookhout's credit that he sought and insisted upon a thoroughly professional instructional staff. Because of Bookhout's efforts, the Bethlehem Central School

Clarksville School, 1992.

District was developed into six neighborhood elementary school centers, a middle school, and the high school.

At this point, it may be appropriate to turn our attention to the progress of the rest of the original fifteen one-room schools in the town of Bethlehem. Located primarily south and southeast of the Bethlehem Central School District, they extended along routes 9W and 144 as far south as the town of Coeymans. This group consisted of Cedar Hill, Selkirk and North Coeymans, South Bethlehem, Jericho, Feura Bush and Bethlehem Church, Callanans Corners, and Cedar Grove. They remained common school districts until 1947 when they combined to form the Union Free School District No. l. According to their places of residence, pupils attended high school in Ravena, Coeymans, or Albany.

Meanwhile, Ravena and Coeymans had been experiencing problems of overcrowding. In 1945-1947, they operated as the Cooperating  Schools of Ravena and Coeymans, with John Diseroth serving as principal of the junior high in Ravena and Edna Lawson supervising the junior high in the Coeymans former high school building. Finally, in 1947, they combined with Alcove, Coeymans Hollow, Aquetuck, and New Baltimore to form the Ravena-Coeymans Central School District. It soon became apparent that new buildings would be needed, especially a high

Ravena-Coeymans-Selkirk Senior High School, 1992.

followed later by a junior high on the same site, the Albertus Becker Elementary School on 9W north of Beckers Corners, and the Pieter B. Coeymans Elementary School between Coeymans and Ravena. The former Ravena High School became an elementary school.

New Ravena-Coeymans-Selkirk Central School District

A considerable number of residents in the Union Free District, believing that there would be too few secondary pupils to permit the wide range of offerings they desired, proposed establishing a new Ravena-Coeymans-Selkirk Central School District. Eventually the matter came to a vote and in July 1955 the centralization took place. The Union Free District protested the action, but a year later, it was decided that the vote was legal and on July 1, 1956, the new central district became official. In subsequent years a new senior high was constructed on Route 9W,

school. While Ravena and Coeymans were beginning to work on plans, the new Union Free School District decided that it, too, would build a high school and prepare a curriculum for the new school.

Every school district has its educational luminaries. It is important to mention Edward Stanton, who presided over the board of education when the centralization of the Ravena-Coeymans-Selkirk district was effected in 1956. His successor, Prescott Archibald, held the presidency from the late 1950s until quite recently. J. Lyman Roney, over a period of sixteen years, was, in succession, a teacher, guidance director, vice-principal, and principal of the junior-senior high school. Edna Farina helped in the transition as a teacher of business education. In that same department, William Gearhardt combined the duties of chairman and teacher for many years. It would seem that Harry Sturges gave most of his adult life to his career as a teacher of industrial arts. Combining longevity and creative teaching made Dominic Donato outstanding in social studies education. The same can be said for Jane Chworowsky in language arts. Also high on this list is Louis Montelone, a popular and successful health-physical education teacher and varsity coach.

The modernization of the two school districts, which gave public instruction to the students who lived in the town of Bethlehem, followed similar paths. Although Bethlehem Central was the first to move toward consolidating in 1930, Ravena-Coeymans-Selkirk, like its neighbor, later found it necessary to centralize a considerable number of hamlets and districts into one functional system. Interestingly enough, the areas served by the R.C.S. system essentially retain their rural-hamlet qualities, something of a contrast to the suburban flavor of Bethlehem.

Saint Thomas School, 1990.

Catholic Education

During the post-war baby boom, a marked increase in the building of educational facilities had been going on in Delmar. The Reverend Daniel Markham, pastor of Saint Thomas the Apostle parish, faced the problem of limited facilities in a rapidly growing parish. He purchased land for a school and collected the money for an expansive building program, which included a rectory and a church as well as the school. In 1955, Father Markham was transferred to Troy and the Right Reverend Raymond F. Rooney was pastor in 1956 when Saint Thomas School opened. At first the school was housed in the old church, but in February classes were moved to the new building, at 42 Adams Place in Delmar, which opened in 1957. At that time, a kindergarten was added to the school, which contained grades one through five. Grades six through eight were added later, and the children who had been in the 1957 kindergar-

ten were the first to complete their nine years in Saint Thomas, when they graduated in 1966. Sister M. Ann Eleanor, S.N.J.M., was the school's first principal. Because of the foresight and vision of these three individuals and their leadership, St. Thomas the Apostle School became a reality and continues today as an excellent parochial school.

New High School Building

The same pressures of increasing population were being felt in the Bethlehem Central School District. For several years double sessions for the senior and junior high classes indicated the need for a new high school building. The voters' approval was won in June 1951 and the present building opened its doors on January 18,

Bethlehem Central High School, 1992.

1954. The initial enrollment of 418 students comprised grades ten through twelve. The old building, later to become the present Middle School with grades six through eight, served as a junior high and contained grades seven through nine. These new facilities provided a modern school plant and they made possible an extension of course offerings, which in turn helped students to develop their individual talents into marketable skills. New recreational facilities made possible not only varsity team sports but universal participation as well. An impressive library encouraged pupil research. Science labs enabled students to pursue their interests in the physical sciences. Bethlehem Central High School, hereafter called Bethlehem Central, acquired an excellent reputation as a comprehensive institution turning out potential leaders in most walks of life.

The 1950s saw what we can call the maturation of the school district. Spurred on by Sputnik, with the perceived notion that American education had fallen behind its Russian counterpart, the federal government decided on strong measures. Thus followed an impressive set of actions, equaled only by the GI Bill of Rights after World War II. The formation of the National Science Foundation provided teachers a wide range of programs, as did foundation grants, fellowships, state grants, and exchange teaching. Few teachers failed to capitalize on these golden opportunities to upgrade their professional skills. The school program reflected this improvement, although it was not necessarily confined to the mathematics-science area. Particularly at the high school level, a proliferation of electives ensued.

In this renaissance period of public education, teachers, by broadening their own horizons and understandings, extended and enriched the curriculum offerings extensively. Gorden Molyneux and Dominick DeCecco are two examples. Molyneux received a Fulbright Award to study at the American University in Beirut. Under the

Gordon Molyneux, 1964.

Dominick J. DeCecco, 1967.

331

Gladys Newell, 1964.

aegis of the State Department, DeCecco participated in a teacher exchange program at the University of Hawaii's East-West Center, followed by a two-month tour of Japan, Korea, Hong Kong, Taiwan, and Thailand. Together they prepared a course in foreign area studies which helped broaden the scope of the social studies program from American nationalism to intercultural and global thinking. Many of our educators took on leadership roles in professional organizations. Gladys Newell, a luminary in social studies education, was president of the New York State Teachers Association and later a founder of the New York State Council for the Social Studies. Helen Hobbie, high school principal, provided excellent leadership in this historical phase.

Helen Hobbie.

Bethlehem was an early pioneer of "open education" at the elementary level. Led by Joseph Shaefer, principal at the Delmar School, this program permitted students to progress in tune with individual capacities and interests, rather than in step with others in the class. Fred Burdick, principal of the middle school, introduced team teaching as a means of providing a transition period from the self-contained, elementary-level classroom to the individualized student scheduling of a high school. Teams of four teachers each brought the disciplines of English, social studies, mathematics, and science into a core curriculum relationship for any given group of youngsters.

Positive outcomes of these endeavors are easily discernible. Bethlehem Central's graduates have gone on to the nation's prestigious universities. The district has provided a substantial share of winners of National Merit and Regents Scholarships in Albany County. By most criteria, Bethlehem Central is considered an outstanding school district, both by state and regional certifying agencies.

The Co-Curricular Program

Let us turn from academic to the co-curricular program. Bethlehem Central has been blessed with a fine sports program. Arthur Ritchko and John Sodergren have turned out excellent football teams. Kenneth Hodge's high school baseball team is a regular stand-out in Albany County. Basketball continues to be a popular sport and many fans will recall Don Farrell as coach. In two sports, tennis and swimming, the record is incredible. Don Camp's tennis teams broke many records, while Jack Whipple's swimming teams were acknowledged to be the best in the area. The interscholastic varsity programs have been supplemented by freshman and junior varsity teams. The intra-mural programs are wide and extensive. These teams have their counterparts among the girls, who participate in all of the sports, excluding football.

The music department, under Samuel Bozzella's leadership, has given the community a series of fine concerts. An unusually large number of Bethlehem Central students have performed in all-state bands and orchestras. Many students have starred in dramatic and musical comedy productions for the public's enjoyment. This writer best remembers an excellent performance of *Oklahoma!* with a cast comprised of teachers and students.

This all-too-brief glance at the school's co-curricular programs gives credence to the idea that to be educated is to be well-rounded, intellectually informed, physically healthy, and socially mature. The record suggests that our schools have succeeded in these goals.

Still, it would be irresponsible, indeed, to suggest that we in Bethlehem have an educational nirvana. Adolescent behavior, often erratic, has not always followed constructive channels, but conscientious educators have found ways to combat the insidious ravages of substance abuse, particularly alcohol and drugs. In this most unsettling of times, in which the fabric of communication among the generations has been badly frayed, the schools have worked hard to respond. Charles Gunner has been a strong figure in introducing substance abuse education into teaching modes. The middle school has refined a program that centers on self-awareness and social conscience as antidotes to drug experimentation among

young teenagers. Called "Skills for Adolescents," the program helps young students in their quest for maturity.

We are indeed fortunate that Bethlehem has largely been spared the racial conflicts that seared the nation's schools in the inner cities in the 1960s and 1970s. Our racial attitudes probably mirror those of other suburban school districts. Nevertheless, the district has made a consistent effort to inject multi-cultural insights into the curriculum. Specific units of study on the cultures of Native Americans, Africans, and Asians, as well as ethnic patterns in American history, have been in place since the 1960s. Since Bethlehem is predominantly a community of Caucasians and middle-class residents, the Bethlehem Central faculties have strived to insure that students' world views embrace cultural pluralism.

Bethlehem's public school history can be viewed with pride. From the most humble of beginnings, civic lay leadership has provided the ground floor for the impressive educational edifice that we have today. The various boards of education, whose members have served without pay and whose sole motivation has been community enlightenment, should not be ignored. Consider, for example, the tireless efforts of these Board of Education leaders with ten or more years of service:

Clarence Crocker	1930-1940
Walter Tiedeman	1930-1941
Clinton Hartzell	1931-1942
John E. Glenn	1942-1959

Russell Freeman	1946-1956
Price Chenault	1946-1957
Walter Zimmerman	1950-1960
Daniel P. Dryden	1950-1963
Ralph A. Holmgren	1956-1972
Robert K. Bair	1960-1975
John H. Clyne	1964-1985
Bethhold Weinberg	1971-1981
Bernard E. Harvith	1972-present
Sheila Fuller	1978-1991
Marjorie O'Brien	1979-1989

Earl W. Cleaves, 1967.

And we should remember teachers whose long service assisted in the transition to the district we have today. Especially significant are Thomas Preston, Helen Adler, Earl Cleaves, Gladys Newell, Lois Mannheimer, Gladys Hosey, Henry Hall, and many others. Another teacher, Rolland Truitt, helped Eva Marie Saint, a Bethlehem high school graduate, launch her acting career. Particularly noteworthy is Jeanette Earls whose career of forty-one years began in the one-room schoolhouse in Cedar Hill and ended as a mathematics teacher in the junior high school.

Although many outstanding educators have been cited for their contributions, the quality of life in the town of Bethlehem has been enhanced by the efforts of hundreds of other teachers who could not be mentioned in this statement. A listing of the faculty who served the district for five years or more since 1950 can be found in the appendix.

It takes no great amount of introspection to realize that the past flows inexorably into the future. The future is the projected past. L. Jeffrey Baltes, assistant superintendent for curriculum and instructional personnel in the Troy School District, says that

> To be even partially effective, the school and community must be in concert. While we can work to counteract those forces we see as detrimental to our youth, we cannot change the fabric at the very foundation of society itself. [14]

The present superintendent of schools, Dr. Leslie Loomis, together with a steering committee of teachers, students, parents, and community members, has provided us with a blueprint for the future in a statement, "The Future Directions."[15] The flavor of the statement is integrative, in both a curricular and human relations sense. As for learning, interdisciplinary approaches and global understandings are stressed. Learning goals would be reached through a healthy school-community relationship. Teachers and students would share with administrators and community citizens in developing academic and socially-related programs. In a larger society "fraught with poverty, substance abuse, a deteriorating family structure, and a value system which is changing more rapidly than the images on our television screens,"[16] the future of the Bethlehem Central

School District would hinge on the efforts of all segments of the community pulling together in a reconstruction of our social and educational lives.

In the 200-year history of Bethlehem, the town has been transformed from a series of crossroads to rural hamlets and, finally, to a mix of commercially developed villages with a suburban flavor. In this long interval, the ties that connect schools and community remained steady. Accordingly, schools had little difficulty in adjusting to new social needs. But how easy it is to forget that community means just that. It is essential that parents and adults show concern for all children. The great unfinished business for the Bethlehem Central School District is to maintain a harmony and balance, a meeting of the minds on purposes and philosophy among citizens, teachers, and school administrators that has served Bethlehem well in the past.

The Library

No one institution in American life attests more strongly to the vitality and the spirit of volunteerism in the United States than does the public library. In the 1830s, Alexis de Tocqueville, French commentator on American life, was struck by the American genius for organizing private citizens to accomplish public ends. Volunteers have been the lifeblood of our social history, a fact easily overlooked in our preoccupation with personal gain.

First public library building in Delmar, ca. 1920.

As Americans emigrated westward, they took with them a philosophy of cooperative group action. Societies began to organize in the various arts and sciences, including literary bodies, the embryonic nuclei for public libraries. In the East, local groups not associated with government circles continued to flourish. Here in Bethlehem, a prototype of American volunteerism was the Delmar Progress Club.

The Progress Club, in addition to its many other interests, was vitally concerned with the level of public literacy. Not content with private libraries as a mechanism for public enlightenment, its members, on May 14, 1913, decided to organize the Delmar Free Library Association.[17] The meeting, held in the home of Mrs. Ira Boynton, drew up a constitution signed by nineteen women residents of Delmar. Its first slate of officers included Mrs. James R. Huested, president, Mrs. Frank

Sharpe, vice president, and Mrs. Ira Boynton, secretary-treasurer. The constitution stipulated that only Progress Club members could belong to the organization.

From this early beginning, a library was quickly established to serve the general public. It opened on August 16, 1913, in the schoolhouse at the corner of Kenwood Avenue and Adams Street, later to become the Masonic Temple. It was a one-room affair, located on the second floor of the school. Volunteers from the Progress Club would administer the library for the next eighteen years. The Board of Regents of the State University of New York gave the association a provisional charter on July 2, 1913. Its first book order of $1,193.19 was given to Baker and Taylor, an establishment that still receives orders for books and video cassettes for the present library. Interestingly enough, a major financial source was the publishing and sale of a family directory for Delmar by a committee of the Progress Club. In 1915, the library shelves contained just 899 book titles.[18]

The women of the Progress Club were given a stunning surprise in November of 1915. This was an offer from the estate of George C. Adams of a parcel of land located on the corner of Adams Street and Hawthorne Avenue to be used for the construction of a library building. The association's trustees at first demurred over certain demands and restrictions in the offer. These obstacles were quickly overcome. Walter Pember, Delmar architect, drew up plans for the building and, in the spring of 1917, the town of Bethlehem had its first public library building. On Novem-

ber 15, 1917, an absolute charter was granted by the Regents. Through private contributions and fund raisers organized by the Progress Club, a total of $3,342.60 was raised to pay for the building. The mortgage on the building was $1,135.06[19] By this time, the Progress Club was being assisted by other volunteers, an arrangement that would remain in effect until 1931.[20]

As Bethlehem entered the 1930s, it was becoming obvious that the volunteer structure was diminishing. Accordingly, the trustees empowered Mrs. Frances Blake and Mrs. Allen Humphrey to negotiate with the school board of the Central Rural District No. 6. On May 5, 1931, the library was taken over by the school district. All monies required for library maintenance and supplies were to be provided by the school district through public taxation. A board of trustees for the library was elected, an arrangement that holds to this day. Mrs. Eula Hallam became the town's first librarian, the custodian of some 2,750 books.[21]

The Bookmobiles

Attesting to the still essentially rural (and automobileless) character of the town was the purchase, in 1931, of a truck to be used as a bookmobile. According to the *Knickerbocker News* of December 9, 1931, this was the first bookmobile operated by a school district to be founded in New York State. The bookmobile made its first trip on that day, carrying 400 books, and driven by Mrs. Eula Hallam. Twice-weekly trips were scheduled, covering the entire thirty-four

"Babe, the Blue Ox." Shipped to the Soviet Union in 1959.

was at its hottest, it was significant that Bethlehem was selected to promote intercultural understanding between Russians and Americans. The Bookmobile was taken out of service in 1976 and replaced by a van, which was used to deliver library services to shut-ins.[23]

By the 1950s it was obvious that the demands on the library were exceeding its capacity to provide effective service. In 1953, the school district voted in favor of a $75,000 addition to the original building, which was constructed in 1917. John N. Brownrigg, Jr., drew up the architectural plans, together with Dr. Theodore C. Wenzl and the Friends of the Delmar Library Committee. Opening on August 1, 1954, the new building was about twelve times larger than the original. The expanded structure contained a community room. Without funds for furnishing the room, the trustees turned to the Progress Club. Now with 280 members, the club raised some $1,282.70 through a community auction. Thus, the room was furnished, and we had another example of how private American volunteerism works to accomplish public ends.

square miles of the school district. In 1942, the original truck was replaced by "Moby Dick," a huge Mack truck lined with book shelves, desks, and magazine racks. Four routes were established, a total run of sixty-four miles. Moby Dick could carry up to 1,000 books to the far reaches of the district.[22]

In 1958, Moby Dick was replaced by "Babe, the Blue Ox," an International Harvester truck with a capacity for 3,000 books. The bookmobile was shipped to the Soviet Union in 1959, as part of the exhibit of American community life at the Moscow World's Fair. In an era when the Cold War

Present Bethlehem Public Library, 1970.

New Bethlehem Public Library planners, 1970. Left to right: Barbara Rau, Carol Alric, Marion Bardole, and Mary Wasserbach.

The Friends of the Library Committee, already working in the background, decided that the time was ripe for a more effective relationship with the trustees and library staff. On September 16, 1954, nine local citizens—Charles Armstrong, Mrs. F.W. Flinton, John Hotaling, Earl S. Jones, Mrs. Joseph B. Lindsey, Jr., Mrs. John B. McMillan, Peter Muirhead, Dr. M.L. Tainter, and Mrs. Richard C. Taylor—met in order to form a more official and permanent type of committee structure, the Friends of the Library. Nevertheless, this first community of "friends" gradually disappeared. In 1984, a second friends of the library committee was formed. The friends, active in planning seminars, study-discussion groups, and musical programs, remain to this day a vital force in the ongoing programs of the library.

The library grew by leaps and bounds. Barbara Hotaling tells us that the 1931 book circulation of 10,700 had expanded to 204,944 by 1964.[24] Parenthetically, book circulation for 1988 was 451,269. During the 1960s, the library employed nine full-time librarians. The full-time staff for 1992 was twenty-seven.

All these statistics suggest that the library's facilities were no longer adequate to meet the needs of the community. Working hand-in-hand with the friends and the Bethlehem Central School District, the trustees planned an entirely new building, to be located at 451 Delaware Avenue, in Delmar. Contracts for the new construction totaled some $1,145,000, to be financed by the Bethlehem Central School District. Ground-breaking ceremonies were held on September 2, 1970. The architect was Harold Geyer.

The New Multi-Media Center

The new library building, opened in May 1972, made possible by a small army of volunteers who moved books, supplies, and equipment from the old facility to the new. The building was dedicated formally on June 4, 1972, at a ceremony conducted by Dr. Theodore Wenzl. Bethlehem now had a multi-media center. The new physical structure made possible not only the main stacks and circulation desks, but a children's reading room, a reference section, facilities for housing myriad audio-visual materials, and special rooms for community affairs, including a small auditorium-meeting room. The old facility, at the corner of Adams Place and Hawthorne Avenue, was then converted to the central administration and board of education offices of the school district. This was completed in the summer of 1972. In the fall of that year the dual facilities of library and school administration assumed their present-day contours.

With the arrival of cable television in 1977, when Adams Russell cable service was awarded the franchise serving the Town of Bethlehem, public access channels became available. According to Mrs. Hotaling, the library at first produced programs to be broadcast over the channel operated by the franchiser. The library purchased its own production equipment and in the early 1980s offered to house the public access channel. With the cooperation of the Bethlehem Historical Association, Bethlehem Channel prepared a program on local history and began its broadcasting career with a showing of that program and a reception on June 3, 1984. TV 31/Bethlehem continues to broadcast regularly.

Another luminary in the library's history was Barbara Rau. This indefatigable worker was our librarian from 1955 to 1984, serving in both the old and the new facilities. Barbara Rau directed a staff of over twenty members, with an additional thirty part-time workers. She was replaced by Barbara Mladinov in 1984, who remains head of the library.

By 1988, the library had become a thoroughly professional operation. Working smoothly with the school district, it served the community in many ways. With a budget of $1.6 million, the library had a collection of books, slides, records, cassettes, and other materials numbering 196,125 items. By 1991, the circulation of books, magazines, and audio or video recordings had grown to 532,000. A staff of eighteen librarians and sixty-three full- and part-time clerical workers answered questions, counseled job-seekers, shelved books, arranged programs, prepared book lists, assisted community groups, and otherwise performed a wide variety of duties.

In addition to these everyday services, the library has provided special programs of note. These include musical recitals, poetry readings, and book discussions. A particularly popular program has been the summer series, Evenings on the Green, with guest stars featured in musical events. Pre-schoolers enjoy story hours each week.

First to third graders look forward to film programs and story hours each month. Adult groups hold a Great Books discussion session twice monthly. Community groups are invited to use the various rooms, including the kitchen.

The public library has been an important ingredient in Bethlehem's community life. Starting as a private, volunteer organization of women, it has grown to a large public enterprise made possible by general taxation and the backing of many enthusiastic supporters. As we look into the future, we can expect a broadening range of services as the needs of the community continue to grow.

The schools and library are twin pillars in Bethlehem's educational structure. Throughout the town's history, a high degree of community cohesiveness has made it possible for these institutions to weather social changes and to accommodate new challenges. The schools have changed from small one-room affairs supported by decen-

tralized hamlets to a tightly knit professional operation. In the school year 1988-1989, the school budget exceeded $22 million, which, with the library budget of $1.6 million, brought expenditures close to the $25 million mark. The two institutions, combined, employed nearly 600 workers. Nearly 3,803 students attended our schools. Their needs were served by about 319 professional educators. An additional 221 nonprofessional employees were needed. By any standard, this is an enormous enterprise for a town the size of Bethlehem. Looked at only in narrow economic terms, the schools and library provide a base of economic activity that would be sorely missed if their services were to be cut back. However, in the larger sense of community health, Bethlehem's educational programs provide its citizens the intellectual and recreational services that living in the 1990s requires. As we peer into the future, may the residents of the town of Bethlehem continue to exert the same quality of social vision that their forbears provided.

13 Military Heritage

Although history records no occasion on which the land within the borders of the town of Bethlehem served as a battlefield for war, Bethlehem's rich heritage is inextricably linked with that of the nation's military legacy. Throughout its history, in times of both war and peace, Bethlehem provided many of its sons and daughters for the nation's armed forces. In addition to the hundreds of individuals from the town who served in the ranks in the period from the Revolutionary War to the end of the Civil War, the town's fertile agricultural base provided much needed supplies to state and federal military forces. The role of local governments in the nation's military affairs has been largely overlooked by historians, but the cooperation and participation of towns like Bethlehem has always been essential to the maintenance of the nation's defense.

The Colonial Period

Throughout most of the colonial period, New York's position in the British Empire was extremely important. As Michael Kammen noted in his study, *Colonial New York*, while the province played a relatively minor role in King George's War (1744-1748) it thereafter became a linchpin among the continental colonies.[1] New York generally, and the area between Albany and Ticonderoga in particular, became a critical sector during the French and Indian War. In the period from 1755 to 1760, Albany was the center of British operations in North America. During the governorship of Admiral George Clinton (1743-1753), the structure of political alignments in Albany underwent major upheaval. As a British official, Governor Clinton was obligated to pursue a vigorous war effort against the French. He found, however, that New York merchants enjoyed an extensive trade with the French West Indies and that Albany merchants and their political allies promoted neutrality in an effort to maintain peaceful Indian relations and keep the fur trade routes open to Montreal. When military involvement became unavoidable in 1746, a coalition of Albany traders and New York merchants organized in opposition to Clinton's rule.[2] Underlying their vocal opposition to escalating involvement in the Crown's imperial war was an understanding that a committed war effort would require a significant raise in taxes. Such taxes would hit merchants and traders hard, but the situation was made worse by the common perception that the collected taxes were not being appropriately utilized for the colony's defense.

Colonists in the area surrounding Albany had learned a hard lesson during King George's War when a party of French and Indians destroyed the village of Saratoga in 1745, killing and capturing more than 100 residents, and in 1748, when Indians burned the settlement at Schenectady. In both instances—and in scores of others the colonists could recount with enmity—the British regulars sent to protect the colonists failed to provide an appropriate defense for the settlers of the New World. Michael Kammen writes that this arrangement "was fairly characteristic of imperial indifference to colonial concerns during much of [the] period."[3] It was this legacy, in the next two decades of increased taxation, that would go a long way toward inspiring revolutionary thoughts in the minds of the merchants and traders and others of means. It was left to these men and women of intelligence and learning to question why a crown which had all but abandoned its colony, save to exploit its riches, deserved any tribute whatsoever. The seeds of revolution were sown in this era of expansive growth and ever increasing self-reliance.

Bethlehem in the Revolution

Most published accounts describing Bethlehem's role in the American Revolution tend to minimize the town's manpower contributions to that struggle. Howell and Tenney's volume on the *History of the County of Albany* went so far as to state that the "territory now included in the township of Bethlehem cannot boast of many patriotic deeds, nor enter upon her record the names of many of her citizens who were active participants in that bloody strife which gained our independence as a nation."[4]

While it may be true that the town's agricultural heritage may have caused the town's citizens to be more interested in farming than in the political dispute being waged against the British crown, the image of the town's residents exempting themsleves from the struggle has been much exaggerated. Throughout the country, the conflict between the North American colonies and Britain was extremely divisive. Neighbor was often pitted against neighbor, and both patriot and Tory suffered in the politically charged environment. In Bethlehem, citizens loyal to the crown gathered in secret to foil the patriot cause.[5] While the historical record does not indicate that any great damage was inflicted upon the town by either Tories or their Indian allies, it is purported that there was a Tory camp and rendezvous on the banks of the Vloman Kill along Mead's Lane.[6]

Although some Bethlehem residents remained loyal to Britain, a large number left their homes and fields to enlist in the patriot forces. Upon the request of the Committee of Correspondence, Albany County organized seventeen regiments of militia under the laws of 1775. The rolls of these patriot units carried the names of many Bethlehem men. Among them were Lt. Col. Francis Nicoll of the 3rd Regiment, First Rensselaerwyck Battalion (later a Deputy to the Provincial Congress in 1776 and Senator in 1797); Major Barent Staats of the Fifth Company; Captain Gerrit Vandenbergh, Lt. Peter Van Wie, Lt. Wouter Becker and Ensign Abraham Slingerland of the Fourth Company; Lt. Dirck Becker, Lt. John Van Wie, and Ensign George Hogan. Other local men found on Revolutionary rosters include Cornelius Vanderzee, John Winne, Peter Boice, George Colenburg, Hugh Jolly, Zimri Murdock, Andrew Conning, Frederick Britt, Patrick Callanan, William Winne, Tunis

A detailed biographical sketch of Conrad Soop was published in *Landmarks of Albany County*.[8] According to this volume, Soop was born in Philadelphia on October 10, 1745. His parents had emigrated from Wurtenberg, Germany, to America under the patronage of Queen Anne in the early 1700s. In May 1774, Conrad Soop married Elizabeth Becker of Schoharie and purchased a farm in Bethlehem. He had scarcely settled there with his young wife when he was called to shoulder a musket in defense of the emerging nation. He was made a lieutenant in Captain Jurian Hogan's company of the 4th Regiment, and later transferred to Captain Ten Eyck's company of the 5th Regiment, a unit with which Soop served during all of its engagements on the northern frontier and at Burgoyne's surrender following the battle of Saratoga. At the close of the war, Soop returned to his farm where he enjoyed the blessings of a large family and long life. His wife died in 1842 in her eighty-eighth year and Soop died in his 102nd year on September 28, 1847.

Memorial plaque to Revolutionary War soldier.

Grave of Francis Nicoll at Cedar Hill.

Slingerland, Solomon Russell, John Sager, John Oliver, Aaron Oliver, Arie Van Wie, David Niver, and Conrad Soop. The last two listed were officers who were present at British General John Burgoyne's surrender at Stillwater on October 27, 1777.[7]

War of 1812

Just a few years after the close of the Revolution, the United States and Great Britain became embroiled in yet another dispute, this time a struggle over America's rights on the high seas. Although much of the War of 1812, otherwise known as "Mr. Madison's War," was fought on water, most of the battles that were fought on land were waged in New York State. The story of Sackett's Harbor and Lundy's Lane are best left to the volumes that provide fine accounts of the battles, but it is enough to say that Bethlehem men were in the ranks at both engagements. Howell and Tenney's history reports that, during the War of 1812, "a fair quota was sent from this township, who served with credit to themselves, and others returned with honors won in the service."[9] Undoubtedly the best known of the town's residents who served in this contest was Solomon Van Rensselaer, a major general in the New York State militia, whose Cherry Hill mansion was then situated within the town's borders. Van Rensselaer commanded the New York State militia during the War of 1812 and enjoyed a successful political career after its close, serving as lieutenant governor of the State and as United States congressman. Other townsmen who served during the war included Walter Vanderzee, Peter W. Ten Eyck, Jacobus Vroman, Captain Garret van Wie, Peter Boice, James Bailey, Jacob Soop, John C. Jarvis, John Adams, James Wiltsie, Frederick Rowe, John Callanan, Simon Kilmer, William Patterson, Captain John Hogan, Joshua Babcock, Marcus Lasher, John Oathout, Alexander Frasier (drummer), and Jacob Hilderbrant. [10]

The Era of Expansion

In the years that followed the War of 1812, the expanding and industrializing American nation focused largely on internal affairs and development. In some ways this rapid development bypassed the town of Bethlehem, whose residents continued the agricultural enterprises they had pursued in the years prior to the Revolution. However, as the United States government began to move toward the creation of an empire in the 1830s and 1840s, the town was once again called upon to support a national war effort. Today the Mexican War is often dismissed as little more than a brash example of American imperialism, but in 1845 it was an expression of the nation's epic quest for manifest destiny, a powerful political and socioeconomic program that would attempt to claim all of North America on behalf of the United States with little regard for those who might stand in the way. It was a bold proposal that the nation saw partially fulfilled in the controversial war with Mexico (1845-1848). The war with Mexico severely tested the nation's political system, dividing North and South in an argument over how the new territories gained by the war should be utilized. Southern politicians desired the new land for the expansion of slavery, while Northern interests worried about the consequent increase in Southern power and influence over governmental affairs should the new territories someday enter the Union as slave states.

One who was strongly opposed to the war was Congressman John I. Slingerland (1804-1861), who was born and lived almost all of his life in Bethlehem. Slingerland was a devoted Whig (and later a Republican) who rose to prominence in the New York State Assembly during the early 1840s and was elected to the United States House of Representatives in 1847. He was an advocate of temperance and strongly in favor of federally-funded internal improvements (a political argument centered primarily on the question of which entity, the state or federal government, should fund the construction of roads and bridges), positions he shared with Abraham Lincoln, another Whig who served in the Thirtieth Congress. In a speech delivered before Congress on June 22, 1848, Slingerland denounced the administration of President James K. Polk, charging that although the President denied the federal government's role in effecting internal improvements on the local level,

> he can lavish millions in a useless and bloody war. He can give the whole revenues of the country, and burden the people with immense debt, to wrest from the hands of the Mexicans her possessions. He has no scruples when blood and money are to be lavished for the ignoble purposes of an unconstitutional war. While we have a domain of rich and virgin soil, scarcely trodden by the foot of man, and which is in the highest degree inviting to the agriculturist, and furnishing to enterprise the

> most ample field of exercise, the President employs the revenues of the nation to obtain possession of rocky mountains and sandy deserts, which will defy all the efforts of industry to render useful. Such blind and fatal policy would excel belief, were it not continually in exercise before our eyes. If this is the fruit of the boasted Democracy that is heralded over the land, I'll none of it. What has it brought us? War and death.[11]

Bethlehem Organizes to Meet the Challenge

In so distant a fight the town of Bethlehem could not have a very significant role, but at least one military training camp was established on the level farm fields within the town. The site of this training camp, on the old Haswell Farm, still survives where Routes 32 and 9W meet. Historical accounts indicate that the land surrounding the house was used as a military training ground as early as 1812 and that Colonel John Moore of Bethlehem trained troops there during the Mexican War. Accounts do not indicate why this particular area was selected as a training ground, but if the Haswell fields were utilized by village volunteers and militia in the years before the outbreak of the Mexican War, this tradition of military usage probably rendered it a natural site for subsequent training. This hypothesis is accorded some support by Howell and Tenney's narrative, which reported in 1888:

The military spirit of the township is buried in the past; no organizations of this character exist. Formerly the State militia and a uniformed company, the "Bethlehem Grays," and a company of cavalry, were the pride of the people, and the military drills and parades of this company were attended by every person who had leisure. The usual drill, on the first Monday in September, was a gala day, which terminated in a grand entertainment and ball at night.

The Grand Review, or General Training, was a day of anticipation and preparation by old and young for weeks before the great event took place. On this day—about the middle of September of each year—the military organizations of several towns forming a brigade met at a central location and were reviewed by superior officers. It was a veritable holiday. All who could possibly attend seemed to enjoy the occasion with a freedom and independence now no longer permitted. Wagons, stands and booths were numerous and well supplied with eatables of many kinds; pumpkin pies and gingerbread in great abundance, loads of fruit, nuts, candies and sweet cider were dispensed to the hungry and thirsty.[12]

This image of the militia closely coincides with that provided by Phillip Shaw Paludan in "*A People's Contest:*" *The Union and Civil War 1861-1865*. In documenting the contributions the militia made in fulfilling the minuteman ideal of the citizen army in American society, a response to the standing armies of Europe that had its origins in Colonial days, Paludan noted that during the ante-bellum period

the minuteman ideal gained vitality in thousands of Northern communities. Acting under state authority, towns, villages, and cities organized militia, which became an important part of everyday life. A combination of fraternal organization, police force, and public entertainers, these groups elected their own officers, chose their own uniforms, and regulated administration. They held picnics, balls, and contests, sponsored reading rooms and lecture series, and of course, mustered for annual parades and for important town events. In more rural areas, that is, in much of the North, militia units served predominately as social organizations. Their functions gave them prestige and linked the community in their allegedly bellicose duties.[13]

The Haswell Farm

In addition to its service during the War of 1812 and the Mexican War, the Haswell farm was also reputed to have served as a military training camp during the Civil War.[14]

Although no full-scale archeological dig has ever been undertaken on the site, several sections of the farm were searched with a metal detector by the author in 1979. Despite claims that military relics, a bayonet, and some military horse equipage bearing the U.S. insignia had been found on the land over the last fifty years, no military items were included among the mostly farm-related artifacts that were recovered in this cursory search. This result does not necessarily end speculation that the land was used for military purposes. It is known that because of concerns about disease and overcrowding in Albany, many volunteers were sent to camps outside of the city. The selection of the Haswell farm is reasonable as it would have offered excellent road access to Albany and to the Hudson River and perhaps because of its previous usage as a militia training ground. Indeed, most primary accounts of soldiers who passed through the Albany area during the Civil War years indicate that the river was used as the main avenue for transporting the new volunteers to the front.

Still, all of this would make for a fairly tentative case in documenting the Haswell farm as a military training camp were it not for the graves of several Union soldiers that were found on the property. Although the graves were once marked with individual stones, only one stone, long ago removed from its original location and now broken into six pieces, remains. It bears the name of M. W. Daniels, who died June 10, 1861, aged twenty-seven years. In 1979, a former owner of the Haswell house, the late Harold VanDerpoel, recalled that the stone was removed from the area near where the Delmar By-Pass now runs and that the graves of several other soldiers were once located in this same vicinity. He recalled that one of the gravestones had a small wire basket hanging from it which was filled with several Civil War bullets and personal effects. VanDerpoel also related that many of the graves had wrought-iron GAR markers next to them. The GAR, or Grand Army of the Republic, was a postwar veterans organization that sought to preserve the memory of the nation's Union Civil War soldiers. Mr. VanDerpoel remembered that during the 1920s an elderly lady frequently came to the farm to put flowers on the Daniels grave. She indicated that she was the soldier's sister from western New York, and that Daniels had died of disease before leaving for the front. When, according to Mr. VanDerpoel, construction crews bulldozed the old cemetery to grade for the Delmar By-Pass, he recovered the Daniels stone in

M. W. Daniels gravestone on the Haswell Farm.

hopes that a family member might return to retrieve it someday. The VanDerpoel family still has the stone and a GAR marker that was removed from one of the grave sites.

Since the rediscovery of the Daniels gravestone in 1979, the author made periodic attempts to obtain Daniels's military service records. Beyond providing information about the soldier's identity, it was hoped that the information could also be used to confirm historical claims regarding the military usage of the Haswell farm, as well as document the Union regiment that encamped on the site. The author's efforts were largely unsuccessful, however, until the spring of 1992, when the military record for Martin W. Daniels was located in the New York State Archives. This record indicated that Daniels was a twenty-seven-year-old private serving in Company H of the 16th New York Infantry when he died of disease on June 10, 1861.

Based on the archival information about Daniels's military service, the regimental records of the 16th New York Infantry were also consulted. This research uncovered a published account of the unit's Civil War service, entitled *From Bull Run to Chancellorsville*, authored by Brigadier General Newton Martin Curtis. The volume

Lt. Albert M. Barney, 16th New York Infantry.

contains a detailed chronicle of the regiment's formation and history and provids solid documentation of the military encampment that was established at Bethlehem in 1861. General Curtis wrote:

> On June 1st, the regiment [16th New York Infantry] in company with the Twenty-eighth New York, under Colonel [Duncan] Donnelly, was moved into camp at Normand's Kill, Bethlehem, and commenced life under canvas. On the 15th, uniforms were received; this acquisition did much to improve the health and spirits of the men.... On Sunday, the 16th of June, the regiment was paid for the time it had been in the State service. Governor [Edwin] Morgan reviewed the regiment on the 24th, and was entertained with a sham battle; the final charge was made with vociferous cheers, and the review might properly have been called "a howling succcess." On the morning of the 25th, six hundred old Springfield muskets, of the same pattern as the hundred and fifty previously supplied, were issued, and in the afternoon the regiment marched to Albany and took passage on a steamer for the city of New York, arriving at the foot of Fourteenth Street early on the morning of the 26th.[15]

The 16th New York Infantry went on to fight in many battles of the Union Army of the Potomac. When the regiment was mustered out at Albany in May 1863, its battle flag carried the honors of Bull Run, the Peninsula, Fredericksburg, and Chancellorsville on its tattered banner.

Further evidence of the Bethlehem Civil War encampment was discovered as a result of inquiries into the history of the 28th New York Infantry, a regiment that General Curtis indicated shared the Bethlehem site with his unit. A rare volume, entitled *A Brief History of the Twenty-Eighth Regiment, New York State Volunteers*, contains an interesting account of the Bethlehem training camp, that was named "Camp Morgan" in honor of New York Governor Edwin Morgan. After arriving in Albany in early May 1861, the regiment was soon ordered out of the city to the Bethlehem encampment occupied by the 16th New York. The regimental history records that on

Detail of Civil War flag from Slingerlands.

> June 1st came the welcome order to move to Camp Morgan—about three miles from the city and one from the river. This was the regiment's first march, and was not that long, but many of the men think they never had a harder one. They were unused to the march, and especially not yet accustomed to moving in light marching order. They had yet to learn how few things are absolutely necessary, and all were burdened with articles supposed to be essential. These were very soon reduced in number, or cast aside altogether. The day was hot and dusty, and many stragglers were brought up by the rear guard.

> The camp was adjoining the Sixteenth New York Regiment, which had just been organized and was in command of Colonel Davies. Here commenced the life in tents, which continued throughout the entire service, except when houses were occupied at Hancock [Va.] for a short time, the next winter. This was a welcome change from the irksome barracks' life of the last few weeks.

> The experience at Camp Morgan was varied, and these should have been the happiest days of the regiment, but

were, without doubt, the most discontented ones. Here the men found it much more difficult to steal past the guards than at the barracks, but passes were issued, and frequent visits were made to the city.

The following was the daily routine: Reveille at five A.M. Roll Call at five thirty. Drill five-thirty to six-thirty. Breakfast seven. Guard Mount, eight. Sick Call, nine. Drill, ten to eleven-thirty. Dinner, twelve. Drill, two to three-thirty. Dress Parade, five. Supper, six. Roll Call, nine. Taps and Lights Out, nine-thirty.

The Bethlehem cook-house was situated outside the camp, and the men marched there for meals. The food

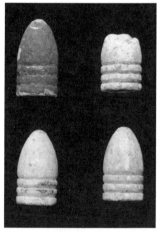

Civil War 58 cal. minie balls recovered from Virginia.

was substantial, and had it been better served no complaints could have been justly made. Dissatisfaction was often shown by drumming on tin cups, when passing near Colonel Davies' tent. This was soon stopped, by the offenders being put in the guardhouse. June 15th the first issue of clothing was made, and proved very acceptable to many. On leaving home, the men had been told not to bring extra clothes, as uniforms and clothing would be drawn on arriving at Albany. But the days and weeks passed, and the old garments were getting not only threadbare, but in many cases in rags. An organization, known as the "Ragged Cadets," was formed. No person was eligible to membership, whose clothing was not badly worn. While to be an officer required more holes than cloth. These "R.C.'S" as they were styled, had daily parades, causing much laughter and fun. As soon as the men drew their overcoats, the companies paraded, presenting the comical sight of regulation coats of blue, covering trousers of nearly every color....

The drills and dress parades improved daily, and seemed fine to raw recruits, but they were simply a burlesque on subsequent attainments.

The sick call soon became an important one, as the mumps broke out in camp, and many were taken ill. Every member of the regiment was vaccinated; the surgeon remarking that this was the first blood the men had shed in defense of their country.

Boxes of delicacies from home continued to arrive, and were always received with great pleasure. The Debating Society, organized at the Barracks, was continued in a large tent, loaned by citizens of Albany, through the influence of N. Ward Cady, a member of Company D. Other meetings, religious, temperance and social, were held in the tent, and were of much interest, being always well attended....

On June 12th one of the happiest experiences of Camp Morgan life occurred; when a beautiful flag was raised at the colonel's tent, with speeches and patriotic songs.

On June 24th the long expected and welcome order came to be "off for the war." At one o'clock tents were struck at the firing of a cannon, and, with the cheers of the Sixteenth New York Regiment, the members of the Twenty-eighth left camp, and marched in the heat and dust, through the city to the steamboat landing, where they embarked on two barges, lying at the wharf in waiting.[16]

The Civil War: A Divided Nation Goes to War

The Civil War years were undoubtedly an exciting time in Bethlehem's history. Although sources published prior to this volume suggest that no record of the town's participation in the war was ever compiled, the author's research in the collection of the New York State Archives now provides cause to revise that appraisal. After the close of the Civil War, the New York State Legislature approved a measure (Chapter 690 of the Laws of 1865) requiring town clerks in the State to compile a complete record of the services of their residents during the war.[17] It had long been thought that the town of Bethlehem did not comply with this measure. Howell and Tenney reported in 1888 that because the Bethlehem town clerk "neglected to comply with the law...the town is defrauded of a valuable historical record, which cannot, at this time, be compiled or collected with accuracy."[18] It can now be conclusively stated that the Bethlehem town clerk's records of Civil War service do exist and are on file with the other records submitted by communities from throughout the State. The archival records contain a great deal of valuable information about the town residents who served in the Civil War.

In total, Bethlehem gave 149 of its townsmen (or about 3% of its 1860 population) to federal service. Of this number, the majority were German-born (64), with the second largest number having been born in Albany County (36). The largest number of Bethlehem soldiers enlisted in 1862

Pvt. William H. C. Frazier, 91st New York Infantry.

for the purpose of paying fifty dollar cash bounties to the men who enlisted. The bounty system was used by many communities throughout the North to encourage enlistments and fill quotas established by the State government. Following the passage of the federal Enrollment Act in March 1863, communities that could not fill their assigned quotas would be compelled to participate in the draft. In 1862, town supervisor Albertus W. Becker established an enlistment office in the south end of the City of Albany to help fill Bethlehem's quota of forty men. The majority of these recruits were assigned to the company being organized by David Burhans that was later received into United States services as part of the 43rd New York Infantry. During the winter of 1862-1863, supervisor Becker, together with Peter Vanderzee and Justus Haswell, visited the Regiment in its camp at Hall's Hill, Virginia.

Of the 149 soldiers who served from the town of Bethlehem eleven (or 7.4%) deserted, sixteen died of disease, twelve (8%) were killed in action and three died in Confederate prisons. Two soldiers were listed as missing in action with no further record. In all, twenty-eight soldiers were wounded in action and presumably recovered from their wounds.

Gravestone of Lt. Leonard Lasher, Co. H, 43rd New York Infantry.

(67) and 1861 (42). Only six Bethlehem men enlisted in 1865 and only eight enlisted in 1863. The remaining twenty-six enlisted in 1864. Town records indicate that in 1862 the town of Bethlehem raised by voluntary subscription a total of $2,690.50

occupations. There were twelve carpenters and eleven moulders in the ranks. Perhaps the most surprising finding was reference to black soldiers that enlisted from the town. The records contain the service histories of nine black men ranging in ages from sixteen to thirty-one. Of those who indicated their marital status, four reported that they were single and four responded that they were married. Of the total number of black soldiers from Bethlehem, seven indicated that they were born in Albany County and two said that they were born below the Mason/Dixon line (one in Virginia and one in Maryland). Seven of the black soldiers said that they were laborers by occupation, employed on the Hudson River boats that docked near Van Wies Point.

The town can claim no famous Civil War generals among her sons, but many of the soldiers who marched away from its borders did achieve some measure of distinction. Prominent among them was Captain David Burhans of the 43rd New York Infantry, who helped organize a company of the Regiment and served admirably until his death in battle at Spotsylvania, Virginia, on May 10, 1864, and John G. Vanderzee of the 44th New York Infantry regiment. This regiment was organized to avenge the death of Colonel Elmer Ellsworth, and its members were specially selected by the communities of New York State. At more than six feet tall and eager to serve, Vanderzee was the town's clear choice to serve in the regiment. Vanderzee served as a color sergeant and later as an officer in the regiment. Captain John Bailey of the 177th New York Infantry also

Capt. David Burhans, Co. H, 43rd New York Infantry. Killed at Spotsylvania, Virginia in 1864.

On the enlistment rolls fifty-four of the Bethlehem soldiers listed their occupations as laborers, with farmers accounting for thirty-six additional

served with honor. Bailey graduated from Union College in 1861 and immediately enlisted in the Union army. As regimental adjutant, Bailey took part in the battles of Amity River, Pouchatula, and the siege of Port Hudson. Following his military career Bailey entered politics, serving as a member of Congress (1878-

Portrait of John Bailey.

President Lincoln issued his call for troops in July 1862. He died, like all too many of his generation, from the effects of disease shortly after arriving at the front. At age thirty-one he left a wife and two children to mourn him. His brother, Charles Van Allen, was a printer with the *Albany Cultivator* newspaper. He enlisted at the same time as Jacob but in a different regiment, the 113th New York Infantry. He remained with this unit until June 16, 1864, when he was captured by the Confederates near Petersburg, Virginia. He was sent to the dreaded Andersonville Prison in southwest Georgia, where he died September 18, 1864. In a letter to Governor Reuben E. Fenton written by his company commander shortly after the war, Van Allen was recommended for a lieutenant's commission. In praise of Van Allen, Captain Norman Moore remembered that he was "a brave and faithful soldier, always ready to do his duty, and when in battle, he was never known to shirk; and I never had occasion even to reprimand him.... He was in every battle in which his regiment was engaged."[19]

Grave marker of John Bailey.

1881) and as United States consul to Hamburg (1881-1885). He also served as a delegate to the Republican National Convention in 1888.

Although distant from the battlefield, Bethlehem did not escape the terrible tragedy of the war. Of the local stories that emerged from the struggle, one of the saddest concerned Jacob and Charles Van Allen, two brothers from the town who both died in the service of their country. Jacob Van Allen was a school teacher who enlisted in the 110th New York Infantry shortly after

Although most of the Bethlehem soldiers served in the 177th New York Infantry and 7th New York Heavy Artillery, men were scattered among many different New York regiments. Records in the New York State Archives indicate that Bethlehem men served primarily in the 91st New York Infantry, the 43rd New York Infantry, and the 41st New York Infantry, but also in the military units of other states with enlistments credited to the town's required quota. The black soldiers from Bethlehem, who were barred from service in the white units, served primarily in the 26th United States Colored Troops, a regiment that was formed at Riker's Island, New York Harbor, in February 1864. The unit served mostly in South Carolina and Georgia and lost a total of 145 men during its term of service. After observing the 26th Regiment during the Union advance on Johns and James Islands outside Charleston, South Carolina, Major General John G. Foster recanted his earlier misgivings about the use of black troops, claiming, "I am now relieved of apprehension about the military aptitude as to this class of troops and believe with active service and drill, they can be made thorough soldiers.".[20]

The Impact of War

Considering its 1860 population of 5,644, the enlistment of 149 men from Bethlehem must have had a noticeable impact on the residents who remained on the homefront. The costs of war are often measured only in the statistics that record the numbers of those who failed to return home. A glance at the enlistment rolls clearly indicates that there were other costs as well. Beyond the thirty-three men who died during their term of military service and did not return to Bethlehem when the war ended, there were probably others whose wounds of a physical or psychological nature left them severely debilitated. The notation on one local soldier's application for a post-war disability pension spoke for many in its evaluation that the war "had left him a broken man forever." Individuals who had been raised to

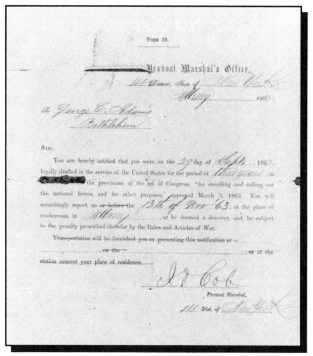

Civil War draft notice for Bethlehem citizen, dated May 1863.

work hard and live long within the town's borders and who accepted the nation's call to arms found their lives dramatically changed by war. There exist no measures save the personal stories that remain, to preserve the memory of their sacrifices. Although many of these stories have been lost to history, it can be deduced from those who survived that the war had a tremendous impact upon the town, both on those who marched away in uniform and on those who were left behind. As it tested the nation at large, so too the Civil War exerted great social pressure on the town. Wars of such dimension are never fully played out on the grand stage, but in their great drama they are all-encompassing, reaching out from far-off places with names like Bull Run and Gettysburg, and invading the quiet sanctuary of sleepy places like Bethlehem, exacting a toll on the youth and life of the community. The Civil War took more from the town than any contest that had been waged previously. Long after the conflict had ended, Bethlehem would remember and honor the memory of its Civil War soldiers.

GAR Veterans Medal.

While it is uncertain when the town's last Civil War veteran passed to his final rest, the January 3, 1936, issue of the *Albany County Post* carried the headline, "Civil War Veteran Succumbs at Elsmere Home." The accompanying story related that Charles Secor, Civil War veteran of 3 Bedell Avenue, Elsmere, died at his home on Saturday, December 28, at the age of ninety years. The paper noted that Secor was a member of Post 45, GAR, and had enlisted in Company A, 9th New York Artillery, in 1864 when only nineteen years old. He was discharged on account of disability at Baltimore's Jarvis Hospital on June 2, 1865. The paper recalled that Secor's most famous engagement was the battle of Cedar Creek, and, that he was to be buried in the Prospect Hill Cemetery at Guilderland.

Westward Expansion and the Displacement of a People

The years immediately following the end of the Civil War found the nation struggling with some important internal questions. As Americans journeyed westward, encouraged by the Homestead Act of 1860, the Native American population was increasingly displaced. In the East, the so-called "Indian problem" was dispatched in the years following the Revolutionary War. Indeed, by 1842, New York State had negotiated treaties with the Iroquois Nation which placed the six tribes that comprised the Iroquois Confederacy on state-established reservations. In the West, however, the United States government and the Native American population were locked in a bitter struggle for control of the land. During the Civil War, when national resources were poured into the military effort against the Confederacy, only a token military force operated on the western frontier. After the war, this situation changed dramatically as national attention turned to the vast quantities of untapped natural resources available west of the Mississippi.

As the post-Civil War armies were fairly limited in size, only a small number of Bethlehem residents served in the ranks. One interesting story from this period concerns a young enlisted man known locally as Gerrit H. Niver, who served in Lt. Col. George A. Custer's famed 7th United States Cavalry and was killed at the Little Big Horn battle on June 25, 1876. Niver, who was born in Bethlehem on February 1, 1846, enlisted in

Grave marker of Gerrit H. Niver.

the 7th Cavalry on October 2, 1873, at age twenty-seven, in New York City. He listed his occupation as farmer and the enlistment records indicate that he had blue eyes, brown hair, and was 5'7" in height. [21] Interestingly enough, Niver is carried on the official rolls of the 7th Cavalry as Gerrett H. Van Allen, an alias that family tradition claims was selected so that Niver's ill mother would not suffer if he did not return from his western expedition. Apparently both Gerrit and his brother Conrad went west in the 1870s under assumed names. According to the family, Conrad worked as an Indian trader under the name John Eddy, and lost an arm out west. When he returned home he brought the news of his brother's death and some photographs of the Little Big Horn battlefield. Niver was one of three Albany County men who died with Custer at the Little Big Horn. Although a monument to Niver's memory was erected in the family plot at the Elmwood Cemetery in Selkirk, it does not, as some have suggested, mark his final resting place. According to Dr. Kenneth Hammer, a Custer scholar who has written a study about the men who died at the Little Big Horn, Niver is probably buried in one of the unknown graves on the battlefield. His name is listed on the Custer battle monument as Garrett Van Allen.

The "Battle of Slingerlands"

Little is known of the participation by local men in the Spanish-American War but the period did mark one of the more interesting chapters in the town's military past. In a book privately published in 1935, entitled *Seventy-Five Years With the Tenth Regiment Infantry, New York National Guard*, Major Clarence Martin chronicled the details of some military maneuvers that were held in the town in 1895, three years before the outbreak of the war. These maneuvers were conducted under the operational title "the battle of Slingerlands." Major Martin recalled that:

> On the fourth day, August 22, the battalion neared its objective, Slingerlands. The sun was up and hot when the march started at 9 a.m. and a rather fast pace was set. There were several cases of sore feet and a few cases of exhaustion before the camping place was reached at 11:30 o'clock. It was not until 3 o'clock that dinner was served but it was worth waiting for when the mess call finally sounded. Just as the meal was over, Fred Hinckel showed up with a load of beer but Colonel Fitch put it on ice and kept it there until supper time.

There was an early reveille on the morning of August 23. Company D had its breakfast and marched out of camp. Details from the other companies were sent out on every road. There were rumors afloat that the enemy was approaching in numbers and the battalion could not let that happen without knowing something about it and sent out scouts. It was said that the enemy was after the beer which was left over from the night before.

The scouts did not find the enemy, for he suddenly appeared on the top of the hill overlooking the camp in the person of Captain Denison and the members of Company D and they fired a volley of blank cartridges right into the battalion. The slaughter was terrible. The sharpshooters of the enemy had singled out the staff officers, who made good targets because of their gaudy uniforms.

Colonel Fitch ordered Major Stackpole to deploy his battalion and attack the enemy. As the battalion moved forward the enemy charged down the hill directly into it, but in doing so lost its left wing. A soldier who had sore feet was placed as guard over the prisoners. The right wing retreated, the battalion sent in its reserves, drove back the beer seeking enemy, and Slingerlands was saved.[22]

The "battle" of Slingerlands was a bloodless affair, a military exercise which turned sideshow. Still, the operation was not without purpose in training its participants for the battlefield. Many of the guardsmen involved in the operation later served in the Spanish-American War. George E. Graham, a member of the Tenth Battalion, was the Associated Press reporter aboard Commodore Schley's flagship, *Brooklyn*, during the battle of Santiago Bay. Graham's critical wire service account of the fight inspired a Congressional investigation into the affair. While Major Martin's memoir serves as a humorous footnote in the annals of local history, it is tragic to realize many of these summer soldiers soon found themselves tested by disease and by the battlefield in Cuba, Puerto Rico, and the Philippines. [23]

Bethlehem and the "War to End All Wars"

During World War I the town backed the military effort with vigor. Of the soldiers who served in the armed forces from Bethlehem during the "war to end all wars," several offer unique insights into the history of the town during this period. Dr. Thomas M. Holmes was one of Bethlehem's more prominent residents who served in the war. A graduate of Union College and Albany Medical College, Dr. Holmes enlisted during World War I for service with the United States Army Medical Corps, but instead was sent over to France to serve as a surgeon with the British Expeditionary Force. Awarded the Purple Heart with an oak cluster when he was wounded by an artillery shell that burst near his battlefield dressing station, Dr.

Holmes served with distinction at the front. A fascinating letter preserved in the family papers of Ms. Evelyn Frazier of Slingerlands, which was sent by Dr. Holmes to her grandfather, William H. C. Frazier, a veteran of the Civil War, [24] provides an exciting account of Dr. Holmes's service at the front. In the letter dated October 26, 1917, Holmes writes:

> I suppose you have begun to think that I have forgotten all about you by waiting so long before writing you. Well I have been some busy man since I arrived doing one thing and another. Had a fine trip over except for the short time that a Sub tried to get us. After landing I knocked about for a little and finally was assigned to a field ambulance. The duty of a field ambulance is to render first aid to wounded and evacuate them as quickly as possible. So you can see that we are constantly within the firing zone. You folks at home cannot realize what a huge tremendous affair this war is. You have to see it to ever have any conception of its magnitude. At first the noise of the cannon annoyed me a great deal but it is marvelous how after a little one becomes accustomed to war and all its methods etc. Have been up to the front line several times and had a good look at what is called "No Mans Land" and it is well named such. I had a good look at the Hun and his method of doing things one day while returning from the front a couple of shells fell near me but by the time they exploded I was on the ground flat so missed being injured.
>
> In spite of fact that this life is much different than that at home I enjoy my work immensely and feel at home only when attending a wounded or sick man.
>
> The weather here is quite cold and rainy and at times have difficulty keeping warm and comfortable. Have left our tents for huts as the cold weather has started in. At times I get quite lonesome for home and all my old friends but I realize that I am like millions of others who are having the same experience.
>
> There are many things I would like to write to you but dare not so I will keep it until I return and when I do we will have a good "old chat" and compare notes of this war with those of the Civil in which you so gallantly displayed yourself. The poor fellows now training at home better realize what they will have to confront when they arrive here. I suppose you have noticed in papers about the advances that have taken place over here. Well

I have had the pleasure of taking part in one of those big shows during which time I attended hundreds of wounded including many German prisoners. Some of the boys who came over with me are in the Hospital having been wounded.[25]

Dr. Holmes returned to Bethlehem after the war, and was employed as a physician for the New York Central Railroad. He later established a medical practice in Delmar. He became involved in politics and served as the leader of the Bethlehem Republican Party for more than twenty-five years. He also was a founding member of the Last Man's Club, a World War I veterans' group.

Local Man's Death Inspires Memorial Organization

It is impossible in the limited amount of space available to provide similar profiles of each of Bethlehem's World War I veterans, but at least some brief mention must be made of the military service of Nathaniel Adams Blanchard, in whose honor American Legion Post 1040 in Delmar is named. Blanchard was just a teenager when he enlisted in the United States Army and was sent to France with the American Expeditionary Force. He was killed in action on November 9, 1918, only two days before the armistice was signed, while serving with the 307th Infantry, 77th Division.[26] When a group of local veterans met at the Delmar

Fire Hall in 1930 with the intention of organizing an American Legion post in the town, they chose to honor Blanchard by naming the post in his memory. It was only fitting, as Blanchard had been born in the structure when it served as the Adams Hotel. Nathaniel Adams Blanchard Post 1040 was chartered December 8, 1930, and has been serving the needs of local veterans ever since.

The Last Man's Club of Bethlehem

Following the close of World War I, many veterans continued the fellowship they had enjoyed in the service by establishing Last Man's Clubs. The concept was based on similar organizations founded by veterans of the War of 1812. Meetings would be held annually in which members would renew their friendships and remember comrades who had passed away since the club's inception. Sixty World War I veterans gathered in Bethlehem on January 21, 1939, to establish a local Last Man's Club. A bottle of 1924 cognac was placed in a hand-crafted mahogany casket, a roster of the club's membership was placed with the bottle, and the men agreed to meet once annually until the last five surviving veterans would come together for a final meeting and drink a toast in honor of their departed comrades. The organization continued until the early 1970s when thinning ranks forced discontinuation of the club. On September 15, 1988, however, the last three surviving members

Bethlehem Last Man's Club, 1939.

of some 1,200 men and women from the town who served the nation in the military during World War II and who were strongly supported by the town's residents. In May 1942, a card party was held to raise money for gifts for the town's soldiers. As a result, a cash gift was sent to each Bethlehem man and woman in uniform. Later, in November of the same year, a memorial board containing the names of those residents in the armed forces was erected at the corner of Delaware Avenue and Oakwood Place by patriotic citizens. [28]

of the club—Norman Bender, Durrell Krause, and Winthrop Robinson—gathered to lift a final toast to the deceased members. Winthrop Robinson, a veteran of the 51st Pioneer Infantry and first commander of the Blanchard post was presented with the vintage bottle. [27]

Throughout the course of the war the *Albany County Post* documented the triumphs and tragedies experienced by Bethlehem families. In 1943, the paper related that Mrs. William Waldbillig had sold $1,993.05 in war bonds since May 1942. These bonds were sold at the public library and at local card clubs. In 1944, the paper reported that the family of Staff Sergeant K. Willey of South Bethlehem was notified of his death in battle in the South Pacific. In July 1944, the paper related the sad news of a War Department telegram received by Mr. and Mrs. Edward J. Bennett of 18 Stratton Place, Delmar, which indicated that their son, Private Clifford E. Bennett, had been killed in action on February 28, 1944. In all, thirty Bethlehem men died in the service of their country during World War II. In addition to persons who served the nation in uniform, many others provided important contributions as members of the Red Cross, Civil Defense, and other agencies assisting in the war effort. [29]

World War II Mobilizes Town Resources

When the United States was attacked at Pearl Harbor on December 7, 1941, at least two Bethlehem men were present in uniform. Newspaper accounts published a few days after the attack reported that Private Edward P. Piper of the 64th Coast Artillery and Private Gordon Palmer of the United States Signal Corps were "feeling fine and doing all right." Piper and Palmer were just two

Memorial Day parade, May 30, 1945.

served as adjutant to Major General Delmar T. Spivey, the highest ranking officer in the camp, and as editor of the camp newspaper, *The Kriegie Times*. The newspaper was merely a ploy to obtain a printing press so that the POWs could forge passes to assist in the escape attempt. The breakout of seventy-nine prisoners from Sagan on March 24-25, 1944, is remembered as one of the classic stories of World War II. Mulligan remained at the camp until it was liberated by General Patton. For his service at Stalag III, Mulligan received the Bronze Star. On General Spivey's orders, Mulligan buried photographs throughout the compound that had been taken with a camera smuggled into the camp. He recovered the photographs after he was liberated. Following his release, Mulligan wrote a report for the Pentagon on the treatment of prisoners of war, utilizing the documentary evidence he had gathered. Shortly before his death, Mulligan contributed his archives of photographs to Time-Life Books for their World War II publication, *Prisoners of War*. [30]

One who performed great service in preserving the history of the conflict was former town historian Thomas E. Mulligan, Jr. During World War II, Mulligan served as an officer in the U.S. Army Air Corps and flew twenty-four bombing missions over Germany until he was shot down during a raid on the Ruhr Valley in 1943. Mulligan spent two years as a prisoner of war in Stalag Luft III, at Sagan, Germany, where British and American air force officers developed the plan which became known as "The Great Escape." During his imprisonment, Mulligan

Thomas E. Mulligan with Civil War historian Bruce Catton.

From Korea to the Present

Since the close of World War II, the nation has issued other calls that have been answered by Bethlehem residents. During the Korean conflict, more than 350 men and women from the town served in the armed forces and at least four—Alva L. Bleau of Selkirk, John P. Conlon of Delmar, Donald Snyder of South Bethlehem, and Henry J. Stephany of Selkirk—did not return. The Korean conflict period was characterized by increasing fears associated with the rise of communism throughout Europe and the potential for nuclear war. Town residents reacted to these concerns with the construction of basement bomb shelters, the imposition of disaster preparedness training in the schools, and the reactivation of civil defense organizations. During the summer of 1950, town supervisor John M. Oliver established at Selkirk an aircraft observation post to be manned on a twenty-four hour basis. Town response was enthusiastic and, by October 1950, several hundred residents had volunteered for service.

The frustrations of the Korean conflict experience gave way to still greater dissension during the 1960s, when many town residents were called to serve in the Vietnam conflict. Although it is unknown how many townspeople served during the Vietnam conflict, records compiled for the Albany County Vietnam Veterans' Monument indicate that nine Bethlehem soldiers were casualties of this undeclared war. The sacrifices of Robert Abbott, Dean B. Allen, James C. Bink, Charles Burkett, Jr., Jared A. Frisbie, Henry Klien, Jr., James Picarazzi, Thomas Ryan, and Major Richard A. Kibbey will not be forgotten.[31]

Major Richard A. Kibbey, a graduate of Bethlehem Central High School, began his military career in the ROTC program at Rensselaer Polytechnic Institute. After enlisting in the United States Air Force, Major Kibbey was assigned to Patrick Air Force Base in Florida. It was from this base that he departed on a rescue mission into Vietnam. His helicopter was shot down over North Vietnam on February 6, 1967. Of the six member crew, only one was rescued. Major Kibbey continues to be listed in official military records as "missing in action."[32]

Like many communities across the nation, Bethlehem was sharply divided in its support for the war in Vietnam. In 1966, a group of concerned veterans, under the leadership of Alexander J. Woehrle, formed an organization called "The Committee that Cares" to provide support for local men and women serving in the armed forces. The organization sent monthly packages to Bethlehem soldiers serving in Vietnam and helped provide assistance to the families left behind. Initiated as a project of the Blanchard American Legion Post, by the spring of 1967 the association had branched out to include most of the veterans', civic, and church groups in the town.[33] In March 1971, the committee received a letter from President Richard M. Nixon acknowledging their valuable work. The letter, dated March 16, 1971, and typed on White House stationery was addressed to Ms. Virginia A. Bailey and read:

> The support which you and the members of your organization have expressed for our country's goals in southeast Asia means a great deal to me and to all of America's fighting men in Vietnam. I greatly appreciate your message, and I want to assure you that I will continue to make every effort to enhance the security of our servicemen and to obtain a just and lasting peace.[34]

Although the divisive nature of the conflict was not often reported in the pages of *The Spotlight*, the October 16, 1969, edition featured a front page article by a recently discharged Vietnam veteran, David Esmond, in opposition to the war.

Bethlehem Veterans' Memorial in Delmar.

I believe that armed forces has a legitimate role in national defense, but we are not defending our nation in Vietnam. We are destroying it. We are squandering our resources, we are killing Americans, we are killing Vietnamese. We are not fighting for freedom and democracy in Vietnam. We are fighting for a corrupt regime which rules by whim, which jailed the runner up in its presidential campaign, which supports a police force which lives on extortion. We are not defeating communism in Vietnam. We are aiding it by providing new recruits — the survivors of families killed in our bombing raids in the south, the peasants we have herded into detention camps, the women and old people our troops have offended or mistreated.[35]

Throughout the course of the Vietnam conflict *The Spotlight* recorded general news of interest about soldiers stationed overseas but did not print the obituary notices of Bethlehem men killed in the conflict. The January 28, 1971, issue of *The Spotlight* carried a lengthy story about Private Peter F. Rossman, a 1969 graduate of Bethlehem Central serving with the 1st Air Cavalry Division in Vietnam. The article described the young man's celebration of Christmas at a jungle fire base some sixty miles north of Saigon. Private Rossman observed that Christmas consisted of an incredible proliferation of Christmas trees mounted atop the bunkers and gun pits. Presents

from home were distributed and one soldier received an assortment of musical instruments and sheet music while another opened up a package containing a female mannequin's leg, complete with nylon stocking and baby blue garter. The men enjoyed an evening worship service among the ammunition boxes and later cooked a holiday feast consisting of shrimp, roast turkey, stuffing, and apple pies. Private Rossman ended the article with a Christmas wish from one of his companions: "All I want for Christmas is my life, my wife and my home. Something I'll have next year. God willing."[36]

In addition to those noted earlier, an incomplete listing of Bethlehem men who served on active duty in Vietnam includes Lt. Ross Dalrymple, Lt. William R. Pearson, Keith Becker, James F. Thomas, Kenneth Wells, Ensign James Hulihan, and Lt. Colonel Stephen G. Olmstead, USMC.

The men and women of Bethlehem have had a role in every military conflict in which the nation has been involved. From the Revolutionary experience of 1776 to the desert warfare of the Persian Gulf, Bethlehem has contributed hundreds of men and women to the armed services. A memorial monument in honor of those who served and those who made the supreme sacrifice

Frank Litto sculpture, Bethlehem Veterans' Memorial.

was dedicated at the Veterans Memorial Park in 1964. A patriotic eagle sculpture, designed by artist Frank Litto, was placed atop the monument in 1965. It serves as a fitting tribute to those residents who left the town to become an important part of the nation's military heritage.

14 Chronology

The reader is now familiar with events in the history of the town of Bethlehem. This chronology attempts to place these events among others which took place in a larger area—the colony (later the county and state) the nation and the world.

Events come in many sizes—from major political or social upheavals to small, homey happenings important in their own times but now trivial. Some of each type are included here to illustrate our town's place in the world and to give us insight into the experiences of our predecessors.

The events are listed in columns—local events headed by the "Bethlehem" sign logo and other events headed by the world map. Local events described in the text are included with the exception of the founding dates of local organizations, which are listed in "Community Organizations in Brief" in the appendix.

	BETHLEHEM	World	
		About 28,000 B. C.	Asians crossed land bridge into North America.
	Wisconsin Glacier covered most of New York State.	About 18,000 B. C.	
	The glacier receded, leaving a huge lake (now known as Lake Albany).	About 15,000 B. C.	
		About 12,000 B. C.	Ice age ended.

Lake Albany began to drain. Spruce and fir forests covered the area and the climate was cold and dry.	About 11,000 B. C.	
Ice Age hunters quarried flint and made stone tools on a hilltop site in West Athens in nearby Greene County.	About 8500 B. C.	Ice Age hunters roamed New York State in search of edible wild plants, fish and game.
Early Archaic Indian hunting parties camped at the confluence of the Vloman Kill and Hudson River in Cedar Hill.	After 6500 B. C.	Mexican natives were growing corn, avocados, beans, squash, and other plants for food.
Vergennes phase Indians returned to the confluence of the Vloman Kill and Hudson River regularly during the spring and summer seasons as did the cultures that followed.	After 3500 B. C.	Cuneiform writing developed in the Middle East. Wheeled vehicles in use in Sumeria. Potter's wheel used in Mesopotamia.
Vosburg phase Indians were using stone ulu knives and cylindrical pestles to prepare food.	After 3000 B. C.	Sumerians were growing barley, baking bread, making beer, and using manufactured coins. Egyptians were building pyramids.
Sylvan Lake phase Indians were using a narrow flint point for hunting, a major improvement over wide points of earlier centuries.	After 2200 B. C.	Egyptians were using papyrus for writing material. Village life developed in Mexico.
River phase Indians were using weighted spear-thrower and spear (atlatl) to increase velocity of their spears.	After 1900 B. C.	Horses used to draw vehicles in Middle East. Percussion instruments added to Egyptian orchestral instruments.
Snook Kill phase Indians were starting fires by striking flint against iron pyrite nodules, a major improvement over the bow drill of earlier centuries	After 1500 B. C.	Hittites were using guitar, lyre, trumpet, and tambourine with religious dances. Court dances in Egypt were accompanied by the harp.
Orient phase Indians developed better ways of preparing food in more sophisticated vessels.	After 1000 B. C.	Knowledge of shipbuilding considerably advanced in Mediterranean and Scandinavian countries. Confucius, born in 551 B.C., developed a system of moral values and responsible behavior.
Adena/Middlesex culture migrates to Bethlehem from Ohio in small numbers.	After 300 B. C.	Ball games, dice-playing, and board games played by Romans.
Owasco/Mahican Indians were experimenting with growing corn, beans, and squash, encouraging larger, more permanent settlements in Bethlehem and in nearby areas.	After 1300 A. D.	Aztecs founded city of Tenochitlan (Mexico). Black death devastated Europe. Mechanical clock installed at Strasbourg Cathedral.

	After early 1600s	Five Iroquois nations, the Mohawks, the Oneidas, the Onondagas, the Cayugas, and the Senecas, were united in a league for the common defense.
Henry Hudson anchored near Bethlehem on September 17; returned to Europe September 23.	1609	Dutch merchants established a trading post in Japan.
	1612	Tobacco seeds were brought to Jamestown, Virginia, from South America.
New Netherland Company granted monopoly to trade in area of Hudson River. Fort Nassau erected on Westerlo Island just east of the mouth of the Normanskill.	1614	Glass industry developed in England. Sir Walter Raleigh wrote *The History of the World.* Copper coins in use throughout Europe.
Fort Nassau destroyed by a spring flood but a new trading post was established on the mainland.	1617	Willebrord Snellius established technique of trigonometrical triangulation for cartography.
	1620	Plymouth Colony founded.
	1621	Dutch West India Company chartered.
Fort Orange built on the west shore of the Hudson River just north of Westerlo Island. Eighteen families settled near the fort to raise supplies of food.	1624	The Dutch arrived in New Amsterdam.
Commander of Fort Orange joined Mahican war party against the Mohawks.	1626	Peter Minuit bought Manhattan Island from native chiefs and the city of New Amsterdam was founded (New York City).
Mahicans driven from the Bethlehem area after a war with the Mohawks.	1628	
Establishment of private colonies in New Netherland permitted by the West India Company; Kiliaen van Rensselaer became patroon of Rensselaerswyck.	1629	
Mahicans began to sell land to Dutch settlers. First settlers, Rutger Hendrickz and Brant Peelen, arrived in Rensselaerswyck.	1630	Pirates settled in Tortuga (West Indies). Massachusetts Bay colony founded.
Sawmills established on the Normanskill.	After 1631	Construction of the Taj Mahal (India).

	1632-1654	Catholics settling in southern Maryland were given freedom to practice their religion.
Brant Peelen renewed his contract with the patroon and can be considered first permanent resident of what is now Bethlehem.	1634	
	1635	Boston Latin School founded (Boston, Massachusetts), oldest public secondary school for boys in the United States.
	1636	Japanese ports closed and most foreigners expelled. Harvard College founded (Cambridge, Massachusetts). Rhode Island and Providence Plantations founded by Roger Williams.
Pieter Cornelissen and Albert Andriessen Bratt arrived to build sawmills. Bratt soon left to raise tobacco and trade furs.	1637	
Fur trade opened to private citizens.	1639	First printing press in North America (Cambridge, Massachusetts).
	1640	Southampton, Long Island, first English settlement in New York founded.
Johannes Megapolensis contracted with the patroon to lead divine services in 1642.	1642	Massachusetts School Law required each town to provide instruction in reading for all children.
Brant Peelen died.	1644	
	1647	Massachusetts law required establishment of an elementary school in each town of fifty or more families, a Latin school in each town of 100 or more families.
Evert Noldingh permitted by patroon to teach in the patroonship.	1648	Iron works in Saugus, Massachusetts, produced up to eight tons per week.
First appearance of the name Bethlehem (on January 21 in a court ruling).	1649	
Mahicans continued to sell land to the Dutch.	1652	First coffee house opened in London.
Uprising of Esopus Indians led to building of a block house in Bethlehem.	1662	
	1664	Dutch surrendered New Amsterdam to the English. New Amsterdam renamed New York and the village of Beverwyck near Fort Orange renamed Albany.

Hendrick Gerritse Van Wie built his home (the site is now Van Wies point).	1679	Reformed Church Classis of Amsterdam allowed formation of a classis in the colonies.
Rensselaerswyck was given status of an English manor.	1685	
Albany granted a monopoly in fur trade, causing Bethlehem settlers to turn to agriculture and sawmilling.	1686	
The patroon introduced lifetime leasehold system to tenants who previously had to renew leases every year or so.	About 1688	
"Glorious Revolution" — King James II succeeded by William and Mary but failure of the monarchs to send governors to New York led to anarchy in the colony.	1688	Pennsylvania Quakers protested against slavery.
Inhabitants of Bethlehem ordered to build a fort for protection in case of invasion from Canada.	1689	
	1689-1697	King William's war in the upper Hudson Valley resulted from conflict between England and France.
	1690	French and Indians burned the settlement at Schenectady.
As many as forty families were living in the Bethlehem area.	1691	Religious freedom granted to all except Catholics in Massachusetts.
	1700	The *Selling of Joseph* by Samuel Sewell was first published American protest against slavery.
	1701	Yale University (at the time Yale College) founded.
	1702-1713	War of Spanish Succession (Queen Anne's War).
	1702	First daily newspaper, *The Daily Courant*, published in London.
Legislation passed by the New York Colonial Assembly provided for annual elections of town supervisors, assessors, and tax collectors.	1703	St. Petersburg, Russia, founded.
	1704	*Boston News-Letter* published weekly.
	1706	First presbytery in North America established.
	1707	England and Scotland united to form Great Britain.

The Abbey Hotel built on Route 144 in Glenmont (razed in 1961).	About 1710	
Rensselaer Nicoll inherited an estate on the Vloman Kill near the Hudson River.	1719	*The American Mercury* published in Philadelphia.
	1721	Regular postage service established between London and New England. *Brandenberg Concertos* composed by Johann Sebastian Bach. Swiss immigrants introduced rifles to America.
Marriage of Elizabeth Salisbury and Rensselaer Nicoll.	1730	
	1731	Subscription library founded by Benjamin Franklin in Philadelphia.
	1732	Theater opened in Covent Garden in London. First theatrical performance in New York City (by a London company).
Nicoll-Sill house (the Bethlehem House) built for Rensselaer and Elizabeth Nicoll.	About 1735	
	1742	*A Short Treatise on the Game of Whist* published by Edmond Hoyle.
	1744	First printed rules for the game of cricket (England).
Timothy (a hay crop) was being cultivated on local farms.	By 1746	
Bethlehem's first supervisor, Philip Van Rensselaer, born.	1747	
Red clover was being cultivated on local farms.	By 1749	
	1750-1800	Introduction of power-driven machinery to weave fabrics.
Albany was supply center of British military operation in North America during the French and Indian War.	1754-1763	French and Indian War.
	Late 1700s	Europeans began to explore the interior of Africa.
	1754	First iron-rolling mill (Hampshire, England).

James Selkirk born in Scotland (Selkirk emigrated first to Galway and then to Bethlehem). The hamlet of Selkirk was named for Selkirk's family.	1756	Cotton velvets first made (Lancashire, England).
Reformed Protestant Dutch Church at Bethlehem and Jericho formed.	1763	
English language used by the Dutch in the area who wanted to participate in trade with the English.	After 1763	
	1764-1790	James Watt perfected a steam engine.
	1765	Chocolate manufacture began in the United States (Dorchester, Massachusetts).
Map identifies 127 households in the Rensselaerswyck. Two hundred ninety-seven names appear on town tax list: 200 Dutch, 40 British, 39 German, 18 French.	1767	
Philip Van Rensselaer, later first supervisor of the Town of Bethlehem, married Maria Sanders.	1768	
English adopted as the liturgical language of the local Dutch Reformed churches.	1770	
Albany County divided into districts; the Bethlehem area was within the district called the Manor of Rensselaerswyck.	1772	
Eight counties created from original area of Albany County.	1772-1809	
	1773	Boston Tea Party protested English taxes on colonies. London stock exchange founded.
John Haswell, Sr., original settler of Houcks Corners, arrived from England and established a farm which stretched from Elsmere Avenue to Elm Avenue on both sides of Feura Bush Road and Murray Avenue.	1774	
Albany County organized seventeen regiments of militia. Purported Tory camp and rendezvous on the banks of the Vloman Kill.	1775-1783	American Revolution.

Presbyterian missionary preached out-of-doors under two oak trees near the site of the present New Scotland town hall.	1776	
Bethlehem residents David Niver and Conrad Soop were present when British General John Burgoyne surrendered at Stillwater.	1777	Lavoisier proved that air consists principally of nitrogen and oxygen. New York State Constitution adopted.
The district of Rensselaerwyck divided into the East District and the West District, called East Manor and West Manor.	1779	
Protestant Dutch Reformed Church of New Salem formed.	1783	
	1784	First use of gas for lighting (France). First Episcopal bishop in the United States installed. Methodist Episcopal Church in the United States formed.
	1785	Cast-iron plowshare patented in England.
Mansion at Cherry Hill built by Philip Van Rensselaer.	1786-1787	
	1787-1788	United States Constitution written and ratified.
Presbytery of Suffolk (Long Island) organized a mission church in New Scotland.	1787	
Town of Watervliet established. (Bethlehem was included in this area.)	1788	
	1789	Episopal Church in the United States organized. Society of Tammany founded in New York City, became Tammany Hall, Democratic political machine in the nineteenth century. First cotton factory (Manchester, England).
	1789-1799	French Revolution.
	1790	United States population was 3,929,000.
First Presbyterian church building erected in New Scotland. Jerusalem Reformed Church built on the road between Unionville and Feura Bush. Mead farm established on Meads Lane between Route 32 and Delaware Avenue.	1791	First Bank of the United States founded. New York Hospital opened.

Methodist residents of Bethlehem attended the Old Stone Church near Coeymans.	1791-1792	
	1791-1824	Latin American wars of independence.
	1792	New York Stock Exchange founded.
Town of Bethlehem established on land taken from the town of Watervliet.	1793	Cotton gin invented by Eli Whitney.
First town meeting of the Town of Bethlehem held at the house of Henry Burhans on April 10. Philip Van Rensselaer chosen first supervisor and John Van Derheyden first town clerk.	1794	
New York State Legislature appropriated $50,000 annually for public education. Albany County's share was $3,975. First pastor installed at the Presbyterian Church in New Scotland.	1795	
Early Haswell family house built at Houcks Corners. Albany Schenectady Turnpike Company incorporated.	1797	Cast-iron plows became available.
Philip Van Rensselaer died.	1798	
	1799	Rosetta stone found in Egypt (enabled scholars to translate hieroglyphics). Beginning in July, newborn children of slaves automatically freed under New York State law.
Albertus Becker homestead at Beckers Corners built.	1800	United States population was 5,308,000.
	1802	First practical steamboat, the tug *Charlotte Dundas*, built by William Symington (Scotland).
	1803	New York State Bank chartered in Albany (later State Bank of Albany, now part of Fleet Bank).
Albany and Bethlehem Turnpike charted (a portion was renamed South Pearl Street in 1870).	1804	First successful use of a railway steam locomotive (Wales).
The Albany and Delaware Turnpike charted (renamed Delaware Avenue in 1870).	1805	
	1807	Steamboat *Clermont* traveled from New York to Albany on the Hudson River.

	1808	Slaves under sixty-five freed by New York State law.
Town population was 4,430.	1810	United States population was 7,204,000. Process for canning food developed.
New York State militia commanded by Solomon Van Rensselaer during the War of 1812. At least twenty men from Bethlehem served.	1812-1814	War of 1812.
	1813	*Pride and Prejudice* written by Jane Austin.
	1814	First practical steam locomotive (Great Britain).
	1815	Crushed stone roads constructed in Great Britain.
	1819	First steamship, the *Savannah,* crossed the Atlantic without passengers or cargo as safety was doubted, but by the 1820s and 1830s regular crossings were being made.
One hundred fifty-five common schools in Albany County.	1820	United States population was 9,638,453.
	1820-1880	Development of gas lighting systems for streets and buildings.
Name of the Reformed Protestant Dutch Church at Bethlehem and Jericho changed to the Reformed Dutch Church of Bethlehem.	1821	Troy Female Seminary founded (now Emma Willard School).
Members of the Old Stone Church (Methodist) who lived in Bethlehem built a church near Beckers Corners.	1823	Rugby football invented (England).
The Onesquethaw Presbyterian Church between Meads Corners and Tarrytown formed by members who left the Presbyterian Church at New Scotland.	1824	Royal Society for the Prevention of Cruelty to Animals founded (London).
The congregation of the Jerusalem Reformed Church on the road between Unionville and Feura Bush divided into two congregations: the Union Church at Unionville and the Jerusalem Church at Feura Bush.	1825	Erie Canal opened. First public railroad (England).
	1826-1838	John James Audubon published *Birds of North America* (in England; American edition published in 1839).
State law provided for election of justices of the peace in towns.	1827	All slaves emancipated in New York State.

Ice harvesting business on the Hudson began. (Ice dealers were listed in the *Tri-Village Directory* as late as 1949.)

1828 First Baedeker travel guide published. Baltimore and Ohio Railroad constructed (first passenger and freight railroad in the United States).

1829 Steam engine, *The Rocket*, first successful adaptation of a steam engine for a railway (England).

Town population was 6,082. Methodist fellowship formed in Adamsville (Delmar).

1830 United States population was 12,860,702.

Albany Seed Store opened in Albany (evolved into Price Greenleaf in Delmar, opened in 1961).

1831 Slave rebellion in Virginia led by Nat Turner.

1831-1847 Reaping machine developed and manufactured by Cyrus McCormick.

Town of New Scotland established on land taken from the town of Bethlehem.

1832 First American coeducational college (Oberlin, Ohio) encouraged enrollment of women and blacks. First horse-drawn trolleys in New York City. First American schools for the blind opened in Boston and New York City.

Erastus Corning, great-grandfather of the twentieth-century mayor of the city of Albany, established a farm between Route 9W and Route 144. Cedar Hill post office established (merged with Selkirk post office in 1901).

1833 Beginning of the Whig party in the United States.

Dock owned by Peter G. and Henry Van Wie leased to the Hudson Steamboat Co. to serve as the Albany passenger terminal. First Presbyterian Church of Bethlehem formed on Krumkill Road in North Bethlehem.

1835 Phineas T. Barnum's first exhibition. Samuel Colt patented repeating pistol.

Nathaniel Adams arrived in what is now Delmar.

1836 Siege of the Alamo. Texas declared independence from Mexico.
1837 Panic lead to economic depression in the United States.

Reformed Protestant Dutch Church formed when the Onesquethaw Presbyterian Church dissolved its relationship with the Presbytery. Nathaniel Adams opened the Adams House Hotel.

1838

1839 Goodyear discovered process of vulcanization of rubber.

Nathaniel Adams established a post office in what is now Delmar. Name Adamsville apparently began to be used at this time.

1840 Samuel F. B. Morse patented telegraph. United States population was 17,063,353.

Joel B. Nott of Bethlehem served as president of the New York State Agricultural Society.

1841 — First wagon train left Missouri for California. Oberlin College granted first degree to a woman in the United States. (Although the college opened in 1832, the first women matriculated for the regular college course in 1837.)

The Adamsville branch of the Unionville Reformed Church formed. Town population was 3,238.

1842 — Chinese ports opened for British trade. Treaties between New York State and the Iroquois established reservations. Railroad connected Boston and Albany. Ether first used as an anesthetic in surgery.

John Babcock, first known physician in the town of Bethlehem, practiced medicine.

1842-1876

1844 — First normal school (teacher training school) in New York State opened in Albany. Safety match invented (Sweden).

Methodist Church building near Beckers Corners taken down and a new building built in South Bethlehem (now South Bethlehem United Methodist Church).

1845 — Knickerbocker Base Ball Club of New York codified rules of baseball.

New State Constitution put an end to lifetime leaseholds in other manors, but left Van Rensselaer Manor unchanged. Building made from timbers of the Methodist Episcopal Church near Beckers Corners dedicated as the First Methodist Episcopal Church of Bethlehem at Janes Corners (South Bethlehem). Grand View Farm operated by Cornelius V. and Caroline Lasher Baker.

1846 — Potato famine in Ireland. Sewing machine invented.

Troops were trained for the Mexican War by Colonel John Moore of Bethlehem at a camp on the Haswell Farm on the old Albany-Bethlehem Turnpike (Routes 32 and 9W). The farm is believed to have served as a training camp during the War of 1812 and the Civil War also. Congressman John I. Slingerland denounced U.S. participation in the Mexican War.

About 1846

1846-1848 — Mexican War.

New York State legislation provided for incorporation of plank road and turnpike construction companies.

1847 — First use of chloroform as an anesthetic (England).

1849 — California gold rush.

	1849-1855	Amelia Bloomer published the *Lily* advocating women's rights including dress reform.
Horse powered mowing, reaping, and threshing machines began to replace hand-held tools. Town population was 4,102.	1850	Jenny Lind, "The Swedish Nightingale," toured the United States. United States population was 23,191,876.
Most of the leaseholds in Van Rensselaer Manor sold to the leaseholders.	1850-1860	
The hamlet of Glenmont called Frazertown. South Bethlehem Plank Road (now 9W) chartered.	1851	Maine and Illinois began to enforce prohibition against liquor.
Post office at Normanskill (Slingerlands) established by William H. Slingerland. Slingerland family vault erected.	1852	Wells, Fargo and Co. founded. *Uncle Tom's Cabin* by Harriet Beecher Stowe published.
Methodist Church built in Adamsville (Delmar).	1852-1853	
	1854	Republican party founded.
Town industry consisted of five coach and wagon factories, three sawmills, two gristmills, a plaster mill, a blacksmith shop, a tannery, and a broom factory, altogether employing forty-seven.	1855	
South Bethlehem called Kimmeys Corners for Philip Kimmey who settled there around 1825. David and Elizabeth Onderdonk Mead established a farm on Creble Road south of Delmar.	1856	
Cedar Hill School building built (enlarged and redesigned in 1907, used as a school until 1960 and occupied by the Bethlehem Historical Association in 1965). New Scotland turnpike (the Hurstville road) ran from Lydius Street (Madison Avenue) in Albany through Slingerlands, New Scotland, and New Salem to Schoharie. The Academy of the Sacred Heart opened in mansion purchased in 1858 by the Catholic Diocese of Albany at Kenwood.	1859	Charles Blondin crossed Niagara Falls on a tightrope. First oil well drilled (Titusville, Pennsylvania). John Brown (abolitionist) raided U.S. arsenal at Harper's Ferry, West Virginia. Charles Darwin published his theory of evolution.
Town population was 2,646 men, 2,505 women. 1,806 children were attending fifteen schools in Bethlehem.	1860	United States population was 31,443,321.

	1860-1880	Louis Pasteur's study of bacteria led to the development of pasteurization of food and vaccination to provide immunization against disease.
Hurstville settled by William Hurst who built Hurst's Hotel (known as the Log Tavern).	1861	
One hundred forty-nine soldiers from Bethlehem served in the Civil War; 42 were killed.	1861-1865	Civil War in the United States.
	1862	Steam plow used in the Netherlands.
Albany and Susquehanna Railroad operated through Adamsville and Slingerlands to New Scotland (acquired by Delaware and Hudson Canal Company in 1866).	1863	Machine gun invented (patented by Richard Jordan Gatling and called the Gatling gun).
Albany street railway ran on South Pearl Street to the hamlet of Kenwood. Mount Pleasant Cemetery established just west of South Bethlehem on Route 396. Bethlehem farmers produced: 210 bushels of gain 14,217.5 tons of hay 97,902 bushels of potatoes 34,061 bushels of apples 106,135 pounds of butter 298,013 pounds of pork	1864	Gettysburg Address and Emancipation Proclamation. Travelers Insurance Company founded (Hartford, Connecticut). Roller skating introduced to the United States. Travers stakes run at Saratoga racetrack. First salmon cannery in the United States (Washington, California).
Bethlehem farms totaled 32,673.75 acres and livestock consisted of: 1,213 horses and colts 1,382 cows 2,986 sheep and lambs, producing 6,946.5 pounds of wool 638 other animals	1865	Railway sleeping cars designed. First train holdup (North Bend, Ohio). Antiseptic surgery introduced.
	1869	Wyoming territory granted suffrage to women.
	By 1870	Steam powered plows and threshing machines were being used.
Land between the Normanskill and the Albany city limits annexed by the City of Albany. Cedar Hill Ice Company formed to harvest ice from the Hudson River. Corning Iron Company founded on Westerlo Island. Town population was 6,950. Community of Normanskill renamed Slingerlands.	1870	Standard Oil Company founded by John D. Rockefeller. Great Chicago fire. United States population was 38,558,371.

Methodist Church building at Adamsville torn down and a new church building was built in Slingerlands (now Community United Methodist Church).

| 1870-1914 | European colonial expansion in Africa and Asia. |

| 1871 | P.T. Barnum's "The Greatest Show on Earth" opened in Brooklyn. |

| 1872 | First woman presidential candidate, Victoria Woodhull, nominated by the Equal Rights party (women were not, however, permitted to vote in most states). |

New Methodist Church building built in Adamsville (now First Methodist Church). Beckers Corners Post Office established (merged with Selkirk in 1899).

| 1873 | First practical typewriter marketed. |

| 1874 | Tennis introduced in the United States. |

Three hundred fifty-eight farms (31,540 acres) in Bethlehem.

| 1875 | |

The *Ironweed* house (featured in the motion picture, *Ironweed*)built by Albert I. Slingerland for Charles D. Hammond, superintendent of the Delaware and Hudson Railroad. James B. Lyon of Cedar Hill founded a printing business in Albany (became part of Williams Printing Company in 1923). Gerrit H. Niver of Bethlehem killed with Custer at the Little Big Horn.

| 1876 | Battle of the Little Bighorn. First words spoken over the telephone by Alexander Graham Bell. |

| 1877 | Bell Telephone company formed. |

American District Telegraph Company formed in Albany. Albany City Iron Works started production with two blast furnaces at the north end of Westerlo Island in the Hudson River.

| 1878 | Milking machine invented. First telephone exchange operated (New Haven, Connecticut). |

Cornelius H. Slingerland started printing business in Slingerlands, incorporated as Slingerlands Printing Company in 1910.

| 1879 | Thomas A. Edison patented an incandescent lamp. |

Map indicates the New York Sand and Facing Company was located in Glenmont next to the West Shore Railroad.

| 1880 | Game of Bingo invented. United States population was 50,189,209. |

| 1882 | Bank of Japan founded. |

Peter Callanan, Dr. J. R. Davidson, Philip Scharbauer, and John Newton Briggs established a gravel quarry (later Callanan Road Improvement Company). Hudson River Telephone Company served Albany (joined New York Telephone Company in 1910). Selkirk post office opened.	1883	Brooklyn Bridge opened. Buffalo Bill Cody presented first "Wild West Show."
First recorded transaction involving the mining of moulding sand in the area.	1884	
	1884-1885	First metal frame skyscraper (Chicago, Illinois).
Gas lighting provided by several companies in the area.	Late 1880s	
	1885	First successful four cycle gasoline engines for automobile built by Karl Benz and Gottlieb Daimler.
The Hudson River Telephone Company (begun in 1883) provided communication from Albany to the Abbey Hotel, Cedar Hill, Hurstville, Slingerlands, and Delmar. Delmar, (then Adams Station) was the largest community in the town with a population of 360; Slingerlands was next with 230.	1886	
Normansville Free Chapel built, now named the Normansville Community Church.	1889	
	1890	Ellis Island opened. Daughters of the American Revolution founded. United States population was 62,979,766.
Slingerlands renamed Ruxton but again named Slingerlands after appeal by the Slingerland family.	1891	Trans-Siberian Railroad construction began. Zipper invented.
	1892	Thomas A. Edison built the first central station to generate and distribute electricity (New York City).
	1893	Thomas A. Edison demonstrated first commercial motion picture projector.
Military maneuvers called "the battle of Slingerlands" took place. Peter Callanan received first road building contract and incorporated a stone crushing business.	1895	First professional football game in United States (Latrobe, Pennsylvania). Safety razor invented.
	1896	First modern Olympics (Athens). Klondike gold rush.

	1898	Spanish-American War.
Whipple bridge erected over the Normanskill in Normansville.	Around 1900	
Edward J. Bedell, M.D., elected town supervisor.	1900	Carry Nation led her first raid against a saloon in Wichita, Kansas. United States population was 76,212,168.
	1901	United States Steel Corporation founded.
Suburban Water Company formed by William Henry Slingerland in Slingerlands (purchased by the town in 1927). Hurstville post office replaced by rural free delivery.	1902	
	1903	Ford Motor Company founded. Wright brothers made first successful flight. Boston won first baseball World Series from Pittsburgh, five games to three.
The South Bethlehem Telephone Co. incorporated. Acquired by New York Telephone in 1923.	1904	Construction of Panama Canal began. Foreign steamship lines charged $10.00 for Atlantic crossing in steerage.
	1906	San Franscico earthquake. Publication of Upton Sinclair's *The Jungle* led to Federal Food and Drugs Act providing measures to ensure the safety of foods and medication sold to the public.
	1907	Boy Scouts founded. Mother's Day first celebrated in Philadelphia, Pennsylvania. First daily comic strip published (*Mr. Mutt*, later *Mutt and Jeff*).
Summer house of Governor Glynn built (now owned by the Bethlehem Chapter of the Benevolent and Protective Order of the Elks No. 2233). Parish of St. Thomas the Apostle formed in Delmar.	1907-1908	
St. Stephen's Mission established in Elsmere with services conducted by priests from the Cathedral of All Saints in Albany (Episcopal).	1908	First Ford Model T (original price of $850.00 was by 1925 reduced to $290.00).
Speed limits for automobiles in the town were 15 mph on roads and 4 mph on bridges. Explosion at Callanan stone crushing plant.	1909	National Association for the Advancement of Colored People founded. Manufacture of Bakelite, first plastic.

The Church of St. Thomas the Apostle incorporated in Delmar and a church building was constructed. Flight by Glenn Curtiss from Westerlo Island to New York City.

Farm established by Joseph and Margaret Cross on Route 144 in Glenmont, later managed by Bernard and Edward Mocker.

Name of the Reformed Dutch Church of Bethlehem changed to First Reformed Church of Bethlehem. Christian Strohmaier farm established on the corner of Elsmere Avenue and Feura Bush Road.

Account book started by Daniel Bennett for his plumbing business. Members of the Delmar Progress Club formed the Delmar Free Library Association and opened a public library in the Delmar School house at the corner of Kenwood Avenue and Adams Street (now the Masonic Temple). Blacksmith shop opened by the Lehmann family in Selkirk (now Lehman's Garage—the oldest continuously run family business in Bethlehem). *Family Directory* issued in Delmar to raise money for the new library.

Clayton Le Gallez submitted proposal for wiring a house, beginning LeGallez Electric Co.

Land on Westerlo Island from which Glenn Curtiss flew to New York City purchased by the City of Albany. Delmar Free Library had a collection of 899 titles.

New Delmar Free Library building opened at the corner of Adams Street and Hawthorne Avenue (now the Bethlehem Central School District office). Town assessment rolls listed 157 farms and 32 businesses.

Nathaniel Adams Blanchard of Delmar was killed in action only two days before the armistice ended fighting in World War I. Tri-Village Bus Service operated by Frank Hungerford (sold to United Traction Company in 1934).

1910 — Halley's Comet observed. Father's Day established in Spokane, Washington. United States population was 92,228,496.

1911 — Triangle Shirt Waist Company fire killed 144 sweatshop workers in New York City. First practical self-starters for automobile developed by Charles F. Kettering.

1912 — Steamship, *Titanic*, sunk; 1,513 drowned. F.W. Woolworth Company formed. Republic of China established.

1913 — Armory Show of modern art held in New York City. Income tax authorized by Constitutional Amendment (sixteenth).

1914 — Panama Canal opened.

1914-1918 — World War I.

1915 — Farm tractor developed by Henry Ford.

1917 — United States entered World War I. Bobbed hair became fashionable for women. Bolshevik Revolution in Russia. Earliest jazz recording (jazz music began to develop in the United States in the nineteenth century).

1918 — Daylight savings time introduced in the United States.

| | 1919 | League of Nations formed. Eighteenth Constitutional amendment ratified and Volstead Act passed prohibiting the manufacture, sale, transport, or import of "intoxicating liquors." |

Town population 4,200. Heath's Dairy established by William H. Heath (sold to N. Barry Dancy in 1985).

1920 — Nineteenth constitutional amendment ratified giving women the right to vote. First commercial radio broadcast (Pittsburgh, Pennsylvania). United States population was 106,021,537.

First town historian, Harriet C. D. Wiltsie, appointed.

1921

William H. Heath began home delivery of milk from his dairy.

1922 — Emily Post published her book on etiquette.

St. Stephen's Mission became St. Stephen's Episcopal Church.

After 1922

New York Telephone became sole provider of telephone service in the town. Engineering and surveying business, established by Edward Boutelle, involved in many local building projects.

1923

1923-1928 — Process for freezing foods developed by Clarence Birdseye.

New York Central Railroad opened a freight classification yard in Selkirk.

1924 — Spin dry washing machine invented. George Gershwin composed *Rhapsody in Blue*.

Delmar School building built at the corner of Delaware Avenue and Borthwick Avenue (served as elementary and high school at the time and has been the Bethlehem town hall since 1980.)

1925 — Knee length skirts were popular. The Charleston was a favorite dance.

Henry and Helen Zdgiebloski established a farm on Elm Avenue.

1926

Water District #1, town of Bethlehem, purchased Suburban Water Co. Delmar-Elsmere Sewer District formed (served about 90% of the town of Bethlehem by 1969).

1927 — Charles Lindbergh flew across the Atlantic Ocean. First sound moving picture (*The Jazz Singer*) released.

Viaduct over Normanskill improved travel between Albany and Bethlehem. New York Telephone began operating dial switching system in the town.

1928 — China unified by Chang Kai-shek. First scheduled television broadcast (Schenectady, New York). Albany County airport opened in Colonie. Amelia Earhart first woman passenger on a flight across the Atlantic Ocean.

| | 1929 | The Great Depression in the United States. |

Nathaniel Adams Blanchard American Legion Post 1040 was chartered in Delmar. Work began on the *Tri-Village Directory*; first edition was ready for distribution in 1932. The Bethlehem Central School District No. Six formed from schools in Delmar, Slingerlands, Elsmere, Houcks Corners, Bethlehem Center, Glenmont-Normansville, and Van Wies Point. Haswell family established a roadside stand on their farm on Feura Bush Road. Two hundred fourteen farms (17,506 acres) in Bethlehem.

1930 — Grant Wood painted *American Gothic*. United States population was 123,202,624.

The Delmar Free Library turned over to the school district when volunteer Progress Club members could no longer maintain operation. The library purchased the first bookmobile to be operated by a school district library in New York State.

1931 — Empire State Building and George Washington Bridge opened.

Bethlehem's first central high school built on Kenwood Avenue (now the Middle School). Delmar streets named, street signs erected and houses numbered. Delmar Lutheran Mission formed under the direction of St. Paul's and St. Matthew's Mission Society of Albany. First *Tri-Village Area Directory* published.

1932 — Amelia Earhart made a solo flight across the Atlantic Ocean.

1933 — Adolph Hitler appointed German Chancellor.

Save Supply Corporation formed by William Bennett, Earl Vadney, and Harold Williams, Sr. Name changed to Security Supply Corporation in 1936.

1934

Three hundred eight Bethlehem farms had a total of 46,394 chickens.

1935 — United States Congress passed Social Security Act providing benefits for retired workers; amended it to provide for their dependents in 1939.

1936 — Novel *Gone with the Wind* published.

Farm established by Konrad and Anna Laidig Koch near Route 396 in South Bethlehem. Sandy Creek Farm on Wemple Road in Glenmont established by Minor and Mabel Winans Newell and their son, Ernest. State legislation disbanded private road companies and made all roads public highways.

1938 — Radio broadcast *War of the Worlds* frightened listeners all over the United States on Halloween. Forty-hour work week established in the United States.

| | 1939 | World War II. Pan-American Airways began regularly scheduled flights between the United States and Europe. Nylon stockings introduced. Film *Gone With the Wind* released. The Great Depression ends. |

Bethlehem Printing Company formed to purchase Slingerlands Printing Company (closed in 1946 and the building was converted to apartments). Present Delmar post office building opened. One hundred five Bethlehem farms reported a total of 36,579 chickens. One hundred forty eight farms reported 1,450 milk cows. Town population 9,782.

1940 — United States population was 132,164,569.

Private Edward Piper and Private Gordon Palmer were present during the bombing of Pearl Harbor. Bethlehem designated as a "First Class Town." David Main appointed first Chief of Police.

1941 — The United States entered World War II after the Japanese attacked Pearl Harbor.

William B. Phipps elected first town councilman.

1942

South Albany Airport built by William Van Valkenberg (operated by Santo Italiano from 1959-1971 and incorporated by a local group in 1978).

1942-1946

Alcove Full Gospel Church organized, now named Mount Moriah Assembly of God Church. Sunnybrook Farm established by Charles and Virginia Elmendorf Waldenmaier. Town Planning Board established. (Howard P. Paddock was first chairman.) First town zoning laws passed.

1943 — Musical *Oklahoma!* and film *Casablanca* produced. Zoot suit popular. Jitterbug was popular dance.

Staff Sergeant K. Willey of South Bethlehem and Private E. Bennett were killed in action in World War II. In all, thirty Bethlehem men were killed in the war.

1944

1945 — Atomic bomb dropped on Hiroshima, Japan.

Selkirk Moulding Sand Company incorporated (sand business no longer profitable after 1960). Town Recreation Commission established.

1946

Bethlehem Church Reforestation Commission established by The First Reformed Church of Bethlehem to maintain a preserve on land given to The Reformed Protestant Dutch Church of Bethlehem and Jericho by Stephen Van Rensselaer in 1795 (known as the Van Rensselaer Forest and Wildlife Preserve). The Union Free School District No. 1 formed from schools at Cedar Hill, Selkirk, and North Coeymans, South Bethlehem, Jericho, Feura Bush and Bethlehem Church, Callanans Corners and Cedar Grove. Ravena-Coeymans Central School District formed from schools at Ravena, Coeymans, Alcove, Coeymans Hollow, Aquetuck, and New Baltimore. Town employees included in the New York State Retirement System.

Normanside Airport operated by Dominic J. Chiore and Santo Italiano.

An Albany County Farm Report (published in 1953) shows 1,841.6 acres farmed in Bethlehem with 1,125 acres producing corn, nearly 500 acres producing wheat, 43.4 acres producing melons, 174.2 acres producing vegetables, and forty-three farms producing fruit—172 acres producing 5,977 bushels of apples and thirty-five bushels of pears. Toll Gate Restaurant established in Slingerlands near site of toll gate on the plank road.

Niagara Mohawk Power Corporation was formed by the consolidation of several lighting and gas companies to provide lighting in a wide area including Bethlehem. Bethlehem farms reported 38,626 chickens, 91 farms reported 924 milk cows. The number of farms totaled 163 with 14,070 acres. First town board meeting held in the new Town Hall at 393 Delaware Avenue (the former Adams Hotel) on December 30. $1000.00 funding for recreation included in town budget.

More than 350 Bethlehem men and women served in the armed forces during the Korean War. Henry J. Stephany and Alva L. Bleau of Selkirk, John P. Conlon of Delmar, and Donald Snyder of South Bethlehem were killed in action.

1947 — Jackie Robinson was first black major league baseball player in the twentieth century. First supersonic airplane flight.

1947-1954

1949 — People's Republic of China established.

1950 — United States population was 151,325,798.

Early 1950s — Rock 'n' roll music appeared.

1950-1953 — Korean War.

| | 1950s-1960s | African colonies gained independence. |

Present membership of the town board (the supervisor and four elected councilmen) established. First town police car purchased.

1951 — First coast-to-coast television broadcast in the United States.

Niagara Mohawk steam generating plant constructed in Glenmont.

1952

1953 — Color television broadcasts began in the United States. Korean War ended.

A new addition to the Delmar Public Library increased the Library's size by about twelve times. New Bethlehem Central High School building opened with 418 students in grades ten through twelve. New York State Thruway opened. 3 Farms Dairy formed from "Sandy Creek Farm," Bernard and Edward Mocker's farm on route 144 (in Glenmont) and Neil Goes' farm in Cedar Hill.

1954 — Public school segregation outlawed by supreme Court ruling, Brown v. Board of Education.

Delmar Presbyterian Church began as a mission church of the Albany Presbytery. Christian Science services held in member's houses. Community Lutheran Church formed.

1955 — Civil rights movement began with Montgomery, Alabama bus boycott.

Name of the Community Lutheran Church changed to Bethlehem Lutheran Church and new church building dedicated. Glenmont Chapel Association, later the Glenmont Community Church (Reformed), organized. The Union Free School District No. 1 joined the Ravena-Coeymans Central School District to form Ravena-Coeymans-Selkirk Central School District. St. Thomas School opened in Delmar; new building at 42 Adams Place opened in 1959.

1956 — Interstate highway system began with passage of Federal Aid Highway Act. Musical *My Fair Lady* produced.

Present church and parish buildings of St. Stephen's Episcopal Church dedicated.

1957 — Russia launched the first space satellite (Sputnik). Terms "beat", "beatnik", and "beat generation" originated.

Proposal to add fluoride to town water supply defeated 1,571 to 915.

1958 — United States satellite launched.

A new bookmobile purchased by the Delmar Public Library in 1958 was exhibited at the Moscow World's Fair. Town planning board authorized to approve subdivision developments.

1959 — Alaska and Hawaii admitted to statehood.

Town population was 18,936.	1960	United States population was 179,323,175.
Lincoln party, a faction of the Republican party, formed.	1961	First United States manned space flight.
Present building of the Church of St. Thomas the Apostle dedicated.	1962	Environmental movement began with publication of *Silent Spring* by Rachel Carson.
Albertus W. Becker Elementary School built.	1962-1963	
Building of the First Church of Christ, Scientist, dedicated.	1963	Artificial heart developed.
	1964	Attack on U.S. destroyer in the Gulf of Tonkin led to legislation allowing the president to wage war in Vietnam.
Town master plan written after two years of study.	1965	U.S. Marines sent to Vietnam. Ralph Nader published *Unsafe at Any Speed* warning consumers about dangerous automobiles. Social Security act amended to provide health care through Medicare and Medicaid.
Bethlehem Community Church formed. New York State Police barracks at Beckers Corners opened. General Electric Plastics plant opened in Selkirk.	1966	Legislation established Medicare to provide health care for Americans 65 and over. National Organization for Women (NOW) formed.
Callanan family ownership of the Callanan company ceased with the sale of the company to Penn Dixie Company. Hurstville and Karlsfeld annexed by the City of Albany.	1967	
Efforts made to pass legislation to prevent dogs running at large. First ordinance, passed in 1967, proved difficult to enforce. Later ordinance, passed in 1977, provided for penalties and fines for violations.	1967-1977	
First meeting of the Albany County Legislature was held, January 1. Edward H. Sargent, Jr., represented the Town of Bethlehem, the thirty-sixth legislative district. Bethlehem Community Church building dedicated.	1968	
	1969	Woodstock music festival at Bethel, N. Y.
	1970	United States population was 203,302,031.

A new building at Delaware and Borthwick avenues opened by the Delmar Public Library, now called Bethlehem Public Library.	1972	Break-in at National Democratic Committee office in Washington, D. C. (the "Watergate break-in"). *Fiddler on the Roof* longest running Broadway show in history.
The number of Bethlehem residents who served during the Vietnam conflict is not known; nine Bethlehem soldiers are memorialized on the Albany County Vietnam Veterans' monument as casualties. Elm Avenue Park opened. Heath's Dairy offered garden plots for rent to the public (fourteen participants in 1973; 260 by 1980).	1973	Peace treaty signed with Vietnam. U.S. ground troops withdrawn from Vietnam.
	1974	Scandal resulting from the Watergate break-in led to resignation of President Nixon.
Emmanuel Community incorporated by three Catholic charismatic prayer groups, purchased the former retreat center in Glenmont. Henry Hudson Park opened.	1975	
Solid Rock Family Outreach Center church building built. St. Michael's Chapel established by a group of traditional Catholics. Faith Evangelical Lutheran Church formed by members who had left the Bethlehem Lutheran Church. Owens-Corning started producing fiberglass insulating material in Selkirk.	1976	
AIRCO Industrial Gases plant opened in Selkirk.	1977	
Former Delmar Elementary School reopened as Bethlehem town hall. Town population at 24,296.	1980	United States population was 226,542,203.
Town Department of Public Works established.	1981	First space shuttle flight launched by the United States.
Adams Hotel building, former town hall, renamed the Joseph T. Weingold Building, renovated to serve as the headquarters of the Association for Retarded Children, Inc.	1983	
A public access television channel began broadcasting from the Bethlehem Public Library.	1984	
Emmanuel Community, now nondenominational, became Emmanuel Christian Church.	1986	

October 1987 snowstorm caused much damage and, in some areas of the town, a week-long power outage. Town highway department managed the clean-up without exceeding the budget as many neighboring communities were forced to do. Delmar Chabad Center, Hasssidic Jewish outreach organization, founded.	1987	
Town Senior Services department established.	1989	
Faith Evangelical Lutheran Church disbanded; many members transferred to the Lutheran Church of the Holy Spirit in Albany. Lord of Life Lutheran Mission formed in South Bethlehem. Town population 27,552. Town police force accredited under the New York State Law Enforcement Accreditation Program.	1990	Iraq invaded Kuwait. United States population was 248,709,873.
"Pooper-scooper" law passed. Full valuation assessment of real property instituted as required by state law.	1991	Communist government in the Soviet Union overthrown and the Soviet Union broke into many individual autonomous states. United States participated in the Persian Gulf War against Iraq.
New Slingerlands post office opened.	1992	

Efforts have been made to ensure that all dates listed in this chronology are accurate. It has, however, proved difficult to pinpoint the exact dates of some events. Ideas, trends, and even inventions are responses to needs and they develop over a period of time and are used and tested until they succeed in meeting needs. The compiler hopes that the events listed will help the reader understand the events his predecessors in the town of Bethlehem saw happening around them and the trends and developments which affected them.

Reference Notes to the Chapters

Chapter 1: BURIED SECRETS

1. William A. Ritchie, personal communication, 1983.

2. William A. Ritchie and Philip Lord, Jr., undated chart; *Major Aboriginal Projectile Points in New York State.*

3. Virginia L. French, Goes farm site field notes, 1985.

4. Jeffrey D. Hubbard, M.D., personal communication, 1986.

5. Ritchie, personal communication, 1986.

6. Robert E. Funk, personal communication, 1986.

7. Elementary school pupil, Greenville, N.Y., personal communication, 1987.

8. Floyd I. Brewer, Goes farm site field notes, 1987.

9. Marie Svoboda, *Plants that American Indians Used*, 1967, Field Museum of Natural History.

10. Funk, personal communication, 1988.

11. Funk, personal communication, 1988.

12. Funk, *Recent Contributions*, 249.

13. Funk, personal communication, 1988.

14. Ritchie and Funk, *Aboriginal Settlement Patterns*, 59.

15. Stephen Brown and Clark Galloway, personal communication, 1991.

16. Ritchie, *Archaeology of New York*, 202.

17. Ritchie, personal communication, 1986.

18. Bill of Sale for Land in Bethlehem, 1652, Albany Institute of History and Art, McKinney Library.

19. Van der Donck, *New Netherlands*.

20. Elementary school pupil, Greenville, N.Y., personal communication, 1987.

21. Van der Donck, *New Netherlands*, 79-80.

22. Van der Donck, *New Netherlands*, 86-87.

23. Robert S. Grumet, five part series on local Indian history, in *Hudson Valley Magazine*, January-June 1991.

24. Grumet, part 2.

25. Grumet, part 3.

26. *A Proud Heritage.*

Chapter 2: COLONIAL BEGINNINGS

1. Or perhaps 43° 00', since the latitudes as reported by Emanuel van Meteren (Dutch consul at London where Hudson arrived after his voyage) seem to be off by twenty minutes. Either figure would place the anchorage several miles north of the modern marker erected in Bethlehem's Henry Hudson Park to commemorate the event.

2. The visitor is probably the Dutch mate, whose name we do not know, rather than the English mate, Robert Juet.

3. Emanuel van Meteren, "On Hudson's Voyage, 1610," and Robert Juet, "The Third Voyage of Master Henry Hudson, 1610," in Jameson, *Narratives of New Netherland*, 7, 22-23.

4. Johan de Laet, "New World," 1625, 1630, 1633, 1640 in Jameson, *Narratives of New Netherland*, 47.

5. Jameson, *Narratives of New Netherland*. Writer-explorer Johan de Laet saw the fort and has left us this description. Van Cleef was a veteran adventurer who made twelve trips to the New World.

6. Brodhead, *History of the State*, 1:82; O'Callaghan, *History of New Netherland*, 1:78.

7. Nicolaes van Wassenaer, "Historisch Verhael," 1624-1630, in Jameson, *Narratives of New Netherland*, 84-85.

8. Brodhead, *History of the State*, 1:182.

9. The English equivalent, patron, no longer conveys the same prestige in modern usage; Italian *padrone* perhaps still does.

10. Van Laer, *Bowier Manuscripts*, 154, 157-58.

11. Gehring, *Land Papers*, 2-3; van Laer, *Bowier Manuscripts*, 158-61, 805-6.

12. Cottamack, Nawanemit, Abantsene, Sagiskwa, and Kanamoack (the spelling of their names varies considerably from one document to the next).

13. In another transcription called Secktanook.

14. Gehring, *Land Papers*, 2-3; van Laer, *Bowier Manuscripts*, 166-69. The clerical copy from which *Land Papers* was translated gives the year erroneously as 1631, however, this is clearly the purchase confirmed by the Indians at Manhattan in August 1630.

15. The sale was certified in May. The Indians were listed as Papsicene, Kemptas, Nancoutamhat, and Sickenosen.

16. Gehring, *Land Papers*, 4; van Laer, *Bowier Manuscripts*, 181, 196-201.

17. The northern portion of the island is now part of the port of Albany; the southern end is still within Bethlehem's bounds.

18. Van Laer, *Bowier Manuscripts*, 169-70, 197-99, 223.

19. Van Laer, *Bowier Manuscripts*, 308, 49.

20. Van Laer, *Bowier Manuscripts*, 208-11.

21. Van Laer, *Bowier Manuscripts*, 806, 808.

22. Van Laer, *Bowier Manuscripts*, 822.

23. Van Laer, *Bowier Manuscripts*, 286.

24. Van Laer, *Bowier Manuscripts*, 286-87.

25. Van Laer, *Bowier Manuscripts*, 427.

26. Van Laer, *Bowier Manuscripts*, 559, 665, 806.

27. David Pietersz de Vries, "Korte Historiael ende Journaels Aenteyckeninge," 1633-1643 (1655), in Jameson, *Narratives of New Netherland*, 206-7.

28. Van Laer, *Bowier Manuscripts*, 809, 459-60.

29. Of course, the name Schuyler was not applied to the flats until their purchase by Philip Pietersen Schuyler in 1672.

30. Van Laer, "Translation of the Letter," *Dutch Settlers Society*, 26.

31. Johannes Megapolensis, Jr., "A Short Account of the Mohawk Indians," in Jameson, *Narratives of New Netherland*, 170.

32. Van der Donck, *New Netherlands*, 32. The English title incorrectly makes a plural of New Netherland.

33. Van Laer, *Correspondence of Jeremias van Rensselaer*, 406.

34. The Mill Creek is now confined to a storm drain in the city of Rensselaer.

35. Van Laer, *Bowier Manuscripts*, 186-89, 222, 309, 807.

36. A third partner also signed but never fulfilled his obligations under the contract.

37. He spelled his name both as Bratt and Brat.

38. The following account is based upon Christoph, *Albert Andriessen Bradt*.

39. Robert G. Cooney, "Bradt Records from Amsterdam," *New York Geneological and Bibliographical Record*, 118:3 (July 1987), 133-34.

40. Van Laer, *Bowier Manuscripts*, 833.

41. Van Laer, *Court of Rensselaerswyck*, 32-33, 35-36, 86, 88, 89.

42. Van Laer, *Court of Rensselaerswyck*, 90, 101, 106; van Laer, *Bowier Manuscripts*, 777, 833.

43. Van Laer, *Bowier Manuscripts*, 742, 736.

44. Van Laer, *Court of Rensselaerswyck*, 198; van Laer, *Bowier Manuscripts*, 777-79.

45. Van Laer, *Court of Albany, Rensselaerswyck, and Schenectady*, 2:183: van Laer, *Correspondence of Maria van Rensselaer*, 135.

46. Van Laer, *Court of Rensselaerswyck*, 140.

47. Pearson, *Early Records*, 4:73. Before the year was out, Claess's widow, with four young children to support, married Jan Tyssen Goes.

48. Van Laer, *Correspondence of Jeremias van Rensselaer*, 295; Pearson, *Early Records*, 3:165-67; van Laer, "Protocol of Dirck van Schelluyne," *Dutch Settlers Society*, 12-13.

49. For an account of him, see van Laer, "Settlers of Rensselaerswyck," *Dutch Settlers Society*, 22-24.

50. Jeremias had succeeded his brother, Jan Baptist, as director in 1660.

51. Van Laer, *Correspondence of Jeremias van Rensselaer*, 357-58, 386, 406-7, 445-45; van Laer, *Correspondence of Maria van Rensselaer*, 132.

52. Danckaerts, *Journal*, 215.

53. Van Laer, *Correspondence of Jeremias van Rensselaer*, 444-45.

54. Van Laer, *Correspondence of Maria van Rensselaer*, 95,

115, 147-48, 185-86. Gerritsen's move is mentioned by O'Callaghan, *History of New Netherland*, 1:433.

55.   Sometimes called Cornelis Segers, Junior, to distinguish him from other Cornelis Cornelissens. He was also known as Young Kees or by the diminutive Keesie to distinguish him from his father; both father and son were also known as Kees Wip (or Wyp), the meaning of which is uncertain.

56.   Presumably this was one of the two creeks which Route 144 crosses in Glenmont between Retreat House Road and Feura Bush Road. That would place this farm behind Cabbage Island, immediately south of Westerlo Island.

57.   Jeremias van Rensselaer, "Account Book;" van Laer, *Court of Rensselaerswyck*, 212; van Laer, *Correspondence of Jeremias van Rensselaer*, 176, 222.

58.   Van Laer, *Correspondence of Jeremias van Rensselaer*, 406-9.

59.   Van Laer, *Court of Albany, Rensselaerswyck, and Schenectady*, 1:183-84, 2:139; Jeremias van Rensselaer, "Account Book."

60.   Van Laer, *Correspondence of Maria van Rensselaer*, 28, 39, 113, 116, 130, 133; van Laer, *Court of Albany, Rensselaerswyck, and Schenectady*, 3:261; Pearson, *Early Records*, 3:520.

61.   Van Laer, *Correspondence of Maria van Rensselaer*, 132-35, 157, 170.

62.   Gehring, *Fort Orange Court Minutes*, 159; van Laer, *Court of Fort Orange and Beverwyck*, 1:185.

63.   Van Laer, *Court of Fort Orange and Beverwyck*, 2:192 or Gehring, *Fort Orange Court Minutes*, 437.

64.   Van Laer, *Court of Albany, Rensselaerswyck, and Schenectady*, 2:141,284, 3:47; van Laer, "Protocol of Dirck van Schelluyne," *Dutch Settlers Society*, 12-13.

65.   Van Laer, "Albany Notarial Papers," *Dutch Settlers Society*, 11-12.

66.   Van Laer, *Bowier Manuscripts*, 550, 824-25.

67.   Van Laer, *Bowier Manuscripts*, 824-25.

68.   Van Laer, *Court of Rensselaerswyck*, 67-68.

69.   Van Laer, *Bowier Manuscripts*, 561, 825; van Laer, *Court of Rensselaerswyck*, 17, 33, 44-46, 57, 75. He was charged for a farm from 1642, barn from 1644, and hay barrack from 1645, but for a dwelling house only from 1646, so he did not live on the farm for the first four years that he worked it.

70.   Van Laer, *Court of Rensselaerswyck*, 41-43, 45.

71.   Van Laer, *Court of Rensselaerswyck*, 59.

72.   Credit for this discovery should be given to Florence A. Christoph.

73.   In an early Indian deed, it is called the Sakax.

74.   Van Laer, *Court of Rensselaerswyck*, 97.

75.   Van Laer, *Court of Rensselaerswyck*, 100-101.

76.   Pearson, *Early Records*, 1:171, 3:406-7, 519-20.

77.   Van Laer, *Bowier Manuscripts*, 819, 823-24; van Laer, *Court of Rensselaerswyck*, 106-7.

78.   Van Laer, *Correspondence of Jeremias van Rensselaer*, 222.

79. Jeremias van Rensselaer, "Account Book."

80. O'Callaghan, *Documentary History of the State*, 2:51.

Chapter 3: LIFE IN AN ENGLISH COLONY

1. Many of Rensselaerswyck's records for this time period were destroyed in a fire in 1911, and it is uncertain when lifetime leases were first offered. Some writers have credited Kiliaen's mother, Maria van Cortlandt van Rensselaer, with influencing him in this decision, and if they are correct, then the first lifetime leases were offered in 1687 or 1688. Kiliaen became manor lord upon the death of his cousin (also named Kiliaen), which occurred on or about February 22, 1687; Maria died January 24, 1689.

2. The assembly had eighteen representatives from nine constituencies (counties and manors) in 1691, thirty-one representatives from fourteen constituencies by 1775.

3. Kim, *Landlord and Tenant*, 235-38.

4. There were three patroons between 1719 and 1769, each of whom died young.

5. Kim, *Landlord and Tenant*, 211, 238.

6. Hamilton, *Itinerarium*.

7. Dutch original in the Albany Institute of History and Art, with translation by Charles T. Gehring.

8. The text has 'haystacks', which makes no sense. We presume the error is with the translator.

9. Kalm, *Travels*, 332.

10. Kalm, *Travels*, 356, 611-13.

11. Johnson, *Papers*, 211.

12. Hamilton, *Itinerarium*, 87-89.

13. Hamilton, *Itinerarium*, 73.

14. Hamilton, *Itinerarium*, 74.

15. For the observations in this paragraph, I am indebted to the late historian and museum curator, Robert G. Wheeler.

16. Hamilton, *Itinerarium*, 89.

17. The editor of the *Itinerarium* supposed that he stayed on Papscanee Island, but that is on the east side of the river and Hamilton could not have walked from there to Albany.

18. Hamilton, *Itinerarium*, 80-81.

19. Christoph, *Upstate*, 48-61.

20. According to Peter Kalm, among others.

21. Christoph, *Upstate*, 148-206, 213-18.

22. Albany County Clerk's office.

23. Schermerhorn Island, formerly held by William Pietersen van Slyck, nicknamed Neef (Dutch for nephew).

24. "Kees Oom," Dutch for Uncle Kees, a nickname of Cornelis Teunissen van Vechten.

25. Sill, "Papers."

26. No record has been found of their wedding, which probably occurred at the Anglican Church in New York City where Rensselaer's father had been a vestryman for many years. The early marriage records of that church were lost in a fire. We assume the couple was married in 1730, their first child being baptized at the Reformed Church in Albany on February 21, 1731.

27. "Miscellaneous Manuscripts," (#26) New York State Library. In the same collection is a Dutch letter to Nicoll from his wife's uncle, Jacob Marius Groen, (#23).

28. Johnson, *Papers*, 13, 211.

29. Kalm, *Travels*, 342.

30. Kalm, *Travels*, 332.

31. Kalm, *Travels*, 335.

32. Kalm, *Travels*, 334.

33. Hamilton, *Itinerarium*, 90.

34. Kalm, *Travels*, 342.

35. Kalm, *Travels*, 335-36.

36. "Bethlehem, a town in Albany co. New York, very fruitful in pastures, and has large quantities of excellent butter." In Morse, *The American Gazetteer*.

37. Kalm, *Travels*, 334-35.

38. Kalm, *Travels*, 346-47, 605.

39. Variously spelled. A footnote in the Johnson, *Papers*, 13:183, indicates that 'suppan' was made with corn and beans.

40. Johnson, *Papers*, 211.

41. Kalm, *Travels*, 346-47, 605, 629.

42. Kalm, *Travels*, 606-7, 349.

43. Kalm, *Travels*, 614-15.

44. Johnson, *Papers*, 211.

45. Kalm, *Travels*, 316.

46. Kalm, *Travels*, 343, 346, 614.

47. Kalm, *Travels*, 346, 615.

48. Hamilton, *Itinerarium*, 75.

49. Johnson, *Papers*, 197.

50. Kalm, *Travels*, 629.

51. Kalm, *Travels*, 333-34.

52. Hamilton, *Itinerarium*, 78.

53. Hamilton, *Itinerarium*, 89-90.

54. Kalm, *Travels*, 614.

55. The boundary between Albany and Bethlehem has been moved several times since then; both Cherry Hill and Schuyler Mansion are now well within the city of Albany.

56. In addition to the close relationships given above, it

should be noted that Francis Nicoll and Philip Van Rensselaer were related more distantly to Philip Schuyler and his wife and to the patroon.

57.   His will was proved April 6, 1790. One cannot imagine why the family would wait until 1790 to prove the will unless 1790 was when he died.

58.   In 1767 he was living in Albany. Christoph, *Upstate*, 18.

59.   Blackburn, *Cherry Hill*, 1.

Chapter 4: BETHLEHEM IN THE NEW NATION

1.   Selkirk, *James Selkirk (1756-1820) and His Descendents.*

2.   Werner, *Civil List*, v.p.

3.   Morse, *The American Gazetteer.*

4.   Howell and Tenney, *History of the County*, 73.

5.   Howell and Tenney, *History of the County*, 779.

6.   "Maude's Travels" in Munsell, *The Annals of Albany*, 3:131-32.

7.   People continued to apply the title to the manor lords, although it had no legal status once Rensselaerswyck ceased to be an independent colony.

8.   New York passed a law in 1799 (several times amended and refined) for gradual emancipation. Any child born to a slave after July 4, 1800, was to be free but would have to work for a certain number of years (comparable to indentured service) for the owner of the parents. All slaves were to be freed by 1827. The former owner would be responsible for the upkeep of any unable to care for themselves; this provision was inserted to deal with unscrupulous persons who would give freedom to the aged and infirm in order to be rid of them.

9.   While we do not attempt to discuss the history of communities which are no longer part of Bethlehem, it should at least be noted here that Bethlehem at one time included the communities of Callanans Corners (in part), Clarksville, Feura Bush (originally Jerusalem), New Salem, Helderberg, New Scotland, New Scotland Station, Onesquethaw (at one time called Tarrytown), and Unionville (formerly Union Church).

10.   Spafford, *Gazetteer of the State*, 51.

11.   Haydon, *Upstate Travels*, 62.

12.   Spafford, *Gazetteer of the State*, 51.

13.   Spafford, *Gazetteer of the State*, 51.

14.   The house is described by Kenney, *The Gansevoorts of Albany*, 136-37. The book also contains much information about Leonard Gansevoort.

15.   Spafford, *Gazetteer of the State*, 51.

16.   Howell and Tenney, *History of the County*, 796-97.

17.   Howell and Tenney, *History of the County*, 798.

18.   Spafford, *Gazetteer of the State*, 51.

19.   "Maude's Travels" in Munsell, *The Annals of Albany*, 3:131-32.

20.   Howell and Tenney, *History of the County*, 798.

21. Morse, *The American Gazetteer*.

22. A useful work on the subject is by Booraem, *Republican Party in New York*.

23. Howell and Tenney, *History of the County*, 209-20.

24. Spafford, *Gazetteer of the State*, 51.

Chapter 5: BUSINESS AND INDUSTRY

1. Douglas Campbell, "Historical Fallacies Regarding Colonial New York." Address delivered before the Oneida Historical Society, Utica, NY, January 14, 1897. New York State Library.

2. Christoph, *People of the Town*, 262-64.

3. Van Laer, *Court of Albany, Rensselaerswyck, and Schenectady*, 1:337. Cruyff also spelled as Cruyf and Cruiff.

4. Pearson, *Geneologies of the First Settlers*, 80.

5. Kenney, *Albany: Crossroads of Liberty*, 11.

6. Christoph, *People of the Town*, vii.

7. Jacob S. Markle, "History of the Township of Bethlehem." In Howell and Tenney, *History of the County*, 790.

8. Jacob S. Markle, "History of the Township of Bethlehem." In Howell and Tenney, *History of the County*, 791.

9. Map, "Portion of Albany County and City of Albany," ca. 1880, Bethlehem Public Library.

10. Bennett, *Times Remembered*, 1-4.

11. Kimball, *The Capital Region*, 2:374.

12. Bethlehem Historical Association, *Ice Harvesting* (videotape). Bethlehem Public Library.

13. "Assessment Roll: Town of Bethlehem, 1917." Bethlehem Town Hall.

14. "Minutes of Town of Bethlehem," book dated 1794. Bethlehem Town Hall.

15. "Minutes of Town of Bethlehem," book dated 1892-1917.

16. *Laws of the State of New York*, Twentieth Session (printed by Thomas Greenleaf), 467.

17. *Proceedings of the Common Council of the City of Albany*, A.D. 1870, 6-7.

18. *Laws of the State of New York*, Twenty-Seventh Session (printed by John Barber), 323.

19. Parker, *Landmarks of Albany County*, 489.

20. *Laws of the State of New York*, Twenty-Seventh Session (printed by John Barber), 330.

21. Bennett, *Times Remembered*, 17.

22. Bennett, *Times Remembered*, 18.

23. *Laws of the State of New York*, Twenty-Eighth Session (printed by John Barber), 63.

24. *Proceedings of the Common Council of the City of Albany*, A.D. 1870, 81.

25. *Laws of the State of New York*, Seventieth Session (printed by Charles Van Benthuysen), 1:216.

26. *Laws of the State of New York*, Seventieth Session, 1:225.

27. "Certificate of Incorporation," The South Bethlehem Plank Road Company.

28. *Laws of the State of New York*, Sixty-First Session (printed by E. Croswell), 254.

29. "Bethlehem Highway Department," report of town roads at end of 1989. Measurement of state and county road lengths by author from the map of Bethlehem by Jimapco, Inc., 1989.

30. Shaughnessy, *Delaware & Hudson*, 60.

31. Harsha, *Noted Living Albanians*, 151.

32. Shaughnessy, *Delaware & Hudson*, 196.

33. *The Spotlight*, May 10, 1979.

34. *New York Times*, May 30, 1910.

35. *Proceedings of the Common Council of the City of Albany*, A.D. 1915, 2:7-8.

36. Albany Port Commission, *The Port of Albany* (dedication booklet, June 6-7, 1932), 29.

37. *Consolidated Laws Service*, "Town Law," Section 130.

38. "Minutes of Town of Bethlehem," 1947, 177.

39. *The Spotlight*, November 14, 1984.

40. The Suburban Water Company, *The Suburban Water System* (pamphlet dated December 26, 1918), Town Historian files.

41. W.B. Eddy, "Telephone Development in Albany" (*The Telephone Review*, October-November, 1911), 247.

42. *Albany County Post*, November 21, 1930.

43. Niagara Mohawk Power Corporation, "The Niagara Mohawk Story 1823-1983," company reference manual, 398.

44. "Niagara Mohawk Story," 1.

45. Niagara Mohawk, "Niagara Mohawk's Albany Steam Station" (undated company pamphlet).

46. "The Callanan Road Improvement Company 1883-1949," unpublished company manuscript, author unknown. Town Historian files.

47. *CRH Annual Report 1988*.

48. *Albany County Post*, November 21, 1930.

49. Alice Porter, "Delmar Then and Now 1926-1974," unpublished manuscript. Bethlehem Public Library.

50. Spinosa, interview with author, September 29, 1991 (unpublished transcript). Bethlehem Public Library.

51. *Albany Times Union*, December 1, 1928.

52. *Albany County Post*, April 18, 1930.

53. Howell and Tenney, *History of the County*, 642.

54. Penn Central, "Alfred E. Perlman Yard" (undated

company brochure). Town Historian files.

55. *The Spotlight*, October 1, 1986.

56. *The Spotlight*, April 18, 1974.

Chapter 6: HOUSES OF FAITH

1. Andrews, *Dictionary of American History*, 810.

2. Roger W. Stump, "The Evolution of Albany's Religious Landscape," in Roberts and Cockrell, *Historic Albany*, 3.

3. Van Laer, *Bowier Manuscripts*, 63.

4. Van Laer, *Bowier Manuscripts*, 208.

5. Jacob S. Markle, "History of the Township of Bethlehem," in Howell and Tenney, *History of the County*, 783.

6. Van Woert, *First Reformed Church of Bethlehem*, 41. Mitford M. Mathews defines thimble-skein as "a conical sheath for the spindle of an axle...." (*A Dictionary of Americanisms on Historical Principles*, entry "thimble," 1723). He defines skein as "A metal thimble protecting the spindle of a wooden axle" (1553). In the *Oxford English Dictionary*, a thimble-skein is defined as "a skein for an axle made in tubular form...." (entry "Thimble"); an example of its use is, "When [the axle- spindle is made] of wood, it is strengthened by metallic straps called skeins, and sometimes by a conical sheath called a thimble-skein." *The Oxford English Dictionary* defines skein as "A metal head or thimble protecting the spindle of a wooden axle" (entry "skein").

7. Christoph, *People of the Town*, 1.

8. Bennett, *More Times Remembered*, 70.

9. Martha Slingerland, interview with author, September 2, 1992.

10. Martha Slingerland, interview with author, September 2, 1992.

11. Beatrice L. Potter, "History of the Delmar Reformed Church from 1841 to 1991," unpublished manuscript, Delmar Reformed Church, 1.

12. Slingerland and Moak, *Jacob Moak*, 76.

13. Bennett, *More Times Remembered*, 70.

14. Meads Corners is on Route 32, also known as Indian Fields Road; Tarrytown is on Route 301, between Clarksville and Meads Corners.

   Onesquethau, with the local title of Tarrytown, is a hamlet about one and a half miles south of Clarksville. It is said to have received its local appellation from the fact that there was once a large building known as "the Castle" in which was kept a tavern which became the resort of idle and dissolute persons who would "tarry" there until unseemly hours. (Parker, *Landmarks of Albany County*, 552-53.)

   The late Harold W. Thompson, folklorist and former professor of English at the New York State College for Teachers (now State University of New York at Albany) and Cornell University, however, has another explanation:

   Nobody feels sure about the name of the city of Tarrytown [in Westchester County], although many like to believe that farmers used to tarry there at an old inn on the present Post Road. Washinton Irving has helped along this interpretation:

This name was given, we are told, in former days, by the good housewives of the adjacent county, from the inveterate propensity of their husbands to linger about the village tavern on market days.

I should like to accept this casual naming, but science demands that I add the weighty opinion of President Ernest Griffen of the Westchester Historical Society that the name derives from *tarwe*, a Dutch word for wheat. (Thompson, *Body, Boots & Britches*, 452-53.)

The name of New Scotland's Tarrytown may also derive from Dutch *tarwe*.

15. Bennett, *More Times Remembered*, 69.

16. Bennett, *More Times Remembered*, 34.

17. Manuscript of church history, Glenmont Community Church office.

18. "Our Heritage," Bicentennial publication, Presbyterian Church in New Scotland, N.Y., 39.

19. "Our Heritage," 41-42.

20. Bennett, *More Times Remembered*, 70.

21. Jacob S. Markle, "History of the Township of Bethlehem," in Howell and Tenney, *History of the County*, 784.

22. Jean Felt, "A History of Delmar Presbyterian Church," (April 1991), in *Parish Handbook*, February 1992.

23. Felt, "A History of Delmar Presbyterian Church."

24. Bennett, *More Times Remembered*, 50.

25. Bennett, *More Times Remembered*, 50.

26. A history of the church tells us that

The entrance to the church faced the street and the pulpit was also on the same end of the building. By this arrangement tardiness brought its own punishment, as such offenders were forced to face the audience, who undoubtedly stared at them with self-righteous complacency.

This fact prevented the front pews being empty, as is too often the case today, as these seats must have seemed to the late arrivals to be places of refuge where they might more quickly end the trying ordeal.

The seats were the old-fashioned, straight backed sort, which were not conducive to comfortable slumber. As was customary in those days, the brethren and sisters sat on opposite sides of the church. (*Eighty Years of Methodism in Delmar*, 6-7.)

27. *Board of Trustees: Secretary (1834-1914)*, manuscript records, archives, Slingerlands Community United Methodist Church, entry for October 3, 1871.

28. *Board of Trustees*, entry for February 24, 1872.

29. *Board of Trustees*, entry for April 14, 1873.

30. Charles A. Schade was also responsible for renovations of and other additions to the Slingerlands Community United Methodist Church as well as to the Slingerlands fire house. He and Gilbert Van Auken of Delmar were the architects of a major addition to the Slingerlands Elementary School.

31.   *The Spotlight*, February 28, 1980.

32.   Conference is a term which was used originally by John Wesley, the founder of Methodism, to denote an annual meeting of church officials from a certain geographical location. Bethlehem's three Methodist churches are members of the Troy Conference, which includes northeastern New York and all of Vermont.

33.   Ruth Cunningham, R.S.C.T., "Life Through 125 Years (1852-1978)," archives, Convent of the Sacred Heart, Albany, 5.

34.   Parker, *Landmarks of Albany County*, 267. John Tracy, a prominent business man in Albany, was by 1863 the sixth richest man in the city; see Bowers, *Albany's South End*, 32.

35.   Craigie, *Kenwood*, 7.

36.   Cunningham, "Life Through 125 Years," 9-10.

37.   Brochure published on the occasion of the dedication on September 16, 1962, of the present St. Thomas Church.

38.   Brochure published on the occasion of the dedication on September 16, 1962, of the present St. Thomas Church.

39.   Father J. Vida Elmer, *The Smoke of the Antichrist*, (1983), St. Michaels Chapel, 2-3.

40.   Bennett, *More Times Remembered*, 115.

41.   Church brochure (November 1961).

42.   *The Spotlight*, March 31, 1977.

43.   *Albany Times Union*, May 31, 1992.

44.   Roseberry, *Flashback*, 98-99.

45.   Jacob S. Markle, "History of the Township of Bethle hem," in Howell and Tenney, *History of the County*, 786.

46.   Thomas Davidson, "A Comprehensive History of the Development of the Kenwood Area," 1966, 17. Bethle-hem Public Library.

47.   Parker, *Landmarks of Albany County*, 498; Jacob S. Markle, "History of the Township of Bethlehem," in Howell and Tenney, *History of the County*, 785.

48.   Information from notes written June 25, 1957, in files of the Bethlehem Public Library, by Mrs. William M. Scrafford (born Grace M. Creble), former resident of Normansville and member of the church, and from Mr. and Mrs. Edwin A. Tompkins, present church members, to author, July 1992.

49.   "Historical Sketch," quoted in *Christian Science*, 24.

50.   Information from Brenda Winnie, church secretary, to author, July 1992.

51.   Statement of purposes and aims of Emmanuel Chris-tian Church by Royal and Mary Cutler, to author, July 1992.

52.   *Jehovah's Witnesses*, 8.

53.   *Jehovah's Witnesses*, 14-15.

54.   Van Laer, *Bowier Manuscripts*, 208.

55. Robert S. Alexander, "Albany's Dutch Church," in Roberts and Cockrell, *Historic Albany*, 66-67.

56. Andrews, *Dictionary of American History*, 180.

57. Morris, *Encyclopedia of American History*, 114.

58. Morris, *Encyclopedia of American History*, 114.

Chapter 7: COMMUNITY ORGANIZATIONS

1. Floyd Brewer, "Community Organizations in Brief," 1989 (data gathering form; summary in appendix).

2. Wilcoxen, *Seventeenth Century Albany*, 122.

3. Wilcoxen, *Seventeenth Century Albany*, 122.

4. M.R. Clowe, "Recipe from Grandmother Slingerlands Cookbook," 1750. Bethlehem Public Library.

5. "Albany Committee on Safety, Minutes, 1777," original transcript, Albany Institute of History and Art.

6. "Quacks and Pretenders," in *Albany Journal*, March 2, 1789.

7. Dancing School advertisement, in *Albany Journal*, May 12, 1788.

8. Brewer, "Community Organizations in Brief."

9. Flossie Smith, personal communication, 1989.

10. "Book of Strays 1794-1823." Town of Bethlehem archives.

11. Brewer, "Community Organizations in Brief."

12. Delmar Progress Club constitution.

13. Lions Club promotional publication, undated.

14. Allison Bennett, "Brief History of the Tawasentha Chapter, Daughters of the American Revolution," 1992.

15. "Minutes of Town of Bethlehem," February 1964.

16. Howard Gmelch, personal communication, 1989.

17. Howard Gmelch, personal communication, 1989.

18. American Association of Retired Persons. News Bulletin, 1972, 8:4.

19. J. Robert Hendrick, Jr., personal communication, 1991.

20. Brewer, "Community Organizations in Brief."

21. Holly Billings, personal communication, 1990.

22. Robert Alexander, personal communication, 1990.

23. *Life*, ca. 1955. Photograph of Delmar Men's Orchestra in rehearsal.

24. Ralph Mead, personal communication, 1990.

25. Delmar Community Orchestra constitution, 1990.

26. "Corps Drums up Interest in Colonial-Style Music," *The Spotlight*, August 15, 1990.

27. "Bicentennial Pageant Program," 1976, Town of Bethlehem.

28. "Sewing Group Plans Card Party," *Altamont Enterprise*, February 18, 1960.

29. MacDonald, *No Idle Hands*, 248.

30. Brewer, "Community Organizations in Brief."

31. Bennett, *Times Remembered*, 49.

32. Adrian B. Arnold, personal communication, 1992.

33. Irving VanWoert, Bethlehem Tomboys scrapbook, 1989.

34. Linda Burtis, "Still Playing the Game," *Times Union*, December 16, 1990.

35. Wyman Osterhout, personal communication, 1992, to John B. Guertze from a member of the first Boy Scout troop in Bethlehem.

36. Ralph T. LaBarge, personal communication, 1991.

37. "Fifth Annual Girl Scout Yearbook," 1928, 47.

38. Brewer, "Community Organizations in Brief."

39. Virginia Cornell, 1992. *Tri-Village Directory* history file.

40. Kenneth E. McNary, 1992. Elsmere Fire Department scrapbook.

41. Minutes of meetings, Selkirk Fire Department, 1928.

42. Minutes of meetings, Selkirk Fire Department, 1928.

43. Comment by Reverend Charles Kaulfass, minutes of meetings, Selkirk Fire Department, 1931.

44. Minutes of meetings, Selkirk Fire Department, 1956.

45. Minutes of meetings, North Bethlehem Fire Department, 1952.

46. *The Spotlight*, February 19, 1992.

47. Brewer, "Community Organizations in Brief."

48. Kenneth Ringler, "From the Supervisor's Desk," 1992, 18:1.

Chapter 8: CHANGING FAMILIES

1. Woodrow Wilson, excerpts from speech made to prospective citizens, 1915. Undated notes.

2. Christoph, *Albert Andriessen Bradt*, 9.

3-10. Peter R. Christoph, unpublished family notes, 1988.

11. "Minutes of Town of Bethlehem," April 15, 1797.

12-15. Peter R. Christoph, unpublished Slingerland family notes, 1988.

16. Excerpts from the *Congressional Globe*, 1847-1848, John I. Slingerland papers, Town of Bethlehem archives.

17. "Record of Manumission of Slaves: 1799-1827," Town of Bethlehem.

18-21. John I. Slingerland account book, 1854.

22. Floyd Brewer, Slingerland family vault site, field notes, 1981.

23. Mendel-Mesick-Cohen Architects, "The Nicoll-Sill House: A Historic Structure Report," 1976

24. Floyd Brewer, Ann Jacobs, and Eleanor Norrix, interim report on bottle finds at the Nicoll-Sill estate, 1989. BethlehemArcheology Group.

25. Brewer, Jacobs, and Norrix, interim report.

26. Floyd Brewer, Nicoll-Sill field notes, 1986.

27. Floyd Brewer, Nicoll-Sill field notes, 1988.

28. "Record of Manumission of Slaves."

29. Bennett, *Times Remembered*, 7.

30. Gutman, *The Black Family*, 3.

31. Undated advertisement in *Harper's Bazaar*. New York: Harper & Brothers, 1883.

32. Marti-Ibanez, *History of American Medicine*, 75.

33. Tony Catalano, undated interview notes, 1987.

34. "Minutes of Town of Bethlehem," undated research notes of author.

35. "Minutes of Town of Bethlehem," 1909.

36. "Ninety Years of the Good Housekeeping Institute," *Good Housekeeping*, February 1990, 74-155. New York: The Hearst Corporation.

37. Marjorie Terrell, personal communication, 1989.

38. Christoph, *People of the Town*.

39. Christoph, *People of the Town*.

40. Allison Bennett, "Glass Greenhouses and Geraniums," *Altamont Enterprise*, August 23, 1974.

41. Bennett, *Times Remembered*, 61.

42. Bennett, *Times Remembered*, 61.

43. Edward W. Boutelle, "Property Owners at Delmar and Elsmere," 1930.

Chapter 9: FROM OXEN TO DIESEL

1. Holbrook, *Down on the Farm*.

2. Van Laer, *Bowier Manuscripts*, 159.

3. Van Laer, *Bowier Manuscripts*, 161, 805-6.

4. Van Laer, *Bowier Manuscripts*, 57, 198-99, 308-9.

5. Van Laer, *Bowier Manuscripts*, 199-200.

6. Van Laer, *Bowier Manuscripts*, 63, 199, 210, 308-9.

7. Van Laer, *Bowier Manuscripts*, 199.

8. Carrier, *Beginnings of Agriculture*, 154.

9. Carrier, *Beginnings of Agriculture*, 154, 158.

10. Van Laer, *Bowier Manuscripts*, 186-88, 212.

11. Van Laer, *Bowier Manuscripts*, 805-6, 813-14, 817, 823.

12. Van Laer, *Bowier Manuscripts*, 810.

13. Van Laer, *Bowier Manuscripts*, 809-810.

14. Van Laer, *Bowier Manuscripts*, 736, 774, 837.

15. Van Laer, *Bowier Manuscripts*, 772-73, 845. Cruyf also spelled as Cruyff and Cruiff.

16. Van Laer, *Bowier Manuscripts*, 775-77.

17. Van Laer, *Bowier Manuscripts*, 775-77.

18. Carrier, *Beginnings of Agriculture*, 23.

19. Carrier, *Beginnings of Agriculture*, 97.

20. Carrier, *Beginnings of Agriculture*, 43, 48-49, 58, 92, 94-95, 97.

21. Keller, *Life Along the Hudson*, 30, 32.

22. *World Book Encyclopedia*, 797.

23. Keller, *Life Along the Hudson*, 32.

24. Wilstach, *Hudson River Landings*, 64

25. *World Book Encyclopedia*, 794.

26. Wilstach, *Hudson River Landings*, 67.

27. *World Book Encyclopedia*, 804.

28. Howell and Tenney, *History of the County*, 776.

29. Cousins, *Hog, Plow and Sith*, 11-12.

30. Ellis, *History of New York*, 164.

31. Ellis, *History of New York*, 164.

32. Cousins, *Hog, Plow and Sith*, 2.

33. Wetterau, *Book of Chronologies*, 193.

34. Wetterau, *Book of Chronologies*, 193.

35. Wetterau, *Book of Chronologies*, 193.

36. Carrier, *Beginnings of Agriculture*, 240-41.

37. Howell and Tenney, *History of the County*, 609.

38. Carrier, *Beginnings of Agriculture*, 155.

39. Ellis, *History of New York*, 170.

40. Ellis, *History of New York*, 171.

41. Howell and Tenney, *History of the County*, 335.

42. Howell and Tenney, *History of the County*, 330.

43. *Agricultural Society*, (1846), 50-52.

44. *Agricultural Society*, (1846), page after 3, 18, 111-18.

45. *Agricultural Society*, (1854), 948.

46. *Agricultural Society*, (1854), 369-70.

47. *Agricultural Society*, (1854), 370,

48. Ellis, *History of New York*, 171.

49. Ellis, *History of New York*, 171.

50. Holbrook, *Down on the Farm*, 102.

51. Howell and Tenney, *History of the County*, 765-796.

52. *Topographical Atlas*, 7.

53. *Topographical Atlas*, 7.

54. Robert Frazier's ledger, copy.

55. Howell and Tenney, *History of the County*, 798.

56. Howell and Tenney, *History of the County*, 799.

57. Grange manuscripts, Bethlehem Public Library.

58. Arthur, *State Grange*, 9.

59. Grange manuscripts, Bethlehem Public Library.

60. Arthur, *State Grange*, 132-34.

61. Arthur, *State Grange*, 130.

62. Ellis, *History of New York*, 497.

63. John Mead, personal communication, 1992.

64. Ellis, *History of New York*, 496-97.

65. Howell and Tenney, *History of the County*, 79; Parker, *Landmarks of Albany County*, 488.

66. Richard Thayer and Margaret Heath, personal communication, 1992.

67. Thomas Newell, personal communication, 1992.

68. Bernard Mocker, personal communication, 1992.

69. Marion Koch, personal communication, 1992.

70. Harry Garry, personal and written communication, 1992.

71. Waldenmaier, Charles and Charles Jr., personal communication, 1991.

72. Waldenmaier, personal communication, 1991.

73. Bennett, *Times Remembered*, 40-41.

74. Richard Hale, personal and written communication, 1992.

75. Warren and Marie Read, personal communication, 1992.

76. M.C. Bond, "New York Census Data by Counties, 1950 Census of Agriculture and Long-Time Changes," Department of Agricultural Economics, New York State College of Agriculture, Cornell University, Ithaca, 7, 9, 11.

77. Bond, "Census Data," 12-13.

78. Bond, "Census Data," 5.

79. John Scharff, personal communication, 1991.

80. Bond, "Census Data," 1.

81. *The Spotlight*, March 18, 1992.

82. *Memoirs of the Board of Agriculture*, 9.

83. *American Agriculturist, Farm Directory*, 25-118.

84. *American Agriculturist, Farm Directory*, insert.

Chapter 10: WILL OF THE PEOPLE

1. Kammen, *Colonial New York*, 38.

2. Flick, *History of the State*, 5:6.

3. Hon. Frank C. Moore, "Early History of Town Government in New York State," *The Consolidated Laws of New York, Annotated, Town Law*, Brooklyn, New York, 1936, vii.

4. Van Laer, Bowier Manuscripts, 740-743.

5. "Journal of the Notes and Proceedings of the General Assembly of the Colony of New York," New York, 1766, 2:388. New York State archives.

6. Kenney, *The Gansevoorts of Albany*, 113.

7. Kenney, *The Gansevoorts of Albany*, 119.

8. *Laws of the State of New York*, (printed by Thomas Greenleaf, 1797), 2:163.

9. *Laws of the State of New York*, (Greenleaf), 2:91.

10. *Laws of the State of New York*, (Greenleaf), 2:166.

11. Howell and Tenney, *History of the County*, 80.

12. *Colonial Laws of New York*, 498.

13. *Colonial Laws of New York*, 539-542.

14. *Laws of the State of New York*, Eleventh Session, 770.

15. *New York Consolidated Laws Service*, 1976, "Town Law," Section 130.

16. Blackburn, *Cherry Hill*, 1.

17. Invitation list, handwritten manuscript, New York State Historical Society archives, New York City.

18. *The Spotlight*, June 8, 1967.

19. *Albany County Post*, May 7, 1948.

20. "Minutes of Town of Bethlehem," April 10, 1947.

21. "Minutes of Town of Bethlehem," December 30, 1950.

22. *Albany Daily Evening Times*, April 13, 1881.

23. *Albany Evening Journal*, April 12, 1848.

24. *Albany Argus*, April 11, 1856.

25. "The Lincoln Story," unknown author, Delmar, 1961. Town Historian files.

26. *The Spotlight*, November 9, 1961.

27. *Journal of Albany County Legislature of Albany County New York 1968*, Albany, 1969, 1.

28. Scrapbook, Women's Republican Club of Bethlehem. Bethlehem Public Library.

29. Cross, interview with author, April 22, 1992.

30. *The Spotlight*, May 14, 1964.

31. Van Laer, *Minutes of the Court (1678-1673)*, 2:16.

32. *Colonial Laws of New York*, 1:29.

33. *The Spotlight*, August 29, 1957.

34. "Minutes of Town of Bethlehem," December 6, 1930.

35. *The Spotlight*, February 2, 1967.

36. *Laws of the State of New York*, Fiftieth Session, 173.

37. "Minutes of Town of Bethlehem," January 2, 1942, November 6, 1951.

38. *Laws of the State of New York*, First Session, 1:15-16.

39. "History of Planning Board," undated, Howard Paddock Papers in Bethlehem Public Library.

40. "Town of Bethlehem Master Plan," Bethlehem Town Hall.

41. "Minutes of Town of Bethlehem," 1957, 276.

42. *Albany County Post*, July 30, 1937.

43. *Laws of the State of New York*, 1945, Chapter 556.

44. "Minutes of Town of Bethlehem," March 25, 1946; May 23, 1946.

45. "Minutes of Town of Bethlehem," February 24, April 17, May 28, June 13, 1947; and October 26, 1949.

46. William Fuller, interview by Margaret Sherman, October 12, 1988. Tape recording, Town Historian files.

47. "Minutes of Town of Bethlehem," September 17, 1969.

48. *Historian's Guide*, A Handbook for Local Historians, The University of the State of New York, 1982, Edmund J. Winslow, Local Historians in New York State, 1.

49. Ruth F. Dickinson, Special Report to Town Board, December 1965.

50. "Minutes of Town of Bethlehem;" 1974, 1983, 1988, 1990.

51. Karen Pelletier, memorandum of senior services history, 1992, Town Hall.

Chapter 11: HAMLETS: A BICENTENNIAL TOUR

1. Phelps, *Albany Handbook* for 1881, 40.

2. [Whish], *Albany Guide Book*, 72.

3. Blackburn, *Cherry Hill*, 1.

4. Munsell wrote that Philip Van Rensselaer was so appointed by Robert Livingston, Esq., "to purchase barreled pork for the use of the Continental army." (*The Annals of Albany*, 7:218).

5. Munsell, *Collections*, 475.

6. Munsell, *Collections*, 475.

7. [Worth], Random Recollections, 8.

8. [Whish], *Albany Guide Book*, 122.

9. In 1824, Spafford mentioned "the hamlet of Rensselaer's mills [Kenwood], at the mouth of Norman's kill, two miles and a half [below the city of Albany]" (Munsell, *The Annals of Albany*, 303; reprinted from Spafford's *Gazetteer of the State*).

10. Thomas Davidson, "A Comprehensive History of the Development of the Kenwood Area," 1966, 1. Bethlehem Public Library.

11. French, *Gazetteer*, 163.

12. Jacob S. Markle, "History of the Township of Bethlehem." In Howell and Tenney, *History of the County*, 783.

13. Davidson, "Kenwood Area," 17.

14. *Bethlehem Chronicle*, September 12, 1959.

15. Concerning the Normanskill gorge at this point: "Water cascades between rock walls one hundred and fifty feet high. The area is geologically unique. Millions of years ago, molten lava intruded vertically through the shale bedrock to produce a 'volcanic dike' which can still be seen at the bottom of the gorge. Also, chert, a rock similar to flint, is found here, and was used by the Indians for arrowheads and tools" (1977 "Drive it Yourself Tour of Albany County," 11).

16. Davidson, "Kenwood Area," 19.

17. Bethlehem Historical Association, "Ice Harvesting," (videotape). Bethlehem Public Library.

18. Davidson, "Kenwood Area," 21.

19. Parker, *Landmarks of Albany County*, 496.

20. Parker, *Landmarks of Albany County*, 3:86.

21. [Whish], *Albany Guide Book*, 26.

22. Parker, *Landmarks of Albany County*, 489.

23. "6th Albany County Drive It Yourself Tour," brochure, 1967, 4-5.

24. The notorious Overslaugh in the Hudson River near Cedar Hill, was one of several hindrances to navigation which made it necessary for large ships to dock at Cedar Hill rather than at Albany. *The Oxford English Dictionary* (entry "Overslaugh") explains that the word is an adaption of Dutch *overslag* from *overslaan* to pass over, omit, pass by, and by means to stop the course or progress of, to bar, obstruct, hinder.

25. Outstanding among the buildings designed by Marcus T. Reynolds are the Flemish Gothic Delaware and Hudson Railroad Building (1915) and its attached Journal Building (1916), inspired by the Cloth Hall at Ypres, Belgium, both in downtown Albany. These buildings now house the central administration offices of the State University of New York (see *Albany Architects*, 19).

26. Ruth Mendel, "Bethlehem Elks Meet in Historic Landmark," *The Helderberg Sun*, March 7, 1978.

27. There is a monument to Dr. MacDonald with a statue of him in the park in Cobleskill, his home town, commemorating his generous assistance in the building of the hospital there (Bennett, *More Times Remembered*, 7).

28. "Ice Harvesting," videotape.

29. Taken from a typescript by Harry C. Dinmore, Jr., 1935, who employed, among several sources of information, recollections of Mr. Duncan H. Sill, a family descendent, and Mr. Sill's article on Caesar in the *New York Geneological and Bibliographical Society Record*, January 1925. The typescript is in the McKinney Library of the Albany Institute of History and Art. See

also, Bennett, *Times Remembered*, 8.

30. Selkirk, *James Selkirk (1756-1820) and His Descendents*.

31. Jean Lyon, personal communication, 1991.

32. Phelps, *The Albany Handbook for 1881*, 40.

33. Phelps, *The Albany Handbook for 1881*, 40.

34. John Slingerland, Daily Journal for 1867, entry for January 9. John Slingerland's manuscript "Daily Journals for 1867 and 1868" are in the possession of his great- granddaughter, Betsey Anrews Mullens Tolman of Slingerlands. She has graciously given the author permission to use quotations from them.

35. Parker, *Landmarks of Albany County*, 490.

36. See for example, the Jimapco map of Bethlehem, 1989. Also, a newspaper obituary stated "A graveside service will be at the Evangelical Protestant Cemetery, Hurstville." *The Spotlight*, July 1, 1992.

37. [Whish], *Albany Guide Book*, 40.

38. *The Spotlight*, June 9, 1977.

39. *The Spotlight*, February 15, 1989.

40. Slingerland, "Daily Journal," July 18, 1867.

41. Slingerland and Moak, *Jacob Moak*, 87.

42. Harold Bullock Slingerland studied under the Slingerlands artist, Edward Buyck, whose home was on McCormack Road near the intersection with New Scotland Avenue.

43. The Peach Festival tickets were given to the Slingerlands Community United Methodist Church by Howard and Jean Clayton, long-time members of the church.

44. Slingerland, "Daily Journal," April 4, 1868.

45. The newspaper articles in this DAR scrapbook in the Bethlehem Public Library are, for the most part, not dated; this one probably was published around 1910.

46. "1976 Drive it Yourself: Three Tours of Albany County," 20.

47. Jacob S. Markle, "History of the Township of Bethlehem." In Howell and Tenney, *History of the County*, 781.

48. Parker, *Landmarks of Albany County*, 493.

49. Richard A. Allen, "Whipple Cast- and Wrought-Iron Bowstring Truss Bridge 1867," *A Report of the Mohawk- Hudson Area Survey*, 135-50. With reference to the inventor's name, Squire was his given name, not a title.

50. "The Tale of Three Centuries," Town of Bethlehem, Women's Republican Club, April 25, 1967. A student of place-names has concluded that the settlement of Elsmere in Cherry County, Nebraska, was "probably named after Mrs. Humphry Ward's onetime popular novel entitled Robert Elsmere" (Lilian L. Fitspatrick, *Nebraska Place- Names*, 37).

51. *Topographical Atlas*, surveyed by Beers, 17. See also the hand-drawn plat accompanying "Abstract of The Title of Part of the Groesbeck farm at Elsmere, Albany County, N.Y.," which shows the location of the rail-

road station in Elsmere, Groesbeck Avenue, and land owned by John Groesbeck.

52. Newspaper article, ca. 1904, in files of the Bethlehem Public Library.

53. Jacob S. Markle, "History of the Township of Bethlehem." In Howell and Tenney, *History of the County*, 781.

54. This record book of the Trustees of the Second M.E. Church of Bethlehem, labeled "Board of Trustees: Secretary (1834 to 1914)," is in the archives of the Community United Methodist Church of Slingerlands. For example, in this record book, it was reported (entry for July 7, 1871) that "The elder [in the Methodist Church in Slingerlands] read a paper from Adamsville."

55. *The Spotlight*, August 18, 1982.

56. Alice Porter, "Delmar Then and Now 1926-1974," 5. Bethlehem Public Library.

57. Letter from Barbara Somers to Mr. Schaefer of Hamagrael School, dated November 30, 1982. Bethlehem Public Library.

58. *The Spotlight*, February 14, 1980.

59. Porter, "Delmar Then and Now," 9.

60. Charlotte Wilcoxen, "How Did It Get Its Name?" In *Commemorative Program of Albany's Spirit of '76 Celebration*. Albany: City and County of Albany, American Bicentennial Commission, July 1-4, 1976.

61. Clarke, "Place Names of Albany," 44.

62. Stewart, *American Place-Names*, 132. H.L. Mencken notes that there are twelve Delmars in the United States; "The name of one of them is in the blend of *Delaware* and *Maryland*; the name of another (in Iowa) was made by using the names (i.e., the initials of the names) of six women who accompanied an excursion that opened the railroad from Clinton, Iowa" (Mencken, *The American Language*, 537-38; see also the one-volume abridged edition by Raven I. McDavid, Jr., 653).

63. Jacob S. Markle, "History of the Township of Bethlehem." In Howell and Tenney, *History of the County*, 781.

64. The author received much of this information on Selkirk from Allison Bennett, historian and native of the hamlet.

65. Letter dated March 9, 1900, from Perry G. Heath, First Assistant Postmaster General of the United States to Edward K. Selkirk.

66. Letter dated June 2, 1930, from Postmaster General Brown of the United States to Edward K. Selkirk.

67. A flyer in Mrs. Kelly's files describes a network of transportation YMCAs throughout the country, a service most people would know about only if they worked for the railroad. The first Railroad YMCA was built in Detroit in 1878.

68. These paragraphs on Beckers Corners were written by Floyd Brewer, the present author's friend and colleague, and the general editor of this bicentennial volume; he has given permission to include them in this chapter.

69. Jacob S. Markle, "History of the Township of Bethle-

hem." In Howell and Tenney, *History of the County*, 780.

70. Bennett, *More Times Remembered*, 50.

71. Bennett, *Times Remembered*, 21-22. "1976 Drive It Yourself: Three Tours of Albany County," 21.

72. Jacob S. Markle, "History of the Township of Bethlehem." In Howell and Tenney, *History of the County*, 780.

73. Jimapco map of Bethlehem, 1989.

74. Parker, *Landmarks of Albany County*, 491.

75. "A Map of the Manor Renselaerwick," surveyed by John R. Bleeker, 1767; a copy of this map is in the frontspiece in Munsell, *The Annals of Albany*, V. Albertus Becker's house is number 131 on the Bleeker map.

Chapter 12: SCHOOLS AND LIBRARY

1. Commager, *Documents of American History*, 26-28.

2. Fiske, *Dutch and Quaker Colonies*, 1:21.

3. Wilcoxen, *Seventeenth Century Albany*, 31.

4. Howell and Tenney, *History of the County*, 248.

5. Kenney, *Stubborn for Liberty*, 86.

6. Kammen, *Colonial New York*, 244.

7. Kammen, *Colonial New York*, 249.

8. Howell and Tenney, *History of the County*, 264.

9. Bennett, *A Brief History*, 19.

10. *The Bethlehem Chronicle*, September 12, 1959.

11. Bethlehem Historical Association, *Schoolhouse of History* (video cassette). Bethlehem Public Library.

12. Sloane, *The Little Red Schoolhouse*, undated and unpaged research notes.

13. Sloane, *The Little Red Schoolhouse*, undated and unpaged research notes.

14. L. Jeffrey Baltes, "Perspective," in *The Sunday Times Union*, April 30, 1989.

15. Bethlehem Central School District, *Highlights*, April 1989.

16. Baltes, *Times Union*, April 30, 1989.

17. Free Library Association, Secretary's Book 1913-1917, Delmar, New York, 11.

18. Barbara Hotaling, "A History of the Library," Bethlehem Public Library.

19. Hotaling, "History," 12.

20. Hotaling, "History," 12.

21. Hotaling, "History," 13.

22. Hotaling, "History," 13.

23. Hotaling, "History," 13.

24. Hotaling, "History," 14.

Chapter 13: MILITARY HERITAGE

1.   Kammen, *Colonial New York,* 305.

2.   Kammen, *Colonial New York,* 305-6.

3.   Kammen, *Colonial New York,* 307.

4.   Howell and Tenney, *History of the County,* 791-92.

5.   Howell and Tenney, *History of the County,* 792.

6.   Bennett, *A Brief History,* 23.

7.   Listing compiled from Van Woert, *History of the First Reformed Church* and from various local cemetery records included in Christoph, *People of the Town.*

8.   Parker, *Landmarks of Albany County,* 345.

9.   Howell and Tenney, *History of the County,* 792.

10. Howell and Tenney, *History of the County,* 792 and Van Woert, *History of the First Reformed Church,* 17.

11. [Slingerland], "Speech" 7.

12. Howell and Tenney, *History of the County,* 792.

13. Paludan, "A People's Contest," 46-47.

14. An abandoned road south of the Haswell Farm known locally as Kitchen Road, purportedly gained its name during the Civil War when soldiers used to gather here from the training ground to receive their daily rations. This story was told to the author in 1979 by the late Thomas E. Mulligan, former town historian and devoted student of military history.

15. Curtis, *Bull Run to Chancellorsville,* 28.

16. Boyce, *Twenty Eighth Regiment,* 13-15.

17. Chapter 690 of the *Laws of the State of New York,* 1865, required town clerks to "fill out the complete record of all officers and soldiers who have entered the military service, and the names of all officers and seamen from the town since April 15, 1861."

18. Howell and Tenney, *History of the County,* 792.

19. Clark, *The Heroes of Albany,* 816-17.

20. *Time-Life Books,* "Echoes of Glory," 276.

21. Information on Niver/Van Allen was gained from correspondence with Custer and Little Big Horn scholar, Kenneth Hammer, during the Spring of 1985.

22. William F. Howard, "When They Fought the Battle of Slingerlands," *The Spotlight,* October 10, 1984.

23. Howard, "When They Fought," 4.

24. For an account of Frazier's Civil War sevice, see William F. Howard, "Pvt. Frazier's War," *The Spotlight,* August 22, 1984.

25. Original letter in the possession of Ms. Evelyn Frazier, Slingerlands, N.Y.

26. Undated obituary clipping in the Jessie Golden Scrapbook, author's collection.

27. Records of the Last Man's Club, Bethlehem Historical Association collection.

28. Clipping in the Golden Scrapbook.

29. Miscellaneous clippings from the *Albany County Post* included in the Golden Scrapbook.

30. Undated *Albany Times Union* clipping in the author's collection.

31. The names of Capital District residents who were killed during the Vietnam Conflict were published in *Hardcopy for the Common Good*, February 1989.

32. "Parents of MIA Major to Speak," *The Spotlight*, October 16, 1969.

33. *The Spotlight*, March 2, 1967.

34. *The Spotlight*, January 28, 1971.

35. David Esmond, "Vietnam Veteran Explains His Views," *The Spotlight*, October 16, 1969.

36. *The Spotlight*, January 28, 1971.

Bibliography

Albany Architects: The Present Looks at the Past. Albany: Historic Albany Foundation, 1978.

American Agriculturist, Farm Directory and Reference Book of Albany and Rensselaer Counties, New York, 1916. New York: Orange Judd Co., 1916.

Andrews, Wayne, ed. Concise *Dictionary of American History.* New York: Charles Scribner's Sons, 1962.

Arthur, Elizabeth L. *The History of New York State Grange, 1934-1960.* State Grange Historian.

Bennett, Allison. *Times Remembered: Chronicles of the Towns of Bethlehem and New Scotland, New York.* Delmar, New York: 1984.

————. *More Times Remembered: Chronicles of the Towns of Bethlehem and New Scotland, New York.* Delmar, New York: 1987.

————. *The People's Choice: A History of Albany County in Art and Architecture.* Albany County Historical Association, 1980.

————. *Town of Bethlehem, Albany County, New York: A Brief History.* 1968. Reprint, 1970.

Blackburn, Roderic H. *Cherry Hill: The History and Collections of a Van Rensselaer Family.* Albany: Historic Cherry Hill, 1975.

Boeraem, Hendrik. *Formation of the Republican Party in New York.* New York: New York University Press, 1983.

Bowers, Virginia B. *The Texture of a Neighborhood: Albany's South End, 1880-1940.* 1991.

Boyce, Charles William. *A Brief History of the Twenty-eighth Regiment, New York State Volunteers.* Buffalo: Mathews-Northrup Co., 1896.

Brodhead, John Romeyn. *History of the State of New York.* Rev. ed. 2 vols. New York: Harper & Brothers, 1871.

Carrier, Lyman. *The Beginnings of Agriculture in America.* New York: McGraw-Hill Book Co., 1923.

Christian Science: A Report for the '90s. Boston: The Christian Science Publishing Society, 1990.

Christoph, Florence A. *Upstate New York in the 1760s.* Camden, Me.: Picton, 1992.

Christoph, Peter R. *Albert Andriessen Bradt: A Norwegian Settler in Rensselaerswyck.* Sarasota, Fla.; Albany, N.Y.: Bradt Family Association.

Christoph, Peter R., and Florence A. Christoph, eds. *Records of the People of the Town of Bethlehem: Albany County New York 1698-1880.* Bethlehem Historical Association, 1982.

Clark, Rufus P. *The Heroes of Albany: A Memorial of the Patriot Martyrs of the City and County of Albany.* Albany: S.R. Gray, 1866.

The Colonial Laws of New York: From the Year 1664 to the Revolution. 3 vols. Albany, New York, 1894.

Commager, Henry Steele, ed. *Documents of American History.* New York: Appleton-Century-Crofts, 1948.

Cousins, Peter H. Hog, *Plow and Sith: Cultural Aspects of Early Agricultural Technology.* Dearborn, Mich.: The Edison Institute, 1973.

Craigie, Cornelia. *Kenwood: The First Hundred Years 1853- 1953.* Albany: Convent of the Sacred Heart, 1953.

Curtis, Newton Martin. *From Bull Run to Chancellorville.* New York: G.P. Putman's Sons, 1906.

Danckaerts, Jasper. *Journal of Jasper Danckaerts, 1679-1680.* Ed. Bartlett Burleigh James and J. Franklin Jameson. New York: Charles Scribner's Sons, 1913.

Dictionary of American Biography. 27 vols. New York: Charles Scribner's Sons, 1943-1965.

Dictionary of American History. Rev. ed. 8 vols. New York: Charles Scribner's Sons, 1976.

Ellis, David M., et. al. *A History of New York State: A Revision of A Short History of New York State.* Ithaca, New York: Cornell University Press, 1967.

The Encyclopedia Americana. International ed. 30 vols. Danbury, Conn.: Grolier, Inc., 1990.

The New Encyclopaedia Britaninnica. 15th ed. 32 vols. Chicago: Encyclopaedia Britainnica, Inc., 1988

Fiske, John. *The Dutch and Quaker Colonies in America.* 2 vols. New York: Houghton Mifflen Company, 1902.

Flick, Alexander C., ed. *History of the State of New York.* 10 vols. New York State Historical Association. New York: Columbia University Press, 1933-37.

French, J.H. *Gazetteer of the State of New York.* Syracuse: R. Pearsall Smith, 1860.

Funk, Robert E. *Recent Contributions to Hudson Valley Prehistory.* Albany: The University of the State of New York, 1976.

Gehring, Charles T., trans. and ed. *Fort Orange Court Minutes, 1652-1660.* Syracuse: Syracuse University Press, 1990.

———. *Land Papers, 1630-1664.* Baltimore, Geneological Pub., 1980 (Series: New York Historical Manuscripts: Dutch).

Grun, Bernard. *The Timetables of History: A Horizontal Linkage of People and Events (Based on Werner Stein's Kultufahrplan).* New, updated ed. New York: Simon & Schuster, 1979.

Gutman, Herbert G. *The Black Family in Slavery and Freedom: 1750-1925.* New York: Pantheon Books, 1976.

Hamilton, Alexander. *Hamilton's Itinerarium, Being a Narrative of a Journey from Annapolis, Maryland through Delaware, Pennsylvania, New York, New Jersey, Connecticut, Rhode Island, Massachusetts, and New Hampshire from May to Septemebr 1744, by Doctor Alexander Hamilton.* Ed. by Albert Bushnell Hart. St. Louis: William K. Bixby, 1907.

Harsha, David Addison. *Noted Living Albanians and State Officials: A Series of Biographical Sketches.* Albany: Weed, Parsons & Co., 1891.

Haydon, Roger, ed. *Upstate Travels:British Views of Nineteenth-Century New York.* Syracuse: Syracuse University Press, 1982.

Holbrook, Stewart, commentary. *Down on the Farm: A Picture Treasury of Country Life.* New York: Crown Publishers, Inc., 1954.

Howell, George R. and Jonathan Tenney, assisted by Local Writers. *History of the County of Albany, N.Y. from 1609 to 1886.* New York: W.W. Munsell & Co., 1886.

"Indian deeds of September 12, 1652 and July 9, 1661" (unpublished manuscripts, EL670-24, EL670-4, with trans. by Charles T. Gehring). Albany Institute of History and Art.

Jameson, J. Franklin, ed. *Narratives of New Netherland, 1609-1664*. New York: C. Scribner's Sons, 1909 (reprint New York: Barnes & Noble, 1967).

Jehovah's Witnesses: United Doing God's Will Wordwide. Brooklyn: Watchtower Bible and Tract Society of New York, Inc., 1986.

Johnson, William. *Papers of Sir William Johnson*. Ed. by Milton W. Hamilton, and others. 14 vols. Albany: University of the State of New York, 1921-65.

Kalm, Peter. *Peter Kalm's Travels in North America*. Ed. by Adolph B. Benson. New York: Wilson-Erickson Ind., 1937 (reprint, New York: Dover, 1987).

Kammen, Michael. *Colonial New York: A History*. New York: Scribner's, 1974.

Keller, Allan. *Life Along the Hudson*. Tarrytown, N.Y.: Sleepy Hollow Restorations, 1976.

Kenney, Alice P. *The Gansevoorts of Albany: Dutch Patricians in the Upper Hudson Valley*. Syracuse: Syracuse University Press, 1969.

Kim, Sung Bok. *Landlord and Tenant in Colonial New York: Manorial Society, 1663-1775*. Chapel Hill: University of North Carolina, 1978.

Kimball, Francis P. *The Capital Region of New York State: Crossroads of Empire*. 3 vols. New York: Lewis Historical Publishing Co., 1942.

MacDonald, Anne L. *No Idle Hands: The Social History of American Knitting*. New York: Ballantine Books, 1988.

Marti-Ibanez, Felix, ed. *History of American Medicine: A Symposium*. New York: MD Publications, Inc., 1959.

Mathews, Milford M., ed. *A Dictionary of Americanisms on Historical Principles*. Chicago: The University of Chicago Press, 1951.

Maude, John. "Maude's Travels." J. Munsell, *The Annals of Albany*. vol.3. Albany: J. Munsell, 1852.

Memoirs of the Board of Agriculture of the State of New York. Vol.1 Albany: 1821. Albany Institute of History and Art.

Mencken, H.L. *The American Language*. 4th ed. New York: Alfred A. Knopf, 1936.

Mencken, H.L. *The American Language*. Abridged 1 vol. ed. by Raven I. McDavid, Jr. New York: Alfred A. Knopf, 1963.

"Miscellaneous Manuscripts." New York State Library. (unpublished manuscripts, AT7003, items 23, 26).

Morris, Richard B., ed. *Encyclopedia of American History*. New York: Harper & Brothers, 1961.

Morse, Jeridiah. *The American Gazetteer*. Boston: S. Hall, Thomas & Andrews, 1797.

Munsell, J. ed. *The Annals of Albany*. 10 vols. Albany: J. Munsell, 1850-59.

———. *The Annals of Albany*. 10 vols. Vols. 1-4, expanded 2d ed., 1869-1871.

Munsell, Joel, ed. *Collections on the History of Albany, from its Discovery to the Present Time*. 4 vols. Albany: J. Munsell, 1865-1871.

The New York Public Library Desk Reference. New York: Webster's New World, a Stonesong Press Book, 1989.

Oberlin Course Catalog 1991-1992. Oberlin, Ohio: Oberlin

College, 1991.

O'Callaghan, E.B. *Documentary History of the State of New York.* 4 vols. Albany: Weed, Parsons, 1849-51 (octavo ed.); 1850-51 (quarto ed.).

————. *History of New Netherland.* 2 vols. New York: Appleton, 1848.

Paludan, Phillip Shaw. "A People's Contest." *The Union and Civil War, 1861-1865.* New York: Harper & Row, 1989.

Parker, Amasa J.,ed. *Landmarks of Albany County New York.* Syracuse, New York: D. Mason & Co., 1897.

Pearson, Jonathan. *Contributions for the Geneologies of the First Settlers of the Ancient County of Albany, 1630-1800.* Reprint from Albany, 1872 volume in George Peabody Department of the Enoch Pratt Free Library, Baltimore. Baltimore: Geneological Publishing Co., Inc., 1978.

Pearson, Jonathan, trans. and ed. *Early Records of the City and County of Albany and Colony of Rensselaerswyck.* 4 vols. (vol. 2-4 rev and ed. by A.J.F. van Laer). Albany: J. Munsell, 1869, University of the State of New York, 1917- 19.

Phelps, H.P. *The Albany Handbook for 1881.* Albany: Chas. van Benthuysen & Sons, 1880.

A *Proud Heritage: Native American Services in New York State.* Albany: New York State Department of Social Services, 1989.

Reinfeld, Fred and Burton Hobson. *Catalogue of the World's Most Popular Coins.* 9th. ed. Syracuse: Sterling Publishing Co., 1976.

Ritchie, William A. *The Archeaology of New York State.* Rev. Harrison, N.Y.: Harbor Hill Books, 1980.

Ritchie, William A. and Robert E. Funk. *Aboriginal Settlement Patterns in the Northeast.* Albany: The University of the State of New york, 1973.

Roberts, Anne F. and Marsha W. Cockrell, eds. *Historic Albany: Its Churches and Synagogues.* Albany: Library Communications Services, 1986.

Roseberry, C.R. *Flashback: A Fresh Look at Albany's Past.* Susanne Dumbleton, ed. Albany: Washington Park Press Ltd., 1986.

Selkirk, Theodore K., comp. *James Selkirk (1756-1820) and His Descendents.* Cincinnati: 1962 (rev. by Lenora R. Levy, 1972).

Shaughnessy, Jim. *Delaware & Hudson: The history of an important railroad whose antecedent was a canal network to transport coal.* Berkeley: Howell-North Books, 1967.

Sill, Dunkin. "Papers." New York Historical Society.

[Slingerland, John I.] "Speech of Hon. John I. Slingerland, N.Y. on Internal Improvements, the War and Land Monopoly, Delivered in the House of Representatives of the United States, June 22, 1849." Washington, D.C.: J. & G.S. Gideon, [1849].

Slingerland, Martha and Grace Moak. *Jacob Moak of New Scotland and His Descendents 1720-1990.* Albany, 1990. Based on Elizabeth Janet Mc Cormick, *Descendents of Jacob Moak of New Scotland,* 1942. Bethlehem Public Library.

Sloane, Eric. *The Little Red School House.* Garden City, N.Y.: Doubleday & Co., 1972.

Spafford, Horatio Gates. *A Gazetteer of the State of New York.* Troy: B.D. Packard and author, 1824. (Reprint from original provided by Troy Public Library). Interlaken, N.Y.: Heart of the Lakes, 1981.

Stewart, George R. *American Place-Names*. New York: Oxford University Press, 1970.

Time-Life Books. "Echoes of Glory: Coins and Equipment of the Union, 1991.

Topographical Atlas of the Counties of Albany and Schenectady, New York. Surveyed by S.N. and D.G. Beers and Assistants. Philadelphia: Stone & Stewart, 1886.

Trager, James, ed. *The People's Chronology: A Year-By-Year Record of Human Events from Prehistory to the Present*. New York: Holt, Rinehart and Winston, 1979.

Transactions of the N. Y. State Agricultural Society: With an Abstract of the Proceedings of the County Agricultural Societies and of the American Institute. Vol. 6,(1846). 1847.

Transactions of the N. Y. State Agricultural Society: With an Abstract of the Proceedings of the County Agricultural Societies. Vol. 14 (1854). 1855.

Van der Donck, Adriaen. *A Description of the New Netherlands*. trans. by Jeremiah Johnson. New York: New York Historical Society, 1841 (rep., Thomas F. O'Donnell, ed., Syracuse: Syracuse University Press, 1968).

Van Laer, A.J.F., trans. and ed. "Albany Notarial Papers, 1666-1693." *Dutch Settlers Society of Albany Yearbook*, XIII, 1937-38.

———. *Correspondence of Jeremias van Rensselaer, 1651-1674*. Albany: University of the State of New York, 1932.

———. *Correspondence of Maria van Rensselaer, 1669-1689*. Albany: University of the State of New York, 1935.

———. *Minutes of the Court of Albany, Rensselaerswyck, and Schenectady*. 3 vols. Albany: University of the State of New York, 1926-32.

———. *Minutes of the Court of Fort Orange and Beverwyck*. 2 vols. Albany: University of the State of New York, 1920-23.

———. *Minutes of the Court of Rensselaerswyck, 1648-1652*. Albany: University of the State of New York, 1922.

———. "Protocol of Dirck van Schelluyne, Secretary of the Colony of Rensselaerswyck, 1660-1665." *Dutch Settlers Society of Albany Yearbook*, XVI, 1940-41.

———. "Settlers of Rensselaerswyck, 1659-1664." *Dutch Settlers Society of Albany Yearbook*, V, 1929-30.

———. "Translation of the Letter from Arent van Curler to Killiaen van Rensselaer." *Dutch Settlers Society of Albany Yearbook*, III, 1927-28.

———. *Van Rensselaer Bowier Manuscripts*. Albany: University of the State of New York, 1908.

Van Rensselaer, Jeremias. "Account Book, 1659-1668." (unpublished manuscript), New York State Archives.

Van Woert, H.S. *History of the First Reformed Church of Bethlehem, New York 1763-1913*. Albany: J.B. Lyon, 1913.

Werner, Edgar A. *Civil List and Constitutional History of the Colony and State of New York*. Albany: Weed, Parsons, 1883.

Wetterau, Bruce. *The New York Public Library Book of Chronologies*. New York: Prentice Hall, 1990.

[Whish, John D.] *Albany Guide Book*. Albany: J.B. Lyon Co., 1917.

Wilcoxen, Charlotte. *Seventeenth Century Albany: A Dutch Profile*. Albany Institute of History and Art, 1984.

Wilstach, Paul. *Hudson River Landings.* Port Washington, N.Y.: Ira J. Friedman, Inc., 1969.

The World Almanac and Book of Facts. New York: World Almanac, 1992.

The World Book Encyclopedia. 22 vols. Chicago: World Book, Inc., 1990.

The World Book Encyclopedia. 22 vols. Chicago: World Book, Inc., 1992.

[Worth, Gorham A.] *Random Recollections of Albany from 1800 to 1808: with some additional matter.* 2d. ed. Albany: Charles Van Benthuysen, 1850.

Credits

116   Courtesy Paul R. Brustman, Mohawk and Hudson Chapter of the National Railway Historical Society.

117   Courtesy General Electric Company.

118   Photograph by Ryland H. Hewitt.

Chapter 6. HOUSES OF FAITH

123-126   Photographs by Ryland H. Hewitt.

128, 130   Photographs by Ryland H. Hewitt.

135   Courtesy *The Spotlight*.

136   Courtesy Bethlehem Public Library.

137   Photograph by Ryland H. Hewitt.

138   Photograph of church courtesy Bethlehem Public Library; photograph of missionary saints by Ryland H. Hewitt.

139, 141   Photographs by Ryland H. Hewitt.

143   Courtesy Normansville Community Church.

144, 145   Photographs by Ryland H. Hewitt.

146   Courtesy Solid Rock Family Outreach Center.

147   Photograph by Ryland H. Hewitt.

Chapter 7. COMMUNITY ORGANIZATIONS

151   Courtesy Bethlehem Masonic Lodge 1096.

152   Mason's Past Master's Jewel courtesy Bethlehem Masonic Lodge 1096, photograph by

Chuck McKinney; Bethlehem Cemetery photograph by Ryland H. Hewitt.

154   Delmar Progress Club photograph by Benjamin French; Lions Lighting the Community courtesy Red Goyer of the Lions Club.

156   Courtesy Alice Boutelle.

156   Courtesy Bernard Kaplowitz, director of Bethlehem Republican Club.

157   Photograph of Jean Lyon and Mary Elizabeth Van Oostenbrugge by Ryland H. Hewitt.

158   Courtesy Jon Jameson.

159   Courtesy Howard Gmelch.

162   Courtesy Bethlehem Public Library.

164   Courtesy Elaine McLain, *The Spotlight*.

165   Courtesy Joanne Kimmey.

166   Courtesy Patricia DeCecco.

168   Courtesy Kathleen and Bernard Kaplowitz.

169   Photograph of Adrian Arnold courtesy Mr. Arnold; photograph of Bethlehem Tomboys courtesy Irving Van Woert, M.D.

170   Courtesy Adele Parsons.

172   Courtesy John B. Geurtze.

173   Photograph by Chuck McKinney.

174   Girl Scout photograph courtesy Hudson Valley Girl Scout Council; photographs of Alice Porter Boutelle and of membership card courtesy Mrs. Boutelle.

175   Photographs courtesy William Campbell, American Legion Post 1040.

177   Photograph by Ryland H. Hewitt.

179   Courtesy Dorothy and Henry Kleinke.

180   Courtesy Kenneth E. McNary, Elsmere Fire Company A.

181   Courtesy Charles Wickham, Jr., Selkirk Fire Company 1.

182   Courtesy Ann C. Leonard.

183   Courtesy Charles Wickham, Jr., Selkirk Fire Company 1.

185   Courtesy Barbara Asprion, Town Supervisor's Office.

Chapter 8. CHANGING FAMILIES

190, 192   Courtesy Bethlehem Public Library.

193   Courtesy office of Bethlehem Town Historian.

194   Photograph of Nicoll-Sill home by Tom Knight, Knight Photographic Services; photograph of ceramics by Chuck McKinney.

195   Photographs by Chuck McKinney.

196   Photograph by Tom Knight, Knight Photographic Services.

197   Courtesy office of Bethlehem Town Historian.

198   Photographs courtesy Ruth Blackmore.

199   Photograph of probable key by Chuck McKinney.

200   Photographs of halfpenny and hair dye bottles by Chuck McKinney; photograph of artifacts by Floyd I. Brewer.

201   Medicine vial photograph by Floyd I. Brewer; photographs of John Babcock, M.D., and his medicine kit and pillbox by Chuck McKinney courtesy Bethlehem Historical Association.

202   Courtesy Bethlehem Historical Association.

203   Courtesy office of Bethlehem Town Historian.

204   Photograph of Richard Kimmey courtesy Alice Boutelle; insurance company sign photograph by Ryland H. Hewitt.

205   Three Glenn photographs courtesy Joanne Kimmey; photograph (lower right) courtesy Bethlehem Historical Association.

206   Photographs (top) courtesy Mary Elizabeth Van Oostenbrugge; photographs (bottom) courtesy Bethlehem Public Library.

207   Photographs (left) by Chuck McKinney; photograph (right) courtesy Bethlehem Public Library.

208   Courtesy Joanne Kimmey.

209   Illustration (top) courtesy Lindsay Boutelle, (bottom) courtesy Barbara Carkner.

210   Courtesy Helen and Evelyn Frazier.

211   Courtesy Marjorie Terrell.

213   Courtesy Slingerlands Community United Methodist Church.

214   Illustration (left) courtesy William Howard, (right) courtesy office of Bethlehem Town Historian.

215   Courtesy Barbara Carkner.

218   Photographs of Adams and Blanchard families courtesy Ruth Blanchard Dalton.

Chapter 9. FROM OXEN TO DIESEL

226, 229   Photographs by Ryland H. Hewitt.

232   Courtesy Richard and Margaret Heath Thayer.

235, 236   Courtesy Richard and Margaret Heath Thayer.

238-246   Photographs by Ryland H. Hewitt.

248, 249   Courtesy Warren "Pete" and Marie Mead.

252   Courtesy Town of Bethlehem Historical Association.

258   From the *American Agriculturist Farm Directory and Reference Book*, Albany and Rensselaer Counties, New York; map courtesy Library of Congress.

Chapter 10. WILL OF THE PEOPLE

260   Located in lobby of Bethlehem Town Hall.

262   Photograph of portrait of Philip Van Rensselaer, located in Bethlehem Town Board meeting room; photograph of John M. Oliver courtesy office of Behlehem Town Historian.

263-265   Courtesy office of Bethlehem Town Historian.

268   Photograph by Ryland H. Hewitt.

269   Courtesy office of Bethlehem Town Historian.

275   Photograph of Elm Avenue Park sign by Ryland H. Hewitt; photograph of Henry Hudson Park plaque by Joseph A. Allgaier.

276   Photographs of Ruth F. Dickinson and of certificate courtesy office of Bethlehem Town Historian.

277   Courtesy Karen Pellettier.

Chapter 11. HAMLETS: A BICENTENNIAL TOUR

The maps on pp. 279, 290, 299, 305, and 312 were composed and produced by Kristi Carr.

Photographs by Ryland H. Hewitt: pp. 280, 285-288, 291, 292, 297, 308, 309, 313, and 314.

294   Photograph courtesy Dr. and Mrs. Robert H. Deily.

296, 298   Courtesy office of Bethlehem Town Historian.

301   Courtesy Bethlehem Public Library.

303   Adams House postcard courtesy William Howard.

304   Courtesy office of Bethlehem Town Historian.

310   Painting by Rita Buttiker (1992), member of Bethlehem Art Association.

311   Courtesy office of Bethlehem Town Historian.

318   Photographs of carriage house and sign by Ryland H. Hewitt; photograph of Delmar Fire Department

courtesy Tom Howard; photograph of Essex house by Chuck McKinney.

Chapter 12. SCHOOLS AND LIBRARY

321   Photograph of District 3 School courtesy Bethlehem Public Library; photograph of Cedar Hill School courtesy Town of Bethlehem Historical Association.

322   Photograph of Cedar Hill School graduates courtesy Martin J. Cross, Jr.; photograph of eighth grade, Selkirk School, courtesy Bethlehem Public Library.

323   Photograph of Slingerlands School courtesy Helen and Evelyn Frazier; photograph of Delmar Public School courtesy Bethlehem Public Library.

324   Photograph of School District No. 6 courtesy Bethlehem Public Library.

325   Photographs by Ryland H. Hewitt.

326   Photograph of Hamagrael School courtesy Bethlehem Public Library; photograph of sign by Tom Knight, Knight Photographic Services.

327   Photograph of Olin Bouck courtesy Bethlehem Senior High Library; photograph of Middle School by Ryland H. Hewitt; photograph of Hamilton H. Bookhout courtesy Bethlehem Senior High Library.

328, 329 Photographs by Ryland H. Hewitt.

330   Photograph of Saint Thomas School courtesy the school; Bethlehem Central High School logo by Kristi Carr, Central Administration Office, Bethlehem Central School District.

331   Photograph of Bethlehem Central High School by Kristi Carr; photographs of Gordon Molyneux and Dominick J. DeCecco courtesy Bethlehem Senior High Library.

332, 334 Photographs courtesy Bethlehem Senior High Library.

335-338 Photographs courtesy Bethlehem Public Library.

Chapter 13. MILITARY HERITAGE

343   Photographs by Benjamin French.

347, 348 Author's collection.

349   Photograph by Ryland H. Hewitt.

350   Author's collection; photograph of minie balls by Chuck McKinney.

352   Photograph of Pvt. Frazier courtesy Helen and Evelyn Frazier; photograph of gravestone, author's collection.

353-355 Author's collection.

356   Courtesy Barbara Carkner.

357   Author's collection.

361   Courtesy Bethlehem Historical Association.

362   Courtesy American Legion Post 1040.

363   Author's collection.

364, 365 Photographs by Ryland H. Hewitt.

Biographical Notes

Mary A. and Richard A. Ahlstrom, associate editors-publication and design, have been Delmar residents for twelve years. Mary was born in Jersey City, New Jersey, grew up and attended school in Manhattan and

met Richard when they both worked for the *New York Daily News*. Mary attended Westchester Community College, Manhattanville College, and the University of Connecticut. Richard, born in Brooklyn, New York, earned bachelor's degrees in history from Brooklyn College and management from Carnegie Institute of Technology. Richard was employed in management positions at the *New York Daily News* for eighteen years and the Gannett Westchester Rockland Newspapers for eleven years. Richard and Mary have six children, Ann Marie, William, Mary Carol, Susan, Richard, and Christina. They are publishers of the Spotlight Newspapers and owners of Newsgraphics Printers.

Joseph A. Allgaier, associate editor-style, and author of the chapters on business and government, is Bethlehem's town historian and a thirty-year resident of Delmar. The son of Joseph and Maria Allgaier, he was born in Brooklyn where he attended parochial and public schools. Allgaier earned a bachelor's degree in engineering from Pratt Institute and

a master's degree from the Rennsselaer Polytechnic Institute. He married Jacqueline Platten in 1958, and they raised three children in Bethlehem, Joseph G., Barbara, and Karen. He retired in 1988 after almost four decades in management positions with New York Telephone and NYNEX.

Floyd I. Brewer, editor, coauthor of the prehistory chapter, and author of the chapters on families and community organizations, has lived in Bethlehem for twenty-six years. The son of Mary Estey and Elwood T. Brewer of Bridgewater, Maine, he had three

years of undergraduate work at the University of Maine at Presque Isle before earning a bachelor's in history at the University of Maine at Gorham. After three years in the United States Air force during World War II, Brewer earned a master's degree and a doctor of education degree in guidance and student personnel administration at Teachers College,

Columbia University. He married Coleen Hamilton in 1944. They have two children, Jeffrey H. and Mark A. He worked as an administrator and professor at three institutions of higher education prior to his retirement from the University at Albany in 1983.

Marie S. Carlson, compiler of the chronology chapter, has lived in Bethlehem most of her life. The daughter of A.W. and Fan Schmidt, she was born in Albany, but attended public schools in Bethlehem. Carlson earned a bachelor's degree from Mount Holyoke College and a master's degree in library science from the New York State College for Teachers,

now the University at Albany. She married C. Theodore Carlson III in 1952, and they have two children, Robin and Paul. She has been on the staff of the Bethlehem Public Library for twenty-four years, and is currently reference librarian and a specialist in local history and genealogy.

Kristi Carr, assistant editor-copy, has been a Delmar resident for eight years. Born in The Dalles, Oregon, the daughter of Gordon and Melva Rapp, she grew up in the Midwest. She holds a bachelor's degree in journalism from the University of Missouri. In 1971 she married Bradley G. Carr. They have two sons, Brian and Seth. For the past seven years, she has been director of information for the

Bethlehem Central School District and editor of the *Bethlehem Central Highlights* newsletter.

Peter R. Christoph, associate editor-research and author of the three overview chapters (two through four), has lived in Selkirk since 1965. He is editor of the New York Historical Manuscripts series which is being published by Syracuse University Press, and has edited ten books. He was curator of manuscripts and special collections at the New York State Library for twenty  years, during ten of which he also served as director of the New Netherland Project to translate colonial Dutch records. He is a graduate of Hartwick College and holds the degrees of master of arts and master of library science from the University at Albany. The son of Hajo and Matilda Christoph, he is a native of Castleton-on-Hudson. He married Florence Weaver in 1959 and they have three children, Daniel, Richard, and Annalise.

Thomas R. Collins, author of the chapter on schools and the library, was born in Newark, New Jersey, the son of Raymond and Marion Collins. Following service in the United States Navy during World War II, he graduated from Trenton State College and earned a master's in history and social studies from Columbia University. Collins married  Marjorie Lakness in 1945, and the couple raised two children in New Jersey, John and Susan. He was a secondary school teacher in New Jersey and Long Island for twenty-seven years as he pursued advanced graduate studies at Columbia University. He served as supervisor of social studies in the Bethlehem Central School District for several years and ended his work career with four years abroad, first in Teheran, Iran, and then two years of teaching in a Department of Defense high school in Okinawa, Japan, prior to his retirement in 1982.

Ross Everett Gutman, assistant editor-copy, is a retired dental surgeon who has lived in Delmar since 1959. The son of Henry and Marie Gutman, he was born in New York City. Gutman earned a doctor of dental surgery degree from New York University and a master's degree in public health from Columbia University. He married Margaret Hoole in 1952 and they have a

daughter, Carol Marie. Margaret teaches in the Albany public school system. Major Gutman was chief of a United States Army dental clinic during World War II, and in charge of dental services in a New York City Health Department district. Later, he directed  a United States Public Health Service preventative dentistry program in New York State and was administrator of school dental programs with the New York State Education Department for twenty-six years before his retirement in 1981.

Ryland Hugh Hewitt, associate editor-graphics and author of the chapters on hamlets and religious institutions, has been a resident of Slingerlands since 1966. He was born in Elmira, New York, the son of Ryland H. and Marion S. Hewitt. He earned a bachelor's degree in English, a master's in dramatic literature, and a Ph.D. in phonetics and linguistics from Cornell University. He married Rowena E.  Fairchild in 1949 and they have three children, Roxanne, Rebecca, and Ruth. He has taught English and speech courses at Colgate University, Mount Union College, Bates College, and the University at Albany, where he was also director of the Northeastern New York Speech Center. During the mid-1960s, he was a Fulbright lecturer in English at the University of Jordan in Amman. After his retirement from the University at Albany, he was cofounder and director of the Capital Area Speech Center in Albany.

William F. Howard, author of the military chapter, is a lifelong resident of Bethlehem as were his parents, William G. and Laura Bailey Howard. He is a graduate of the University at Albany and was a Herbert H. Lehman fellow while earning a master's degree from the Graduate School of Public Affairs, the University at Albany. Howard married Paulette  Morgan in 1968. He has written extensively on American history subjects. Howard is an elected fellow of the Company of Military Historians and a founding member of the Capital District Civil War Roundtable. He is employed as a labor, civil service, and pensions analyst by the New York State Assembly.

Emrie Davis LaBarge, assistant editor-copy, was born in Acadia, Florida, the daughter of Margaret R. Scott and Herbert T. Davis, Jr. She earned a bachelor's degree in history from Emory University and a master's in school counseling from the State University of New York at Buffalo. She married John S. LaBarge in 1972. They lived in Pittsford, New York, for twelve years before moving to Bethlehem in 1984. They have three children, Elizabeth, John, and James. LaBarge is currently employed by Castle Computers in Latham as a salesperson and computer trainer for Macintosh equipment.

Charles D. (Chuck) McKinney, associate editor-publication and design, and coauthor of the prehistory chapter, grew up in Mount Vernon, Illinois, the son of Margaret Arnold and Clifford I. McKinney. He earned bachelor's and master's degrees in geology and geography from Southern Illinois University at Carbondale. McKinney married Barbara-Ann Siems in 1966. She is currently a home and career skills teacher in the Albany public schools. They have two children, Mark and Ryan, and have lived in Bethlehem since 1978. He held several regional planning and governmental consultant positions in Missouri, Illinois, Vermont, and Connecticut before accepting employment with the New York State Energy Research and Development Authority. He is currently employed as an economic development specialist by the New York State Department of Economic Development.

Carol Zdgiebloski Northrup, author of the farm chapter, is a lifelong resident of Bethlehem, and now lives across the road from her family's Elm Avenue farm in Selkirk. The farm was

established by her grandparents, Henry and Helen Zdgiebloski in 1926, and was continued by her parents, Dorothy Sitterly and Peter P. Zdgiebloski. She married Daniel A. Northrup in 1964 and has three children, Leah M., Daniel A., Jr., and Barbara J. She continued to help out on the family farm while her children were growing up. Northrup is currently attending Maria College and is employed by the New York State Education Department.

Jean Lyon and Eleanor Turner, research assistants, have worked as a team since the beginning of the written phase of this project in 1986. The daughter of Mary Miscampbell and Thomas T. Murray, Jean was born in Canada and moved to Al-

bany when she was four years old. She attended Saint Agnes School, Skidmore College, and the Tobe-Coburn School of Fashion Design and Merchandising in New York City. She married Robert L. Lyon in 1944 and has two children, Lisa and Michael. Lyon was administrator of the Albany Medical Personnel Pool for eight years before her retirement in 1984. She is a charter member of the Bethlehem Historical Association and a long-term anchor for the association's work at the Schoolhouse Museum. Eleanor Turner was born in Coeymans, the daughter of Ernest W. and Edith Wiltsie Payne. She married Milton R. Turner in 1940 and has two children, Dennis and Gwen. She worked in the office of the Albany Steel and Iron Works Supply Company between 1967 and 1983, when she retired. Her knowledge of the history of local families has served her well in her work with this project.

> *Special thanks are due to the wives and husbands mentioned above who answered inumerable phone calls about bicentennial history drafts, kept track of papers and, in some instances, proofed the various drafts written by their spouses.*

Supervisors and Town Clerks over the Ages

SUPERVISORS

1794 - 1797	Philip Van Rensselaer
1798 - 1803	Jacob Ten Eyck
1804 - 1818	David Delong
1819 - 1820	David Burhans
1821	Henry L. Mead
1822 - 1825	William N. Sill
1826 - 1827	Mathew Bullock
1828 -	Garret Hogan
1829 - 1830	James Alexander
1831 - 1832	Leonard G. Ten Eyck
1833	William N. Sill
1834	Leonard G. Ten Eyck
1835	David Springsteed
1836 - 1837	James B. Wands
1838 - 1839	Joshua F. Babcock
1840 - 1841	Abner Udell
1842 - 1844	Andrew Vanderhyden
1845	Francis Shafer
1846 - 1847	John McHarg
1848 - 1850	Jeremiah Mead
1851 - 1852	Elias Milbanks
1853	George F. Imbrie
1854	John Patterson
1855 - 1858	Leonard G. Ten Eyck
1859 - 1861	John Wilkes
1862	Albertus W. Becker
1863 - 1866	William Kimmey
1867 - 1870	George C. Adams
1871 - 1874	Albertus W. Becker
1875 - 1876	John W. Wemple
1877	W. Chauncey Hotaling
1878 - 1880	William L. Flager
1881 - 1882	W. Chauncey Hotaling
1883 - 1885	John L. Winne
1886 - 1888	Garrett Vanderpool
1889 - 1893	John Patterson, Jr.
1894 - 1895	William H. Slingerland, Jr.
1896 - 1899	William Blodgett
1900 - 1909	E. J. Bedell, M.D.
1910 - 1923	Charles D. Niver
1924 - 1931	Alton C. Rowe
1932 - 1941	Ray F. Arthur
1942 - 1959	John M. Oliver
1960 - 1974	Bertram E. Kohinke
1975 - 1977	Harry H. Sheaffer
1978 - 1984	Thomas V. Corrigan
1985 - 1989	J. Robert Hendrick
1990 -Present	Kenneth J. Ringler, Jr.

TOWN CLERKS

John Van Derheyden	1794-1797
Henry Vanderzee	1797-1801
James Wands, 2nd	1801-1802
John Van Derheyden	1802-1804
John H. Burhans	1804-1806
James Wands, 2nd	1806-1809
John Van Derheyden	1809-1810
John J. Moak	1810-1814
Garritt Hogan	1814-1818
James B. Wands	1818-1822
William Dickson	1822-1825
Frederick Markle	1825-1826
John Reid	1826-1827
Garritt Hogan	1827-1828
David Chesebrough	1828-1829
Daniel McEwan	1829-1831
John Reid	1831-1832
Daniel McEwan	1832-1833

Henry B. Haswell	1833-1835		Isaac Bulger	1869-1870
David J. Burhans	1835		Daniel Walley	1870-1871
John V.L. Burhans	1835-1838		Wendell Bender	1871
Jacob Springsteed	1838-1840		E.M. Van Auken	1874-1876
Edward S. Willett	1840-1841		Thomas T. Winnie	1876-1880
Alexander F. McGill	1841-1842		Edwin Hotaling	1880-1883
Hiram Babcock	1842-1845		Charles A. Niver	1884-1884
Henry Creble	1845-1846		Henry V. Long	1884-1893
James W. Bender	1846-1847		Oscar Haswell	1893-1897
John Birch	1847-1850		D. R. Udell	1897-1901
David P. Kimmey	1850-1853		Rodman R. Allen	1901-1903
Hiram Hotaling	1853-1854		Clinton Longdon	1904-1907
David Couse	1854-1855		George T. Coughtry	1908-1910
William Kimmey	1855-1856		George H. Coughtry	1910-1917
David M. Niver	1856-1858		Stiles W. Conning	1918-1919
Richard C. Maine	1858-1859		Albert M. Reynolds	1920-1923
John G. Hotaling	1859-1862		Ray F. Arthur	1924-1931
Washington Groesbeck	1862-1863		Edward W. Boutelle	1932-1939
John J. Bradt	1863-1864		Robert F. Westervelt	1940-1963
Eli Bell	1864-1865		Margaret Kneff	1964-1970
William Sible	1865-1866		Marion T. Camp	1971-1985
John Simpson	1866-1867		Carolyn M. Lyons	1985-1991
George Prindle	1867-1869		Kathleen A. Newkirk	1992-Present

Lists of names in the appendix are not included in the index. Since long lists of names are fraught with potential for error, it is our hope that readers will provide us with evidence of the correct spelling of misspelled names and notify us of names omitted from the lists.

TOWN OF BETHLEHEM
— 1993 —

SUPERVISOR
Kenneth J. Ringler, Jr.

COUNCIL
Sheila Fuller
M. Sheila Galvin
Charles A. Gunner
Frederick C. Webster

BETHLEHEM TOWN BOARD *Left to Right:* M. Sheila Galvin, Charles A. Gunner, Kenneth J. Ringler, Jr., Fredrick C. Webster, and Sheila Fuller.

Town Clerk: Kathleen A. Newkirk

Receiver of Taxes: Kenneth P. Hahn

Superintendent of Highways: Greg A. Saggendorph

Assessor: M. David Leafer

Director, Senior Services: Karen K. Pellettier

Parks & Recreation: David B. Austin

Secretary to the Supervisor: Barbara A. Asprion

Board of Appeals: Charles B. Fritts

Police Department: Chief Richard J. LaChappelle

Town Historian: Joseph A. Allgaier

Comptroller: Judith E. Kehoe

Commissioner of Public Works: Bruce H. Secor

Town Planner: Jeffrey Lipnicky

Building Inspector: John H. Flanigan

Data Processing Manager: Jeffrey A. Dammeyer

Community Relations: Marilyn Corrigan

Planning Board: Martin L. Barr

Jutice Department: Justice, Peter Bishko, Justice, Peter C. Wenger, Court Clerk, Barbara J. Hodom

Town Attorney: Bernard Kaplowitz

Community Organizations in Brief

Adamsville Ancients Fife & Drum Corps. 1988. *Purpose:* to promote the enjoyment and preservation of ancient (Colonial) music. *Early leaders;* **James Willey**, director; **Beth Thompson**, business manager; **Beth Willey, Carol Willey, Vincent Thompson.** *History consultant:* **Beth Thompson.** *Membership:* 8-start, 18-peak, 18 in 1990.

American Association of Retired Persons-Tri-Village Chapter 1598. 1973. *Purpose:* To provide fellowship and services for senior citizen members and the community in keeping with the motto-"To Serve, Not to be Served". *First officers:* **Arthur Ahr**, president; **Alfred Davies**, vice president; **Helen Davies**, secretary; **Elizabeth Klapp**, corresponding secretary, and **James E. Van Buren**, treasurer. *History consultants:* **George W. Chesbro, John Gardiner, J. Robert Hendrick.** *Membership:* 158-start, 400-peak, 300 in 1990.

American Legion Post 1040- Nathanial Adams Blanchard Post. 1930. *Purpose:* to uphold and defend the Constitution of the United States of America, to care for needy veterans and their families and to serve the community, state, and nation. *First officer:* **Winthrop P. Robinson**, commander. *History consultants:* **Charles J. O'Hara, Alexander J. Woehrle.** *Membership:* 150-start, 850-peak, 700 in 1990.

American Legion Post 1040 Ladies Auxiliary- Nathanial Adams Blanchard Post. 1931. *Purpose:* to assist the American Legion and to offer aid to veterans and their children. *First officers:* **Winifred Butler**, president; **Florence Holmes, Mrs. Newell Steward**, and **Helen Piper**, vice presidents; **Edna Lauer**, secretary, and **Thelma Jones**, treasurer. *History consultant:* **Barbara Whitney.** *Membership:* 42-start, 210-peak, 186 in 1990.

Arachne Weavers. 1973. *Purpose:* to accommodate weavers who wish to exchange weaving skills for personal satisfaction and growth. *Organizer and history consultant:* **Janet S. Nyquist.** *Membership:* 12-start, 30-peak, 30 in 1990.

Audubon Society of New York State- Hollyhock Hollow Sanctuary. 1940. *Purpose:* to preserve a bird and wildlife sanctuary in its natural state for the enjoyment of the public. *Benefactors and organizers:* **Robert Rienow and Leona Train Rienow** in consultation with **Ronald Dodson**, president of the Audubon Society of New York State. *History consultant:* **John J. Santacrose.** *Membership:* 100-start, 500-peak, 500 in 1991.

Benevolent and Protective Order of the Elks- Bethlehem Lodge 2233. 1961. *Purpose:* to provide the members with fraternal, patriotic and benevolent opportunities in the community. *Early officers:* **John A. Buehler, Sr., Albert A. Danckert, Gerard A. Langhauser, Allen T. Murphy, William J. O'Neil, Stuart Stephany, David Weisheit**, and **Luther A. Williams.** *History Consultant:* George A. DeSormeau. *Membership:* 150-start, 1000-peak, 600 in 1990.

Benevolent and Protective Order of the Elks 2233 - Ladies Auxiliary. 1962. *Purpose:* to support Bethlehem Elks programs and objectives. *First officer:* **Barbara Alexander**, president. *History consultant:* **Joane M. DeSormeau.** *Membership:* 110-peak, 67 in 1991.

Bethlehem Archaeology Group. 1982. *Purpose:* to carry out archaeological and historical research for the Town of Bethlehem and to publish the findings in three books: *Bethlehem Revisited: A Bicentennial Story, Bethlehem Diary* and *The Archaeology of Bethlehem, New York. First officers:* **Ralph B. Wood**, president; **Adrienne R. Gordon**, vice president; **Ann S. Jacobs**, secretary-treasurer; **Floyd I. Brewer**, field director and editor of publications. *History consultants:* **Florence A. Christoph, Roy A. Dietert, James T. Engleman, Benjamin and Virginia French, Edward D. Homiller, Jeanne Knouse, Bernard Lamica, Jean M. Lyon, Charles D. (Chuck) McKinney, Nanci Page**, and **Eleanor E. Turner.** *Membership:* 8-start, 28-peak, 17 in 1991.

Bethlehem Area Ministerial Association. 1979.(An out-growth of the Tri-Village Clergy Association which was organized in the 1940s). *Purpose:* to provide opportunities for area ministers and other church leaders to discuss and support ecumenical church projects and related church matters. *History consultants:* **Larry Deyss** and **Charles H. Kaulfuss.** *Membership:* 7-start, 10-peak, 10 in 1991.

Bethlehem Art Association. 1966. *Purpose:* to stimulate public interest, understanding, and appreciation of fine art and to provide a forum for artists to exchange ideas, conduct exhibitions, and support worthy community projects. *Early leaders:* **Margaret G. Foster, Barbara Wooster,** organizers; **Johanna Saper,** president; **Joseph Robinson,** vice president; **Patricia Baruch,**treasurer; **Rita Wiepert,** corresponding secretary; **Evelyn Sanders,** recording secretary. *History consultants:* **Florence Becker, John Hotchin, Eunice Hunter, Joan Krathaus, Colleen Kriss, Lillian Longley, Virginia Remington Rich,** and **Dorothy Smith.** *Membership:* 25-start, 88-peak, 88 in 1991.

Bethlehem Bicentennial Commission. 1988. *Purpose:* to plan and implement a celebration for the town of Bethlehem's bicentennial in 1993. Initially spearheaded **by Sue Ann Ritchko** and **Cynthia Wilson,** co-chairs, the leadership role was assumed by **J. Robert Hendrick** in 1990. He was assisted by **Joseph Allgaier,** town historian; **Floyd Brewer,** editor of publications; **Marty Cornelius,** business liaison; **Dominick DeCecco,** school liaison; **Robert Johnson,** treasurer; **Bernard Kaplowitz,** town attorney; **Robert Kerker,** commemorative booklet; **Barbara Muhlfelder,** public relations; **Ann Patton,** community liaison; **Pieter Van Derzee,** special projects; and **Sue Zick,** events. *Membership:* 12-start, 12-peak, 12 in 1992.

Bethlehem Babe Ruth League. 1955. *Purpose:* to provide opportunities for participation in league and inter-league baseball for thirteen to fifteen year-old Bethlehem citizens with an emphasis on good sportsmanship, courage in defeat, and modesty in victory. *Organizers:* **Robert S. Barned, John B.**

Geurtze, Robert M. McAmmond, Elmar L. Morway, William G. Reuter, Edmund A. Steere, Albin A. Studler, and **John F. Toohey Jr.** *First officers:* **Tom Yovine,** president; **Richard Van Wormer,** district administrator. *History consultants:* **John B. Geurtze, Edward** and **Marie Miles.** *Membership:*...start, 110-peak, 130 in 1991.

Bethlehem Business Women's Club. 1951. *Purpose:* to promote friendships and the interests of women in the local business and professional community. *First officers:* **Helen R. Knowles,** president; **Lucille Williams** and **Gladys Glander,** vice presidents; **June Lake** and **Alma Hoffmeyer,** secretaries; *History consultants:* **Elizabeth Geurtze, Patricia Bannan, Alice Boutelle, Dorothy Brown, Evelyn Essex, Nellie Evans, Dorothy Kelleher, Evelyn Sanvidge.** *Membership:* 25-start, 60-peak, 57 in 1990.

Bethlehem Cemetery Association. 1865. *Purpose:* to plan and supervise the development and maintenance of a cemetery. *First officers:* **John Van Allen, M.D.,** president; **Jacob Hotaling,** vice president; **Reverend J. Lansing Pearse,** secretary; **John H. Booth,** treasurer; **George C. Adams, George M. Bender, Ancel Crocker, Robert Frazier,** and **Albert Slingerland,** trustees. **Mr Adams** was appointed superintendant of the cemetery. *History consultant:* **Gilbert O. Drake.** Trustee *Membership:* 9-start. 9-peak. 9 in 1991.

Bethlehem Central Children's Theatre Association. 1938. *Purpose:* to provide children in the elementary grades with a variety of experiences in the performing arts. *Early leaders:* **Ann Olford,** organizer; **Hamilton Bookhout, Edith Dappert, Mrs. Richard Kraft, Mrs. Henry MacMillan,** and **Mrs. V.A.(Catherine) Van Volkenburgh.** *History consultants:* **Joan Barron, Elizabeth Deily, Marie Musgrove,** and **Nancy Smith.** *Membership:* 6-start, 30-peak, 30 in 1990.

Bethlehem Chamber of Commerce. 1954. (an outgrowth of the former **Bethlehem Business Men's Association** which was formed in 1949). *Purpose:* to keep the members up-to- date on new developments and to promote the civic and economic vitality of the community. *First officers:* **Charles Oliver**, president; **William Schoonmaker**, vice president; **Alfred Peterson**, secretary and **Lucille Williams**, treasurer. *History consultant:* **Alan Hilchie**. *Membership:* 60-start, 450- peak, 450 in 1991.

Bethlehem Citizens for Responsible Planning. 1987. *Purpose:* to advocate effective and consistent planning in the Town of Bethlehem. *First officers:* **John Finn**, president; **John Smolinsky**, vice president; **Roberta Poneman**, secretary and **Jean Ducar**, treasurer. *History consultant:* **Roberta Poneman**. *Membership:* 8-start, 270-peak, 270 in 1990.

Bethlehem Conscript Society. 1875. *Purpose:* to pursue and recover horses stolen from the members. *First officers:* **Albertus W. Becker**, treasurer; **William Kimmey**, vice treasurer; **John J. Mull**, **John F. Shafer**, and **Isaac Van Allen**, auditors. Membership figures unavailable.

Bethlehem Festival Fund (originally the **Bethlehem Community Christmas Festival**). 1942. *Purpose:* to focus attention on the true spirit of the holiday season and to encourage citizens to help the needy. *Early leaders:* **Mrs. Sydney L. Smith**, organizer and **Rolland R. Truitt**, musical director. *History consultants:* **Helen Denny**, **John** and **Phyllis Flandreau**, **Richard Haverly, Sr.**, **Gregory Jackson**, and **Joanne Kimmey**. Served by a Board of Directors; now twelve members, four officers, and three advisory committee members.

Bethlehem Garden Club. 1965. *Purpose:* to promote interest in gardening, conservation and community beautification with flowers. *First officers:* **Phyllis LeMaitre**, president; **Helen Waller**, vice president; **Signe Klusman**, secretary and **Edith Miller**, treasurer. *History consultants:* **Ruth H. Bruso, Phyllis Harwood, Dorothy B. Hill, Eunice Hunter**, and **Constance Strong**. *Membership* 20-start, 80-peak, 80 in 1990.

Bethlehem Grange 137. 1874. *Purpose:* to advance the eco-nomic, social, and political interests of farmers in the Town of Bethlehem and surrounding towns. *First Master:* **Jurian Winne**. *History consultants:* **Henry Meyer** and **Helen Raynor**. *Membership:* 30-start, 305-peak, 211 in 1991.

Bethlehem Junior Grange 115. 1929. *Purpose:* to teach community work, arts and crafts, and Grange rituals through social programs. *First master:* **David A. Mead**. *History consultant:* **Helen Raynor**. *Membership:* 14-start, 65-peak, 27 in 1991.

Bethlehem Lions Club. 1955. *Purpose:* to help the hearing and visually impaired and other needy community interests under the motto, "We Serve." *First officers:* **John B. Heidel**, president; **A. Scott Rowe, Emilio Montrose** and **Burton W. Miller**, vice presidents; **Harold E. Williams**, secretary-treasurer. *History consultants:* **Robert DeGrof, Michael Murphy**, and **Mr. Suparmanto**. *Membership:* 29-start, 58-peak 37 in 1991.

Bethlehem Masonic Lodge. 1820. *Purpose:* to bring men together for fellowship and to encourage individual integrity, charitable contributions, and good citizenship. *Early officers and charter members:* **Joshua Babcock, John H.Burhans, Abram Drummond, Peter Esmay, Henry B. Haswell, John Haswell, John Kelderhouse, John P. McHarg, Nathaniel Sawyer,** and **John W. Wands**. *Membership:* 10-start. Termination information not available.

Bethlehem Masonic Lodge 1096. 1928. *Purpose:* to bring men together for fellowship and to encourage individual integrity, charitable contributions and good citizenship. *First officers:* **Robert T. Martin**, master; **Howe K. Cassavant**, senior warden; **J. Walter Hotaling**, junior warden; **Edward J. Slingerland**, treasurer; **DeForest S. Dunlop**, secretary; **George C. Porter**, senior deacon; **W. Jack Weaver**, junior deacon; **Stanley R. Crocker**, senior master of ceremony; **William S. Stafford**, junior master of ceremony; **Leon M. Adkins**, chaplain, **Edward H. Marsh**, marshall; **Walter F. Sherman**, senior steward; **Fred H. Blessing**, junior steward; **William Vogel**, organist, and **Frank R. Stevens**, tiler. Additionally, **Clarence T. Dolson**

and **Henry E. Hauf** served as trustees. *History consultant:* **Alan C. Lewis.** *Membership:* 95-start, 490-peak, 300 in 1990.

Bethlehem Men's Republican Club. 1961. *Purpose:* to advocate and promote principles of political and social conduct for which the Republican Party stands. *First officers:* **Charles H. Redmond,** president; **Raymond Brownell,** vice president; **Arthur E. McCormick,** secretary; **Vincent P. Herzog,** treasurer; **Otto Deheus,** town Republican chairman and **Bertram E. Kohinke,** town supervisor. *History consultants:* **David Austin, Bernard Kaplowitz, Brian M. Murphy, Robert K. Oliver,** and **Paul A. Wagner.** *Membership:* 300 start, 550 peak, 550 in 1990. Note: this group merged with the Bethlehem Women's Republican Club in 1992. The new group is called **The Bethlehem Republican Club.**

Bethlehem Music Association. 1975. *Purpose:* to provide music enrichment opportunities for students not normally offered in the schools. *First officers:* **Mrs. Bailey Bloom,** president; **Kathleen Kaplowitz,** vice president; **Barbara Meinert,** secretary; **Bette Shaw,** treasurer and **Samuel S.Bozella,** music supervisor. *History consultants:* **Anna C. Birdsey, Kathleen Bragle, Ann Leonard.** *Membership:* 36-start, 300-peak, 300 in 1991.

Bethlehem Opportunities Unlimited. 1984. *Purpose:* to provide alternatives for teenagers to drug and alcohol use and abuse. *First officers:* **Holly Billings,** president; **Anthony Bango** and **Constance Cunningham,** vice presidents; **Linda Carotenuto,** secretary; and **Philip Maher,** treasurer. *History consultants:* **Holly Billings, Megan Bugler,** and **Elizabeth Iseman.** *Membership:* 30-start, 270-peak, 245 in 1990.

Bethlehem Mutual Protective Association. 1909. *Purpose:* to protect the members against violations of the law and to guard against theft, trespass, and mischief. *First officers:* **W.F. Wheelock,** chairman; **J.W.F. Neef,** chief of police; **William A. Glenn,** attorney and counsel. *Membership:* 15-start, 440-peak. Uncertain membership when group disbanded ca. 1936.

Bethlehem Senior Citizens, Inc. 1955. *Purpose:* to provide social and cultural enrichment experiences for Bethlehem citizens over the age of fifty-five. Early leaders (when the group was under Lion's Club and Bethlehem Central School sponsorship): **Vivian Bennett, William Gatgen, Ralph Hoag, Jesse Ressimini,** and **Leonard Smith.** The first executive committee was formed in 1958: **Harry Bender,** president; **Clara Forkel,** vice president; **Mrs. Glen Wehrle** and **Blanche McNary,** secretaries; **Stanley Snyder,** treasurer; and **Mary Mason,** historian. *History consultants:* **Joyce Becker** and **Karen Pelletier.** *Membership:* 73-start, 259-peak, 259 in 1991.

Bethlehem Soccer Club. 1978. *Purpose:* to promote the game of soccer through an intra-club program and the Capital District Youth soccer League. *First Officers:* **George Tilroe,** president; **Charles Guinn,** vice president; **Janet Morris,** secretary; and **Arthur Guarino,** treasurer. *History consultant:* **Gerald J. Docteur, Dominick Matarrese,** and **William Silverman.** *Membership:* 14-start, 1500-peak,1500 in 1990.

Bethlehem Sportsmen's Club. 1946. *Purpose:* to promote and defend the wise use of natural resources, to sponsor a rifle club in which safe gun- handling and responsible behavior are taught, and to promote shooting sports and sports camaraderie. *First officers:* **Harold Ochner,** president; **Edward Kuhl,** vice president; **Charles Quay,** secretary; **Edward Hehre,** treasurer; **Millard Brimmer, Frank Burke, John Doyle, Sr., Henry Hershenroder, Robert Rayburn, Otis Williams, M.D.,** and **Donald Williamson,** directors. *History consultants:* **Norman Elfeldt** and **John E. Manne, D.D.S..** *Membership:* 20- start, 200-peak, 160 in 1990.

Bethlehem Support Group for Parents of Students With Handicapping Conditions. 1987. *Purpose:* to provide of emotional support, information, and advocacy to parents and guardians of students with any type of handicapping condition. **Jeanette Koch,** organizer. *History consultant:* **Gail S. Moon.** *Membership:* 25-start, 35-peak, 35 in 1990.

Bethlehem Tennis Association. 1966. *Purpose:* to promote the playing of tennis through tournaments and junior development programs. *Early leaders:* **Maynard B. Parsons**, organizer; **Thomas Stevenson**, president; **Wayne F. Fry**, vice president; **Karen Korngold**, secretary; **Douglas Ferguson**, treasurer; **Donald M. Camp**, instructor. *History consultants:* **Donald M. Camp, David L. Ernst, Michael W. Hampton,** and **Adele M. Parsons.** *Membership:* 96-start, 460-peak, 460 in 1991.

Bethlehem Tomboys. 1972. *Purpose:* to organize fast-pitch softball experiences for young women in Bethlehem. *First officers:* **John Castiglione**, president; **Sally Castiglione**, vice president; **Sally Abele**, secretary; **Fred** and **Jean Frattura, Rex Hornbrook, Nancy Richter,** and **Robert Ruckterstuhl**, directors; **Irving Van Woert, Jr.**, coach. *History consultant:* **Irving Van Woert Jr.** *Membership:* 141-start, 315-peak, 180 in 1990.

Bethlehem Volunteer Ambulance Service. 1956. *Purpose:* to provide basic life support and ambulance service for residents in the hamlets of Glenmont, Selkirk, and South Bethlehem. *First officers:* **Charles Sullivan**, president; **Vincent Lyons**, vice president; **Adelaide Weiseburn**, secretary; and **Carlton Chesbro**, treasurer. *History consultant:* **Richard T. Stangle.** *Membership:*...start, 76-peak, 76 in 1992.

Bethlehem Women's Republican Club. 1926. *Purpose:* to work toward advancing the best interests of the state and nation through the agency of the Republican Party, and to uphold and promote Republican principles. *First officers:* **Ruth M. Miner**, organizer and president; **Nettie Glenn**, vice president; **Eleanor Andrews**, secretary; **Thelma Comstock**, treasurer. *History consultants:* **Deborah Maher, Kathleen Noonan,** and **Cynthia Wilson.** *Membership:* 15-start, 2,000-peak, 167 in 1991. Note: this group merged with the Bethlehem Men's Republican Club in 1992. The new group is called the **Bethlehem Republican Club.**

Boy Scouts of America, Delmar Troop 16. Fort Orange Council. 1912. *Purpose:* to provide boy scouts with character-building, citizenship training, and physical fitness through use of the outdoors as a classroom. *Early leader:* **Charles Stine**, scoutmaster. *History consultant:* **John B. Geurtze.** *Membership:* 24-peak. Termination information unavailable.

Boy Scouts of America -Delmar Troop 71, Uncle Sam Fort Orange Council. 1974. *Purpose:* same as Troop 16 above. *First Leaders:* **Roger E. Dandeneau**, scoutmaster; **Ralph T. LaBarge**, assistant scoutmaster; **Richard VanWoert**, chairman of the organizing committee; **James D. Daley**, pastor and adviser. *History consultants:* **Ralph LaBarge** and **Richard Switzer.** *Membership:* 5-start, 29-peak, 11 in 1990.

Boy Scouts of America - Delmar Troop 75, Fort Orange Council. 1930. *Purpose:* same as Troop 16 above. *First leaders:* **George Henry Blakeslee, Jr.**, scoutmaster; **John A. Beaumont**, assistant scoutmaster; **Walter F. Henkel, Jr.**, chairman of the organizing committee; **Leon M. Adkins**, pastor and advisor. *History consultants:* **Charles D.(Chuck) McKinney, Susan** and **Robert Tangorre.** *Membership:* 11-start, 50 -peak, 50 in 1991.

Boy Scouts of America - Elsmere Troop 1, Fort Orange Council. 1919. *Purpose:* same as troop 16 above. **Kenneth Swallow** scoutmaster; **Herman Lieblich**, assistant scoutmaster. *History consultant:* **Robert Allen Baldwin.** *Membership:* 5-start, 5-peak, 5 when disbanded in 1919.

Boy Scouts of America - Elsmere Troop 58, Fort Orange Council. 1920. *Purpose:* same as Troop 16 above. *First leaders:* **Carl L. Wehrle**, scoutmaster; **Harold Geurtze**, assistant scout master; **William J. Knowles**, chairman of the organizing committee. *History consultants:* **Kenneth S. Bauer, Dennis Green, Kathleen Newkirk.** *Membership:* 12-start, 27-peak, 15 in 1990.

Boy Scouts of America - Selkirk Troop 1. Fort Orange Council. 1919. *Purpose:* Same as Troop 16 above. Organizer: **Charles Mallery**; scoutmaster: **James Killough.** *History consultant:* **Kenneth Van Allen.** *Membership:* around 14.

Boy Scouts of America - Selkirk Troop 81, Fort Orange Council. 1949. *Purpose:* same as Troop 16 above. *Early leader:* C.L. Klahn, chairman of the organizing committee. **History consultants: Jeffrey Ball, Dudley Moon,** and **Robert J. Selover.** *Membership:* 8-start, 25-peak, 23 in 1991.

Capital District Civil War Roundtable. 1984. *Purpose:* to promote interest in the Civil War through lectures and field trips. *First officers :* **Michael Aikey,** president; **Robert Mulligan,** vice president; **William Howard,** secretary; **Richard H. Davis,** treasurer; and **James Corsaro,** editor of publications. *History consultant:* **William Howard.** *Membership:* 45-start, 125-peak, 125 in 1992.

Delmar Athletic Club. ca. 1904. *Purpose:* to field athletic teams in several sports in both intramural and inter-city leagues. Early participants: **George Spawn, Sr.,** coach; **Harry Bender, Dudley Boutelle, Robert Carrick, Thomas Carrick, Roy McCormick, Edward Mockrie, Scott Palmer, Crannell Sprong, Clarence Van Wie,** and **Charles Williams.** *Membership:* figures not available.

Daughters of the American Revolution - Tawsentha Chapter. 1907. *Purpose:* to perpetuate the memory and spirit of American independence, to uphold the spirit of the U.S. Constitution and to foster genuine patriotism and love of country. *Early leaders:* **Mrs. Calvin W. Edwards,** first regent; **Mrs. F.S. Blessing, Mrs. W.H. Coughtry.** *History consultants:* **Mrs. William D. (Allison) Bennett, Mrs. Warren Creel,** and **Mrs. Eleanor Turner.** *Membership:* 114-peak, 73 in 1990.

Delmar Business Men's Association. 1949. *Purpose:* to promote trade, commerce and good customer relationships. *First president:* **Arthur Starman.** *Officers in 1952:* **Donald Terry,** president; **Charles Oliver,** vice president; **Lucille Williams,** secretary; and **Chester Hawley,** treasurer. *Membership* in 1952: 45.

Delmar Camera Club. 1957. *Purpose:* to provide the members with opportunities to develop skills in photography as a hobby or vocation. *First officers:* **William C. Bennett,** president; **Russell Deneger,** secretary- treasurer; **Father Charles Kaulfuss,** black and white print chairman; **Kenneth Smith,** color print chairman; **John D. Brown** membership chairman; **Mrs. Kenneth Smith,** social chairman. *History consultants:* **Amelia R. Andersen, Florence Becker,** and **Benjamin French.** *Membership:* 46-start, 46-peak, 20 in 1990.

Delmar Choral Society. 1928. *Purpose:* to provide opportunities for Bethlehem residents to sing serious music and to present programs for enjoyment of Bethlehem area citizens. *Early leaders:* **Ethel Dewire,** accompanist and conductor; **Mrs. Henry S. Manley,** president; **Mrs. George Maclay,** vice president; **Mrs. Jack Weaver,** secretary; and **Dr. Paul B. Brooks,** treasurer. *Membership:* 24-start. Disbanded in the late 1930s.

Delmar Community Orchestra -formerly the Delmar Men's Orchestra. 1940. *Purpose:* to provide opportunities for amateur musicians to play in a group and to bring live music to groups such as nursing and retirement homes. *Early musicians:* **Rolland Truitt,** music director; **Carlton Gordon, Charles Lacy.** *History consultants:* **Ralph Mead, Robert McGowan,** and **Millie Stahl.** *Membership:* 7-start, 56-peak, 50 in 1990.

Delmar Concert Orchestra. 1928. *Purpose:* to provide opportunities for citizens to play musical instruments, particularly in a support role for Delmar Choral Society concerts. *First leader:* **Donald W. Dewire,** music director. *History consultants:* **George Alfred Lansing, Sr.,** and **Claude White.** *Membership:* 16-start, 29-peak, Disbanded in late 1930s.

Delmar Craft Club - originally the Delmar Evening Unit (Home Bureau). 1946. *Purpose:* to stimulate interest in and to offer instruction in a variety of home crafts. *First officers:* **Mrs. Lincoln Petersen,** chairman; **Mrs. William Foss,** vice chairman; **Mrs. Arlington Smith,** secretary-treasurer. *History consultants:* **Dorothy Hinsdale** and **Edrie M. Pregent.** *Member-*

ship: 9-start, 135-peak, 45 in 1990.

Delmar Fire Department, Inc. - formerly Delmar Fire Company Chemical No. 1. 1911. *Purpose:* to provide fire protection for the hamlet of Delmar and advanced life support for tri-village residents. *Early leaders:* **Edward J. Bedell, E.P. Burnham,** and **Hiram W. Cowlbeck,** organizers; **Alton C. Rowe,** captain; **Hiram W. Cowlbeck,** clerk; **George E. Geager,** treasurer; **W. Scott Palmer,** first lieutenant, **Ira Boynton,** second lieutenant; **F.A. McMillen, C.E. Mochrie,** and **C.F. Williams,** trustees. *History consultant:* **LeRoy J. Cooke,** *Membership:* 34-start, 62-peak 62 in 1991.

Delmar Dolphins Swim Club. 1964. *Purpose:* to provide the members with a competitive swim program with an emphasis on teaching strokes for meets and competitions. **Early leader: Raymond Sliter,** coach. *History consultants:* **Margaret Byrd** and **John Whipple.** *Membership:* 25-start, 175-peak, 50 in 1990.

Delmar Progress Club. 1901. *Purpose:* to promote an intelligent interest in literature, art, science, philanthropy and the vital questions of the day. *Early leaders:* **Miss Elva Hinman Dyer,** organizer; **Carolyn Rouse,** president; **Elizabeth Connors, Nettie Glenn,** and **Mrs. Edward Mochrie** held various positions in the early years. *History consultants:* **Lois H. Dillon** and **Margaret B. Zimmerman.** *Membership:* 11-start, 350-peak, 350 in 1990.

Delmar Sunday Morning Running Group. 1981. *Purpose:* to provide an opportunity for local runners to meet on a weekly basis to run for pleasure, exercise and/or to prepare for races. *Early leader:* **Doris Davis,** organizer. *History consultants:* **Doris Davis, Robert MacDowell, Robert Salamone, Henry Steadman, Judith** and **Thomas Swazey,** and **Alan Via.** *Membership:* 4-start, 20-peak, 20 in 1990.

Echoes Baseball Team (Slingerlands). 1890. *Purpose:* to arrange practice and tournament play for residents who enjoy the game of baseball. *Prominant players:* **Brate Babcock, William Burns, Frank Hitchcock, Edward Joselin, "Yocky" Oliver, Harry McCormack,** and **George Remmey.** *History consultant:* **Alice Boutelle** and paper based on an interview with John Oliver. No membership statistics available.

Elmwood Cemetery. 1860. (Bethlehem Rural Cemetery Association). *Purpose:* to organize and develop a rural cemetery association under a state law (April 27,1847) authorizing incorporation. *First officers:* **Peter Niver,** president; **Lewis Meyers,** secretary-treasurer; **John Babcock, Zachariah Riker, Robert Selkirk, Daniel P. Winne,** trustees. *History consultants:* **Kenneth H. Malary, Herbert Strumpf,** and **Marie Vadney.** *Membership:* 6-start, 9-peak, 9 in 1991.

Elsmere and Delmar Sewing Circle. 1902. *Purpose:* to provide the members with opportunities to share ideas about sewing and knitting and to make useful items for the needy. *Early participants:* **Mrs. William Furman, Mrs. Henning, Mrs. Lucius Reed, Mrs. Rourke, Mrs.Harry Shill** and **Mrs.Elsworth Van Wie. Agnes Bender,** and **Mrs. George Casey** joined the group a little later. *Membership:* 8-start, 30-peak, 30 when group disbanded in 1978.

Elsmere Fire Company A. 1922. *Purpose:* to preserve and protect life and property from and during any fires occurring within the Elsmere Fire District. *First officers:* **Peter N.A. Klein,** chief and chairman of the Board of Fire Commissioners; **H.B. Case,** captain and member of the Board; **E.B. Scrafford,** 2nd lieutenant; **G.B. Wells,** 3rd lieutenant; **W.S. Stafford,** clerk; **E. Orvis,** treasurer; and **F.A. Hunsdorfer,** member of the Board. *History consultants:* **J. Robert Hendrick, Jr., Kenneth E. McNary, James Reagan,** and **Richard S. Webster.** *Membership:* 40 active and 190 associate members at start, 70 active and 250 associate members at peak, 70 active and 250 associate members in 1992.

Embroiderers' Guild of America, New York Capital District Chapter. 1967. *Purpose:* to foster the highest standards of excellence in the practice of the art of embroidery through an active program of education and study. *History consultant:* **Gertrude (Hallenbeck) Cashvan.** *Membership:* ca. 35-start, 236-peak, 210 in 1992.

Five Rivers Limited. 1973. *Purpose:* to promote and support educational programs at the Five Rivers Environmental Center. *Early resource leaders:* **Robert Budlinger** and **Dr. Vincent Schaeffer.** *First officers:* **Dr. Robert Nurnberger,** president; **Sigrid Newell,** secretary; **Erastus Corning,** treasurer. *History consultant:* **Dr. Robert S. Alexander.** *Membership:* 9-start, 480-peak, 480 in 1990.

4 H Groups in Bethlehem. 1946. *Purpose:* to help young people from seven to nineteen years of age become self-sufficient, creative, responsible citizens through a variety of programs and educational experiences under the group's watchwords - head, hands, heart and health, and motto, "To Make the Best Better." Early leaders of groups that remained together over ten years: **Marion Shelmerdine,** among others, Delmar Stitch and Chatter Girls - 1946-1959; **Helen Prusik,** Elm Avenue Elves-1954-1963; **Helen Olson,** Jolly Homemakers - 1957-1971. *History consultants:* **Joan Prusik Adams, Jean Olson Lucey, Carol Zdgiebloski Northrup.** *Membership:* strong in the 1950s and 1960s, declining in recent years.

Friends of the Bethlehem Public Library. 1984. *Purposes:* to increase public awareness of the functions and services of the library, offer cultural and educational programs of interest to the community, help the library implement specific projects, and to sponsor interaction between the library and other community organizations. *First officers:* **Frederic Adler,** president; **Eleanor Haywood,** secretary; **Robert O'Neil,** treasurer; **Jean** and **Morton Adell, Patricia Meldrum, Donald MacHarg, Virginia Woodward,** and **Irving Zeitz,** trustees. *Membership:* 30-start, 315-peak, 315 in 1990.

Glenmont Homemakers (founded as the **Glenmont Home Bureau**). 1945. *Purpose: to* create projects for the improvement of home and family life. *Early leaders:* **Mrs. Thomas Sanvidge,** organizer; **Mrs. John Muller,** chairman; **Harriet Metz,** vice president; **Elizabeth Stoffels,** secretary; and **Kathryn Nolan,** treasurer. *History consultant:* **Alice Wiggand.** *Membership:* 21-start, 60-peak, 55 in 1990.

Hadassah - Bethlehem Chapter. 1987. *Purpose:* to improve education, medical care, and youth rescue programs in this country and abroad, especially in Israel. *First officers:* **Amy Sonne** and **Irene Rosenthal,** co- presidents; *History consultant:* **Shelly Liebman.** *Membership:* 150-peak, 150 in 1991.

Hudson Valley Girl Scout Council - Delmar Troop 1. 1917. *Purpose:* to inspire girls with the highest ideals of character, conduct, patriotism and sevice to help them become happy and resourceful citizens. *Early leaders:* **Dorothy Best, Helen Karpel, Jane MacConnel, Mrs. Allen Merselis, Miss Ruth M. Miner, Mrs. Elmer L. Morway, Miss Beverly Tonkin, Mrs V.A.Van Volkenburgh.** *History consultants:* **Ms. Terri A. Fox, Bonnie Stone.** *Membership:* figures unavailable.

Hudson Valley Girl Scout Council - Delmar Troop 33. ca. 1925. *Purpose:* same as Troop 1 above. *Leaders in the 1930s:* **Captains Mabel Barton** and **Florence Wilcox, lieutenants Dorothy Barton,** and **Alice Porter.** *History consultants:* **Alice Porter Boutelle** and **Florence Wilcox Reynolds.** *Membership:* ca. 12-start, 21-peak, disbanded in the 1940s.

Hudson Valley Girl Scout Council - Glenmont Troop 315. 1963. *Purpose:* same as Troop 1 above. *Early volunteeer staff:* **Joy Ford,** leader; **Dorothy Starkweather,** assistant leader. *History consultants:* **Joy Ford** and **Marcelle M. Olsen.** *Membership:* 11-start, 50-peak, 10 when troop disbanded in 1984.

Hudson Valley Girl Scout Council - Hammagrael Troop 321. 1958. *Purpose:* same as Troop 1 above. Organized by **Margaret Lilly** with assistance from **Evelyn Drake.** *History consultant:* **Margy-Jo Lilly Borofsky.** *Membership:* figures not available.

Hudson Valley Girl Scout Council - Selkirk Troop 48. ca 1934. *Purpose:* same as Troop 1 above. *Troop leader:* **Jessie Winne.** *History consultant:* **Allison Bennett.** Membership figures not available.

Knights of Columbus. 1951. *Purpose:* to promote and conduct educational Catholic religious programs and help with social welfare for the good of the community. *First officers:* **Richard K. Rudolph,** grand knight; **Ambrose F. Brennan,** deputy grand knight; **Harry Desmond,** warden; **Paul Coty,** financial secretary; **Harry Kohls,** treasurer; **Donald Gallagher,** advocate; and **Ray McGuire,** chancellor. *History consultant:* **Richard K. Rudolph.** *Membership:* 80-start, 80-peak, 35 in 1991.

Kiwanis Club. 1940. *Purpose:* to help needy individuals and groups under the motto, "We Build." *First officer:* **Dr. S. Benjamin Meyers,** president. *History consultants:* **Charles Fritts, Benjamin L. Meyers,** and **Charles Waggoner.** *Membership:* start, 70-peak, 20 in 1990.

Ladies Auxiliaries - Bethlehem Fire Departments. Organized soon after the dates shown for individual companies. *Purpose:* to assist the companies in handling telephone calls, correspondence, fund-raising, and social events for the members, and to aid firemen in numerous ways for effective fire protection to all of the hamlets throughout Bethlehem. *History consultant:* **Arcola Leonard.** *Membership:* varies with the individual company.

Light of Bethlehem - Independent Order of Good Templars 118. 1879. *Purpose:* to aid citizens in abstaining from alcohol through group support. *Early leaders:* **Joseph S. Baumes, W.C.T.,** and several members of the Baumes family in Cedar Hill, organizers. *Membership:* 13-start. Termination information unavailable.

Normanside Country Club. 1926. *Purpose:* to provide a golf course, clubhouse and related facilities enabling the members to enjoy the game through individual play and tournaments,

and to further friendships in a social/athletic setting. *Founder:* **William A. Glenn.** *Other leaders:* **Dr. Edward J. Bedell, Fred M. Earing, Walter P.R. Pember.** *First elected president:* **William A. Mansfield.** First president of Normanside Corp.: **Dr. Thomas M. Holmes.** *History consultants:* **Joseph A. Allgaier** and **James Kurposka.** *Membership:* 325 single and family memberships in 1992.

North Bethlehem Fire Department. 1947. *Purpose:* to provide fire protection service to the hamlet of North Bethlehem. *Early leaders:* **Stephen B. Fliegel,** chief; **Robert Devine,** president; **D. Cady Herrick II,** legal adviser; **Elizabeth Schloupt,** president of the Ladies Auxiliary. *History consultant:* **William James, Jr.** *Membership:* 120-start, 120-peak, 22 in 1992.

Order of the Eastern Star # 818 (Onesquethaw Chapter). 1928. *Purpose:* to support the work of Onesquethaw Masonic Lodge 1096 and needy charities. *Early matrons:* **Emma Ellsworth, Edna Tiedeman, Florence Dolson, Emma Hafley, Evelyn Higby, Anna Wilcox, Edith Herbage, Maude Hafley,** and **Mildred Terwilliger.** *History consultants:* **Flossie Smith** and **Shirley A. Lewis.** *Membership:* 8-start(and 86 more initiated in 1928) 180-peak, 180 in 1991.

Pop Warner Football. ca. 1963. *Purpose:* to provide football and cheerleading experience for Tri-Village youth between the ages of 9 and 14 years. *Early leaders:* unknown. *History consultants:* **Theresa Deyo** and **Thomas Walmsley.** *Membership:* 170-peak, 170 in 1991.

Quilters United in Learning Together (QUILT). 1977. *Purpose:* to share ideas and expertise in quilting. *Early leader:* **Charlotte Rinehart,** instructor. *History consultants:* **Ann Jacobs** and **Margaret Tubbs.** *Membership:* 47-start, 185-peak, 185 in 1990.

Rotary Club of Delmar. 1957. *Purpose:* to provide opportunities for the members to support high vocational standards, community service and international understanding. *First officers:* **Lowell H. Gypson,** president; **Chester L. Hawley,** vice president; **Leslie Edsall**, secretary; **Raymond A. LaMoy**, treasurer; **J. Coolidge Hand, Paul F. Laffey, Robert Martin**, and **Robert S. Miller**, directors. *History consultant:* **Raymond A. LaMoy**. *Membership:* 24-start, 32-peak, 24 in 1990.

Second Milers. 1964. *Purpose:* to offer the members opportunities for social fellowship and exposure to the issues and problems of the day through enlightened speakers. *Early leaders:* **Earl S. Jones** and **Dr. Robert Thomas**, organizers; **Howard W. Davenport**, president. *History consultants:* **Col. Howard R. Gmelch, Robert E. Patton**, and **A. Neil Smith**. *Membership:* 20-start, 200-peak, 190 in 1990.

Selkirk Fire Department - Company 1. 1926. *Purpose:* to provide fire protection service for the hamlet of Selkirk. *Early leaders:* **T.B. Van Derzee**, commissioner and chief; **William T. Fletcher, Neil D. Hyde, Walter Miller**, and **Michael H. Mangini**, commissioners. *Membership:* 5-start, 40 peak, 33 in 1991.

Selkirk Fire Department - Company 2. 1952. *Purpose:* to provide fire protection service for the hamlet of Glenmont. *First officers:* **John Hoose**, chief; **August Spaziano**, first assistant chief; **Robert Wiggand**, second assistant chief; **Alfred Relations**, secretary; **Robert Pauley**, treasurer, *Membership:* 24-start, 42-peak, 40 in 1991.

Selkirk Fire Department - Company 3. 1956. *Purpose:* to provide fire protection service for the hamlet of South Bethlehem. *Early leaders:* **Harold L. Williams**, district chief; **Gerard Wisenburn**, chief; **Ivan Baker**, first assistant chief; **Willard Griffen**, second assistant chief; **Ernest Hahn** and **Laird Robinson**, secretaries; and **Frank With**, treasurer. *History consultants for all three companies:* **Louis J. Picarazzi, Pieter Van Derzee** and **Charles Wickham**. *Membership:* **34-start, 38-peak, 36 in 1991.**

The Slingerlands Community Players. 1952. *Purpose:* to produce plays for school, civic and Bethlehem area audiences

and to present plays through the Quarto Players (a group within the Players) to audiences in the northeastern United States. *First officers:* **Ruth Wilbur**, organizer and coach; **Morris Schaeffer**, president; **Sylvester J. Bower**, vice president; **Mary F. Nugent** and **Ruth Oliver**, secretaries; **Mrs. Sylvester J. Bower**, treasurer; and **William E. Zimmerman**, business manager. *History consultants:* **Katherine DePorte** and **Joanne G. Kimmey**. *Membership:* 18-start, 70-peak, 40 when disbanded in 1979.

Slingerlands Fire Department. 1928. *Purpose:* to provide fire protection service for the hamlet of Slingerlands. *Early leaders:* **George Fowler**, chief; **Frederick Oliver** and **Charles Sanders**, assistant chiefs; **E. J. Nicholson**, secretary; and **John Carroll**, treasurer. *History consultant:* **Earl G. Lenhardt**. *Membership:* 38-start, 41-peak, 44 in 1992.

Town of Bethlehem Historical Association. 1964. *Purpose:* to stimulate an appreciation of the town's historical heritage and to discover, collect, and preserve material that illustrates local history. *Organizing participants in 1964:* **Norma L. June**, chairman; **Allison C. Bennett, Ruth E. Dickinson, Ruth E. Funk, Jean M. Lyon, Townsend R. Morey, Jr., S. Vint Van Derzee**, and **Mary Elizabeth Van Oostenbrugge**. *First officers in 1965:* **J. Phillips Campbell**, president; **Constance Loucks**, vice president; **Jean M. Lyon**, secretary; **Townsend R. Morey, Jr.**, treasurer; and **Meredith Clapper**, chairman of the Museum Committee. *Additional history consultants:* **Charles** and **Evelyn Alford, Peter** and **Florence Christoph, Charles** and **Marjorie Crangle, Mrs. Edward R. Dillon Jr., Miss Marjorie A. Terrell, Richard** and **Margaret Thayer, William** and **Mary Tinney, James** and **Ann Vandervort, James** and **Eleanor Weidemann**, and **Marie Weidemann**. *Membership:* 15-start, 254-peak, 254 in 1991.

Tri-Village Directory Association. 1930. *Purpose:* to issue an information dirctory for Delmar, Elsmere, and Slingerlands. *Prime mover:* **Mrs. Alton C. (Caroline) Rowe**, who was assisted by the Ladies Aid Society in the church. *History consultant:*

Virginia Cornell. *Membership:* 443- peak, 443 in 1992.

Tri-Village Little League. 1954. *Purpose:* to promote sportsmanship, teamwork, and skill in the game of baseball. *First officers:* Arthur L. Fleahman Jr., president; Robert H. Rice, vice president; Frederick Potter, treasurer; and Edward Bayer, secretary. *History consultants:* Adrian Arnold and Peter Meyer. *Membership:* 60-start, 630-peak, 620 in 1992.

Tri-Village Squares. 1983. *Purpose:* to provide opportunities for the members to learn and practice western square dancing. *Early leaders:* Duane Silver, instructor; Bernard and Antionette DeLeo, co-presidents; George and Diane Gravlee, co-vice presidents; Beatrice and Irving Grossman, co-secretaries; Kenneth and Jean Marriott, co-treasurers. *History consultants:* William and Barbara Sippel. *Membership:* 18-start, 55-peak, 55 in 1990.

Tri-Village Welcome Wagon (formerly Tri-Village Newcomers Club). ca. 1953. *First officers:* Mrs. Robert Schreck, president; Mrs. Gomer Davis and Mrs. William Osborne, vice presidents; Mrs. Howard Bartlett, secretary; and Mrs. Gordon Carvill, treasurer. *History consultants:* Cheryl Cook, B. J. Moreen, Barbara Riegel, and Marjorie Thurlow. *Membership:* 20- start, 200-peak, 140 in 1990.

Veterans of Foreign Wars - Bethlehem Memorial Post 3185. 1946. *Purpose:* to strengthen comradeship among the members and to support patriotic activities. *First officer:* James Austin, commander. *History consultants:* Robert Conti, Allen Cornes, Ralph Gregory, Carl W. Rappe, Thomas Skultety, Ronald Trevett. *Membership:* 60-start, 150-peak, 120 in 1990.

Veterans of Foreign Wars - Bethlehem Memorial Post 3185 Ladies Auxiliary. 1947. *Purpose:* to support the work of VFW Bethlehem Memorial Post 3185 and others in need. *First officer:* Hazel Martin, president. *History consultants:* Frances Gatnam, Gail Larvia, Valerie Mosley, Marie Privler, Karla Skultety, Mary Trevett. *Membership:* 21-start, 77-peak, 61 in 1991.

Village Stage. 1984. *Purpose:* to entertain, enrich and educate Bethlehem area audiences in the field of drama. *First officers:* Patricia B. DeCecco, president; Lars Allanson, vice president; Dorothy Brown and Muriel Welch secretaries; Jo Ann Davies, treasurer; William Schoonmaker, legal adviser and trustee; Ann Marie Dullea, Judith Lamprecht, and Helen Scott, trustees. **Membership:** 120-start, 135-peak, 95 in 1990.

Village Volunteers Fife and Drum Corps (originally Village Fire Fifers). 1956. *Purpose:* to perpetuate the traditions of early American martial music and to provide opportunities for young people and adults to accept responsibility and set goals together. *Early leaders:* Lois and William F. Bub, Mr. & Mrs. Carl Benenati, and Robert Mulligan, Jr. *History consultants:* Robert Mulligan, Jr., and Kathleen Quinlan. *Membership:* 15-start, 67-peak, 36 in 1991.

Village Wonders. 1901. *Purpose:* to train Bethlehem youth in the game of baseball and to arrange games with other teams. *First staff and players:* "Bugs" Whitman, manager; Clarence Houck, president; DeWitt Simmons, scorekeeper; Ira Pier, captain and pitcher; Arthur Callan and Charles Callanan, catchers; John Oliver, first base; Clarence Earl, second base; Charles Pier, shortstop; Willis Redden, third base; Bert Sager, left field; Howard Sager, center field; and Kenneth Boutelle, right field. *History source:* paper written by Ted Boutelle in consultation with Ira Pier and John Oliver. **Membership:** 13-start. Team disbanded ca. 1915.

Bethlehem Men and Women in the Military

REVOLUTIONARY WAR:

Becker, Dirck
Becker, Wouter
Boice, Peter
Britt, Frederick
Callanan, Patrick
Colenburg, George
Conning, Andrew
Hogan, George
Jolly, Hugh
Murdock, Zimri
Nicoll, Francis
Niver, David
Oliver, Aaron
Oliver, John
Russell, Solomon
Sager, John
Slingerland, Abraham
Slingerland, Tunis
Soop, Conrad
Staats, Barent
Vandenbergh, Gerrit
Vanderzee, Cornelius
Van Wie, Arie
Van Wie, John
Van Wie, Peter
Winne, John
Winne, William

WAR OF 1812:

Adams, John
Babcock, Joshua
Bailey, James
Boice, Peter

Callanan, John
Frasier, Alexander
Hilderbrant, Jacob
Hogan, John
Jarvis, John J.
Kilmer, Simon
Lasher, Marcus
Oathout, John
Patterson, William
Rowe, Frederick
Soop, Jacob
Ten Eyck, Peter
Vanderzee, Walter
Van Rensselaer, Solomon
Van Wie, Garret
Vroman, Jacobus
Wiltsie, James

CIVIL WAR:

Able, John Wing
Ackerman, Christian
Adams, William S.
Aikens, John
Albert, John
Albert, Joseph
Albright James
Andes, Frederick
Apply, John
Arch, John
Arnold, Chester
Arnold, John
Arnold, Leonard
Bailey, George R.
Bailey, John M.
Bailey, John E.

Bailey, Robert H.
Bashwinger, Frank
Bashwinger, Joseph
Bateman, Edward
Bell, Cook
Bendall, Isaac
Bender, John
Berger, Henry
Bender, Wendell W.
Betz, Jacob
Biel, Robert
Bienan, George
Boice, Andrew
Boice, Jacob
Boniker, Jacob
Bradford, Eugene
Bradt, Adam
Bradt, Francis
Bradt, Henry
Bradt, John
Bradt, William
Brayton, Theodore
Breche, Joseph
Broaker, Nicholas
Brooks, Sylvester
Brooksby, James
Brown, Erastus
Brown, George
Brown, Michael
Blaser, John
Bleeker, Thomas S.
Blowers, Jospeph
Buerger, David
Burhans, David *
Burnside, William H.
Carknard, Andrew B. *

Carter, John
Calla, John
Canary, John
Caswell, James
Carpenter, Theodore
Chambers, Walter
Chandler, Warren D.
Clark, William
Coats, John
Cole, Daytus
Cook, William
Coons, Peter
Coons, Jacob
Copps, Godfrey
Cothran, William
Cregan, John
Curdy, Andrew
Daniels, Martin
Davis, E.W.
DeFreest, John
Denick, Nathaniel
Dexter, Charles
Dickson, Peter
Dingman, Asa
Doyle, Farrell
Drummer, August
Dunn, Charles
Dunn, George
Dunny, Charles
Earles, James
Eckert, Charles
Elgenheiser, John
Engler, John
English, John
Everling, John A.
Farrell, Patrick

Feeney, James
Feeley, John
Feeley, C. Lagrange
Fisher, John
Fitzgerald, John
Fitzpatrick, William
Flanders, Charles
Frazier, Daniel C.
Frazier, William
Frazier, Jacob
Frick, Christian
Fullman, Peter
Gable, Charles
Grebb, Joseph
Grey, Benjamin
Grey, Walter
Glass, George
Hagadorn, Peter
Hahn, William
Harrigan, William
Harwinger, Joseph
Hall, Robert Lewis
Hallenbeck, George
Hare, Adam
Hart, Thomas
Hart, John
Hertzog, Christopher
Herring, James *
Hesley, John J.
Hilton, Nicholas J.
Hoag, Samuel
Hoffman, Jacob
Hoffman, Charles
Hoffman, John
Hofman, Jacob
Houghtailing, David
Houser, Frederick
Huyck, Garret W.
Jackson, Jacob

Jackson, Jerrod
Jackson, Robert
Jackson, Samuel
Johns, Julius
Kana, John
Kana, Lawrence
Karens, John
Karknard, Richard
Kechner, Frank
Keeler, Jacob
Keeler, John
Keeler, Peter
Kelder, David
Kennedy, Andrew
Kimmer, John
Kimmer, Joseph
Kimmer, Robert
King, Thomas
Kirkhim, Theodore
Kirkhim, Thomas
Klein, Russell
Koernicke, Martin
Koons, William H.
Kramer, Andrew
Kramer, Jacob
Krank, Augustus
Krank, George
Krank, John A.
Krank, Joseph K.
LaCoy, Jacob
LaGrange, William J.
Lape, John L.
Lasher, Garret
Lasher, Leonard
Lasher, Joseph
Lanby, Joseph
Lembrocht, Alfred
Lenty, Joseph
Limback, John

Limback, Paul
Loesh, John
London, George
London, Michael Thomas
Long, Conrad
Long, John *
Marenis, Jacob
Marenus, David
Marenus, George
Marsden, William
Marsh, Frank
Martse, Christopher
Masen, George
McCullock, Conrad
McCormick, David
McCormick, George A.
McCormick, John Henry
McCormick, Samuel
McCormick, William M.
McEwin, Valentine
McGown, John
McRea, William
Meim, Lambert
Melius, Dewitt
Merisert, George
Merisert, Hernry
Merisert, Michael
Merrifield, William
Meyers, George
Mitler, Charles
Miller, Francis
Miller, Valentine
Moat, Thomas
Mosher, William A.
Myers, Andrew
Myers, John
Myers, Philip
Myers, William
Negelin, Thomas

Newhaus, Charles
Neydorff, Conrad A.
Newman, John
Niver, Edgar M.
Noxon, Robert G. *
Oliver, Aaron J.
Oliver, Andrew
Oliver, George W.
Osterhout, Henry O. *
Pangburn, John
Peterson, Jospeph
Platte, Bleeker
Pflager, John P.
Pommer, John
Radley, Aaron
Radley, Rushmore
Radley, William H.
Radliff, James
Radliff, Lewis
Rehm, Charles
Riley, James
Riley, Patrick
Rist, John
Rosekrans, Albert
Rosekrans, Leonard
Russell, Frederick
Russell, John
Russell, Joseph
Russell, William N.
Sager, Conrad
Sager, John A.
Sausbier, August
Schamehorn, Charles
Schindler, Max
Schindler, Richard
Schindler, William
Schneider, Peter
Schramm, Theodore
Sciss, Andrew

Sharp, George
Sharp, Matthew W.
Shieferdecker, Frederick A.
Shillford, Matthew *
Shutts, John
Skinger, Gustavus
Sigsby, William
Sitt, William
Silsby, Henry T.
Sitterly, Peter
Slingerland, Alvin
Slingerland, James T.
Slingerland, John Henry
Slingerland, William
Smith, Lewis H.
Smith, Philip
Staats, Jacob I.
Steel, William
Stremfill, John L.
Stultz, John *
Stumpf, William
Sumner, August
Sweet, William H.D.
Taylor, Peter *
Tilson, John S.
Tomkins, Gustus
Tomlinson, Edward
Tummler, Johann
Ulrich, Christian John
Vackmaster, Valentine
Van Allen, Charles *
Van Allen, Jacob *
Vanderpool, Garrett H.
Vanderpool, Isaac
Vanderzee, John Gurnsy
Vanderberg, W.H.
Van Hoesen, Peter
Van Steenburg, John E.
Van Wormer, Alfred

Van Wormer, James
Van Zandt, Elijah
Van Zandt, Frederick
Van Zandt, Henry
Van Zandt, Isaac
Van Zandt, Peter
Wahleber, Frederick
Waldie, James
Waley, Charles E.
Waley, John G.
Walker, Stephen *
Wallace, Frank
Welling, Hiram
Wemply, David P.
Werter, John
Westervelt, William Henry
White, Mark
Whittle, George
Whitman, Augustus
Wicks, George
Wippel, Michael
Wiley, George
Wiley, James A.
Williams, Samuel
Wiltsie, Soloman
Winne, Peter
Wise, John
Wistler, Barthold
Worker, Lewis
Wright, Mayor
Wynkoop, Peter A.
Yooz, Gottfried
Young, Matthew

WORLD WAR I:

Angell, Joseph
Baer, Thaddeus
Barber, Clifton

Barnes, P.
Bender, Norman
Blanchard, Nathaniel
Blessing, Fred
Bowen, Ward
Bowers, William
Brasure, John
Bresnahan, Edward
Britton, Walter
Brown, Alfred
Brown. George
Burnham, Lester
Butler, Ralph
Carr, J. Benson
Christopherson, Fred
Cochrane, William
Condon, Edward
Coughtry, James
Cowlbeck, Hiram
DeHeus, Otto
Deitz, Burr
Desso, Ernest
Dewey, Robert K.
Dysinger, Fred
Ertel, John
Fairlee, Ira
Flannery, Frank
Flint, William
Fowler, George
Gabriel, Alexander
Gardiner, Charles
Gilbert, Howard M.
Goddard, Charles
Goebel, Fred
Hague, John
Halsdorf, Marshall
Hartnett, William
Haswell, Richard
Henderson, Charles

Hertz, Joseph
Hevenor, E. Earle
Hewett, George
Higby, Leonard
Holland, Paul
Holmes, Florence
Holmes, Dr. Thomas M.
Hoopam, Cadle
Hungerford, Fred
Hungerford, Myron
Isdell, Irving
Jones, Earl
Keelan, Harry
Krause, Durrell
Lamson, John
Lauer, George
Lilly, Avrid
Luckrow, Harmon
Long, William
Mang, Harry
Martin, John
McMillan, Norman
McNutt, Clyde
McQuirk, Earl
McQuirk, Ray F.
Milbrandt, Adolph
Miller, Russell
Montgomery, James
Mullens, Dr. Clarence
Murray, Joseph
Oliver, Charles
Oliver, John
Ottman, Frederick
Paddock, Howard
Parker, Harry
Phillips, H. Deane
Pinkerton, Fred
Piper, Edwin
Pitcher, Ervin

Potter, Edgar
Prue, Milton
Reamer, Arthur
Reuter, George
Rider, Duglas
Robinson, Winthrop
Rowe, Alton, Jr.
Sampson, William
Sanders, Charles
Scaliza, Anthony
Seymour, James
Sharpe, Peter
Smith, Frederick
Smith, Guy B.
Spinosa, Vincent
Stewart, Rev. Newell
Streeter, H. Grey
Swarthout, Harry
Thompson, Willard
Tripp, Lynn
Van Liew, Roland
Weber, Warren
Weddell, Ernest
Wells, Joseph
Whitney, Clifford
Whitney, Frederick
Willard, Frank
Wood, Bernard

WORLD WAR II:

Abell, John P.
Abley, Marie
Adams, James
Adams, John Frank
Adams, Richard N.
Adams, William C. *
Adams, Frederick B.
Adriance, J. William

Agar, Charles C.
Agar, Charles C., Jr.
Agar, James T.
Aiken, Ralph C.
Airey, James L.
Aiken, Ralph C.
Airey, James L.
Alden, John
Alexander, Harvey
Alexander, Daniel A.
Allen, Charles H.
Allen, Louis A.
Allen, Richard F.
Allen, Walter R.
Allen, William E.
Allen, John F.
Altimari, James A.
Anderson, C. Brook
Anderson, Robert E.
Andrews, Harold F.
Angell, Robert B.
Apgar, George W.
Argus, Phillip
Armentrout, L. Lyman
Arnold, Harrison A., Jr.
Arnold, Adrian
Arntstein, Franklyn W.
Arthur, Donald F.
Arthur, Raymond B.
Augustine, Caly E.
Aylward, Harry B.
Babbitt, Robert D.
Babbitt, Richard R.
Bacher, Edwin J.
Bachmann, Alvin B.
Bahn, Gertrude I.
Bailey, Dwight P.
Bailey, Kenneth H.
Bailey, Richard J.

Bailey, William C.
Bailey, Francis
Bain, Kenneth J.
Bainer, Edward C.
Bainer, Henry R.
Bainer, Howard J.
Barachini, Neil
Barker, Stanley T.
Barker, Stephen M.
Barkhuff, Harold C.
Barnard, Alvin W.
Barnett, William F.
Barrett, Oscar
Bartlett, Robert
Barton, Scott L.
Basch, Alfred
Bastian, Joseph J., Jr.
Bates, Alexander J., Jr.
Bates, Harold L.
Bates, Walter
Bauer, Louis C.
Baxter, Jack
Beard, David B.
Beatty, Wallace G.
Begy, Jack
Behr, Carl M., Jr.
Behr, Hilda
Beller, Peter A.W., Jr.
Ben Fonte, Patrick J.
Benedetto, Orlando
Bennett, Clifford E. *
Bennett, Edward J., Jr.
Bennett, Richard
Bennett, Ronald
Bennett, William C., Jr.
Bennett, William D.
Bennett, William M.
Bentz, Frank P.
Bercharlie, Anthony

Bercharlie, John
Berman, Irving E.
Betts, Richard H.
Biernacki, Stanley A. *
Bilyieu, Douglas
Birchenough, Robert M.
Bird, Samuel E.
Bishop, Clinton H.
Blanchard, John A.
Blanchard, Marcus
Blanchard, Ruth M.
Blankenhorn, Charles W. *
Blatner, Henry L.
Bliesath, Ernest, Jr.
Blocksidge, Edwin L.
Blocksidge, Richard J.
Bloodgood, J.A.
Bloodgood, Arnold J.
Bloodgood, George A., Jr.
Bloodgood, Gerturde R.
Bogart, Willard A.
Boldue, Leopold L.
Boldue, Lomer F.
Bombenck, Phillip V.
Booth, William H.
Borst, Donald J.
Borst, Niles W.
Bourke, John J.
Boutelle, Edward W., Jr.
Boutelle, Lindsey
Bowen, Donald C.
Bradt, Claude A.
Bradt, George W.
Bradwell, Albert S.
Brate, Donald C.
Brayton, Kenneth G.
Brennan, Thomas H.
Briggs, Donald W.
Brisson, Daniel

Brockley, James C.
Brockley, John J.
Brockley, Leo J., Jr.
Brookmiller, Harold
Brooks, George L.
Brown, Leslie F.
Brown, Harry L.
Brownell, W. Van Kirk
Brumfield, William S., Jr.
Bryant, Leland O.
Buchaca, Robert
Buchanan, Kenneth D.
Buckley, Donald L.
Bump, Gardiner
Burgess, Harry
Burgess, Joseph J.
Burgess, Milton
Burhans, Willis G.
Burke, Frank J.
Burke, James E.
Burke, William G.
Burnes, Robert E.
Burns, Esther M.
Burns, Jerome M.
Bushey, Donald
Butler, Barent M.
Butman, George J.
Butts, George
Butts, George J.
Butz, Andres
Butz, Edward
Butz, Karl
Cady, James R.
Campbell, Delevan S.
Cantwell, Joseph E.
Caple, Forest E.
Cargill, Harvey D. *
Cargill, William S.
Carl, Clyde L.

Carlin, Catherine
Carmer, Henry S.
Carnell, Edwin B.
Carnell, John R.
Carney, Lawrence B.
Carpenter, Robert H.
Casey, Clifford H.
Cassavant, Donald H.
Catlin, George
Childs, Jack
Chisholm, Clifford V.
Christensen, Albert
Clisham, John
Clyne, John Joseph
Coburn, Robert S.
Cole, Arthur M.
Cole, Caroline B.
Cole, William E., Jr.
Coleman, George
Collett, Alfred R.
Collins, Francis J.
Colonna, Victor C.
Colwell, Edward J.
Comet, Lester
Condon, Reid W.
Conklin, Calvin E.
Conklin, Jeanne D.
Conrad, Charles
Conrad, Harold K.
Contento, Arthur M.
Cooke, Donald F.
Cooke, LeRoy J.
Cookingham, Herman V.
Coombs, Richard W.
Cornell, Nathaniel A.
Cornell, Warren S.
Cornes, Allen L.
Corning, Edwin, Jr.
Corr, Francis J.

Corsi, Rocco
Covey, Nelson L.
Cowan, Frank E.
Cowing, William A.
Croes, Peter G., Sr.
Cromwell, Raymond J.
Cromwell, Robert M.
Cronk, Donald M.
Crook, William D.
Cross, Newell C.
Crossman, Everett A.
Crowder, Everett A.
Cruttenden, Lawrence L.
Cunningham, William J.
Curran, George A.
Cushing, Francis
Dahl, George J.
Daley, Percy D., Jr.
Dane, Thomas H.
Daniels, Eugenia
Dappert, Anselmo F.
Darbecker, Nettie
Dare, Thomas
Darrow, Daniel P.
Davis, Richard E.
De Ronde, John A.
de Shaw, Richard E.
Decker, James G.
Decker, Robert K.
Delong, Donald W.
Delskowicz, Victor
Denman, Pauline A.
Denney, Raymond F.
Denney, Robert L.
Denney, William
Derby, Ralph A., Jr.
DeTiere, Elmer F., Jr.
Devoe, Wilson J.
Dibble, John J.

Dieter, Alvin A.
Dieter, James J., Jr.
Dietz, Arthur P.
Dillehunt, Donald B.
Dillhunt, Charles E.
DiMura, Fortune A.
DiMura, Frank C.
DiPierro, Cosomo
Dixon, Sydney H.
Dixon, William E.
Dobbs, Wiley A.
Dodge, Frederick F.
Doetsch, William F.
Doherty, Carolyn
Doherty, Matthew S.
Dollard, John G.
Domermuth, Richard
Donato, Anthony
Donato, Dominick
Donato, Louis
Donato, Samuel
Doran, Winfield
Dorsman, Cornelius
Drake, Gilbert O.
Drake, William D.
Driscoll, James V.
Drislane, John J.
Drislane, William J.
Duffek, Imrick C.*
Dugan, William J., Jr.
Dunn, James
Dunston, William A.
Dupree, Floyd B.
Dutton, Herman G.
Dutton, Thomas
Dutton, William
Dysinger, Robert E.
Dzeobecki, Alexander
Dzeobecki, Frank

Earl, Andrew F.
Eastman, Fred P.
Easton, John V.
Eck, Emmanuel J., III
Ecker, George W.
Edgcumbe, Douglas
Egnasher, Joseph F.
Elliott, Francis R.
Emmons, Norman A.
Engel, Howard B.
Engett, John
Ercole, Anthony A.
Ercole, George D.
Erkson, Robert L.
Ertel, George L.
Ertel, John F.
Evans, George F.
Ewing, Dwight F.
Ewing, Leland
Fahrenkopf, Norbert
Fales, Allen R.
Fanning, James O.
Farber, Leonard L.
Felgentreff, Raymond
Fendt, Leslie K.
Ferguson, John B.
Ferriere, Benjamin
Ferris, Joseph
Feth, Martin
Fick, John R.*
Filkins, Ellsworth G.*
Fink, Louis H.
Finley, Reid W.
Finley, Thomas L., Jr.
Fisher, Lloyd C.
Fisher, Ralph L.
Flagg, Myron D.
Flandreau, John H.
Flanigan, John H.

Fleahman, Arthur L.
Flint, William S.
Flood, John E.
Fogarty, William M.
Forkell, Kurt A.
Foster, Robert R.
Fourman, Luther G.
Frank, Rudolph, Jr.
Franz, Norman
Freeman, Charles M.
Freeman, Wilmer B.
French, Donald I.
Frick, Earl
Frick, John D.
Fromma, Charles
Fryer, Roger J.
Fuchs, Herman G., Jr.
Fullager, William A.
Fuller, Marlin S.
Gabriels, Alexander, Jr.
Gabriels, John J.
Gainor, John E.
Gait, John P.
Gall, Ernest
Gall, Gerhardt
Gallup, Allen D.
Ganter, Harvey G.
Ganter, Warren P.
Gardner, Robert M.
Garrison, Philip
Garrison, Ralph S., Jr.
Garrison, Robert
Gensick, Anthony R.
Geurtze, Harold
Gibbo, Royal M., Jr.
Gibbs, Robert S.
Gibson, Charles, II
Gibson, Edward J.
Gibson, Edward L., Jr.

Gibson, Robert W.
Gibson, William W., Jr.
Gifford, Kenneth H.
Gilbreth, William
Gillett, Roy L., Jr.
Gimlick, Russell W.
Ginter, Edward C.
Ginter, John P.
Glasstetter, Donald
Glasstetter, Robert J.
Gleason, John E.
Glenn, W. Oliver
Goca, Paul T.
Gochee, Harry O., Jr.
Goeldner, Kenneth F.
Golden, Ray M., Jr.
Golding, Ward E.
Goldring, Janet
Granato, Andrew V.
Grant, Benjamin
Grant, Robert E.
Green, James W.
Greene, George J.
Greenfield, Milton L.
Greenwood, Alvin W.
Gresen, Arthur A.
Griffin, LeRoy, Jr.
Griffin, William D.
Grim, Gerald M.
Grim, John S.
Grinnell, Carroll C., Jr.
Grinnell, William S.
Gudz, William
Gundlach, Alfred F.
Guy, Frederick
Guyer, Ralph L.
Hackell, Ernest M.
Hagen, B.S.
Hagman, Carl A.

Haight, Jacob P.
Haines, Delbert W.
Hall, Frank G.
Hall, Henry J.
Hall, Howard L.
Hall, Thomas J.
Hallock, Franklin W.
Halsdorf, Donald
Halsdorf, Henry J.
Halsdorf, Paul D.
Hamann, Arthur
Hamilton, Douglas K.
Hamilton, George
Hamilton, Robert
Hamilton, Walter
Hammett, Frank U., Jr.
Hand, Robert N.
Hanley, John E.
Hannaway, William
Hannay, Donald E.
Hanson, Edward
Harbeck, Howard E.
Harden, Adolph
Harder, Harold D., Jr.
Harrig, George A.
Harting, Alfred F.
Hartnett, William R.
Hartzell, Clinton H., Jr.
Hartzell, Graham B.
Hatfield, George E.
Hathaway, John
Hauf, John E.
Hault, John B.
Hausburg, Edward W.
Haverly, Edward H., Jr.
Hayes, Dean J., Jr.
Hayes, Robert C.
Hayes, William I.
Hayner, Robert L.

Hays, Clinton B.
Haywood, William F., Jr.
Heath, William L.
Heatley, Harvey M.
Hehre, Edward
Heim, Herman F.
Hempstead, Clarence
Hempstead, Orin
Hempstead, Vincent
Henderson, John H.
Henderson, Parker J.
Henkel, Richard C.*
Henkens, Jacob J.
Henry, Neil A.
Herrick, Benjamin S.
Herrick, Charles A.
Herrick, D-Cady, II
Herrick, Newell F.
Hicks, Robert St.J.
Higby, Leonard G.
Hinke, Robert
Histed, Edgar
Hitchcock, Dwight C., Jr.
Hoffman, Harold
Hoffman, John C.
Hoffman, Robert E.
Hogancamp, Allen F.
Hollenbeck, Hollis E.
Holmes, James W.
Honan, Walter A.
Hood, John P.
Horn, Jacob E.
Horn, Richard
Hotaling, Burton L.
Hotaling, Donald
Hotaling, Earl C.
Hotaling, Horace H.
Hotaling, Jesse E.
Hotaling, John J.

Hotaling, Leighton
Hotaling, Staats E.
Hotaling, Wesley H.*
Hotaling, William L.
Hotaling, Wynton T.
House, Daniel W.
House, Paul D., Jr.
Hover, James E.*
Howarth, James A.
Howarth, Richard J.
Howd, Frank
Hritz, Andrew A.
Huerter, Richard H.
Hughes, John F.
Humphrey, Clayton D.
Humphrey, Warren E.
Hunsdorfer, Richard A.
Huntoon, Calvin B.
Hurley, Joseph B.
Igoe, James E.
Isdell, Fred R.
Isdell, Nelson L.
Isdell, Robert C.
Isenman, John
Jackson, Robert A.
Jacobson, James D.
Jagereski, Eugene
Jakway, George F.
Jamieson, George R.
Jane, Jane S.
Jenkins, Jasper L.
Jensen, Louis J.
Jensen, Robert W.
Jeram, Francis T.
Jeram, Frederick T., Jr.
Jeram, Lawrence W.
Jeune, Warren M.
Johnson, Gale P.
Johnson, Luther M.

Johnson, Peter B.
Johnson, Victor L.
Johnston, William, Jr.
Jones, Donald M.
Jones, Earl S., Jr.
Jones, John
Jones, Kilmer
Jones, Le Roy
Jones, Leonard L.
Jones, Norman
Jones, Ralph D.
Jones, Reginald F.
Jones, Richard M.
Jordan, Howard L.
Jordan, James F.
Joslin, Margaret D.
Karl, William E.
Karl, William F.
Karwelat, Arthur
Kass, Fred J.
Kass, Herbert
Kavoukian, Martin
Kearney, Edward J., Jr.*
Keaveney, James E.
Keefer, Earl H.
Keller, Lyndon M.
Kelp, Harold W.
Kemp, Robert C.
Kenyon, Joseph J., Jr.
Keyser, Darwin
Kibbe, John P.
Kilbourne, Cecil E.
Killion, Maxine
Killough, Joseph R.
Kimball, Russell
King, Charles H.
King, George A.
King, Glenn A.
King, Robert C.

Kinney, Louis M.
Kinns, Edwin
Kirk, Raymond L.
Kiszka, Vincent A.
Kitchen, William A.
Klein, Karl J.
Kleinhans, Floyd
Kleinhans, Harold
Kleinhans, Kenneth B.
Kleinke, Henry L.
Klett, Henry N., Jr.
Klink, Irving C.
Knapp, Christopher C.
Knapp, Frederick V.
Knapp, Kenneth A.
Knapp, Mathew G., Jr.
Knapp, Phillip D.
Knapp, David *
Knowles, Ernest J.
Knowles, William F.
Knowlson, Walter T.
Koechling, Harold
Kohinke, Bertram E.
Kohls, Harold W.
Kolb, Francis
Kolb, Harvey
Kolber, George J.
Kommit, Lester
Kositzka, Charles W.
Krajca, Fred F.
Kramer, John J.
Krause, Edward
Krichbaum, Elmer C., Jr.
Krouse, Henry A.
Krull, Robert C.
Kryzykowski, Joseph
Kukuk, Frank H.
Kunz, Charles E.
Labrie, Louis P.

LaFay, Frank
LaFon, Waldo
Lagerstedt, John H.
Lang, H. Beckett
Langer, Walter C.
Langford, Herbert B.
Languish, Otto J.
LaPointe, Henry D., Jr.*
Lapp, Fred
Laremore, Richard T.
Lattin, Robert D.
Lauer, Charles
Laurence, William M.
Lauterborn, Raymond J.
Lavery, Harold V.
Lawrence, Orville E.
Lawton, Arthur
Layton, Bruce
LeBesco, Michael G.
Lefevre, Daniel P.
Leggett, William H.
Lehmann, Albert J., Jr.
Leighton, T. Howard
Lennon, Roger B.
Leonard, Boynton C.
Leonard, James F.
Leonard, Kenneth M.
Leonard, Thomas L.
LeSeroned, Robert
Lestrange, Robert W.
Lewis, John G.
Liebich, Herman
Lill, John P.
Ling, Halstead C.
Livermore, Armon, Jr.*
Lockrow, Bart E.
Lomax, Richard
Long, Charles B.
Long, Richard

Lorio, Lucille
Loux, Arthur
Loux, Joseph
Luce, Paul A.
Luck, William D.
Ludwig, Harold W.
Lutz, Edward A.
Lynch, Richard A.
Lyon, James B., III*
Lyon, Robert L.
Lyon, Robert P.
Lyon, William Thompson
Lyons, Francis J.
MacDonald, Raymond C.
MacDonald, Richard
MacDonald, Richard E., Jr.
MacDowell, Robert L.
Machmann, Alvin B.
MacKenzie, Leonard C., Jr.
MacKinnon, Roderick P.
MacKinnon, Malcom B.*
Maclay, Geoffrey
MacRae, Colin D.
MacRae, Donald C.
Magee, Edward M.
Maher, James B.
Maher, William
Maier, Roger A.
Main, Carol
Malanga, Larry C.
Malanga, Ralph, Jr.
Malary, John H.
Mallory, Harold
Malone, Joseph L.
Mang, Harry H.
Mangini, John M.
Many, James L.
Mardolillo, Salvador
Markell, Herbert, Jr.

Marshall, John E.
Martin, Charles B.
Martin, Charles G.
Martin, David W.
Martin, Fortis M.
Martin, Frank
Martin, Frederick W.
Martin, Henry V.
Martin, John L.
Martin, John W., Jr.
Martin, Kenneth J.
Martin, Leland F., Jr.
Martin, Marjorie
Martin, Robert C.
Mason, Raymond
Mason, William R.
Mathias, Mary M.
Mattice, Edward B.
Mattox, Richard
Maxwell, Cyrus
Maxwell, Edward W.
Maynard, William J.
McArthur, Lawrence B.
McAuliffe, Chester
McCann, Joseph A.
McCauley, Henry E.
McClintock, Carl
McClintock, John C.
McCormack, Roy, Jr.
McCredie, Donald P.
McFarland, Frank J.
McGrath, Robert
McGuire, John F.
McGuire, Lawrence D.
McGuirk, Donald R.
McGuirk, Joseph E.
McIntosh, Willis, Jr.
McLaughlin, Ann
McLeod, Charles E.

McMillen, Floyd J.
McMillen, Gerald L.
McNary, Earl
McNary, Kenneth E.
Meany, Edward F.
Meany, John P.
Meehan, Thomas C.
Melco, Christopher
Melco, Peter
Menges, Roger G.
Miller, Edward A.
Miller, Harold E.
Miller, Joseph
Miller, Michael J.
Milvo, Charles F.
Milvo, John D.
Mizener, Clifford
Mizener, LeRoy
Moak, Ernest
Moak, Roger J.
Moak, William
Moecker, Herman E.
Montgomery, James
Montysko, Joseph W.
Moody, Harold A., Jr.
Moody, Jean A.
Moody, Theodore W.
Moore, Amos D.
Moore, Arnold C.
Moore, John C.
Moore, Kenneth R.
Moore, Raymond C.
Moore, William M.
Morehouse, George W.
Morris, George D.
Morris, Harold
Morrison, Donald H.
Morrison, Francis L.
Morse, Gordon H.

Morse, Harry
Morse, Stanley W.
Mosall, Milton W.
Moselle, George
Moses, Lawrence R.
Mosher, Ralph H.
Mosher, William
Mosher, William R.
Mosmen, Arnold F.
Mott, George S., III
Mott, James S.
Mulholland, James A.
Mulholland, William D.
Mullens, Robert S.
Muller, Joseph C.
Murray, Gifford J.
Murray, Gilbert
Murray, John L.
Murray, Philip R.
Myers, Harold F.
Myrick, George C.
Myrick, George C., Jr.
Nardolillo, Salvador
Nasholds, Russell Z.
Nasner, Francis J.
Nasner, Paul
Nasner, John P.*
Neal, Virginia P.
Nellegar, James J.
Nellegar, Joseph B.
Neri, Albert H.
Neri, Peter
Newcomb, N. Davis
Newcomb, Philip K.
Newkirk, Alfred T.
Nichols, Daris G.
Nichols, Norman B.*
Nicholson, Elwood J., Jr.
Niles, Gibson

Niles, Richard W.
Niver, Gerrit M.
Nolan, Francis J.
Nolan, Joseph H.
Noonan, William
Northrup, Arnold D.
Noyes, Robert S.
O'Brien, Donald*
O'Connell, Charles
O'Donnell, Morgan J.
O'Rourke, Arthur
O'Toole, Lawrence W.
Oates, Richard G.
Obenauf, Walter H.
Obie, Malcolm
Ochs, Rudy H.
Ogden, George H.
Olenhouse, Earl E.
Oliver, Chester T.
Oliver, George
Oliver, Robert K.
Oliver, William H.
Oliver, Charles E.
Oppenlander, George H.
Ormsbee, John R.*
Osborne, Lincoln B.
Osborne, Thomas D.
Osterhout, Charles L.
Osterhout, Frank C.
Osterhout, Ralph J.
Otten, Kenneth
Ottman, Thomas M.
Ottman, James A.
Paddock, John D.
Paige, Harry W.
Palmer, Charles
Palmer, Gordon
Palmer, Harry G.
Palmer, Jack K.

Palmer, William W.
Palmer, James W., Jr.*
Pappalau, John J.
Parker, Elwyn G.
Parker, Everett L.
Parks, James G.
Pastori, Ramon V.
Patten, Harmon S., III
Patterson, Allen L.
Patterson, Richard M.
Patterson , Robert
Patterson, Thurbert
Paul, John R.
Pauley, William R.
Payette, Henry M.
Peck, George W.
Peck, Paul H.
Peeney, Charles F.
Pelter, Alfred
Pelton, Cornelius H.
Pelton, LeRoy
Peltz, Philip
Peltz, William L., Jr.
Pember, Edward K.
Perez, Robert C.
Perry, Alfred E.
Peters, Frederick F.
Peters, William F.
Petersen, Andrew, Jr.
Peterson, James H.
Peterson, William
Phillips, Dean H.
Phillips, Henry G.
Phillips, Merton H.
Phillips, William E.
Phillips, William F.
Piazza, Florence L.
Piazza, George O.
Picarazzi, George L.

Picarazzi, Perry
Pier, Perry W.
Pietropaoli, Orlando
Pillsbury, Richard C.
Pillsbury, Russell H.
Pinkerton, Romaine A.
Piper, Edwin B., Jr.
Pittz, Vincent J.
Playford, James R.
Playford, Leonard
Ploski, Leo S.
Porter, William R.
Pospishil, Joseph
Potter, Albert D., Jr.
Potter, Edgar D., Jr.
Potter, Thomas M.
Powers, John E.
Powers, Joseph C.
Powers, Robert J.
Powley, Benjamin
Preska, Victor R.
Price, Ernest
Price, Frank T.
Price, Howard G.
Prince, Lennox C.
Prior, Daniel
Prue, Arthur A.
Pryor, Edward M.
Przysiecki, Roman C.
Quattrine, Ennio
Queen, Lillian V.
Quintana, Manuel, Jr.
Rabineau, William R.
Radliff, Alfred C.
Radliff, Wilbur W.
Randall, Thomas
Rankin, James
Rapazzo, Joseph
Raymond, Allan W.

Raymond, Leonard
Raymond, Philip D.
Read, S. Merrill
Reed, Frederick I.
Reeve, Roland B.
Rehbaum, Robert W.
Reinisch, Melvin T.
Relyea, Raymond A.
Remele, Kermit Evans
Remele, Robert T.
Rendo, Wallace G.
Rengler, Frederick J.
Reynolds, Roger A.
Ribero, Earl B.
Richardson, Wayland F.
Richey, Robert E.
Richter, Bodo
Rienow, Robert
Riley, Francis S.
Riley, John H.
Risley, Edward
Ritter, William M.
Robbins, Donald H.
Robert, Robert E.
Roberts, Brooks H.
Robertson, Hammond
Robertson, John A.
Rogers, George P.
Rohr, Harold
Rolston, Mary
Rolston, William H.
Roninson, Earl
Rook, Douglas L.
Root, Gordon
Rope, Frederick T.
Rosboro, Frederick C.
Rosbrook, Seth
Rosen, Gerald
Rowe, Alton Scott

Rowe, Russell
Rude, Philip H.
Rukwid, Edmund J., Jr.
Sack, Irving
Sager, Donald
Sager, Elmer E.
Sager, Gilbert
Sahloff, Joseph G.*
Salisbury, Louis V.
San Souci, Arthur
Sanborn, Alvah W.
Sanders, Charles
Sanefski, Donald A.
Sanefski, Richard H.
Saunders, Robert
Saunders, William P.
Schaap, Leonard A.
Schaffer, Frederick
Schaffer, George, Jr.
Schaffner, Marjorie
Schielding, Raymond W.
Schifferdecker, Gerald B.
Schillaci, John J.
Schneider, Rosemarie
Schoen, Helmuth O.
Schoenbeck, John G.
Schoonbeck, John William
Schoonmaker, William J.
Schramm, Harry W.
Schultes, Richard, Jr.
Scoons, Albert J.
Scoons, Clarence
Scoons, Donald G.
Scott, James LeRoy
Seaburg, Paul S.
Seaburg, Wendell
Seaburg, Wiley D.
Segur, William S.
Senning, William C.

Sequin, Alfred L.
Setford, Dale S.
Severino, Joseph J.
Shaffer, Alvin G.
Shaffer, Frederick
Shaffer, George
Shaw, Gene L.
Sherman, Robert W.
Shutter, Richard J.
Silliman, Henry William
Simmons, Arthur T.
Simmons, James C.
Simmons, Robert N.
Simmons, William E.
Simmons, Thomas J.
Simon, Max R.
Simon, Richard
Simon, Robert
Simpson, Frederick L.
Sitterly, Arthur J.
Sitterly, Joseph H.
Skinner, Harold C.
Skinner, Walter L.
Slawson, Arlene M.
Slingerland, Claude
Slingerland, Harmon C.
Slingerland, Howard J.
Smallman, Theodore R.
Smart, Wallace F.
Smith, Asa H.
Smith, Charles L.
Smith, Clarence E.
Smith, Donald E.
Smith, Frank H., Jr.
Smith, Frederick H.
Smith, Gerald G.
Smith, Guy A., Jr.
Smith, Harlan E.
Smith, Harry A.

Smith, Henry S.
Smith, James A.
Smith, James E., Jr.
Smith, Joseph
Smith, Kenneth R.
Smith, Loren D.
Smith, Ralph H.
Smith, Richard K.
Smith, Sanford F., III
Smith, Sherman K.
Smith, Walter R.
Smith, William
Smith, William E.
Snider, Andrew L.
Sniffen, Kenneth E.
Snook, Robert C.
Snyder, Alton E.
Snyder, Charles
Snyder, Everett C.
Snyder, Everett H.*
Snyder, Howard S.
Snyder, Willis H.
Sonsterud, Edgar E.
Sonsterud, Norris E.
Sorn, William W.
Southworth, Theodore C.
Spatz, Peter
Spawn, George D.
Spence, Donald P.
Spencer, Richard M.
Spencer, Roy
Sperry, Kenton F.
Sperry, Page W.
Sperry, Thomas
Spinosa, Thomas
St. Lucia, Charles H.
Stalker, Oscar H.
Steede, Raymond J.
Steele, Richard W.

Steltz, Alice
Steltz, Keith
Steltz, Russell
Stephany,Henry J.
Stephens, Irving
Stephens, Richard
Stevenson, George B.
Stiles, Claud
Stipe, Everett
Stoklas, Nicholas P.
Stolz, Frederick W.
Stott, James L.
Strait, Harry A.
Straub, Jack F.
Streeter, Leslie M.
Streeter, Walter C.
Strope, James E.
Strope, Walter A.
Stubbs, Frank C.
Stutsrim, George W.
Stutt, Thomas G.
Sullivan, Dennis J.
Sullivan, Francis J.
Sutter, Richard E.
Sutton, Neil V.*
Svolos, Peter A.
Swartout, Frank E.
Swartout, Harry A.
Sweeney, Ralph C.
Tatro, Donald F.
Tatro, Henry E.
Tauss, Julius
Taylor, Clayton F.
Taylor, George W.
Taylor, Harold G.
Taylor, Robert B.
Tebbutt, Edward C.
Tebbutt, James G., Jr.
Ten Eyck, Andrew

Thomas, Donald F.
Thomas, Joseph A.
Thompson, John C.
Thompson, John M.
Thompson, Mary E.
Thompson, Richard F.
Thorn, John B.
Thorne, Belmont L.
Throope, Wallace E.
Tibbits, Trafford N.
Tice, Edward
Tice, Eugene F.
Tice, Ruth
Tice, William
Tiedeman, Jean
Tiedeman, Walter D., Jr.
Tilroe, Dexter
Timmons, Alfred C.
Todd, John R.
Tolman, Edith
Tolman, Leland L.
Tolman, Mason
Tomchin, John M.
Tomlinson, Arthur H.
Tompkins, Leonard, Jr.
Tougher, William H.
Tozzi, Enio A.
Traeger, Christopher F.
Treiber, Henry, Jr.
Truitt, Rolland R.
Tubbs, Kenneth E.
Tubbs, Charles F.*
Tull, L. Emerson
Tull, Laurence S.
Turner, Byron L.
Turner, George I., Jr.
Turner, Jessie F.
Twichell, Paul S.
Vaccariello, Dominick J.

Vadney, Earl D.
Valek, Joseph W.
Van Alstyne, Floyd
Van Alstyne, Freeman
Van Alstyne, Herman C.
Van Alstyne, Kenneth
Van Cott, Willis
Van Denburg, Alvin, Jr.
Van Denburg, Harry
Van Duren, Thomas
Van Dusen, John A.
Van Dyke, Clifford
Van Hoven, Alfred R.
Van Kempen, Frederick P.
Van Liew, Roland, Jr.
Van Loan, Roland C.
Van Loon, William H.
Van Oostenbrugge, John C.
Van Patten, Grant
Van Valkenberg, Francis
Van Valkenburg, Toule
Van Woert, Ralph P.
Van Zandt, Welles K.
Van Zandt, William E.
Van Zandt, William K.*
VanAllen, Howard C.
VanAllen, John R.
VanAllen, Robert
Vandenburgh, William H.
Vanderwerken, Donald
Van Derzee, Newton B., Jr.
Vella, Louis M.
Ventura, Charles F.
Venus, Karl W.
Vincent, Franklin G.
Vitillo, Otto A.
Vogel, Willis
Vogel, Willis R.
Volk, George G.

Voorhees, James, Jr.
Vorce, Raymond B.
Vroman, Thomas B.
Vrooman, Jason C.
Vrooman, Wesley S.
Wade, Elizabeth A.
Wade, William
Wagner, Eleanor E.
Wakeman, Roland C.
Waldo, John A.
Walker, B.E.
Walker, George M.
Wall, Andrew B.
Wallace, Donald C.
Wallace, William H.*
Walsh, William C.
Walter, James E.
Walworth, Fayette C.
Warner, Frederick B.
Wasserbach, John A.
Wasson, Martin F.
Waterbury, Walter A.
Weaver, Lillas J.
Weaver, William J., Jr.
Weber, Dr. George W.
Webster, Gordon V.
Weekes, Willard
Welch, Franklin H.
Wells, Austin B.
Wells, Bradford H.
Wells, Edmund I.
Wells, George A.
Wells, Joseph B.
Wells, Mac C.
Wells, Valentine K.
Welsh, Charles S.
Welter, Lawrence F.
Welter, Leonard, Jr.
Wenger, George F.

Werner, Kurt
West, C. Richard
West, Kenneth E.
Westbrook, Henry W.
Wey, John
Whan, William A.
Wheeler, Edward A., Jr.
Whitbeck, Carmon
Whitbeck, Randall K.
Whitcomb, Henry L.
White, Benjamin W.
White, Edgar H.
White, Edward T.
Whitlock, James
Whitting, Ray
Wickham, Herbert G.
Wiedemann, James F.
Wilcox, Donald C.
Wiley, Richard
Wilkes, Henry O.
Wilkes, Morgan E.
Wilkes, Willard, Jr.
Wilkie, Allen L.
Wilkie, Edythe P.
Wilkie, Leighton K.
Wilkins, Floyd D.
Willard, Frank A.
Willey, Allen L.
Willey, John F.
Willey, Clarence K.*
Williams, Carl A.
Williams, Edward T.
Williams, Rocco J., Jr.
Wilsey, James E.
Wilson, Alton H.
Wilson, Richard B.
Wilson, Robert C.
Wiltsie, Franklin
Winne, Mary

Wirasnik, Charles F., Jr.
Wirasnik, William A.
Wise, Elmer H.
Wisenburn, Gerald
Wisenburn, Grace
Wisenburn, Lewis, Jr.
Woehrmann, Fred
Woehrmann, Harry M.
Wogastske, Doris J.
Wolfe, Harry
Wood, Edwin W.
Wood, Paul O.
Wood, Philip R.
Wood, Thomas G.
Woodin, Stanley W.
Woods, John P.
Worden, Edward C.
Wright, Edward T.
Wright, Robert E.
Wright, Robert S.
Wright, Walter S., Jr.
Wright, Stanley A.*
Wriston, George W.
Wulse, Henry, Jr.
Wynkoop, William
Yeomans, Harold W.
Young, Owen W.
Young, Richmond C.
Zawar, Hans A.
Zawar, Robert
Zdziebloski, John M.
Zdgiebloski, Joseph A.
Zdgiebloski, Peter
Ziehm, Raymond H.
Zimmer, Marshall O.
Zimmerman, Wilson H.
Zorn, Ralph

KOREAN WAR:

Adams, Russell
Agar, Richard E.
Angell, Edward
Applegate, Gerald
Arkley, John
Arkley, Robert J.
Asprion, Mathew J.
Bachman, Alvin
Bailey, Ivan
Bailey, Robert L.
Bainer, Henry
Bainer, John
Bainer, Robert J.
Bangert, Robert E.
Barends, Frederick W.
Barkhuff, Graham
Bauer, Robert
Bedell, Arthur W.
Behr, Julian
Bercharlie, Anthony
Betts, Richard
Bleau, Alva L.*
Bodgett, Marvin
Bohen, John
Bonapart, Claude A.
Boomhower, Ernest R.
Borger, Paul
Bradt, Donald J., Jr.
Brasure, John E.M.
Brown, Richard L.
Byrnes, Lester
Campbell, Milford E.
Carroll, James
Casey, Arthur F.
Christie, Donald R.
Clausen, Bernard L.
Coburn, Guy

Collins, Robert J.
Conlon, John P.*
Conlon, Joseph E.
Constantine, Angelo
Cook, Robert A.
Coon, Robert E.
Coulson, Thomas H.
Covey, Henry J.
Cowen, Peter A.
Cox, A. Fletcher, Jr.
Crandall, James E.
Creifelds, Robert
Curran, John
Debravalskas, John P.
Dahl, Donald S.
Davenport, Edward
Davis, C. Richard
Day, Roger U.
Denson, Francis
De Vellis, Francis
De Witt, John E.
Doherty, James
Doran, Paul J.
Downey, Thomas J.
Drobner, Daniel
Drobner, Everett
Duclos, Charles P.
Ertel, Thomas J.
Ewing, William D.
Fink, Howard C.
Foster, Gibbs C.
Franks, Graham P.
Furbeck, Warren
Fursman, Lewis F.
Gabriel, Richard
Gabriels, Robert D.
Gail, Julius J.
Gallup, Thomas L.
Gantz, Robert J.M.

Gerber, Joseph R.
Gillespie, Frederick
Glenn, Creighton
Goodspeed, Walter
Grant, Richard W.
Green, Robert
Griffin, Robert A.
Gundell, Henry F.
Hagen, Allen
Haight, Henry C.W.
Halter, Robert
Hammond, Donald
Haverly, Edward H., Jr.
Haverly, Richard B.
Higby, Paul N.
Hillman, William C.
Hodgkins, David H.
Hodgkins, Robert C.
Hoffman, Alan C.
Holcomb, Peter
Holland, Ernest
Holland, Raymond
House, Paul D., Jr.
Humphrey, Clayton
Humphrey, Raymond K.
Huntington, James C., Jr.
Irish, James M.
Jensen, Floyd M.
Jensen, Lewis K.
Johnson, William E.
Jones, Llewelyn, Jr.
Kaser, Paul
Kass, George W., Jr.
Keel, Robert
Kelly, Henry M.
Kimball, Russell A.
King, Roland
Kirk, George E., Jr.
Kirk, Raymond L.

Knox, Dale B.
Kraft, Richard A., Jr.
Krause, George E.
Kross, Kenneth B.
Kunz, Robert P.
Lake, John
Lasher, Gerald
Lassonde, Maynard W.
LeFevre, Louis
Leon, John
Loeschner, Theodore R., Jr.
Lohrey, Theodore H.
Lozzi, Ezio
Ludwig, Robert A.
Lyon, Bruce
MacIntosh, Earl A.
McGee, James W.
McHugh, Arthur C., Jr.
McKinney, Alice Ruth
Magee, Milton B., Jr.
Maloney, Jeanne D.
Manning, Gerald F.
Many, James L.
Marsh, Edward S.
Martin, Frank E.
Martin, Duncan S.
Martin, Gerald
Martin, James H.
Martin, LeRoy, Jr.
Mattice, Ward A.
Matott, Charles
May, Francis M., Jr.
Mead, Douglas C.
Metchick, Harry
Mickits, Robert B.
Miller, John E.
Miller, Philip A.
Mirabile, Joseph M.
Mitchell, Carol

Mitchell, L.
Mizener, William F.
Moody, Harold W.
Moody, Theodore W.
Moore, Dana
Morrison, Donald H.
Murphy, Thomas S.
Murtagh, John J.
Muzzey, Ernest F., Jr.
Naslund, Edwin
Nelson, Stanley F.
Neumann, Richard
Newell, Edward F., Jr.
Nicholson, David A.
Oaks, Dudley, Jr.
O'Brien, Richard
Olmstead, Stephen
Ordway, Doncaster R.
Oropallo, Ralph
Padula, Joseph
Pape, Joseph S.
Parks, James G.
Perry, Walter R.
Peterson, Harry W.
Phillips, Ernest
Phillips, Merton H.
Phillips, William
Picarazzi, Louis
Picarazzi, R.D.
Plummer, David G.
Potter, Albert
Pound, Russell, Jr.
Powers, Del Herbert
Prince, Lennox B.
Prior, Joseph
Prior, Robert J.
Pyle, George
Radcliff, Frank
Rankin, Duncan A.

Raymond, Roy V., Jr.
Rees, Edward
Reid, Robert M.
Rhodes, Harold F.
Rivkin, Dewey
Rivkin, William
Rooney, Andrew E., Jr.
Ross, Edward A., Jr.
Rossi, Michael
Rukwid, Paul D.
Rutherford, John
Sabol, Edward J.
Sapsuzian, Leon, Jr.
Sargent, Rodney E.
Scepkowski, Henry, Jr.
Schaming, Peter, III
Schraa, William, III
Schubert, Frederick
Schwarze, William
Scoons, Clifford
Seaburg, Carman T.
Selkirk, Charles
Sheldon, Richard
Sippling, Millerd L.
Slingerland, William F.
Smith, Donald J.
Smith, Robert
Snyder, Donald*
Snyder, Milton, Jr.
Spangenburg, William
Stalker, Oscar H.
Stephany, Henry J.*
Studler, Albin A., Jr.
Stutsrim, William H.
Sutter, Irvin O.
Swartfigure, George W.
Tozzi, Ezio
Van Deusen, Richard N.
Van Valkenburg, Richard A.

Van Wormer, Theodore A.
Veino, Milford A.
Vitillo, Nicholas
Wait, Samuel
Walter, Gerald E.
Webb, Robert M., Jr.
Weber, Fred C.
Weber, William R.
Weidman, Victor
Weiler, Robert E.
Wells, Mac C.
Westervelt, George
Westervelt, Robert
Whitlock, James
Whitlock, Robert H.
Whitmore, Robert C.
Wiley, William A.
Williams, Charles
Williams, Harold E., Jr.
Williams, Peter J.
Williamson, Andrew, Jr.
Williman, Charles G.
Winne, Wallis G.
Wirasnik, Charles J., Jr.
Wolfe, Richard S.
Woodhead, Albert A.
Woods, William R.

VIETNAM CONFLICT:

Abbot, Robert *
Allen, Dean B. *
Applebee, Peter
Banahan, James L.
Bardelli, Edward J. Jr.
Barends, Frederick W.
Barriere, Ronald O.
Barry, Duncan A.
Becker, Keith

Bell, Ronald J., Sr.
Benton, Jim, III
Berry, James J.
Bink, James C. *
Blaber, Richard
Blanchard, Arthur P.
Bressett, Donald L.
Briand, Virginia E.
Burkett, Charles, Jr.*
Carroll, William J.
Clark, Colin P.
Conti, Robert G.
Corson, Stephen C.
Cunningham, Matthew J.
Curtiss, William C.
Czajak, Edward F.
Dalrymple, Ross
Davis, Robert J., Jr.
Day, Royce W.
DeWilde, Dale E.
Decker, E., Jr.
Demarest, Wesley
Duff, David
Esmond, David
Evangelista, Joseph
Fahey, Thomas P.
Farina, Matthew A.
Forster, James M.
Fournier, Alfred W., Jr.
Frazier, Peter J.
Frazier, Thomas L.
Frisbie, Jared A. *
Germann, Anthony F.
Grandy, George W.
Gutman, Joseph C., Jr.
Hayes, Edward J., Jr.
Heineman, Robert K., Jr.
Helligrass, Robert J.
Henry, Charles J.

Hogan, James B., Jr.
Holligan, Frederick J.
Hollner, John F., III
Hulihan, James
Johnson, Wayne R.
Jones, H.W.
Joralemon, Paul W.
Kalendek, Raymond F.
Kavanagh, Michael J.
Kibbey, Richard A. (MIA)
King, Bill
Klein, Henry, Jr. *
Kollarits, Bela, Jr.
Kurtick, Edward F.
Lenhardt, George H.
Mann, Stephen E.
Maxwell, Lee W.
McDonald, William F.
McMahon, Daniel P., Jr.
Miller, Kenneth R.
Moran, David J.
Mosmen, Arnold F., Jr.
O'Keefe, Timothy K.
Olmstead, Stephen G.
Pearce, William C.
Pearson, William R.
Picarazzi, James *
Pratt, Douglas E.
Rarick, Charles T.
Rauch, Gary L.
Richardson, Eric H.
Rinaldi, Vincent D.
Roberts, Paul F.
Rossman, Peter F.
Ryan, Thomas *
Schultes, Robert
Skultety, Thomas C.
Sleurs, Jospeh W.
Stephens, Robert L.

Strumpf, John W.
Swanson, Roger A.
Toussaint, Jon T.
Trevett, Ronald D.
Van Amerongen, Peter
Van DeLoos George, Joseph P.
Van Derzee, Pieter S.
Vogel, John A.
Walsh, Brian P.
Wilkinson, Richard
Williamson, John A., Jr.
Winchester, Earl B.

* — Killed in service

Faculty/Professional Staff of the Bethlehem Central Schools with Five or More Years in the District

NAME	YEARS	POSITION	NAME	YEARS	POSITION
Ableman, Edna	1947-75	Elementary, Slingerlands	Bender, Christina	1975-92	Middle, Basic Skills
Adler, Helen	59-77	H.S., Language Arts	Berberich, Robert	56-62	H.S., Driver Education
Agars, Mary	83-92*	Middle, Mathematics	Bergan, Elizabeth	79-91	Middle, Music
Aidala, Judith	79-84	Elementary, Slingerlands	Berman, Sadie	51-70	Elementary, Hamagrael
Aidala, Gregory	73-78	Middle, Mathematics	Bida, Mary	58-71	Principal, Slingerlands
Alec, Rudi	62-68	Elementary, Hamagrael	Biernacki, Theodore	79-92	Elementary, Music
Allen, Florence	58-78	Elementary, Delmar	Bish, Carl	68-74	Middle, Language Arts
Almindo, Susan	83-92	Elementary, Glenmont	Blackmore, Mae	63-79	H.S., Guidance
Anderson, Dorothy	70-92	Middle, Mathematics	Blanchard, Mary	76-91	H.S., Music
Anderson, Ruth	65-86	Elementary, Elsmere	Bloom, Gytelle	67-92	Elementary, Hamagrael
Applebee, Robyn	81-92	Elementary, Clarksville	Bobbins, Phyllis	71-76	Middle, Guidance
Archer, Therese	63-80	Elementary, Hamagrael	Boehm, Catherine	57-71	Elementary, Librarian
Arnold, Ruth	45-61	Nurse, Teacher	Boggs, Karen	70-92	Middle, Guidance
Artz, Annilee	68-74	Middle, Reading	Bordick, Felicia	82-92	Elementary, Glenmont
Assael, Zachary	79-92	H.S., Mathematics	Bonacker, George	46-71	Principal, Delmar
Atkinson, Thomas	59-89	H.S., Science Supv.	Bookbinder, Harold	62-73	Assistant Superintendent
Auerbach, Philip	50-63	H.S., Guidance	Bookbinder, Kathy	61-73	Elementary, Psychology
Austin, Bruce	57-86	H.S., Guidance	Bookhout, Hamilton	38-64	Supervising Principal
Averell, Helen	54-64	Elementary, Hamagrael	Bosworth, Candice	71-92	Middle, Science
Bain, Harry	50-59	H.S., Social Studies	Bover, Roland	64-90	Elementary, Clarksville
Backer, Anne	84-92	Elementary, Slingerlands	Boyer, Leslie	65-92	Elementary, Social Studies
Bailey, Jack	71-92	Elementary, Clarksville	Bozzella, Beverly	81-92	Middle, Music
Baker, Anne	61-72	Elementary, Clarksville	Bozzella, Samuel	63-92	Supervisor, Music
Baker, Richard	54-82	Middle, Science	Brandt, Marion	53-68	Middle, Basic Skills
Baker, Seena	70-76	Elementary, Clarksville	Braverman, Jesse	74-92	Middle, Basic Skills
Bango, Anthony	74-92	H.S., Reading	Brooks, Edward	54-77	H.S., Social Studies
Barclay, Anna	78-85	Elementary, Reading	Brown, Cherryl	78-92	Elementary, Hamagrael
Barnes, Louella	53-66	Elementary, Elsmere	Brown, Donald	64-70	Elementary, Glenmont
Barron, Joan	71-86	Elementary, Librarian	Brown, Herman	62-86	H.S., Social Studies
Bartley, Katherine	83-92	Elementary, Clarksville	Brown, Hugh	56-73	H.S., Business Education
Bassotti, Richard	72-92	H.S., Assistant Principal	Brown, Mary Jane	85-92	H.S., Special Education
Bauder, Geraldine	56-72	Elementary, Music	Brown, Ralph	62-89	H.S., Social Studies
Baxter, Janet	65-92	Middle, Foreign Language	Browne, Catherine	55-61	School Psychologist
Beck, Marie	54-69	Elementary, Slingerlands	Burda, Rosemarie	79-92	H.S., Mathematics
Behrens, George	56-86	Elementary, Speech	Burdick, Frederick	57-92	Middle, Principal

*All 1992 listings are for continuing employees

Burkart, Patricia	1982-92	Middle, Nurse
Burlingame, Marion	54-74	Elementary, Elsmere
Buyer, Richard	63-90	Middle, Social Studies
Bylsma, Karen	86-92	Elementary, Glenmont
Camp, Donald	46-78	H.S., English
Capobianco, Mary	85-92	Elementary, Glenmont
Cappiello, Jane	71-92	Middle, Science
Carmody, Mary	71-92	Middle, Food Service
Caron-Moriarity, Gayle	84-92	H.S., Guidance
Carr, Suzanne	67-82	Elementary, Music
Catalano, Ida	65-84	H.S., Foreign Language
Cavalieri, Alfredo	58-78	District, Music
Cesta, Anita	46-72	H.S., Foreign Language
Cherny, Audrey	60-66	Junior High, Phys. Ed.
Ciavardoni, Kelly Ann	84-92	Elementary, Glenmont
Clark, Richard	51-67	Junior High, Social Studies
Clarke, Leona	67-73	Junior High, English
Clausen, Anna	53-65	Junior High, Home Economics
Cleaves, Earle	47-80	H.S., Science
Clement, Patricia	85-92	Elementary, Clarksville
Cleveland, William	68-92	H.S., Social Studies
Cohen, Donald	54-61	Junior High, Mathematics
Cole, Karen	86-92	Middle, Language Arts
Collins, Anna	51-60	Elementary, Hamagrael
Collins, Ethel	68-76	Elementary, Hamagrael
Collins, Thomas R.	71-76	Supervisor, Social Studies
Collins, Thomas W.	57-62	Elementary, Elsmere
Collins, Wilma	53-68	Junior High, Librarian
Collis, Delbert	53-73	Business Administration
Connolly, Ann	73-92	Middle, Language Arts
Conroe, Constance	51-79	Elementary, Music
Cons, Ruthann	66-75	School Psychology
Conway, Barbara	59-68	H.S., Business Education
Cook, Margaret	68-92	Elementary, Clarksville
Copeland, Arthur	70-92	Elementary, Hamagrael
Corson, Christine	77-92	H.S., Mathematics
Coslick, Ronald	63-68	Junior High, Math
Cowling, Alison	69-81	H.S., Language Arts
Cox, Barbara	84-92	Elementary, Hamagrael
Cronin, James	1960-70	Elementary, Delmar
Cronk, Margaret	80-92	Elementary, Reading
Crummey, Betty	64-81	H.S., Language Arts
Crysler, Maria	54-73	Elementary, Delmar
Cummings,Shirley	52-66	Junior High, Language Arts
Cunningham, Susan	85-92	Clarksville, Nurse
Cunningham, Thomas	68-92	H.S., Science
Curran, Margaret	68-72	Elementary, Slingerlands
Curtin, Patricia	68-92	Middle, Social Studies
D'Agostino, Sharon A.	86-92	Elementary, Clarksville
Dagneau, Ellen	71-92	H.S., Librarian
Dale, Gale	71-92	Elementary, Hamagrael
Dale, Virginia	71-92	Elementary, Slingerlands
D'Arcangelis, Howard	68-92	Middle, Language Arts
Darrone, Natalie	68-86	H.S., Mathematics
Darrow, Manda	44-71	Elementary, Elsmere
Daves, Nancy	77-92	H.S., Nurse
Davies, JoAnn	71-92	Supervisor, Occupation Ed.
Dean, Lucy	55-66	Elementary, Clarksville
DeCecco, Dominick	58-92	Supervisor, Social Studies
deHart, June	78-92	Elementary, Hamagrael
Daily, Elizabeth	66-72	Elementary, Librarian
DeMaria, Teresa	83-92	Elementary, Elsmere
DeMeo, John	81-92	H.S., Physical Education
Dempsey, Kathy	77-92	Elementary, Elsmere
Derosia, Gale	71-92	Elementary, Art
DiMuria, Susan	86-92	Social Worker
Dingman, Virginia	71-76	Elementary, Hamagrael
Dinova, Margaret	69-92	H.S., Language Arts
Ditton, Ruth	56-79	Elementary, Slingerlands
Donnelly, Peter	62-77	H.S., Guidance
Doyle, Alice	56-71	Elementary, Slingerlands
Doyle, Marilyn	84-92	Remedial Reading
Doyle, Ruth	56-70	Elementary, Glenmont
Dryden, Elizabeth	70-77	Elementary, Hamagrael
Duffy, Eugene	71-91	Supervisor, Language Arts
Dufur, Evelyn	78-85	H.S., Home Economics
Duquette, JoAnn	81-92	H.S., Mathematics
Earls, Jeanette	31-68	Junior High, Math

Eckhardt, Patricia	1966-88	Elementary, Elsmere
Eddington, Fannie	60-71	Supervising, Science
Ellery, Barbara	61-86	H.S., Social Studies
Elliott, Mary	62-76	H.S., Business Education
Elliott, Richard	63-68	Junior High, Social Studies
Ellis, Patricia	77-92	Hamagrael, Nurse
End, Helen	56-83	Elementary, Slingerlands
Englander, Katherine	86-92	Middle, Art
Eppleman, Ann	60-92	H.S., Language Arts
Erkson, Grace	39-73	Principal, Glenmont
Esmond, Irwin	53-71	Junior High, Guidance
Esmond, Julia	54-70	Elementary, Glenmont
Evans, Francis	74-92	Elementary, Glenmont
Everett, Delmer	58-73	Business Administrator
Facetti, Corinne	64-77	H.S., Foreign Language
Fairbanks, Elizabeth	61-66	Junior High, Language Arts
Falco, Valarie	87-92	Elementary, Clarksville
Falvey, John	46-76	Principal, Hamagrael
Farrell, Donald	49-77	H.S., Physical Education
Farrell, Joseph	66-92	H.S., Music
Farrell, Linda	63-92	Middle, Home Economics
Feisthamel, Jane	66-78	Middle, Social Studies
Feldman, Jane	82-92	Middle, Science
Feldman, Richard	58-90	H.S., English
Fernandez, Odilia	62-71	Elementary, Art
Fiordilino, Robert	68-92	Middle, Mathematics
Fish, Peter	86-92	Middle, Technology
Fiser, Margaret	63-79	Elementary, Elsmere
Fisk, Bernadene	74-92	Elementary, Hamagrael
Fitzpatrick, Eugene	60-92	H.S., Guidance
Flanagan, Margaret	48-70	Elementary, Elsmere
Flanders, A. Lee	70-75	Elementary, Glenmont
Fleming, Patricia	78-85	Elementary, Glenmont
Flieri, Nina	55-73	Elementary, Reading
Flinton, Doris	54-66	Elementary, Reading
Flynn, Sandra	77-86	H.S., Business Education
Foley, Dorothea	71-92	Elementary, Slingerlands
Forman, Carol	69-79	Middle, Art
Forrest, Carol	62-81	Elementary, Hamagrael
Franze, August	1958-66	Elementary, Hamagrael
Franze, Grace	55-92	Elementary, Hamagrael
Freeman, Jilda	75-92	Elementary, Specialist
Freeman, Nancy	52-76	Elementary, Delmar
Fuller, Velma	70-91	Elementary, Glenmont
Fuller, William	69-92	Elementary, Phys. Ed.
Furey, John	82-92	H.S., Physical Education
Gallagher, Judith	74-92	Middle, Reading
Ganey, Santa	63-76	Junior High, Music
Gangi, Salvadore	68-86	H.S., Music
Garbowitz, Barbara	72-80	Speech Therapy
Gatto, Mary	57-62	Junior High, Math
Gaura, Nicholas	70-73	Elementary, Glenmont
Gerber, Joseph	51-68	Elementary, Hamagrael
Gibbons, Phillip	77-92	Supervisor, Mathematics
Gilboard, Louis	70-92	Middle, Language Arts
Gillespie, Susan	58-64	Elementary, Hamagrael
Glatz, Roberta	57-77	H.S., Foreign Language
Gorman, Leonard	62-69	Elementary, Slingerlands
Gorman, Olive	68-82	Junior High, Math
Gorman, Richard	56-92	H.S., Mathematics
Graham, Madeleine	70-77	H.S., Mathematics
Grapka, Barbara	86-92	Elementary, Special Education
Gregonis, Gregory	59-66	Junior High, Science
Guerrera, Joseph	54-71	Supervisor, Physical Education
Guiliano, James	69-88	H.S., Language Arts
Guillet, Gwen	87-92	Elementary, Guidance
Gunner, Charles	73-88	H.S., Principal
Gunner, Keith	86-92	H.S., Science
Gunther, Elsa	53-72	Elementary, Delmar
Guyon, Lorraine	85-92	Clarksville, Music
Guzior, Eloise	77-92	H.S., Psychologist
Hafley, Patricia	53-61	Elementary, Elsmere
Hajeck, Suzanne	85-92	Elementary, Slingerlands
Hall, Henry	37-68	H.S., Mathematics
Hammer, Gary C.	67-92	Middle, Mathematics
Harrington, Nelson	66-92	Middle, Physical Education
Hart, Thomas	64-69	H.S., Science
Hase, Edwina	61-82	Elementary, Elsmere

Hawley, Frances	1945-68	Elementary, Elsmere
Hawthorne, Ruth	59-77	Elementary, Librarian
Haywood, Eleanor	58-70	Junior High, Language Arts
Heath, Penelope	72-81	Elementary, Slingerlands
Heicklen, Muriel	66-72	Elementary, Education
Hermann, Jeanne	65-82	Elementary, Delmar
Hermann, Richard	52-84	Principal, Elsmere
Hitchcock, Thomas	67-92	H.S., Mathematics
Hoagland, Jean	67-84	Elementary, Hamagrael
Hobbie, Helen	56-73	H.S., Principal
Hodge, Kenneth	68-92	H.S., Physical Education
Hogan, Peter	73-92	Elementary, Physical Education
Holmes, Linda	67-70	Elementary, Clarksville
Holmgren, Margaret	51-84	Elementary, Elsmere
Holt, Margaret	47-69	Elementary, Delmar
Hooper, Linda	71-77	Elementary, Elsmere
Hopkins, Helen	63-73	Elementary, Elsmere
Hopkins, Kim	83-92	Middle, Technology
Hosey, Dorothy	42-75	Elementary, Delmar
Hosey, Gladys	47-71	H.S., Business Education
Howe, Gladys	42-77	Elementary, Glenmont
Hughes, Julia	57-79	Junior High, Nurse
Hughes, Margaret	61-78	Elementary, Glenmont
Hughes, Mary Jane	82-92	Elementary, Elsmere
Hughes, Mildred	66-82	Elementary, Hamagrael
Hughes, Richard	65-92	H.S., Science
Hungerford, Bernard	55-66	Elementary, Phys. Ed.
Hungerford, Muriel	54-92	Elementary, Clarksville
Hunter, Vivian	60-84	Middle, Guidance
Hunter, William	68-80	H.S., Language Arts
Hyde, Joan	68-86	Elementary, Hamagrael
Isenberg, Diane	87-92	Elementary, Elsmere
Ives, Eunice	63-76	Elementary, Clarksville
Ives, Sammie	56-68	Elementary, Hamagrael
Jablon, Bert	55-61	Junior High, Social Studies
Jackson, Carol	69-76	Middle, Foreign Languages
Jantschi, Edward	55-60	Junior High, Music
Jensen, Constance	63-92	H.S., Foreign Language
Jeram, Elaine	63-92	Elementary, Clarksville
Jerry, Jocelyn	1963-92	H.S., Language Arts
Joachim, Andrew	68-92	H.S., Science
Johnstone, Mary	60-81	H.S., Home Economics
Jongedyk, Mary	54-67	Junior High, Science
Judd, Paulette	71-76	Middle, Physical Education
Judge, Cheryl	77-92	Elementary, Hamagrael
Kallop, Jean	54-80	Elementary, Elsmere
Kanter, Gloria	66-91	Middle, Social Studies
Karl, John	64-92	H.S., Social Studies
Karp, Max	55-86	H.S., Assistant Principal
Keetz, Frank	68-90	H.S., Social Studies
Kelly, Grace	52-67	Elementary, Elsmere
Kerr, Jean	62-79	Junior High, Math- Science
Ketchum, Frederick	53-62	Junior High, Language Arts
Ketchum, Jean	57-62	Elementary, Glenmont
Kimes, Judith	85-92	Elementary, Clarksville
Kinsley, William	48-68	Principal Junior High
Kinum, Rosemarie	64-70	Elementary, Hamagrael
Klett, Geraldine	61-78	Elementary, Nurse
Knight, Charlotte	63-73	H.S., Mathematics
Knox, Douglas	64-70	Elementary, Glenmont
Koban, Betty	72-92	Middle, Art
Kozma, Helen	70-80	H.S., Guidance
Kraft, Sally	46-80	H.S., Language Arts
Kreidler, Ruth	62-73	Elementary, Clarksville
Kullman, Warren	55-77	Supervisor, Science
Kung, Catherine	57-80	Elementary, Glenmont
LaBate, Michelle	82-92	H.S., Special Education
Lambert, Robert	56-71	Supervisor, Language Arts
Lamere, Clifford	67-91	H.S., Science
Lapetina, Susan	71-79	Middle, Language Arts
Lawrence, Donna	76-82	Elemenetary, Music
Lawrence, Jane	64-74	Elementary, Delmar
Lawson, Joan	56-76	Elementary, Art
Leder, Arthur	86-92	Elementary, Elsmere
Lennox, Virginia	64-73	Elementary, Elsmere
Lephart, Clarence	56-62	H.S., Physical Education
Lewis, Eugene	57-91	Middle, Art
Lincoln, Alice	54-74	H.S., Nurse

Linford, Barbara	1973-92	Middle, Keyboarding
Livesy, Mona	65-72	Elementary, Elsmere
Long, Frances	42-66	Elementary, Clarksville
Loomis, Dr.Leslie	87-92	Superintendent of Schools
Lornell, Betty	67-80	Social Worker
Lowe, Virginia	71-77	Principal, Slingerlands
Lubert, Stuart	68-72	Junior High, Science
Lussier, Mary	68-92	Middle, Physical Education
MacDonald, Webster	58-70	H.S., Art
MacCulloch, Cheryl	70-92	Principal, Clarksville
MacKenzie, Richard	73-92	H.S., Learning Disabled
Mackey, Nancy	77-92	Middle, Foreign Language
Mahaffey, Margaret	38-70	Elementary, Delmar
Malloy, Elizabeth	87-92	Glenmont, Special Ed.
Mannheimer, Lois	43-81	Middle, Social Studies
Martini, Betty	55-60	Elementary, Hamagrael
Masino, Andrew	85-92	Supervisor, Art
Mayne, Edna	63-69	Junior High, Language Arts
McAllister, Shirley	78-92	Elsmere, Nurse
McAndrews, J. Briggs	73-92	Assist. Superintendent
McCarthy, Joann	86-92	Elementary, Clarksville
McGibbon, Margaret	63-73	Junior High, Guidance
McGraw, Ruth	61-69	Elementary Librarian
McLaughlin, Margaret	86-92	Elementary, Glenmont
McNitt, Sara	53-66	Elementary, Delmar
McNiven, Diane	79-92	Elementary, Slingerlands
Mead, Carole	56-63	Elementary, Glenmont
Melanson, Mona	72-79	Middle, Guidance
Miller, Charlene	82-92	Elementary, Hamagrael
Miller, Constance	66-88	Elementary, Elsmere
Miller, Merle	63-92	H.S., Business Education
Miller, Richard	57-62	Junior High, Director Recreation
Mitchell, Mary Ann	83-92	H.S., Guidance
Moise, Sarah	73-92	Elementary, Speech Therapy
Molyneaux, Gordon	59-88	H.S., Social Studies
Momot, Arthur	55-61	Elementary, Clarksville
Moomaw, Richard	64-70	Superintendent of Schools
Moore, Heidi	66-82	H.S., Foreign Language
Morand, Mary D.	68-81	H.S., Guidance
Morrison, William	1953-86	Middle, Science
Mossin, Rachel	58-68	Elementary, Hamagrael
Muntz, Mary A.	63-72	H.S., Social Studies
Murphy, David	61-92	Principal, Slingerlands
Musgrove, Marie	72-88	Elementary, Librarian
Nealon, Nicolas	83-92	H.S., Media Center
Nehring, James	86-92	H.S., Social Studies
Nestlen, Judith	68-76	Middle, Language Arts
Nestlen, Richard	67-92	Middle, Social Studies
Nevens, Muriel	72-92	Elementary, Music
Newell, Gladys	33-71	Supervisor, Social Studies
Ninness, William	70-92	Elementary,Physical Education
Noller, Sally	54-61	Elementary, Librarian
Norelli, Rosemary	74-92	H.S., Mathematics
North, Doris	54-73	H.S., Social Studies
Nuzzo, Virginia	68-85	Elementary, Hamagrael
Nyilis, John	62-92	H.S., Driver Education
O'Brien, Maureen	77-92	H.S., Business Education
O'Brien, Michelle	82-93	H.S., Special Education
O'Hara, Nancy	71-80	Elementary, Art
Oliver, Joanne	45-78	Elementary, Delmar
Oro, Marion	73-86	Elementary, Elsmere
Otis, Gladys	54-71	Elementary, Music
Pace, David	87-92	Middle, Science
Pace, Jeannette	69-92	H.S., Art
Palmer, Elaine	56-75	Elementary, Glenmont
Palmer, Helen	52-63	Elementary, Delmar
Pardoe, Marcia	63-90	Elementary, Glenmont
Parry, Judith	85-92	Elementary, Glenmont
Patchen, Anne	61-71	Elementary, Nurse
Patterson, Nancy	62-87	Elementary, Hamagrael
Perkins, Eileen	78-92	Slingerlands, Nurse
Peters, Robert	70-92	H.S., Industrial Arts
Peterson, Elvira	54-61	Elementary, Nurse-Teacher
Philips, Mignonne	77-92	Elementary, Clarksville
Phillips, Elizabeth	42-77	Elementary, Slingerlands
Phillips, Sara	68-76	Elementary, Music
Pickett, Isabel	72-82	Middle, Foreign Language
Pickett, Fred	67-91	H.S., Librarian

Pierson, Robert	1964-91	H.S., Business Education	Ritchko, Arthur	1958-84	H.S., Physical Education
Pinchback, Patricia	84-92	H.S., Guidance	Roberts, Asta	68-92	H.S., Language Arts
Piper, Shari	87-92	Elementary, Elsmere	Robillard, Donald	64-92	Elementary Principal
Platel, Dorann	61-68	Elementary, Hamagrael	Robinson, Richard	62-73	H.S., Assistant Principal
Platt, Joan	81-92	H.S., Foreign Language	Robinson, Wayne	63-90	Middle, Science
Pleasure, Edith	66-71	H.S., Language Arts	Rodgers, Francis	63-89	H.S., Assistant Principal
Pook, Doris	51-67	Junior High, Language Arts	Rosenfeld, Peter	69-78	Middle, Science
Polley, Jean	65-71	Junior High, Home Economics	Rosenfield, Marcia	61-67	Elementary, Elsmere
Poplaski, Richard	68-92	H.S., Social Studies	Rossi, Michael	68-92	Middle, Mathematics
Powell, Judith	85-92	Glenmont, Nurse	Rossuck, Richard	60-71	Elementary, Hamagrael
Preston, Thomas	47-83	H.S., Social Studies	Rothaupt, Karen	65-86	Middle, Science
Post, Henric	72-92	H.S., Art	Rounds, Charlotte	70-92	Elementary, Slingerlands
Prue, Milton	53-63	H.S., Science	Rutnick, Mary Jo	72-92	Elementary, Clarksville
Pryle, Ann	53-85	Junior High, Foreign Language	Rutschmann, Chris	86-92	Middle, Physical, Education
Quackenbush, Cathy	71-92	Middle, Science	Ryan, Dian	69-92	Middle, Mathematics
Quackenbush, Roger	66-92	H.S., Science	Ryan, Alexia	87-92	Middle, Science
Quinn, Doris	56-79	H.S., Mathematics	Salamone, Helen	86-92	Elementary, Slingerlands
Rapaport, Robin	82-92	H.S., Language Arts	Salamone, Robert	74-92	Elementary, Physical Education
Rathjens, John	57-88	Middle, Guidance	Sanders, Evelyn	59-69	Junior High, Art
Ray, Marie	64-84	Elementary, Delmar	Scanlon, Judith	66-91	Elementary, Hamagrael
Rawitsch, Peter	81-92	Elementary, Glenmont	Schade, Christine	87-92	Elementary, Hamagrael
Reardon, Ann	51-76	Elementary, Reading	Schaefer, Joseph	71-92	Principal, Hamagrael
Reed, Cathy	86-92	Elementary, Slingerlands	Schaefer, Cathy	71-92	Elementary
Reed, Charles	86-92	H.S., Science	Schelling, Mary	38-70	H.S., Social Studies
Reich, Stanley	55-84	Supervisor, Art	Schenmeyer, Shirley	68-92	Middle, Librarian
Reid, Mary	71-86	Elementary, Clarksville	Schmitt, Claire	31-65	Junior High, Special Education
Reissig, Harold	42-77	Supervisor, Mathematics	Schmitt, Marie	35-69	Elementary, Elsmere
Renison, Harriet	56-66	Elementary, Glenmont	Schwarz, Louise	82-92	H.S., Music
Restifo, Alfred	51-91	Middle, Mathematics	Segal, Diane	86-92	H.S., Art
Reynolds, Jeffrey	75-86	Elementary, Slingerlands	Seim, Dorothy	66-86	Elementary, Nurse Teacher
Rezzemini, Jessie	54-71	Junior High, Phys. Ed.	Seymour, Victoria	72-83	Elementary, Clarksville
Ricciardelli, Sheryl	81-91	Elementary, Glenmont	Shaloum, Aaron	58-82	Middle, Industrial Arts
Rice, Edward	57-76	Elementary, Music	Shartzer, Norman	67-92	H.S., Science
Rice, Jeannette	80-92	Middle, Health	Shaves, Carmita	54-68	Junior High, Language Arts
Rice, Roberta	70-92	H.S., Science	Shea, Debora	78-87	Elementary, Glenmont
Richards, Mary	63-90	H.S., Language Arts	Sheldon, Hilda	46-67	H.S., Librarian
Rider, Steven	82-92	Middle, Mathematics	Sherman, Nancy	54-80	Elementary, Elsmere
Ries, Deborah	62-66	Junior High, Mathematics	Shogan, Johanna	87-92	Middle, Language Arts
Rightmeyer, John	87-92	Middle, English	Skevington, Gladys	39-63	H.S., Language Arts

Sliter, Raymond	1962-91	Supervisor, Physical Education
Smith, Clarissa	55-69	H.S., Guidance
Smith, Carol	70-92	Elementary, Elsmere
Smith, Flossie	31-71	Elementary, Librarian
Smith, George	77-92	Middle, Music
Smith, Grace	68-91	Elementary, Clarksville
Smith, Joanne	81-92	H.S., Special Education
Smith, Nancy J.	86-92	Elsmere, Librarian
Smith, Nancy R.	66-92	Middle, Physical Education
Snider, Glenn	66-86	H.S., Science
Sobolewski, Gail	86-92	Middle, Math
Sodergren, John	73-92	H.S., Health
Solberg, Nancy	87-92	Elementary, Hamagrael
Solnick, Arlene	62-92	Elementary, Slingerlands
Sorenson, Dorothy	55-76	Elementary, Nurse
Spain, Clarence	73-91	Director, Professional Services
Spelich, Louis	58-86	H.S., Art
Stafford, Jean	67-92	H.S., Physical Education
Stagnitta, George	64-91	Middle, Assistant Principal
Stark, Denise	85-92	H.S., Foreign Language
Stephany, Doris	56-73	Junior High, Bus. Education
Stephany, Ray	54-73	Elementary, Principal
Stewart, Merelyn	83-92	Elementary, Slingerlands
Stewart, Mildred	43-69	Elementary, Delmar
Stoker, Warren	67-92	Middle, Social Studies
Storch, Phillip	69-74	Middle, Music
Stout, Elsie	48-68	Junior High, Math
Straw, Thomas	87-92	H.S., Social Studies
Streiff, Jane	68-92	H.S., Librarian
Superko, Arlene	56-67	H.S., Guidance
Sykes, Esther	43-70	Junior High, Science
Symula, David	62-92	H.S., Science
Taber, Geraldine	49-78	Elementary, Elsmere
Tallcott, Margaret	52-61	Elementary, Delmar
Talmadge, Barbara	77-92	Middle, Mathematics
Terhune, Donald	36-59	H.S., Agriculture
Terranova, Marilyn	81-87	Elementary, Gifted
Textores, Elfrieda	55-86	H.S., Social Studies
Thacher, Elizabeth	79-92	Middle, Foreign Language
Thayer, Virginia	1954-59	Elementary, Nurse Teacher
Thomas, Nancy	87-92	Elementary, Glenmont
Tibbetts, Elizabeth	66-78	Junior High, Reading
Tobler, Leonard	86-92	Elementary, Music
Todak, Joseph	49-60	Junior High, Art
Tompkins, Virgil	56-62	H.S., Principal
Treby, Judith	66-72	Junior High, Foreign Language
Truitt, Rolland	36-64	Supervisor, Music
Turner, Sidney	61-91	H.S., Language Arts
Ulion, Ann	70-92	Middle, Social Studies
Ulion, Terry	70-92	H.S., Social Studies
Ungerman, Annette	63-73	H.S., Social Studies
Valenti, Marilyn	84-92	Elementary, Reading
VanDemark, Paul	57-90	Middle, Health
VanderHeide, Ralph	77-92	Supervisor, Foreign Language
VanDuzer, Carol	69-92	Middle, Science
Varriale, Donna	66-92	Middle, Social Studies
Vendetti, Pio	65-89	H.S., Industrial Arts
Venter, Kathleen	71-79	H.S., Business Education
Villa, Richard	81-92	H.S., Guidance
Vincent, Frances	84-92	Middle, Physical Education
Vogel, Eleanor	65-80	Elementary, Elsmere
Volk, Ann	56-70	Elementary, Slingerlands
Wadsworth, Bruce	68-92	H.S., Science
Wagner, Florence	53-60	H.S., Home Economics
Walencik, Thomas	70-80	H.S., Mathematics
Wallace, Diane	74-92	Middle, Basic Skills
Walts, Carol	71-92	H.S., Physical Education
Walts, Dale	68-80	H.S., Physical Education
Watthews, Thomas	60-92	H.S., Science
Webster, Eugene	58-89	H.S., Social Studies
Weiss, Dorothy	56-89	Elementary, Glenmont
Weitzman, Janet	66-92	Middle, Language Arts
Wendth, Julie	80-92	H.S., Physical Education
Wernick, Sandra	57-62	Elementary, Music
Westervelt, Margaret	64-76	H.S., Business Education
Westfall, Sandra	70-92	H.S., Mathematics
Whipple, Jack	68-89	H.S., Assistant Principal
Whiting, Esther	52-69	Elementary, Clarksville

Whitney, Dorothy	1974-92	Principal, Elsmere
Wiedemann, Marie	45-68	Elementary, Glenmont
Wilkinson, Ruth	69-92	Elementary, Hamagrael
Williams, Hubert	66-92	Elementary, Elsmere
Wiltse, Maureen	73-92	Elementary, Elsmere
Wiltsey, Helen	66-74	Elementary, Glenmont
Withers, Sandra	70-92	Elementary, Elsmere
Woehrle, Mary	69-80	Middle, Language Arts
Woller, Catherine	86-92	Elementary, Elsmere
Wood, David	74-81	Middle, Foreign Language
Woytowick, Donald	1965-71	Elementary, Delmar
Wuinee, Edward	72-77	H.S., Foreign Language
Xeller, Janice	72-92	Elementary, Resource Room
Xeller, Peter	71-92	Elementary, Slingerlands
Yacobian, Richard	59-76	Junior High, Music
Yeara, Claudia	87-92	Elementary, Glenmont
Yeara, James	85-92	H.S., English
Yencha, Mary	71-92	Middle, Social Studies
York, Magdalene	60-73	H.S., Music
Zinn, Lawrence	71-85	Superintendent of Schools
Zwicklbauer, Franz	73-92	Assistant Superintendent

Maps

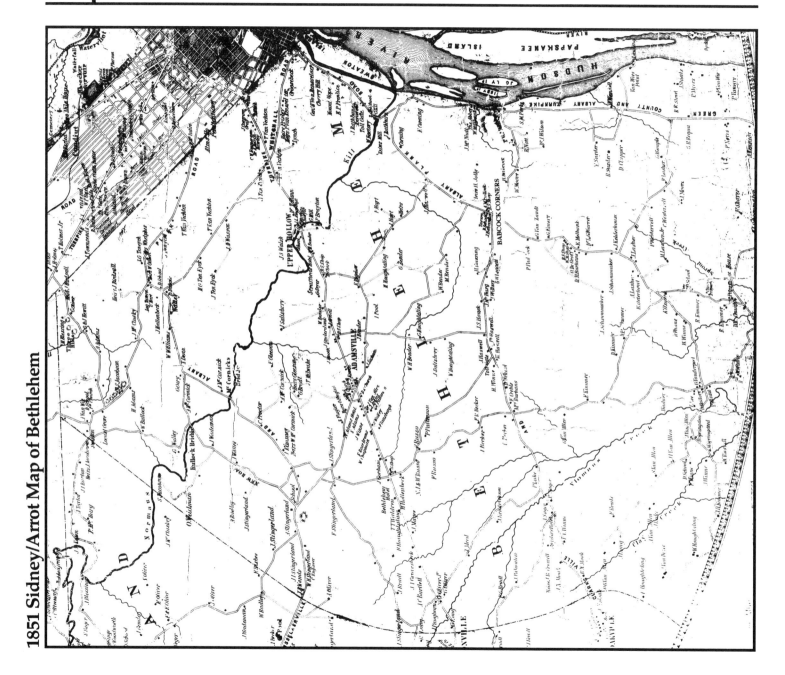

1851 Sidney/Arrot Map of Bethlehem

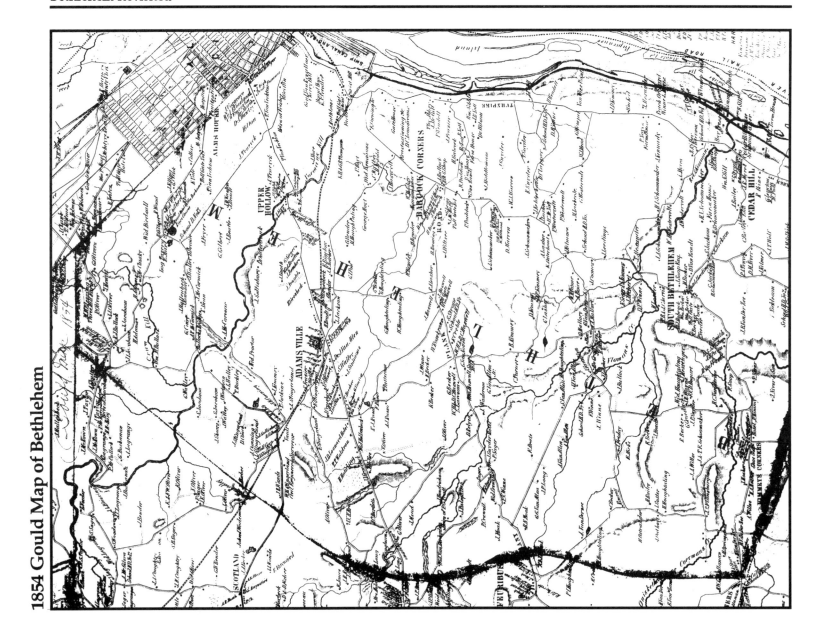

1854 Gould Map of Bethlehem

1866 Beers Map of Bethlehem

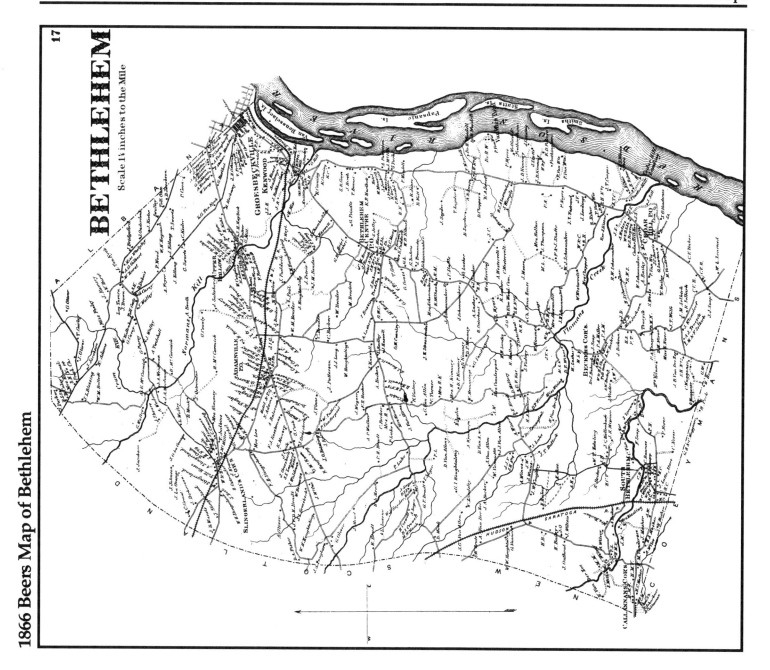

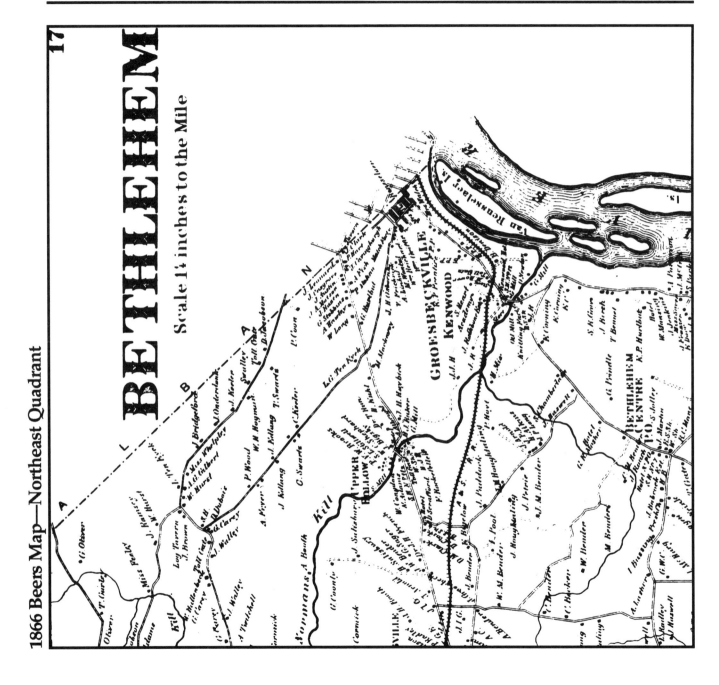

1866 Beers Map—Northeast Quadrant

BETHLEHEM

Scale 1½ inches to the Mile

17

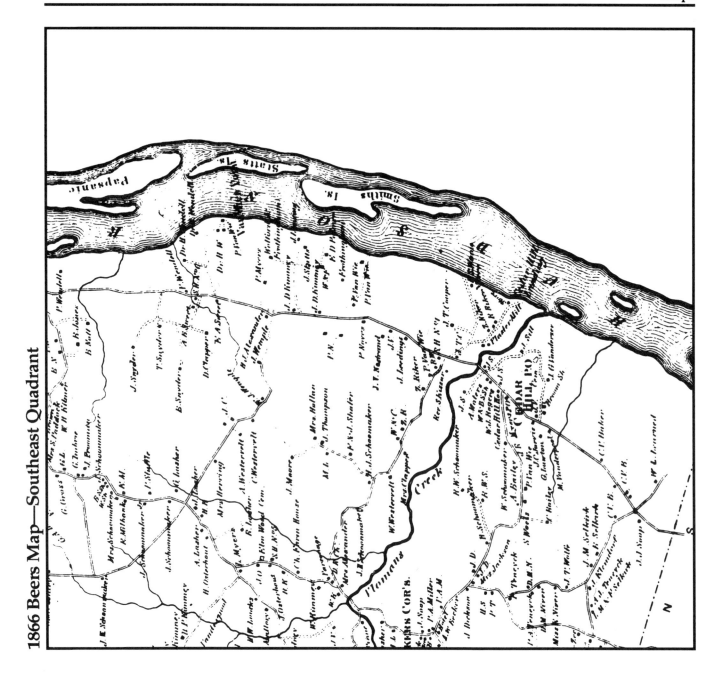

1866 Beers Map—Southeast Quadrant

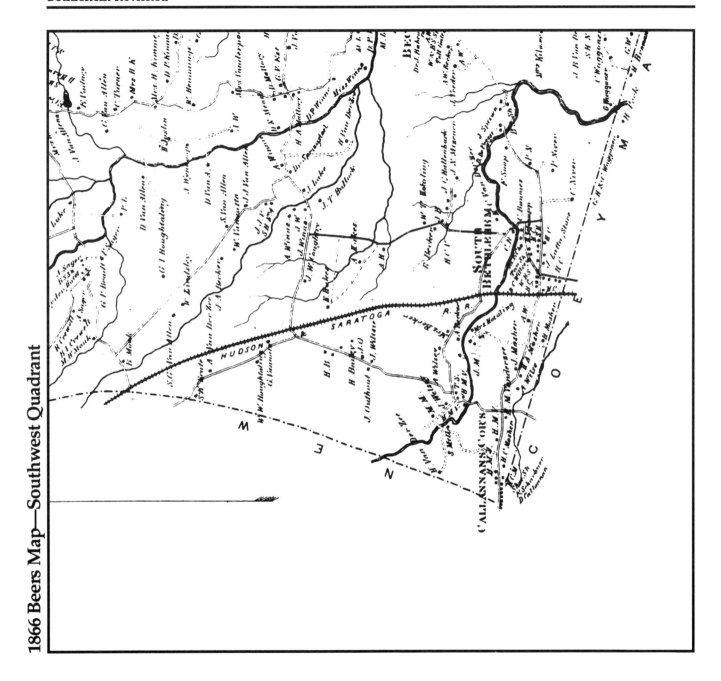

1866 Beers Map—Southwest Quadrant

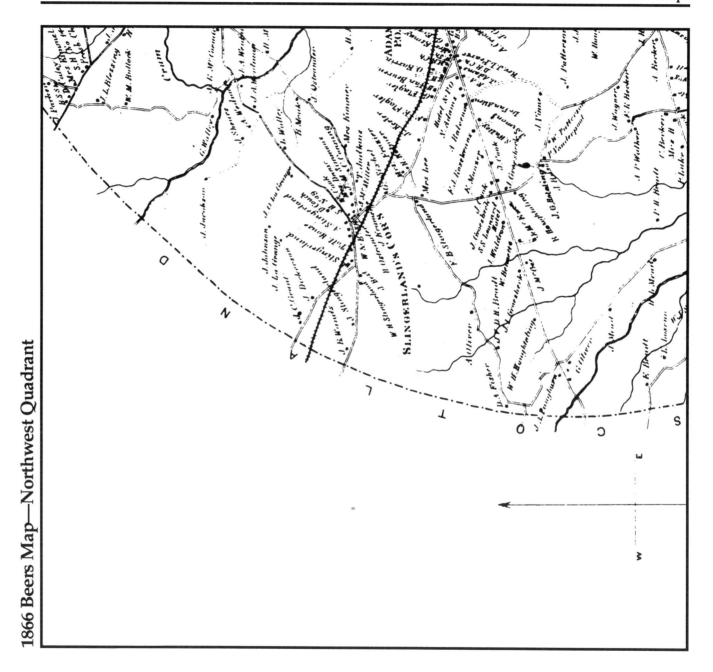

1866 Beers Map—Northwest Quadrant

Index

H